Dissociative Identity Disorder

Dissociative Identity Disorder: Theoretical and Treatment Controversies

Edited by

Lewis M. Cohen, M.D.
Joan N. Berzoff, MSW, Ed.D.
Mark R. Elin, Ph.D.

JASON ARONSON INC.
Northvale, New Jersey
London

This book was set in 10 point Palacio by TechType of Upper Saddle River, New Jersey, and printed and bound by Haddon Craftsmen of Scranton, Pennsylvania.

Copyright 1995 by Jason Aronson Inc.

10 9 8 7 6 5 4 3 2 1

Library of Congress Cataloging-in-Publication Data

Dissociative identity disorder : theoretical and treatment
  controversies / edited by Lewis M. Cohen, Joan N. Berzoff, and Mark R. Elin.
    p. cm.
  Includes bibliographical references and index.
  ISBN 1-56821-380-8
  1. Multiple personality. I. Cohen, Lewis M. II. Berzoff, Joan N.
III. Elin, Mark R.
  [DNLM]: 1. Multiple-Personality Disorder. WM 173.6 D6134 1995]
  RC569.5 M8D55 1995
  616.85′236 – dc20
  DNLM/DLC
  for Library of Congress   94-32539

Manufactured in the United States of America. Jason Aronson Inc. offers books and cassettes. For information and catalog write to Jason Aronson Inc., 230 Livingston Street, Northvale, New Jersey 07647.

Dedicated to the memory of Sydney D. Berzoff, Vera Cohen, and Irving A. Cohen.

L.C., J.B.

Dedicated to Jeanne, Stephen, Jessica, and Andrew.

M.E.

CONTENTS

Acknowledgments   ix

Contributions   xi

Introduction   xv

Part I: Does Dissociative Identity Disorder Exist?

1   **The Manufacture of Personalities: The Production of Multiple Personality Disorder**   3
Harold Merskey

2   **Correspondence: Reactions and Replies**   33
Maeve Lawler-Fahy
Ann Chande
Harold Merskey
Paolo Novello and Alberto Primavera
Frank W. Putnam
G. A. Fraser
Alfonso Martinez-Taboas and Margarita Francia
David Spiegel
Harold Merskey

3   **A Sociocultural Analysis of Merskey's Approach**   57
Alfonso Martinez-Taboas

4   **The Validity and Reliability of Dissociative Identity Disorder**   65
Colin A. Ross

Part II: Theoretical Controversies

5   **Gullible's Travels, or The Importance of Being Multiple**   87
Michael A. Simpson

6   **A Skeptical Look at Multiple Personality Disorder**   135
August Piper, Jr.

7   **Dissociative Identity Disorders and the Trauma Paradigm**   175
Denise J. Gelinas

8   A Developmental Model for Trauma   223
    Mark R. Elin

9   Diagnosis of Dissociative Identity Disorder   261
    Colin A. Ross

10 Cultural Variations in Multiple Personality Disorder   285
    Deborah Golub

11 Allegations of Ritual Abuse   327
    David K. Sakheim

12 Current Controversies Surrounding Dissociative
    Identity Disorder   347
    Richard P. Kluft

                Part III: Treatment Controversies

13 Misalliances and Misadventures in the Treatment
    of Dissociative Disorders   379
    Seth Robert Segall

14 Current Treatment of Dissociative Identity Disorder   413
    Colin A. Ross

15 Consequences of Arriving at the Diagnosis of Multiple
    Personality Disorder   435
    Alan E. Siegel

16 Treatment of Character or Treatment of Trauma?   447
    Joan Berzoff and Jaine Darwin

17 Vicarious Traumatization: Countertransference
    Responses to Dissociative Clients   467
    Karen W. Saakvitne

18 Treatment of Multiple Personality Disorder in a
    Community Mental Health Center   493
    Ellen Nasper and Tracy Smith

19 The Role of the Client's Partner in the Treatment of
    Multiple Personality Disorder   509
    Mark A. Karpel

Credits   543

Index   545

ACKNOWLEDGMENTS

The authors wish to acknowledge the following people and institutions for their support, inspiration, and good humor throughout the preparation of this book.

The inspiration for this manuscript was a conference entitled "Multiple Personality Disorder: Critical Issues and Controversies," that was held at Baystate Medical Center in Springfield, Massachusetts in the spring of 1993. The conference was organized by Drs. Cohen and Elin and was sponsored by the Department of Psychiatry, with the assistance of an educational grant from Ciba-Geigy. Joanna Barnett, Director of Continuing Education, was instrumental in its planning and operation. Benjamin Liptzin, M.D., chairman of the department, provided his full support and leadership for this successful event, and it was sensitively introduced by Lisa Uyehara, M.D.

Many of the authors represented in this book spoke that day; other chapter contributors were subsequently recruited on the basis of their expertise and willingness to stake out an opinion amidst the heated controversies. *The British Journal of Psychiatry* graciously allowed us to reprint Dr. Merskey's article and ensuing correspondence. Each of the correspondents likewise provided copyright permission or wrote additional material for this volume. We were thereby able to gather an international roster of authors, and would like to thank all of them for their enthusiasm and tolerance in this exciting and occasionally grueling process.

We also wish to thank the Brown Foundation and the Clinical Research Institute of the Smith College School for Social Work, which provided an educational and research grant. We thank Muriel Poulin who served as our administrative assistant/typist and devoted painstaking hours to seeing this project through, and Deborah Best for her much-needed secretarial assistance. We want to acknowledge the support of Ann Hartman, the former Dean of the School for Social Work, who granted sabbatical time to Professor Berzoff.

In addition, we thank our families, including Toby Tider, Felice Grunberger, David Cohen, Barbara Shapiro, and Myra Berzoff, for their unending encouragement and love. We want to thank our sons, Zeke Berzoff-Cohen and Jake Berzoff-Cohen who tolerated their parents' occasional unavailability and moodiness. Their precious sweetness and merriment often made it difficult for us to turn the computer on. We thank our dear friends for lending their caring, wisdom, and support, including Cynthia and Bob Shilkret, Gerry and Steffi Schamess, Jaine Darwin, Adin DeLacour, Vivien Weiss, Wendy Salkind, Patti Kates, Liz Bigwood, Arthur Krim, and Richard Meyer. We are also intellectually indebted to Marge Bayes, Kathryn Basham, Ellie Hackett, Ned Cassem, George Murray, Donna Greenberg, and the late Tom Hackett.

Finally, we appreciate the opportunity provided by Baystate Medical Center, Smith College School for Social Work, and Jason Aronson, Inc., to publish this controversial academic book. It has been a real pleasure to produce the kind of book that we would want to read—one that sometimes rocked us with laughter, other times touched us with pure sentiment, and much of the time left us thoughtfully stimulated.

Lewis M. Cohen, M.D.
Joan N. Berzoff, MSW, Ed.D.
September 29, 1994
Pine Island Lake, Westhampton, MA

Many persons were helpful, instrumental, or enthusiastic supporters of this book. I can express my gratitude to only a few of them. I wish to acknowledge my teachers and mentors, Drs. Mardi Horowitz, Philip Grossi, Robert Wallerstein, John Steinhelber, Stephen Hinshaw, Sidney Blatt, Alexander Peer, Colin Ross, and Richard Kluft for their wisdom, advice, and support through the years. The library staff at Baystate Medical Center gave unselfishly of their time, energy, and individual expertise. Kathy Houle devoted herself to the arduous task of typing, in an efficient, patient, and caring manner. Finally, I owe a special debt to all the contributors to this book.

Mark R. Elin, Ph.D.
September 28, 1994
Baystate Medical Center, Springfield, MA

CONTRIBUTORS

Editors:

Lewis M. Cohen, M.D., Director, Psychiatric Consultation Service, Baystate Medical Center, Springfield, MA, and Clinical Assistant Professor, Department of Psychiatry, Tufts Medical School, Medford, MA.

Joan N. Berzoff, M.S.W, Ed.D., Co-Chair Doctoral Program and Associate Professor, Smith College School for Social Work, private practice, Northampton, MA.

Mark R. Elin, Ph.D., Clinical Psychologist/Neuropsychologist, Department of Psychiatry, Baystate Medical Center, and Clinical Instructor, Department of Psychiatry, Tufts Medical School, Medford, MA.

Authors:

Jaine Darwin, Psy.D., Clinical Instructor in Psychology, Department of Psychiatry, Harvard Medical School, and Clinical Supervisor, Victims of Violence Program, The Cambridge Hospital, private practice, Cambridge, MA.

Denise J. Gelinas, Ph.D., Lecturer in Psychology, Department of Psychiatry, Harvard Medical School, Cambridge, MA, and private practice, Northampton and Springfield, MA.

Deborah Golub, Ed.D., A.T.R., Part-time Faculty, Smith College School for Social Work, Northampton, MA, and Visiting Scholar/Researcher, Division of Transcultural Psychiatry, School of Medicine, McGill University, Montreal, Canada.

Mark A. Karpel, Ph.D., Lecturer in Psychology, Department of Psychiatry, Harvard Medical School, Cambridge, MA, and private practice, Northampton and Springfield, MA.

Richard P. Kluft, M.D., Director, Dissociative Disorders Unit, Institute for Pennsylvania Hospital, and Clinical Professor, Department of Psychiatry, Temple University School of Medicine, Philadelphia, PA.

Alfonso Martinez-Taboas, M.A., Ph.D.(C), Caribbean Center for Post-Graduate Studies, Institute for Scientific Investigations, San Juan, Puerto Rico.

Harold Merskey, M.D., F.R.C.P.(C), F.R.C.Psych, F.A.P.A., Professor of Psychiatry Emeritus of the University of Western Ontario, Director of Research, London Psychiatric Hospital, London, Canada.

Ellen Nasper, Ph.D., Director of Intake, Greater Bridgeport Community Mental Health Center, and Assistant Clinical Professor, Department of Psychiatry, Yale Medical School, New Haven, CT.

August Piper Jr., M.D., private practice, Seattle, WA.

Colin A. Ross, M.D., Director of the Dissociative Disorders Unit, Charter Hospital, Dallas, TX.

Karen W. Saakvitne, Ph.D., Clinical Director and Director of Post-doctoral Training at The Traumatic Stress Institute, and The Center for Adult and Adolescent Psychotherapy, South Windsor, CT.

David K. Sakheim, Ph.D., Clinical Consultant, Trauma Resolution Program, Elmcrest Hospital, Portland, CT, and private practice, South Windsor, CT.

Seth R. Segall, Ph.D., Assistant Clinical Professor of Psychology, Yale School of Medicine, New Haven, CT, and private practice, Waterbury, CT.

Alan E. Siegel, Ed.D., Clinical Director, Department of Psychiatry, The Cambridge Hospital, and Lecturer on Psychology, Department of Psychiatry, Harvard Medical School, Cambridge, MA.

Michael A. Simpson, M.B., B.S., M.R.C.S., L.R.C.P., M.R.C.Psych, D.P.M., Director of National Centre for Psychosocial and Traumatic Stress, and Professor of Psychiatry, Medical University of South Africa, Pretoria, South Africa.

Tracy Smith, M.S.W., Director of Mobile Crisis Unit, Greater Bridgeport Community Mental Health Center, Bridgeport, CT, and private practice, New Haven, CT.

Correspondents:

Ann Chande, M.B., F.R.C.P.C., Brockville, Ontario, Canada.

Margarita Francia, M.A., Ph.D.(C), C.P.C. San Juan Capistrano Hospital, Trujillo Alto, Puerto Rico.

George A. Fraser, M.D., Director, Anxiety and Phobic Disorders Clinic, Royal Ottawa Hospital, Ottawa, Ontario, Canada.

Maeve Lawler-Fahy, M.B., M.R.C.,Psych, F.R.C.P.(C), Brockville, Ontario, Canada.

Paolo Novello, M.D., Assistant Neurologist, Department of Neurology, University of Genoa, Italy.

Alberto Primavera, M.D., Assistant Neurologist, Department of Neurology, University of Genoa, Italy.

Frank W. Putnam, M.D., Senior Scientist, Laboratory of Developmental Psychology, National Institute of Mental Health, Bethesda, MD.

David Spiegel, M.D., Professor of Psychiatry and Behavioral Sciences, Stanford University School of Medicine, Stanford, CA.

INTRODUCTION

"Sacred cows make the tastiest hamburgers."
—Facetiously attributed to Gandhi,
and actually stated by Abbie Hoffman.

As the opening quotation suggests, this book embraces the belief that the controversial nature of Dissociative Identity Disorder has much to teach us about psychiatric diagnosis and treatment. The book's nidus was a provocative article by Harold Merskey that appeared in the *British Journal of Psychiatry* and was titled "The Manufacture of Personalities: The Production of Multiple Personality Disorder." By reviewing the historical literature that Merskey maintained was rife with misdiagnosis and error, the article audaciously challenged the existence of the disorder. Emphasizing that widespread publicity in North America made it impossible for cases to arise without having been influenced by suggestion or prior preparation, Merskey argued that MPD posed a distraction from good patient care. He concluded that "the value and good sense of psychiatry become suspect as wonders multiply" (p. 29, this volume).

The correspondence subsequently published in the *British Journal of Psychiatry* demonstrated I was not alone in having been stimulated by Merskey's position. In April of 1993, Drs. Merskey and Ross were the keynote speakers at a conference sponsored by Baystate Medical Center, at which they were given an opportunity to debate this controversial subject.

My colleague, Lisa Uyehara, M.D., framed the conference issues as follows:

> In the last decade interest in our field has proliferated in various aspects of trauma studies. Awareness of the pervasive underestimation of childhood trauma in the past and its sequelae has contributed to an atmosphere of advocacy about some of these issues. Multiple Personality Disorder in particular has aroused both great interest and great skepticism. We are divided into those who see the disorder often, those who do not believe that the syndrome arises spontaneously, and then in the middle a lot of us like myself who have never diagnosed MPD and aren't quite sure what to think.
>
> I would like to present a moment which occurred late in a therapy hour— I think not an unusual moment. The patient, in her fifth year of intensive psychoanalytic psychotherapy, has an extensive history of childhood trauma,

including maternal physical abuse and paternal incest, and employs some dissociative defenses along with more neurotic defenses. After disclosing a painful new detail about the sexual experiences with her father, she was overwhelmed with affect and panicked about leaving my office. As we talked about how she would manage until the next session, the patient stated, "I don't feel that I am the one in control of myself." I paused for a beat before asking in my usual way, "What do you mean?" She went on to talk about feeling two aspects of herself, one which functioned at school and within her family and thought she would be OK, and one which felt that she must do something drastic to avoid the psychic pain she was in. She did not know which aspect would prevail.

Did the patient's statement, "I'm not the one in control" offer a door into a multiple personality which I refused to open by not asking who was in control? Or would my doing so have reified a way of her speaking about her experience—concretizing the metaphor? Did my neutral question allow her to describe her experience without interference from me, or did I lose an opportunity to present a better way to understand her.

Why the intense controversy about this particular diagnosis? Is disbelief in the diagnosis an uncontrolled countertransference reaction evoked by a dramatic, bizarre, and frightening clinical picture? Or are there legitimate intellectual and critical reasons to entertain doubts?

Psychiatric diagnosis may be regarded as an evolving social construction embedded in history, culture, and politics. On an individual level, diagnosis involves complex interactions between a clinician and patient which inevitably organize and impart meaning to the way each of them sees the patient's difficulties, whether the diagnosis is diabetes, schizophrenia or MPD.

There is broad agreement that dissociative phenomena, including autohypnosis, out of body experiences, self anesthesia, and amnesia are common in patients who have been traumatized. Perhaps the disagreement is not about the fragmented identities of patients who suffer from dissociative symptoms, but is about how the disorder exists in the mind of the therapist, and consequently what develops between therapist and patient.

We need to ask how our notions about this syndrome fit into our general models of psychological functioning. Do we consider dissociative symptoms like other psychological symptoms, such as the paralysis of the hysteric, the distorted body-image of the anorexic, or the delusions of the paranoid? In these instances, we try, I believe, to recognize the reality of the belief for the patient, while holding its "as if" character in our minds. Do we step from an attitude of "as if" to "is" when it comes to the alter personalities of MPD, or experiences of forgetting and not knowing? Although many proponents of the diagnosis caution against regarding the alters as real people, the language about the phenomena regularly slips into making these intimations. Where do we draw the line between the therapist's understanding of the patient's experience, and his participation in a pathological self-construction? And how do we conceive of individual responsibility for one's mental life, including defenses and unconscious processes, when we speak of a person as not having executive control? In considering treatment, is the therapist's interest in the complexity of the dissociative phenomena necessary to their integration, or can it produce further fragmentation in patients prone to split off segments of their experience?

A diagnosis which confronts us with such perplexing questions about the nature of consciousness, the unconscious, perception and memory, developmental processes, and the relative permeability of psychic defenses surely can enhance and be enhanced by psychoanalytic metapsychology. For example, can MPD phenomena be understood on some continuum with Winnicott's idea of the "false self"? What is the role of fantasy in dissociative phenomena?

The exponential rise in reported cases of MPD and the wide variations among clinicians in the frequency of diagnosing the disorder demand an explanation. Lenore Terr, who has worked extensively with child and adult trauma victims, considers dissociative reactions common but MPD rare . . . [O]thers have seen dozens of cases of MPD. Is this a rare disorder that is being overdiagnosed by some who are fascinated by the diagnosis? Is this a common disorder, which has been misdiagnosed or undiagnosed for decades? Is this a once rare disorder become common today because some confluence of social forces has produced dramatic increases in the prevalence of the most extreme forms of childhood trauma?

Supporters and skeptics of this diagnosis share an important characteristic. In this age of biological psychiatry, they are all believers in the power of therapy and the therapeutic relationship. The supporters emphasize the importance of the therapist's respect for and understanding of the patient's experience, and ask whether doubts about the diagnosis stem from countertransference anxiety. The skeptics remind us of the intense needs of some patients to comply with their therapists' interests, and warn us of the potential dangers of our countertransference enthusiasms. Judging from my perusal of the literature, this diagnosis has stimulated an intense and impassioned debate. I hope we will pursue our inquiries and arguments in a spirit of mutual respect and understanding that whatever our disagreements, we are all searching for the best ways to be helpful to our patients.

During the succeeding year, while I edited the chapters of this book, Dr. Uyehara's remarks have continued to echo in my thoughts. Encounters with people diagnosed with Dissociative Identity Disorder (DID), or its progenitor, Multiple Personality Disorder (MPD), invariably transform therapists into enthusiasts or skeptics. This is a book written by both skeptics and enthusiasts, and it will alternately enrage and delight readers who have themselves struggled with the diagnosis and treatment. It should also be valuable to individuals who have previously not given much thought to the disorder, but are curious about the intense debate, theoretical ramifications, and extreme feelings that it evokes. Lastly, the book should be entertaining; this is not a desiccated subject and the contributors were given free rein to express their opinions about the various controversies.

In 1994 the very name and diagnostic criteria of multiple personality disorder were altered. DID (or MPD) is currently being held up to public and professional scrutiny, and its continued existence in the psychiatric lexicon will depend on the arguments and research being generated. For practitioners and patients, DID is an important but beleaguered disorder. It is immutably welded to the more general subject of trauma and abuse, and sits in the eye of a media storm. In the United States it is impossible to be shielded from celebrity confessions on talk shows, exposés in journalistic/documentary programs, dramatic books and lurid magazine articles, or the classic movies on the subject.

Meanwhile in court, lawyers joust over issues of culpability in cases ranging from that of a student whose alter plagiarized, to that of a serial murderer pleading insanity on the basis of DID. Our judicial system is also determining whether therapists have committed malpractice and negligence if they diagnose and treat this disorder when the patient later decides that she did not actually have DID.

Another highly publicized and related topic of legal contention is "false memory syndrome." Here, patients are trying to secure justice for early sexual abuse; families are trying to respond to what they allege are untrue accusations. One of our contributors views the families as the victims of human rights violations. On the other hand, another author sees the organization that represents families as being on a vindictive witch-hunt directed at mental-health practitioners. The use of hypnosis or intravenous barbiturates in the exploration of possible abuse and reconstruction of past events have likewise become the focus of legal, ethical, and scientific debate. Intense reactions, including puzzlement and ridicule, are also being evoked by accusations of satanic ritual abuse and by accounts of alien abductions.

Our society is undergoing a transformation in which truth is being battered, deconstructionism is in vogue, and more people are making statements that are blatantly delusional, fabrications, or outright falsehoods. For example, in recent months our local newspaper has reported on two separate public rallies that were held in support of a 13-year-old black Muslim student who claimed she was a victim of racist threats and assault, and a young lesbian woman who stated that she was intentionally struck by a motor vehicle containing occupants who shouted slurs and profanities. There was also a report of strange lights in the sky that many presumed to be a UFO. The newspaper subsequently published articles revealing that the teenager concocted her story, the young woman was intoxicated and her account has been contradicted by witnesses, and two local businessman with ties to the airport and a tavern have been selling alien-invader-related T-shirts and paraphernalia, while taking credit for the hoax.

In the midst of the societal turmoil, this book offers a thoughtful and occasionally heated forum for academicians and skilled clinicians to grapple with some of these related issues while focusing on the existence of DID, its prevalence, etiology, and treatment modalities.

Colin Ross has categorized certain individuals and practitioners as being enthusiasts of the DID diagnosis. We have been fortunate to marshal the efforts of a pantheon of authorities in this field as our supporters. In addition to their eloquent theoretical arguments, the chapters on treatment controversies should be of practical value to enthusiastic readers. The therapy described is not the same treatment that was publicized five or ten years ago. Trauma and dissociative disorder therapies have been evolving, and they are likely to be most efficacious when adhering to traditional principles of solid clinical practice. Awareness of the problems and controversies should greatly assist further refinement of these treatments.

This book is also for the self-proclaimed skeptics. Until now, they have not had a published volume of their own, and have had to base arguments on a few scattered journal articles and editorials. Skeptical readers will be greatly stirred by the lucid arguments of the international group of contributors. Their chapters will leave readers feeling increasingly dubious and suspicious of the burgeoning DID literature, the limitations of its research, and the resulting therapeutic cottage industry.

This book is divided into three sections. Part I frames the debate at its extremes, by beginning with the original article by Harold Merskey and the responses that appeared in subsequent volumes of the *British Journal of Psychiatry*. Contact was made with the authors of these letters, who all graciously agreed to their inclusion in this book, and in several cases sent additional material. Their letters are remarkably heartfelt and direct, while Harold Merskey's replies manage to be both learned and witty. This section sets an international context for the book, which has drawn its authors from the United States, Canada, the Caribbean, England, Italy, and South Africa.

Colin Ross, who is a transplanted Canadian to the United States, rounds off the section by acknowledging the political nature of psychiatric nosology, and by providing an erudite discussion of the validity and reliability of DID. He cites the "pervasive fixed negative cathexis in psychiatry of the term *multiple personality disorder*," and describes the attempt in the *DSM-IV* to alter this by the formulation of *dissociative identity disorder*.

Part II amplifies and extends the debate by beginning with two lively chapters that excoriate the theoretical tenets of DID, and manage to do this with logic and great humor. Michael Simpson has written a sparkling manuscript that darts from "*Gullible's* Travels" to "the myth of the immaculate *perception*," to Tinkerbell and the Malleus Maleficarum. August Piper, Jr., energetically lashes into the diagnostic weaknesses, malpractice risks, problems with hypnosis, and financial aspects of the treatment accorded to people diagnosed with dissociative identity disorder. Both authors have written devastating reviews of the psychiatric literature.

The following three chapters represent a shift from skepticism to enthusiasm, and cogently demonstrate how the dissociative disorders can be understood according to new models or paradigms. Denise Gelinas attempts to get beyond the controversies by accepting them as a natural and predictable part of knowledge development. She cites Thomas Kuhn's structure of scientific revolutions to explain that the DID controversies are a subset of ongoing paradigm shifts in mental health over trauma theory. Like Merskey, she excavates the historical roots of the dispute, citing Janet, Freud, and Lindemann, among others. Unlike Merskey, she finds a compelling historical context for DID and MPD.

Mark Elin has created a developmental model for trauma that encompasses the dissociative disorders. Elin brings to bear an expertise in neuropsychology and psychodynamic therapy. He synthesizes a vast literature, including memory, cognition, and epilepsy, as well as object relations theory. These theories are integrated into a useful therapeutic model.

Colin Ross is one of the preeminent psychiatrists in the field of dissociative disorders, with expertise as a researcher, theoretician, and clinician. He was a keynote speaker at the Baystate conference, and has contributed three chapters to this volume. In the second of these, he reviews the empirical and theoretical data that support the validity and reliability of the DID diagnosis.

However, a debate limited to the existence or iatrogenesis of DID can only end in a cul-de-sac. Perhaps of greater interest are the more subtle differences and problems that have emerged from trying to conceptualize and work with trauma and dissociative disorders. For example, none of us is so myopic that we cannot appreciate the cultural and political influences on the creation and recognition of psychiatric disorders. Alfonso Martinez-Taboas provides a refreshing social contructivist and epistemological perspective of DID. In Part II, Deborah Golub surveys an impressive body of anthropological and cultural literature. In her chapter she sweeps through time and space to highlight the universality versus culture-boundedness of the behaviors called DID.

Few would disagree that there is a need for an empathic clinical stance coupled with scientific neutrality, but David Sakheim takes on the daunting task of applying this approach to the topic of satanic ritual abuse. His chapter is one of several that carefully explore highly controversial topics in a remarkably balanced manner.

Richard Kluft, in the final theoretical chapter of this section, has attempted to review many of the controversies with both dignity and objectivity. Relying on his extensive clinical experience, acumen, and appreciation for the nature of paradigm shifts, he argues that DID does exist, has existed, and must be treated. However, he is not bashful in his criticism of therapists who iatrogenically worsen DID by prematurely breaking through amnestic barriers, by the overuse of "journaling," or by excessive preoccupation with mapping the personality system. He is refreshing in his acknowledgment of the painful clinical reality that naturalistic, iatrogenic, and factitious features can be found in the same patient.

Part III revolves around the treatment controversies. Seth Segall, a skilled and sensitive psychologist, has focused on the misalliances and misadventures that can occur in treatment with patients who have dissociative disorders. His chapter stresses the need to maintain the time-honored and carefully evolved traditional *treatment framework*, and describes how easily patients and therapists can deviate from this path. It is a pleasure to have an articulate accounting of the principles of good therapy.

Colin Ross's treatment chapter will surprise any clinician who is fixated on the primitive, dangerous, and outmoded treatment techniques that were in vogue several years ago. His rational approach—with its attention to cognition and behavior, its lack of reliance on hypnosis, and its emphasis on helping patients to function—is completely consistent with excellent clinical practice.

This part also offers case examples illustrating various aspects of the treatment controversies. Alan Siegel describes a composite case that highlights the difficulties faced by a patient who is encouraged by her therapist to embrace an identity as a "multiple." This philosophy may be helpful for some individuals, and there is certainly a vibrant community of support groups and self-help publications (including a children's book to explain "why mother sometimes behaves as if she were different people"). However, Siegel's conclusion is that this therapeutic intervention is harmful and counterproductive, and that even well-intentioned therapists slip into fixed and problematic transference relationships. His case serves as a morality tale for how things can go awry.

Joan Berzoff and Jaine Darwin successively followed the same patient over fifteen years. Berzoff conducted a psychoanalytically based treatment of character pathology, while Darwin subsequently emphasized the sequelae of early trauma history and thereby uncovered a DID. The dilemmas and tribulations of the two treatments and the differences that emerge when borderline and dissociative pathology are focused upon, provide an unsettling lesson about the importance of diagnosis in the treatment process.

Karen Saakvitne has turned her attention to the countertransference issues that confront therapists who work with this patient population. The consistent theme of the chapter is that good trauma therapy is good theory-based psychotherapy. The author delineates some of the elements of psychoanalytic trauma therapy that derive from her experience with DID clients. She examines the purposes served by dissociation and, importantly, attends to the ways in which therapists can address their own vicarious traumatization.

Ellen Nasper and Tracy Smith consider how community mental health clinics can deliver treatment to the most severely ill clients with DID. They have been confronted with patients whose illnesses often appear to be schizophrenic. Nasper and Smith describe how community mental health can ideally address the needs and demands of patients with extreme and disabling dissociative pathology.

Most therapists are sufficiently overwhelmed by the multitude of emerging alters that the notion of couples therapy seems inconceivable (and certainly unmanageable). Mark Karpel has dared to inquire whether therapists should involve the DID client's partner in treatment. He asks about the concerns, benefits, and liabilities, and whether couples work should be carried out by separate therapists. Beginning with the "forgotten partner," he elegantly moves through a typology of relational patterns and describes various ways and advantages of involving partners in treatment.

Let me conclude by mentioning some of the decisions that influenced this book. While most of the authors participated in the original conference, many were recruited on the basis of their long-standing interest and expertise in the field. Authors selected a controversial topic and could be as succinct or prolix as they felt necessary. Some of the resulting chapters are obviously tightly focused, while others demonstrate the extent to which their authors could become consumed by this endeavor.

Chapters were written during the nosological transition time when MPD became DID. Although it would have been a simple matter to have swept through the manuscripts substituting the *DSM-IV* terminology, we chose to leave the terms used by the contributors. While the name MPD has itself become controversial, it is still burned into our society's consciousness and our psychiatric literature. The reception of the newly coined DID remains unclear.

Last, I speak on behalf of my fellow editors in expressing our gratitude for the seriousness displayed by our authors and am delighted that a scholarly work frequently managed to include the elusive but necessary ingredient of humor. We anticipate that this controversial book will evoke intense reactions among its readers, and sincerely hope that for most it will be a source of enjoyment and edification.

                                                              —Lewis M. Cohen

I

Does Dissociative Identity Disorder Exist?

1

The Manufacture of Personalities: The Production of Multiple Personality Disorder

Harold Merskey

Unprecedented numbers of cases of Multiple Personality Disorder (MPD) have been diagnosed, mainly in North America, since 1957. Widespread publicity for the concept makes it uncertain whether any case can now arise without being promoted by suggestion or prior preparation. In order to determine if there is any evidence that MPD was ever a spontaneous phenomenon, a series of cases of MPD from the earlier literature has been examined, with particular attention given to alternative diagnoses which could account for the phenomena report and to the way in which the first alternate personality emerged. The earlier cases involved amnesia, striking fluctuations in mood, and sometimes cerebral organic disorder. The secondary personalities frequently appeared with hypnosis. Several amnestic patients were trained with new identities. Others showed overt iatrogenesis. No report fully excluded the possibility of artificial production. This indicates that the concept has been elaborated from the study of consciousness and its relation to the idea of self. The diagnosis of MPD represents a misdirection of effort which hinders the resolution of serious psychological problems in the lives of patients.

THE CURRENT CLINICAL PICTURE OF MULTIPLE PERSONALITY DISORDER

Multiple personality disorder (MPD) is defined in *DSM-III-R* as:

A. The existence within the person of two or more distinct personalities or personality states (each with its own relatively enduring pattern of perceiving, relating to, and thinking about the environment and self). B. At least two of these personalities or personality states recurrently take full control of the person's behaviour. [American Psychiatric Association 1987]

Putnam (1989), one of the authors of this definition, says that there is a patient profile that should suggest MPD. The core features are a profusion of psychiatric, neurological, and medical symptoms; a host of diagnoses; and a failure to respond to treatment for those diagnoses. The symptoms include depressed mood, suicidal attempts and ideas, impaired concentration, fatigue, sexual difficulties, crying spells, and insomnia. *Often* there is enough superficially to suggest the diagnosis of major affective disorder. Nightmares are prominent, along with terrifying hypnagogic and hypnopompic hallucinations. Closer inquiry discloses that the depression is more labile than is usual with major affective illnesses and that there may be several mood swings each day. Amnesia or time loss may affect as many as 90 percent, and fugue episodes and feelings of depersonalization occur in more than 50 percent. There is sleepwalking in many subjects, anxiety, phobic symptoms, substance abuse, and hallucinations during the day as well. Self-mutilation occurs in about a third of the patients. The life history is almost always marked by sexual abuse. A great majority of patients are women.

Some patients declare their diagnosis. Otherwise, says Putnam (1989), the therapist who wishes to "elicit alter personalities" should ask gentle questions about whether the patient has ever felt like more than one person, searching for another part, and ultimately asking, "Do you ever feel as if you are not alone, as if there is someone else or some other part watching you?" (p. 90). In the event of a response the therapist looks for "any . . . attribute, function or description to use as a label to elicit this other part directly." This is a very clear and honest statement, but with such an approach there is a likelihood that the therapist will produce the phenomenon.

The more dramatic examples of this syndrome attract much attention, ranging from *The Three Faces of Eve* (Thigpen and Cleckley 1957) to an unfortunate 27-year-old waitress in Oshkosh, Wisconsin, who claimed to have forty-six different personalities, of whom six were sworn in and gave testimony in a trial (Daniels 1990). Publicity must also be suspected of producing such events.

Many of these patients have had terrible experiences and awful problems in their lives. The argument of this chapter is not whether or not the patients need treatment—they do—but rather under what label and with which ideas.

QUESTIONS AND CONTROVERSIES

The foregoing picture is sanctioned by *DSM-III-R* and has many supporters in North America but is viewed with skepticism by others and is rarely, if ever, found in Japan (Takahashi 1990) or Britain. Occasionally clinicians (Allison and Schwartz 1980, Kluft 1982) mention patients with twenty or more personalities. *DSM-III-R* states that 100 personalities can occur in one person. Fahy (1988) argued that the literature lacks information on the reliability of diagnosis, prevalence, or the role of selection bias, that iatrogenic factors may contribute to MPD, and that there is little evidence from genetic or physiological studies to suggest that it presents a distinct psychiatric disorder. Hacking (1986) suggests that the idea of multiple personalities "was largely invented by doctors, but later became a spontaneous way in which to express unhappiness." Aldridge-Morris (1989) calls it an exercise in deception and sees it as a cultural phenomenon.

Some clinicians working on dissociative memory disorders encounter inordinate numbers of cases of MPD. Others report none. Ljungberg (1957) found none among 381 patients with overt hysterical symptoms. In eighty-nine cases of classic dissociative or conversion disorder (Merskey and Buhrich 1975) I encountered no MPD. In thirty-six years I found none among many more patients with conversion disorders. One patient dissociated and talked to herself in a detached fashion. In that instance the genesis of MPD was carefully avoided. Another, under the care of a colleague, declared she had reported her multiple personalities to please the doctors who first told her that that was her condition. Mayer-Gross and colleagues (1954, 1977) said that multiple personalities were always artificial productions, due to medical attention and literary interest. Sim (1981) likewise gives a sceptical report. Chodoff (1987) noted the rarity of cases in his own practice and that of colleagues. Fahy and colleagues (1989) reported a patient who fulfilled the diagnostic criteria for MPD. She had seen the film *The Three Faces of Eve* and had read the book *Sybil* (Schreiber 1973). Directing her attention away from the "alternate personalities" led to their decline.

With each favourable step in the public discussion, more cases have occurred. The problem is whether MPD represents a valid syndrome. Simpson (1989) remarks critically upon the enthusiasm of its protagonists. Aldridge-Morris (1989) suggests that it is unhelpful to regard it as a discrete clinical entity and that it is being grossly overdiagnosed.

The disproportionate numbers of female patients (e.g., 90 percent in the report of Ross and colleagues [1990]) raise a question as to whether this is a natural phenomenon related to sex or a social product due to earlier ill-treatment or other forces. It may result from abuse of individuals, or from encouragement to comply with a special role, or from both such causes.

THE INCREASING NUMBER OF CASES

Scepticism about the diagnosis has increased by this great growth in numbers of cases. The pattern of this growth is noteworthy. The first supposed case of MPD recorded in detail is that of Mary Reynolds of Pennsylvania (Mitchell 1816, Plumer 1860, Mitchell 1888). The initial report by Mitchell (1816) is thirdhand and brief. Plumer (1860) described the history six years after the patient's death, from interviews with her relatives. S. W. Mitchell described the case again in 1888 from Plumer's report and from the papers of his father, J. K. Mitchell. He also reinterviewed the same relatives Plumer had consulted. About that time there was lengthy discussion of several cases, specially by Azam (1876, 1887, 1892), Janet (1887, 1888, 1889), James (1890), Prince (1908), and Sidis and Goodhart (1904). Prince (1908) cited some twenty-four reported cases. He held that in the more fully developed forms the secondary or "disintegrated" personality would approximate that of normal life and might pass before the world as mentally healthy.

Hacking (1986) has argued that MPD was created, as it were, in 1875. In the first three-quarters of the nineteenth century there were only a few notable cases, such as that of Mary Reynolds. Thereafter there was much discussion, especially in France where the concepts supported the views of positivist philosophers and psychologists such as Ribot, who gained ascendancy in French academia. More cases were described, including the retrospective descriptions in detail by Azam in 1876 of his own case from 1858, by Mitchell of his father's case, and Leonie and others by Janet. After Prince's book in 1908 the numbers increased again. Taylor and Martin (1944) identified seventy-six cases occurring over 128 years, and suggested there might be as many more.

In 1954 Thigpen and Cleckley reported a case. Their book *The Three Faces of Eve* appeared in 1957, and a film was made of it. From that point cases multiplied. Boor (1982) recognized seventy-nine reports after 1970. *DSM-III-R* established a category for MPD in 1987. Kluft (1982) mentioned 130 such patients, of whom he had treated 70. Bliss had seen 100 cases, and Jeppsen another 50 (Bliss and Jeppsen 1985). Putnam and colleagues (1986) reviewed 100 cases. Ross (1987) found an incidence of 4.4 percent among his patients and claimed that MPD can be readily discovered with a reliable and valid screening instrument (Ross 1989).

A BASIS FOR EVALUATION

In light of the growth in numbers and some of the increasingly improbable stories associated with MPD it seemed worthwhile to seek a further method by which to probe the origin of the phenomenon. One of the most explicit discussions is given by Sutcliffe and Jones (1962). They considered various conceptions of multiple personality—as a diagnostic fashion, as a product of shaping in therapy, as a product of hypnotic suggestion, as stimulation, and as an extension of characteristics found in normal personalities.

We now have a strong diagnostic fashion for the topic in some countries. Hypnotic suggestion accompanies innumerable reports. Simulation is always possible but, if therapists can create the condition by suggestions, the need for simulation is slight. Explanation by an extension of normal personalities is disputable since the patterns presented are distinct.

I noticed some examples in which shaping by therapy was the most plausible explanation (Prince 1908, Janet 1911) and therefore examined a sample of the literature for information on other diagnoses and on the moments of emergence of secondary personalities. It appeared that the historical context of ideas on the topic might cast light on its growth. This seems all the more important because lately the potential for artificial production of the phenomenon has been facilitated by publicity and by *DSM-III-R*, so that patients appear with foreknowledge of the pattern. This chapter presents observations on the diagnosis of classic cases and the origins of the extra personalities.

CONCEPTUAL PRESUPPOSITIONS

Diagnosis in medicine is heuristic and variable (Merskey 1986). Some diagnoses are preferable to others because the conditions seem to originate independently of doctors or social demands, or because they are more successful in prognosis or in explaining etiology, or—most important—because they are the most helpful guides to treatment. They may be influenced by psychological factors or by social expectations, whether we are talking about cancer pain, endogenous depression, or post-traumatic stress disorder. However, it is reasonable to reject those diagnoses that most reflect individual choice, conscious role playing, and personal convenience in problem solving, provided we have alternatives that are less troublesome intellectually, and not morally objectionable. Hence I am evaluating MPD as a diagnosis with the implicit view that certain other diagnoses are acceptable alternatives. Mania, certain depressive illnesses, schizophrenia, obsessional neurosis, and even some conversion or dissociative symptoms arise in very many cases of MPD without medical induction or social facilitation. This necessitates review of the diagnosis of MPD. Some authors have already maintained that MPD is produced by the interest of doctors and others.

SAMPLE OF CASES

I examined a series of descriptions of early cases that were accessible to me and that presented relevant data. All, or almost all, the prominent cases from Europe and North America have been covered, as well as some that are less well known. However, cases such as that of Sorgel (an early nineteenth-century criminal with epilepsy and automatism) or of Mesnet (a soldier who had a left parietal bullet wound and a transient right paresis) have been omitted since Myers (1903) and Sutcliffe and Jones (1962) have taken them to be subject to organic cerebral disorders. The cases of Dufay and Bellanger, summarized by Gilles de la Tourette (1887), are also not discussed, as they appear to be fugues or simple hypnotic states.

Those examined and their sources are as follows: Gmelin's report (1791) and that of Despine (1840); Reynolds as described by Mitchell (1816), Plumer (1860), Weir Mitchell (1888), and William James (1890); the cases of Skae (1845) and Mayo (1845); the cases of Azam (1876, 1887, 1892); Camuset (1882); Richet (1883); Bourru and Burot (1885); Pierre Janet (1887, 1888, 1889, 1907, 1911, 1913); Rochas (1887); Jules Janet (1888); Proust (1890); James (1890) and Hodgson (1891), who both described the Reverend Ansel Bourne; Daily (1894); Prince (1900, 1908) on Miss Beauchamp; Sidis and Goodhardt (1904) on the Reverend Thomas Hanna; Hart (1912); Cory (1919); the long article by W. F. Prince (1916) on the Fischer case; Lipton (1943); a paper and book by Goddard (1926, 1927); a book by Franz (1933); and the discussion by Lewis (1953).

Five recent volumes and a paper concerning five individuals have also been examined (Hawksworth and Schwarz 1977; Horton and Miller 1972; Peters and Schwartz 1978; Schreiber 1973; Sizemore and Pittillo 1977; Thigpen and Cleckley 1957), all of which give information on the emergence of the phenomenon; Allison and Schwarz (1980) described still more cases, although incompletely.

I reviewed this material for psychiatric conditions with which MPD might be confused, or which might promote it, and the way in which the second personality emerged. This discussion of cases occurring since 1957 is intended to be illustrative and not comprehensive.

PROMINENT EARLY CASES

Benjamin Rush mentioned the earliest known possible cases of MPD (Carlson 1981). Ellenberger (1970) states that case histories of MPD began to appear in mesmerist writings and, later, in the medical literature only after the disappearance of the phenomena of possession, although cases of exorcism and possession sometimes still occur (McKellar 1979; Peters and Schwarz 1978). Ellenberger (1970) cites Gmelin's 1791 report of a German woman aged 20, in Stuttgart, who was impressed by refugees from the French Revolution and their aristocratic manners. She "suddenly 'exchanged' her own personality for the manners of a French-born lady . . . speaking French permanently, and German as would a French-born woman" (p. 127). Sufficient context is not available to evaluate this case for its onset. French and German states alternated with loss of memory for each other. "With a motion of his hand Gmelin was easily able to make her shift from one personality to another" (Ellenberger 1970, p. 127). Despine (1834) reported a case of alternating states in an 11-year-old Swiss girl, Estelle, who had been diagnosed as having a spinal paralysis and severe pains, which ultimately responded to "magnetism." A comforting angel, Angeline, talked to Estelle in her magnetised condition, advising support for her whims. The angel prohibited all foods that Estelle disliked and ordained that she should have anything she desired, including snow. The angel said, "Let her act according to her whims; she will not take advantage of the situation" (pp. 34–39). The book provides no evidence for a second personality.

The first report on Mary Reynolds describes two independent states of consciousness, the first appearing after sleep. Some of her changes followed the anticipated pattern of the mesmerizers of the day, when they produced "somnambulism" (i.e., hypnotism). Nevertheless, one also finds embedded in the descriptions some striking material which suggests manic-depressive illness. For example, Plumer (1860) wrote as follows:

> In her first state she was quiet and sedate, sober and pensive, almost to melancholy, with an intellect sound though rather slow in its operations, and apparently singularly destitute of the imaginative faculty. In her second state she was gay and cheerful, extravagantly fond of society, of fun, practical jokes, with a lively fantasy, and a strong propensity for versification and rhyming. . . . In her natural state the strange double life which she led was the cause of great unhappiness. She looked upon it as a severe affliction from the hand of Providence, and dreaded a relapse into the opposite state, fearing that she might never recover from it and so might never again in this life know the friends of her youth, nor her parents, the guardians of her

childhood. . . . In the abnormal state, though the prospect of changing into her natural state was far from being pleasant to her, yet it was for different reasons. She looked upon it as passing from a bright and joyous into a dull and stupid phase of life.

Mitchell (1888) confirmed Plumer's account with Mary's relatives, the Reverend Dr. John V. Reynolds and his brother Mr. William Reynolds. Using material that also appears in the earlier reports, he portrayed Mary Reynolds as having a profound sleep, after which she awakened in a state of unnatural consciousness. Her memory had fled. "All . . . that remained to her was . . . a few words." She had to be taught their significance, who were her relatives and friends, and her duties. She quickly relearned reading and writing.

Formerly she had been melancholy, taciturn and reserved, but now she was jocose and unrestrained. She had no fear of rattlesnakes, copperheads or bears . . . in this peculiar state. Mary's parents had no control whatever over her. She was very fond of exercising her ingenuity, inventing tricks at the expense of theirs, . . . for the purpose of enjoying a laugh and causing others to join in it, at the ludicrous figure in which she never failed to make them appear.

After five weeks she reverted to her former state, which alternated with the new condition at intervals of varying length for fifteen or sixteen years. Once her natural disposition returned "her melancholy was deepened by the information of what occurred." When she was cheerful her buoyancy of spirits was so great that no depression was produced; in her other state she was quiet and shy, and there were times when she manifested an unusual degree of nervousness and restlessness. When she was 35 or 36 the alternations ceased, leaving her "permanently in her second state" until she died, aged 61.

Apart from the amnesia, this case resembles bipolar affective illness. However, Mary apparently awoke with an amnesia and communication was employed to build up her knowledge of the world. During reeducation the original pattern may be reintroduced or new patterns encouraged. So much must depend upon the response by others that it is unlikely that anyone waking with a hysterical amnesia would develop a new personality without assistance. In fact, Reynolds kept her identity but changed her mood. Mitchell described her later phase as a gradual change "from a gay hysterical mischievous woman, fond of jests and subject to absurd beliefs or delusive convictions, to one . . . sobered down to levels of practical usefulness."

At the reading of Mitchell's paper, Dr. H. C. Wood said that *double consciousness* was about as bad a term as could be selected. He compared the case with that of a lady who suffered from melancholia and who alternated between being rather coarse and rude and thoroughly disregarding the rights of others on the one hand and suffering from the deepest religious melancholia on the other. In the same discussion, C. K. Mills said that the case resembled "insanity of double form," which we would now call manic-depressive illness (Carlson 1984).

The case of Skae (1845) is a further striking example of such bipolar illness. The patient was a man of regular and retiring habits, and extremely temperate, who "commenced with the usual symptoms of dyspepsia" which gradually passed into "hypochondriacism" and then into a state "bordering between hypochondriasis and mental alienation." At the height, "feelings of gloom and despondency were at the same time developed: the most trifling errors of the past were magnified into crimes of unpardonable magnitude, and the future was contemplated with the utmost dread." He spent much time reading and incessantly turning through the Bible, sat up the greater part of every night, lay in bed during the day, and "under the influence of the bodily distress and mental despondency . . . he not infrequently spoke of drowning himself, or of throwing himself out of a window, and on several occasions begged earnestly that he might have his razors." After nine or ten years the symptoms, which had been aggravated somewhat on alternate days, became distinctly periodic:

> On each alternate day, the patient is affected in the manner just described and will neither eat, sleep nor walk, but continues incessantly turning the leaves of a Bible, and complaining piteously of his misery. On the intermediate days he is, comparatively speaking, quite well, enters into the domestic duties of his family, eats heartily, walks out, transacts business, assures everyone he is quite well, and appears to entertain no apprehension of a return to his complaints.

This is evidently a patient who began with depression and dependency and moved into a regular fluctuation from cheerful indifference to depression on alternate days. The case of Mayo (1845) is only described briefly but also resembles a bipolar disorder, a dull, quiet phase contrasting with one of extreme excitement.

In Europe most early cases showed only so-called dual consciousness. Authors such as James (1890) and Janet (1889, 1911) were interested in dissociative phenomena as a means to understanding the operations of the conscious mind. Independent personalities were of secondary importance initially. When they were proposed, it was often done overtly. Jules Janet

(1888), the brother of Pierre, hypnotized Blanche W., a patient with hysterical symptoms, at the Salpetriere, and restored normal function. This lady appears in the family picture reproduced by Owen (1971) and by Goetz (1987) of Charcot demonstrating hysterical dystonia. Janet says, "She willingly accepted the name Louise, which I suggested to her," but she still regarded herself as Blanche. More personalities with strong delineation emerged only later. Greaves (1980) states that the description of multiple selves appeared in the twentieth century. There are hints, however, in several famous French cases.

Azam (1876, 1887, 1892), a professor or surgery interested in hypnotism, described Felida X. at the age of 47 after thirty-two years of observation. She had convulsions and was hysterical, and "was industrious, intelligent, and of a serious, almost sad, character" (Azam 1876). In what was taken to be her basic condition,

> she thinks unceasingly about her morbid state which causes solemn preoc-cupations, and suffers from sharp pains in several parts of the body especially the head. The symptom called hysterical nail (i.e., sharp localized pain in the head) is prominent. One is particularly impressed by her somber manner and the lack of desire which she has to speak; she responds to questions but that is all. [Azam 1876]

Azam describes how then almost every day without any apparent cause or any excitement, she enters her second condition. Suddenly, after a pain in the temple, she falls into a profound sleep which lasts from two to three minutes. Then she wakes, merry and laughing. She hums a tune as she goes on with the work she is engaged upon, makes jokes with those about her, and does not suffer from the neuralgic pains of her supposedly ordinary state. "In this state, which we call the second condition, Felida has a complete knowledge of the whole of her life" (Azam 1892). "For the last nine or ten years the period of the second conditions has diminished in time of duration to lasting a few hours only and appearing only every 25 to 30 days. So that Felida is almost cured, and will be perfectly so at . . . the menopause."

Azam (1892) denied the diagnosis of dual personality, and explained "doubling of consciousness" in terms of somnambulism. The correct diag-nosis today might be a rapid-cycling bipolar state modified by cultural expectations.

Pierre Janet described a number of cases, particularly Leonie, Lucie, Rose, Marie, and Marceline. Leonie had been much treated previously by "magnetisers." Janet (1888) writes, "the magnetisers called her Leontine during somnambulism and recognizing that they had reason to give a new name I kept it" (p. 260). In 1889 he was to say, "Formerly we gave the subject different forenames . . . condition of Leonie, condition of Leontine, etc. The confusion caused by this practice was recognized. Now following Azam, we will say condition 1, condition 2, condition 3, for each subject" (pp. 86–87). He then identified patients in different states according to the pattern Lucie 1, Lucie 2, Lucie 3, etc.

Leonie 1 knew only of herself; Leonie 2 (Leontine) knew of herself and of Leonie 1, of whom she said: "That good woman is not myself. She is too stupid" (Janet 1913, p. 113). A third Leonie emerged who knew of herself and of both the others. The early history of how Leonie 2 emerged is lost, but obviously suspect of production by her magnetisers. Janet seems to have rediscovered her through automatic writing produced in response to a posthypnotic suggestion made over two months previously. There was a letter in her normal style of Mme. B (the original name of Leonie) and another one on the back of the page signed by Leontine, saying how much trouble Leonie was giving Leontine (Janet 1888, pp. 252–253). Leonie was hypnotized repeatedly from 1869 onwards and by Janet himself many times at least from 1885 onwards. Myers (1903) describes her as Janet's classic case of factitious secondary personalities.

Janet (1887) describes at length his practice with Lucie, a much younger girl with a history of many hysterical symptoms. In this principal description, repeated and varied somewhat two years later (Janet 1889), he distinguishes between three phases: the original individual, a hypnotized state, and another character who emerged under automatic writing. In his 1889 volume and later editions (Janet 1913, p. 87) he describes hypnotizing Lucie and establishing this state of altered awareness, which he called Lucie 2. One day she failed to obey the hypnotic suggestion and, to augment her response, he made hypnotic passes on Lucie 2 as if she were not already hypnotized. After various changes, a new personage, Lucie 3, emerged.

The following exchange occurred with Lucie under hypnosis and through automatic writing.

"How are you?"
"I don't know."
"There must be someone there who hears me."
"Yes."
"Who is it?"
"Someone other than Lucie."
"Ah indeed. Another person. Would you like us to give her a name?"
"No."
"Yes. It would be more convenient?"
"All right. Adrienne."

"Very well, Adrienne. Do you hear me?"
"Yes."

Janet (1913) adds: "Without a doubt I suggested the name of the personage and gave it a lot of individuality but we saw how much it develops spontaneously . . . this naming of the unconscious personage greatly facilitates the experiences" (p. 318). Janet was nevertheless convinced that although these hypnotic states were often imperfect and rudimentary, they could also constitute a new existence, more complete than the normal existence of the individual. The life or vitality of a psychological system, in favorable circumstances, would constitute different personalities with various hypnotic somnambulistic states. However, the act of asking a hypnotized subject if someone else is there clearly encourages the production of an artificial entity. Janet (1913) actually also declares about these subjects, "We consider that we have been able to establish, even to produce at will, somnambulisms which are completely the same as those of Felida" (p. 178). Binet (1891) made a telling comment about the above exchange with Lucie: "It is plain that M. Janet by christening this unconscious person, and more still, by declaring that someone must exist in order to answer him, aided materially in the formation of a person; he himself created her by suggestion."

Rose and Marie, like Leonie and Lucie, had numerous variations under hypnosis. The exact origin of these cases and their second forms of personality is either dubious or is not described in detail in any of the original sources listed here. However, all had hysterical symptoms and multiple changes under hypnosis. Janet (1913) describes Lucie and Marie, asserting their identity. One says, "It is I Lucie but you have changed me," and Marie says, "It is still always me . . . but not at all the same thing" (p. 131). Janet goes on to remark that Deleuze had observed that some somnambulists talk of themselves in the third person.

Janet (1907, 1911) had another case, which he called an "artificial Felida," referring to the moods of depression in both cases. Janet (1907) wrote of "a double personality . . . produced artificially . . . in 1887 a young woman of 20, whose name was Marceline, entered the hospital. . . . For several months past she had not taken any food [and] had reached the last stage of emaciation" (pp. 86ff).

Marceline was fed under hypnosis. After hypnosis she forgot what had happened. She could not get out of bed and had retention of urine, which hypnosis relieved without catheters. Repeated hypnosis kept her lively, cheerful, intelligent, and active by day. At night she was allowed to relapse, inert and immobile. The treatment begun by Jules Janet in 1887 was continued by his brother Pierre for over ten years.

Janet (1907, 1911) never gave Marceline another name. He studied differences between the two phases in which memory, mood, and behavior alternated, but the individual was still the same person. At times Marceline fell into profound depression. Janet (1911) finally concluded that "dual personality is the hysterical form of periodic depression." The strongest reason for calling Marceline an "artificial Felida" was the indication of alternating retarded or withdrawn states, and cheerful, alert ones. We may wonder how many other cases of recurrent depression have been cast in a pattern of dissociative disorder from Mary Reynolds onwards. Certainly, a relationship between hysterical symptoms and depression has been suggested on other grounds as well (Slater 1965; Merskey 1979).

Felida (Azam 1876, 1887, 1892) and Janet's cases (Janet 1889, 1911), offer nineteenth-century instances where more than two such conditions emerged. In Felida a frequent state of an elevated mood alternating with the primary personality was observed, and briefly a third state in which the patient had some terror. In Leonie all three personalities had similar names, and the secondary personalities had knowledge of those revealed earlier. Lucie, Marie, and Rose resemble Leonie. I suggest that there is so much evidence of active shaping of Janet's cases that it would be unjustified to accept any of them as spontaneous examples of MPD without strong positive evidence for the syndrome, which is lacking. We also see that Leonie came to Janet fully formed by magnetisers, the naming of individual personalities was a practice that he took from them, and there is open acknowledgment of pressure on his other subjects to develop secondary personalities. On occasion he appears to indicate this for all his cases, not only Marceline, who is frankly described as an "artificial Felida."

Another leading French case, Louis V., described by Camuset (1882), Bourru and Burot (1885) and Myers (1886), is complicated and varied, with hysterical paralysis, mood changes, and a motive to avoid punishment. The emergence of the personality change is also not described in detail. Richet (1883) describes women with partial striking amnesias. He says of his cases however that they have lost the memory of their personality. They gave to their *moi*, forms which were different from their real forms. He sees this as a transformation of personality for which it was enough to pronounce one work with sufficient authority. He describes the activities of M in different roles of peasant, actress, general, priest, and nun. Another patient is a general, sailor, old woman, little girl, and pastry cook. These cases appeared to be frank examples of play acting under the command of the hypnotist rather than any form of spontaneous alternate personalities.

Similar dramatic changes were obtained by Rochas (1887), who presents a case where a change of name and role was produced by posthypnotic suggestion. On the other hand the case of Proust (1890) was a lawyer with hysterical fugues, easily hypnotized, convicted of dishonesty, and pardoned on the grounds of automatism. None of these cases shows a valid pattern of independent personalities and Proust presents his case only as one of automatism.

Daily (1894) described a melodramatic case with initial head injuries and clairvoyance. According to Daily, both George M. Beard and W. A. Hammond denied the validity of his case. Janet (1907) wrote about it: "The history is strangely related: you feel in it . . . an exaggerated seeking after surprising and supranormal phenomena. Mollie Fancher . . . at least five persons, who have very poetical pet names: Sunbeam, Idle, Rosebud, Pearl, Ruby. . . . The complication of this case is very amusing" (pp. 84–85).

Many early cases had evidence of organic disease. Among fourteen cases before 1905 at least two, and possibly three, had significant evidence of brain damage while another three had evidence of epilepsy (Sutcliffe and Jones 1962). Other patients had fugues or somnambulistic states or were hypnotized, although some of the remaining cases were said by Sutcliffe and Jones to demonstrate true MPD. An embarrassing failure to recognize an organic element appears later in a case described by Franz (1933).

Thus it appears that the leading nineteenth-century cases were examples of bipolar illness (Reynolds, Skae's patient, Felida), organic cerebral disorder (Myers 1903, Sutcliffe and Jones 1962) or hypnotic induction. The latter was sometimes overt and frequently persistent, if less obvious.

THE TURN OF THE CENTURY

The Reverend Ansel Bourne of Rhode Island (Hodgson 1891; James, 1890) was an itinerant preacher who disappeared from home. Two weeks later a man calling himself A. J. Brown rented a small shop at Norristown, Pennsylvania. Some seven weeks subsequently he woke in a fright and asked where he was. He said that his name was Ansel Bourne; he was entirely ignorant of Norristown. Under hypnosis he recalled the lost initial two weeks, which included visits to Boston, New York, and Philadelphia, resting, reading, and looking around. Coons (1984) denies this was a case of MPD and emphasizes the misdiagnosis of many early cases.

This case seems to represent a fugue in which the patient established a new identity. Unlike most MPD cases the persistence of the role was brief and the alternate state was less happy or lively than the usual secondary and tertiary personalities which are described. Stengel (1941) noted the importance of depression in many fugue states.

The Reverend Thomas Carson Hanna was born in 1872 (Sidis and Goodhart 1904). On April 15, 1897, he fell from his carriage and was picked up unconscious. Large doses of strychnine were administered hypodermically, and on waking the Reverend Hanna appeared to be offering to push one of his physicians. He was strong but was overcome and bound with straps. He lay quiet and the straps were removed, after which it was recognized that he had lost his speech and appeared to be in a state of "complete mental blindness." He was reeducated, like an infant. In May 1897 the observers (Sidis and Goodhart 1904) remarked: "No memory of his previous life spontaneously occurs to him. The time of his accident may therefore be considered as the boundary line between two distinct and separate lives of the same individual. . . . We may say *two personalities* dwell within the same individual" (p. 135, my emphasis).

The Reverend Hanna was investigated through dream analysis, interview, and hypnosis. He was encouraged to establish recollections. Incidents from his past life were recalled, or reconstructed (or created). After two months the personalities were reconstituted, apparently spontaneously, in a state resembling mental stupor. No second personality is described, only the recall of primary experiences alternating with the impaired awareness of the external world associated with an amnesia, possibly organic initially, with hysterical elaboration.

The most famous case is that of Christine (Sally) Beauchamp. Prince described her first in 1900, reported her at length in 1905 in the first edition of *The Dissociation of Personality*, and extended the description subsequently in 1908 and 1920. Before Prince's case, most examples were patients with episodes of altered consciousness in which information about the world and themselves was merely reduced, or individuals who entered into a second mood state or condition of activity.

THE BIRTH OF SALLY

Prince ultimately described four different personalities in his patient. It is instructive to examine his description of "the birth of Sally" from Miss Beauchamp. He first presents the contents of a hypnotic session in which he was taxing her with not remembering material she had clearly referred to on previous occasions. He then says that he was startled to hear her, when hypnotized, speak of herself in her waking state as "she." He writes (the emphasis is mine):

> but now the hypnotic state, for the first time, used the pronoun "She," in speaking of her waking self, as if of a third person; but used "I," of herself in

hypnosis. The tone, address, and manner were also very different from what they had been . . . my experience of this case entirely contradicted the view that I had held up to this time. My conviction had been growing that so-called personalities, *when developed through hypnotism*, as distinct from the spontaneous variety, were purely artificial creations . . . in opposition to this view the personality known as B III, or Chris, which first made its appearance during hypnosis . . . originated and persisted against my protests and in spite of my skepticism . . . asked . . . who "she" was. The hypnotic self was unable to give a satisfactory reply.

"You are 'She,' " I said."
"No, I am not."
"I say you are."
Again a denial.

I made up my mind that such an artifact should not be allowed to develop. I pursued her relentlessly in my numerous examinations, treated the idea as nonsense, and refused to accept it. . . .
Finally:

'Why are you not 'She?' "
"Because "she" does not know the same things that I do."
"But you both have the same arms and legs, haven't you?"
"Yes, but arms and legs do not make us the same."
"Well, if you are different persons, what are your names?"
[On another occasion they spoke as follows:]
"Listen, now you say you are Miss Beauchamp."
"Yes." . . .
"The last time we talked you said you were not Miss Beauchamp."
"You are mistaken. I did not. I said nothing of the sort."
"Yes, you did."
"No."
[Prince 1908, pp. 26ff]

McDougall (1948) observes: "It has been suggested in the course of Prince's long and intimate dealings with the case, involving as it did the frequent use of hypnosis . . . he may have moulded the course of its development to a degree that cannot be determined. This possibility cannot be denied."

Perhaps Prince did not discourage multiple personality as much as he suggests. Despite his statement to the latter effect, he asked for names, and he strongly reminded the patient of another "she." We cannot know what would have happened had he ignored minor discussion of the patient's self in the third person.

AFTER MORTON PRINCE

Bernard Hart (1912) had a patient who had an angry outburst followed by a partial amnesia. He was told in psychotherapy that he was like a person who was not whole, sometimes like four-fifths of the whole individual, sometimes like one-fifth chipped off. Hart says that the one-fifth man underwent a rapid development, and was subsequently a much more complicated person than on the occasion of his first appearance.

The more prominent cases in this period were mostly described in America. Doris Fisher (Prince 1916) is reported in a rambling fashion. The emergence of the first personality is associated with strong hints of possession and hysterical delirium or sleep. Two secondary personalities are said to have emerged at the age of 3 when the patient was physically ill treated. The information given is essentially retrospective as well as jumbled.

Goddard (1926, 1927) met Norma-Polly when she was 19 and an established patient with at least two different phases of personality. Good reasons are given for emotional disturbance in this patient's life but the process of appearance of the second personality is not specified. A strong hint is offered on page 115 (1927), where it is suggested that at the age of 18 the patient had the opportunity to visit a sister, aged 4, who was being very well cared for, when she was not. She would have been expected to imagine herself in her sister's place. Such legitimate wishes could have developed into the evolution of a personality with another name. However, the proof of this is lacking. Hacking (1991) has obtained evidence that Norma was admitted to a psychiatric hospital in 1923 with a diagnosis of mania, although Goddard claimed she had been cured.

One of the most interesting cases is briefly described by Cory (1919). A young woman sitting alone in the house at the piano felt as if something said to her, "take a deep breath," and the sound of singing which she had never heard before came from the same direction and frightened her. Just before the song she had shuddered and felt as if something had possession of her; she went to the kitchen to get a drink then and asked, mentally, who was it that sang, and she acquired another name. It was several weeks however before this other person learned to emerge or to submerge the original personality of the patient. This appears to have been a daydream or wish for fulfillment of another role partly granted by the unconscious. The new person began to speak garbled Spanish, which fitted the needs of that personality. On close inspection this case looks rather like one that might have to be treated as an example of conscious fantasy. It is also not outlined in very much detail.

MISDIAGNOSIS AND OVERT PRODUCTION

The case of Franz (1933) reflects partial misdiagnosis. The patient suffered from a confusional state due to neurosyphilis and then contracted malaria, which probably halted the syphilis, or slowed it down, but left brain damage. The original physicians did not recognize the diagnosis of neurosyphilis. The patient moved to America and was examined and reported by Franz (1933) simply as a case of MPD. Before the book appeared the patient returned to England, gave evidence of manic-depressive syndrome, was admitted to Maudsley Hospital in London in 1931, and was shown to have positive serology for general paresis of the insane. After treatment with induced malaria, he still showed some (organic) memory disturbance (Lewis 1953). Lewis provides a compelling argument that this patient had some organic brain change and hysterical symptoms at the time that he was diagnosed as a case of MPD. The conclusion of Sutcliffe and Jones (1962) and the organic evidence in the case of Thomas Hanna were noted above.

Sara, the case of Lipton (1943), had repeated attacks of amnesia. Lipton wrote: "In discussing . . . violent behavior with the . . . staff, as well as with Sara, one was constantly saying, 'Sara changed again,' or 'Sara had one of her violent spells,' or some similar expression. . . . It was decided to call the patient by another name, Maud, when she appeared different . . . this was merely for convenience."

A determined effort was made to be kind and considerate to Maud. Soon two different personalities emerged. Sara was mature and intelligent, with an IQ of 128. Maud had an IQ of 43. Numerous other differences developed. Later, a third personality emerged. "She identified herself as Sara and denied the existence of any other personality as did the other two. She was dubbed Ann. . . . The failure to discover Ann in seven months of observation in the hospital, for a time even after diagnosis of dissociated personality was made, is evidence of the skill with which the various personalities 'covered up'." The question arises to what extent a similar manufacture occurs with other cases, albeit less obviously. Frank suggestions were remarked upon previously, with hypnosis by Pierre Janet (1889, 1911), and Jules Janet (1888), as well as the highly questionable evolution of Hart's case.

RECENT CASES: FROM EVE TO BILLY MILLIGAN

Christine Costner Sizemore, called Eve by Thigpen and Cleckley (1957), also provided her own versions of events (Sizemore and Pittillo 1977). She was seen for headaches as an outpatient. She seemed to be "neat, colourless, gentle, humble, not under-nourished" (Thigpen and Cleckley 1957). During one interview she spoke of a voice she heard, apparently wishing to say more and finding herself at a loss for adequate expression. The medical authors (1957) write:

> Eve seemed momentarily dazed. Suddenly, her posture began to change. Her body slowly stiffened until she sat rigidly erect. An alien, inexplicable expression then came over her face . . . suddenly erased into utter blankness. . . . Closing her eyes she winced. . . . A slight shudder passed over her entire body.
> Then the hands lightly dropped. She relaxed easily. . . . There was a quick reckless smile. In a bright, unfamiliar voice that sparkled, the woman said, 'Hi there Doc!'
> With a soft and surprisingly intimate syllable of laughter, she crossed her legs, carelessly swirling her skirt . . . in a manner which was playful and somehow just a little provocative.

Sizemore says that after the discussion of hearing voices she changed.

> As she sat . . . eyes downcast, unable to hide her pain, she moaned softly, then slowly the head raised, straight and proud; the sparkling eyes gazed back at him sardonically.
> "Hi Doc," she chirped, changing the tired droop of her body to a sensuous slouch with one almost imperceptible wiggle.
> She asked the doctor for a cigarette, which he gave to her hesitantly. He lit it for her and said,
>
> "Who are *you*?"
> "I'm me," she flipped.
> "And what is your name?" he pursued.
> "I'm Chris Costner."
> "Why are you using that name instead of Chris White?"

Thigpen and Cleckley described their case as Eve White who altered to become Eve Black. The patient described herself as Chris White who altered to become Chris Costner. Costner was her maiden name and there were substantial marital difficulties.

Dr. Thigpen witnessed a dissociative episode. The important difference between the two accounts is that Eve used her maiden name, a point not very evident in *The Three Faces of Eve*. We can see denial of the marriage, for reasons well described by both doctor and patient. A different pose and set of attitudes were adopted but this might not have been another personality; it was an affirmation of a previous (real) single state, which the patient regretted leaving. However, the patient's account does partly support the earlier psychiatric account. Sizemore indicates that as Miss Costner, she denied having a child and defended herself by saying that her body might have had the baby, but not when she was in it. In any case, once the decision was made to accept a denial of marriage as a second personality, a different pattern followed. From then on, Sizemore had repeated dissociative episodes and ultimately she described up to twenty-two different personalities.

Sizemore was emaciated and depressed on admission. Her childhood as described included some frightening experiences, but not childhood abuse, unlike nearly all recent cases.

Elizabeth (Congdon et al. 1961) described a spontaneous change. This came after *The Three Faces of Eve*. No report is given about inquiry into possible knowledge she might have had concerning MPD. Since the widespread publicity about *The Three Faces of Eve* and *Sybil*, all subsequent cases are suspect of being prepared by prior information.

Horton and Miller (1972) reported the case of Gloria, a very disturbed 16-year-old with varied moods, fainting turns, and somnambulism, who said one day, "Four years ago, I . . . went by the name of Sue," and ultimately described four different personalities. Preferring a different name probably served her as a springboard for new personalities.

Sybil (Schreiber 1973) was 1.65 m (5 feet 5 inches) tall, and weighed 34.5 kg (79 lbs.) when, after repeated amnesias, she entered treatment with Dr. Wilbur. Early in treatment she read many psychiatric case histories. During one session she abreacted violently, regressed in her age, changed her accent, and spoke atypically and ungrammatically. She described an incident in which a child was killed. Dr. Wilbur said to her, "Who are you?" She answered, "I'm Peggy."

Peggy then admitted to living with Sybil and her mother, but denied that she was the daughter of Sybil's mother. The doctor concluded that Sybil was a case of MPD.

Sybil's mother was probably psychotic, treated her appallingly, and called her by different names which she preferred (e.g., Peggy). Victor (1975) held that Wilbur persuaded Sybil to believe in extra personalities, but the patient's reading in the existing literature may also have contributed.

Both of the last two cases had conscious awareness of the adoption of different imaginary roles. Henry Hawksworth had five personalities, also adopted consciously (Hawksworth and Schwarz 1977). The second appeared when he was 3 years old and persisted for forty years. He was abused and later suffered from marked depression, elation, and abuse of alcohol. He pretended that another version of himself, an imaginary playmate Johnny, lived inside a ventriloquist's doll. Even if he blamed Johnny for his misdeeds he recognized that he himself still got punished at home and at school. Hawksworth recalls being in the playground, thinking of himself as Dana. His teacher said:

> "Henry Hawksworth, you are to report to the principal's office immediately."
> "Yes, Ma'am," said Dana, uncertain why the principal would want to see him.

He was punished for bad language, spoken by Johnny.

In this case serious adult misbehavior occurred, alternating with phases of sober, calm, settled, and successful work as a law-abiding citizen. The adoption of multiple personalities was conscious and grew out of child-hood fantasies with an obvious motive, which are also presented as overtly conscious. There is also another difficulty. Like others in this group, the story is not always told consecutively, like a psychiatric history, but often in the screenplay, flashback pattern.

Christina (Peters and Schwarz 1978) was terribly abused. A brutal father killed one of her baby siblings, terrorized her mother, and raped her when she was 5. She lost consciousness or recollection, and woke in an orphanage as Marie. She became an alcoholic and a drug addict, fantasized about spirits, and believed she was possessed. Her doctor claimed to have exorcised her. Afterwards, he introduced her to the idea of multiple personalities and she developed them. As a child she had retreated into an alternative identity. Her adult condition was taught to her.

W. S. Milligan (Keys 1981) committed repeated rapes. He was found not guilty by reason of insanity, that is MPD, and has been kept in a psychiatric forensic institution. In his first year of life he was in and out of hospitals. His alcoholic father committed suicide. A brutal stepfather physically and sexually abused him when he was 8 or 9 years old. From the age of 3 years and 8 months he had an imaginary playmate. At one time he wanted to play with his baby sister, but his mother said he could not do so. When bored, he went to sleep and when he woke he had the identity of Christene, who could play with the baby. It is not clear if this was an unconscious switch. By the age of 9, he had six other imaginary identities, seemingly often conscious. Every situation called for a new role, for example Adalana, a girl, who would enjoy washing dishes when it was required.

Eve and Sybil had depression, severe anorexia, and hysterical amnesias or fugues. The first appearance of a secondary personality in Eve was an episode of denial of her marital relationship. We are not informed if she knew of MPD before the change. Once she became a case of MPD the stage was set for twenty-two individual forms to emerge. Thigpen and Cleckley (Thigpen 1984) have been reluctant to diagnose subsequent cases, but Eve has been the model for hundreds more, perhaps for all the cases that followed.

Before the full adult syndrome emerged, Christina had direct instruction from her doctor about multiple personality. Elizabeth followed Eve. Sybil probably read descriptions of MPD and was persuaded by her therapist, at least in part. Hawksworth, Milligan, Sybil, Christina, and Gloria consciously used their alternate roles for emotional relief, or social advantage. Eve's case has the most convincing descriptions and yet a doubt remains. In her case it is uncertain whether there was prior knowledge of the concept of MPD. On the other hand, it does not appear to have been ruled out; there is a strong lead to another explanation; the childhood experience is not apparently typical; and the more skeptical we become about personality number 22, the more we may question the first alternate. The case of Milligan also raises doubt but its reliability has already been strongly questioned (Thigpen 1984).

In these cases the role of a secondary personality, at any age, developed out of depression or severe emotional conflict, and as a protection from experiences that could not otherwise be tolerated. In most or all of them, spontaneous origin of anything that we should call MPD, without some prior awareness of the disorder, is either doubtful or disproved. This need not imply malingering—that is, the conscious adoption of a symptom in order to achieve a deliberate or unfair benefit, ordinarily at the expense of others or society. Here the patient, with some awareness, adopts a role which at least part of the environment favors.

Cases like that of Reverend Ansel Bourne suggest that brief spontaneous second identities may emerge in vulnerable individuals with the help of depression and environmental stress. Secondary identities may appear in others like Gloria, Sybil, or Henry Hawksworth as a result of fantasies of imaginary companies, social encouragement, or some combination of these items. However, the persistence of such discrete identities, if any, is not evident without artifactual medical, psychological, or social processes noted above.

Lastly, among case reports, Allison and Schwarz (1980) describe several patients. Their first presented fully formed. Analysis of her process suggested spontaneous developments as a child but the origins of the adult patterns are not clear. Another patient was treated by exorcism. No example in the book, which is written for the general reader, is convincing.

Greaves (1980) notes that Christine Beauchamp (Prince's case) had four personalities; others have had sixteen (Schreiber 1973), twenty-two (Sizemore and Pittillo 1977), and even thirty-five (Allison and Schwarz 1980).

Kluft (1982) described sixty cases in some detail, of whom only eleven had two personalities, eight had 305 personalities, twenty had six to ten personalities, nineteen had eleven to twenty personalities, and two more than twenty personalities. Hilgard (1988) observed that such numbers "as well as those reported by several others, are bound to raise doubts about diagnoses."

DISCUSSION

The early cases show limited development of dual consciousness. Their changes are related to fluctuations of mood, anorexia, hypnotism, overt suggestion, or organic disease. Dual personality as distinct from dual consciousness is sometimes explicitly denied (Azam 1887).

James, Azam, and Janet were concerned with somnambulism, awareness, automatic behavior, attention, memory, dissociation, and ultimately recognition of the self and awareness of the self. These topics were prominent for Herbert Spencer in his book *The Principles of Psychology* in 1855, and are described by Coupland (1892) among others. They continue into the twentieth century (Myers 1903, Stout 1919). The discussion centered on ways to understand the operations of the mind, in quite another direction from the issue of multiple selves.

A number of the early cases raise questions of diagnosis. Three of the most famous have a strong spontaneous streak of bipolar fluctuations or depression persisting for many years (Mary Reynolds, the case of Skae, and Felida X.). Others have a prominent (and generally accepted) organic contribution (e.g., Myers 1903, Sutcliffe and Jones 1962). The cases in the twentieth century of the Reverend Thomas Hanna and Franz Lewis's patient also had undisputed organic problems. All of the cases of Pierre Janet, as well as most of the other French ones, emerged with hypnosis. Marceline was severely anorexic, like Eve and Sybil later. Alcoholism was overt in later cases (Hawksworth, Christina). Louise (Janet 1888) and Sara (Lipton 1943) were openly created, probably like Leonie and several others.

No case has been found here in which MPD, as now conceived, is proven to have emerged through unconscious processes without any shaping or preparation by external factors such as physicians or the media. With respect to this argument, we may have reached a situation comparable to Heisenberg's principle of uncertainty: observation of the phenomenon changes it. If this is true it means no later case probably since Prince, but at least since the film *The Three Faces of Eve*, can be taken to be veridical since none is likely to emerge without prior knowledge of the idea.

It is likely that MPD never occurs as a spontaneous persistent natural event in adults. The cases examined here have not shown any original conditions that are more autonomous than a fugue or a second identity promoted by overt fantasies or conscious awareness. The most that may be expected without iatrogenesis is that an overt inclination for another role could cause the adoption of different conscious patterns of life, as in Cory's (1919) case, or perhaps the case of Horton and Miller. Without reinforcement, such secondary changes would ordinarily be expected to vanish.

Suggestion, social encouragement, preparation by expectation, and the reward of attention can produce and sustain a second personality. Admittedly, if only those physicians who expect the disorder can see it, those who do not believe in it cannot see it. However, like others, I was willing to entertain its existence and never found it myself, neither before the dramatic rise in reported cases nor since. Meanwhile, it is not necessary to treat patients who have had terrible childhoods, and who have conversion symptoms, by developing in them beliefs in additional first personalities. Enthusiasm for the phenomenon is a means of increasing it.

We should consider how patients, and doctors, come to believe in MPD or to present the popular pattern. Four suggestions are appropriate to explain the way in which MPD is created. The first is the misinterpretation of organic and bipolar illness. The second is the conscious development of fantasies as a solution to emotional problems. The third is the development of hysterical amnesia, followed by retraining. The fourth is the creation by implicit demand under hypnosis or repeated interviews. Retraining may arise in a purely dissociative amnesia, or one that is triggered by a head injury or depression but followed by hysterical patterns of memory loss. This learning effect is evident in Mary Reynolds. Mitchell (1888) reported: "The first lesson in her education was to teach by what ties she was bound to those by whom she was surrounded, and the duties devolving upon her accordingly. After a while some striking mood fluctuations were observed between depressed and elated, shy and retiring, or outgoing and overconfident."

Two personalities were not evident here, only two mood states. The natural effort to retrain the individual is described. The same natural effort comes out very clearly in the case of the Reverend Hanna (Sidis and Goodhart 1904). One can imagine the consequences if this patient was in touch with someone who wanted to suggest that he might have thought that he had another mood, characterized, say, by the name William. The potential for creating a new story would have been strong.

Miss Beauchamp is but another example of the fourth scenario. Prince first describes verbatim a gentle argument with his patient, under hypnosis, about what she could recall and what not. As he attributed the power of recollection to her, she presumably began to distance herself, under hypnosis, from that power and role. Ultimately, in one of her sessions under hypnosis, she used the word "she" for herself at another time, and Prince pounced upon it. Despite his conviction that other selves appearing under hypnosis were produced by suggestions, he explored the question as to "who" she was and then said "you are she." Despite her denial, he persisted with his assertion and went on, in due course, to ask her for the name of the other personality and, later, to remind her of "she." Today patients are better trained. Spanos and colleagues (1986) obtained telling experimental evidence that procedures employed routinely to diagnose MPD encourage and legitimate enactments of the syndrome.

The change that occurred in Eve, as she describes it, is less impressive in a significant particular than the way in which it was described by Thigpen and Cleckley (1957). If she did indeed principally deny her married status, choosing her maiden name once more, and secondarily defended her decision by denying associated items, the creation of the secondary personality was not a complete transformation. The development of the condition in some of the other cases in childhood is a kind of conscious make-believe, by necessity, and may be carried through with insight into adult life. Again, this does not amount to spontaneous, functioning alternate personalities who should be granted a life of their own for pragmatic, legal, or therapeutic purposes.

A relevant human mechanism appears in patients with paralyzed limbs or dysfunction of a part. A patient with hemi-ballismus, unable to control the erratic and violent movements of her left arm, described it separately as "George." The tendency to distance oneself from an unpleasant phenomenon is common and easy to adopt. MPD offers a mode of separating, splitting, and isolating particular subjective problems. However, the evidence so far implies that it requires assistance.

Proponents of the diagnosis of MPD point to the high frequency of sexual abuse in the histories of sufferers. In Canada, Ross and colleagues (1990) found that 90 percent of 102 patients were so affected, while a national survey (Committee on Sexual Offenses Against Children and Youth 1984) indicated some sexual abuse by touching or attempted assault in 45.6 percent of females. This includes incidents of exposure or threatened abuse. Sexual abuse in childhood is not specific to a particular diagnosis. Walker and colleagues (1988) reported that 64 percent of patients with chronic pelvic pain had a history of sexual abuse, whereas 23 percent of a control group had comparable experiences; many patients with pelvic pain also had symptoms of a type associated with depressive and somatic complaints. The frequency of childhood deprivation and other abuse in current patients with symptoms related to hysteria has been recognized from some time in discussions of hospital addiction and simulated illness (Merskey 1979). As investigators have tended to emphasize sexual abuse as a criterion for the diagnosis of MPD, it is hardly surprising that the phenomenon has increased in their sample, but the definition of the diagnosis in terms of sexual abuse cannot serve as a proof of the independent existence of the condition.

More recently, larger series of cases have been published and the journal *Dissociation* (June 1989) has dealt specifically with the question of iatrogenesis. Several arguments are offered to deny the occurrence, or importance, of iatrogenesis. Among them, Ross and colleagues (1989) claim that iatrogenic production of MPD by specialists in dissociation has not been reported in the literature. The analysis here of the most prominent cases shows otherwise. The same authors also suggest that because they have found no important demographic differences between the MPD patients of psychiatrists with many cases and psychiatrists with few cases, this means that those with many cases are not producing them differentially. This argument is not a proof of validity, only consistency in selection. Likewise, reliability of diagnosis (Ross 1989) is not proof of validity. Kluft (1989) mentions the worsening of MPD by inept therapy. Yet the authors of the relevant section of *DSM-III-R* allow up to 100 alternate personalities in a case, and Kluft (1982) has himself reported nineteen patients with eleven to thirty personalities and two with more than thirty personalities.

Recent cases are not appropriate subject matter to explore the question of suggestion, since they have all been open to it in developed countries. Some cases recently reported from India also indicate the influence of the cinema in producing rather facile fugue states (Adityanjee et al. 1989). Instead, we should require that early cases, and any late cases that might be thought to have escaped the pervasive influence of the media, or iatrogenesis, should show spontaneous origin without any reasonable doubt.

It is always open, of course, to any particular investigator to say, "My patient had no training, arose naturally, and was not prepared by me." Fortunately, or otherwise, that position has been undermined by widespread knowledge of the concept. If the case were to be provided, it should have been done with Eve at the latest, and it was not. The concept of MPD should be seen now as, at best, a byway in the history of ideas.

ILL-EFFECTS OF THE DIAGNOSIS

Many of the patients have had awful experiences, with an extensive history of child abuse, and they need attention and treatment, but the diagnosis of MPD may not give the best treatment.

The diagnosis of MPD need not exclude other diagnoses, but it is likely to distract attention away from them. Alcoholism or depression may be better treated by directing attention to the problems with drink or using nonaddictive medication. The diagnosis of MPD (or production of it) may hinder the most appropriate action and damage treatment. Chodoff (1987) writes that in two cases demonstrated on videotape, he was struck by the bolstering of defenses—with a stultifying effect on psychotherapeutic progress—exerted by concentration on the characteristics of the individual personalities rather than the patient's underlying conflicts. Whether the patient needs management of social relationships, the resolution of conflicts in psychotherapy, the recognition of physical illness, or the prescription of medication, the process of treatment will not be helped by extraneous diagnoses.

Another ill effect also exists. The value and good sense of psychiatry become suspect as wonders multiply.

Acknowledgment: Ms. Mai Why provided extensive biographical help.

REFERENCES

Adityanjee, Raju, G. S. P., and Khandelwal, S. K. (1989). Current status of multiple personality disorder in India. *American Journal of Psychiatry* 146:1607–1610.

Aldridge-Morris, R. (1989). *Multiple Personality. An Exercise in Deception.* London: Lawrence Erlbaum.

Allison, R., and Schwarz, T. (1980). *Minds in Many Pieces.* New York: Rawson Wade.

Diagnostic and Statistical Manual of Mental Disorders (1987). 3rd ed., rev. Washington, DC: American Psychiatric Association.

Azam, E. E. (1876). Amnésie périodique, ou doublement de la vie. *Revue Scientifique,* deuxième série, 10:481–489.

———— (1887). *Hypnotisme, Double Conscience, et Altérations de la Pérsonnalité.* Paris: Bailliere.

———— (1892). Double consciousness. In *A Dictionary of Psychological Medicine,* vol. 1, ed. D. Hack Tuke, pp. 401–406. London: Churchill.

Binet, A. (1891). *Alterations of Personality,* ed. D. N. Robinson, 1977, p. 146. Georgetown University Publications of America.

Bliss, E. L., and Jeppsen, E. A. (1985). Prevalence of multiple personality disorder among in-patients and out-patients. *American Journal of Psychiatry* 142:250–251.

Boor, M. (1982). The multiple personality epidemic. Additional cases and references regarding diagnosis, etiology, dynamics, and treatment. *Journal of Nervous and Mental Disease* 170:302–304.

Bourru and Burot (1885). De la multiplicité des états de conscience. *Revue Philosophique* 20:411–416.

Camuset, L. (1882). Un cas de doublement de la personnalité. *Annales Medico-Psychologiques* 7:75–86.

Carlson, E. T. (1981). The history of multiple personality in the United States: I. The beginnings. *American Journal of Psychiatry* 138:666–668.

_____ (1984). The history of multiple personality in the United States: Mary Reynolds and her subsequent reputation. *Bulletin of the History of Medicine* 58:72–82.

Chodoff, R. (1987). Multiple personality disorder. *American Journal of Psychiatry* 14:124.

Committee on Sexual Offences against Children and Youth. (1984). *Report.* Ottawa, Canada: Ministry of Supply and Services.

Congdon, M. H., Hain, J., and Stevenson, I. (1961). A case of multiple personality illustrating the transition from role-playing. *Journal of Nervous and Mental Disease* 132:497–504.

Coons, P. (1984). The differential diagnosis of multiple personality. *Psychiatric Clinics of North American* 7:51–67.

Cory, C. E. (1919). A divided self. *Journal of Abnormal Psychology* 14:281–291.

Coupland, W. C. (1892). Philosophy of mind. In *A Dictionary of Psychological Medicine*, vol. 1, ed. D. Hack Tuke, pp. 27–49. London: Churchill.

Daily, A. H. (1894). *Mollie Fancher. The Brooklyn Enigma.* New York: Mary J. Fancher.

Daniels, A. (1990). *Daily Telegraph* November 13, p. 17.

Despine, Pere. (1834). *De l'emploi de magnétisme animal et des eaux minérales dans le traitement des maladies nerveuses, suivi d'une observation très curieuse de guerison de névropathie.* Paris: Germer, Bailliere.

Ellenberger, H. (1970). *The Discovery of the Unconscious.* New York: Basic Books.

Fahy, T. A. (1988). The diagnosis of multiple personality disorder. A critical review. *British Journal of Psychiatry* 153:597–606.

Fahy, T. A., Abas, M., and Brown, J. C. (1989). Multiple personality. A symptom of psychiatric disorder. *British Journal of Psychiatry* 154:99–101.

Franz, S. I. (1933). *Persons One and Three. A Study in Multiple Personalities.* New York: McGraw-Hill.

Gmelin, E. (1791). *Materialen für die Anthropologie I.* Tübingen: Cotta.

Goddard, H. H. (1926). A case of dual personality. *Journal of Abnormal and Social Psychology* 21:170–191.

_____ (1927). *Two Souls in One Body. A Case of Dual Personality.* New York: Dodd, Mead & Co.

Goetz, C. G. (1987). *Charcot the Clinician. The Tuesday Lessons.* New York: Raven.

Greaves, G. B. (1980). Multiple personality 165 years after Mary Reynolds. *Journal of Nervous and Mental Disease* 168:577–596.

Hacking, I. (1986). The invention of split personalities. In *Human Nature and National Knowledge*, ed. A. Donagan, A. N. Petrovich, Jr., and M. V. Wedin, pp. 63–85. Dordrecht: Reidel.

_____ (1991). Two souls in one body. *Clinical Enquiry* 17:838–867.

Hart, B. (1912). A case of double personality. *Journal of Mental Science* 58:236–243.

Hawksworth, H., and Schwarz, T. (1977). *The Five of Me.* Chicago: Henry Regnery.

Hilgard, E. R. (1988). Professional skepticism about multiple personality. *Journal of Nervous and Mental Disease* 176:532.

Hodgson, R. (1891). A case of double consciousness. *Proceedings of Social Psychical Research* 7:221–257.

Horton, P., and Miller, D. (1972). The etiology of multiple personality. *Comprehensive Psychiatry* 13:151–159.

James, W. (1890). *Principles of Psychology*, vol. 1. New York: Henry Holt.

Janet, J. (1888). L'hystérie et l'hypnotisme d'après la théorie de la double personnalité. *Révue Scientifique* 41:616–623.

Janet, P. (1887). L'anesthésie systematisée. *Révue Philosophique* 23:449–472.

_____ (1888). Les actes inconscients et la mémoire. *Revue Philosophique* 25:238–279.

_____ (1889). *L'Automatisme Psychologique.* Paris: Alcan.

_____ (1907). *The Major Syndromes of Hysteria.* New York: MacMillan.

_____ (1911). *L'Etat Mental des Hystériques.* Paris: Alcan.

—— (1913). *L'Automatisme Psychologique*, 7th ed. Paris: Alcan.

Keyes, D. (1981). *The Minds of Billy Milligan*. New York: Random House.

Kluft, R. P. (1982). Varieties of hypnotic intervention in the treatment of multiple personality. *American Journal of Clinical Hypnosis* 24:230–240.

—— (1989). Iatrogenic creation of new alter personalities. *Dissociation* 2:83–91.

Lewis, A. J. (1953). Hysterical dissociation in dementia paralytica. *Monatschrift für Psychiatrie und Neurologie* 125:589–604.

Lipton, S. (1943). Dissociated personality: a case report. *Psychiatry Quarterly* 17:45–56.

Ljungberg, L. (1957). Hysteria. *Acta Psychiatrica Scandinavica* (suppl. 112).

Mayer-Gross, W., Slater, E. T. O., and Roth, M. (1954). *Clinical Psychiatry*. London: Cassell.

—— (1977). *Clinical Psychiatry*, 3rd ed. London: Bailliere, Tindall.

Mayo, T. (1845). Case of double consciousness. *London Medical Gazette, New Series*, 1:1202–1203.

McDougall, W. (1948). *An Outline of Abnormal Psychology*, 6th ed. London: Methuen.

McKellar, P. (1979). *Mindsplit*. London: Dent.

Merskey, H. (1979). *The Analysis of Hysteria*. London: Bailliere, Tindall.

—— (1986). A variable meaning for the concept of disease. *Journal of Medicine and Philosphy* 11:215–232.

Merskey, H., and Buhrich, N. A. (1975). Hysteria and organic brain disease. *British Journal of Medical Psychology* 48:359–366.

Mitchell, S. L. (1816). A double consciousness, or a duality of person in the same individual. *Medical Repository (New Series)* 3:185–186.

Mitchell, S. W. (1888). Mary Reynolds: a case of double consciousness. *Transactions of the College of Physicians, Philadelphia* 10:366–389.

Myers, A. T. (1886). The life-history of a case of double or multiple personality. *Journal of Mental Science* 31:596–605.

Myers, W. H. F. (1903). *Human Personality and Its Survival of Bodily Death*, vol. 1. London: Longmans Green.

Owen, A. R. G. (1971). *Hysteria, Hypnosis and Healing: The Work of J. M. Charcot*. London: Dennis Dobson.

Peters, C., and Schwarz, T. (1978). *Tell Me Who I Am Before I Die*. New York: Rawson.

Plumer, W. S. (1860). Mary Reynolds: a case of double consciousness. *Harper's Magazine* 20:807–812.

Prince, M. (1900). *The Problem of Multiple Personality*. Paris: International Congress of Psychology.

—— (1908). *The Dissociation of Personality*, 2nd ed. London: Longmans Green.

Prince, W. F. (1916). The Doris case of quintuple personality. *Journal of Abnormal Psychology*:73–122.

Proust, A. (1890). Automatisme ambulatoire chez un hystérique. *Révue de l'Hypnotisme, Psychologie et Physiologie* 4:267–269.

Putnam, F. W. (1989). *Diagnosis and Treatment of Multiple Personality Disorder*. London: Guilford.

Putnam, F. W., Guroff, J. J., Silberman, E. K., et al. (1986). The clinical phenomenology of multiple personality disorder: review of 100 recent cases. *Journal of Clinical Psychiatry* 47:285–293.

Richet, C. (1883). La personnalité et la mémoire dans le somnambulisme. *Revue Philosophique* 15:225–2442.

Rochas de, A. (1887). Hypnotisme et changement de personnalité. *Revue Philosophique* 5:330–333.

Ross, C. A. (1987). Inpatient treatment of multiple personality disorder. *Canadian Journal of Psychiatry* 32:779–781.

_____ (1989). *Multiple Personality*. New York: Wiley.

Ross, C. A., Norton, G. R., and Fraser, G. A. (1989). Evidence against the iatrogenesis of multiple personality disorder. *Dissociation* 2:61–65.

Ross, C. A., Miller, S. D., Reager, P., et al. (1990). Structured interview data on 102 cases of multiple personality disorder from four centers. *American Journal of Psychiatry* 147:596–601.

Schreiber, F. R. (1973). *Sybil*. Chicago: Henry Regnery.

Sidis, B., and Goodhart, S. P. (1904). *Multiple Personality*. Reprint. New York: Greenwood.

Sim, M. (1981). *Guide to Psychiatry*. Edinburgh: Churchill Livingstone.

Simpson, M. A. (1989). Multiple personality disorder. *British Journal of Psychiatry* 155:565.

Sizemore, C. C., and Pittillo, E. S. (1977). *I'm Eve*. New York: Doubleday.

Skae, D. (1845). Case of intermittent mental disorder of the tertian type with double consciousness. *Northern Journal of Medicine* 4:10–19.

Slater, E. (1965). Diagnosis of "hysteria." *British Medical Journal* 1:1395–1399.

Spanos, N. P., Weekes, J. R., Menary, E., et al. (1986). Hypnotic interview and age regression procedures in the elicitation of multiple personality symptoms: a simulation study. *Psychiatry* 49:298.

Spencer, H. (1855). *The Principles of Psychology*, 3rd ed. London: University Tutorial Press.

Stengel, E. (1941). On the aetiology of fugue states. *Journal of Mental Science* 87:572–599.

Stout, G. F. (1919). *Manual of Psychology*, (3rd Edition). London: University Tutorial Press.

Sutcliffe, J. P., and Jones, J. (1962). Personal identity, multiple personality and hypnosis. *International Journal of Clinical Experimental Hypnosis* 10:231–269.

Takahashi, Y. (1990). Is multiple personality disorder really rare in Japan? *Dissociation* 3:57–59.

Taylor, W. S., and Martin, M. F. (1944). Multiple personality. *Journal of Abnormal Social Psychology* 39:281–330.

Thigpen, C. H. (1984). On the incidence of multiple personality: a brief communication. *International Journal of Clinical Experimental Hypnosis* 32:63–66.

Thigpen, C. H., and Cleckley, H. M. (1954). A case of multiple personality. *Journal of Abnormal Social Psychology* 9:135–151.

_____ (1957). *The Three Faces of Eve*. New York: McGraw-Hill.

Tourette, Gilles de la (1887). *L'hypnotisme et les états analogues au point de vue medico-legal*. Paris: Pion, Nourrit.

Victor, G. (1975). Sybil: grande hystérie ou folie à deux? *American Journal of Psychiatry* 132:202.

Walker, E., Katon, W., Harrop-Griffiths, J., et al. (1988). Relationship of chronic pelvic pain to psychiatric diagnoses and childhood sexual abuse. *American Journal of Psychiatry* 145:75–80.

2

Correspondence:
Reactions and Replies

Editor's Note: The following correspondence responding to Dr. Merskey's article appeared in several sections of the British Journal of Psychiatry. *Permission to publish this material has been generously granted by the BJP and the individual authors. Several authors provided additional material, which is noted in the text.*

BRITISH JOURNAL OF PSYCHIATRY (1992)
161:268–284.

Sir: I am angered by Merskey's article, "Manufacture of Multiple Personality Disorder" (*BJP* March 1992 160:327–340), just as I was by Fahy's review on the same subject (BJP September 1988 153:597–606). I did my psychiatric training in Galway in the early 1980s and immigrated to Canada in 1986. At that time I was also very sceptical of the diagnosis of multiple personality disorder (MPD) but that has changed in my last six years of practice; through diagnosing and treating people with MPD and other sequelae of sexual abuse, and attending conferences on the subject, I now have no doubts that such an illness exists.

Recognizing that diagnosis is important, sometimes we forget that there can be different levels of illness within the one diagnosis. For example, if somebody fractures a leg, it can be a simple fracture, compound fracture, clean fracture, or fragmented fracture. One of these fractures needs more treatment or longer treatment than the others. Why can psychiatrists not recognize that just because somebody has a certain diagnosis, this does not preclude that the patient cannot have other illnesses concurrent with their primary diagnosis. Instead of arguing over the existence of multiple personality disorder or dissociation, we should recognize that dissociation exists in different degrees and continue to treat the victim, who is traumatized, rather than leave [him or her] without treatment while we argue over the validity of the diagnosis.

Dissociative Identity Disorder seems to be a compartmentalization of abuses at different points in a person's life. By accessing these memories we break down the walls of these compartments, thus opening them up into each other, and we do this through psychotherapy, writing, collages, and art work. As each wall is removed, we work through the blocked feelings and emotions and we allow that patient to start functioning as a unit again. Some of my patients talk through one of their components at all times and others express feelings, emotions, and memories through individual components. It is imperative that we do not lose sight of the fact that it is one person and one body, and our objective is to help that person to function as a unit again.

Depending on the trauma suffered, some patients are more compartmentalized than others. I do not see this as unique because I believe that all of us have compartments and blocked memories. If accessed through regression, hypnosis, or a life-event trigger, we react with whatever emotion of coping mechanism that was learned when that situation was experienced initially.

Dr. Merskey comments on the pattern of growth of the diagnosis of MPD in recent years. Many of the patients who have been suffering for years from multiple personality disorder have previously been diagnosed as schizophrenic because they hear voices in their head. As the psychiatric knowledge has increased, the emerging pattern of their current life situation and their past history does not fit that of a diagnosis of schizophrenia. In my opinion, this is one of the reasons we have an increase in the diagnosis of multiple personality disorder. This is very similar to the increase in the diagnosis of manic-depressive psychosis a number of years ago. Once the psychiatric knowledge in that field increased, many people were rediagnosed from schizophrenia to manic-depressive disorder. The same controversy has not emerged within the psychiatric literature over this reclassification as it has with the diagnoses of multiple personality disorder. I wonder if this is because many psychiatrists are unable to look at the dynamics associated with the diagnosis of MPD and the consequences of abuse.

One of the other difficulties for some psychiatrists is that many of the patients fitting into this category are from the upper social class and it is a painful reality to come to terms with the fact that such severe abuse is occurring within our own stratum of society.

I am also concerned that many of the people who talk about dealing with issues of abuse are female feminists. These therapists are often as rigid as the therapists who refuse to recognize the existence of dissociation.

Psychiatrists and mental health professionals should be aware that many males in our population are equally traumatized. Males have more difficulty recognizing the trauma, coming forward, and expressing their feelings.

I do not use hypnosis in diagnosing or treating this or any other condition, nor would I even think of suggesting this diagnosis at the initial interviews. I have found that patients are so ashamed of their symptoms, of their feelings, of hearing voices in their head, of their loss of memory, and of feeling that they are a freak or are going crazy, that they think I will not continue to treat them if they disclose these phenomena. I have found that patients are often in treatment for many months to years, testing and learning to trust me before they are willing to share their secrets and the diagnosis of MPD is finally made. In my opinion, it is not the diagnosis that we treat but the patient as a whole. The diagnosis should not change our method of treatment. The treatment of choice is in-depth psychotherapy to explore the abusive background, and thus help patients to free themselves and take control of their own lives.

Maeve Lawler-Fahy
Ontario, Canada

Sir: Merskey writes about the production of multiple personality disorder. As a fellow Canadian psychiatrist I feel compelled to write and advocate an entirely contrary position, one that is shared by the majority of psychiatrists of my personal experience. Writing this letter is especially important as it is my impression, based on contacts with British colleagues, that they are not yet totally familiar with MPD. There may be a large populations with MPD in Britain, unrecognized and untreated. The bias of the articles that appear in the *Journal* about MPD would seem to support this.

My first acquaintance with a patient subsequently diagnosed as MPD was during my first days as a psychiatrist resident on a long-term rehabilitation unit. There was absolutely no experience on this unit, either by the consultant psychiatrist or the staff, with the diagnosis. During my undergraduate medical training (in Britain in the 1960s) MPD had never been mentioned. Neither the patient or myself had seen the movie *Eve* or read *Sybil*. I had four months of accumulating historical data and clinical observations that did not fit the many psychiatric diagnoses that had been made, before I started learning about dissociative disorder.

I found my patient totally consistent with the descriptions appearing in the literature, and continued to parallel descriptions in the writings and workshops that have blossomed over the past six years. How could I have induced a classic case when I had absolutely no notion of what that might mean? I believe Dr. Merskey is correct when he writes "MPD offers a mode of separating, splitting and isolating particular subjective problems," but I believe that the etiology is in the horrific childhood experiences of these patients, not in [their] response to suggestions by a therapist. The extensive clinical experience with MPD in childhood supports this.

I cannot follow the logic of the argument that to diagnose MPD may hinder the most appropriate treatment. Surely accurate diagnosis in any illness has always been the first step in management! MPD is a treatable condition with an optimistic prognosis if recognized and managed appropriately. The emphasis should be on better preparing psychiatrists to be familiar with treatment options.

Dr. Merskey may fear that he may be so distracted by the exciting diagnosis that he will forget basic principles of biopsychosocial management and neglect to treat coexisting conditions. It is not my experience that those of us who are comfortable working with MPD patients do this. We do indeed treat the whole patient.

Ann Chande
Ontario, Canada

Editor's Note: The following additional comments were contributed by Dr. Chande for this book.

It seems to me that you become a believer in MPD when you treat your first case. Then the absolute consistency of the facial appearance, voice, mannerisms, posture, personal history, coping style, interpersonal relatedness, handwriting, and special talents of each discrete personality state convinces you that there really is within one single person apparently separate and autonomous personality states exchanging control. There have been a number of occasions in my personal experiences with patients when it seemed that there was a discrepancy in the history as I remembered it and as it was represented in the therapy session. When I would later check back in my notes, the patient was always accurate, a consistency that would be impossible to maintain if it was not based on a solid enduring personality stature. A totally consistent history of each individual alter dating back to childhood or infancy unfolds gradually.

I worked with a patient for a number of months as a first-year psychiatric resident, having no knowledge of MPD myself; the patient had an entirely different diagnosis. Even after it was recognized that this patient had MPD, the information readily available on that disorder was limited. I met and worked with helper alters, protective alters, child alters, alters who were keepers of the unendurable feelings, and the inner-self helper, before I learned that what I was discovering with this patient was totally consistent with that which the leaders in the field were describing in books, articles, and workshops. It is impossible for me to reconcile my personal reality and experience with Dr. Merskey's view that this is an iatrogenic disorder created by the expectations of the patient and therapist.

Also, in talking to families and friends of patients recently diagnosed with MPD, it is obvious that these close contacts have been recognizing the switches for a long time and that the diagnosis finally provides a plausible explanation for the turmoil and confusion that the personality exchanges have been producing. There are many psychiatrists working with children with a diagnosis of MPD. Dr. Merskey does not give an explanation for how he thinks it could be induced, shaped, and scripted in this population.

It is hard to imagine what secondary advantages there could be for either the therapist or the patient in the iatrogenic creation of MPD. In my mind there is nothing glamorous or titillating about the diagnosis. Rather it is an indication that the patient has creatively used dissociation as a child to survive horrendous and prolonged victimization, usually involving physical, mental, and sexual abuse. The therapist knows that a major focus in therapy will be to facilitate the recovery and abreaction by the patients of the brutal horrors of their early life. This is an extremely painful process both for the patient and for the therapist alike. It is difficult to remain dispassionate in the presence of someone who has been severely and inhumanly violated. It may be that denial of MPD is a resistance by the therapist to acknowledging the extent to which our cruel society is savaging our children.

Uncomfortable feelings of horror, grief, rage, and helplessness are generated in the presence of a victim, and perhaps resonate with known or unknown earlier abuse experiences of our own. Questioning the validity of MPD is a way to avoid, disbelieve, deny, and retreat from such patients and to rationalize withdrawing from the challenge of the extremely difficult and painful therapy involved with helping the patients work through their dissociated abuse histories.

By not being accurately diagnosed for MPD, the patient risks being misdiagnosed with schizophrenia, schizoaffective disorder, bipolar disorder, or borderline personality disorder, and then getting inappropriately treated with medication or behaviorial restrictions and suffering further abuses in the psychiatric system. These wrong diagnoses then deny the patient the opportunity for an uncovering psychotherapy that would access and abreact their horrendous histories, repressed feelings, and tissue memories. The process of this type of psychotherapy facilitates internal understanding and leads to the breakdown of the amnestic barriers and ultimately to integration and unification of the multiple personality system. MPD is a hopeful diagnosis of a treatable condition and it is a privilege to be a witness, as a therapist, to this healing journey, especially with a patient who was chronically disabled and who becomes totally functional.

Of course, I am not suggesting that there might not be a concurrent diagnosis such as depression, anxiety, personality disorder, substance abuse, medical illness, and so forth, that needs to be a focus of management. One treats a person, not a diagnosis. Other issues such as social support, shelter, and current relationships may need attention or referral. I deeply resent Dr. Merskey's closing remarks in his article when he suggests that those of us (unlike him) who are treating patients with MPD are likely to be distracted by the diagnosis and forget the principles of a comprehensive biopsychosocial approach.

Psychiatrists with their comprehensive training are very well suited to be able to integrate all aspects of treatment. It is our responsibility to take a leadership role. As we waste our energy and time quibbling about whether or not MPD is manufactured or real, other disciplines—some very well trained and competent, but others, dangerously incompetent—are setting up treatment centers and programs and taking leadership away from us.

The need for treatment is outstripping the resources available to the patients. My challenge to Dr. Merskey is to devote an equal investment of effort to study live patients (such as those on Dr. Ross's unit) as he has done researching those long dead. He can acquire the expertise in diagnosis and treatment that has evaded him to this point in his professional career. Then he can join the ever-growing body of psychiatrists who are working with this challenging but extremely courageous and inspiring group of people. If we meet with an open, humble, and flexible attitude we will learn much from each other.

DR. MERSKEY REPLIES

Dr. Chande indicates that the majority of Canadian psychiatrists of her acquaintance accept the concept of multiple personality disorder (MPD). My experience differs and extends to Canadian, British, United States, and Australian psychiatrists, and the majority with whom I have discussed the issue are skeptical of the validity of the disorder. Orne and Bauer-Manley (1991) observe polarization between ". . . a relatively small group of therapists . . . reporting large numbers of cases (increasingly with large numbers of 'personalities' in each case) and other who believe that if MPD occurs spontaneously at all, it does so extremely rarely." We do not know the proportions of support for this diagnosis at the present time, but it is controversial, a point made in the discussion of it in ICD-10. I accept that Dr. Chande did not induce her "classic case," but the risk of her patient being influenced by the media is not limited to seeing the two films in question, and prior contacts may also have been relevant.

The diagnosis of MPD is not always a distraction from treating other conditions. However, in practice that is how Chodoff (1987) has observed it to work and that is my observation and that of my colleagues in four cases that we have prepared for publication. These are the first four alleged cases that we have seen to date. Their treatment was not helped by a diagnosis of MPD, and their management would have been better if the basic principles of biopsychosocial management had been employed in their cases.

Dr. Chande is sweeping in suggesting that if the logic of my argument is accepted, every medical and psychiatric diagnosis is suspect. Some diagnoses, like schizophrenia, have increasing amounts of corroborative physical and prognostic evidence, and we should also look at the striking success of appropriate treatments in conditions like depressive disorders and anxiety states. Comparable results do not appear to be obtainable with the diagnosis of multiple personality disorder as a result of treatments directed to that diagnosis. There are other diagnoses which I agree could be suspect, including hysterical symptoms mimicking organic disease in patients who have seen cases of physical disorder. (Charcot's cases of hysteria and the history of shell shock in the First World War provide excellent examples.) However, I doubt if many who use the diagnoses of schizophrenia, endogenous depression, and obsessional neurosis, among others, will see much resemblance between these conditions and those where suggestion has been so prominent.

I wish to reiterate that many of the patients who are not diagnosed as having multiple personality disorder appear to have substantial problems in their early lives and current adjustment, and in their personalities. In-depth psychotherapy may well help them, but the benefits of producing and reuniting disparate personalities have not been demonstrated.

Dr. Fahy surmised that I felt this article would be more acceptable to British than to North American psychiatrists. She is right, but no doubt she is aware of the high standing of the *British Journal of Psychiatry*, which is widely read in North America.

I would like to take the opportunity to clarify a point in my article. The clarification has to do with *The Three Faces of Eve*. I wrote that there was an important difference between the psychiatrist's account and the patient's account in the presentation of her maiden name, saying that the point was not evident in the psychiatrist's account. That is correct, but the fact that the patient reverted to her maiden name was not concealed by Thigpen and Cleckley (1957). However, they only report it a page later in parentheses and do not discuss the choice of name there, so that the importance of this item is lost in their text.

I did not always disbelieve in MPD. I thought it might occur as a rare event. The astonishing growth of improbable cases prompted me to look more closely at the phenomenon, and it was only then that I came to the conclusion that there was no veridical evidence that would be adequate to support the diagnosis, and the mere spread of enthusiasm for it had itself served to make it impossible to prove that it existed. Such a diagnosis deserves to be characterized by the term *doxogenic disease* which has been used until not long ago (Dorland 1957) to characterize illnesses due to the patients' own mental conceptions (from *doxa*, meaning opinion, and *genes*, to produce). In this case the opinions are largely received as a result of external influences which are medical, journalistic, literary, broadcast, and theatrical.

H. Merskey
Ontario, Canada

REFERENCES

Chodoff, P. (1987). Multiple personality disorder. *American Journal of Psychiatry* 144:124.
Dorland. (1957). *Dorland's Illustrated Medical Dictionary*, 23rd ed. Philadelphia: W. B. Saunders.
Orne, M. T., and Bauer-Manley, N. K. (1991). Disorders of self: myths, metaphors, and the demand characteristics of treatment. In *The Self: Interdisciplinary Approaches*, ed. J. Strauss and G. R. Goethals, pp. 93–106. New York: Springer-Verlag.
Thigpen, C. H., and Cleckley, H. M. (1957). *The Three Faces of Eve*. New York: McGraw Hill.

ADDITIONAL CORRESPONDENCE: BRITISH JOURNAL OF PSYCHIATRY (1992) 161:415–429.

Sir: We read with interest the article by Merskey (*Journal* [March 1992] 160:327–340), in which he examined a number of cases of multiple personality disorder (MPD) from the earlier literature in order to determine whether there is any evidence that MPD was ever a spontaneous phenomenon.

Since human behavior can be understood if we have sufficient informa-tion about a person's development—his biological, psychological, and sociological history—(Ewalt et al. 1957) we would direct attention toward inheritance of ancestral beliefs in the etiology of psychopathology. In particular, we would underline the concept of soul in an anthropological context.

Frazer (1922) reports a number of races in which there was a belief that several souls were harbored in the same body. For example, he reports that the Caribbeans believed that there is a soul in the head, another in the heart, and others in all the points in which there is an arterial pulse. The Indian Hidatsa interpreted the phenomenon of agony, supposing that man has four souls that leave the body in succession. The Daiachi of Borneo and the Malesian believed that every man has seven souls and the Alfur of Minahassa (Celebes) believed that there are three souls. The Indians of Laos supposed that the body is the seat of thirty souls.

The shamanic trance may be considered as a primitive form of hypnosis. It is noteworthy that in individuals suffering from MPD, nightmares are prominent, along with terrifying hypnagogic and hypnopompic hallucina-tions. These phenomena are similar to the terrifying visions that sometimes appear in the shamanic trance.

Evidently, these primitive beliefs, and subsequently the religious be-liefs, show evocative similarities with MPD, and suggest the presence of univocal elements of thought with different types of behavior, with respect to different times and places.

We conclude with two remarks. First, since the developmental history of our species casts an unmistakable shadow on our mental lives, the comprehension of psychopathological behavior may be facilitated by an ethnological approach. Second, in a multicultural Europe, the transcultural approach to clinical problems is more and more necessary (Cox 1991).

Paolo Novello and Alberto Primavera
Department of Neurology
University of Genoa, Italy

REFERENCES

Cox, J. L. (1991). Transcultural psychiatry. *British Journal of Psychiatry* 158:579–582.
Ewalt, J. J. B., Strecker, E. A., and Erbaugh, F. G., eds. (1957). The development of a normal personality. In *Practical Clinical Psychiatry*, 8th ed., p. 3. New York: McGraw Hill.
Frazer, J. G. (1922). *The Golden Bough. A Study in Magic and Religion*, pp. 799–801. London: Macmillan.

Sir: The recent questions and concerns raised in the *Journal* about the "unprecedented numbers" of cases of multiple personality disorder (MPD) diagnosed in North America require a response.

Although the diagnosis of MPD has received attention and support in Europe and Latin American, there is a strong resistance in Britain to accepting this conditions. There it is argued that MPD is: (a) a misdiagnosis of organic conditions or bipolar illness, or (b) created by iatrogenic suggestion, or (c) induced in suggestible patients by popularized accounts in the media.

The arguments against the validity of MPD made thus far in the *Journal* rely on examination of historical or dramatized accounts of the condition and inexplicably fail to examine the large number of modern scientific studies published in reputable journals. These increasingly sophisticated studies, using standardized measures and structured diagnostic interviews available to all interested professionals, have documented the existence of a complex psychiatric syndrome that is frequently misdiagnosed. The growing professional acceptance of MPD in North America is a response to these scientific studies and not to the reports in the mass media, which are largely a by-product of the resurgence in professional interest.

The arguments made in the *Journal* are specious in that they do not account for why the particular symptom of having two or more alter personality states should be so tractable to suggestion or contamination effects. The other symptoms expressed by MPD patients are taken at face value—as are those of most psychiatric patients. Why should asking a patient if he has ever felt as if there were another part or side to him be more likely to induce an alter personality than, for example, creating hallucinations or ruminations by inquiring if he has ever heard voices talking to him when no one else was present or had thoughts that occurred over and over again that he could not get out of his head? Why should one symptom be suggestible and another not?

The argument that MPD is produced by merely reading *Sybil* or seeing the movie *The Three Faces of Eve* is likewise flawed. A number of dramatic psychiatric disorders, such as anorexia nervosa, bulimia nervosa, obsessive-compulsive disorder, and bipolar illness, are daily topics in books, magazines, newspapers, films, radio, and television. Are all of these conditions produced by suggestions from the mass media? Of course not! Why is MPD singled out as being uniquely susceptible to media contamination compared with other psychiatric disorders? Arguments based on postulated suggestions and contamination effects should be tabled until critics can convincingly demonstrate a specificity of suggestion and contamination for alter personality states and MPD compared with other psychiatric symptoms and disorders.

British critics of MPD frequently assert that these cases are not seen in England. Patients meeting *DSM-III* criteria for MPD have been described in the *Journal*—although the authors chose to give them other diagnostic labels (Fahy et al. 1989, Bruce-Jones and Coid 1992). Ian Hacking has documented that early historical cases fitting the MPD template were described in Britain well before the first French cases were reported toward the end of the nineteenth century (Hacking 1991). MPD, as defined by *DSM-III/DSM-III-R* criteria, does indeed exist in Britain.

The real question is why British academic psychiatry chooses to ignore the peculiar disturbance in identity characteristic of these patients. This is the critical difference between the British and North American positions. North American interest in MPD does not represent an infatuation with *DSM-III-R* diagnosis per se. Rather, it reflects a clinical belief that direct interaction with the alter personality states provides a more effective therapeutic approach to certain symptoms. A reading of the North American clinical literature—as opposed to the sensationalized popular press accounts—quickly demonstrates that reputable clinicians do not believe that the alter personalities represent distinct people. The North American model advocates a therapeutic approach that balances interventions made with the person as a whole with interventions directed toward specific alter personality states associated with pathological behavior.

Whether the North American model is more therapeutic than the British model remains an open question for the present. Preliminary reports do suggest efficacy for the North American approach compared with prior non-MPD treatment of these patients. If the North American model of MPD were merely a fad and conferred no therapeutic advantages it would have melted away by now and have been replaced by another faddish diagnostic label. The continuing increase in the numbers of MPD cases reflects our clinical experience that this model, and the therapeutic interventions associated with it represent an effective treatment approach to a very difficult group of patients. Future debate should focus on the crucial question of therapeutic efficacy rather than on diagnostic labels. It is what we can do to help our patients and not what we call them that is important.

Frank W. Putnam
National Institute of Mental Health, Bethesda, MD

REFERENCES

Bruce-Jones, W., and Coid, J. (1992). Identity diffusion presenting as multiple personality disorder in a female psychopath. *British Journal of Psychiatry* 160:541–544.

Fahy, T. A., Abas, M., and Brown, J. C. (1989). Multiple personality. *British Journal of Psychiatry* 154:99–101.
Hacking, I. (1991). Double consciousness in Britain 1815–1875. *Dissociation* 4:134–146.

Sir: Dr. Merskey argues that being diagnosed as having MPD would be better managed with the "view that certain other diagnoses are acceptable alternatives: mania, certain depressive illnesses, schizophrenia, obsessional neuroses . . ." Each of these alternatives is a primary diagnosis according to both *ICD-9* and *DSM-III-R*, and these must *all* be diagnosed if also present and must be accounted for in the treatment plan. But to selectively leave out the dissociative symptoms would be to ignore another primary *ICD-9* and *DSM-III-R* diagnosis, that of MPD. This would lead to absolutely no management of the trauma leading to the dissociation (be it sexual abuse or any other overwhelming trauma). None of his alternative diagnoses offers any specific therapy for the abuses that lead to MPD.

Dr. Merskey argues that to be able to fully understand MPD he must study cases unadulterated by the mass media. To do this he refers to various cases in the last century as well as the turn of this century. Unfortunately, he harks back to a time when no theories had been agreed upon as to what exactly constituted MPD. He quotes cases from such sources as the well-respected *Discovery of the Unconscious* by Henri Ellenberger (1970).

Dr. Merskey perhaps might have seriously reconsidered his approach to this paper had he heeded Ellenberger's caveat: "One should be cautious in the study of old case histories, which have not always been recorded with the care one would wish for today" (p. 134).

As the arguments come closer to our own years, it is suggested that Eve (Thigpen and Cleckley 1957) has been a model for all subsequent MPD cases. Such a whimsical statement is hardly worthy of mention in a scientific journal. It should be taken into account that Thigpen and Cleckley have admitted only to treating this one case of MPD. Even then they did not adequately understand the full complexity of Eve's dissociation. On the basis of the treatment of one patient, they can hardly be considered to be experts on MPD management or diagnosis.

Dr. Merskey then mentions the work of Dr. Nicholas Spanos. Dr. Spanos's case study of college students who successfully feigned MPD symptoms is frequently quoted, and unfortunately is just as often misinterpreted as evidence against the reality of MPD. Merskey writes that the experiment utilized procedures employed routinely to diagnose MPD. This is not true. The procedures employed were based on a single case of a forensic interrogation of a murderer (Kenneth Bianchi) who claimed to be suffering from MPD. There was nothing routine about this procedure. As for the Spanos and colleagues (1986) experiment, I believe there are findings that must be seriously considered. These are (a) that MPD symptoms may be suggested by leading interview techniques and that (b) some people may adopt a "role from a variety of quite different sources (movies, books, gossip)" and then go on to "seek legitimization" from friends and mental-health professionals. Some may even "be convinced by their own enactment." What, in effect, Spanos and colleagues show is that we need to be (a) cautious of the iatrogenic creation of MPD symptoms and (b) aware of the possibility of factitious disorder (Munchausen syndrome). The misinterpretation arises when the above observations of Spanos and colleagues are used to suggest that *all* cases presenting with MPD symptomatology are either iatrogenic or factitious. Perhaps this problem could be resolved if we added a diagnostic category for "iatrogenic MPD syndrome." As well we must pay far more attention to the possibility of increased presentations of factitious disorder at a time when there is such a considerable awareness of sexual abuse in the public domain. For MPD therapists to underestimate the effect of the media would be as incautious as proposing that the media is the *cause* of the entire phenomenon. Spanos's study should stand as a wise warning to overzealous therapists, but it does not in any way rule out the reality of MPD.

In Canada we are witnessing an alarming number of disclosures of incidents of sexual abuse. There have been numerous recent convictions relating to sexual abuse by the caretakers in our society, including priests, Christian brothers, teachers, and parents. Some of these crimes were committed decades ago, but the victims dared not tell due to their shame and the rightful fear that they would not be believed. A colleague of mine recently told me that two boys in a reform school had reported to him sexual abuses to them and others by the male clergy who ran the school. These disclosures were fifteen years ago. He discounted their stories (subsequently shown to be true), assuming secondary gain to be their underlying motive.

Only in 1990 did this psychiatrist realize the grave error he had made, and he now wonders about the years of suffering he might have prevented for the two had he heard rather than judged them. We can no longer ignore the fact of extensive abuse to children. The numbers in Canada are shockingly high, and I doubt very much that Britain can cast any stones in our direction.

If MPD syndrome can be induced by careless therapeutic techniques (and I accept that it is possible), then one can surely understand that the *actual* disorder can be caused by a much more severe error, that of traumatic ongoing child abuse. The patients we are seeing with the worst problems are not those with a recent onset of dissociation symptoms, that is, due to therapist error/suggestion, but rather those who have been dissociating since childhood with extensive amnesia relating to severe traumas, be it sexual, physical, or emotional. Such a group of patients does exist! The time has come to understand that iatrogenesis of an MPD-like syndrome is a possibility but it is *not* the whole answer. Let us learn the important differences between "iatrogenic MPD syndrome" and the much more debilitating "trauma produced MPD." We must be able to treat them *both* properly, as well as the Munchausen syndrome.

The value and good sense of psychiatry become suspect when we direct patients' attention away from their concerns of having alternate personalities and turn to old, outdated textbooks to justify our denial of accurate diagnosis and treatment.

Yours sincerely,
G. A. Fraser, M.D., F.R.C.P.(C)
Director, Anxiety and Phobic Disorders Clinic
Royal Ottawa Hospital, Canada

REFERENCES

Ellenberger, H. (1970). *The Discovery of the Unconscious*. New York: Basic Books.
Spanos, N. P., Weekes, V. R., Menary, E., et al. (1986). Hypnotic interview and age regression in the elicitation of multiple personality symptoms: a simulation study. *Psychiatry* 49:298–311.
Thigpen, C. H., and Cleckley, H. M. (1957). *The Three Faces of Eve*. New York: McGraw Hill.

Editor's Note: Drs. Merskey and Fraser (and Drs. Ross and Francois Mai) debated this subject during the 1992 Annual Meeting of the Canadian Psychiatric Association. The following comments were made by Dr. Fraser at that time.

Dr. Merskey has admitted to never having seen a case of MPD in thirty-eight years of practice! This was one of the sad facts of the debate. That is, that we had to debate with two physicians (Drs. Merskey and Mai) who had not managed one full case of MPD between them. I would have preferred to debate with someone who had not discouraged the presentation of varying personality states but rather had successfully managed at least one or two cases meeting *DSM-III-R* criteria and, based on clinical observations during the course of the therapy, had concluded that what was presented clinically was invalid.

Of a comment by Merskey, I stated that if knowing or reading about Sybil or Eve meant (because of contamination by suggestion) that MPD could not longer be diagnosed, then Shakespeare's *Macbeth* which portrays compulsive hand washing (to get rid of blood) means obsessive-compulsive disorder can never again be diagnosed.

As for Dr. Mai's rare experience with MPD in his four years in Ottawa, I pointed out that in the past three and a half years I had 157 referrals for assessment of MPD (in the same city in which Dr. Mai practices). I asked the audience, "If you suspected a patient of MPD and you lived in Ottawa, who would you send the referral to—Dr. Mai, or me?"

Of MPD being a North American phenomenon, as suggested by Merskey, I stated that it is not usual that a diagnostic recognition trend must begin somewhere. Would one have discounted psychoanalysis by saying it was a Viennese or Austrian phenomenon?

I ended by pointing out that MPD treatment techniques such as guided imagery in dissociative state patients represented a new breakthrough in psychotherapy, which should be welcomed and not ridiculed or discounted without appropriate professional study.

G. A. Fraser, M.D., F.R.C.P.(C)

Sir: We want to offer some comments on Dr. Merskey's article. Dr. Merskey concludes that MPD is a product of suggestions and social encouragement. In our view, his main arguments are seriously flawed Our criticisms are outlined below.

First, there is not a single psychopathological diagnostic entity, that we know of, that would be discarded as mere suggestion because of some sort of public knowledge of the disorder.

Secondly, Kleinman (1988) and many other renowned anthropologists have cogently argued that psychiatric diagnoses derive from categories, which themselves are congeries of psychological, social, and biological processes. Quoting Kleinman: "Categories are the outcome of historical development, cultural influence, and political negotiation. Psychiatric categories . . . are not exception" (p. 12). From a social constructionist viewpoint, Merskey's assertion that MPD has to emerge "without any shaping or preparation by external factors such as physicians or the media," has no sense (Martinez-Taboas 1991). As remarked by many taxonomists, there is no such thing as a culture-free or context-free taxonomy. Merskey's undue emphasis on such diagnostic pureness, free of the influence of historical and cultural factors, is not only naïve, but is also consonant with the sort of "immaculate perception" of the logical positivists, which has been under heavy attack by modern epistemologists (Manicas and Secord 1983, Millon 1991).

Thirdly, Merskey's contention that the diagnosis of MPD usually does not afford the patient the best treatment is ill-founded. In fact, he does not present any type of evidence to sustain his claim. Here, in Puerto Rico, we have treated two female patients who, before their MPD diagnosis, were diagnosed as schizophrenics for more than a decade. Both of them had multiple suicide attempts, self-mutilations, were unemployed, and had numerous psychiatric admissions. After their correct diagnosis of MPD, both patients are again working and are finally coping with their lives in an adequate way.

Alfonso Martinez-Taboas and Margarita Francia
Department of Psychology
University of Puerto Rico

REFERENCES

Kleinman, A. (1988). *Rethinking Psychiatry: From Cultural Category to Personal Experience*. New York: Free Press.

Manicas P. T., and Secord, P. F. (1983). Implications for psychology of the new philosophy of science. *American Psychologist* 38:399–413.

Martinez-Taboas, A. (1991). Multiple personality disorder as seen from a social constructionist viewpoint. *Dissociation* 4:129–133.

Millon, T. (1991). Classification in psychopathology: rationale, alternatives, and standards. *Journal of Abnormal Psychology* 100:245–261.

Editor's Note: Dr. Spiegel's letter appeared later in the British Journal of Psychiatry (Jan. 1993) 162:126. and did not include a reply from Dr. Merskey.

Sir: Dr. Merskey reviews historical literature on cases of multiple personality. He reaches the conclusion that they can be accounted for as an iatrogenic creation based on (a) misdiagnosis of organic or bipolar illness, (b) the conscious development of fantasies, (c) hysterical amnesia and retraining, and (d) explicit or implicit hypnotic suggestion or other forms of therapist persuasion. The article is more like one side of a debate than a scientific review of the literature. In every case in which there is insufficient information, a common problem in reviewing historical case material, the author concludes that the possibility of contamination by therapist suggestion is indeed a probability. The author seems to take particular delight in highlighting the "embarrassing failure" of American psychiatrists to make a proper diagnosis, a deficiency remedied when the hapless patient is fortunate enough to return to Great Britain.

Dr. Merskey acknowledges that many of the patients in these studies have various dissociative symptoms such as dissociative amnesia. If they do in fact have real dissociative symptoms, then the disagreement is really about phenomenology, that is, a failure of integration of memory rather than a more pervasive failure of integration of aspects of identity.

While such skepticism can help to strengthen diagnostic procedures, this article constitutes an unusual attack on the diagnostic abilities of psychiatrists who make the diagnosis of MPD. It is true that patients prone to dissociative disorders are generally highly hypnotizable and therefore unusually vulnerable to direct or indirect suggestion. Nonetheless, to argue that all of this form of psychopathology can be accounted for by misdiagnosis, and accidental or deliberate suggestion, is at variance with a wealth of data that suggests otherwise. The author concedes in his diatribe the existence of genuine dissociative psychopathology independent of iatrogenesis.

We intend to include a tightened version of the diagnosis of multiple personality disorder in the fourth edition of the *Diagnostic and Statistical Manual* of the American Psychiatric Association. In addition to some changes in language, we are reintroducing the requirement that the dissociative amnesia be part of the syndrome in order to make the diagnosis. We strongly encourage further research in this complex but important area of psychopathology.

David Spiegel
Stanford University School of Medicine
Stanford, California

DR. MERSKEY REPLIES

Drs. Novello and Primavera find historical and anthropological parallels with secondary personalities. Their observations are of interest. Dr. Fraser, on the other hand, wishes to reject historical data, while Dr. Putnam offers Hacking's nineteenth-century cases to prove the existence of MPD in Britain. The additional British cases were the patient of Dyce (Dewar 1823) and those of Dunn, Ward, and Browne. Dyce's patient reflects the quite conventional trance states of the period and the other three, as documented by Hacking (1992), are similar. Hacking presents them to emphasize the "cascade" effect whereby one report in the literature in turn produces several more—just like today.

Dr. Putnam asserts that it is specious not to explain why two or more alter personality states should be so tractable to suggestions or contamination effects. Hysterical symptoms are so notoriously prone to suggestion that Babinski even wanted to change the name to *Pithiatism*, meaning an illness due to the suggested idea (Babinski and Froment 1918, p. 26).

Hypnotism is institutionalized suggestion and, even if he is not using hypnotism, Dr. Putnam overtly recommends procedures which are an open invitation to his subjects to dissociate into secondary personalities. Not surprisingly, once the breach is made, patients and practitioners feel free to enlarge the numbers. From her original three, sanctioned by her doctors, Eve went on to twenty-two. The practice hardly existed at first, and now has the approval of *DSM-III-R* for up to 100 personalities or fragments thereof. Dr. Putnam is a leading member of the committee that recommended this and seems to accept the result as realistic.

The lurid popular accounts seem to me to be quite close to the position which Dr. Putnam adopts with lots of personalities occurring in only one person. Fraser (1991) bases part of his techniques on one of them, Billy Milligan. There is a more important issue in this respect, in that when the consequences of the current definition seem to be under pressure, we are offered a new formulation, which talks about interventions directed "towards specific alter personality states associated with pathological behaviors," gliding away from the reified constructs with which the behavior is propagated, although even this latest formulation could still hardly come into being without the *DSM-III-R* concept.

Dr. Fraser suggests that making an alternative diagnosis would leave out dissociative symptoms and provide "absolutely no management of the trauma. . . ." This assumes that some aspect of a case has to be in the diagnosis in order to be treated. We need only look at concern with suicidal ideas, which rarely figure in a diagnostic label, to realize that non sequitur.

Dr. Putnam defends the scientific standards of modern MPD by reference to "increasingly sophisticated studies, published in reputable journals." If that is a logical position, we should never submit another article to a reputable journal in order to correct or advance previous positions. Tom Fahy (1988), in his critical paper in this journal, found little value in that literature and, in my reading, it has not changed. We need not dispute that the syndrome can be found reliably with agreed criteria. An actor's performance of specific parts will be highly reliable repeatedly, in front of hundreds of people, but will not establish a fictional character as an individual who lives or who has lived. Nor can the problems of other diagnoses release the proponents of MPD from their difficulty.

I pointed out in my article that "it is reasonable to reject those diagnoses which most reflect individual choice, conscious role playing, and personal convenience." The conditions that Dr. Putnam cites as receiving media attention were all recognized repeatedly before now and have not been found to be misleading initial creations, as I have found MPD to be (which does not mean that some, such as anorexia nervosa, are unlikely to be increased by publicity). Dr. Putnam's claim that MPD is not created by reading *Sybil* or seeing *Eve* can be left to readers to evaluate, taking note that at least the dramatized stories of Eve were presented as truthful expansions of Thigpen and Cleckley's 1954 article.

Dr. Putnam raises a more interesting dilemma with regard to hallucinations in schizophrenia. Careful practitioners try to elicit hallucinations indirectly, or merely to confirm what has been reported independently and spontaneously. The nature of hallucinations, if declared, is tested by nondirective questions, for example, about content and the nature of the voices. With ruminations—as perhaps everyone agrees—the problem is not suggestibility, but a lack of it combined with reticence. In substance, the elicitation of MPD is irremediably flawed.

I would again draw the attention of the reader to Dr. Putnam's description of his procedure. To me, it reads much like the interview in Spanos and colleagues' (1986) experiment which Dr. Fraser says is nonstandard. When Dr. Putnam does not get a direct acknowledgment of feeling like more than one person, he asks the patient, "Do you ever feel is there is some other part [side, facet, etc.] of yourself that comes out and does or says things that you would not do or say?" or "Do you ever feel as if you are not alone, as if there is someone else or some other part watching you?" He also recommends that, in certain circumstances, a clinician can ask whether it would be possible to meet with another part. "Can this other part come out and talk with me?"

Spanos asked his intended artificial subjects to play someone called either Harry or Betty who is accused of murder and is going through a full psychiatric interview. Subjects were told the following, "I've talked a bit to Harry [Betty], but I think that perhaps there might be another part of Harry [Betty] that I haven't talked to, and I would like that other part to come to talk to me. Would you talk to me, Part, by saying 'I'm here'?" This was taken from a direct report of the interrogation of an accused (and subsequently convicted) murderer. The subjects were further asked:

(a) "Part, are you the same as Harry/Betty, or are you different in any way?"
(b) "Tell me about yourself."
(c) "Do you have a name I can call you by?"
(d) "What is your function within Harry/Betty?" and so forth.

I do not understand how Dr. Fraser can suppose that there is not a great similarity between these two procedures, apart from the fact that one was understood to be experimental. I might also note that Dr. Putnam (Putnam 1989) approves of another extreme technique, that of Richard Kluft, who stresses suspected MPD patients by extended interviews of several hours. Dr. Fraser (1991) himself recommends hypnosis, or that patients be invited to imagine being at a table with empty chairs and to fill the chairs with their other personalities. All this speaks for itself in terms of the overt message that is being given to the patient and the degree of suggestion that distinguishes this label from others.

Currently, neither Dr. Putnam nor I can predict the survival or demise of MPD, but it is salutary to recall that, at the end of the nineteenth century, MPD extended prominently to spiritism (see Hacking 1992), which declined into scientific disrepute because of the excesses of its supporters. This risk is inherent in a diagnosis which is driven by enthusiasm and unrestrained by realistic limits.

Like Drs. Fraser and Putnam, Drs. Martinez-Taboas and Francia have overlooked my relativist position about diagnosis (Merskey 1986) to which I drew explicit attention in my *Journal* article. But a relativist position does not mean that all conceptual elaborations have the same value or utility. Drs. Martinez-Taboas and Francia are, of course, to be congratulated on the good results they have obtained after rescuing two patients from a wrong diagnosis, as I hope they will congratulate others on improved treatment after the rediagnosis of supposed MPD.

My most important point in this discussion has remained unchallenged. If MPD is so very susceptible to artificial production, how can we ever know that it is veridical? We cannot. But since we now may recognize that those early cases, which might have been credible MPD without the help of suggestion, are also either immensely unreliable, or clearly something else, there is no point in this magical, doxogenic diagnosis.

REFERENCES

Babinski, J., and Froment, J. (1918). *Hysterical or Pithiatism and Reflex Nervous Disorders in the Neurology of War*, trans. J. D. Rollestone, ed. E. F. Buzzard. London: University of London Press.

Dewar, H. (1823). Report on a communication from Dr. Dyce of Aberdeen to the Royal Society of Edinburgh. On uterine irritation and its effects on the female constitution. *Transactions of the Royal Society of Edinburgh* 9:366–379.

Fahy, T. (1988). The diagnosis of multiple personality disorder. A critical review. *British Journal of Psychiatry* 153:597–606.

Fraser, G. A. (1991). The dissociative table technique: a strategy for working with ego states in dissociative disorders and ego-state therapy. *Dissociation* 4:205–213.

Hacking, I. (in press). Multiple personality disorder and its hosts. *History of Human Sciences*.

Merskey, H. (1986). Variable meanings for the definition of disease. *Journal of Medicine and Philosophy* 3:215–232.

Putnam, F. W. (1989). *Diagnosis and Treatment of Multiple Personality Disorder*. London: Guilford.

Spanos, N. P., Weekes, J. R., Menary, E., et al. (1986). Hypnotic interview and age regression procedures in the elicitation of multiple personality disorder: a simulation study. *Psychiatry* 49:298–311.

Thigpen, C. H., and Cleckley, H. M. (1954). A case of multiple personality. *Journal of Abnormal Social Psychology* 9:135–151.

Editor's Note: Dr. Merskey provided the following comments for this book in June 1994.

In little more than a year since the Baystate Medical Center conference was held some very instructive information has become available. The practice of Dr. Ross, which Dr. Chande has advocated, was filmed for a program of the Canadian Broadcasting Corporation (CBC, Fifth Estate, November 9, 1993). Female patients in romper suits were seen engaging in profoundly demeaning regressive behaviour with his encouragement as an alleged treatment for their multiple personalities and to eradicate their distress at their childhood abuse. Many who have seen this program have felt that, to put it mildly, the practice in question encouraged patients to reduce themselves to an infantile level which was unhelpful to them. The interviewer stated that according to a book proposal obtained by the Fifth Estate [the name of the program], Dr. Ross and his patients believed that a CIA plot existed, going all the way back to the 1940s. Dr. Ross said, "They are taken to special training centres, where these different techniques, like sensory isolation and deprivation, flotation tanks, hypnosis, various memorization tasks, virtual reality goggles, hallucinogenic drugs, and so on, are used on them to try and deliberately create more alter personalities that can hold information." The interview included his claim that the reason that there are people who are now dissenting against his type of therapy was that they worked for the CIA as programmers of children whose memories he is now uncovering in therapy.

In the same program Dr. Herbert Spiegel reported for the first time his opinion of the case of Sybil who was referred to him for additional treatment by Dr. Cornelia Wilbur. He said, "When she worked with me she would ask me now, when we wanted to go to a certain period of life, 'Well, shall I become Flora or can I just say it?' I didn't know what she meant at first. Well she said, 'Well, when I'm with Dr. Wilbur, she wants me to be that person.' And I said, 'Well if you want, you can, but you don't have to if you don't want to.' So with me, she didn't have to be these personalities." Dr. Spiegel agreed that the personalities were "created by the therapist." This provides additional—and I believe incontrovertible—evidence to support the suspicion I voiced in my 1992 article that the case of Sybil was an artificial one.

At the time I only had the published information on her knowledge of psychology upon which to rely, in addition to the general implausibility of the reports by therapists in this field.

A significant number of recanters has also now become available and at least eighty are known to the False Memory Syndrome Foundation. These recanters have rejected the beliefs of childhood abuse that were inculcated in them either during the course of therapy for alleged MPD, or in the process of the induction of false memories by therapists who were, at the very least, overenthusiastic and misguided.

The field of MPD has thus become even more shabby in the light of the additional evidence that is now becoming available. Its logical validity had previously been attacked by Fahy (1988) and by Aldridge-Morris (1989). At the time of the conference I was able to present orally some parts of the trenchant scholarly critique technique which Dr. Piper (1994) has made of the whole theoretical concept of MPD and the pretensions of its practitioners, and which is now published.

One argument that has not been dealt with much by the critics of MPD is the suggestion that the vividness and strength of the clinical phenomenon that is manifest when MPD is studied in patients is an unequivocal demonstration of its validity. Dr. Chande makes this sort of claim in her addendum. Again, it has to be repeated that actors can be just as convincing and that the cognitive psychologists who have been studying memory problems point out how individuals have been repeatedly persuaded to believe that things happened which did not happen and gave their stories with the air of utmost conviction. These strong clinical impressions unfortunately cannot stand up to a critical analysis of the nature of what happens, either in the leading cases—including some still alive—or any others.

We are now witnessing alarming numbers of disclosures of incidents of sexual abuse in Canada and the same is certainly true in the United States. It has become apparent that the most dreadful allegations of abuse by parents and persons in positions of trust have been made on the basis of flimsy evidence and in response to pressure by therapists. The United States in particular, but also Canada, now faces a human rights' problem of considerable proportions, since many innocent people have been accused and more are being not merely prosecuted but persecuted. Notorious incidents such as the accusation against a cardinal in Chicago, since withdrawn, have contributed to making it harder to convict the genuinely guilty. This is clearly one of the most serious consequences for society of the unbridled encouragement to fantasy in the production of MPD and allied phenomena. What began as an aberration, or set of aberrations, in psychiatry, has become part of a grievous issue of human rights.

REFERENCES

Aldridge-Morris, R. (1989). *Multiple Personality. An Exercise in Deception*. London: Lawrence Erlbaum.

Fahy, T. A. (1988). The diagnosis of multiple personality disorder. A critical review. *British Journal of Psychiatry* 154:99–101.

Piper, A., Jr. (1994). Multiple personality disorder: A critical review. *British Journal of Psychiatry* 164:600–612.

3

A Sociocultural Analysis of Merskey's Approach

Alfonso Martinez-Taboas

The comments in this chapter expand on a previously published critique (Martinez-Taboas and Francia 1992) of Harold Merskey's article, "The Manufacture of Personalities: The Production of Multiple Personality Disorder" that is reprinted in this book. Page numbers will refer to Chapter 1 of this volume.

From my standpoint two major themes appear in Merskey's (1992) article: (1) that historical and well-known cases of multiple personality disorder (MPD) can be dismissed as the product of misdiagnosis and other artifacts, and (2) that MPD is an iatrogenic sociocultural artifact, because in every modern case we cannot completely eliminate the influence of the "widespread publicity for the concept" (p. 3).

I would like to analyze in a critical manner the tacit assumptions behind Merskey's second theme and to demonstrate that such a thesis is highly inadequate from an epistemological and cultural psychology viewpoint (Schweder 1991). I will not comment on Merskey's first postulate because, in my opinion, his highly selective and fragmentary synopsis of historical cases is unconvincing.

MERSKEY'S THESIS FROM A SOCIAL CONSTRUCTIONIST AND EPISTEMOLOGICAL VIEWPOINT

According to Merskey (1992), MPD "never occurs as a spontaneous persistent natural event in adults" (p. 26). From the start, I have some grave misgivings with regard to Merskey's requirements and terminology. For example, what is to be understood by "spontaneous"? Without social influence? And, what is a "natural event"? An event "decontaminated" or decontextualized from culture and society?

Let us quote a few passages from Merskey:

> Recent cases are not appropriate subject matter to explore the question of suggestion, *since they have all been open to it in developed countries. Some cases recently reported from India also indicate the influence of the cinema.* . . . [p. 28, my italics]
>
> If this is true it means that no later case, probably since Prince, but at least since the film *The Three Faces of Eve*, can be taken to be veridical *since none is likely to emerge without prior knowledge of the idea.* . . . [p. 25, my italics]
>
> No case has been found here in which MPD, as now conceived, is proven to have emerged through unconscious processes *without any shaping or preparation by external factors such as physicians and the media.* [p. 25, my italics]

To put it succinctly, Merskey will not accept the ontological reality of MPD if: (a) the case is reported in a developed country, (b) if the clinician suspects and tries to listen for the disorder, (c) if the clinician and/or patient has had any prior knowledge of that idea.

From a social constructionist viewpoint (Martinez-Taboas 1991) Merskey's position is deeply flawed. First, it is becoming widely recognized that psychiatric categories are not natural things out there waiting impatiently for a psychiatrist to discover their "true," "natural," "spontaneous," and "uncontaminated" expression (Fabrega 1992, Millon 1991, Morey 1991, Suppe 1989, Ware and Kleinman 1992). This point is cogently expressed by Kleinman (1988):

> Psychiatric diagnoses are not things, though they give name and shape to processes involving neurotransmitters, endocrine hormones, activity in the autonomic nervous system, and thoughts, feelings, and behaviors that show considerable stability. Rather, psychiatric diagnoses derive from categories. They underwrite the interpretation of phenomena which themselves are congeries of psychological, social, and biological processes. Categories are the outcome of historical development, cultural influence, and political negotiation. Psychiatric categories . . . are no exception. [p. 12]

Millon (1991) presents a similar position:

> No classification in psychopathology today is an inevitable representation of the real world. . . . Because classification is a human artifact, not every one of its terms needs to be linked to observable events. . . . Unrealistic standards of empirical anchorage, particularly in the early stages of taxonomic construc-

tion, often discourage the kind of imaginative speculation necessary to decode and to integrate elusive phenomena. [pp. 246, 249–250]

It seems clear that Merskey is vainly searching for an impossible objective: the documentation of a psychiatric disorder (e.g., MPD) decontaminated from culture, society, and other human transactions that culminate in a category. This aseptic approach is reminiscent of the outmoded epistemologic stance of the logical positivists. For the logical positivists of the 1930s, 1940s, and 1950s, true or natural knowledge was essentially an objective given of nature. For that reason this epistemological stance came to be known as "the received view" (Polkinghorne 1983). According to this, the scientist only had to attune his instruments or categories to the realities of the phenomena. Consistent with this posture, all external influences (political, cultural, historical, sociological) were extraneous to the scientific inquiry.

Fortunately we understand today that this type of objectivism is naïve and misguided. There is wide consensus that this kind of epistemology is moribund among philosophers and historians of science (Giere 1988, Laudan 1977, Longino 1990, Manicas and Secord 1983, Newton-Smith 1981, Popper 1974, Suppe 1989, van Fraassen 1985).

So, my first critique of Merskey's thesis is that one of his pivotal and basic arguments (e.g., that MPD has to emerge naturally and without external influence) will not receive a favorable hearing in this postmodern period, especially among many social scientists and philosophers of science. Contrary to Merskey's contention, every category in psychiatry *is* the product of a complex interplay between cultural, social, psychological, and biological variables (Greenwood 1991). *There is no compelling reason why MPD has to be the exception.* Or as Hahn (1984) concisely puts it:

The events which happen to persons (or in which persons participate) have multiple *aspects*, for example, physical, chemical, physiological, psychological, anthropological, and environmental. Each aspect forms a system of interacting elements. . . . The systems are more or less open, since the interaction of their elements is both influenced by and itself influences phenomena which are not in that system. . . . Instead of asking whether some phenomenon or event is physiological or psychological or social, it assumes the phenomenon or event to have at the same time physiological, psychological, and social aspects. [p. 20]

A second point that is highly relevant to Merskey's position is that there are numerous reasons to think that many psychiatric disorders are not only shaped or molded by culture (Westermeyer 1985), but are also mainly constituted by culture, history, and society (Bracken 1993, Nilchiakovit et al., 1993). Fabrega (1992) expresses this idea forcefully: "Culture is not only responsible for the 'surface' content of behavior but also for part of its structure, that is, the nature of conflicts, stresses, and the patterning of psychological defenses brought to bear on the conflicts all influence content as well as form" (p. 99).

From a social constructionist view, culture and consciousness make each other up. It is a basic tenet of constructionism that the processes of con-sciousness may not be uniform across the cultural regions of the world. As Kleinman (1988) expresses it: "Mental health and illness, we may conclude, are inseparable from the social world" (p. 63). Cushman (1991) further remarks: "Constructionists, therefore, suggest that psychologists should embrace the inevitable and study local, historical, and particular phenom-ena and the indigenous psychologies of the multitude of cultures on earth" (p. 208).

Psychopathologies such as suicide, personality disorders, agoraphobia, bulimia, anorexia nervosa, somatization disorders, alcoholism, drug abuse, and other psychiatric categories are deeply ingrained and constrained by culture, society, and history (Greenwood 1991, Kleinman 1988). From a social constructionist view, such categories are not artificial, iatrogenic, or the product of suggestion. They are deeply intrinsic products and ways of how at a particular point in time and place a complex interplay of biopsychosocial variables synergistically creates the ideal conditions for the emergence of serious and distinct psychopathologies. MPD could be a temporal and historical phenomenon of our times, but not for the reasons Merskey thinks (incompetence of a therapist, spurious iatrogenesis, hys-terical suggestion). I have argued that MPD will be fairly visible in societies with an individualistic (vs. collectivist) outlook of the self; where culture and society expose their members to high-risk situations (abuse of chil-dren, sexual abuse) that facilitate the development of MPD; and where the self is nonporous to external influences (e.g., spirits, magic, possession). According to this last point, the dissociative experience that is used to protect the fragile self will be channeled as a by-product of *internal* psychic factors (Lewis-Fernandez, in press).

A third reason that points to a serious weakness in Merskey's arguments is that his core criticisms are nonfalsifiable. This point is highly relevant in this discussion because many philosophers of science and methodologists argue that it is highly appropriate to present one's hypothesis in a falsifiable manner. But this task is impossible in Merskey's thesis. A few of his sentences will illustrate this point.

> Since the widespread publicity about *The Three Faces of Eve* and *Sybil*, all sub-sequent cases are suspect of being prepared by prior information. . . . [p. 22]

Eve's case has the most convincing descriptions and yet a doubt remains. In her case *it is uncertain whether there was prior knowledge of the concept of MPD*. . . . [p. 24]

It is always open of course to any particular investigator to say, 'My patient has had no training, arose naturally, and was not prepared by me.' Fortunately, or otherwise, that position has been undermined by widespread knowledge of the concept. [p. 28].

Quotes such as these invite some comment. First, Merskey is again searching for indubitable knowledge—or what the logical positivists called apodictic knowledge. It seems important once again to mention that in the last two decades it has been widely recognized by epistemologists that the search for apodictic knowledge is a spurious endeavor. All human knowledge is fallible, incomplete, and has an uncertain ring around it (Laudan 1977, Popper 1974). Merskey's fanciful case, where it can be established with certainty that "there was no prior knowledge of the concept of MPD" is misguided and somewhat futile.

Secondly, Merskey leaves no room for a worthwhile debate when he holds to the position that no modern case of MPD can be ascribed to a natural course since the general public and mental health providers know of the disorder.

Some years ago I detected a case of MPD in a 16-year-old female. She lived in a rural portion of Puerto Rico, was practically blind, and could not recall hearing about MPD and its characteristics. Similarly, Dr. Mauricio Sierra, a psychiatrist working in Colombia, recently told me (personal communication, 1992) that he had detected MPD in a 15-year-old Indian girl who resides in a rural and isolated part of his country.

Could examples such as these refute Merskey's thesis? Not at all! Merskey would contend that maybe those patients had no previous idea of MPD, but their therapists did. So, even if one encounters a potential case where the person is totally ignorant of the concept of MPD, *there has to be a person who has to recognize its manifestation*. And that person usually is the therapist. But, in order to recognize and diagnose MPD, the clinician has to have some previous notion or knowledge of the disorder. We must remember that MPD is a psychiatric category, which means that like any other category, it is not to be captured instantaneously and without the special social process that implies the learning of psychiatric nomenclature. The totally naïve clinician who by an immaculate act recognizes a case of MPD without learning first that such a clinical entity has a place in psychiatry is a fictional character. Competent and expert clinicians are those who have developed sensitive knowledge and experience with the subtleties and vagaries of a determined category.

CONCLUSIONS

In the last six years I and an increasing number of clinicians have detected some thirty cases of MPD in Puerto Rico. Many of those patients had gone undetected by previous mental health professionals. Some of the patients were given spurious diagnostic labels (epilepsy, schizophrenia, psychotic depression) and treated without any noticeable benefit. Our clinical experience is totally at odds with Merskey's armchair opinion, when he says that the diagnosis of MPD iatrogenically complicates the clinical condition and prognosis of the patient. What I and a number of colleagues have corroborated time and again is that with a proper diagnosis MPD patients can finally put together their shattered lives and obtain marked symptomatic relief.

In summary, Merskey examines MPD from an epistemological stance that has been repeatedly denounced on logical and empirical grounds. Merskey's irrefutable and aseptic view of MPD is not the proper approach to study or understand the complexities of dissociative disorders.

REFERENCES

Bracken, P. H. (1993). Post-empiricism and psychiatry: meaning and methodology in cross-cultural research. *Social Science and Medicine* 36:265–272.

Cushman, P. (1991). Ideology obscured: political uses of the self in Daniel Stern's infant. *American Psychologist* 46:206–219.

Fabrega, H. (1992). The role of culture in a theory of psychiatric illness. *Social Science and Medicine* 35:91–103.

Giere, R. N. (1988). *Explaining Science*. Chicago: University of Chicago Press.

Greenwood, J. D. (1991). *Relations and Representations*. London: Routledge.

Hahn, R. A. (1984). Rethinking "illness" and "disease." In *South Asian Systems of Healing*, ed. E. V. Daniel and J. F. Pugh, pp. 1–23. Leiden: E. J. Brill.

Kleinman, D. (1988). *Rethinking Psychiatry*. New York: Free Press.

Lauden, L. (1977). *Progress and Its Problems*. Los Angeles: University of California Press.

Lewis-Fernandez, R. (in press). The role of culture in the configuration of dissociative states. In *Dissociation: Culture, Mind and Body*, ed. D. Spiegel.

Longino, H. (1990). *Science as Social Knowledge*. New York: Basic Books.

Manicas, P. T., and Secord, P. F. (1983). Implications for psychology of the new philosophy of science. *American Psychologist* 36:399–413.

Martinez-Taboas, A., and Francia, M. (1992). Correspondence. *British Journal of Psychiatry* 161:417–418.

Merskey, H. (1992). The manufacture of personalities. *British Journal of Psychiatry* 160:327–340.

Millon, T. (1991). Classification of psychopathology. *Journal of Abnormal Psychology* 100:245–261.

Morey, L. C. (1991). Classification of mental disorder as a collection of hypothetical constructs. *Journal of Abnormal Psychology* 100:289–293.

Newton-Smith, W. (1981). *The Rationality of Science*. London: Routledge.

Nilchiakovit, T., Hill, J. M., and Holland, J. C. (1993). The effects of culture on illness behavior and medical care. *General Hospital Psychiatry* 15:41–50.

Polkinghorne, D. (1983). *Methodology for the Human Sciences*. Albany: State University of New York Press.

Popper, K. (1974). Replies to my critics. In *The Philosophy of Karl Popper*, ed. P. A. Schlilpp, pp. 961–1197. La Salle, IL: Open Court.

Shweder, R. A. (1991) *Thinking Through Cultures*. Cambridge, MA: Harvard University Press.

Suppe, F. (1989). *The Semantic Conception of Theories and Scientific Realism*. Chicago: University of Illinois Press.

van Fraassen, B. C. (1985). Empiricism in the philosophy of science. In *Images of Science*, ed. P. M. Churchland and C. A. Hooker, pp. 245–308. Chicago: University of Chicago Press.

Ware, N. C., and Kleinman, A. (1992). Culture and somatic experience. *Psychosomatic Medicine* 54:546–560.

Westermeyer, J. (1985). Psychiatric diagnosis across cultural boundaries. *American Journal of Psychiatry* 142:798–805.

4

The Validity and Reliability of Dissociative Identity Disorder

Colin A. Ross

Dissociative identity disorder (DID), formerly called multiple personality disorder, is one of the five dissociative disorders listed in *DSM-IV* (1994), and has been listed as a separate disorder with operationalized diagnostic criteria for fourteen years, since the appearance of *DSM-III* (1980). In *DSM-IV*, DID is an exclusion criterion for the diagnosis of dissociative disorder not otherwise specified, and conversion disorder is classified as a somatoform disorder. In *ICD-10* (1992), by contrast, DID is still called multiple personality disorder and is listed under "Other dissociative [conversion] disorders."

In *ICD-10* (1992) the section on dissociative disorders includes the conversion disorders and is titled "F44 Dissociative [conversion disorders]." It includes dissociative amnesia, dissociative fugue, trance and possession disorders, dissociative disorders of movement and sensation, dissociative motor disorders, dissociative convulsions, dissociative anesthesia and sensory loss, mixed dissociative [conversion] disorders, other dissociative [conversion] disorders, and dissociative [conversion] disorder, unspecified. Outside North America, conversion is understood as a form of dissociation: "The common theme shared by dissociative [or conversion] disorders is a partial or complete loss of the normal integration between memories of the past, awareness of identity and immediate sensations, and control of bodily movements" (p. 151).

In *DSM-IV* (1994), conversion is excluded from the definition of dissociation: "The essential feature of the Dissociative Disorders is a disruption in the usually integrated functions of consciousness, memory, identity, or perception of the environment" (p. 477).

These differences between *DSM-IV* and *ICD-10* highlight the fact that attitudes toward certain mental disorders, and the way they are classified, are highly political in nature. There are no definitive research data supporting the placement of conversion disorder among the somatoform disorders or the dissociative disorders, so the decision is made differently in *DSM-IV* and *ICD-10* based on ideology and the vestigial effects of Freudian theory. This could not occur in a truly scientific classificatory system.

Any discussion of the validity and reliability of DID must be based on an understanding that insufficient data exist to establish definitively or refute the scientific reality of the disorder. It is important to grasp the fact that proving that DID is not valid requires data, and cannot be accomplished by anecdotal case arguments or at an ideological level. This is as true for DID as it is for all other mental disorders.

Discussion of the validity and reliability of DID cannot proceed rationally if the disorder is treated as a special case. To be valid and reliable, DID must meet the same criteria for reliability and validity as are applied to all other psychiatric disorders. It must be studied with the same methodology, and the same logical arguments must apply. In this chapter I will describe the procedures required to establish or refute the reliability and validity of DID, and describe the existing data, which although not definitive, clearly weigh in the direction of the disorder being real. Before doing so I will briefly review the clinical concept of DID, and then will list the kind of arguments that cannot be part of a rational scientific discussion of the reliability and validity of DID, just as they cannot be accepted in any serious conversation about the reality of any other disorder. DID is subject to differential pseudoarguments against its validity because of hostile countertransference toward it, but this level of intellectual function needs to be set aside for serious study to continue. I will close by reviewing evidence from CIA and military mind-control research about the difficulty of creating artificial DID and differential amnesia barriers.

THE CLINICAL CONCEPT OF DISSOCIATIVE IDENTITY DISORDER

The name of this disorder was changed to DID in *DSM-IV* in an effort to neutralize the pervasive fixed negative cathexis in psychiatry of the term *multiple personality disorder*. The hope was that by changing the name the argument that the disorder cannot be real because it is not possible to have more than one personality could be circumvented. Whether this will prove to be a successful political strategy or not, time will tell.

There are only a few basic concepts to grasp about DID. The first is what I call the *central paradox of DID*. What is the nature of the reality of the disorder? The reality of the disorder exists at a metalevel. What is real about DID is that it is both real and not real at the same time. This being so, debates about whether the disorder is real or not real are misconceived and futile when they are conducted at the primary level rather than at the metalevel. DID is not real in the sense that it is not possible to have more than one personality, or more than one person inside the same body. The identities or personality states are not concretely, physically, or literally real—they are not composed of matter, and do not occupy physical space. They are constructs, enactments, devices, or internal autohypnotic structures, depending on one's choice of vocabulary. Skeptics who think they are arguing against the reality of the disorder by pointing out that it is not real in this sense are missing the point.

DID is real in the sense that individuals meeting *DSM-IV* criteria for the disorder have complex, chronic dissociative symptoms that are not better accounted for by any other diagnostic criteria set in *DSM-IV*. These symptoms antedate first contact with a mental-health professional, can be observed in children, and are virtually identical in Canada, the United States, the Netherlands, and Japan (Boon and Draijer 1993, Ross et al. 1990, Steinberg 1994). However, DID being real in this operationalized diagnostic sense does not refute the coexisting fact that the disorder is not concretely real in a biomedical or physical sense.

DID is a little girl imagining that the abuse is happening to somebody else. It is a developmentally protective illusion that actually functions to buffer the organism from the overwhelming impact of unmodulated trauma, occuring in an interpersonal field from which there is no escape. Where would the child get the idea of creating an alternate identity to be the victim of the trauma, or to escape, have greater strength, or acquire other survival skills? This idea is everywhere in the child's environment, in cartoons, in video games, in movies and books, and on the school playground. Transformation of identity is a ubiquitous theme in the popular culture of North America, as it is around the world.

The highly dissociative child amplifies this basic survival strategy by inserting an amnesia barrier between herself and the newly created identity, so that now not only is the abuse not happening to me, I don't even remember it. The ability of the human mind actively to create defensive amnesia barriers is so well recognized in the literature on hypnosis and combat trauma that it doesn't require debate or referencing, and can be taken as a given.

Because the abuse is chronic and repetitive, the dissociation is reinforced and the dissociated internal structures are crystallized until they acquire a compelling subjective quality of separateness. To repeat, this is not a literal reality, it is a subjective illusion, but for the illusion to work as a survival strategy it must be subjectively compelling. If the little girl said to herself consciously that she was merely pretending to have someone else inside, and could really remember the abuse, then the dissociative structure wouldn't function as a way of containing the traumatic affect—to be developmentally protective, the illusion must be subjectively compelling.

The signs and symptoms of the disorder, which I will review in a subsequent chapter, flow logically from the intrapsychic structure of the disorder, which is the existence of abnormally personified and dissociated subsystems within the psyche, between which there are varying degrees of amnesia, and which take turns being in full or partial control of the body. No other clinical model in psychiatry accounts so elegantly for so much otherwise disparate clinical data. What is hard to grasp or accept about this model? What is so threatening about it? Why is it so important to some professionals that DID not be real? These are questions I cannot answer fully, despite a decade of thought about the problem.

CLASSES OF ARGUMENT WHICH ARE NOT SCIENTIFIC OR LOGICAL

I used to think that the main source of resistance to DID was unwillingness to accept the endemic nature of childhood physical and sexual abuse, neglect, and their long-term consequences. To understand the reality of DID is to understand the reality of childhood trauma and its effects. Although I still think this, I am giving increasing weight to cultural resistance to *polypsychism*: I believe that the dissociative continuum, rather than going from normal dissociation, at the left-hand end, to DID, on the right-hand end, actually starts at a different point in our culture (Ross 1992). The statistical norm in our culture is an abnormal form of pseudounity—healthy multiplicity is in the middle of the spectrum, with DID at the far-right end. Resistance to the reality of DID, then, is primarily a defensive adherence to pathological pseudounity: accepting the reality of DID means accepting the pathology of the pseudounity.

Whatever the exact dynamics and motives, the pervasive use of arguments against the reality of DID, which could never be published in a leading psychiatry journal if directed at depression or schizophrenia, implies to me that the issues at stake for the skeptics are not really scientific, and that something is being acted out in terms of DID, when the real issues remain disguised. The theme of the cultural conflict between pseudounity and polypsychism is dealt with repeatedly in a book entitled *Dissociation: Culture, Mind, and Body,* edited by David Spiegel (1994).

At the Canadian Psychiatric Association meeting in Montreal in September, 1992, Dr. George Fraser and I debated against Dr. Harold Merskey and Dr. Francois Mai on the reality of DID. Dr. Mai opened his remarks by stating that he was going to take an epidemiological approach to the problem, and then cited a number of general population surveys that did not report any cases of DID. He regarded this as evidence against the reality of the disorder, and in favor of its iatrogenic nature when diagnosed by enthusiasts. My response to Dr. Mai was to point out that the structured interviews used in these studies did not inquire about dissociative symptoms or make dissociative diagnoses. Imagine if such an argument were made anywhere else in medicine—for instance if chest pain were "proven" to be an iatrogenic artifact by general population surveys that did not inquire about chest pain. Clearly, this level of argument would simply be inadmissable elsewhere in medicine.

In the discussion following the debate, an audience member objected that I was using a continuous measure, the Dissociative Experiences Scale (Bernstein and Putnam 1986, Carlson et al. 1993) to make a categorical diagnosis. He said that this violates the logic of science. My reply was to point out two things: First, the Beck Depression Inventory and Hamilton Depression Scale are routinely used in drug studies to establish cutoffs for entry into the study, though the scores by themselves do not confirm a diagnosis of clinical depression. Second, less than five minutes earlier, I had presented data in which only 17 percent of 1051 clinical subjects scoring above 30 on the DES had a clinical diagnosis of DID. Since I had just made this point, failure to hear seemed to me to have been based on an active subconscious effort not to listen.

Another audience member objected that individuals in the dissociative disorders field are diagnosing all sexual abuse survivors as having DID, and that this is obviously bad practice. I agree fully that it would be bad practice: the problem is that there is no one in the world who is actually doing this. I pointed out that I myself have published research (Ross 1991) in which only 20 percent of individuals in a general population sample reporting childhood physical and/or sexual abuse met criteria for a dissociative disorder of any kind. In no other area of psychiatry are these kinds of straw man arguments allowed or used against the validity of a disorder.

Similarly, for no other disorder would it be possible to publish four case examples of false positive diagnoses in a national level journal. Yet the *Canadian Journal of Psychiatry* recently published a paper of this kind by Dr. Merskey and his colleagues (Freeland et al. 1993). In his abstract he states that "four cases are presented in which an unjustified diagnosis of multiple personality disorder was made" (p. 245). In none of the case histories is sufficient clinical data presented to rule in or out any *DSM-IV* diagnosis. One cannot tell which disorders from *DSM-IV* these individuals have, and which they do not have. The paper therefore has no meaningful content. Imagine trying to publish a paper in which four false positive diagnoses of schizophrenia were revised to bipolar mood disorder, with insufficient information included to rule in or out either diagnosis. Such a paper wouldn't even be sent out for review by the journal editor, and could not be published even as a letter to the editor. Even if one conceded that all four cases were true examples of false positive diagnoses of DID, this would prove nothing, since all *DSM-IV* diagnostic criteria sets generate false positives. Dr. Merskey's paper functions at a level of analysis that is incapable of contributing anything to the literature. The fact that a paper at this level could not be published about any other disorder proves that the motivation for its publication is ideological, not scientific.

Similarly, anecdotal case arguments from the nineteenth century are irrelevant to a scientific analysis of the validity of a disorder. For instance, there had been no diagnoses of schizophrenia made in all of human history at the end of the nineteenth century. It would be inconceivable to use this fact as an argument against the validity of schizophrenia. Similarly, panic disorder did not exist in the nineteenth century, and it would not be hard to find false positive diagnoses of neurasthenia and shell shock in the older literature.

Another argument used against the reality of DID is so impressionistic that it would be disallowed in any other area of psychiatry. This is the often made claim that most of the diagnoses are being made by a small number of enthusiasts (Merskey et al. 1994). This claim is inadmissable for two reasons: first, it is made without any supporting data and, second, it is refuted by the facts. This argument was correct in 1980, but is simply out of date in 1994. For instance, in 1989 I published a series of 236 cases reported to me by 203 different clinicians (Ross et al. 1989a). In less than three years, our Dissociative Disorders Unit at Charter Health System of Dallas has received referrals from hundreds of different clinicians in Canada, Australia, and all parts of the United States, and the referral sources work in all sectors of the mental-health field, from Stanford University to Harvard University to private practice. I personally give workshops and lectures to several thousand mental-health professionals per year, the majority of whom have made independent DID diagnoses. Casual acquaintance with the mental-health field in 1994 establishes that DID has been independently diagnosed by a minimum of thousands of mental-health professionals, and probably tens of thousands. Even the data gathered by Dr. Mai (1992) and presented at the Canadian Psychiatric

Association debate refute this argument. Dr. Mai found that about 30 percent of Canadian psychiatrists responding to his survey had made an independent diagnosis of DID. I pointed out that this survey, if done ten years ago, would have yielded a figure of a few percent, and if done ten years from now would likely yield a figure of 90 percent. Since there are over 30,000 psychiatrists in North America, Dr. Mai's figures, if they are valid and representative, suggest that about 10,000 psychiatrists in North America have made an independent DID diagnosis. Yet Dr. Merskey continues to state, in a letter to the editor of the *Canadian Journal of Psychiatry* (Merskey et al 1984) that it is a small number of enthusiasts who diagnose the great majority of cases" (p. 245).

Another argument mounted against the validity of DID is that the existence of a reported history of childhood trauma is used tautologically to support the diagnosis. This is not possible logically because there are no trauma items in the *DSM-IV* criteria for the disorder. Further, the argument actually applies to adjustment disorders and posttraumatic stress disorder, but would never be used against them because the tautology would be ridiculed by the majority of psychiatrists. Why is the same class of argument applauded when used against DID, but ridiculed if used against any other disorder? Could this be possible in a truly scientific field, or debate?

Another problem in the debate about the reality of DID, which does not actually function within psychiatry at a level that I would call a debate, is that disbelievers often cannot distinguish between a hypothesis and an argument. In a scientific debate, one makes a hypothesis, then marshals evidence and arguments to support the hypothesis. In the pseudodebate about the reality of DID, hypotheses are simply insisted upon, as if they were arguments. For instance the contention that DID is a cultural artifact strongly influenced by the media is a hypothesis, not an argument—where are the data, or the compelling arguments, to support the hypothesis? There are none. Since the movie *Rain Man*, one could hypothesize, all idiot savant cases are media artifacts—one would need to provide evidence supporting the hypothesis, otherwise it is no more than an opinion.

The media-artifact hypothesis about DID illustrates the pervasive phenomenon, which is intellectually dishonest, of differential application of charges to DID, which could as easily be made against any psychiatric disorder, but isn't. What is the argument supporting the differential sensitivity of DID to media influence and artifact? It is a tautology and a bias, masquerading as an argument—the "argument" is that DID patients are differentially suggestible and hysterical, but this is an assumption that proves the artifactual nature of the disorder by a tautology, in the absence of any differential empirical data. It might be true that DID patients are differentially susceptible to media artifact but this is an *empirical* question, not something that can be resolved by ideological assertion.

Another differential failure of psychiatry regarding DID is the level of scholarship that is permitted in disbeliever papers about DID. These can be published with content which is purely ideological and anecdotal in leading journals like the *British Journal of Psychiatry* with failure to reference, discuss, or analyze the relevant empirical research literature (Fahy 1988, Merskey 1992). With respect to the *British Journal of Psychiatry*, one can construct a 2 × 2 table in which DID disbeliever papers of low methodology and intellectual level are published, while schizophrenia disbeliever papers of similar quality would not even be sent out for review. Schizophrenia believer papers of good methodology get published, while DID papers of similar quality do not. It is clear that this table is not the result of disinterested intellectual inquiry into the nature of human psychopathology.

In summary, these are types of argument and evidence that are simply not relevant to deciding the reliability and validity of DID or any other disorder. Demonstrating that DID is *not* valid and reliable requires methodologically adequate research with large numbers of subjects and statistical analysis—the purpose of such research, like any truly scientific inquiry, is to find out what is going on in nature, not to back preconceived ideological positions. The fact that low levels of pseudoargument about the reality of DID are allowed in psychiatry is a symptom of the failure of liberal arts education in our culture.

A STUDY TO ESTABLISH THE VALIDITY AND RELIABILITY OF DID

Having just made a purist argument about the nature of scientific research, I believe it is important to acknowledge that scientists are always interested in a particular theory and point of view, as I am. My point of view is that DID will prove to be a valid and reliable disorder, and that all the existing data point in that direction. What distinguishes the scientist from the ideologue is the scientist's committment to the *process*, as opposed to the *outcome*. Naturally, the scientist is hoping that his theory is correct, but if he is more wedded to his theory than to understanding nature, he will never be a truly creative scientist. This is my attitude, and I view myself as no more invested in the DID-is-real outcome than the DID-is-not-real outcome, at the primary level, because I am interested in its reality at the metalevel. Therefore I do not experience myself as engaged in a meaningful conversation with disbelievers.

I have designed a project to investigate the reliability and validity of all the dissociative disorders, including DID. The project will involve administering an assessment battery to 300 subjects in treatment for drug and alcohol abuse and dependency. This population has been selected because it contains a large number of subjects with undiagnosed dissociative disorders who are not invested in having dissociative disorders, do not expect such diagnoses to be made, and are not under the care of clinicians who diagnose dissociative disorders. There are no discernible demand characteristics to have a dissociative disorder in place in this clinical setting, and in fact there are institutionalized counterpressures strongly in favor of false negative dissociative diagnoses. In Canada, out of 100 subjects with chemical dependency problems, 43 met criteria for a dissociative disorder on the Dissociative Disorders Interview Schedule (Ross 1989, Ross et al. 1989b) including 14 with DID (Ross et al., unpublished data). At Charter Health System of Dallas, the frequency of clinically undiagnosed dissociative disorders in chemical dependency inpatients, when they are interviewed with the DDIS, is just under 60 percent, including 18 percent with DID.

The project design is to have four independent interviewers interview the 300 subjects. All will be blind to the dissociative status of each subject and the findings of the other interviewers, and the subjects will be blind to whether they have dissociative disorders, since dissociative diagnoses are not made clinically on the Unit. One interviewer will administer the DES and DDIS. A second interviewer will administer the Structured Clinical Interview for *DSM-IV* Dissociative Disorders (SCID-D) (Steinberg 1993, 1994; Steinberg et al. 1990) and the borderline personality disorder section of the Structured Clinical Interview for *DSM-III-R* (Spitzer et al. 1990). The SCID-D manual is well enough regarded in psychiatry that it is published by the American Psychiatric Press, and Dr. Steinberg's research is supported by the National Institute for Mental Health.

A third interviewer will administer the Diagnostic Drawing Series, a simple art-therapy method for diagnosing DID, which has promising potential. A fourth interviewer will do clinical interviews to rule in or out each of the dissociative disorders and borderline personality disorder. The SCID-II section on borderline personality disorder has been included because I am interested in the interactions of childhood trauma, dissociation, and borderline diagnostic criteria. There will be DID subjects with and without borderline personality disorder, and borderlines with and without non-DID dissociative disorders in sufficient numbers for analysis.

This study will result in a meaningful scientific statement about the validity and reliability of the dissociative disorders, including DID. I predict that the results will support the validity of DID, but will publish them and revise my thinking if they do not. This project, combined with SCID-D multicenter research already underway and described by Dr. Steinberg elsewhere (1994), will allow for meaningful scientific conclusions to be drawn well before the end of the decade. Once a substantial body of research has been published, if the results are as I predict, extreme disbeliever positions will simply become eccentric. Dr. Steinberg's work in developing the SCID-D is a major and serious piece of programmatic research, comparable in methodology, originality, and thoroughness to anything being done in psychiatry today.

HOW DOES ONE ESTABLISH THE VALIDITY AND RELIABILITY OF A PSYCHIATRIC DISORDER?

The procedure for establishing the reliability of any given psychiatric disorder is well accepted and straightforward. Merskey and colleagues (1994) states that "the proponents of MPD have produced figures for high reliability in this condition but this is no more than may be obtained by an actor giving a convincing performance of something or other" (p. 246). In fact, it is a difficult task to establish the reliability of a psychiatric disorder, and requires a sustained research effort. For instance, the average inter-rater reliability for all Axis I disorders on the SCID is 0.68 (Spitzer et al. 1990), including a kappa for schizophrenia which is exactly average at 0.68. If it is so easy to establish the reliability of a disorder, why, in one study, did investigators using state of the art structured interviews for diagnosing borderline personality disorder fail to reach the minimum cutoff for establishing the reliability of the disorder, with a maximum kappa of 0.52?

Reliability is the degree of agreement between different raters as to who does and does not have a given disorder. If two clinicians independently interview 100 subjects, and agree in every single case who does and does not have DID, then inter-rater reliability as measured by a statistic called Cohen's kappa is 1.0. If they disagree in every single case, kappa is −1.0. If they agree half the time, as they would by flipping coins, kappa is 0. To be reliable, a diagnosis must have a kappa of at least 0.60—kappas above 0.70 are good, and above 0.80 excellent. The highest kappa on the SCID is for agoraphobia at 0.92.

Inter-rater agreement can take several forms, including agreement between two clinicians, between two structured interviews, or between a structured interview and clinical diagnosis. Another form of agreement is test-retest reliability in which the same test is administered to the same subjects at different points in time to demonstrate the temporal stability of the findings. In psychiatry, clinical diagnosis is used as the gold standard throughout the full range of *DSM-IV* disorders.

Reliability is determined in psychiatry by comparing the clinical diagnoses of trained expert subspecialist clinicians to structured interview diagnoses. This is the standard machinery of the science. If one were to use Dr. Merskey as the clinical diagnostician in such a study, he would find that no subjects have true DID. Kappa would be 1.0 if all the subjects did not have DID on structured interview, it would be −1.0 if all had structured interview DID, and 0.0 if half did, so there would be no point in doing the study: the results would be an artifact of the number of subjects with structured interview diagnoses of DID, and could be predicted in advance. If I wanted to demonstrate that the reliability of DID is high, I would simply present Dr. Merskey with a pool of subjects of whom only a small minority had DID on structured interview. Therefore clinicians of Dr. Merskey's persuasion make it scientifically impossible ever to establish whether DID is or is not reliable. It is important to emphasize this point— ideologically preconceived closure makes scientific investigation impossible. It is antiscientific.

Unless one has reliability, one cannot have validity. Imagine that one expert has written a book on how to treat borderlines, while another has written a book describing a distinctly different method of treating narcissists. Both books and both treatment methods will be meaningless unless the two authors can agree on who is a borderline and who is a narcissist.

Validity is a more complex concept and more difficult to establish. There are various subtypes of validity such as face, concurrent, and construct validity, and I will not go into these in detail here. Face validity simply means whether the construct or disorder makes sense on its face, that is, at an intuitive or common-sense level. For Dr. Merskey, DID has no face validity, while for me it has high face validity. Face validity, however, is only the simplest beginning stage of scientific research into validity. Restricting analysis and discussion to ideologically driven disagreements about face validity brings scientific inquiry to a halt at its most primitive level.

For practical purposes, from a clinicians's perspective, a diagnosis is valid if it leads to a differential treatment that benefits individuals with the disorder more than other treatments. The diagnosis becomes meaningful and valid if it makes a difference in the afflicted individual's life. My clinical experience tells me that DID has by far the highest treatment validity of any chronic complex mental disorder. The curious thing is that Dr. Merskey's clinical experience tells him that the diagnosis has negative treatment validity, that it results in regression, harm, reinforcement of the sick role, and artifactual symptoms. Both of these are anecdotal opinions and choosing the correct one will not be possible until adequately designed treatment outcome studies have been conducted. Preliminary financial analyses on small numbers of subjects suggest that the financial savings due to early diagnosis and specific treatment of DID could range in the order of $250,000 per case (Ross and Dua 1993). My question for Dr. Merskey is whether it is clinical experience or his ideology that is driving his opinion, since he nowhere provides evidence of having attended at a dissociative disorders unit, sat in on treatment, reviewed videotaped treatment sessions of recognized experts, or attended trainings by leading experts.

In research terms, validity is established if different structured interviews, self-report measures, and clinical diagnoses are consistent with each other, in other words, if the gold standard of clinical diagnosis is supported by a variety of research tools and methodologies. In clinical medicine, different gold standards such as X-rays of broken legs and sputum cultures of pneumonia patients are available, which we do not have in psychiatry. For instance, the inter-rater reliability and validity of a compound fracture of the femur are so obvious that research on the question isn't required. In general medicine, a disorder can be fully valid even though there is no effective treatment—an example of such a disorder is cancer of the pancreas. Therefore, although treatment is the ultimate goal, the absence of definitive treatment outcome studies for DID does not mean that we cannot establish its diagnostic validity.

EXISTING DATA ON THE VALIDITY AND RELIABILITY OF DID

What data currently exist and what is their quality? It is clear that the quantity of data is still small compared with that for other areas of *DSM-IV*, therefore definitive conclusions cannot be reached at this time. However, all existing data point to the reliability and validity of DID, and there are no published scientific research studies that indicate that the disorder is not legitimate. I will not attempt an exhaustive review of the literature, and will concentrate on the DES, SCID-D, and DDIS. The Dissociation Questionnaire developed by Vanderlinden (1993) in Europe has good reliability and has been used in a variety of studies that confirm the research findings in North America.

If DID is valid and reliable, it should not be limited to North America. Its key structural features should have been observed in a variety of cultures, with the specifics of the different cultures having a pathoplastic effect primarily at the level of content. This is the accepted understanding of schizophrenia, for instance, in which differences in the content of the delusions vary according to culture, but the core and structural components of the disorder are relatively invariant.

Arguments that DID is culture-bound, artifactual, and limited to North America are differentially applied to DID in a way that is not done for other disorders. There is in fact overwhelming and abundant evidence that the key elements of DID are universal and have been recognized throughout history (Kirmayer 1994, Lewis-Fernandez 1994, Ross 1989, Suryani and Jensen 1993). These elements are switches of executive control in which another entity takes control of the body, and varying degrees of amnesia. This basic property of the human mind is the foundation of DID, and also of a wide range of ecstatic, trance, and possession states which have been recognized from time immemorial, and subcategorized by the Catholic Church as *lucid possession* and *somnambulistic possession*.

In North America, these fundamental dissociative abilities of the human mind are harnessed to cope with severe, chronic childhood trauma. Because our culture is comparatively secular and individualistic, the created identities tend to be secular and personified as human beings. Nevertheless, even in North American DID, in a series of 236 cases, 28.6 percent included personality states identified as a demon, 28.1 percent states identified as another living relative, and 20.6 percent states identified as a dead relative (Ross 1989, Ross et al. 1989a). Called *parental introject alters* clinically, these personality states are commonly understood by the patients as literal discarnate intrusions of the spirits of dead relatives (Ross 1994). In two general population surveys (Ross and Joshi 1992), 2–3 percent of adult respondents in North America reported possession experiences and channeling discarnate entities through themselves while in a trance state. These findings and a vast anthropological literature clearly establish the phenomenological and structural overlap between DID and mediumship, possession, and a variety of other universally recognized dissociative states.

What about clinically diagnosed DID outside North America? Small numbers of cases have been diagnosed in many different countries (Coons 1994). However this does not counter the view that North America is experiencing an artifactual epidemic. So far no systematic research has been done outside North America that detected prevalences of DID in clinical populations markedly different from those in North America. The most extensive research has been done in the Netherlands using a Dutch version of the SCID-D (Boon and Draijer 1993), and the finding is that DID is common and has the same profile as in North America. The same is true of DID in Japan detected in a screening study with Japanese translations of the DES and DDIS (Berger et al 1992). The opinion that DID is limited to North America will disappear as research accumulates over the next decade, though diehard extremists will maintain that the hysterical epidemic has simply spread.

DID is not diagnosed outside North America because clinicians are ideologically opposed to recognizing the disorder, are not trained in its detection, and do not inquire systematically about its symptoms. Clinical populations anywhere in the world could be screened with translated versions of the DES, SCID-D, and DDIS—one can guess my prediction as to the results. In the absence of such research, all opinions are merely political in nature.

Both the DDIS and SCID-D have reliabilities for the diagnosis of DID in the range of 0.95–0.96, which is higher than that for any other psychiatric disorder. Although the quantity of data are as yet small, and replications are required, this finding is true of the SCID-D in both North America and Europe. To illustrate with the DDIS, in 196 subjects with clinical diagnoses of DID, the DDIS made the diagnosis in 95.4 percent of cases, which is a sensitivity higher than that of structured interviews for schizophrenia. In over 500 subjects without clinical diagnoses of DID, the false positive rate for DDIS diagnoses of DID has been under 1 percent—if these 696 subjects are pooled, the overall kappa for rate of agreement between structured interview and clinical diagnosis is 0.96.

The rate of false positive diagnoses of DID made by the DDIS, in my clinical experience, is lower than the rate of false positive diagnoses made by clinicians referring to our Dissociative Disorders Unit at Charter Health System of Dallas. For instance, I have had patients referred to me with clinical diagnoses of DID whom I considered to have Munchausen's syndrome, schizotypal personality disorder, dissociative disorder not otherwise specified, and schizoaffective disorder. In Canada I was referred a patient whose sole diagnosis was premenstrual syndrome.

What about the performance of the DES as a screening instrument for DID? In a study conducted at seven research centers and involving 1051 subjects Carlson et al. (1993) demonstrated that the DES performs at the state of the art in psychiatry as a screening measure and has high validity. A simple cutoff score of 30 on the DES resulted in a sensitivity of 74 percent and a specificity of 80 percent for the diagnosis of DID. The study involved sophisticated statistical analyses including a receiver operating-characteristic curve, and a computer algorithm for best predicting status as DID or non-DID based on weighted item scores. No meaningful critique of the validity of DID can be undertaken that does not focus in detail on the methodology of this study. Data reviewed in that paper and elsewhere by

Carlson (1994) establish the reliability and validity of the DES at the state of the art in psychiatry.

Scientific study of the DES no longer focuses on its clinical utility as a screening measure for DID, which has been established, but rather on questions such as the stability of its factor structure in different populations.

In summary, although the existing data are not definitive, the burden of proof lies on extreme disbelievers to establish through scientific studies that DID is not valid and reliable, since the existing data point to the opposite conclusion. Meaningful criticisms of the existing literature must be scientific in nature and must focus on details of methodology, sample size and bias, and related concerns.

HOW EASY IS IT TO CREATE DIFFERENTIAL AMNESIA OR ARTIFACTUAL DISSOCIATIVE IDENTITY DISORDER?

An implicit assumption of the extreme disbeliever position about DID is that it is relatively easy to create artifactual DID through demand characteristics, leading questions, and differential reinforcement of patient re sponses. This is not actually the case, and we have empirical evidence based on extensive mind-control research funded by the CIA and military intelligence agencies demonstrating the difficulty of creating secure amnesia barriers and dissociated personality states. Much of this information is still classified, but that which is available makes the point adequately. Military intelligence personnel would be delighted, I am sure, if they could create amnesia barriers in their operatives as easily as such barriers are alleged to be created in civilian therapists' offices. The disbeliever argument is absurd from the point of view of anyone with extensive experience in civilian treatment of naturalistically occurring DID, or intelligence experience in the artificial creation of DID.

For instance, Dr. Ewen Cameron conducted research for the CIA at the Allan Memorial Institute in Montreal under the mind-control program called MKULTRA (Collins 1988, Marks 1979, Thomas 1989, Weinstein 1990). Among other projects, he attempted to create differential amnesia in patients with schizophrenia, and claimed positive results. He claimed that by depatterning an individual (Cameron 1956) he could create differential amnesia for delusional and psychotic symptoms that occured during a period of active illness, and that the disorder did not relapse as long as the amnesia was maintained (Cameron 1960). What effort was required to produce this amnesia?

In his paper entitled "Production of Differential Amnesia as a Factor in the Treatment of Schizophrenia," Cameron (1960) describes his procedure:

> The usual treatment plan employed is to put the patient on prolonged chemical sleep and immediately to start electroshock therapy in the form of Page-Russell treatments twice a day. The average length of sleep is 15 to 30 days, although some patients have been treated up to 65 days in continuous sleep with a 3-day awakening period. The average amount of ECT given is 20-30 electrical treatments, but a number of the patients have received considerably more than this.[p. 27]

For those not familiar with this literature, a Page-Russell ECT treatment involved giving six electric shocks to the brain per treatment instead of the usual one. I personally reviewed records from the Allan Memorial Institute on a patient who was admitted under Dr. Cameron in March 1963 at age 25, and discharged in early September 1963, after she had turned 26: from May to September she received 102 ECT treatments. This woman continues to the present to be amnesic for her entire life from age 26 back. For the first year after being released from the Allan Memorial Institute she was profoundly neuropsychologically impaired, having been unable to state her name, the year, or the location during the course of her hospitalization, and having at one point been incontinent of urine and feces. There has never been any hint of psychosis in this woman, and she probably had dissociative disorder not otherwise specified prior to admission under Dr. Cameron. At discharge, Dr. Cameron instructed her husband not to talk about her past, to expose her to her family as little as possible, and to make her initiate all relearning of cognitive skills, which included reading, cooking, driving, and recognizing her children, all of which she managed successfully over a year. This is the technical difficulty and scale of intervention required to produce and maintain differential amnesia in clinical patients.

What about the difficulty of creating even simple dual personality for intelligence purposes? G. H. Estabrooks (1971), who identifies himself as having been a psychological warfare expert during the First and Second World Wars, describes the extensive effort over periods of months required to create an enduring dual personality for intelligence purposes. This is very different from the transient creation of a laboratory analog of some features of DID in college students. Military intelligence experts in psychological warfare, working under the financial and military pressures of war with willing and carefully selected subjects, were well aware of the difficulty of creating the secure, enduring intrapsychic structure called an *alter personality*. It is simply not plausible that Estabrooks would have gone to all this effort if the task was so easy. Estabrooks (1943) wrote a major textbook of hypnosis, which went through many editions and which included a chapter on psychological warfare. This account, however, is taken from a popular article (Estabrooks 1971).

> During World War II, I worked this technique with a vulnerable Marine lieutenant I'll call Jones. Under the watchful eye of Marine intelligence I split his personality into Jones A and Jones B. Jones A, once a "normal" working Marine, became entirely different. He talked communist doctrine and meant it. He was welcomed enthusiastically by communist cells, was deliberately given a dishonorable discharge by the Corps (which was in on the plot) and became a card-carrying party member.
>
> The joker was Jones B, the second personality, formerly apparent in the conscious Marine. Under hypnosis, this Jones had been carefully coached by suggestion. Jones B was the deeper personality, knew all about the thoughts of Jones A, was a loyal American and was "imprinted" to say nothing during conscious phases.

One can see that, from a military intelligence point of view, the proposition that an enduring dual personality can be created by a civilian psychotherapist in a few sessions is laughable. Yet the extreme disbeliever position is that complex cases with many personalities and complex amnesia barriers of many different types have been created unwittingly and with ease in tens of thousands of individuals carrying this diagnosis in North America today. The hypothesis that a substantial number of DID diagnoses are purely artifactual has no empirical support and has face validity for a diminishing number of professionals.

CONCLUSIONS

Is DID a valid and reliable diagnosis? That is a scientific question that can be answered only by scientific methods. It cannot be answered by anecdotal case arguments, ideological assertion, tautology, or vote. Scientific research may yield either a positive or a negative answer; however, the existing data point toward a positive conclusion. Extreme disbeliever arguments about the reality of DID, as they exist currently in psychiatry, are conducted at a low intellectual level, in ignorance of the central paradox of the disorder, and in dissociation from the existing data. They clearly do not represent disinterested intellectual inquiry and are symptoms of institutionalized hostile countertransference toward DID within psychiatry.

From a general sytems theory perspective, DID is not peculiar to the human psyche, because it is a mode of dyfunctional system organization that can occur in any system in the universe. The core features of DID, from a systems perspective, are the existence of abnormally dissociated subsystems that act as if they are not segments of the larger system, and which display radical failures of information transfer between subsystems. From this perspective, DID affects *DSM-IV*, federal governments, corporations, and many other systems. When subsystems fail accurately to differentiate self and other, and launch destructive attacks on other subsystems within human patients with DID, we call this DID. When the same thing occurs in the immune system, we call it an autoimmune disorder. The greater validity of DID is that it provides a window into dysfunctional systems of all kinds—insights from the psychotherapy of DID might be harnessed to yield isomorphic repair mechanisms for other dissociated systems.

REFERENCES

Diagnostic and Statistical Manual of Mental Disorders (1980). 3rd ed. Washington, DC: American Psychiatric Association.
_____ (1994). 4th ed. Washington, DC: American Psychiatric Association.
Berger, P., Saito, S., Ono, Y., et al. (1992). Dissociative symptomatology in an eating disorder cohort in Japan. Paper presented at the Japanese Stress Science Conference, Tokyo.
Bernstein, E. M., and Putnam, F. W. (1986). Development, reliability, and validity of a dissociation scale. *Journal of Nervous and Mental Disease* 174:727-735.
Boon, S., and Draijer, N. (1993). *Multiple Personality Disorder in the Netherlands*. Amsterdam: Swets and Zeitlinger.
Cameron, D. E. (1956). Psychic driving. *American Journal of Psychiatry* 112:502-509.
_____ (1960). Production of differential amnesia as a factor in the treatment of schizophrenia. *Comprehensive Psychiatry* 1:26-34.
Carlson, E. B. (1994). Studying the interaction between physical and psychological states with the Dissociative Experiences Scale. In *Dissociation: Culture, Mind and Body*, ed. D. Spiegel, pp. 41-58. Washington, DC: American Psychiatric Press.
Carlson, E. B., Putnam, F. W., and Ross, C. A. (1993). Validity of the Dissociative Experiences Scale in screening for multiple personality disorder: a multicenter study. *American Journal of Psychiatry* 150:1030-1036.
Collins, A. (1988). *In the Sleep Room. The Story of CIA Brainwashing Experiments in Canada*. Toronto: Lester & Orpen Dennys.
Coons, P. M. (1994). Reactions to four cases of supposed multiple personality disorder: evidence of unjustified diagnosis. *Canadian Journal of Psychiatry* 39:243-244.
Estabrooks, G. H. (1943). *Hypnotism*. New York: E. P. Dutton.
_____ (1971). Hypnosis comes of age. *Science Digest*, April, 44-50.
Fahy, T. A. (1988). The diagnosis of multiple personality disorder: a critical review. *British Journal of Psychiatry* 153:597-606.

Freeland, A., Manchanda, R., Chiu, S., et al. (1993). Four cases of supposed multiple personality disorder: evidence of unjustified diagnosis. *Canadian Journal of Psychiatry* 38:245–247.

The ICD-10 Classification of Mental and Behavioural Disorders. Clinical Descriptions and Diagnostic Guidelines (1992). Geneva: World Health Association.

Kirmayer, L. J. (1994). Pacing the void: social and cultural dimensions of dissociation. In *Dissociation: Culture, Mind, and Body*, ed. D. Spiegel, pp. 91–122. Washington DC: American Psychiatric Press.

Lewis-Fernandez, R. (1994). Culture and dissociation: a comparison of *ataque de nervios* among Puerto Ricans and possession syndrome in India. In *Dissociation: Culture, Mind, and Body*, ed. D. Spiegel, pp. 123–167. Washington, DC: American Psychiatric Press.

Mai, F. (1992). Resolved: Multiple personality disorder is misleading and counterproductive as a diagnostic category. Paper presented at the Canadian Psychiatric Association Annual Meeting, Montreal.

Marks, J. (1979). *The Search for the Manchurian Candidate*. New York: W. W. Norton.

Merskey, H. (1992). The manufacture of personalities. The production of multiple personality disorder. *British Journal of Psychiatry* 160:327–340.

Merskey, H., Freeland, A., Manchanda, R., et al. (1994). The authors respond. *Canadian Journal of Psychiatry* 39:245–246.

Ross, C. A. (1989). *Multiple Personality Disorder. Diagnosis, Clinical Features, and Treatment*. New York: John Wiley & Sons.

_____ (1991). Epidemiology of multiple personality disorder and dissociation. *Psychiatric Clinics of North America* 14:503–517.

_____ (1992). The dissociated executive self and the cultural dissociation barrier. *Dissociation* 5.

_____ (1994). *The Osiris Complex. Case Studies in Multiple Personality Disorder*. Toronto: University of Toronto Press.

Ross, C. A., and Dua, V. (1993). Psychiatric health care costs of multiple personality disorder. *American Journal of Psychotherapy* 47:103–112.

Ross, C. A., Heber, S., Norton, G. R., et al. (1989b). The dissociative disorders interview schedule: a structured interview. *Dissociation* 2:169–189.

Ross, C. A., and Joshi, S. (1992). Paranormal experiences in the general population. *Journal of Nervous and Mental Disease* 180:362–368.

Ross, C. A., Kronson, J., and Hildah, K. Unpublished data.

Ross, C. A., Miller, S. D., Reagor, P., et al. (1990). Structured interview data on 102 cases of multiple personality disorder from four centers. *American Journal of Psychiatry* 147:596–601.

Ross, C. A., Norton, G. R., and Wozney, K. (1989a). Multiple personality disorder: an analysis of 236 cases. *Canadian Journal of Psychiatry* 34:413–418.

Spiegel, D. (1994). *Dissociation: Culture, Mind, and Body*. Washington, DC: American Psychiatric Press.

Spitzer, R., Williams, J., and Gibbons, M. (1990). *Structured Clinical Interview for DSM-III-R*. Washington, DC: American Psychiatric Press.

Steinberg, M. (1993). *Interviewer's Guide to the Structured Clinical Interview for DSM-IV Dissociative Disorders (SCID-D)*. Washington, DC: American Psychiatric Press.

_____ (1994). Systematizing dissociation: Symptomatology and diagnostic assessment. In *Dissociation: Culture, Mind, and Body*, ed. D. Spiegel, pp. 59–88. Washington, DC: American Psychiatric Press.

Steinberg, M., Rounsaville, B. J., and Cicchetti, D. V. (1990). The structured clinical interview for *DSM-III-R* dissociative disorders: preliminary report on a new diagnostic instrument. *American Journal of Psychiatry* 147:76–82.

Suryani, L. K., and Jensen, D. J. (1993). *Trance and Possession in Bali. A Window on Western Multiple Personality, Possession Disorder, and Suicide*. Kuala Lumpur: Oxford University Press.

Thomas, G. (1989). *Journey into Madness. The True Story of Secret CIA Mind Control and Medical Abuse*. New York: Bantam.
Vanderlinden, J. (1993). *Dissociative Experiences, Trauma and Hypnosis*. Delft: Eburon.
Weinstein, H. M. (1990). *Psychiatry and the CIA: Victims of Mind Control*. Washington, DC: American Psychiatric Press.

II

Theoretical Controversies

5

Gullible's Travels, or The Importance of Being Multiple

Michael A. Simpson

The movement's anti-empirical features are legion. They include its cult of . . . personality; its casually anecdotal approach to corroboration; its cavalier dismissal of its most besetting epistemic problem, that of suggestion; its habitual confusion of speculation with fact; its penchant for generalizing from a small number of imperfectly examined instances; its proliferation of theoretical entities bearing no testable referents; its lack of vigilance against self-contradiction; its selective reporting of raw data to fit the latest theoretical enthusiasm; its ambiguities and exit clauses, allowing negative results to be counted as positive ones; its indifference to rival explanations and to mainstream science; its absence of any specified means for preferring one interpretation to another; its insistence that only the initiated are entitled to criticize; its stigmatizing of disagreement as "resistance," along with the corollary that . . . all such resistance constitutes "actual evidence in favour of the correctness" of the theory. . . .

Frederick Crews

THE NATURE OF MPD

Frederick Crews was writing about classical psychoanalysis; but his comments are remarkable and exactly apposite to the field of MPD. Before it is possible to contemplate how one should manage the sort of patients so ardently described as having MPD, it is necessary to understand the many things that are misconceived and odd about the diagnosis and its attendant literature.

Multiple personality disorder is a very curious condition. Its basic characteristics, according to its own fond literature, show a unique pattern of peculiarities. Its literature's claims to be scientific are hard to justify. In this chapter, we will examine some of the fundamental features of the malady, its literature, and its claims. It is probably the most controversial diagnosis in current vogue. Although its adherents tend rather petulantly to dismiss the serious criticisms it arouses, it will become clear that there is a decidedly sound basis for such criticism, and that its critics have never been effectively refuted. We will examine the scientific status claimed by writings on the subject by its apologists, and some alternative explanations of the phenomena in question.

Let me begin by declaring what I am *not* challenging. I have no doubt whatsoever that many people have major inconsistencies within their personality structure and between their behaviors on different occasions. The experience of multiplicity within one self is rather commonplace to the self-perceptive. As the character Bernard (in Virginia Woolf's *The Waves*) says: "I am not one person; I am many people." But it is the one "I" who is many. Similarly, Walt Whitman wrote: "I am large, I contain multitudes"; but it is quite clear that the individual "I" contained the multitudes. Oscar Wilde (Ellman 1987) said, "I am certain that I have three separate and distinct souls." William James (1890) quoted Faust saying that "two souls dwell within his breast." The experience of being *like* separate souls is both common and normal. But claiming special rights and benefits on this basis is neither.

Similarly, I do not doubt that there are a number of highly suggestible and unhappy people who, after encountering enthusiasts of MPD, come to display the sort of features commonly described as representing MPD. Let us not waste any time disputing these facts. But I do strongly challenge the proposition that there is a common, naturally occurring, and universal disorder, arising without substantial pathoplastic input from the media, enthused therapists, amateur zealots, and other marketers and profiteers, and strong cultural priming; that anything much about the condition has been established with reasonable scientific certainty by rational scientific method; that the theories of causation so far advanced are convincing or helpful; and that the gross therapeutic overindulgence and patient pandering, which seem to have become common, are useful forms of intervention.

I do consider that MPD is a rum phenomenon, significantly unlike most, if not all, other diagnoses in modern usage. Its distribution is abnormal, resembling that of a culture-bound disorder linked to American psychobabble culture. Its incidence is irregular, and has waxed and waned markedly over the last 150 years, showing a consistent relationship to the degree of publicity given to multiplicity in popular media.

For the sake of economy, I will often refer to the views of the composite orthodox MPD establishment as the MPD-ites, for, unlike most other areas of medical, psychiatric, and psychological endeavor, the latter-day MPD movement shows many of the features of a religious, or other, cult. There is not sufficient space to consider fully the schisms and variances within the field, though the strong personal allegiances, the reliance on apostolic pronouncements in place of hard data, and the prevalence of discipular and proselytizing behavior among followers and converts reminds one of medieval apostasies and sects: the Kluftites and the Coonies, Putnamists, Braun-shirts, and Rossites. (If it be thought that I might be exaggerating the degree of personality cult arising, one should note such signs as the collecting of "Kluftisms" [Goodwin and Attias 1993].

The response of MPD-ites when their beliefs are challenged is typically that of cult-members rather than scientists. As Festinger and colleagues wrote (1956) in their classic study of the extent to which individuals and groups can contort common sense in order to preserve the purity of their belief system from invasion by mere facts:

> A man with a conviction is a hard man to change. Tell him you disagree and he turns away. Show him facts or figures and he questions your sources. Appeal to logic and he fails to see your point. We have all experienced the futility of trying to change a strong conviction, especially if the convinced person has some investment in his belief. We are familiar with the variety of ingenious defenses with which people protect their convictions, managing to keep them unscathed through the most devastating attacks.

They pointed out that when someone has such committed beliefs and takes irrevocable public actions based on them, and then meets "evidence, unequivocal and undeniable evidence, that his belief is wrong," then "the individual will frequently emerge, not only unshaken, but even more convinced of the truth of his beliefs than ever before. Indeed, he may even show a new fervor about convincing and converting other people to his view."

THE DUTY OF SKEPTICISM

The skepticism I express is my scientific duty—there are so many busy "iconoblasts" about that the role of iconoclast is biologically necessary.

Skeptical views are widely shared though less often expressed publicly or in print. It is highly significant how many of the luminary leaders of international psychiatry and psychology have avoided the controversy, but have failed to acknowledge MPD as common or important. Skepticism is notable in the World Health Organization's latest (1992) classification system, *ICD-10*, derived from extensive international consensus development, which remarks: "If multiple personality disorder . . . does exist as something other than a culture-specific or even iatrogenic condition, then it is presumably best placed among the dissociative group"; and adds, "this disorder is rare, and controversy exists about the extent to which it is iatrogenic or culture-specific . . . subsequent changes . . . occur during sessions with a therapist that involve relaxation, hypnosis, or abreaction."

Many of those authorities who have commented on MPD have maintained skepticism. Mayer-Gross and colleagues (1960) wrote of MPDs that they "are always artificial productions, the product of the medical attention that they arouse." Even Thigpen and Cleckly (1984) wrote with disquiet of the "epidemic" of MPD cases after they reported Eve (1957), and record that they found only one other case they considered genuine among tens of thousands referred in the thirty years after Eve. They wrote of patients traveling from therapist to therapist, finding one who believed them, and competing with other patients to have the most personalities. "Unfortunately, there also seems to be a competition among some therapists to see who can have the greatest number of multiple personality cases."

Skepticism is not only recent; even early pioneers of the field had serious doubts about the premises accepted by fervent current believers. Janet (1920) did not regard MPD as an important new syndrome, predicting that it would be of more academic than clinical interest, and so rare that "it is unlikely that you will have to occupy yourselves with it in practice." Braun (1984a) acknowledged that it was Janet who first suggested that MPD could be created by hypnosis; and Janet also raised the possibility of role playing to please the therapist, openly stating his belief that some of his patients were playing and acting (Decker 1986, van der Hart and Horst 1989). Even in the 1880s there was reaction against it, authors pointing out cases where alters were conveniently created to avoid responsibility for unacceptable behavior. (MPD-ites emphasize the unacceptable behavior of others, not that of their clients.) Overinvolvement by the therapist, including counter-transference anomalies, have been notable from the start of the literature, and Prince's obsession and infatuation with the case of Christine Beauchamp was widely recognized.

The current wave of concern about MPD, and especially its purported link to child abuse and even to unproven claims of satanic cult abuse, is strongly reminiscent of the witchcraft scares of earlier centuries. Then, too, uncorroborated claims made by children after prolonged questioning that local people were witches became increasingly believed, until they over-reached themselves in the extent and attribution of their claims, and became disbelieved (e.g., Notestein 1968, Richardson and Best 1991).

THE INCIDENCE OF MPD

Ross (1989), like so many of the enthusiasts of the diagnosis, complains that MPD is "vastly underdiagnosed," despite the recent exponential increase in the numbers receiving the diagnosis, and argues in favor of "overinclusive diagnostic criteria" as "in the best interests of patients." Hard data to justify such views is absent.

Ross estimated the point prevalence of MPD in urban North America as between 1 in 50 and 1 in 10,000 persons, deriving these figures by unscientific extrapolation from his personal experience in Winnipeg, where he estimated that about 5 percent of university students have MPD. (Perhaps they should pay extra tuition fees?) Even Modestin (1992a) admits that there are practically no reliable data on MPD prevalence, and that studies such as that of Bliss and Jeppsen (1985) are based on a markedly biased sample, while other estimates (Ross et al. 1990, Schafer 1986) "are not substantiated by any appropriate data."

Guesstimates of incidence are extraordinarily unrealistic projections based on invalid extrapolation from incidences noted in highly selected and atypical groups, usually patients at centers where figures widely renowned for their interest in MPD are located. Proper epidemiological studies should have been possible by now, and, within such a growing and profitable market, affordable.

Nakdimen (1992), without data, emotionally claims that the average MPD patient "has had to suffer the condition for literally a quarter of a century before being correctly diagnosed, and that most such patients never get diagnosed." The number of MPD patients who never get diagnosed is equal to the number of angels who can dance on the tip of a pin: wholly unknowable, and decided only by blind faith.

No reliable and valid figures of incidence have yet been published. Yet sequential claims suggest a very rapidly growing number of patients have been receiving this diagnosis in recent decades. No convincing explanation has been given for this rapid rise, or for the high incidence being claimed.

The amount and severity of trauma is not increasing commensurably with the rapid inflation in case numbers. If the increase is, as is implied, due to the superb diagnostic skills of the minority of clinicians who use the diagnosis, then the remaining 99 percent of their colleagues must be stunningly obtuse and negligent, to miss so many cases of so common and dramatic a plight. But with increases of hundreds of percent per year, are the skills of these MPD clinicians really growing at that rate? This in itself would be an achievement unique in medical history, and one demanding serious study in its own right.

If MPD is truly, as asserted by its proponents, a common result of chronic childhood trauma (child abuse, or as Ross [1990] later admitted, war, famine, or disaster); and, if one allows the unproved qualification Ross added in his 1990 response to Simpson (1989), even if such trauma had this effect "only within a window of vulnerability ending in early adolescence": why, in peaceful Winnipeg (where one recalls no major wars, famines, or disasters, and the incidence of child abuse is surely no higher than in other comparable communities) does Ross find so many cases (5% of his university students, plus his many other cases) while we in Africa haven't yet been able to find a case? And why has there been no report of a massive epidemic in Europe, following the Second World War?

Ross (1989) confidently suggested that "by the year 2000, most mental health professionals will probably have diagnosed at least one case of MPD." With only six years to go, and many millions of us still to achieve that milestone, an enormous number of new cases are needed—unless Ross's estimate relied on many of us sharing the experience of individual cases. The World Health Organization called for "Health for All" by 2000; Ross seems to have called for MPD for all by the year 2000. Yet, contradicting himself in the same book, Ross expresses fear that MPD may once again fall into obscurity and "disrepute" in the next decade or two.

THE SEX DISTRIBUTION OF MPD

The sex distribution of cases is distinctive. Putnam and colleagues (1986) reported that 92 percent are female; and other reports are consistent. Like hysteria, MPD is predominantly a diagnosis of women, made by men. There have been untested suggestions that there are large numbers of male cases in prison, but no convincing reports of any large number of male cases being assessed there. The claim that men with MPD end in prison rather than in therapy (at least parole from prison is more likely than from MPD therapy!), though pathetically easy to test, has never been substantiated. The claim has appeared several times in articles, apparently supported by citing three papers (two by Putnam) that actually contain no data whatsoever to support the hypothesis, merely repeating the empty assertion. Putnam (1989) makes the same claim, but only supports it by citing similar statements by himself, Bliss, Greaves, and Boor.

I can locate only one study of cases in jail (Bliss and Larson 1985), exclusively of thirty-three male sex offenders, of whom 21 percent were classified as MPD by the generous *DSM-III* criteria, with another 18 percent called "possible" MPD. (What a uniquely elastic diagnosis! Even I might have "possible" MPD. But none of me agrees with this.)

This is typical of the MPD literature: convenient hypotheses are stated as if they have been proved, and no realistic attempt is subsequently made to test them. The uncritical reader, however, especially if unable to pursue and read the references, and to discover that they contain no supporting data, is often given the impression that these are established facts, rather than guesses.

THE DISTRIBUTION OF CASES
AMONG CLINICIANS

I have also pointed out the epidemiologically strange dispersal of MPD, with the gross lack of a normal distribution. One rarely meets a clinician who, over a significant period of time, has seen just one case. "The vast majority of talented, sensitive, observant clinicians have never seen a case at all" (Simpson 1989), while a very small number of clinicians report the great majority of cases.

Coons (1990) and Ross (1990) fiercely rejected Simpson's views (1989), without providing data. Coons (1990) asserted that MPD is common in many parts of the world—on the basis of his correspondence. Apparently the clinicians with whom he corresponds fail to get reports of their findings published in any refereed journals, for reasons not made clear.

Coons (1990) made a deeply peculiar claim, regrettably misleading. Responding to Simpson's comment that the majority of cases are reported by a small number of clinicians, he says that "the 211 case reports in the English literature have been reported by 180 different clinicians." This is simply unbelievable, and he owes us a detailed paper proving this astonishing assertion. He would have great difficulty showing that there were only 211 papers on MPD, by 180 clinician-authors. But in 1986, Coons had estimated that 6,000 cases had been diagnosed in North America (Coons 1986, also cited in North et al. 1993). His claim is untenable, and shows highly selective inattention to the noisiest of the literature. Far more cases have been reported, and most of the reports have come from a very much smaller number of authors.

The numbers quoted shift and overlap confusingly. In 1982, Kluft reported 70 cases (Kluft 1982); yet in 1984, he (1984a) refers to a "research series" of 73 cases he had described in a conference paper back in 1979! Also in 1984 (Kluft 1984b) he referred to 73 cases reviewed retrospectively, and "over 100 cases" studied prospectively. Yet, in the same year (1984c) Kluft reported having interviewed 171 cases, saying that 117 sought treatment with him. Later papers by Kluft refer to still more cases of MPD he has seen and reviewed.

Various other authors have reported significant numbers of patients (not claiming these were the only MPD patients they'd ever seen). Coons himself (1984) reported 10 cases; Horevitz and Braun (1983) discussed 33 cases; Bliss (1984) reported on 70, stating that he had personally seen 100 in 4 years, later confirming this total (Bliss 1986); Morton Prince collected some 20 cases (Prince 1906a,b); Putnam et al. (1986) reviewed 100 cases; Ross (1989; also Ross et al. 1989b) reported a series of 236. I could continue, but it is clear that when three authors can report over 500 cases, Coons's attempt to refute my hypothesis is incomprehensible.

Some prolific authors on MPD, like Putnam and Kluft, also seem to collect and report on other clinicians' cases. This makes it impossible, from the data supplied, to be sure how many clinicians have seen how many cases, and how many cases may have seen reported several times in different publications.

Yet, as Merskey's brilliant review reminds us (1992), not only do the vast majority of psychiatrists and psychologists see no cases, but even some of those specially studying dissociative disorders have reported none. He cited several studies of hundreds of patients with dissociative/ hysterical/conversion disorders, among whom MPD was not found. Chodoff (1987) also noted the rarity of the state.

INFLATION IN THE NUMBER OF ALTERS

When I said that the number of alters tend to grow in therapy (Simpson 1989), this conclusion was fiercely rejected by some. Yet Ross himself (1989), and North and colleagues (1993) have proved my assertion of the steady inflation in the number of alters. From the last century to the 1940s, most cases reported were dual; from 1944 on, three or more were typical; Putnam reported a series with a mean of 13.3 alters (Putnam et al. 1986), and Ross's own series had a mean of 15.7. Boon and Draijer (1993) reported a mean of 18.4 personalities. More recent reports (e.g., Dell and Eisenhower 1990) described a mean of 24.1. Ross et al. (1989a) described a case with 300 alters; and Spencer (1989) claimed more than 400. Kluft apparently holds the record, recording more than 4,500 reported alters (1988). As Braude (1991) comments: "One can only wonder about the accuracy of such an estimate". . . .

Spanos (1986), and Spanos and colleagues (1986) support my view, while Sutcliffe and Jones (1962) commented on "the most luxurious growth and long life of additional personalities" in psychotherapy, calling Eve's escalation of alters "therapy nurtured."

No one has given a coherent explanation of *why* there should have been such a dramatic increase in the number of alters. It absolutely cannot be due to increasing severity of the early trauma, as there is no evidence that the extent or severity of the trauma or abuse experienced by patients has changed significantly over the decades.

MPD AND AGE: LACK OF REPORTS IN CHILDHOOD AND OLD AGE

Despite the great many assertions that these problems start in early childhood, there is a great lack of reliable and convincing reports of cases in children. Snowden (1988) wrote a paper called: "Where Are All the Childhood Multiples?" Too often there has been reliance on later reports by an adult patient that they were symptomatic in childhood, rather than on clear cases in children. There are only a few reports on MPD and children, brief and unconvincing. Peterson (1990) refers to twenty-one case reports in eight papers, including his own, and I have located only a very few further reports (cf. Fagan and McMahon [1984], Kluft [1984d, 1985a,b, 1986], Malenbaum and Russell [1987], McMahon and Fagan [1993], Riley and Mead [1988], Snowden [1988], Waters [1989], and Weiss et al. [1985]. Yet, according to the theory of MPD, it should be common and clear in children. In fact most, if not all, of the child cases reported (the details are often too sketchy to allow full analysis) fail to meet even the broad, vague, and generous criteria for MPD, and are described as "incipient MPD," or as showing "precursors or manifestations of MPD." Typical of this field, Peterson (1990) proposes to solve this problem by special criteria for childhood MPD, even more broad, and generously including other well-recognized aspects of childhood psychopathology.

MPD in old age has been even more comprehensively absent. Only Kluft (1984c) has referred to older cases, claiming that 15 percent are aged 40–49, 6 percent 50–59, and 3 percent over 60; but his percentages are unreliable, being based on a series of only thirty-three cases, of which perhaps eight were beyond their thirties. Why is there a dearth of reports of older cases of MPD? Do cases "burn out"? Or do older people have more fruitful ways to spend their time? Or are MPD therapists uninterested in the old?

THE RACIAL AND SOCIAL CLASS DISTRIBUTION OF MPD

Though race is generally ignored or unreported in the MPD literature, the great majority of cases seem to be white (Putnam 1989). Why? Surely African-Americans are, according to all available statistics, more traumatized than whites, at all ages. A ready explanation of this finding is that African-American patients have less ready access to prolonged, preferably subsidized or sponsored, psychotherapy, and that the white therapists who dominate the field are less likely to engage with black patients in the necessary prelude to the production of elaborated MPD.

There is also a distinct lack of data provided on the social class and financial background of MPD patients. No case descriptions seem to be of lower-class, poor, or homeless patients, and the great costs of treatment (and the lack of patients reported from outside of private practice) imply that at least the treated patients are of relatively high social class and have healthy financial support. This would support my hypothesis (Simpson 1989) that one of the characteristics of MPD is that it occurs principally in the context of the availability of lengthy psychodynamic psychotherapy affordable by the subject. Where the health care system or health insurance does not sponsor such indulgence, the condition simply does not occur.

The omission of so much routine demographic data in the large MPD literature is startling and unjustifiable; while we are told certain things about MPD patients with monotonous repetitiveness, there are many perfectly basic things we simply do not know about them.

THE INTERNATIONAL DISTRIBUTION OF CASES

The dispersal of cases internationally is also distinctive. MPD is a North American epidemic, with sporadic reports from a very few clinicians with similar viewpoints to the American clinicians (often with North American training or similar influence). It is rarely seen in Japan (Takahashi 1990), or in Britain. Aldridge-Morris (1989), after writing to the Bulletins of the

British Royal College of Psychiatrists and the British Psychological Society seeking cases, received only four replies, from clinicians who thought very tentatively that they might have seen six cases among them. Only two cases have been reported in the modern British literature (Cutler and Reed 1975, Fahy et al. 1989), and both reports expressed doubt as to whether the phenomena could be considered a psychiatric disorder. I have repeatedly sought cases in the South African media and at major clinical facilities, and have carefully questioned a range of psychiatrists from East Europe, Asia, and elsewhere in Africa, but have been unable to locate any cases.

Boon and Draijer (1991, 1993) described MPD patients in the Nether-lands, as did van der Hart and Boon (1990); but these three references may give a misleading impression of widespread interest and involvement. These publications also follow the common practice of other MPD litera-ture: sequential papers refer to increasing numbers of patients, but the actual patients appear to overlap significantly between the individual articles, obscuring the actual total numbers involved.

Modestin (1992a,b) reported Swiss responses to a questionnaire. Only 60 percent of the psychiatrists polled responded clearly, but only 679 of these 770 responded on the issue of whether they had seen cases of MPD; only nineteen indicating that they had done so, four of these being unsure of their diagnosis. Modestin claimed on this basis that 3 percent of Swiss psychiatrists had treated one or more cases of MPD. In fact, even including the uncertain cases, only 2.46 percent of those responding, and only 2.8 percent of those responding specifically to this question, indicated this. It is more appropriate to exclude those not sure of their diagnosis, which brings the percentage down to 2 percent of those answering this question, and 1.8 percent of the overall respondents. The two who had never heard of MPD before reading the questionnaire should also be excluded (surely their diagnosis was unreliable) dropping the proportions having treated MPD to 1.77 percent and 1.56 percent respectively. As it is highly unlikely that any of those who bothered to complete the questionnaire but omitted to answer this question had actually treated a case, the best estimate of Swiss psychiatrists who have treated MPD is actually 1.56 percent.

Only 655 responded as to whether they had seen a case in their entire career (it is not clear whether they could respond positively if they had seen an American case demonstrated or on video, which would be irrelevant to the issue of cases occurring in Switzerland). Only sixty-three indicated that they had, which Modestin counted as a 10 percent response: although eight had never heard of the concept before receiving the questionnaire (making their sightings unconvincing); and seventeen had significant doubts about the diagnosis. Considering only the thirty-eight sure of the diagnosis of what they had seen, this would mean that only 5.8 percent of those answering this question, and only 4.9 percent of those responding to the study, had ever seen a case.

If these Swiss psychiatrists are actually seeing and treating MPD, they are failing to report cases—even Modestin has not documented cases of his own. One also notes the odd distribution of cases among doctors: one reported seeing twenty current cases, and at least fifty-nine in the past. Modestin modestly calls his overestimate of 0.05 percent to 0.10 percent of patients seen by psychiatrists "the most precise, data-based estimate" of the prevalence of MPD. This is an unacceptable claim: relying only on the memory of those responding, without any standardized, validated diagnostic system having been used, and using guesses as to the total number of patients seen by Swiss psychiatrists—that is hardly precise or data-based.

Martinez-Taboas (1989) described some cases in Puerto Rico. This is hardly outside the boundaries of U.S. psychiatric culture, especially with regard to the training of its physicians and psychiatrists.

There was fierce objection to my emphasis on the peculiarities of geographical distribution of MPD (Simpson 1989), but Ross himself (1989) has admitted that "the treatment of MPD in North America in the 1980s and 1990s is culture-bound . . . and . . . is rarely diagnosed in Great Britain and continental Europe today" and Putnam admits (1989) that "cross-cultural reports are scarce." Altogether, there is no impressive evidence suggesting that MPD might be common in other countries. Arguments on this point are often complicated by MPD enthusiasts generously embracing other culture-bound dissociative disorders in other countries, claiming that these are actually MPD and evidence of its ubiquity. This tactic is analogous to arguing that that because Congo Fever and AIDS are both basically viral diseases, Congo Fever is actually very common.

Again, my concern has historical backing. Even Janet (1907, 1920) noticed that most of even the early cases were from America. Hacking (1991) described MPD as "strictly American with Canadian branch plants" (p.). If one believes the zealots' claims, MPD appears endemic, almost epidemic in the USA: yet what they describe as its purported cause: child abuse, is far more widely distributed.

METHODS OF MAKING THE DIAGNOSIS

MPD-ites frequently assert mass misdiagnosis by their colleagues, assuming that *all* prior diagnoses were wrong, and that their MPD diagnosis is unquestionably correct. Should we automatically believe that the host of previous clinicians were all incompetent, but that the clinician diagnosing MPD is infallible? Such claims are not commonly made in regard to other diagnoses, and would never be allowed publication in scientifically respectable journals without strong supporting evidence. Kluft (1984a) also says that 40 percent of cases presented with only subtle hints, and 40 percent with "no overt signs at all": so the diagnosis *must* emerge from the assessment means used. He has seemed to blame the problem on the miscreant majority of clinicians failing to maintain a high index of suspicion for MPD, but it is arguable that it is just that high index of suspicion that creates the cases. He says it is best to be nonintrusive "initially" (which implies one may save the intrusiveness for later); but says one may press ahead "aggressively" with hypnosis, when time is limited.

BASIC ASPECTS OF DIAGNOSIS

The discussion by Klein and Riso (1993) on the problems of drawing boundaries in psychiatric disorders, and the failure of the sort of data we have been offered to prove the existence of a discrete typological condition, is highly relevant.

Putnam (1987) and others have insisted that MPD must be considered as a superordinate diagnosis superseding all others; but no logical justification, let along adequate data, have been provided for this routinely unexamined assumption. Van Praag (1993) comments: "The only justification they provide is that working with the alternates can provide a therapeutic device that cannot be utilized in the 'unified' individual, a contention which is not backed up by any controlled outcome study. We are back to the traditional psychiatric adage: I think this, thus it is true." In fact, the bald assertion is backed up by no form of data whatsoever.

The MPD literature, and authors such as Putnam, cheerfully instruct us that an inconsistent or even contradictory story is typical. In other words, it is typical to be atypical. Contradiction is never considered potentially to indicate faking, but is taken as proof of genuineness. When the patient denies current or prior features of MPD, or claims to have faked complaints, it is regarded as a "flight into health": so, if he or she denies it, then it must be true.

The MPD literature seems to ignore the well-established matter of experimenter bias and demand characteristics, and similar forces that lead people to find what they expect to find; and the evidence of how accommodating many subjects can be in meeting their assessor's expectations, even without realizing it. Even where there is absolutely no conscious intention on the part of the clinician to influence events, inadvertent cues can have substantial effects. If this is true even for white rats (Rosenthal and Fode 1963), how much more so for a group of selectively the most highly dissociative and suggestible and self-hypnotically talented human subjects available.

There seems to be a studied lack of awareness of the impact of the observer's beliefs and needs on the phenomena described, something that must be assumed (and carefully controlled for) within the behavioral sciences, as it has been well recognized in the physical sciences. As Heisenberg (1959) wrote: "We have to remember that what we observe is not nature in itself, but nature exposed to our method of questioning."

THE FACTOR OF COACHING AND TRAINING

There is considerable evidence that coaching and shaping of the patient's presentation occurs, with strong pressure exerted to get the patient to accept the diagnosis of MPD. Patients say they "couldn't believe" the diagnosis at first; but "finally accept" it. Pat, for example (Cohen et al. 1991), recalls: "Very early on he started: 'You were abused,' he would flatly, though gently, say to me. And I, just as flatly . . . would tell him no, it had not been so. . . . 'You were abused,' he continued to say. . . . I felt I had, at all costs, to defend against those words, 'You were abused.' " Then after about a year of therapy, she became convinced she had been abused and that she had MPD. From her description, the "abuse" she identified to oblige the therapist was pathetic: she "remembered" having been left alone for "hours" as an infant (highly dubious recall) and was "a disappointment" to her father, apparently not receiving enough attention for her taste demands. It is offensive to the really abused to call such limited disappointments by the same name. By these criteria, everyone alive was abused. Many such reports reflect very strong pressure being brought upon patients to accept the therapist's views.

Leslie (also in Cohen et al. 1991), joined an incest survivor's group, where the leader, a specialist in MPD, gave members a reading list including *Sybil*, *When Rabbit Howls*, *The Minds of Billy Milligan*, *Prism*, *Andrea's World*, and others. This would constitute a training program in how to grow multiple personalities. Cathy's therapist gave her many articles about MPD to read and reread, and others describe getting copies of the proceedings of MPD conferences, and articles by Kluft, and avidly reading them. One writes: "My therapist educated me, so by the time we decided I had MPD, I knew a lot." Kim describes her therapist giving her journal articles on dissociative disorders, and also read Putnam's book on MPD.

Ross (1989), among others, writes of the use of video, of showing videos of the different alters and the switches between them to all alters, and of having patients watch educational videos about MPD. He remarks: "This can be helpful and may act as a kind of vicarious group therapy."

THE ISSUE OF SUGGESTION AND IATROGENESIS

Fahy (1990) commented on how readily Coons and Ross dismiss out of hand any possibility of iatrogenesis. He suggests, as do I, that short-lived benign dissociative personality disturbance may occur, but contends that "to attain the complexity of psychopathology seen in American cases of MPD, some element of reinforcement from therapists, relatives or the media is necessary." The extent to which these possibilities are denied, ignored, and explained away by American MPD researchers is truly remarkable.

Ross (1989) claims that his flawed 1989 paper (Ross et al. 1989a) gives evidence against the iatrogenesis of MPD. The study is based on double hearsay. He collected 236 cases from other people's questionnaires—thus basing it on what other doctors chose to tell him about what their patients chose to tell them about what might have happened. Subgroups of patients were selected on grounds not fully clarified or defended. Then Ross proposed the logically unappealing argument that the more experienced the therapist, the more he ought to be influencing his patients to show signs they wouldn't otherwise show. Thus he expected differences between cases seen by MPD specialists and by MPD believers who had seen fewer cases. As all cases had to meet the same criteria for the diagnosis of MPD, it seems very unlikely that any differences *following* diagnosis would be seen—which is just what he found. My argument is that the peculiar doctor–patient relationship would reduce natural variations, and produce a more stereotyped clinical picture, which is what Ross's unsoundly argued paper confirmed. This was no proof of the absence of artifact, but merely a demonstration of the consistency of the artifactual product. There was no good explanation of why the two groups should be expected to differ, or of what difference was to be anticipated.

Then, typical of the distraction techniques used in MPD papers, Ross solemnly tells us that the groups did not differ in age, sex, marital status, or number of children—but why on earth would they? Such features are hardly open to artifactual influence by the doctors, at least not in the manner we envisage it! There was no difference between the groups in the percentages meeting each of the diagnostic criteria for MPD—but why should there be? They all had to achieve the diagnosis and meet the criteria, or they would not have been studied!

He lays much emphasis on the assertion that some patients "(had) not been hypnotized," ignoring the fact that, as Bliss established, such patients self-hypnotize so rapidly and easily that it is difficult for a psychiatrist to manage to hypnotize them first.

The numbers cited by Ross and his colleagues (1989a) are odd, and simply do not add up. Of 214 cases where he received information about hypnosis, 176 had been hypnotized, he says (but then 38 had not been hypnotized, at least not officially). Then he says a further 85 had been hypnotized only after the diagnosis was made, with 56 hypnotized both before and after: this now adds up to only 141 hypnotized, with 35 missing. He seems to compare only three groups, so there is no explanation for the missing numbers.

Yet Ross (Ross et al. 1989a) boasts that after this epochal study, "anyone who wishes to establish the correctness of the iatrogenic theory is going to have to provide very strong data . . . in order to overcome our evidence against iatrogenesis." But iatrogenic theory would predict precisely the results he found!

The common use of leading and repeated questions is problematic. Putnam (1989), for example, comments that if the alter doesn't "pop out" the first time you ask, "it is often necessary to repeat the request several times." He values very long interviews, extending over several hours. At the very least it is known that such a method increases the likelihood of reporting abuse, whether or not it occurred, due to the suggestibility of patients in response to the strong cues indicating that a positive response is expected and desirable. And because patients vary in the extent to which they are vulnerable to such suggestions, this effect will be variable, adding to the unreliability of the method. Because it appears that patients with psychopathology, especially some varieties, are more susceptible to the effects of such questioning, such methods can produce a differential effect, misleadingly suggesting a spuriously greater incidence of such experiences in relation to certain psychopathology.

It should be noted that the methods of examination advocated in the MPD literature closely resemble, in very significant particulars, the methods of coercive interrogation I have reviewed in the context of human rights abuses (Simpson 1993).

Even in rare studies like Boon and Draijer (1991, 1993), where they tried to limit the extent to which the researchers encouraged patients to "recall" childhood abuse, they were not, of course, dealing with naïve, unspoiled patients, virginal to knowledge of MPD theories. The patients had been seen by clinicians suspecting and considering MPD, had already been diagnosed in most cases, and were likely to have been influenced by previous interviews and therapeutic interchanges, not controlled for or documented by the researchers.

Then there is the problem of the common use of hypnosis in diagnosis. In papers arguing that hypnosis plays no part in producing the picture of MPD, we are usually told that it is not used until after the full picture has emerged spontaneously. Yet other authors are more frank. Bloch (1991) admits, "There will be times, however, when the evaluator appropriately decides to pursue hypnotic inquiry prior to spontaneous alter emergence." He says this is indicated when a rapid diagnosis is needed, or when there's enough reason to have already diagnosed MPD, or "when obviously extant alters are avoidant of spontaneous emergence." (How they are "obviously extant" when they have not emerged, is not clear.) This sounds mighty like making the diagnosis prior to the spontaneous emergence of the required signs, and then using a procedure well known to be able to create exactly the missing signs to confirm one's presuppositions. These are methods with a high potential for creating the symptoms, rather than simply eliciting them.

Greaves (1992), sympathetic to MPD, admits the effects of contamination and contagion, the unconscious incorporation of material from other sources within stories individuals earnestly believe to represent their own experience, and agrees that this is common in group therapy and inpatient care of such patients.

THE NATURE OF MPD PATIENTS: FROM THEIR OWN ACCOUNTS

Highly revealing material, supportive of the skeptical case (very well summarized by North et al. 1993) is contained in the popular autobiographical MPD books, but has been largely ignored. Eve, for instance, admitted that she was "having fun being a multiple" (Lancaster and Poling 1958), and after fusing, wrote that "the magic had gone out of my life" (Sizemore 1989). She changed her story several times as to the originating trauma, depending on which of her books one reads. Sybil (Schreiber 1973) made some profoundly unlikely claims, for example, describing in detail incidents occurring when she was 6 weeks and 6 months of age, when ordinary brain development would not allow the formation and recovery of such complex memories. Many of the famed cases had detailed medical and psychiatric knowledge, and even knowledge of each other's cases.

Revealingly, as the survey of biographical accounts by North and colleagues (1993) shows, many MPD patients also claim experiences of ESP, clairvoyance, reincarnation, astral travel, poltergeists, and similar phenomena. This suggests the possibility of similar origins for all these experiences.

Earlier cases of MPD were like Victorian novels and dramas, long-winded and loquacious, contemporary artistry requiring such detail that patients could only manage a repertoire of two or three presentations. This is, in many ways, the Scheherezade Syndrome, whose patients are psychic chameleons. Modern MPDs, however, are more like MTV video-surfers who skim across the many channels of cable TV, zapping between impressionistic scraps of what seem more like the inhabitants of a host of soap operas.

MEDIA INFLUENCES

Coons (1990) wrote that over 700 scientific articles, chapters, and books have appeared on MPD, yet he also said that there had then been a total of 211 case reports. This would seem to represent over 3.3 articles, chapters, or books per patient, surely a psychopathological record.

Putnam (1991) asserts that "perhaps the strongest support for the construct validity of MPD as a diagnosis rests on the well-replicated clinical phenomenology of the disorder." But when the phenomenology is so heavily publicized, when clinicians hand copies of articles and books about it to patients, when it has been graphically enacted and demonstrated repeatedly on network television, this proves nothing except that many people can read and learn.

Prince (1906) thought media influences were shaping the development of MPD in his time: "The fact is that our conception of multiple personality disorder has been derived entirely from those sensational cases. . . . Such cases appeal to the imagination, and, from their very bizarre character, have colored the popular concept of multiple personality." Decker (1986), in her review, showed the effects of literary models in the earlier history of the condition. Even patients of Janet, Breuer, and Freud resembled then popular literary characters.

THE MULTIPLE MULTIPLE PERSONALITY DISORDER DISORDER: PROBLEMS WITH DIAGNOSTIC CRITERIA FOR MPD

Van Praag (1993) reminds us of the unjustifiable haste with which MPD entered *DSM-III* in 1980, without *any* of the testing that was needed before such a step was taken, and without properly documented scientific evidence for the validity of the criteria. Kirk and Kutchins (1992) similarly testify that MPD entered *DSM-III* due to pressure from enthusiasts, in the absence of any quality of necessary data. The inter-rater reliability, and even the validity of the criteria have never been adequately established. But since the inclusion of MPD in *DSM-III* (a product of lobbying rather than science) the very *fact* of its inclusion has been used to argue that MPD *must* exist, and to justify rejecting the views of critics.

Ross and colleagues (1990) described 102 MPD patients, finding in a structured interview that the vast majority had concurrent diagnoses: 91.2 percent major depression, 63.7 percent borderline personality disorder, 60.8 percent somatization disorder, 50 percent substance abuse, and 92 percent suicidal behavior. Others (including North et al. 1993) have confirmed the routine presence of stable sets of symptoms of other diagnoses, which obviously potentially invalidate the claim to autonomous diagnostic status for MPD. As Orne and colleagues (1984) have commented, a continuum of increasingly less stringent criteria, within a concept of a continuum of MPD syndromes and dissociative disorders, makes "the possibility of ever falsifying the diagnosis . . . increasingly tenuous."

There are many problems with the *DSM-III* criteria for MPD, which are mischievously vague. They include "the existence within the person of two or more distinct personalities, each of which is dominant at a particular time." But what is a "personality"? What is "distinct"? And what is "dominant"? Further, "each individual" (presumably each individual "personality," the phrasing is murky) "is complex and integrated with its own unique behavior patterns. . . ." What is "complex," "co-existence," "well-developed," "integrated," or "unique?" These are critically important definitional matters. The part so often played by hypnosis in the creation or elicitation of these phenomena is crucial, but ignored by DSM-III. Other relevant concerns have been raised by many others, including, for example, Ludolph (1985).

As several reviews (e.g., Fahy 1988, North et al. 1993) have shown, MPD patients share many characteristics with malingering, with borderline personality disorder, with somatization disorder/Briquet's syndrome, and with psychopathy. They strongly resemble the patients who used to be diagnosed as hysterical. Yet DSM-III has refused to supply any exclusion criteria to separate MPD from other conditions, notwithstanding the obvious overlap.

Despite the vagueness and generosity of DSM-III criteria, which Ross (1989) admitted "will result in too many false positive diagnoses," Nakdimen (1992) complained that the failure of most psychiatrists to diagnose it means that the criteria "clearly have inadequate diagnostic sensitivity" and should be broadened! The *DSM-IV* proposals, still not based on adequate data, though remaining susceptible to lobbying, make no substantive improvement.

Especially notable was the proposal that "dissociative disorder not otherwise specified" be enlarged still more generously (again in the absence of proper research data) to include cases similar to MPD, but not meeting its criteria, including those in which "not more than one personality state is sufficiently distinct." It thus gives us MPD with only one personality! Are we now to seriously contemplate diagnosing "single personality disorder?"

Others have argued for the existence of "covert multiple personality"; and "ego-state disorder," where ego states tend to experience themselves as parts of one person—which is the normal state of mind. Kluft (1991) described a typology of MPD, incorporating twenty-two varieties, including "Secret MPD . . . Covert MPD . . . Ad Hoc MPD" quasi-roleplaying MPD, ostensible imaginary companionship MPD, and the pseudo-false positive MPD. This is truly the multiple multiple personality disorder disorder!

THE FAULTY NATURE OF THE MPD LITERATURE

As North and colleagues (1993) documented: "the average number of annual publications on MPD prior to 1970 had been fewer than 1, between 1970 and 1980 the number increased a thousand percent, to 9.1. In the next decade (1981–1990) the annual number increased to 59.8 (Goettman et al. 1991)"; this is a vast and exponential rise.

One should note the extreme incestuousness of this literature, that is, the extent to which a small number of authors are cited repeatedly, and cite each other. If we define an inner core of MPD authors such as Bliss, Braun, Coons, Kluft, Ross, Putnam, and Spiegel, the degree of citation of works by them, and each other, or of authors edited by them and each other, is uniquely high. Often 60 percent to 87 percent of the references are by the authors themselves or from within this inner circle. There is also a heavy reliance on unpublished references, which the reader cannot check; and unpublished data, which does not seem to get published, and a pretty consistent lack of replication. A high proportion of the more dramatic claims made and heavily cited are published in journals internal to the MPD movement, such as *Dissociation*, rather than in major, scientifically demanding, independently refereed journals.

One finds clear problems in key articles. For instance Bliss (1986) reports on examining the records of twelve patients, then says "in thirteen subjects collateral evidence was available"; 13 out of 12? Over 108 percent corroboration? How impressive!

There are many recurrent problems which the scientifically literate find in the MPD literature. There is heavy reliance on proof by assertion: It is true because I say so, or because X or Y says so. There is a dominant use of undocumented anecdotes, and the citation of references that simply repeat the same assertion, without providing any further data for it.

PATHOLOGIZING THE NORMAL

An efficient tactic, if one wishes to claim that a pathology is common, is to include a good deal of entirely normal phenomena within the definition or screening method. There is a recent tendency, for instance, to equate dissociative experiences with dissociative disorders. Among the items assessed that can contribute to a diagnosis of dissociative disorder are: failing to recall part of what happened while driving a car, being approached by someone who insists he's met you before, becoming so absorbed in television as to be unaware of one's surroundings, daydreaming, talking aloud to oneself when alone, or failing to attend to part of what someone else is saying. These are entirely routine aspects of normal psychological function, and variation in scores for such items may be more reflective of an individual's capacity for self-awareness and memory for mundane experiences than truly representing disorderly dissociation.

Commonly used and recommended checklists, especially in the field of supposed ritual abuse, contain many totally trivial and absolutely normal features, wrongly suggesting (with no scientific basis) that these typify the ritually abused, or could justify the assumption of prior abuse, the taking of hectic precautions, or starting therapy.

Let us look, for instance, at the absurd checklists issued by Gould (1992), which she says should be used "in the clinical evaluation of *all* children to rule out any possibility of ritual victimization" (my emphasis). These include as grounds for suspicion: the use of baby words for sexual and bodily parts and functions; constipation; resistance to toilet training; a child's interest in urine and feces; imitating the passing of gas; fear of monsters and ghosts, or that something nasty is under the bed, in the closet, or peering in the window; singing songs incomprehensible to the parent, or songs with a you-better-not-tell theme (that includes "Santa Clause Is Coming to Town!"); being afraid of shots (injections); disliking food that is red, orange, or brown (like carrots or pumpkin?); being resistant to authority, biting nails, being accident prone; being clingy or afraid to separate from parents or seeming distant from them (that gets you coming and going!); becoming angry when told what to do or not to do by parents; pretending to kill play figures (what else do you do with toy soldiers?); preferring chase games; and so forth. Has any normal child ever failed to show many of these signs? It is rather the *absence* of these features, falsely claimed to be signs of abuse, that would be signs of abnormality in a child.

THE TINKER BELL SYNDROME

MPD militants also rely on emotional appeals to our duty to believe patients. This argument is the direct equivalent of Peter Pan's appeal to save Tinker Bell by clapping if you believe in fairies! It is charming and quaint, but nothing remotely like science.

I have noted (and the observation has been confirmed and described to me by other observers of this field) how MPD patients, meeting a new clinician, will often begin: "I have MPD. Do you believe in it?" We are also told that "alters" will often refuse to show themselves to an unbeliever. Kluft (1984b) tells us that "sensitive alters" note staff attitudes toward MPD, and seek out those who are accepting, avoiding the skeptics. This would be a wise and typical precaution for fakes as well.

In the book by Cohen and colleagues (1991), the patient, Cathy, insists that therapists must accept what they are told by someone with MPD, and demands "unshakable belief" from the therapist; while Robert urges us to "believe all of what you hear. / Don't search for proof or details."

Ganaway (1989a,b) described MPD patients as displaying "an insatiable need to be believed." Like so many features of MPD, this is *not* seen in undoubted trauma survivors (like Holocaust survivors) but is a caricature of their responses. Yes, for the survivors of the Holocaust, war, and torture we work with, it is often important for them to be able to establish the truth of what occurred, but it is not the predominant drive in clinical practice.

Nor is the demand primarily for repeated iteration of literal belief from the therapist, but more often an interest in the availability of external and objective evidence confirming the events they experienced.

This is what makes MPD the Tinker Bell Syndrome, in which the patient demands continuing, actively demonstrated belief in the syndrome, and in their every assertion, in order to thrive. It would also be wise behavior for someone simulating the condition, so as neither to waste effort nor to run a higher risk of discovery, by exhibiting symptoms to an unbeliever.

"Every time a child says: 'I don't believe in fairies,' there is a fairy somewhere that falls down dead" (Barrie 1928). After Tinker Bell has drunk poison, Peter Pan appeals directly to the audience: "Her light is growing faint, and if it goes out, that means she is dead. Her voice is so low I can scarcely tell what she is saying. She says—she says she thinks she could get well again if children believed in fairies. . . . Do you believe in fairies? Say quick that you believe! If you believe, clap your hands!" And thus the fairy is saved. Am I alone in hearing echoes of Peter Pan whenever it is demanded of me that I believe, unquestioningly, in incredible claims from noncredible witnesses?

THE MYTH OF THE IMMACULATE PERCEPTION

An assumption that every clinician ever involved with the patient prior to the diagnosis of MPD being made was negligent and incompetent is frequently voiced. A typical pattern is shown by Boon and Draijer (1993): "Our patients . . . spent many years in the mental health system before receiving a correct diagnosis." They provide no evidence whatsoever for this extreme opinion, save the extravagant assumption that the diagnosis *they* made was unquestionably correct, while all previous diagnoses, being different from theirs, must be conclusively wrong. Such authors suffer from what I have elsewhere called the myth of the immaculate perception (Simpson 1974). In this instance an acute awareness of the faultiness and uncertainty of every diagnosis but theirs, and of every clinical judgment but their own.

These authors neither sought nor analyzed any data about the exact presentation and symptomatology at the time of previous diagnoses. The description of their methodology is vague, but they seem to have relied on the patient's own reports of previous diagnoses, which is highly unreliable. They make no reference to studying the patient's previous medical records for data before insulting their colleagues. They do not report attempting to make any other diagnosis than MPD and PTSD, and are therefore unable even to exclude any other current diagnoses, let alone to exclude or invalidate any previous diagnosis.

Previous diagnoses are said to include personality disorder—is that inescapably incorrect? Surely most if not all MPD patients do indeed have a personality disorder. On what grounds can these authors claim that this must have been incorrect? Nearly 27 percent were previously diagnosed as suffering from a dissociative disorder, without specifying MPD. On what data and what grounds can they be certain that these patients were *not* suffering from any other dissociative disorder when previously seen? There is no evidence to suggest that MPD patients are somehow immune to other problems that could merit other concurrent or dual diagnoses; therefore, previous diagnoses could have been entirely correct. Nor is there evidence that MPD is unremittingly diagnosable and constantly available for recognition (and there is much evidence to the contrary). Putnam and Loewenstein (1993) unashamedly repeat the assertion that MPD patients were previously treated for "incorrect psychiatric diagnoses."

Kroll (1993) has a more parsimonious explanation for the reiterated claim that the average patient diagnosed as MPD has been in previous therapy for six years or more: "it took the therapists, especially the last one who, by definition, is the 'discoverer' of the underlying nature of the problem, six and a half years to instruct the borderline patient how to become a multiple personality."

Many in the MPD literature (e.g., Goodwin et al. 1990) pathologize their colleagues, explaining our reluctance to believe every assertion made by every patient as due to: "identification with the aggressor, revulsion at child abuse, or anxiety about involvement in a difficult clinical situation that might make the clinician angry or sexually stimulated." The sheer nasty condescension of such remarks is one-sided. If we suggested that MPD zealots get sexual stimulation out of seeking out and believing fantasies of abuse, or identify with the victim, we'd be deafened by their protests. There is a frequent suggestion that we are somehow too faint-hearted to face up to accounts of child abuse. Yet no one seems puzzled that we're able to stomach true and credible stories of torture, the Holocaust, and other appalling cruelties.

MPD adherents often behave like cult members. They do not resemble cool scientists who, should I disagree with what they consider to be self-evident and proven, may think me sadly misguided or mistaken, but would offer me convincing evidence for their point of view. Instead, like cult members, they seem to consider one not merely ill-informed, but *wrong* in the moral sense, heretical, almost wicked. Ross (1989) wrote insightfully that "there is a potential danger of an in-club forming, with little tolerance for dissenting opinion." Well, the club has formed. These doctors are working within a premature assumption of orthodoxy.

THE SCIENTIFIC FAILURES OF THE MPD LITERATURE

Ross (1989) impressively illustrates the problems in his resolutely unscientific, almost antiscientific book, which relies on ex-cathedra assertions that we are expected to accept because he has said them. It is full of dramatic claims devoid of data. For example, we're told that many prostitutes have MPD, and "probably a large number" of AIDS victims, and that "many . . . would potentially stop prostituting if they were diagnosed and treated for their MPD." Of course, they might eat more breakfast cereal, too. He complains that less is spent on MPD than on AIDS research, with an implication that failure to recognize and treat MPD increases the risk of AIDS.

He assures us that "it's safe to say" that the cases reported by himself and Putnam are "reasonably representative of cases currently in treatment in North America." In a questionnaire survey, he reports that 85.5 percent reported abuse, but then says, "when we took the missing data and 'unknown' responses into account, it was possible that the *absence*" of abuse occurred in as few as 3.6 to 4.3 percent of the cases. In other words, if one massages the data, and assumes that *every* case with unknown or missing data was positive, one can produce a higher figure. This is science?

The MPD authors seem pretty universally to ignore the hypothetico-deductive method (and, indeed, other scientific methods of inquiry), especially the principle of falsifiability, which Karl Popper so usefully emphasized (see also Medawar 1982). A scientist tests hypotheses by systematic attempts to refute them; no number of attempts solely to confirm them will ultimately do so. As Magee (1973) comments: if we rejected all falsifying observations, and "kept reinterpreting the evidence to maintain its agreement with our statements, our approach would have become absurdly unscientific." We should not evade refutation by introducing ad hoc hypotheses or definitions, or by refusing to recognize inconvenient experimental results. We need to formulate our theories so as to open them to refutation. It is easy to accumulate a very great many confirming observations of untrue statements or theories without ever proving their truth, or even increasing the probability that they are true.

This is the criterion for statements to be scientific and even to make common sense; otherwise we are engaged in metaphysics. When I read Goodwin psychopathologizing my disbelief in her views (or, even, my failure to accept them unquestioningly), I recall Medawar's comments (1982) that "we obviously cannot accept into science any system of thought . . . which contains a built-in antidote to disbelief: that to discredit [it] is an aberration of thought which calls for psychoanalytical treatment. The critic cannot win against such a contention. . . ."

A major, central, and recurring problem with the MPD concept and its literature is that, while claiming to be scientific and to deal with established facts and certainties, it is resolutely unscientific and nonfalsifiable. If a patient's claim to have been abused decades ago is considered true if she shows all the features typically associated with truth, and *also* if she shows every feature typically associated with falsity, and if the very absence of corroboration cannot prove that it was not so, then we are simply not dealing with a matter of science, but of metaphysical belief. As Popper wrote: "The wrong view of science betrays itself in the craving to be right" (Popper 1963, 1968).

We are repeatedly offered assertions and scolded if we find them unconvincing. We are told that it is *our* task to disprove them, when it is their originator's task, and when they have usually been formulated so as to be immune from disproof. We are told that we must believe in MPD — because it is in *DSM-III*; because Putnam and Kluft say they have seen very many cases; because increasing numbers of cases are being reported; because a small number of people are writing an awful lot of papers about it; and because, if you ask patients they say have MPD a set of questions describing what they call MPD, these often say yes to many of the questions (wouldn't it be strange if they didn't?). But if I defined MPD as "wearing a moustache" I could easily produce a test for MPD with much higher reliability, but no necessary validity whatsoever.

There are regular peculiarities in the uses of data. For example, Kluft (1984a) makes an assertion about what "most psychiatrists" do, supported solely by a citation to himself, with the reference "unpublished data, 1980–1983." And he wonders why we are skeptical? (Simpson, unpublished data, 1968–1994 — but don't look for this item in the reference list at the end of this chapter!).

Schetky (1990) reviewed some of the major problems in such research, all regularly typified in the MPD literature, including: sampling problems; selection bias which is often extreme; extrapolation from very small numbers; use of imprecise or nonstandard means of data collection; lack of standardization and of adequate reliability and validity data of many of the means of screening, diagnosis, or assessment used; lack of appropriate control or comparison groups; the weaknesses of retrospection; lack of uniform definitions; pooling of cases; use of obscure or undisclosed means of data analysis; ignoring of what at times are significantly low response rates; use of unstructured interviews; reliance on second-hand or even more distant sources of data; and difficulty differentiating the effects of the abuse from that of the conditions that predispose to it (such patients are "at risk for emotional problems given their life circumstances regardless of whether or not sexual abuse occurs.")

Andersen (1990) has brilliantly illustrated the range of major method-ological errors that are regrettably common in medical research. Virtually every error he delineates is illustrated, often in very gross form, in the MPD research literature. Among the errors typical in MPD studies but not already mentioned above, are problems with the use of inappropriate research designs: many varieties of bias, a characteristic lack of clearly stated hypotheses, a priori hypotheses or fishing expeditions in which the hypothesis appears to have been chosen after the event to fit the data, an almost total lack of randomization, Hawthorne effects, the Gail fallacy and Berkson's fallacy, the use of inappropriate statistics, and others.

Most of the MPD studies are on odd samples, from which any generalization would be hazardous. They generally seem to be conve-nience samples, of people actively seeking treatment for dissociative-type symptoms, or on the basis of their identification of themselves as victims of earlier abuse. There have been very few follow-up studies, none that are satisfactory.

Many questions still need to be answered. How many integrated patients stay integrated? And for how long? If they are left alone, what happens? Does MPD remit spontaneously? If so, under what circum-stances? What is the natural history of the condition without major intervention? After alters fuse, what other problems are left? There is remarkably little data on the families of MPD patients.

THE INCIDENCE OF CHILD ABUSE RELATED TO MPD: THE DOCTRINE OF THE UNCHALLENGEABLE CONFESSION

Pride (1986) raises important facts generally ignored by scientific studies. For instance, in many states, up to five or more separate incidents of abuse per child are listed separately, so a report of over 1,000 *incidents* may represent only 250 actual victims. No allowance is made for duplication of reports of the same incident to different agencies or on different occasions. Also, reports of substantiation very often do *not* represent only cases where abuse was proven in court, or by independent witnesses or physical evidence. In very many cases this may merely mean that a social worker who heard about the complaint considered it convincing. The definitions of abuse are often so broad, vague, and elastic that ghastly physical abuse and rape can be lumped in with trivial fondling or embracing that may have had no abusive content, intent, or effect. Abuse has, for example, been defined so as to include: "failing to provide sympathy and support"; not allowing a child to watch TV; and children who are "too neatly dressed." In some hands, "abuse" becomes "raising children differently from the way I would."

Then there is what I call the doctrine of the unchallengeable confession. Children, though well known for their enviably rich fantasy and play lives, are assumed always to tell 100 percent truth about abuse. We are told that we must believe the child when he accuses others of abuse, but that when he denies there was abuse, we must *not* believe that—in fact, some seem to assume this to prove that there was abuse.

One of the most mischievous of the unscientific but convenient concepts was the child sexual abuse accommodation syndrome, described by Summit (1983). Never supported by scientific data, it says: abused children tend to contradict themselves, to cover up incidents, to show little emotion afterwards, and to wait a long time before making accusations. As Pride remarks (1986): "In other words, all the evidence typically used to show *no* sexual abuse occurred . . . has now been captured to 'prove' the very opposite. According to this logic, if it looks like a cheeseburger, smells like a cheeseburger, and tastes like a cheeseburger that proves it is *not* a cheeseburger."

MPD AS A CULTURE-BOUND DISORDER

Those who have sought imperialistically to claim the large territory of spirit possession and related states within the MPD empire have wholly missed the most relevant point. Possession *is* a dissociative state (usually relatively brief, because it is not usually encouraged to last long) and it *never ever* occurs except in a believer in such phenomena, usually in the presence of and encouragement of other believers. The belief shapes the form of the dissociative state, just as MPD only thrives in a believer who is among believers.

Too often, Western psychopathology likes to pretend that it is culture-free, as if all "our" views were simply laws of nature, in contrast to the superstitions of others. Vaingloriously, the MPD-ites seem to be trying to claim all possession phenomena as part of the MPD domain; in fact, the reverse is true: MPD is a Western, American-culture equivalent to possession states, with very similar phenomena, colored by the belief system common to MPD patients and their clinicians. Littlewood and Lipsedge (1986) emphasize as typical of such culture-bound syndromes that "the behavior usually has a 'dramatic' quality," and "the individual is not held to be aware or responsible in the everyday sense." The behaviors directly legitimate the status quo rather than explicitly question it. "They permit a constrained display of deviance, often glossed by a local notion of catharsis."

Lewis (1971, 1979) has brilliantly reviewed possession states, and, apart from the principles he elegantly extracts and explicates, I see other generalities clearly apparent from his data, including the neglected point that possession states are often sequalae to trauma, and show interesting similarities to MPD.

Recognition of the role of suggestion and artificial provocation of possession states, and concern with the genuineness of the claims of such states, are ancient and widespread (see, for instance, Oesterreich 1930). Lewis (1971) pointed out that these states are usually restricted to women, and to downtrodden men who are discriminated against in their society, and he sees them as thinly disguised protest movements, often very effective in gaining for the possessed individual a measure of protection, attention, gratification, and exemption from otherwise usual restrictions. MPD functions very similarly in North American society. This alternate view of MPD is discussed at length in my book currently in progress.

Internationally widespread cultural variants of possession states are *not* varieties of MPD. On the contrary, MPD is a secular, Western variety of possession state, adapted to the lack of a predominant, single cultural and religious belief structure in North American culture (and some related parts of European culture). Not based on a single, coherent, religious-cultural belief system, it has evolved a more mundane and secular basis within the widely shared territory of psychobabble (that is, based on popular psychological beliefs which are superficial, unscientific, and firmly based on the marketing principle of confirming whatever the client truly wishes to believe). The true nature of the phenomenon is shown in the alacrity with which the field has embraced the urban legends of Satanism and concerns with cult and ritual abuse. These are widely believed, but backed by an astonishing lack of hard objective evidence (Bromley and Shupe 1981, Ofshe and Watte 1993, Waller 1991). It is also reflected in the development of strong cultlike features within the MPD industry. Interestingly, Kluft (1989) reported that demonic alters are more common among MPD patients whose therapists have religious belief systems.

Others have previously speculated that possession syndrome and MPD might represent cross-cultural variants of the same dissociative disorder in India and the USA (Adityanjee and Khandelwal 1989). Bliss (1986) also considered as similar self-hypnotic phenomena on a larger scale the crusades, dancing manias, witch-hunting, and so forth. The MPD epidemic shows many features of being a modern equivalent. And just as the rapidly growing mass belief in witches at the end of the fifteenth century lead to a large secondary industry of witch-hunters, a renewed role for clergy, and training, as in the Malleus Maleficarum, in the skills of identifying and dealing with witches, so it has been with MPD in our own time.

GULLIBLE'S TRAVELS: ISSUES OF CREDIBILITY, FABRICATION, AND CONFABULATION

Putnam (1989) describes "subtle nuances," signs highly significant in diagnosing MPD, which he calls *grounding*, supposedly the process of adjusting when an alter emerges. These include such trivia as touching the face, pressing the temples, touching the chair one is sitting in, looking around the room, shifting posture, blinking, twitching, touching one's body or a nearby object, and changes in inflection. I have studied very few videos of normal or otherwise afflicted patients who did not regularly show such signs, as they are ubiquitous. I show all those behaviors, as do all normal people, during *any* period of observation.

What has been overlooked is that most of these features tenderly described as diagnostic of MPD closely resemble the nonverbal behaviors typically associated with lying and deception. In reviewing methods of detecting deception, Annon (1988) comments on general body indicators thus:

> Typical indicators of possible deception are increases in body movements; increased postural shifts, unusual frequency of limb and foot movements, stiff and rigid postures, little head nodding, low-level hand movements, considerable movement with feet or legs; increased shoulder shrugs, increased manipulators or adapters (grooming gestures), decreased illustrators, nose touching and mouth covering, fast or shallow breathing, sweating, and frequent swallowing.

The abrupt onset or offset of facial expressions, and increased blinking, are also typical of deceit.

Zuckerman and colleagues (1981) recognize comparable signs. In his chapter, "Detecting Deceit from Words, Voice or Body," Ekman (1985) lists congruous cues to deceit: hesitations, pauses, speech errors, shift in pitch, tone, speed of voice, and so forth. One is probably dealing largely with what Martin Orne and colleagues (1984) called "honest liars," and what I call "sincere liars." These are people who report, with conviction, false memories and confabulations.

Even Ross (1989) remarked that "MPD is an elaborate pretending. The patient *pretends* that she is more than one person, in a very convincing manner. She actually believes it herself." Later he adds: "The creation of alter personalities is an extreme extension of the normal psychic mechanism of everyday malingering."

Putnam (1989) commented on the difficulty in getting a coherent history, saying that "much of the information is inconsistent or even contradictory and it is difficult to obtain a clear chronological sequence of events." He says this is typical, characteristic, of MPD patients; it is also typical of liars or simulators in training. He mentions that the information they provide early in evaluation is "usually vague and lacking in substantive detail." They complain of a bad memory, without showing memory impairment on mental state examination; and may "confabulate information to fill in an otherwise unacceptable gap in memory or to placate the interviewer" (he also cites Kluft in agreement with this). They commonly pretend to know more than they do and will suddenly change the subject. All these behaviors are also typical of liars and noncredible speakers.

Kluft (1993) records the case of a woman who alleged extensive abuse and "described in detail the murder of her husband, and abreacted it with convincing fervor. Ancillary sources were able to demonstrate that the individual alleged to have been killed was alive and well." But such conduct—only in the case of an MPD patient—is excused, and not considered to indicate pathological lying. In fact, this case closely resembles the cases described by Simpson (1978b) as pseudo-bereavement in the Munchausen syndrome.

Ross (1989) explains a lack of real recall of abuse in many cases by suggesting that the abuse is remembered by undetected alters. What a perfectly unscientific, unrefutable theory! The patients *could* have been undetectably anesthetized and abused by undetected Martians (an equivalently scientific explanation) but we have no more reason to believe it. He suggests that the lack of cases in earlier times is because child abuse was rarer, and was less severe or nasty—though there is absolutely no evidence in favor of this assertion. Like so many MPD enthusiasts, he readily believes even the most unlikely stories, like that of the girl whose father supposedly dressed as a woman and stuffed live spiders into her vagina before having intercourse with her. Did he think about how difficult it is to assemble and carry a number of live spiders, and then stuff them into a small vagina? "I believed the story," he tells us proudly.

Kluft's paper (1987a) on the simulation and dissimulation of MPD is an extraordinary indictment of the whole MPD concept. He assures us that apart from the exceedingly generous and vague *DSM-III* criteria, the signs of MPD "often are covert and counterexpectational," and that patients often hide the condition. Thus, presumably, if you meet diagnostic criteria, you have MPD; if you provide the opposite evidence, or vague evidence, or even no evidence, then you may still have MPD. When there is no corroboration of assumed abuse, Kluft explains that "those that know them best may well be tainted informants and are prone to denial" (once again, assertions not proved scientifically). So if there is family confirmation of abuse, you have MPD; and if there is no confirmation, then you probably still have MPD! It is really hard to imagine how one should behave so as to be reliably denied the diagnosis! You *cannot* malinger MPD—whatever you do will be excused by an MPD-ite.

As in so much of the MPD literature, the methodology of this study is vaguely described, uses so much private and unrevealed information as to be impossible to replicate or refute, and the numbers are confusing and contradictory. Extraordinarily, Kluft tests the possibility that MPD patients might be malingering by a nonblind, retrospective, reassessment of his own diagnoses! No attempt was made to examine actual patients. Instead, he apparently relies on written materials from his earlier examinations in which he had not found any of them to be malingering, but in which he may well not have asked all the necessary questions, or recorded all relevant data. He says he reviewed his own material on "over 200" MPD patients he had interviewed (what numerical precision!) plus six for some reason considered to have been faking (we don't know how they achieved that rare status) and one person whose lawyer told him to ask whether he had MPD. A paragraph later he refers to another 46 patients, not explaining where these came from, or how they relate to the others.

Much crucial information was missing or not defined in the records, and he explains his failure to use any other rater by saying that he used his "notes *and recollections*." Peculiarly, he explains his failure to define properly the terms for whose presence he looked, or to attempt quantification, because this "might appear to 'overlegitimize' any findings." I have been able to find no other example in the published scientific literature of a researcher striving to *avoid* "legitimizing" his findings. Surely there can rarely if ever have been a study published so biased against scientific objectivity, proper methodology, or with the odds so heavily loaded against finding evidence of malingering.

But then, astonishingly, Kluft admits that "review of available material showed that *every indicator of lying/malingering was found to occur in genuine mpd patients.*" Every single one of his patients (whose MPD was genuine only according to his own unsupported judgment) showed two or more characteristics of malingerers and liars! And this occurred despite the large number of biases acting against such a finding. How odd, but how deeply revealing, that this finding does not get widely cited in the voluminous MPD literature, unlike so many other of Kluft's findings.

The rest of this astounding paper is devoted to explaining away this embarrassing finding. Without any evidence or argument to justify such a convenient interpretation, he says that though the "overt, emitted phenomena" of both groups may look alike, "they have different origins." He fails to explain the origins of such behaviors in either group, or to supply a shred of evidence that they are of different origin; he merely asserts this. On this flimsy basis, he opines that it may not be of differential diagnostic value to recognize such "malingering/lying-like behavior" when diagnosing MPD! This is truly breathtaking chutzpah. *All* the evidence in his paper is that his own personally diagnosed MPD patients *all* showed behavior typical of liars and/or malingerers, and he suggests we should ignore this!

His closing section contains a series of explanations and excuses for the MPD patient, but also some revealing admissions—that "real" MPD patients often read "voraciously" about MPD; that the classic symptoms are inaccurate; that MPD patients "wish to please" the interviewer; that the "overlap" between the basic phenomena of MPD and the classic indicators of malingering "is extensive and problematic"; that the method of asking questions can allow the patient to figure out the "right" answers to convey "crucial impressions," and to be "led"; and that care should be taken to avoid leading questions, to which MPD patients are also vulnerable. "The stress of trying to prove themselves can induce exaggeration and partial malingering in genuine MPD patients," he adds. In this ingenious way, malingering can be a sign of genuineness. This is diagnosis in wonderland.

He recommends extended interviews, as "unforced" dissociation (!) often emerges after 2½ to 4 hours of continuous interviewing! This allows great amounts of time for the witting and unwitting exchange of suggestion and expectation (and implying that more is sought than anything already provided). As an expert in coercive interrogation (Simpson 1993), I can state that enormous care would be needed in the sort of continuous and extended interrogation he advises to avoid coercion that would otherwise be the effect of this recommended procedure.

Kluft (1984a) reports that 59 percent of his series admitted they had withheld data which might have suggested the diagnosis. He admits that "diagnosis proceeds with the recognition that the patient may defensively withhold or misrepresent data . . . and that confabulation or knowledge misstated as if it were memory . . . may confound matters."

North and colleagues (1993) survey the research on personality tests in MPD, but are far too kind in their interpretation of, and excuses for, the dismal results achieved. High scores on the L Lie scale, F scale, and others suggesting exaggeration or confabulation, are excused with elaborate explanations that are *not* applied to other categories of patients showing similar scores.

A quaint distinction is at times made in discussing MPD between historical truth and narrative truth (e.g., Ganaway 1989a). But these are not alternatives. Only historical truth is veridical. Narrative truth really deals with whether a tale is convincing, realistic, sounds like a truth, and thus serves very different functions.

Glass (1993) similarly repudiates truth: "Whether or not the specifics are historically true, however, is not the issue or the point. What is the point and what is true are the reflections [the patient] carries within. . . ." Jaspers and others judge narrative truths by whether they are meaningful and convincing. This means that many, probably a majority, of lies are narratively true. It deals with artistic/aesthetic quality, not validity.

We are often told that the stories reported by MPD patients *must* be true because they feel convincing and emotionally moving to the observer. In that case, Olivier *was* Hamlet, and Charlton Heston *is* Moses. It's an absurd criterion. As my earlier work has confirmed, when patients with the Munchausen syndrome (e.g., Simpson 1975, 1978a,b) tell tales that are false beyond question, they are characteristically emotionally convincing and move even the professional assessor.

The MPD enthusiasts often construct paper tigers, then argue against assertions we skeptics have never made. For example, we have never said that *all* recollections of abuse are false. But we *do* ask that clinicians and researchers *always* assume that their subjects' memories *could be* distorted and biased, and that some subjects, such as high dissociators, are more likely to have distorted or biased reports, and to be more sensitive to producing or magnifying such reports where the clinician or researcher creates or fails to control a situation in which leading questions, demand characteristics, situational expectations, secondary advantages, and other such factors favor the production of such "recollections."

The paper of Herman and Schatzow (1987) is often the only one cited to defend the credibility of accounts of childhood abuse. They reported, in an atypical group of women self-selected in an "incest survivors" group, that they found "corroborating evidence" in 75 percent. There are methodological problems with this piece (which was published in a psychoanalytic rather than scientific journal); but even if it were perfectly convincing, it cannot be generalized to the point of absolving all other MPD literature from ever needing to establish corroboration again.

The degree of skill needed to fool an examiner has been exaggerated. As Aldridge-Morris (1989) wisely remarked: "It is a harsh truth that human beings devote much of their lives to consistent and utterly convincing deceptions." Braude (1991) argues that while it might be "fairly easy to duplicate some of the more obvious features of multiplicity for short periods of time, it is considerably more difficult to display the full and subtle tangle of behaviors characteristic of MPD, and to do so consistently over an extended period." But most alters in most MPD cases cannot do so, either. Putnam (1986) revealed that short testing periods, 15–20 minutes, are used in MPD patients, "which is generally the upper limit that many personalities can 'hold the body' in a stressful situation." There is no logical reason why this should be so; but faking for longer periods would be difficult.

There's a phoniness and a strong flavor of ham acting about the portrayals one is shown. In one case, a patient lunged out and hit a new nurse, then looked blank, and asked the therapist: "Why did I do that?" Even within the MPD belief system one would expect that if she had enough awareness of the behavior of the alter who hit the nurse to know what had happened, she should have had enough awareness to be able to recall why that alter did it. In fact, as she was told eagerly a little later, one of her personalities, under hypnosis, told the doctor that yet another alter did it because the nurse had the same name as someone who had raped her. But real rape victims absolutely never do that! They may feel uncomfortable on meeting someone who resembles their rapist, and maybe even on meeting someone who simply shares the same surname: but they do not hit perfect strangers, known to be nurses, simply because of a coincidence of surnames. It's a marvelous way to dramatize a concept of MPD, but why should a raped alter behave so unlike a real rape survivor?

So many of the alters I have been shown on videotape (presumably, no therapist chooses his very worst and most unconvincing tapes to show me) as well as some of those I have watched perform in flesh-creepingly embarrassing performances on public television have seemed crude and unconvincing—amateur theatrics. I do not say this as a pejorative comment, but as a carefully considered, scientific description of phenomena I am being urged to take seriously.

I notice that while really early reports of dual personalities seem to describe reasonably complex and rounded portrayals approximating the range of fullness of a normal person's personality (at least to the extent that this is observable in social contacts), with the rapid progression toward very large numbers of personalities, the quality and complexity of each personality seems to diminish. They are more like the very rapid personality sketches of an impressionist — fleeting, very highly stereotyped, and centering on one or two vivid characteristics that will be readily recognizable to the observer, externally visible signs without which the simulation could run the awful risk of passing unnoticed by the necessary observer and validator. Eve's later productions, for example, included one obsessed with collecting bells, another fascinated by turtles, and one who loved strawberries. It's hard to see these as relevant to solving problems of earlier trauma! Intrapsychically irrelevant, such details would be absolutely required by any simulator. These are caricatures, not characters; parodies, not personalities.

All the states are self-dramatizing because all states dramatize the self, in differing roles. Some roles are flamboyant, or ham-acted, and others are not. A great actor, or a great role, leads you, like any other great art, to suspend disbelief, and to be absorbed in it: you ignore its unrealities and accept it for itself. Ham acting, on the other hand, occurs when the technique and method intrude between you and the role you are observing, so that you become aware of the use of method and artifice, rather than art.

Kluft (1984a) refers to alters with different voices, vocabularies, accents, handedness, handwritings, and so forth. These are revealingly superfluous. What intrapsychic function, protective of tender sensitivities from the memories of abuse, are fulfilled by speaking with a different accent, when the average alter functions in the internal life of the patient, and may not spend much time talking to anyone else? And why would two alters necessarily have different handwriting? They write with exactly the same hand. What intrapsychic function could a different handwriting have? Surely the only valid function would be to convince the observer of the genuineness of the multiplicity. However vastly different their intrapsychic utility, if they spoke identically, wrote identically, and showed no dramatic external differences, other people might well fail to be suitably impressed by their multiplicity. Any sensible actor or faker would definitively adopt such superficial differences.

Spanos and his colleagues (1985) argued that MPD patients aren't merely passive victims of unconscious and internal processes, but purposeful and witting participants in creating the roles of their alters, "using available information to create a social impression that is congruent with their perception of situational demands and with the interpersonal goals they are attempting to achieve." They're helped by therapists who encourage, provide information and "stage direction," and validate the creations. The studies of Spanos and his colleagues are convincing, showing that it is quite easy to enact a MPD role, given support and inducement. Spanos, like other experts, sees hypnosis as a state in which one person tries to meet the perceived wishes of another.

THE MYTH OF PHYSIOLOGICAL DIFFERENCES

There are many highly misleading references to "documented physiological differences between personality states in MPD," offered as proof of diagnostic validity. Ross (1989, e.g.) claimed these cannot be fully replicated by normals or actors, which is untrue and unproven—but most of all, untested.

There is very poor science in this literature, but bold claims are made of differences in PET scans, evoked potentials (Larmore et al. 1977, Ludwig et al. 1972, Putnam 1984), voice prints (Putnam 1984), visual acuity, eye muscle balance, visual field size (Miller 1989), galvanic skin response (Bahnson and Smith 1975, Brende 1984, Larmore et al. 1977, Putnam 1984), EEG patterns (Coons et al. 1982, Larmore et al. 1977), electromyography (Larmore et al. 1977), and cerebral blood flow (Mathew et al. 1985).

All of these studies refer to variables that have no demonstrated relationship to *any* meaningful definition of personality nor to any disorder of personality, but which normally vary, and are responsive to mood and arousal levels. So what? Coons and his colleagues (1982) did a tiny study of two MPD patients with Coons himself (a curious choice) serving as the control. They found very little neurophysiologic changes reflecting the various personalities of either patient, but, intriguingly, more marked differences across simulated personalities in the control, Coons! They had to admit the most likely explanation for such differences was "changes in intensity of concentration, mood, and degree of muscle relaxation . . . [and] changes in emotional state."

It is hard to imagine why such studies were ever done, or published. Measurements of parameters known to vary substantially in relation to concentration, mood, and level of arousal, were absolutely certain to vary, rather randomly, in such circumstances, without proving anything about MPD. Despite this very obvious fact, more trivial studies keep being done. Putnam and colleagues (1990) looked, for no convincing reason, at skin conduction differences between left and right sides of the body, and not surprisingly, found no consistent differences. As North and colleagues (1993) summarize this naïve literature, "Some of the control subjects were able to produce 'alternates' with a degree of differentiation equivalent to the most differentiated MPD patients." Amazingly, though, Putnam's group interpreted their non-results to show that alters "are physiologically distinct states of consciousness," cheerfully ignoring the obvious implications of their data. Such authors fail to explain why and how one would expect consistent and significant physiological differences (other than of arousal and mood) within a single body, however many personalities might inhabit it.

Colin Ross and I are very different personalities – sustainably and consistently so. Yet, unless one of us has a specific physical disease, you could not distinguish between us by our pulse rate, or our blood pressure, nor (again, excepting eye pathology in either of us) by visual acuity. It is highly likely that there is far more variation in Colin Ross's pulse rate, blood pressure, GSR, and so forth, within any average day, than there is a difference between us at any particular time.

These peculiar studies were trying to distinguish physiologically between alters (within the same body) in a manner that cannot distinguish between unquestionably different people in different bodies. The measures offered are all able to be varied under hypnosis, and all tend to vary according the individual body's state of arousal.

When we hear that different alters may have different eyeglasses and different responses to the same medication, van Praag (1993) sensibly calls this "a contention created out of the realm of lore and imagination, lacking any empirical foundation." Why not claim that they wear different size shoes?

There are even more astoundingly naïve assertions, however. What is one to make of statements like one, typical of MPD writings, that a 32-year-old man "was transformed into what appeared to be a 5-year-old." Either a miraculous physical metamorphosis occurred, and we should be shown photographs of this miracle, or that author knows some very peculiar-looking 5-year-olds. What he must have meant – the difference is immensely important – is that his 32-year-old patient began *behaving like* a 5-year-old, something very much easier to achieve, and pathetically easy to fake. Bryant and co-workers (1992), for example, write of "physical differences" between personalities, but of course none exist.

POLITICS OF MPD

Patronizingly, Putnam writes (1989): "I have learned to stop arguing with those who, either out of ignorance or malice, attempt to deny the reality of MPD." How rude! If I don't agree with his dogma, he allows me only two options: I am ignorant or malicious! Just as condescendingly, he continues,

"It is sufficient to point them gently toward the *DSM-III-R* and a list of references . . . and let the sheer volume of evidence argue on its own behalf." There's an even larger literature on ghosts, UFOs, fairies and elves—but it does not necessarily prove that they exist.

An epiphenomenon is being used to argue for the reality and validity of the questionable phenomenon: as Fernando (1990) points out, Coons and others who claim that we must believe in MPD because over 700 publications on it have appeared are deeply unconvincing. The mere existence of a quantity of such literature, as opposed to its quality, does not require belief.

MPD zealots frequently complain that they receive insufficient respect and excessive antagonism (cf. e.g., Bliss 1988, Dell 1988, Hilgard 1988a, b, Spiegel 1988, Tozman and Pabis 1989). Yet the MPD literature shows far more contemptuous and arrogant comments by the MPD enthusiasts about the skeptics than the other way around. Bloch (1991) writes that "most clinicians treating MPD learn of the considerable damage and inadvertent mistreatment experienced by MPD clients that is attributable to misdiagnosis, an inevitable result of extreme skepticism by professionals." Typically, no evidence is given of these serious allegations.

Yet another misleading slur must be addressed: Although we skeptics may indeed reject the weaknesses of MPD theories and practices, we do not reject the patients. Interpreting the patient's problems differently from Ross, Kluft, and Putnam, and treating the patient differently from them, is not cruel or unprofessional, ineffective or wicked!

Ross (1989) wrote: "To diagnose MPD is a bit like admitting you believe in UFOs: it calls your professional reputation into question." Tozman and Pabis (1989) complain that MPD receives from the scientific community the degree of respect that ESP does. But why complain of that? Actually, there's better evidence for ESP.

Science isn't like the caucus race in *Alice in Wonderland*, where everybody has won and everyone gets prizes. Science *must* be highly skeptical and demanding of all new claims—the odder the claim, the fiercer the skepticism, or science would be wholly worthless. It is not our skilled skepticism that needs to be defended, but the pathological lack of skepticism of those who repeatedly invoke the name of science to support their opinions.

Simpson (1989) has commented how some of the clinicians who report these cases show an infatuation with the syndrome. They are like new parents, who rarely miss an opportunity to show videos of their uniquely talented offspring, or to tell you of their latest cute trick. Coons (1990) petulantly complained that because I, like the great majority of clinicians on earth, have never found a case of MPD, I should not comment on the subject. He reminds me of a patient who rejected my opinion that it was unlikely that there were flying saucers on his roof, on the grounds that I had had far less experience of Martians than he; but I have never previously met a scientist seeking to reject criticism of a theory on such a basis.

Humphrey and Dennett (1989) wisely comment on "the cliquish, almost cultish character of those who currently espouse the cause of MPD,": "In a world where those who are not for MPD are against it, it is perhaps not surprising that 'believers' have tended to close ranks."

DISSOCIATION AND HYPNOSIS IN RELATION TO MPD

Dissociative experiences are commonplace, and are often shaped in their form and expression by dominant cultural beliefs and expectations where these exist in a traditional or highly publicized form. Depending on the ambient expectations and the responses of others, these may become expressed in various ways. Where such events are culturally expected to be short-lived, they are. Where they are able to attract the interest and continuing attentions and explorations of a fascinated clinician, concentrating on one specific, potentially transient aspect of their shifting patterns, they extend into more elaborate and lasting forms. (Simpson 1989, 1990).

Ross (1989) agrees that dissociation is "a pervasive aspect of normal mental function." In addition, it can be voluntarily induced in a number of ways (Simpson 1977). The various measures of dissociation popularly used in MPD research, as reviewed by North and colleagues (1993) are readily fakable, and distinguishing real from faked scores is not reliable; reported research has shown that students without specialized knowledge of MPD can fake it successfully on such tests.

Erickson and colleagues (1976) emphasized the subtlety and power of indirect hypnosis, of which the subject and even the therapist may be unaware. What they and others describe is very close to what occurs in accounts of MPD, and the *grounding* signs described in the MPD literature are clear signs of trance induction or of change of altered states.

Kluft (1987b) admitted that there's a literature documenting that "phenomena analogous (sic) to MPD can be produced quite readily by hypnosis or any number of interventions" (e.g., Harriman 1942a, b, 1943, Janet 1907/1920, Kampman 1976, Kluft 1982, 1985c, Leavitt 1947, Spanos et al. 1985), but complains that they do not reproduce the syndrome "as an enduring whole." Of course they don't, in the absence of motivation to remain handicapped, and of secondary gain, to continue or prolong the situation. Actually, this is an even more mischievous complaint than it looks. With human subjects, it is unethical for any researcher to ever deliberately produce an enduring illness, so this has not even been attempted. Kluft implies we should read significance in a failure to achieve what has not been tried, and what would be unethical to attempt.

Many others have agreed that hypnosis and suggestion can account for the creation of personalities (Bliss 1988, Braun 1984a, Coons 1988, Herzog 1984, Horevitz and Braun 1983, Kluft 1982, Kohlenberg 1973, Ludwig et al. 1972, McCurdy 1941, Putnam et al. 1986, Ross et al. 1989, 1989a, Spiegel 1988) or of some cases (Coons 1980, Fahy 1988); or by iatrogenesis (Horton and Miller 1972, Ross et al. 1989, Ross et al. 1989a, Silberman et al. 1985, Spiegel 1988, Sutcliffe and Jones 1962).

If we don't all differ widely from birth in our skill at dissociation (a point never studied), it does seem that some children, perhaps traumatized and perhaps for other reasons, become skilled at exercising deliberate control of dissociation, and at being able to deliberately induce it.

Those totally committed to the independent existence of MPD, such as Braun (1984b), Greaves (1980), and Kluft (1982), have declared that the personalities created in the hypnosis studies are not "multiple personalities by any reasonable criteria" (Braun 1984b) which is unfair: they are vastly more like MPD personalities than many of the described productions of accredited MPD patients; they would meet the broader and generous criteria MPD-ites have often requested; and they do not blossom and develop as MPD patients' personalities do because they are terminated by the researcher/hypnotist, and not nurtured, rehearsed, named, and talked to over numerous sessions. Also, they are induced in less suggestible, less manipulative subjects, not especially motivated to captivate the therapist (and with less gullible therapists). Above all, they occur in people who have a life—who have other and better things to do with their time, and thus do not retain and elaborate the hypnotic creations.

Bloch (1991) carries the idea of MPD "as a superordinate diagnosis" to its illogical conclusion, and suggests that subordinate diagnoses include dysthymia, depressive disorders, anxiety disorders, phobic disorders, sexual dysfunctions, avoidant personality disorder, psychosomatic disorders, and others. Little within psychiatry would be left outside the MPD empire!

With the loss of hysteria, MPD emerged. There is always a presentation by which the hysteric, or the dissociation adept, can fascinate the naïve doctor or psychologist, colored by prevailing fashions.

In Robert Louis Stevenson's report on the case of Dr. Jekyll and Mr. Hyde (1877), he explored the insight that the advantage of multiplicity can be the capacity to dissociate the impulsive, selfish, evil impulses within one from the moral strictures of one's conscience, enabling guilt-free indulgence. Jekyll says that he discovered that

> man is not truly one, but only two. I say two, because the state of my own knowledge does not pass beyond that point. Others will follow, others will outstrip me on the same lines, and I hazard the guess that man will be ultimately known for a mere polity of multifarious, incongruous and independent denizens. . . . In my own person, . . . I learned to recognise the thorough and primitive duality of man; I saw that, of the two natures that contended in the field of my consciousness, even if I could be rightly said to be either, it was only because I was radically both. . . . I had learned to dwell with pleasure, as a beloved daydream, on the thought of the separation of these elements. If life would be relieved of all that was unbearable; the unjust might go his way, delivered from the aspirations and remorse of his more upright twin; and the just could walk steadfastly and securely on his upward path, doing the good things in which he found his pleasure, and no longer exposed to disgrace and penitance by the hands of this extraneous evil. It was the curse of mankind . . . that in the agonized womb of consciousness these polar twins should be continuously struggling.

REFERENCES

Adityanjee, R., and Khandelwal, S. K. (1989). Current status of multiple personality disorder in India. *American Journal of Psychiatry* 146:1607–1610.

Aldridge-Morris, R. (1989). *Multiple Personality: An Exercise in Deception*. Hillsdale, NJ: Lawrence Erlbaum.

Andersen, B. (1990). *Methodological Errors in Medical Research*. Oxford: Blackwell Scientific Publications.

Annon, J. S. (1988). Detection of deception and search for truth: a proposed model with particular reference to the witness, the victim, and the defendant. *Forensic Reports* 1(4)303–360.

Bahnson, C. B., and Smith, K. (1975). Autonomic changes in a multiple personality. [Abstract.] *Psychosomatic Medicine* 37:85–86.

Barrie, J. M. (1928). *Peter Pan: The Boy Who Would Not Grow Up*. London: Hodder & Stoughton.

Bliss, E. L. (1984). Hysteria and hypnosis. *Journal of Nervous and Mental Disease* 172:203–206.

_____ (1986). *Multiple Personality, Allied Disorders, and Hypnosis*. New York: Oxford University Press.

_____ (1988). Professional skepticism about multiple personality. *Journal of Nervous and Mental Disease* 176:533–534.

Bliss, E. L., and Jeppsen, E. A. (1985). Prevalence of multiple personality among inpatients and outpatients. *American Journal of Psychiatry* 142:250–251.

Bliss, E. L., and Larson, E. M. (1985). Sexual criminality and hypnotizability. *Journal of Nervous and Mental Disease* 173:522–526.

Bloch, J. P. (1991). *Assessment and Treatment of Multiple Personality and Dissociative Disorders*. Sarasota, FL: Professional Resource Press.

Boon, S., and Draijer, N. (1991). Diagnosing dissociative disorders in the Netherlands: a pilot study with the Structured Clinical Interview for *DSM-III-R* Dissociative Disorders. *American Journal of Psychiatry* 148:458–462.

———— (1993). Multiple personality disorder in the Netherlands: a clinical investigation of 71 patients. *American Journal of Psychiatry* 150(3):489–494.

Braude, S. E. (1991). *First Person Plural: Multiple Personality and the Philosophy of Mind*. London: Routledge.

Braun, B. G. (1984a). Hypnosis creates multiple personality: myth or reality? *International Journal of Clinical and Experimental Hypnosis* 32:191–197.

———— (1984b). Towards a theory of multiple personality and other dissociative phenomena. *Psychiatric Clinics of North America* 7:171–193.

Brende, J. O. (1984). The psychophysiological manifestations of dissociation. *Psychiatric Clinics of North America* 7:41–50.

Bromley, D. G., and Shupe, A. D. (1981). *Strange Gods: The Great American Cult Scare*. Boston: Beacon.

Bryant, D., Kessler, J., and Shirar, L. (1992). *The Family Inside: Working with the Multiple*. New York: W. W. Norton.

Chodoff, P. (1987). More on multiple personality disorder. *American Journal of Psychiatry* 144:124.

Cohen, B. M., Giller, E., and "W," L. (1991). *Multiple Personality Disorder from the Inside Out*. Lutherville, MD: Sidran.

Coons, P. M. (1980). Multiple personality: diagnostic considerations. *Journal of Clinical Psychiatry* 41:330–336.

———— (1984). The differential diagnosis of multiple personality: a comprehensive review. *Psychiatric Clinics of North America* 7:51–67.

———— (1986). The prevalence of multiple personality disorder. *Newsletter of the International Society for the Study of Multiple Personality and Dissociation* 4:6–8.

———— (1988). Psychophysiologic aspects of multiple personality disorder: a review. *Dissociation* 1:47–53.

———— (1990). More on multiple personality disorder. *British Journal of Psychiatry* 156(3): 448–449.

Coons, P. M., Milstein, V., and Marley, C. (1982). EEG studies of two multiple personalities and a control. *Archives of General Psychiatry* 39:823–825.

Crews, F. (1993). The unknown Freud. *The New York Review of Books* 40(19):55–66.

Cutler, B., and Reed, J. (1975). Multiple personality: a single case study with a 15 year follow-up. *Psychological Medicine* 5:18–26.

Decker, H. S. (1986). The lure of nonmaterialism in materialist Europe: investigations of dissociative phenomena: 1880–1915. In *Split Minds/Split Brains: Historical and Current Perspectives*, ed. J. M. Quen, pp. 31–62. New York: New York University Press.

Dell, P. F. (1988). Not reasonable skepticism, but extreme skepticism. *Journal of Nervous and Mental Disease* 176:537–538.

Dell, P. F., and Eisenhower, J. W. (1990). Adolescent multiple personality disorder: a preliminary study of eleven cases. *Journal of the American Academy of Child and Adolescent Psychiatry* 29:359–266.

Ekman, P. (1985). *Telling Lies: Clues to Deceit*. New York: W. W. Norton.

Ellman, R. (1987). *Oscar Wilde*. London: Hamish Hamilton.

Erickson, M. H., Rossi E. L., and Rossi S. I. (1976). *Hypnotic Realities: The Induction of Clinical Hypnosis and Forms of Indirect Suggestion*. New York: Irvington.

Fagan, J., and McMahon, P. P. (1984). Incipient multiple personality in children. *Journal of Nervous and Mental Disease* 172:26–36.

Fahy, T. A. (1988). The diagnosis of multiple personality disorder: a critical review. *British Journal of Psychiatry* 153:597–606.

———— (1990). Multiple Personality Disorder. *British Journal of Psychiatry*, 156, (6):906.

Fahy, T. A., Abas, M., and Brown, J. C. (1989). Multiple personality: a symptom of psychiatric disorder. *British Journal of Psychiatry* 154:99–101.

Fernando, L. (1990). Multiple personality disorder. *British Journal of Psychiatry* 157:150.

Festinger, L., Riecken, H. W., and Schachter, S. (1956). *When Prophecy Fails*. Minneapolis, MN: University of Minnesota Press.

Ganaway, G. K. (1989a). Historical versus narrative truth: clarifying the role of exogenous trauma in the etiology of MPD and its variants. *Dissociation* 2(4):208–215.

———— (1989b). Exploring the credibility issue in multiple personality disorder and related dissociative phenomena. Paper presented at the 4th Regional Conference on Multiple Personality and Dissociative States, Akron, Ohio, April.

Glass, J. M. (1993). *Shattered Selves: Multiple Personality in a Postmodern World*. Ithaca: Cornell University Press.

Goettman, C., Greaves, G. B., and Coons, P. M. (1991). *Multiple Personality and Dissociation, 1791–1990: A Complete Bibliography*. Norcross, GA: Ken Burrow & Co.

Goodwin, J., and Attias, R. (1993). Marginalia. *ISSMP&D News*, April 11, pp. 2, 7.

Goodwin, J., Hill, S., and Attias, R. (1990). Historical and folk techniques of exorcism: application to the treatment of dissociative disorders. *Dissociation* 3:94–101.

Gould, C. (1992). Diagnosis and treatment of ritually abused children. In *Out Of Darkness: Exploring Satanism and Ritual Abuse*, eds. D. K. Sakheim and S. E. Devine, pp. 207–248. New York: Lexington Books/Macmillan.

Greaves, G. B. (1980). Multiple personality: 165 years after Mary Reynolds. *Journal of Nervous and Mental Disease* 168:577–596.

———— (1992). Alternative hypotheses regarding claims of satanic cult activity: a critical analysis. In *Out of Darkness: Exploring Satanism and Ritual Abuse*. eds. D. K. Sakheim and S. E. Devine, pp. 45–72. New York: Lexington Books/Macmillan.

Harriman, P. L. (1942a). The experimental production of some phenomena related to the multiple personality. *Journal of Abnormal Social Psychology* 37:244–255.

———— (1942b). The experimental production of multiple personality. *Psychiatry* 5:179–186.

———— (1943). A new approach to multiple personality. *American Journal of Orthopsychiatry* 13:638–643.

Heisenberg, W. (1959). *Physics and Philosophy: The Revolution in Modern Science*. New York: Harper.

Herman, J. L., and Schatzow, E. (1987). Recovery and verification of memories of childhood sexual trauma. *Psychoanalytic Psychology* 4:1–14.

Herzog, A. (1984). On multiple personality: comments on diagnosis, etiology, and treatment. *International Journal of Clinical and Experimental Hypnosis* 32:210–221.

Hilgard, E. R. (1988). Professional skepticism about multiple personality. *Journal of Nervous and Mental Disease* 176:532.

Horevitz, R. P., and Braun, B. G. (1983). Are multiple personality disorder patients borderline? An analysis of 33 patients. *Psychiatric Clinics of North America* 7:69–87.

Horton, P., and Miller, D. (1972). The etiology of multiple personality. *Comprehensive Psychiatry* 13:151–159.

Humphrey, N., and Dennett, D. C. (1989). Speaking for ourselves: an assessment of multiple personality disorder. *Raritan* 9 (Summer): 69–98.

James, W. (1890). *The Principles of Psychology*. New York: Henry Holt.

Janet, P. (1907). *The Major Symptoms of Hysteria*. New York: Macmillan.

———— [1907] (1920). *The Major Symptoms of Hysteria: Fifteen Lectures Given in the Medical School of Harvard University*. Reprint. New York: Macmillan.

Kampman, R. (1976). Hypnotically induced multiple personality: an experimental study. *International Journal of Clinical and Experimental Hypnosis* 24:215–227.

Kirk, S. A., and Kutchins, H. (1992). *The Selling of DSM: The Rhetoric of Science in Psychiatry.* New York: Aldine de Gruyter.

Klein, D. N., and Riso, L. P. (1993). Psychiatric disorders: problems of boundaries and comorbidity. In *Symptoms of Schizophrenia*, ed. C. G. Costello, pp. 19–66. New York: Wiley.

Kluft, R. P. (1982). Varieties of hypnotic interventions in the treatment of multiple personality. *American Journal of Clinical Hypnosis* 24:230–240.

—————— (1984a). An introduction to multiple personality disorder. *Psychiatric Annals* 14 (1):21–24.

—————— (1984b). Aspects of the treatment of multiple personality disorder. *Psychiatric Annals* 14(1):51–55.

—————— (1984c). Treatment of multiple personality disorder: a study of 33 cases. *Psychiatric Clinics of North America* 7 (1):9–29.

—————— (1984d). Multiple personality in childhood. *Psychiatric Clinics of North America* 7:121–134.

—————— (1985a). Childhood multiple personality disorder: predictors, clinical findings, and treatment results. In *Childhood Antecedents of Multiple Personality Disorder*, ed. R. P. Kluft, pp. 167–196. Washington, DC: American Psychiatric Press.

—————— (1985b). *Childhood Antecedents to Multiple Personality.* Washington, DC: American Psychiatric Press.

—————— (1985c). Using hypnotic inquiry protocols to monitor treatment progress and stability in multiple personality disorder. *American Journal of Clinical Hypnosis* 28:63–75.

—————— (1986). Treating children who have multiple personality disorder. In *Treatment of Multiple Personality Disorder*, ed. B. G. Braun, pp. 79–105. Washington, DC: American Psychiatric Press.

—————— (1987a). The simulation and dissimulation of multiple personality disorder. *American Journal of Clinical Hypnosis* 30(2):104–118.

—————— (1987b). More on multiple personality. *American Journal of Psychiatry* 144:124–125.

—————— (1988). The phenomenology and treatment of extremely complex multiple personality disorder. *Dissociation* 1 (4):47–58.

—————— (1989). Iatrogenic creation of new alter personalities. *Dissociation* 2:83–91.

—————— (1991). Clinical presentations of multiple personality disorder. *Psychiatric Clinics of North America* 14:605–629.

—————— (1993). Integrating ourselves: multidisciplinary co-operation and synergy in the hospital treatment of Multiple Personality Disorder. In *Expressive and Functional Therapies in the Treatment of Multiple Personality*, pp. 273–293. Springfield, IL: Charles C Thomas.

Kohlenberg, R. J. (1973). Behavioristic approach to multiple personality: a case study. *Behavior Therapy* 4:137–140.

Kroll, J. (1993). *PTSD/Borderlines in Therapy: Finding the Balance.* New York: W. W. Norton.

Lancaster, E., and Poling, J. (1958). *The Final Face of Eve.* New York: McGraw-Hill.

Larmore, K., Ludwig, A. M., and Cain, R. L. (1977). Multiple personality: an objective case study. *British Journal of Psychiatry* 131:35–40.

Leavitt, H. (1947). A case of hypnotically produced secondary and tertiary personalities. *Psychoanalytic Review* 34:274–295.

Lewis, I. M. (1971). *Ecstatic Religion: An Anthropological Study of Spirit Possession and Shamanism.* London: Penguin.

—————— (1979). Speaking in tongues and the possession syndrome. In *Psycholinguistics in Clinical Practice: Languages of Illness and Healing*, ed. M. A. Simpson, pp. 56–65. New York: Irvington.

Littlewood, R., and Lipsedge, M. (1986). The "culture-bound syndromes" of the dominant culture: culture, psychopathology and biomedicine. In *Transcultural Psychiatry*, ed. J. L. Cox, pp. 253–273. London: Croom Helm.

Ludolph, P. S. (1985). How prevalent is multiple personality? *American Journal of Psychiatry* 142:1526–1527.

Ludwig, A. M., Brandsma, J. M., Wilbur, C. B. et al. (1972). The objective study of a multiple personality: or, are four heads better than one? *Archives of General Psychiatry* 26:298–310.

Magee, B. (1973). *Popper*. London: Fontana.

Malenbaum, R., and Russell, A. T. (1987). Multiple personality disorder in an eleven-year-old boy and his mother. *Journal of the American Academy of Child and Adolescent Psychiatry* 26:436–439.

Martinez-Taboas, A. (1989). Preliminary observations on MPD in Puerto Rico. *Dissociation* 2(3):128–131.

Mathew, R. J., Jack, R. A., and West, W. S. (1985). Regional cerebral blood flow in a patient with multiple personality. *American Journal of Psychiatry* 142:504–505.

Mayer-Gross, W., Slater, E., and Roth, M. (1960). *Clinical Psychiatry*. London: Cassell & Co.

McCurdy, H. A. (1941). A note on the dissociation of a personality. *Character and Personality* 10:33–41.

McMahon, P. P., and Fagan, J. (1993). Play therapy with children with multiple personality disorder. In *Clinical Perspectives on Multiple Personality Disorder*, eds. R. P. Kluft and C. G. Fine, pp. 253–276. Washington, DC: American Psychiatric Press.

Medawar, P. (1982). *Pluto's Republic (including the Art of the Soluble)*. Oxford: Oxford University Press.

Merskey, H. (1992). The manufacture of personalities: the production of multiple personality disorder. *British Journal of Psychiatry* 160:327–340.

Miller, S. D. (1989). Optical differences in cases of multiple personality disorder. *Journal of Nervous and Mental Disease* 177:480–486.

Modestin, J. (1992a). Multiple personality disorder in Switzerland. *American Journal of Psychiatry* 149:88–92.

——— (1992b). Dr. Modestin replies: multiple personality disorder: a factual error. *American Journal of Psychiatry* 149:(10):1417.

Nakdimen, K. A. (1992). Diagnostic criteria for multiple personality disorder. *American Journal of Psychiatry* 149(4):576–577.

North, C. S., Ryall, J-E. M., Ricci, D. A., et al. (1993). *Multiple Personalities, Multiple Disorders: Psychiatric Classification and Media Influence*. New York: Oxford University Press.

Notestein, W. (1968). *A History of Witchcraft in England from 1558–1718*. New York: Crowell.

Oesterreich, T. K. [1921] (1930). *Possession, Demoniacal and Other, among Primitive Races, in Antiquity, the Middle Ages, and Modern Times*. Translated from the German. London.

Ofshe, R., and Watte, E. (1993). Making monsters. *Society* March-April:4–16.

Orne, M. T., Dinges, D. F., and Orne, E. C. (1984). On the differential diagnosis of multiple personality in the forensic context. *International Journal of Clinical and Experimental Hypnosis* 32:118–169.

Peterson, G. (1990). Diagnosis of childhood multiple personality disorder. *Dissociation* 3(1):3–9.

Popper, K. R. (1963). *Conjectures and Refutations: The Growth of Scientific Knowledge*. London: Routledge & Kegan Paul.

——— (1968). *The Logic of Scientific Discovery*. London: Hutchinson. (originally Logik der Forschung, Vienna 1934).

Pride, M. (1986). *The Child Abuse Industry*. Westchester, IL: Crossway Books.

Prince, M. (1906a). *The Dissociation of a Personality*. New York: Longman, Green.

——— (1906b). Hysteria from the point of view of dissociated personality. *Journal of Abnormal and Social Psychology* 1:170–187.

Putnam, F. W. (1984). The psychophysiologic investigation of multiple personality disorder: a review. *Psychiatric Clinics of North America* 7:31–50.

_____ (1986). The scientific investigation of multiple personality disorder. In *Split Minds/Split Brains: Historical and Current Perspectives*, ed. J. M. Quen pp. 109–125. New York: New York University Press.

_____ (1987). Multiple personality disorder? *Journal of Clinical Psychiatry* 48:174.

_____ (1989). *Diagnosis and Treatment of Multiple Personality Disorder*. New York: Guilford.

_____ (1991). Recent research on multiple personality disorder. *Psychiatric Clinics of North America* 14:489–502.

Putnam, F. W., Guroff, J. J., Silberman, E. K., et al. (1986). The clinical phenomenology of multiple personality disorder: review of 100 recent cases. *Journal of Clinical Psychiatry* 47:285–293.

Putnam, F. W., and Loewenstein, R. J. (1993). Treatment of multiple personality disorder: a survey of current practices. *American Journal of Psychiatry* 150(7):1048–1052.

Putnam, F. W., Zahn, T. P., and Post, R. M. (1990). Differential autonomic nervous system activity in multiple personality disorder. *Psychological Research* 31:251–260.

Richardson, J., and Best, J., eds. (1991). *The Satanism Scare*. Chicago: Aldine.

Riley, R. L., and Mead, J. (1988). The development of symptoms of multiple personality disorder in a child of three. *Dissociation* 1(3):43–46.

Rosenthal, R., and Fode, K. L. (1963). The effect of experimental bias on the performance of the albino rat. *Behavioral Science* 8:183–187.

Ross, C. A. (1989). *Multiple Personality Disorder: Diagnosis, Clinical Features, and Treatment*. New York: John Wiley & Sons.

_____ (1990). More on multiple personality. *British Journal of Psychiatry*, 156, 3:449–450.

Ross, C. A., Miller, S. D., Reager, P., et al. (1990). Structured interview data on 102 cases of multiple personality disorder from four centers. *American Journal of Psychiatry* 147:596–601.

Ross, C. A., and Norton, G. R. (1989). Effects of hypnosis on the features of multiple personality disorder. *American Journal of Clinical Hypnosis* 32:99–106.

Ross, C. A., Norton, G. R., and Fraser, G. A. (1989a). Evidence against the iatrogenesis of multiple personality disorder. *Dissociation* 2:61–65.

Ross, C. A., Norton, G. R., and Wozney, K. (1989b). Multiple personality disorder: an analysis of 236 cases. *Canadian Journal of Psychiatry* 34:413–418.

Schafer, D. W. (1986). Recognizing multiple personality patients. *American Journal of Psychotherapy* 40:500–510.

Schetky, D. H. (1990). A review of the literature on the long-term effects of childhood sexual abuse. In *Incest-Related Syndromes of Adult Psychopathology*, ed. R. P. Kluft, pp. 35–54. Washington, DC: American Psychiatric Press.

Schreiber, F. R. (1973). *Sybil*. Chicago: Henry Regnery.

Silberman, E. K., Putnam, F. W., Weingartner, H., et al. (1985). Dissociative states in multiple personality disorder: a quantitative study. *Psychiatry Research* 15:253–260.

Simpson, M. A. (1974). A mythology of medical education. *Lancet* 1:399–401.

_____ (1975). Munchausen in the IRA. *World Medicine*, pp. 10, 19, 15.

_____ (1977). Self-induced depersonalization. *American Journal of Psychiatry* 134 (12):1449–1450.

_____ (1978a). Munchausen Syndrome. *British Journal of Hospital Medicine* 20:2, 209.

_____ (1978b). Pseudo-bereavement in the Munchausen Syndrome. *British Journal of Psychiatry*.

_____ (1989). Multiple personality disorder. *British Journal of Psychiatry* 155(10):565.

_____ (1990). Multiple Personality Disorder. Pretoria, South Africa: Centre for Psychosocial and Traumatic Stress.

_____ (1993). Traumatic stress and the bruising of the soul. In *International Handbook of Traumatic Stress Syndromes*, ed. J. P. Wilson and B. Raphael, pp. 667–684. New York: Plenum.

Sizemore, C. C. (1989). *A Mind of My Own*. New York: Doubleday.

Snowden, C. (1988). Where are all the childhood multiples? Identifying incipient multiple personality in children. [Summary.] In *Proceedings of the Fifth International Conference on Multiple Personality/Dissociative States*, ed. B. G. Braun, p. 36. Chicago: Rush.

Spanos, N. P. (1986). Hypnosis, nonvolitional responding, and multiple personality: a social psychological perspective. *Progress in Experimental Personality Research* 14:1–62.

Spanos, N. P., Weekes, J. R., and Bertrand, L. D. (1985). Multiple personality: a social psychological perspective. *Journal of Abnormal Psychology* 94:362–376.

Spanos, N. P., Weekes, J. R., Menary, E., et al. (1986). Hypnotic interview and age regression procedures in the elicitation of multiple personality symptoms: a simulation study. *Psychiatry* 49:298–311.

Spencer, J. (1989). *Suffer the Child*. New York: Pocket Books.

Spiegel, D. (1988). Commentary: the treatment accorded those who treat patients with multiple personality disorder. *Journal of Nervous and Mental Disease* 176:535–536.

Stevenson, R. L. (1877). *The Strange Case of Dr. Jekyll and Mr. Hyde*. In *Dr. Jekyll and Mr. Hyde*. London: J. M. Dent & Sons, 1925.

Summit, R. C. (1983). The child sexual abuse accommodation syndrome. *Child Abuse and Neglect* 7:177–193.

Sutcliffe, J. P., and Jones, J. (1962). Personal identity, multiple personality, and hypnosis. *International Journal of Clinical and Experimental Hypnosis* 10:231–269.

Takahashi, Y. (1990). Is multiple personality disorder really rare in Japan? *Dissociation* 3:57–59.

Thigpen, C. H., and Cleckly, H. M. (1957). *The Three Faces of Eve*. New York: McGraw-Hill.

———— (1984). On the incidence of multiple personality disorder. *International Journal of Clinical and Experimental Hypnosis* 32:63–66.

Tozman, S., and Pabis, R. (1989). Further skepticism (without hostility . . . we think). *Journal of Nervous and Mental Disease* 177:708–709.

van der Hart, O., and Boon, S. (1990). Contemporary interest in multiple personality disorder and child abuse in the Netherlands. *Dissociation* 3 (1):34–37.

van der Hart, O., and Horst, R. (1989). The dissociation theory of Pierre Janet. *Journal of Traumatic Stress* 2:397–412.

van Praag, H. M. (1993). *"Make-Believes" in Psychiatry or The Perils of Progress*. New York: Brunner/Mazel.

Waller, P. (1991). The politics of child abuse. *Society* 28(6):6–13.

Waters, F. S. (1989). Non-hypnotic therapeutic techniques in multiple personality in children. [Summary.] In *Proceedings of the Sixth International Conference on Multiple Personality/ Dissociative States*, ed. B. G. Braun, p. 165. Chicago: Rush.

Weiss, M., Sutton, P., and Utrecht, A. J. (1985). Multiple personality in a ten-year-old girl. *Journal of the American Academy of Child and Adolescent Psychiatry* 24:495–501.

World Health Organization (1992). *The ICD-10 Classification of Mental and Behavioural Disorders: Clinical Descriptions and Diagnostic Guidelines*. Geneva.

Zuckerman, M., DePaulo, B. M., and Rosenthal, R. (1981). Verbal and nonverbal communication of deception. In *Advances in Experimental Social Psychology*, ed. L. Berkowitz. New York: Academic.

6

A Skeptical Look at Multiple Personality Disorder

August Piper, Jr.

Most of the published literature on multiple personality disorder (MPD), or dissociative identity disorder (DID), has been written by proponents of the condition.[1] Such one-sidedness is not good for psychiatry, which needs and deserves a healthy and reasoned debate. This chapter reviews diagnosis and treatment, and discusses the deficiencies of much of the present-day thinking about the disorder. The following seven issues are examined:

1. Vagueness, imprecision, and overinclusiveness of the MPD/DID diagnostic criteria;
2. The recent sharp increase in the number of people alleged to have the disorder;
3. Exposure to malpractice risks;
4. Conceptual weaknesses in the theory of pathogenesis and treatment of the condition;
5. Encouragement of regressive and nonresponsible behavior;
6. Financial aspects of treatment;
7. Difficulties related to hypnosis.

IMPRECISE AND OVERINCLUSIVE DIAGNOSTIC CRITERIA

Of all the problems analyzed in this chapter, the weaknesses of the diagnostic criteria in the *DSM-IV* and its predecessor, the *DSM-III-R*, are

---

[1]Although this chapter will discuss the *DSM-IV* criteria for dissociative identity disorder (DID), most references will be to the earlier nomenclature, multiple personality disorder (MPD).

the most critical. The *DSM-IV* criteria for dissociative identity disorder are as follows:

1. The presence of two or more distinct identities or personality states (each with its own relatively enduring pattern of perceiving, relating to, and thinking about the environment and self);
2. At least two of the personality states recurrently take full control of the person's behavior;
3. Inability to recall personal information that is too extensive to be explained by ordinary forgetfulness;
4. Not due to the direct effects of a substance (e.g., blackouts or chaotic behavior during alcohol intoxication) or a general medical condition (e.g., complex partial seizures). Note: In children, the symptoms are not attributable to imaginary playmates or other fantasy play.

The *DSM-IV* has changed the name of the condition from "multiple personality disorder" to "dissociative identity disorder." It remains to be seen whether reliance on identity and the emphasis on dissociation will substantially ameliorate the difficulties that were originally posed by the use of "personality" in the *DSM-III-R*.

The *DSM-IV* does not define "personality" or "personality state," but the *DSM-III-R* text devines personality as "a relatively enduring pattern of perceiving, relating to and thinking about the environment and one's self that is exhibited in a wide range of important social and personal contexts." Personality states "differ only in that the pattern is not exhibited in as wide a range of contexts." There are several problems with such definitions. For example, in how narrow a range can the pattern be exhibited before the examiner may conclude that the behavior is not a manifestation of a personality but rather of a personality state? Is the definition satisfied if the personality state appears only in the therapist's office, for example, or only under hypnosis, or only when the patient is stressed? The criteria are further flawed by the vagueness of the expression "take full control of." How can the clinician recognize, with any reasonable degree of confidence, that a personality has taken control of a patient's behavior? What are the operational definitions of this expression?

Even the major contributors to the MPD literature contradict each other on the definitions of personalities and personality states. Bliss (1984a), for example, believes that personalities have specific and limited functions: "One [personality] thinks but does not feel, another cries but cannot laugh, a third specializes in self-mutilation." However, Braun (1984) disagrees, saying that *fragments* do not have a wide range of mood or affect. In other words, the terms *alter personality*, *personality state*, and *personality fragment* are ill-defined. Since "personality" is so difficult to define, Aldridge-Morris (1989) argues, a useful definition of "multiple personality" is elusive. This observation is important. What is the difference between a "personality state" and the behavior one shows, say, when angry or happy? Franklin (1990) attempts to answer this question by significantly expanding the concepts of dissociation and alter personalities. Even those minor changes in affect, posture, and voice quality that are frequently seen in therapy sessions may, she believes, indicate hidden alters.

It follows that few limits exist to the number of "personalities" one may unearth; the number is bounded only by the interviewer's energy and zeal in searching, and by the interviewer's subjective sense of what constitutes a "personality" (Dinwiddie et al. 1993). The intangibility of alters means that any attempt to answer the question, "how many personalities?" quickly takes on the character of ancient theologians' debates about the number of angels that could sit on the head of a pin (Aldridge-Morris 1989).

The imprecision of terms such as *alter personality* should render suspect the increase in numbers of alters recently found in MPD cases. In the nineteenth century, nearly all reported cases were of dual personalities (Boor 1982). But now, cases average from six to sixteen personalities (Coons et al. 1988, Kluft 1984a, Ross et al. 1989); in one 1982 series almost half the patients had more than ten alters (Kluft 1982). Cases of 100, 300, 400, and 1,000 alternates have now been reported (Coons 1986d, North et al. 1993).

The term *alter personality* means different things to different contributors to the MPD literature. Ross (1990b), for example, says it is a dissociated component of a single personality, a stylized embodiment of conflicted memories, feelings, thoughts, and drives. He believes the patient's mind is no more host to numerous distinct personalities than his or her body is to different people. Bliss (1984a) considers an alter personality to be an obviously imaginary construct. Both these notions are contradicted by the *DSM-IV*, and by several other writers:

> The major identifying characteristic [of MPD is] the presence of separate personalities in a single individual. [Kluft 1984]

> [The cases show] two or more personalities, each of which is so well developed and integrated as to have a relatively coordinated, rich, unified, and stable life of its own. [Taylor and Martin 1944]

In summary, it is difficult to know how to test or prove an assertion that an individual has more than one personality, or how to distinguish clinically between personalities or personality states, when there is no general agreement about what any of these terms mean (Dinwiddie et al. 1993).

With respect to Ross's comment about conflicted mental functions, psychodynamic theory holds that *all* individuals have conflicts. Further, partial dissociation occurs constantly in normal individuals (Spiegel and Cardeña 1991, Thigpen and Cleckley 1984). To some extent all people can be different people under different circumstances; everyone has at least a touch of multiple personality within them (Ludwig et al. 1972). Where then is the line of demarcation between normal and pathological, between normality and multiplicity? Thigpen and Cleckley (1984) answer by urging that the MPD diagnosis be reserved for those very few people who are fragmented in the most extreme manner.

Because no one has direct access to another person's consciousness, the only way to know how people perceive or think about their environment or themselves is to observe their behavior, including their verbal productions (Dinwiddie et al. 1993). Thus, the *DSM-III-R* definition of personality really reduces to a relatively enduring pattern of *behavior* that is exhibited in a wide range of important personal and social contexts. To speak of directly assessing perceptions and thoughts, independently of an individual's speech or behavior, adds nothing to the definition, and implies that clinicians can assess functions they cannot.

If this more modest definition is accepted, then it is immediately clear that multiple personality disorder ceases to be distinguishable from many other psychiatric phenomena. MPD may present with symptoms identical to any of a number of other conditions. For example, Ross (1988) sees a phenomenological overlap between MPD and at least some cases of obsessive-compulsive disorder; Kluft (1991) describes a patient, considered for years to have obsessive-compulsive disorder, who was cured when the true diagnosis of MPD was finally made. Other writers comment on the similarity between the symptoms of MPD and those of schizophrenia (Malenbaum and Russell 1987, Nakdimen 1990), and point out how frequently patients with MPD show Schneiderian symptoms (Putnam 1989, Ross et al. 1989a). MPD patients often meet criteria for somatization disorder (Ross et al. 1989b). They also usually satisfy *DSM-III* criteria for borderline or other personality disorders (Coons et al. 1988, Horevitz and Braun 1984). MPD may resemble rapid-cycling affective disorder (Alarcon 1990); episodic dyscontrol syndrome or intermittent explosive disorder (Fichtner et al. 1990); or depression, mania, bulimia, anorexia, or various anxiety disorders (Putnam et al. 1984). A case of MPD presenting as postpartum depression has been reported (Satel and Howland 1992). The condition may present with hallucinations, delusions, catatonia, or symptoms of a thought disorder (Putnam 1989); self-destructive behaviors or depression (Putnam et al. 1986); post-traumatic stress disorder (Loewenstein 1991); or transsexualism or other psychosexual disorders (Putnam 1989). According to Kluft (1987a), even the blackouts of a recovering alcoholic may suggest unsuspected MPD, and substance abuse of various kinds is common in MPD (Putnam 1989). MPD has been reported to occur in association with complex partial seizure disorder (Drake 1986, Mesulam 1981). There is speculation that male MPD patients display the disorder in antisocial ways, leading to involvement with the courts rather than the mental health system (Bliss and Larson 1985, North et al. 1993, Putnam 1984); indeed, a person who repeatedly engages in criminal behavior could legitimately claim to be demonstrating a relatively enduring pattern of behavior caused by a personality state. Coons (1984) and Kluft (1991a) have both provided long lists of disorders resembling MPD, and the latter encourages the inclusion of MPD in virtually all differential diagnoses. In fact, because MPD patients exhibit a plethora of symptoms similar to all major psychiatric disorders (Bliss 1984a), multiplicity could be advanced as a possible explanation for *any* psychiatric symptom (North et al. 1993).

The fundamental definitions of critical features of the MPD diagnostic criteria are vague, overinclusive, and too dependent on interpretation. Thus, they are what are called *open concepts* (Pap 1953): that is, categories formulated with minimal or no observable referents. Some writers have insisted that efforts be made to relate these categories clearly to the external world of objects and events—to give an explicit, public statement of the meaning of a theoretical term (Hine and Feather 1961). If such efforts are not made, assertions incorporating open concepts tend to be muddled and maddeningly abstract, as, for example, "the archetypal mechanisms of the ego become diffused when libidinous energies overwhelm superego introjects" (Millon 1991, p. 24) or "personalities . . . are alternative ways of configuring aspects of the mental apparatus" (Kluft 1991a, p.). No observable phenomena exist by which such formulations can be evaluated, critically tested, or determined to be false. Thus *one can never determine that the diagnosis of MPD is false*; the assertion that "Smith has MPD" can never be disproved or refuted. The inability to determine whether an assertion is false is not a virtue (as people often think) but a vice. An example will make this clear.

A patient presents with complaints of a circumscribed phobia—say to bathtubs—and has a history of possible childhood sexual abuse. A therapist might say, after several interviews, that the patient has MPD, that the phobia occurs because the patient was abused in bathtubs, and that the phobic symptoms are the manifestation of an alter personality.

How could such assertions possibly be refuted? If the patient denies being abused, the therapist could say that MPD patients often attempt to hide their abuse histories (Putnam 1989). If the patient does not show evidence of other personalities, she would fit the criteria for "secret MPD" (Kluft 1991), in which the alters do not emerge unless the host is alone. Alternatively, she could have "latent MPD" (Kluft 1991a), where the alters are generally inactive but emerge infrequently and then subside, thereby creating a more-or-less brief window of diagnosability. According to Kluft (1987a), many MPD patients experience substantial periods of time in which the various personalities do not emerge overtly; years may pass with little overt dissociative activity (Kluft 1985a, Kluft 1991a). If the patient denies having MPD, the therapist could make any of several claims: that the denial was not unusual, because patients frequently dispute the accuracy of the diagnosis (Loewenstein 1991, Putnam 1989); that denying the diagnosis is a major form of resistance to therapy (Putnam 1989); that patients frequently deny a symptom in one part of the interview and then admit to it in another (Loewenstein 1991); or that people can be multiples without being aware that they are (Weissberg 1993). Even showing absolutely no sign of the disorder does not disconfirm the diagnosis: Kluft (1984b) claims that almost half his patients initially had no evidence of MPD at all. According to Kluft (1985b), overt behavioral phenomena are not basic ingredients of MPD. Instead, MPD's irreducible core is a persistent intrapsychic structure *rather than overt behavioral manifestations* (Kluft 1991a) "What is essential to multiple personality disorder across its many presentations *is no more than* the presence, within an individual, of more than one structured entity with a sense of its own existence" (Kluft 1985a, emphasis added). These open concepts demonstrate why it is impossible to refute an assertion that a patient has MPD: if the "entity" shows itself, then the patient has MPD. But if it fails to show itself, the patient still has MPD—by virtue of the simple presence of an invisible "entity." To speak thus of things unseen is to speak of demons and ghosts, not of science; such language invites derision of our profession.

MPD rarely presents as a freestanding condition. According to Kluft (1987a), "Almost invariably its manifestations are embedded within a polysymptomatic presentation suggestive of one or more commonplace conditions" (p. 367). However, this leads to a difficulty not satisfactorily addressed in the MPD literature. In the absence of reliable tests for the condition, the clinician has no basis for deciding whom to treat for MPD and whom to treat for the disorders that resemble MPD. Given that MPD has such extensive comorbidity, the failure of *DSM-III-R* or *DSM-IV* to specify exclusion criteria for other disorders must be regarded as a serious deficiency (North et al. 1993).

The MPD literature encourages overdiagnosis of the disorder. For example, Kluft's (1985b) comment that "it is productive to err on the side of overconsideration of the diagnosis" invites false-positive diagnoses (p. 6). The American Psychiatric Association (1989) says MPD should be diagnosed whenever its features are present—but the report does not specify *which* features. The practice of employing long lists of questions designed to elicit symptoms, without specifying how many positive responses are required to cross diagnostic thresholds, increases the number of false-positive diagnoses (Dinwiddie et al. 1993). Noteworthy examples of this practice exist (Fagan and McMahon 1984, Hornstein and Tyson 1991, Loewenstein 1991). As one example, Fagan and McMahon's (1984) list of twenty-six signs and symptoms of MPD in children contains items such as having imaginary playmates; being lonely, truant, homicidal, suicidal, sexually precocious, or delinquent; failing to change behavior when disciplined; denying misbehavior even though evidence is obvious; perplexing professionals, and so forth. Loewenstein (1991) reports no fewer than thirty-nine symptoms that suggest MPD. The current MPD literature is oddly silent on the question of the minimum number and kind of symptoms needed for an accurate diagnosis of the disorder; it is difficult to overstate the seriousness of this deficiency.

The risk of overdiagnosing MPD is increased by statements (Putnam et al. 1984) that MPD is a "superordinate" diagnosis:

> Once the diagnosis of MPD is confirmed, it is important to consider it as the superordinate diagnosis even when other symptom clusters seem to predominate. . . . Amnesia, anxiety, mood changes, hallucinations, somatization, and anorexic-bulimic symptoms, among others, generally can be conceptualized as manifestations of different alternate personalities or of interactions between alternate personality states. [p. 175]

It is only a short step from this position to one of considering every psychiatric patient to have MPD. I find no data in the literature to support the idea that symptoms of MPD should be accorded superordinate status. Fahy (1988) likewise criticizes the arbitrary, uncritical and precipitous "inflation of a single symptom, over other coexisting ones, into a final diagnosis," and North and colleagues (1993) point out that there is no good evidence to direct clinicians to preempt a diagnosis such as Briquet's syndrome or borderline personality in favor of a diagnosis of MPD.

In this context, a study by Ross and Norton (1988) is revealing. The authors, by means of a questionnaire, obtained information on 177 patients, all of whom had been diagnosed as having MPD. Of these, 81 had a past diagnosis of schizophrenia and 96 did not. The two groups did not differ in the features of MPD they showed. Although there was no proof that all the patients truly had MPD and not schizophrenia, the study is nonetheless presented as a cautionary lesson: "Clinicians should be aware of the features that lead to a misdiagnosis of schizophrenia, in order not to make that diagnostic error" (p. 40). Such a conclusion reflects an arbitrary and uncritical acceptance of the accuracy of the MPD diagnosis.

To avoid thinking that every patient has MPD, there must be a way to confirm the diagnosis. How does one do this? The experts disagree. According to Coons (1980), the diagnosis cannot actually be confirmed until the clinician observes the dissociation into secondary personalities. However, Putnam (1989) says that meeting a different personality does not settle the diagnostic question:

> That awaits determining that the alter and any others that may subsequently appear are really separate, unique, and relatively enduring entities, rather than transient ego-state phenomena. The therapist will need to determine . . . the extent to which the alters are active outside of the therapy setting . . . the role they have played in the patient's life history, [and] the consistency of the alter personalities over time.

As noted above, alters may not appear for years, and the signs of their emergence may be quite subtle. Thus, even using Putnam's criteria, clarifying the diagnosis of MPD may take years: "Not uncommonly, the diagnostic picture remains unsettled for fairly prolonged periods" (American Psychiatric Association 1989, p. 2212). Putnam's criteria are very difficult to utilize in actual practice. One reason is that he gives no hint of what is meant by "unique entities" or "ego-state phenomena." Another is that it is not made clear how to find out from MPD patients, who are acknowledged, even by proponents, to be very unreliable historians, what the alters do outside of therapy. Finally, the requirement of alter consistency conflicts with both Bliss (1980) and Kluft (1991a), who say that alters may appear just once, to carry out some task, and then vanish.

It seems unacceptable to remain in limbo for years about a patient's diagnosis. Nonetheless, Graves (1989) recommends prolonged periods during which the clinician should avoid making other diagnoses, and instead search "for as long as necessary" to find the hidden dissociative symptoms that will clarify the diagnosis (p. 126). The author, of course, is attempting to perform the logical impossibility of proving a negative. He will treat for, say, a bipolar disorder only when he has proven the absence of a dissociative disorder.

Given the varied presentations of MPD, reliable and accurate ways of confirming the diagnosis are crucial. However, methods used by proponents of MPD are open to the criticism that they suggest symptoms to the patients, and thus bias the examination. As one example, Putnam and associates (1986) report that in about half of their 100 cases, the clinicians either asked to meet a suspected alter, or used hypnosis or barbiturate-facilitated interviews to bring forth the alters. The possibility that such techniques may "lead" the patient is dismissed by Kluft (1991a), who says the clinician should not be constrained by such concerns. Rather than deferring direct questions, he recommends "unapologetic direct inquiry" into the possibility of MPD. I will say more later in the chapter on the question of biasing the patient.

Some efforts have been made to improve the validity of MPD diagnoses. For example, in *DSM-IV*, amnesia has been added as a diagnostic criterion for MPD. This addition accomplishes little, because obviously no one can verify that a person truly does not remember something (Schacter 1986). Other writers have used psychometric tests in an attempt to increase the accuracy of MPD diagnoses (Bernstein and Putnam 1986, Bliss 1984a, Steinberg et al, 1990). However, the tests themselves are validated against *DSM-III* or *III-R* criteria, which, as discussed above, are too unelaborated to allow for precise diagnosis (Dinwiddie et al. 1993, Ludolph 1985). Therefore, the validity of these instruments must be in question. The Dissociative Experience Scale (DES) developed by Bernstein and Putnam (1986), has been criticized by Franklin (1990). He points out that the phenomena included in the scale may very well reflect factors quite different from dissociation, such as imaginative capacity, attention, attribution, and recall. Also, Weiner (1992) notes that all questions in the instrument are scored in the same direction. Thus, anyone with a tendency to say yes to any question—a distinct possibility with MPD patients—would score high on the DES.

These criticisms notwithstanding, the DES has been used in several studies (Loewenstein and Putnam 1988, Ross et al. 1990, Ross et al. 1992). Bernstein and Putnam (1986) and Ross and associates (1990) state that the validity of the DES has been demonstrated, that their studies suggest that dissociative disorders are relatively common in the general population, and that the DES can differentiate MPD from other diagnostic groups. These assertions are not well supported by the evidence. First, the impression is given that the DES truly measures dissociation—that is, that the scale has construct validity. However, I am unaware of any investigation that has provided much evidence of construct validity for the DES (see Frischholz et al. 1990, Ross et al. 1988). Indeed, there is evidence suggesting that the scale *lacks* construct validity. Sandberg and Lynn (1992) examined those subjects with DES scores in the upper 15 percent of their study population—a group expected to be at high risk for a dissociative disorder.

However, only 6 percent of this group actually met criteria for such a disorder. Chu and Dill (1990) also find no correlation between DES scores and either dissociative symptoms or dissociative diagnoses.

Misleading terminology is also found in Bernstein and Putnam's 1986 paper, in which it is claimed that the DES has good construct validity because item scores and scale scores are highly correlated. However, such a correlation is a measure of the homogeneity of the scale, which has little relevance to construct validity of a test (Anastasi 1988). Similarly, the authors state that because item scores on the test differentiate subjects similarly, the DES has good criterion-rated validity. This is incorrect. According to Anastasi (1988), criterion-related validity indicates the effectiveness of a test in predicting an individual's performance in specified activities. Without evidence of construct validity, it is inappropriate to use results from the scale to draw conclusions about the prevalence of dissociative disorders.

Frischholz and colleagues (1990), in their study supporting the reliability and validity of the DES, say that dissociative disorders in the general population are very rare. The authors thus contradict Ross and colleagues' (1992) claim that these conditions may be common in the general population.

Does the DES truly differentiate between MPD and other diagnostic groups? The 1986 Bernstein and Putnam study intends to test this hypothesis, as does a 1993 report by Carlson and colleagues. I believe both studies are flawed, and for the same reasons. First, both use *DSM-III* criteria as external validators. The discussion above has shown, however, that these are too nonspecific to be of value to the researcher. Second, neither study uses a particularly challenging mix of diagnoses. No attempt is made to have the DES discriminate between patients with MPD and those with, say, somatization disorder or borderline personality disorder— a task often quite difficult in clinical practice (Dinwiddie et al. 1993, Kemp et al. 1988). To attempt such a differentiation would be a more stringent test of the scale's construct validity than has hitherto been attempted. Another test that might provide evidence of construct validity would be to compare DES scores of a group of MPD patients before and after treatment; lower scores after successful therapy of the condition would be significant.

Finally, even if it were proven that the DES actually measures dissociation, it is not necessarily true that the dissociation produces the psychopathology: correlation, of course, does not prove causation.

Both Fahy (1988) and, especially, North and colleagues (1993) approach the question of validity of the MPD diagnosis in a manner that makes their conclusions worthy of attention. They both rely on Robins and Guze (1970) and Feighner and colleagues (1972), who established methods of determining diagnostic validity of psychiatric disorders. These methods involve five kinds of procedures. First, the disorder is described clinically. Second, laboratory abnormalities are discovered. Third, the condition is differentiated from other disorders. Fourth, follow-up studies are carried out; and fifth, the family history of the disorder is elucidated. The scientific methodology available now is not sufficiently sophisticated to allow all of these procedures to be carried out for any presently known psychiatric condition. However, MPD in particular fails the all-important third procedure: because of elastic diagnostic criteria and lack of exclusion criteria for other disorders, the condition simply cannot be differentiated from the numerous other psychiatric and medical disorders it resembles.

In conclusion, patients diagnosed by current criteria as having MPD belong to a very heterogeneous group that has poorly demarcated boundaries with many other psychiatric conditions.

THE RECENT SHARP INCREASE IN THE NUMBER OF PATIENTS ALLEGED TO HAVE THE DISORDER

The number of patients diagnosed with MPD has increased exponentially during the 1980s (Ross 1991). At the beginning of the decade the entire world literature contained only about 200 cases, with a mere eight having been reported between 1960 and 1970 (Bliss 1980). Between 1944 and 1969, only fourteen cases were reported (Greaves 1980). In the twenty years prior to 1989, just one case appeared in the British literature (Fahy et al. 1989). Now, however, the MPD phenomenon has reached epidemic proportions (North et al. 1993). Coons (1986a) estimates that 6,000 cases of MPD have been diagnosed in North America alone; Ross (1991) believes that "complex dysfunctional MPD requiring specific psychotherapy" affects about 1 per cent of the population of a major Canadian city (p. 511); Kluft (1985a) polled 70 students at a workshop and discovered that a total of over 260 cases had been seen by members of that group. Putnam and associates (1986) commented that as of that year, more cases of MPD had been discovered within the previous five years than in the preceding two centuries. Fagan and McMahon (1984) predict that soon, a clinician who has *not* recently seen a patient with MPD may expect to have questions asked about his/her diagnostic ability or lack of familiarity with recent literature.

Several writers are skeptical about the striking increase in the alleged prevalence of MPD. For example, in response to a suggestion by Ross (1990c) that 5 percent of all adult psychiatric admissions in Britain or South

Africa would meet *DSM-III-R* criteria for MPD, Fernando (1991) comments that it is incredible that a condition could be this common and yet never once be seen or diagnosed by a majority of psychiatrists on either side of the Atlantic. Similarly, Tozman and Pabis (1989) report that in forty years of practice, they have never seen a legitimate case of MPD. In Modestin's (1992) study, just three psychiatrists—less than 0.5 percent of the total surveyed—contributed 128 of the 221 MPD cases. Modestin suggests these clinicians either evaluated the same clinical phenomena differently from the others, applied the diagnostic criteria differently, or somehow shaped or elicited their patients' symptoms. He also believes this condition is sufficiently uncommon—less than 0.1 percent of psychiatric patients—that several decades of professional experience are needed before a psychiatrist is likely to encounter even one patient with MPD. Finally, Thigpen and Cleckley (1984), who wrote *The Three Faces of Eve*, say that in thirty years they have had hundreds of referrals of patients who were thought to have MPD. Other than Eve, they saw only one case that appeared to be undeniably a genuine multiple personality.

Ross (1991) does not attempt to answer the obvious question of why the number of these cases has increased so dramatically. However, Kluft (1987a) attributes the increase to several factors: more widely disseminated information about MPD; narrowing of the definitions of other conditions, such as schizophrenia, with which MPD may be confused; greater scrutiny of cases where there is failure to respond to appropriate treatment for some other condition; and increased awareness of the hitherto unacknowledged high prevalence of child abuse and incest. There is no way to convincingly refute such suggestions. However, it seems difficult to believe that these factors alone could account for the explosive rise in the number of MPD cases diagnosed in the past few years. It is similarly difficult to ignore the most parsimonious explanation of this phenomenon: that the *DSM-III* diagnostic criteria are elastic enough to accommodate a very broad group of patients, and that some practitioners have begun to uncritically apply these criteria.

MALPRACTICE RISKS

Hardy and associates (1988) warn that clinicians face legal jeopardy if they fail to diagnose MPD in patients with the condition. The authors argue that this disorder has a good prognosis when properly treated, and a poor one when it is not. Thus, they say, failing to make the correct diagnosis deprives a patient of potentially useful treatment; the omission may be compensable at law.

Such an effort to sue a therapist would be particularly misguided, for the following reasons. First, as was discussed above, several fundamental features of MPD are poorly defined; it seems inappropriate to punish a clinician for missing a diagnosis whose features depend so much on interpretation.

Furthermore, Hardy and colleagues (1988) themselves comment that MPD patients may strongly resist giving information the clinician needs to make the diagnosis. People with this condition may deny, confabulate, downplay, or rationalize the phenomena of the disorder (Loewenstein 1991, Putnam 1989). In addition, repression may cause an inability to provide data about two kinds of experiences that are important in making the diagnosis—child abuse and dissociative episodes (Putnam 1989). According to the MPD literature, memories of abuse are often repressed—although the belief that one can selectively block out whole sets of memories, and then retrieve them years later, has recently come under strong attack (Lindsay and Read 1994, Loftus 1993, Wakefield and Underwager 1992). Of course, the clinician might try to corroborate an abuse history by interviewing family members. However, families tend to be poor sources of validation for these episodes (Putnam 1989); if, as often happens, the family denies that the events occurred, the clinician will not know whom to believe. Two critical reviews of retrospective accounts of abuse have recently been published (Brewin et al. 1993, Frankel 1993). Putnam (1989) acknowledges that an independent verification of alleged abuse, which often occurs ten or more years prior to being reported in therapy, is almost impossible for the average therapist to obtain.

Serban (1992) discusses a case that reveals the other edge of the MPD sword. A psychiatrist was sued by a patient who claimed he had falsely diagnosed her as having MPD. As a result of this misdiagnosis, she said, she had failed to be given proper care by her physician. The records showed that during the hospital treatment, she had demonstrated behaviors typical of MPD patients. On some occasions, she would ask for coloring books and crayons, or go to the store with a nurse, giggling like a little girl and asking for candy; on others, she would act "in a whorish manner," behaving seductively and using crude language. At trial, however, she claimed that she had acted out all these behaviors to conform to the physician's diagnosis, which she said came out of nowhere. This case again raises the concerns stated in the first section of this review: given that the patient did show these behaviors, how could the physician have verified that they indeed resulted from various personalities? To put it another way, how could the doctor have determined the patient was malingering? Serban (1992) concludes that either would have been unlikely, unless the clinician had performed an electroencephalogram and had conducted extensive interviews with people who had known the patient in the past.

Significant practical and economic obstacles stand in the way of routine clinical use of these methods. Serban's suggestion to use an EEG study is based on a study by Putnam (1984), in which visual evoked potentials and standard EEGs were compared in MPD patients and simulators. Some differences were seen, but Putnam does not claim that they were sufficiently robust to be of diagnostic value. More recently, Loewenstein and Putnam (1988) state that the vast majority of MPD patients do not have detectable EEG abnormalities; North and colleagues (1993), after examining the data, conclude that no laboratory test will differentiate MPD from other conditions. In any case, it would be impractical to use the EEG to try to "catch" an alter during those unpredictable times when it is "out." There are also obstacles to obtaining data from collateral interviews. What if the patient refuses permission for them? How reliable are the collateral historians? What if the patient has "latent" or "secret" MPD (Kluft 1991a), or if the symptoms have just recently begun (Satel and Howland 1992)? How would such a person meet the burden of providing independent collateral evidence of symptoms prior to contact with a clinician? In addition, since most MPD patients are said to be skilled at dissimulation, and to struggle vigorously to hide their multiplicity (Kluft 1987a), one wonders how useful collateral interviews can possibly be.

Kluft (1987b) reaches a conclusion similar to Serban's. He says that there are no reliable methods of unmasking a patient simulating MPD. He discusses several simulators, and warns that the appearance of lying or malingering may not be of value in distinguishing simulators from genuine MPD patients. In his study, in fact, every indicator of malingering was found to occur in genuine MPD patients. (Weissberg [1993] notes that MPD proponents do not stress the converse of this fact: that the condition is easily faked because genuine and malingered MPD look so similar.) Coons (1991) provides a list of clues suggesting malingering or factitious disorder, but many of these are strikingly similar to the manifestations of non-malingered MPD. For example, one listed clue is that malingerers may have only two or three personality states. However, the usefulness of this clue is diminished by the fact that Putnam and associates (1986) note that the modal number of personalities displayed by *true* MPD patients is indeed three. Another clue is said to be inconsistency in presentations of the alters over a relatively brief period. Kluft (1991a), however, indicates that rapid fluctuation and switching of alters is a hallmark of "extremely complex" or "polyfragmented" MPD. Another clue—lack of dissociative symptomatology prior to the evaluation—seems reasonable, until one is reminded that some MPD patients become overt only when their own children reach the ages at which they themselves had been traumatized, or when their abusers become ill or die (Kluft 1991a, Satel and Howland 1992).

The Kenneth Bianchi case, in which an alleged murderer claimed to have MPD—apparently to pursue a verdict of not guilty by reason of insanity—testifies to the difficulty of distinguishing malingered from actual cases of MPD (Coons 1991). The defendant was examined by no fewer than seven psychiatrists and psychologists—yet they could not reach agreement on the central question of whether the MPD diagnosis was veridical. The patient discussed by Serban (1992) was also interviewed by "several experts," but just as in the Bianchi case, they reached no consensus about the accuracy of the MPD diagnosis. One might therefore legitimately wonder how a busy practitioner, not specializing in MPD treatment, could confidently make the diagnosis if experts, examining patients and their records at leisure, could not. Brick and Chu (1991) discuss a case of simulated MPD, and warn that as a result of recent proliferation of information about MPD in the popular and professional press, the realistic simulation of the condition has become more probable. They, too, acknowledge that detecting such behavior can be difficult. Other writers are more emphatic, asserting that there is little reason to believe that the distinction between true and malingered MPD can be made with an acceptable degree of accuracy (Dinwiddie et al. 1993).

CONCEPTUAL WEAKNESSES IN THE THEORY OF MPD'S PATHOGENESIS

One difficulty—verification of abuse—was mentioned in the preceding section. Another conceptual problem is the paucity of support in the literature for a major theory of the pathogenesis of MPD: that the condition arises as a result of trauma.

Putnam (1989), and Ross (1991) both claim that there is strong evidence linking the development of MPD to severe, recurrent traumatic experiences. So firmly is child abuse linked with the theory of MPD pathogenesis that some investigators have used abuse as a criterion for the diagnosis (Merskey 1992). Ross and associates (1991) call MPD the most complex dissociative response to severe childhood trauma. If this were true, one would expect to see differences in the abuse histories of MPD patients, as compared to those with other psychiatric disorders. However, a history of abuse is by no means uncommon among either in- or outpatients who have a variety of psychiatric diagnoses (Brown and Anderson 1991, Shearer et al. 1990, Swett et al. 1990, Winfield et al. 1990), and it is particularly common in patients with borderline personality disorder (Paris and Zweig-Frank 1992, Western et al. 1990). Furthermore, it is not at all clear that such a history is more likely to be found in patients with the diagnosis of MPD than in others. In fact, the only study to examine this question shows the opposite: patients diagnosed as having borderline personality disorder had a greater prevalence of reported childhood abuse than did those with MPD (Ross 1991, Ross et al. 1990). Finally, a history of sexual abuse appears to be common even in women who do not have psychiatric complaints (Anderson et al. 1993). There is virtually no general domain of symptomatology that has not been associated with a history of sexual abuse (Kendall-Tackett et al. 1993); sexual abuse does not appear to predispose to any one diagnosis (Carlin and Ward 1992, Pribor and Dinwiddie 1992). Investigators in the MPD field tend to conflate all childhood sexual abuse, thus failing to recognize that not all traumatic experiences carry equal weight. The long-term effects of sexual abuse of children differ, depending on many factors: whether penetration occurred, the child's age at the time, whether the abuser was a caretaker or relative, the frequency of the events, whether the abuse was disclosed to parents and what their reaction was, whether force was used, and so forth (Browne and Finkelhor 1986, Ernst et al. 1992, Green 1993, Kiser et al. 1988, Mennen 1993). The MPD research has generally paid insufficient attention to the methodological complexities of childhood sexual-abuse research (see Bifulco et al. 1991, Conte et al. 1991, Green 1993, and Kendall-Tackett et al. 1993, for discussion.) For example, the published papers do not acknowledge the fact that investigators may obtain significantly different figures for the prevalence of childhood sexual abuse, depending on what age limits are set for childhood, whether a narrow or wide definition of the term "sexual abuse" is employed, and whether the data includes or excludes sexual contacts between individuals of approximately the same age.

The literature in this area approaches the problem of the etiology of MPD in a rather simplistic fashion. It gives the impression that childhood trauma, particularly sexual abuse, has been established as the primary cause of MPD, and that severe sexual abuse more or less inevitably leads to the condition (Kluft 1987a). According to Coons (1986c), "Trauma has long been recognized as an essential criterion for the production of dissociative disorders including multiple personality" (p. 457). Ross and colleagues (1991) state that MPD is "a disorder of both males and females arising from physical and sexual abuse of childhood" and that it is "a response to severe childhood trauma" (p. 100); Coons and Milstein (1986) say that the syndrome of multiple personality has been associated with child abuse; and Ross (1991) contends that the dissociative disorders are directly linked to trauma.

In contrast, the broader literature recognizes that sexual abuse is not a single, unitary phenomenon linked to any particularly recognizable syndrome, and acknowledges that such experiences do not necessarily lead to later psychological disturbance (Green 1993, Hussey and Singer 1993). Contributors to the MPD literature make no mention of topics such as factors that protect children from the adverse effects of early negative experiences (Green 1993, Widom 1991). Furthermore, a major methodological flaw in this literature is the failure to separate the effects of abuse from the confounding effects of other life circumstances (Hussey and Singer 1993). An example: One analysis concluded that childhood sexual abuse rarely led to later depression unless the child's environment was violent and neglectful as well (Bifulco et al. 1991). Absent, too, from the published material on MPD is any recognition that some cultures sanction children's sexual activities (Konker 1992). Finally, contributors to the MPD literature insufficiently emphasize the fact that repression and dissociation as responses to trauma—critical elements in the presumed pathogenesis of MPD—are unvalidated theories, against which there is good evidence (Wakefield and Underwager 1992). For example, in one study (Malmquist 1986), no child who had observed a parent's murder repressed the memory; all were preoccupied with the traumatic event and all were plagued by emotions related to it. Terr (1988) reached a similar conclusion in her investigation of children traumatized before age 5: they invariably remembered the trauma.

One final concern about how abuse is analyzed in the MPD literature is that this literature tends to accept all patient reports as true. Of all the studies reviewed here, only Coons and Milstein (1986), and Dell and Eisenhower (1990) attempt to determine the accuracy of such histories. Frankel (1993) agrees that the MPD literature generally provides minimal corroboration of its abuse reports; he expresses serious concerns about unquestioning acceptance of adult reports of childhood events. Ross and colleagues (1991), in an apparent attempt to justify failure to verify these accounts, say that there has not been a single confirmed report of an entirely fabricated abuse history in a patient with MPD. The authors do not make clear how they would confirm that such accounts were fabricated. However, the lack of reports is hardly surprising, since attempting to prove that abuse did *not* occur in a given case would be a formidable logical and practical undertaking.

Bliss and Jeppsen (1985) provide an example of bias toward ready acceptance of such claims. Their randomly selected outpatients had no memory of early traumatic experiences. However, under hypnosis, nearly 20 percent recalled early abuse experiences. The investigators give no evidence that they attempted to verify the accuracy of the histories. In uncritically accepting the veracity of the recollections, the authors pay insufficient attention to professional standards encouraging independent corroboration of hypnotic memories (American Medical Association 1985), as well as to the widely known data on how hypnotized subjects may readily confabulate (Lynn et al. 1989, Orne 1979, Sheehan 1988).

Much empirical evidence shows that memory can no longer be thought of as an archive of accurate, specific, and unchanging information about the past (Bonanno 1990, Suengas and Johnson 1988, Wakefield and Underwager 1992). The research has implications for psychotherapy in general and specifically for the treatment of MPD. A brief discussion of the theory generated by these studies will therefore be presented.

The data contradict the attractive but simplistic notions that people accumulate memories like so much videotaped material; that memories are fixed and unchangeable; and that therapy is an effort to gain access to that hidden, pristine material. The brain does not function in such a fashion (Bonanno 1990). Rather, the studies indicate that memory involves an unceasingly operating procedure during which bits of information are continually altered, reworked, interpreted, and reconstructed during the course of remembering (Loftus and Ketcham 1991). Furthermore, patient recall about the past is affected by interactions with the therapist (Bonanno 1990, Suengas and Johnson 1988), as demonstrated by Smith and Ellsworth (1987). These investigators showed subjects a videotape of a bank robbery and later questioned them about the robbery. The questioner was presented as either naïve to the crime or as an expert on such videotapes. As part of the experiment, the questioner occasionally asked misleading questions. Participants reported less accurate information when the misleading questions were posed by the purported expert. Because therapists are typically viewed by patients as experts, findings such as these indicate that a patient's recollections during therapy will be colored by both the therapist's questions and interpretations (Bonanno 1990).

Thus, psychotherapists do not uncover objective facts and details of a life story, or *historical truth*. Rather, these clinicians aid in producing *narrative truth*, which is a reevaluation of the past in the light of present-day experience as well as a product of the communication between therapist and patient. According to this view, then, it is not the task of therapists to help patients retrieve lost memories (Bonanno 1990).

The foregoing analysis has significant implications for the treatment of MPD as it is usually conducted today. Much of that therapy involves ferreting out hidden memories of past abuse, which the alter personalities guard or hold (Frankel 1993). Clinicians who base their work on patients' memories should beware of suggesting that patients experienced childhood trauma; avoid relentlessly probing for recalcitrant memories; beware of uncritically accepting uncorroborated memories as fact; and be modest about their abilities to distinguish truth from falsity (Frankel 1993, Loftus 1993).

In summary, weaknesses abound in the current theories of the pathogenesis of MPD. North and associates (1993) say that because the nosologic status of MPD is in such disarray, efforts to determine the etiology of the condition are certainly premature.

ENCOURAGEMENT OF REGRESSIVE AND NONRESPONSIBLE BEHAVIOR

Working with a patient as a multiple means working directly with the alter personalities (Putnam 1989). Putnam says therapists may have to ask directly to meet an alter, and may have to repeat the request several times (Putnam 1989). Other writers (American Psychiatric Association 1989, Caul 1984, Congdon et al. 1961) call forth, and speak with, various alters, and Ross (1988) gives friends and relatives of MPD patients training in calling out rational, adult alters. In order to get alters to reveal themselves, Kluft (1987b) recommends extending interviews, sometimes for periods of up to eight hours. During these sessions, those interviewed "must be prevented from taking breaks to regain composure" (p. 115). On at least one occasion, Kluft says it took eight hours for a definitive spontaneous switching of personalities to occur. One writer recommends calling forth a personality by pressing the thumb against the center of the patient's forehead and repeating several times the name of the desired personality, saying, "I want to talk with you" (Fagan and McMahon 1984, p. 32). Ross (1990b) says that the standard mental status examination for auditory hallucinations should include an attempt to engage indirectly the voices in rational conversation by using the presenting part as an intermediary. Caul (1984) urges the alters to talk to each other in what he calls "internal group therapy," where all the members of the group are personalities of the patient.

Putnam (1989) uses a technique called the "bulletin board," which allows the patient to have a "place where personalities can 'post' messages for each other. . . . I suggest that the patient buy a small notebook. . . . Personalities are then instructed to write messages in the notebook to one another" (p. 154). He furthermore recommends that the therapist should interview each alter, taking a history from each one, obtaining their names, sexes, ages, and roles, and asking each if he or she knows of others. He also suggests "mapping the system," by which he means asking the alters to produce a map or diagram of how they fit together; the map is periodically reviewed and new data added. Similar techniques are endorsed by other contemporary writers on MPD (Fine 1991, Kluft 1987a, Ross and Gahan 1988). Other authorities recommend that therapists participate in age-appropriate activities with child alters, such as formal play therapy and trips to McDonald's; child alters are encouraged to work on projects in occupational therapy (Ross and Gahan 1988). The rationale for such interventions is to provide necessary rewards and demonstrate respect for the alter.

In addition to whatever else such techniques may do, they must certainly sanction and reinforce the patient's belief in his or her dividedness, and encourage the production of more symptoms (Simpson 1989). Many writers have warned against showing too much interest in the dissociated personality (Gruenewald 1971), against encouraging ideas of multiplicity in patients by speaking to one of the personalities (Horton and Miller 1972), and against utilizing therapeutic techniques that sanction role-adopting behavior (Cutler and Reed 1975). Sutcliffe and Jones (1962) point out that if certain behaviors are reinforced at their inception, subjects will tend to repeat those behaviors and perform related behaviors. Spanos and associates (1985) note that clinicians vary quite dramatically in the extent to which they encourage and legitimate enactments of multiple identity. They say it is therefore not surprising that some therapists are much more likely than others to discover cases of MPD.

Bowers (1991) believes that the current high frequency of MPD is due in part to publication and dramatization of *Sybil* and similar case studies. Information about MPD is widespread in our culture now, and thus the major components of the role are well known (North et al. 1993). According to the *social role perspective* (Spanos et al. 1985, Spanos 1989), psychotherapists play an important part in the generation and maintenance of this role enactment. The techniques listed above—the "bulletin board," the training in calling out alters, the "internal group therapy," and the like—encourage patients to adopt the role of being a multiple.

Spanos (1989) contends that therapists frequently provide information about how to enact the role convincingly, and, perhaps most important, provide "official" validation for the different identities their patients enact. Then, once patients are publicly identified as multiples, their enactments of secondary personalities are repeatedly validated by others who become aware of their diagnosis (Spanos 1989). Sutcliffe and Jones (1962) state that mutual shaping between clinician and patient clearly accounts for some cases of MPD; in this regard, it is noteworthy that one patient, reported by Ross (1984), fabricated an elaborate account involving an alter because, she said, she wanted to please the therapist. Serban's (1992) patient also claimed to have made up her account. Similarly, Taylor and Martin (1944) conclude that some cases of MPD are apparently caused by suggestion either from the patient, some outside person, from the physician (especially if hypnosis is used), or from more than one source. Greaves (1980) acknowledges that no one seriously discounts the possibility (even the inevitability) of a certain amount of shaping occurring, and the literature abounds with warnings in this regard, particularly as concerns the use of hypnosis.

Some investigators use barbiturate-facilitated techniques, such as the Amytal interview, to uncover buried memories of childhood abuse, or to call forth hidden alter personalities (Hall et al. 1975, Putnam et al. 1986). A recent review points out several problems associated with such procedures (Piper 1994). First, these techniques are highly suggestive to patients. They also significantly disturb the mental processes of those being interviewed. Thus, any information obtained under Amytal and other hypnotics may well be distorted and therefore inherently unreliable. Finally, because of this procedure's reputation as "truth serum," interviewers may easily be misled into believing that what patients say under the influence of the drug corresponds to external fact. In reality, however, the literature shows quite clearly that people undergoing Amytal interviews can and do lie.

One author (Putnam 1992) wonders why asking a patient if he has ever felt as if there were another part or side to him is considered more likely to induce an alter personality than inquiring about voices is to create hallucinations, or inquiring about recurring thoughts is to create ruminations. However, there is a profound difference between standard psychiatric interview procedures—where practitioners take great care not to bias patients' reports—and the techniques for diagnosis and treatment espoused by the leading contributors in the MPD field. It is absurd to maintain that those techniques are not vehicles of grossly overt suggestion to patients. It is equally absurd to believe that in any other branch of psychiatry, one would see a clinician prodding a schizophrenic patient to produce more voices, or taking part in a 4-hour interview with a patient who might possibly be bulimic, to suggest more frequent bingeing.

The intense publicity surrounding the MPD diagnosis makes it highly questionable whether any case of the disorder can now arise without having some component of suggestion or prior preparation (Merskey

1992). Thus, it is unlikely that all recently diagnosed cases of the condition are genuine. A study has recently been published of patients who were previously misdiagnosed as having MPD (Freeland et al. 1993).

The literature on treating MPD is dominated by those advocating the kind of suggestive techniques described earlier. It gives the impression that there is only one proper and effective way to treat the condition. Indeed, a 1993 survey reports clinicians' "unequivocal" and "uniform" endorsement of long-term, twice-weekly psychotherapy facilitated by hypnosis as the best treatment for MPD (Putnam and Loewenstein 1993). In view of the equivocal results of the outcome studies cited later in this chapter, however, such a confident call to therapeutic orthodoxy is premature (Fahy 1989, North et al. 1993).

Fahy and associates (1989) discuss the improvement shown by an MPD patient whose treatment did not involve concentrating on the alternate personalities. Similarly, in several other published reports, nonpsychodynamic treatments of MPD have been said to be effective (North et al. 1993). Also, nondynamic therapies have been useful in treating patients who repeatedly attempt to harm themselves (Liberman and Eckman 1981, Salkovskis et al. 1990). Several writers have published data on nonpsychodynamically based treatments for borderline patients (Linehan et al. 1991, Swenson 1989). Because MPD patients have much in common with borderline and parasuicidal patients, they might respond to similar interventions (North et al. 1993).

It is important to discuss the issue of MPD patients' responsibility for their actions. The term, as used here, implies either blame or obligation — to say that one was responsible for a past act usually means that the actor is blameworthy. Responsibility for future conduct means incurring an obligation to behave in a certain way, and if the obligation is not met, blame will ultimately follow (Halleck 1988).

The concept of MPD has several implications for attributing moral and legal responsibility to those with the disorder (Halleck 1988). Surprisingly, however, the major theoreticians and students of the condition have said almost nothing about this issue (see American Psychiatric Association 1989, Kluft 1987a, and Ross 1990b).

If an MPD patient commits an antisocial act for which he or she claims amnesia, it does at first glance seem offensive to hold that individual blameworthy. If conceptualized as a collection of relatively autonomous personalities, the patient does not have the full resources of the integrated personality available. Thus, he or she has a lessened ability to evaluate the rightness or wrongness of the act (Halleck 1990). Bliss (1980) agrees, warning that in MPD patients, judgment and inhibition are impaired or absent. However, Halleck (1990) urges a closer look. He points out that if society accepts the separateness or autonomy of differing alters, it ceases to describe a morally or legally recognizable person, but rather describes a collection of partial persons who have no collective capacity for responsibility. The collection would be a potentially dangerous entity, because of its limited capacity to control undesirable conduct. This view of MPD patients would justify society's taking coercive action to control them, since it assumes they would not be responsive to the sanctions that influence people who do not have the condition.

Another problem is that the fragmented person approach casts serious doubt on whether the patient has one of the major moral and legal attributes of personhood—the ability to choose. Can such a collection of personalities legally choose to sign (itself? himself? themselves?) into a hospital, voluntarily enter into a sexual relationship, make a legally binding will, or enter into a contract to buy a car? If one truly respects the idea of autonomous personalities, these questions must be answered in the negative. Moore (1984) proposes another approach to the questions of MPD patients' rights. Just as young children are not accorded all the rights of adults, Moore considers MPD patients to be examples of *suspended personhood*—there was but one person before and, if the therapy is successful, there will be again. In the meantime, however, the only answer to the question, "how many persons?" is: none.

Three other little-considered implications of the MPD diagnosis deserve mention (Halleck 1990). First, it is sometimes insufficiently emphasized that when patients say they are "taken over," they can logically only be "taken over" by themselves. Therefore, MPD patients should be held responsible for all their behaviors. Second, fusion of personalities does not require pharmacological or other somatic interventions. Therefore, the patient, even before starting therapy, must have at least a latent *innate* capacity to control dissociation. In other words, any psychotherapist planning to use psychotherapy to achieve personality fusion must believe that the patient can, under proper environmental circumstances, create that fusion. If the patient has this capacity and does not use it, simply because the environment favors multiplicity, then the argument for holding him or her responsible for the undesirable behavior of any of the personalities is strengthened. Third, if nearly all MPD patients try to hide or dissimulate their conditions (Kluft 1987a), then again, they must be able to exercise at least some control over the symptoms. Silberman and associates (1985) tacitly acknowledge this fact. They asked MPD patients to provide at least two alter personalities to participate in a study. Selection of alternates was left to the patient, with the stipulation that the two chosen should have no conscious awareness of each other's experiences. The authors obviously must believe that multiples have enough control over their alters not only to bring them out on demand, but also to produce the "right" ones.

To conclude, the more psychiatry makes extreme claims about MPD, unsupported by critical thinking and clear definitions of terms, the more the value and good sense of psychiatry become suspect (Merskey 1992) by the larger public as well as by the courts. Defendants have attempted to raise MPD as a legal defense (Lewis and Bard 1991), but so far, the courts have not been well disposed to any assertion that MPD exculpates those accused of crimes. In one case, for instance, a court declared itself unwilling to "begin to parcel criminal accountability out among the various inhabitants of the mind" (Kirkland v. Georgia, 304 S.E.2d 561 [Ga. App. 1983]).

THE EXPENSE OF TREATING MPD

Ross and Dua (1993) believe they have one answer to the financial burdens facing the mental-health system. They examined costs of psychiatric care for fifteen patients before and after the diagnosis of MPD was made, and projected these into the future. They conclude that reaching an accurate diagnosis opens the door to cost-effective psychotherapy that adequately treats the disorder. The resulting improvement reduces the time patients spend in treatment; thus, significant financial savings occur. In fact, the writers claim that if their findings could be generalized to all MPD patients, "the psychotherapy of MPD would then be demonstrated to be the most cost-effective mental health intervention known" (p. 110). The evidence supporting these assertions leaves much to be desired.

That the MPD diagnosis invites ballooning mental-health costs can hardly be doubted. There are five reasons. First, numerous patients satisfy the nonspecific diagnostic criteria for MPD; this overdiagnosis increases total costs for mental-health services. Second, because almost no outcome data have been published, it is unclear that psychotherapy for the disorder produces results in a reasonable time. Third, the writings of major proponents of the condition certainly do not suggest that it can be treated in a timely manner. Fourth, few clinicians are likely to duplicate the results claimed by the leading MPD theoreticians. Finally, my experience casts doubt on the idea that treatment of MPD is cost effective.

That MPD is overdiagnosed has been discussed above. There is one consequence of the ease with which so many people can so effortlessly be found to fit the MPD diagnostic criteria: patients newly diagnosed with the condition flood the mental-health system. The increase is already visible, as shown by the figures cited in the second section of this chapter. The costs for treating MPD will rise simply because more people are diagnosed with it (incorrectly, in my view and in that of others [Chodoff 1987, Tozman and Pabis 1989]; once diagnosed, they expect treatment for the disorder.

Furthermore, the children of present-day MPD patients are the MPD patients of tomorrow. Kluft (1987a) advocates that all children of those with the condition should have regularly scheduled psychiatric evaluations to search for incipient cases.

Ross and Dua (1993), as well as others (Bliss and Jeppsen 1985, Putnam et al. 1986), believe that those patients newly assessed to have MPD are already in treatment at the time of the new diagnosis, but have previously been misdiagnosed and therefore treated for the wrong conditions. According to Ross and Dua (1993), costs for undiagnosed MPD are on average very high. However, the savings would be significant, these writers assert, if earlier diagnosis began to occur throughout the mental-health system. This assertion can be true only if psychotherapy of MPD has a better outcome than treatment of the conditions with which it is confused (a doubtful proposition, which I take up in what follows). However, I am unaware of any study that compares the outcome of therapy of MPD with that of these other conditions. Putnam (1989) acknowledges the paucity of outcome data for MPD treatment. Even Ross and Dua's own data do not support the belief that the diagnosis and treatment of MPD result in financial savings: table IV in their article shows a *doubling* of the overall psychiatric health-care costs after the patients were given the MPD diagnosis. Most of this increase resulted from inpatient hospitalizations, the costs of which also doubled after the diagnosis was made.

Ross and Dua's claim of cost savings is worrisome, because in an environment where one cannot confirm that the MPD diagnosis is correct, the claim subtly encourages overdiagnosis of MPD. The encouragement occurs because clinicians believe that by making the diagnosis of MPD, they are diagnosing a condition for which cost-effective and efficacious treatment exists. The availability of novel or effective therapy has biased psychiatric diagnostic practices in the past, probably because physicians want to believe their patients have treatable disorders (Baldessarini 1970, Stoll et al. 1992).

Proponents of MPD frequently point out that the disorder is quite responsive to treatment (American Psychiatric Association 1989). Do the data support this position? I am aware of two studies on the question (Coons 1986b, Kluft 1984a). In the latter investigation, 123 patients started treatment, but only 33 met the investigator's criteria for 27 months of stable fusion. The others had begun to redissociate after variable periods of fusion, had declined or prematurely terminated treatment, could not be contacted at follow-up, had unsuccessful treatments, or were of question-able reliability. In the former report, Coons (1986b) evaluated twenty MPD patients an average of 39 months after they had started treatment. Five were integrated. However, the investigator does not report how long his patients have maintained their fusions, so there is no way to know if the fusions are truly stable.

Thus, if the studies are combined, 38 patients out of the 153 who started treatment had achieved fusion. It is difficult to know how to interpret this figure, because over time, more patients will successfully finish treatment, while at least a quarter of those who were thought to be fused will redis-sociate (Kluft 1984a). Because MPD has intermittent symptoms and a waxing and waning course, prolonged follow-up and reassessment of ther-apeutic gains are essential to be certain that those treated for the disorder maintain their improvement (Kluft 1984a). However, such studies, involv-ing significant numbers of patients with MPD, have yet to be conducted.

As noted above, Putnam (1989) has pointed out the paucity of outcome data for treatment of MPD. Thus, little published evidence supports the idea that psychotherapy of MPD produces timely results at reasonable expense. This is indeed surprising, given that thousands of people since 1980 have been diagnosed as having MPD. It has been suggested that dissociative disorders, including MPD, may affect 5 to 10 percent of the general population (Ross et al. 1990), 5 to 10 percent of inpatients on adult psychiatry hospital units (Bliss and Jeppsen 1985, Ross 1990c, Ross 1991) and perhaps one hundred million people worldwide (Ross 1991). If MPD were this common, and treatment as effective as Ross and Dua (1993) suggest, then proponents of the disorder should easily have been able, during the past decade, to collect reasonable data on the outcome of therapy for MPD.

The MPD literature itself provides further reason for skepticism about the claim that psychotherapy for the condition is cost effective. The type of psychotherapy currently recommended by proponents of MPD fails to yield results within a moderate period of time or at reasonable cost. Kluft (1991b) states that in any six-month period, between 15 and 85 percent of MPD patients will require hospitalizations, some of which, according to Ross (1991), should last for six months or longer. Outpatient care is similarly costly. The treatment advocated for MPD patients is psychother-apy, performed at least twice weekly if possible—daily when the patient is in crisis—with prolonged sessions or inpatient stays provided to deal with difficult and painful material (Coons 1986a, Kluft 1984a, Kluft 1987a).

Even the major contributors to the literature do not expect results quickly. According to Kluft (1984a), favorable prognosis of MPD requires intensive treatment over a protracted period of time. Coons (1986a) says that "due to the lengthy period of time necessary to treat adult [MPD patients], future outcome studies should extend into the 10- to 15-year range." The same author states that the psychotherapy of patients with multiple personality is tedious and time-consuming (Coons 1986a). According to one author, the therapy requires not less than two to five years under ideal conditions (Greaves 1980), but another notes that it may require a decade or more (Coons 1986a, Coons 1986b). It is worth noting that the psychoanalytic treatment of Sybil, one of the early American MPD patients, took nearly eleven years and over 2,300 office visits (Schreiber 1973). In Coons's (1986a) study, only one-quarter of the patients had achieved stable integration after over three years of psychotherapy; one of his patients had been seen four to five times weekly over five years and still had not become fused.

Also, treatment does not end at the time of integration or unification of the personalities, and "patients who leave therapy at this point almost invariably relapse. . . . Many patients require prolonged periods of post-fusion therapy" (American Psychiatric Association 1989, p. 2214). Kluft (1988) says that those who decline postunification treatment usually relapse, and that over 90 percent of patients who achieve unification require more therapy. He strongly cautions against regarding unification as an endpoint in therapy; rather, one to two years of postunification psychotherapy should occur. Kluft (1982) notes that the cure of MPD leaves the patient afflicted with "single personality disorder"—the state in which most patients begin psychotherapy. Interestingly, even after all this therapy, retraumatization leads to relapse in virtually *every* case (Kluft 1987a).

Even these figures may understate the actual amount of time required to treat MPD. Other clinicians are unlikely to achieve Ross and Dua's (1993) degree of success for two reasons. First, Putnam correctly doubts that the successes of a few highly experienced clinicians are representative of the overall treatment outcome of MPD (Putnam 1989). Rather, he believes that because most of Coons's therapists were treating their first MPD patients, those results (Coons 1986a), summarized above, are more likely to reflect the prognosis in real-life clinical practice. Second, Ross and Dua appear to have studied a highly select group of MPD patients, requiring four years to gather just fifteen subjects to study. This is surprising because if MPD truly affected 1 percent of the North American population (Ross 1991), it would seem that a much larger sample could have been collected in that time. Also, several cases were excluded from Ross and Dua's data analysis, but the authors fail to specify how many subjects this affected. Finally, the investigators themselves acknowledge that inpatients with MPD are unlikely to be representative of all individuals with MPD (Ross and Dua 1993).

A final, personal reason exists for skepticism about the claim of cost-effective MPD psychotherapy. Since 1987, I have functioned in several capacities that have brought me into contact with many MPD patients and their treating clinicians: as chair of a hospital's department of psychiatry, chair of two hospital quality assurance committees, and as a psychiatric peer reviewer for several insurance companies. Over the years, these extensive contacts have strongly impressed me with one fact: patients with this disorder rarely seem to improve. This apparent lack of progress persists despite the expenditure of huge sums on their treatment, the amassing of hours of psychotherapy, and numerous hospital stays sufficient to generate charts a foot or more thick in just a few years.

This impression is, of course, vulnerable to the criticism that these failures represent only the least responsive MPD patients, or that my impression reflects a subjective bias. If the criticisms are accurate, however, the time is overdue for major MPD theorists to publish studies demonstrating improvement in a large series of their patients. The research should be published in critically refereed journals. That "many successful clinicians have presented their results in meetings, courses, and workshops, or in other forums besides professional publications" (Putnam 1989, p. 298) is not a persuasive argument. If MPD is truly "entering the mainstream of American psychiatry as a legitimate and important clinical syndrome" (Kluft 1985b, p. 3), then thoughtful proponents of the disorder will subject their views to the same kind of critical scrutiny that is the norm in any other mainstream scientific discipline. I believe such efforts should be a priority—one at least as important as organizing and producing the several conferences on the disorder held each year.

HYPNOSIS AND MPD

An important controversy revolves around the role of hypnosis in the diagnosis and treatment of MPD: can hypnosis create MPD? Some commentators answer in the negative (Kluft 1982, Braun 1984).

Although MPD proponents acknowledge that personified states (Coons 1991) personality fragments (Braun 1984), and numerous multiple personality-like phenomena have been produced under hypnosis (Coons 1986c), they argue that hypnosis produces only a part and not the enduring whole of the clinical picture (American Psychiatric Association, 1989, Braun 1984, Kluft 1987a). Five objections to such a claim come to mind.

One is that the contributors to the MPD literature never state exactly how "personified states," "personality fragments," and "multiple personality-like phenomena" differ from true alters. Some authors believe a true alter should have a memory of its life history (Braun 1984), but in view of the evidence that hypnosis distorts memory (Sheehan 1988, Sheehan et al. 1992), it is unclear how one could obtain an accurate life history from a hypnotized subject. Second, the original research communications indicate that the early investigators clearly believed they had hypnotically induced a true multiple personality (Harriman 1943, Leavitt 1947). I find no evidence that these past investigations should be ignored in favor of the present claim that hypnosis does not cause the symptoms of MPD. Third, as discussed above, the boundaries of the term "multiple personality disorder" are not specified in the literature; it is thus meaningless to speak of the "whole" of the condition. Fourth, both Bliss (1980) and Kluft (1991a) state that personalities may appear only once for a single mission and thereafter remain dormant; therefore, why must MPD symptoms be "enduring?" Finally, and perhaps most important, it strains credulity to believe that MPD could *not* be produced by hypnosis. After all, under the influence of hypnosis, people have even confessed to crimes they did not commit, providing confabulated details of their participation (Coons et al. 1988, Ofshe 1992). There is also one case in which a posthypnotic suggestion apparently led to a bank robbery by a man who had no prior criminal behavior (Deyoub 1984). Greaves (1980), remarking on the potential of hypnosis, says that the range of hypnotic phenomena is as varied as the human imagination. MPD patients are uniformly quite hypnotizable — Bliss (1984b) refers to them as "hypnotic virtuosos." They seem to use self-hypnosis very frequently, and also readily enter externally induced trances (American Psychiatric Association 1989, Herzog 1984, Sutcliffe and Jones 1962). If hypnosis has the potential to cause any other psychiatric sign or symptom, as Bliss (1984b) claims it can, then why should these highly hypnotizable individuals not be able to develop, as a result of hypnosis, the signs of MPD?

For these reasons, it is extremely difficult to believe that hypnosis cannot create, in at least some cases, the symptoms of MPD. Another point should be mentioned: because MPD patients are excellent hypnotic subjects, they must also therefore be quite suggestible (Bowers 1991). This has obvious implications for the conduct of their psychotherapy.

DISCUSSION AND CONCLUSIONS

What conclusions can be reached from the above analysis? First, it is premature to speak of the incidence, prevalence, natural history, pathogenesis, and most appropriate treatment of MPD/DID, until the criteria for diagnosis are revised, tightened, and better clarified. A cogent definition of "personality" would be of immense value. These efforts should be a very high priority for theoreticians of MPD, and it is uncertain as to how useful the shift to DID will be in this regard.

Second, "multiple personality disorder" is a misnomer. It is not even a syndrome, let alone a unique disorder. The core meaning of a syndrome is a combination of symptoms so commonly occurring together that they constitute a distinct clinical picture (Miller and Keane 1987). However, as is indicated in the first section of this review, literally *any* combination of psychiatric symptoms would allow a patient to be included in the category of MPD. Putnam (1991) illustrates this point nicely. He believes that the strongest support for the construct validity of MPD as a diagnosis is its consistent clinical picture—but then says that MPD patients are uniformly found to be polysymptomatic. Even what Putnam calls the "core cluster" of MPD contains several different and nonspecific types of symptoms. In other words, the distinct clinical picture of MPD is that it actually has *no* distinct clinical picture. Such an expansion of the meaning of "syndrome" ultimately robs the word of any meaning at all.

The third conclusion grows out of the second: the MPD/DID diagnosis does not define a homogeneous class. Rather, it refers to a collection of individuals with nonspecific, disparate symptoms (Dinwiddie et al. 1993). Several writers have come to this conclusion, reaching it by different paths. Greaves (1980), Merskey (1992), and Sutcliffe and Jones (1962) point out that many of the early cases apparently had organic pathology, usually epilepsy. Thus, because some modern-day patients are said to have both seizures and MPD (Loewenstein and Putnam 1988), some of today's patients probably have organic pathology (Merskey 1992). Alcoholism and bipolar disorder were prominent in several early examples (Merskey 1992). Fahy (1988), after reviewing the literature, finds little evidence that MPD is a separate diagnosis. Lauer and colleagues (1993) have the same opinion, based on their study of the characteristics of patients diagnosed with either MPD or borderline personality disorder. Weissberg (1993) reviews the treatment of an early psychoanalytic patient, and concludes that present-day MPD is a diagnosis of fashion, like hysteria in nineteenth-century Vienna. Finally, North and associates (1993), after exhaustively examining the data for and against MPD as a separate diagnosis, comment that present knowledge does not sufficiently justify the validity of MPD as a separate diagnosis.

This chapter does not attempt to claim that *no* cases of MPD exist. The antiquity and circumstances of some of the reported cases do not support such a position (North et al. 1993, Taylor and Martin 1944). Sutcliffe and

Jones (1962) conclude that after all schizophrenic, brain-damaged, and epileptic patients are eliminated from consideration, a group remains that cannot readily be assigned to any category other than one fitting the most stringent criteria for the diagnosis of MPD.

The chapter also concludes that mutual shaping of MPD symptoms occurs, between some patients interested in conveying an appropriate impression, on the one hand, and some therapists, on the other, who vigilantly watch for signs of the condition. Hypnosis and suggestion are very likely to play a significant role in the generation and maintenance of MPD phenomena. The examples in this chapter indicate that at least some MPD patients malinger or simulate the disorder. This is not difficult to do: role playing different personalities is simple (American Psychiatric Association 1989).

The true prevalence of MPD can only be conjectural unless and until the condition is better defined. This chapter's discussion and analysis lead to the conclusion that MPD has been overdiagnosed in the past few years. Based on this conclusion, certain assertions that are frequently cited about MPD must be called into serious question. One of these is that MPD patients average six to seven years of mental-health contact before a correct diagnosis is made (Putnam et al. 1986). It is easy to forget how this statement rests on the assumption that MPD patients are diagnosed correctly. In view of the tenuousness of the MPD diagnosis, such an assumption is poorly grounded indeed.

Other questionable assertions are found in the MPD literature, such as: "It is difficult to overemphasize [either] the vulnerability of multiple personality to false-negative diagnosis, [or] the [resulting] cost to the patient. . . . In terms of treatment outcome, the conservative error in regard to multiple personality is the false-positive one" (Greaves 1980, p. 584). These assertions deserve challenge. This chapter has made it clear that MPD is vulnerable to over-, not underdiagnosis. Furthermore, an erroneous MPD diagnosis does significant harm, in that treatment for the actual condition is delayed, and patients are encouraged to embark on long, arduous, and costly therapy. Also, because past sexual abuse is found in virtually every case of MPD, there is a danger that those erroneously diagnosed will be encouraged to believe that they, too, must have been abused, their failure to remember such abuse merely showing that they are "repressing" the memory. These implanted beliefs could cause suicidal thoughts and other long-term adverse effects (Loftus 1993).

This chapter closes with a comment about health-care costs. Using money prudently should be an especial concern for psychiatrists now, when psychiatry is becoming a prime target for the same intensive cost-containment that was imposed elsewhere in medicine (Morreim 1990).

Morreim notes that physicians in all areas of medicine are under pressure to demonstrate the value of what they do, and to utilize cost-efficient clinical routines. Thus, before psychiatry considers asking of society the resources to treat thousands of MPD patients, and putting "pressure on mental health agencies and third-party payers to provide more support" for their treatment (Putnam and Loewenstein 1993, p. 1052), a serious effort to evaluate the efficacy of such treatment should be mounted. Existing MPD outcome studies are marred by equivocal results, brief or unspecified follow-up periods, and small numbers of patients; they do not come close to supporting the kind of dramatic public-policy initiatives advocated by Putnam and Loewenstein (1993). The argument is not whether MPD patients need treatment—they do—but rather under what label, and with which ideas (Merskey 1992).

It is hoped that the foregoing review, by encouraging a more critical evaluation of what is called multiple personality disorder, will assist clinicians in their efforts to help those rare patients who truly should be given the diagnosis, as well as the much larger number who certainly should not.

REFERENCES

Aldridge-Morris, R. (1989). *Multiple Personality: An Exercise in Deception*. Hove, United Kingdom: Erlbaum.

Alarcon, R. D. (1990). Pseudomultiplicity: a clinical manifestation of rapid-cycling affective disorder in borderline personality. *Annals of Clinical Psychiatry* 2:127–133.

American Medical Association Council on Scientific Affairs (1985). *Scientific status of refreshing recollection by the use of hypnosis*. (Journal of the American Medical Association 253:1918–1923).

American Psychiatric Association (1989). *Treatments of Psychiatric Disorders*. Washington, DC: American Psychiatric Association Press.

Anastasi, A. (1988). *Psychological Testing*, 6th ed. New York: Macmillan.

Anderson, J., Martin, J., Mullen, P., et al. (1993). Prevalence of childhood sexual-abuse experiences in a community sample of women. *Journal of the American Academy of Child and Adolescent Psychiatry* 32:911–919.

Baldessarini, R. J. (1970). Frequency of diagnoses of schizophrenia versus affective disorders from 1944 to 1968. *American Journal of Psychiatry* 127:759–764.

Bernstein, E. M., and Putnam, F. W. (1986). Development, reliability, and validity of a dissociation scale. *Journal of Nervous and Mental Disease* 174:727–735.

Bifulco, A., Brown, G. W., and Adler, Z. (1991). Early sexual abuse and clinical depression in adult life. *British Journal of Psychiatry* 159:115–122.

Bliss, E. L. (1980). Multiple personalities: a report of 14 cases with implications for schizophrenia and hysteria. *Archives of General Psychiatry* 37:1388–1397.

——— (1984a). A symptom profile of patients with multiple personalities, including MMPI results. *Journal of Nervous and Mental Disease* 172:197–202.

——— (1984b). Spontaneous self-hypnosis in multiple personality diorder. *Psychiatric Clinics of North America* 7:135–198.

Bliss, E. L., and Jeppsen, E. A. (1985). Prevalence of multiple personality disorder among inpatients and outpatients. *American Journal of Psychiatry* 142:250–251.

Bliss, E. L., and Larson, E. M. (1985). Sexual criminality and hypnotizability. *Journal of Nervous and Mental Disease* 173:522–526.

Bonanno, G. A. (1990). Remembering and psychotherapy. *Psychotherapy* 27:175–186.

Boor, M. (1982). The MPD epidemic: additional cases and inferences regarding diagnosis, etiology, dynamics and treatment. *Journal of Nervous and Mental Disorders* 170:302–304.

Bowers, K. S. (1991). Dissociation, hypnosis, and multiple personality disorder. *International Journal of Clinical and Experimental Hypnosis* 39:155–176.

Braun, B. G. (1984). Hypnosis creates multiple personality: myth or reality? *International Journal of Clinical and Experimental Hypnosis* 32:191–197.

Brewin, C. R., Andrews, B., and Gotlib, I. H. (1993). Psychopathology and early experience: a reappraisal of retrospective reports. *Psychological Bulletin* 113:82–98.

Brick, S. S., and Chu, J. A. (1991). The simulation of multiple personalities: a case report. *Psychotherapy* 38:267–272.

Brown, G. R., and Anderson, B. (1991). Psychiatric morbidity in adult inpatients with childhood histories of sexual and physical abuse. *American Journal of Psychiatry* 148:55–61.

Browne, A., and Finkelhor, D. (1986). Impact of child sexual abuse: a review of the research. *Psychological Bulletin* 99:66–77.

Carlin, A. S., and Ward, N. G. (1992). Subtypes of psychiatric inpatient women who have been sexually abused. *Journal of Nervous and Mental Disease* 180:392–397.

Carlson, E. B., Putnam, F. W., Ross, C. A., et al. (1993). Validity of the dissociative experience scale in screening for multiple personality disorder: a multicenter study. *American Journal of Psychiatry* 150:1030–1036.

Caul, D. (1984). Group and videotape techniques for multiple personality disorder. *Psychiatric Annals* 14:43–50.

Chodoff, P. (1987). More on multiple personality disorder (letter). *American Journal of Psychiatry* 144:124.

Chu, J. A., and Dill, D. L. (1990). Dissociative symptoms in relation to childhood physical and sexual abuse. *American Journal of Psychiatry* 147:887–892.

Congdon, M. H., Hain, J., and Stevenson, I. (1961). A case of multiple personality illustrating a transition from role-playing. *Journal of Nervous and Mental Disease* 132:504.

Conte, J. R., Sorenson, E., Fogarty, L., et al. (1991). Evaluating children's reports of sexual abuse: results from a survey of professionals. *American Journal of Orthopsychiatry* 61:428–437.

Coons, P. M. (1980). Multiple personality: diagnostic considerations. *Journal of Clinical Psychiatry* 41:330–336.

——— (1984). The differential diagnosis of multiple personality. *Psychiatric Clinics of North America* 7:51–67.

——— (1986a). The prevalence of multiple personality disorder. *Newsletter of the International Society for the Study of Multiple Personality and Dissociation* 4:6–8.

——— (1986b). Treatment progress in twenty patients with multiple personality disorder. *Journal of Nervous and Mental Disease* 174:715–721.

——— (1986c). Misuse of forensic hypnosis: a hypnotically elicited false confession with the apparent creation of a multiple personality. *International Journal of Clinical and Exerimental Hypnosis* 36:1–10.

——— (1986d). Child abuse and multiple personality disorder: review of the literature and suggestions for treatment. *Child Abuse and Neglect* 10:455–462.

——— (1991). Iatrogenesis and malingering of multiple personality disorder in the forensic evaluation of homicide defendants. *Psychiatric Clinics of North America* 14:757–768.

Coons, P. M., Bowman, E. S., and Milstein, V. (1988). Multiple personality disorder: a clinical investigation of 50 cases. *Journal of Nervous and Mental Disease* 176:519–528.

Coons, P. M., and Milstein, V. (1986). Psychosexual disturbances in multiple personality: characteristics, etiology, treatment. *Journal of Clinical Psychiatry* 47:106–110.

Cutler, B., and Reed, J. (1975). Multiple personality: a single case study with a fifteen year follow-up. *Psychological Medicine* 5:18–26.

Dell, P. F. (1988a). Professional skepticism about multiple personality. *Journal of Nervous and Mental Disease* 176:521–531.

———— (1988b). Not reasonable skepticism, but extreme skepticism. *Journal of Nervous and Mental Disease* 176:537–538.

Dell, P. F., and Eisenhower, J. W. (1990). Adolescent multiple personality disorder: a preliminary study of eleven cases. *Journal of the American Academy of Child and Adolescent Psychiatry* 29:359–366.

Deyoub, P. L. (1984). Hypnotic stimulation of antisocial behavior: a case report. *International Journal of Clinical and Experimental Hypnosis* 32:301–306.

Dinwiddie, S. H., North, C. S., and Yutzy, S. H. (1993). Multiple personality disorder: scientific and medicolegal issues. *Bulletin of the American Academy of Psychiatry and the Law* 21:69–79.

Drake, M. E. (1986). Epilepsy and multiple personality: clinical and EEG findings in 15 cases. *Epilepsia* 27:635.

Ernst, C., Angst, J., and Földenyi, M. (1993). Sexual abuse in childhood. Frequency and relevance for adult morbidity. Data of a longitudinal epidemiological study. *European Archives of Psychiatry and Clinical Neuroscience* 242:293–300.

Fagan, J., and McMahon, P. P. (1984). Incipient multiple personality disorder in children: four cases. *Journal of Nervous and Mental Disease* 84:26–36.

Fahy, T. A. (1988). The diagnosis of multiple personality disorder: a critical review. *British Journal of Psychiatry* 153:597–606.

———— (1989). Multiple personality disorder (letter). *British Journal of Psychiatry* 154:878.

Fahy, T. A., Abas, M., and Brown, J. C. (1989). Multiple personality: a symptom of psychiatric disorder. *British Journal of Psychiatry* 154:99–101.

Feighner, J. P., Robins, E., Guze, S. B., et al. (1972). Diagnostic criteria for use in psychiatric research. *Archives of General Psychiatry* 26:57–63.

Fernando, L. (1991). Multiple personality disorder (letter). *British Journal of Psychiatry* 158:150.

Fichtner, C. G., Kuhlman, D. T., Gruenfeld, M. J., and Hughes, J. (1990). Decreased episodic violence and increased control of dissociation in a carbamazepine-treated case of multiple personality. *Biological Psychiatry* 27:1045–1052.

Fine, C. G. (1991). Treatment stabilization and crisis prevention: pacing the therapy of the MPD patient. *Psychiatric Clinics of North America* 14:661–675.

Frankel, F. H. (1990). Hypnotizability and dissociation. *American Journal of Psychiatry* 147:823–829.

———— (1993). Adult reconstruction of childhood events in the multiple personality literature. *American Journal of Psychiatry* 150:954–958.

Franklin, J. (1990). The diagnosis of multiple personality based on subtle dissociative signs. *Journal of Nervous and Mental Disease* 178:4–14.

Freeland, A., Monchanda, R., Chiu, S., et al. (1993). Four cases of supposed multiple personality disorder: evidence of unjustified diagnoses. *Canadian Journal of Psychiatry* 38:245–247.

Frischholz, E. J., Braun, B. G., Sachs, R. G., and Hopkins, L. (1990). The dissociative experiences scale: further replication and validation. *Dissociation* 3:151–153.

Graves, S. G. (1989). Dissociative disorders and dissociative symptoms at a community mental health center. *Dissociation* 3:119–127.

Greaves, G. (1980). Multiple personality: 165 years after Mary Reynolds. *Journal of Nervous and Mental Disease* 168:577–596.

Green, A. H. (1993). Child sexual abuse: immediate and long-term effects and intervention. *Journal of the American Academy of Child and Adolescent Psychiatry* 32:890–902.

Gruenewald, D. (1971). Hypnotic techniques without hypnosis in the treatment of dual personality. *Journal of Nervous and Mental Disease* 153:41–46.

Hall, R. C., Le Cann, A. F., and Schooler, J. C. (1975). Amobarbital treatment of multiple personality disorder. *Journal of Nervous and Mental Disease* 161:138–142.

Halleck, S. L. (1988). Which patients are responsible for their illnesses? *American Journal of Psychotherapy* 42:338–353.

———— (1990). Dissociative phenomena and the question of responsibility. *International Journal of Clinical and Experimental Hypnosis* 38:298–314.

Hardy, D. W., Daghestani, A. N., and Egan, W. H. (1988). Multiple personality disorder: failure to diagnose and the potential for malpractice liability. *Psychiatric Annals* 18:543–548.

Harriman, P. L. (1943). A new approach to multiple personalities. *American Journal of Orthopsychiatry* 13:638–643.

Herzog, A. (1984). On multiple personality: comments on diagnosis, etiology, and treatment. *International Journal of Clinical and Experimental Hypnosis* 32:210–221.

Hine, F. R., and Feather, B. W. (1961). Psychiatry and philosophy of science: i. conceptual problems in psychiatry. *Journal of Nervous and Mental Disease* 132:485–496.

Horevitz, R. P., and Braun, B. G. (1984). Are multiple personalities borderline? *The Psychiatric Clinics of North America* 7:69–87.

Hornstein, N. L., and Tyson, S. (1991). Inpatient treatment of children with multiple personality/dissociative disorders and their families. *The Psychiatric Clinics of North America* 14:631–648.

Horton, P., and Miller, D. (1972). The etiology of multiple personality. *Comprehensive Psychiatry* 13:151–159.

Hussey, D. L., and Singer, M. (1993). Psychological distress, problem behaviors, and family functioning of sexually-abused adolescent inpatients. *Journal of the American Academy of Child and Adolescent Psychiatry* 32:954–961.

Jacobson, A. (1989). Physical and sexual assault histories among psychiatric outpatients. *American Journal of Psychiatry* 146:755–758.

Kemp, K., Gilbertson, A. D., and Torem, M. (1988). The differential diagnosis of multiple personality disorder from borderline personality disorder. *Dissociation* 1:41–46.

Kendall-Tackett, K. A., Williams, L. M., and Finkelhor, D. (1993). Impact of sexual abuse on children: a review and synthesis of recent empirical studies. *Psychological Bulletin* 113:164–180.

Kiser, L. J., Ackerman, B. J., Brown, E., et al. (1988). Posttraumatic stress disorder in young children: a reaction to purported sexual abuse. *Journal of the American Academy of Child and Adolescent Psychiatry* 27:645–649.

Kluft, R. P. (1982). Varieties of hypnotic interventions in the treatment of multiple personality. *American Journal of Clinical Hypnosis* 24:230–240.

———— (1984a). Treatment of multiple personality disorder: a study of 33 cases. *Psychiatric Clinics of North America* 7:9–29.

———— (1984b). An introduction to multiple personality disorder. *Psychiatric Annals* 14:19–24.

———— (1985a). The natural history of MPD. In *Childhood Antecedents of Multiple Personality*, ed. R. P. Kluft, pp. 198–238. Washington, DC: American Psychiatric Press.

———— (1985b). Making the diagnosis of multiple personality disorder. *Directions in Psychiatry* 5:Lesson 23, 1–11.

———— (1986). Personality unification in multiple personality disorder: a follow-up study. In *Treatment of Multiple Personality Disorder*, ed. B. G. Braun, pp. 29–60. Washington, DC: American Psychiatric Press.

_____ (1987a). An update on multiple personality disorder. *Hospital and Community Psychiatry* 38:363–373.

_____ (1987b). The simulation and dissimulation of multiple personality disorder. *American Journal of Clinical Hypnosis* 30:104–118.

_____ (1988). The post-unification treatment of multiple personality disorder: first finding. *American Journal of Psychotherapy* 42:212–228.

_____ (1991a). Clinical presentations of multiple personality disorder. *Psychiatric Clinics of North America* 14:605–629.

_____ (1991b). Hospital treatment of multiple personality disorder. *Psychiatric Clinics of North America* 14:691–795.

Konker, C. (1992). Rethinking child sexual abuse: an anthropological perspective. *American Journal of Orthopsychiatry* 62:147–153.

Lauer, J., Black, D. W., and Keen, P. (1993). Multiple personality disorder and borderline personality disorder: distinct entities or variations on a common theme? *Annals of Clinical Psychiatry* 5:129–134.

Leavitt, H. C. (1947). A case of hypnotically produced secondary and tertiary personalities. *Psychoanalytic Review* 34:274–295.

Lewis, D. O., and Bard, J. (1991). Multiple personality and forensic issues. *Psychiatric Clinics of North America* 14:741–756.

Liberman, R. P., and Eckman, T. (1981). Behavior therapy versus insight-oriented therapy for repeated suicide attempters. *Archives of General Psychiatry* 38:1126–1130.

Lindsay, D. S., and Read, J. D. (1994). Psychotherapy and memories of childhood sexual abuse: a cognitive perspective. *Applied Cognitive Psychology* 8:281–338.

Linehan, M. M., Armstrong, H. E., Suarez, A., et al. (1991). Cognitive-behavioral treatment of chronically parasuicidal borderline patients. *Archives of General Psychiatry* 48:1060–1064.

Loewenstein, R. J. (1991). An office mental status examination for complex chronic dissociative symptoms and multiple personality disorder. *Psychiatric Clinics of North America* 14:567–604.

Loewenstein, R. J., and Putnam, F. W. (1988). A comparison study of dissociative symptoms in patients with complex partial seizures, MPD, and posttraumatic stress disorder. *Dissociation* 1:17–23.

Loftus, E. F. (1993). The reality of repressed memories. *American Psychologist* 48:518–537.

Loftus, E. F., and Ketcham, K. (1991). *Witness for the Defense.* New York: St. Martin's.

Ludolph, P. (1985). How prevalent is multiple personality? (letter) *American Journal of Psychiatry* 142:1526–1527.

Ludwig, A. M., Brandsma, J. M., Wilbur, C. B., et al. (1972). The objective study of a multiple personality. *Archives of General Psychiatry* 26:298–310.

Lynn S. J., Weekes J. R., and Milano, M. (1989). Reality versus suggestion: pseudomemory in hypnotizable and simulating subjects. *Journal of Abnormal Psychology* 98:137–144.

Malenbaum R., and Russell, A. T. (1987). Multiple personality disorder in an 11-year-old boy and his mother. *Journal of the American Academy of Child and Adolescent Psychiatry* 26:436–439.

Malmquist, C. P. (1986). Children who witness parental murder: post-traumatic aspects. *Journal of the American Academy of Child and Adolescent Psychiatry* 25:320–325.

Mennen, F. E. (1993). Evaluation of risk factors in childhood sexual abuse. *Journal of the American Academy of Child and Adolescent Psychiatry* 32:934–939.

Merskey, H. (1992). The manufacture of personalities: the production of multiple personality disorder. *British Journal of Psychiatry* 160:327–340.

Mesulam, M. M. (1981). Dissociative states with abnormal temporal lobe EEG: multiple personality and the illusion of possession. *Archives of Neurology* 38:176–181.

Miller, B. F., and Keane, C. B. (1987). *Encyclopedia and Dictionary of Medicine, Nursing, and Allied Health.* Philadelphia: Saunders.

Millon, T. (1991). Classification in psychopathology: rationale, alternatives, and standards. *Journal of Abnormal Psychology* 100:245–261.

Modestin, J. (1992). Multiple personality disorder in Switzerland. *American Journal of Psychiatry* 149:88–92.

Moore, M. S. (1984). *Law and Psychiatry: Rethinking the Relationship.* Cambridge: Cambridge University Press.

Morreim, E. H. (1990). The new economics of medicine: special challenges for psychiatry. *Journal of Medicine and Philosophy* 15:97–119.

Nakdimen, K. A. (1990). Multiple personality (letter). *Hospital and Community Psychiatry* 41:566–567.

North, C. S., Ryall, J. M., Ricci, D. A., and Wetzel, R. D. (1993). *Multiple Personalities, Multiple Disorders: Psychiatric Classification and Media Influence.* New York: Oxford University Press.

Ofshe, R. J. (1992). Inadvertent hypnosis during interrogation: false confession due to dissociative state; mis-identified multiple personality and the satanic cult hypothesis. *International Journal of Clinical and Experimental Hypnosis* 40:125–156.

Orne, M. (1979). The use and misuse of hypnosis in court. *International Journal of Clinical and Experimental Hypnosis* 27:311–341.

Pap, A. (1953). Reduction-sentences and open concepts. *Methods* 5:3–30.

Paris, J., and Zweig-Frank, H. (1992). A critical review of the role of childhood sexual abuse in the etiology of borderline personality disorder. *Canadian Journal of Psychiatry* 37:125–128.

Piper, A. (1994). "Truth serum" and "recovered memories" of sexual abuse: a review of the evidence. To appear in *The Journal of Psychiatry and Law*, Spring 1994.

Pribor, E. F. and Dinwiddie, S. H. (1992). Psychiatric correlates of incest in childhood. *American Journal of Psychiatry* 149:52–56.

Putnam F. W. (1984). The psychophysiologic investigation of multiple personality disorder: a review *Psychiatric Clinics North America* 7:31–39.

———— (1989). *Diagnosis and Treatment of Multiple Personality Disorder.* New York: Guilford.

———— (1991). Recent research on multiple personality disorder. *Psychiatric Clinics of North America* 14:489–502.

———— (1992). Multiple personality disorder (letter). *British Journal of Psychiatry* 161:415–416.

Putnam, F. W., Guroff, J. J., Silberman, E. K., et al. (1986). The clinical phenomenology of multiple personality disorder: review of 100 recent cases. *Journal of Clinical Psychiatry* 47:285–293.

Putnam, F. W., and Loewenstein, R. J. (1993). Treatment of multiple personality disorder: a survey of current practices. *American Journal of Psychiatry* 150:1048–1052.

Putnam, F. W., Loewenstein, R. N., Silberman, E. J., and Post, R. (1984). Multiple personality disorder in a hospital setting. *Journal of Clinical Psychiatry* 45:172–175.

Robins, E., and Guze, S. B. (1970). Establishment of diagnostic validity in psychiatric illness: its application to schizophrenia. *American Journal of Psychiatry* 126:983–987.

Ross C. A. (1984). Diagnosis of multiple personality disorder during hypnosis: a case report. *International Journal of Clinical and Experimental Hypnosis* 32:222–235.

———— (1988). Phenomenological overlap of multiple personality disorder and obsessive-compulsive disorder. *Journal of Nervous and Mental Disease* 176:295–299.

———— (1990a). Structured interview data on 102 cases of multiple personality disorder from four centers. *American Journal of Psychiatry* 147:596–601.

———— (1990b). Twelve cognitive errors about multiple personality disorder. *American Journal of Psychotherapy* 44:348–356.

———— (1990c). Multiple personality disorder (letter). *British Journal of Psychiatry* 156:449.

———— (1991). Epidemiology of multiple personality disorder and dissociation. *Psychiatric Clinics of North America* 14:503–517.

Ross, C. A., Anderson, G., Fleisher, W. P., et al. (1992). Dissociative experiences among psychiatric inpatients. *General Hospital Psychiatry* 14:350–354.

Ross, C. A., and Dua, V. (1993). Psychiatric health care costs of multiple personality disorder. *American Journal of Psychotherapy* 47:103–112.

Ross, C. A., and Gahan, P. (1988). Techniques in the treatment of multiple personality disorder. *American Journal of Psychotherapy* 42:40–52.

Ross, C. A., Heber S., Norton, G. R., et al. (1989a). Differences between multiple personality disorder and other diagnostic groups on structured interview. *Journal of Nervous and Mental Disease* 177:487–491.

―――― (1989b). Somatic symptoms in multiple personality disorder. *Psychosomatics* 30:54–160.

Ross, C. A., Joshi, S., and Currie, R. (1990). Dissociative Experiences in the General Population. *American Journal of Psychiatry* 147:1547–1552.

Ross, C. A., Miller, S. D., Bjornson, L., et al. (1991). Abuse histories in 102 cases of multiple personality disorder. *Canadian Journal of Psychiatry* 36:97–101.

Ross, C. A., and Norton, G. R. (1988). Multiple personality disorder patients with a prior diagnosis of schizophrenia. *Dissociation* 1:39–42.

Ross, C. A., Norton, G. R., and Anderson, G. (1988). The dissociative experiences scale: a replication study. *Dissociation* 2:221–224.

Ross, C. A., Norton, G. R., and Wozney, K. (1989). Multiple personality disorder: an analysis of 236 cases. *Canadian Journal of Psychiatry* 34:413–418.

Salkovskis, P. M., Atha, C., and Storer, D. (1990). Cognitive-behavioural problem solving in the treatment of patients who repeatedly attempt suicide. *British Journal of Psychiatry* 157:871–876.

Sandberg, D. A., and Lynn, S. J. (1992). Dissociative experiences, psychopathology and adjustment, and child and adolescent maltreatment in female college students. *Journal of Abnormal Psychology* 101:717–723.

Satel, S. L., and Howland, F. C. (1992). Multiple personality disorder presenting as postpartum depression. *Hospital and Community Psychiatry* 43:1241–1243.

Schacter, D. L. (1986). Amnesia and crime: how much do we really know? *American Psychologist* 41:286–295.

Schreiber, F. R. (1973). *Sybil.* Chicago: Henry Regnery.

Serban, G. (1992). Multiple personality: an issue for forensic psychiatry. *American Journal of Psychotherapy* 46:269–280.

Shearer, S. L., Peters, C. P., Quaytman, M. S., and Ogden, R. L. (1990). Frequency and correlates of childhood sexual and physical abuse histories in adult female borderline inpatients. *American Journal of Psychiatry* 147:214–216.

Sheehan, P. W. (1988). Memory distortion in hypnosis. *International Journal of Clinical and Experimental Hypnosis* 36:296–311.

Sheehan, P. W., Green V., and Truesdale, P. (1992). Influence of rapport on hypnotically induced pseudomemory. *Journal of Abnormal Psychology* 101:690–700.

Silberman, E. K., Putnam, F. W., Weingartner, H., et al. (1985). Dissociative states in multiple personality disorder: a quantitative study. *Psychiatry Research* 15:253–260.

Simpson, M. (1989). Multiple personality disorder (letter). *British Journal of Psychiatry* 155:565.

Slovenko, R. (1989). The multiple personality: a challenge to legal concepts. *Journal of Psychiatry and the Law* 17:681–719.

Smith, V. L., and Ellsworth, P. C. (1987). The social psychology of eye-witness accuracy: misleading questions and communicator expertise. *Journal of Applied Psychology* 72:294–300.

Spanos, N. P. (1989). Hypnosis, demonic possession, and multiple personality: strategic enactments and disavowals of responsibility for actions. In *Altered States of Consciousness and*

Mental Health: A Cross-Cultural Perspective, ed. C. A. Ward, pp. 96–125. Newbury Park, CA: Sage.

Spanos, N. P., Weekes, J. R., and Bertrand, L. D. (1985). Multiple personality: a social psychological perspective. *Journal of Abnormal Psychology* 94:362–376.

Spiegel, D., and Cardena, E. (1991). Disintegrated experience: the dissociative disorders revisited. *Journal of Abnormal Psychology* 100:366–378.

Steinberg, M., Rounsaville, B., and Cicchetti, D. V. (1990). The structured clinical interview for *DSM-III-R* dissociative disorders: preliminary report on a new diagnostic instrument. *American Journal of Psychiatry* 147:76–82.

Stoll, A. L., Tohen, M., and Baldessarini, R. J. (1992). Increasing frequency of the diagnosis of obsessive-compulsive disorder. *American Journal of Psychiatry* 149:638–640.

Suengas, A. G., and Johnson, M. K. (1988). Qualitative effects of rehearsal on memories for perceived and imagined events. *Journal of Experimental Psychology: General* 117:377–389.

Sutcliffe, J. P., and Jones, J. (1962). Personal identity, multiple personality, and hypnosis. *International Journal of Clinical and Experimental Hypnosis* 10:231–269.

Swenson, C. (1989). Kernberg and Linehan: two approaches to the borderline patient. *Journal of Personality Disorders* 3:26–35.

Swett, C., Surrey, J., and Cohen, C. (1990). Sexual and physical abuse histories and psychiatric symptoms among male psychiatric outpatients. *American Journal of Psychiatry* 147:632–636.

Taylor, W. S., and Martin, M. F. (1944). Multiple personality. *Journal of Abnormal and Social Psychology* 49:135–151.

Terr, L. (1988). What happens to early memories of trauma? A study of twenty children under age five at the time of documented traumatic events. *Journal of the American Academy of Child and Adolescent Psychiatry* 27:96–104.

Thigpen, C. H., and Cleckley, H. M. (1984). On the incidence of multiple personality disorder: a brief communication. *International Journal of Clinical and Experimental Hypnosis* 32:63–66.

Tozman, S., and Pabis, R. (1989). MPD: further skepticism (without hostility . . . we think). *Journal of Nervous and Mental Disease* 177:708–709.

Wakefield, H., and Underwager, R. (1992). Recovered memories of alleged sexual abuse: lawsuits against parents. *Behavioral Sciences and the Law* 10:483–507.

Weiner, A. (1992). The dissociative experiences scale (letter). *American Journal of Psychiatry* 149:143–144.

Weissberg, M. (1993). Multiple personality disorder and iatrogenesis: the cautionary tale of Anna O. *International Journal of Clinical and Experimental Hypnosis* 31:15–34.

Western, D., Ludolph P., Misle, B. A., et al. (1990). Physical and sexual abuse in adolescent girls with borderline personality disorder. *American Journal of Orthopsychiatry* 60:55–66.

Widom, C. S. (1989). Does violence beget violence? A critical examination of the literature. *Psychological Bulletin* 106:3–28.

―――― (1991). The role of placement experiences in mediating the criminal consequences of early childhood victimization. *American Journal of Orthopsychiatry* 61:195–209.

Winfield, I., George, L. K., Swartz, M., and Blazer, D. G. (1990). Sexual assault and psychiatric disorders among a community sample of women. *American Journal of Psychiatry* 147:335–341.

7

Dissociative Identity Disorder and the Trauma Paradigm

Denise J. Gelinas

The variety and intensity of controversies surrounding MPD are striking. What is multiple personality disorder (MPD)? Does it exist? If MPD does exist, what causes it? Is it an artifact of poor treatment, and therefore iatrogenic? If therapists can produce alters, does this necessarily mean that MPD does not exist? Is MPD part of another diagnosis or does it stand on its own? Is it caused by hypnosis? Is dissociation merely self-hypnosis? Should MPD be addressed directly in therapy, or, for fear of exacerbating its symptoms, is it best ignored? Can it be successfully treated?

Attempts to understand the controversies associated with MPD are hampered if discussion is limited to an ahistorical perspective. This cross-sectional view results in the controversies remaining opaque. However, when MPD and its controversies are examined within the context of the history of science, it becomes clear that these controversies were predictable; they are part of processes *intrinsic* to the production and acceptance of knowledge. Applying Thomas Kuhn's (1970a, b) perspective on the evolution of scientific knowledge proves remarkably revealing. There is a striking correspondence between processes identified by Kuhn in the growth of knowledge and the controversies that are currently associated with MPD.

The central thesis of this chapter is that controversies surrounding the existence of MPD represent an extension of the controversy, denial, and suppression that historically have met all investigations of psychological trauma. Further, it will be seen that the greatest controversy, denial, and suppression have occurred when trauma results from interpersonal violence, rather than from accident, natural disaster, or combat. It is predictable that intense controversy would accompany the exploration and treatment of MPD since it is typically precipitated by the most disturbing forms of interpersonal violence.

KUHNIAN PARADIGM FRAMEWORK

Conventionally the growth of knowledge in science has been viewed as cumulative and accretionary. In his classic essays Kuhn (1970a, b) argued that when we examine how science really happens rather than how it is supposed to happen, periods of cumulative, accretionary work (which he calls "normal science") are punctuated by revolutions involving new paradigms.

Paradigms as Solution-Exemplars

Paradigms are important problem solutions that function as "exemplars" (Kuhn 1970a). These concrete solutions are sufficiently unprecedented to attract an enduring group of adherents away from competing modes of scientific activity. The concrete problem solution serves as an analogue, a gestalt with which to "see" new problems as subjects for the application of the model solution.

Anomalies and the Emergence of Paradigms

Kuhn (1970b) identified two kinds of anomalies, or violations, of theory-based expectations. In the first, practitioners in a field gradually become aware that their vision and methods cannot solve certain problems. Intractable problems demonstrate the limitations of their field. The anomalous intractable problem creates a crisis in the field and prompts the emergence of a new paradigm. The best-known example is the replacement of the Ptolemaic earth-centered astronomical system by the emergence of the Copernican paradigm of a heliocentric system.

In other circumstances, anomalies are not intractable problems but surprises — phenomena that should not exist given current theory, but do. This type of anomaly can appear only against the background provided by a paradigm and associated normal science. This kind of surprise emerges only for the person who knows *"with precision* what he *should* expect, [and] is able to recognize that something has gone wrong"* (Kuhn 1970b, p. 65). Recognition of such an anomaly often occurs by accident. The discovery of X-rays is a well-known example. As with many new scientific discoveries, X-rays were greeted with surprise and shock. Scientists were staggered by it. X-rays violated deeply entrenched theoretical expectations and undermined the credibility of previous experiments, which would now have to be repeated. Lord Kelvin pronounced them an elaborate hoax. (Kuhn 1970b).

Recognizing an anomaly is a precursor to the formulation of a new paradigm, but we know very little about what makes it possible for some individuals to recognize anomalies. Noticing anomalies is disruptive to normal science, psychologically uncomfortable, and not what scientists are trained to do. However, individuals who propose new paradigms are usually "men [sic] so young or so new to the . . . field that practice has committed them less deeply than most of their contemporaries to the world view and rules determined by the old paradigm" (Kuhn 1970b, p. 144). Many have come out of left field, that is, they were working in one field and saw the solution to an anomaly in another. Dalton revolutionized chemistry with his atomic theory but he was a meteorologist working on the absorption of gases by water in the atmosphere. He approached the long-standing problem of compounds in chemistry from a different perspective than contemporary chemists, and so was able to see the fixed proportions that had eluded them (Kuhn 1970b).

Small paradigms engender small revolutions. Some paradigms affect only the members of a professional subspecialty. For example, Maxwell's equations regarding the nature of light were no less revolutionary than Einstein's and just as strongly resisted (Kuhn 1970b), but they affected a much smaller professional group. The Copernican heliocentric paradigm, in contrast, was large and engendered a major revolution. Other large paradigms include Aristotle's *Physica*, Ptolemy's *Almagest*, Newton's *Principia* and his *Opticks*, Franklin's *Electricity*, Lavoisier's *Chemistry*, and Lyell's *Geography* (Kuhn 1970b), as well as Darwin's *Origin of the Species* and Einstein's theories of relativity. Every large paradigm has necessitated rejection of one time-honored scientific theory in favor of another that is incompatible with it. It has produced a shift in what are admissible problems and legitimate problem-solutions and has transformed the scientific imagination so that the world is seen differently. "Such changes, together with the controversies that almost always accompany them, are the defining characteristics of scientific revolutions" (Kuhn 1970b, p. 6).

Disciplinary Matrices and Normal Science

Extending the paradigm produces a strong network of conceptual, theoretical, and methodological commitments that define a community of practitioners and enable them to enjoy relative unanimity in problem choice and solutions (Kuhn 1970a). These practitioners and their work commitments are disciplinary matrices (DMs). DMs are what the scientist "describes under such rubrics as 'Ptolemaic astronomy' (or 'Copernican'), 'Aristotelian dynamics' (or 'Newtonian'), 'corpuscular optics' (or 'wave optics')" (Kuhn 1970b, p. 10). Paradigms precede and serve as exemplars for the DMs; thus, the *Principia* was the paradigm for Newtonian dynamics, and the *Almagest* for Ptolemaic earth-centered astronomy. Normal science is scientific activity that follows the paradigm and incrementally creates the DM; it is fundamentally a "puzzle-solving" activity (Kuhn 1970b). According to Kuhn (1970b), "Mopping-up operations are what engage most scientists through their careers. . . . No part of the aim of normal science is to call forth new sorts of phenomena; indeed those that will not fit the box are often not seen at all" (p. 24).

Responses to a New Paradigm

Understanding a new paradigm, the ability to see a problem in a new way and thus solve it, is like the figure-ground experiments in Gestalt psychology, in which a picture can look like one thing, but then be seen as something else. Sometimes, in fact, the viewer can have difficulty getting him- or herself to see it in the original way once he/she has made the gestalt switch to the new view. The ability to see a new paradigm is not a point-by-point translation, but an intuitive, coherent switch. Kuhn (1970b) likens it to a conversion experience and feels that the gestalt switch remains at the heart of the revolutionary process. Some individuals make this gestalt switch and they use and articulate a new paradigm; there are others who resist and reject.

Resistance and Controversy

A new paradigm always precipitates some sort of battle (Kuhn 1970b); rejecters are typically the leading adherents of the old paradigm. Individuals committed to an older theory have everything invested in it and they may have difficulty seeing the new pattern of problems and solutions. They cannot, or will not, make that gestalt switch. The growth of knowledge is replete with examples of this. Copernicans made very few converts for almost a century after his death and Newton's *Principia* was widely rejected, particularly on the continent, for more than fifty years. Kuhn (1970b) notes that Priestley never accepted the oxygen theory. Maxwell's electromagnetic equations were resisted, especially by Lord Kelvin. Dalton's atomic theory was widely attacked and "Berthollet, in particular, was never convinced" (p. 133). Because a new paradigm invalidates part of the scientific work already completed within the old paradigm it requires the reconstruction of prior theory and the reevaluation of prior fact. A new paradigm is not merely an increment to what is already known, but a new way of looking at problems that redefines the universe of problems, data, and solutions. This is an intrinsically revolutionary process that is never welcomed by established individuals in the field and never accomplished overnight (Kuhn 1970b).

Paradigm makers themselves have often been aware of this rejection by adherents of the old school. In the *Origin of the Species*, Darwin wrote:

> I by no means expect to convince experienced naturalists whose minds are stocked with a multitude of facts all viewed, during a long course of years, from a point of view directly opposite to mine. . . . But I look with confidence to the future, – to young and rising naturalists, who will be able to view both sides of the question with impartiality. [Kuhn 1970b, p. 151]

Max Planck wrote that a new truth did not prevail by " 'convincing its opponents and making them see the light' " (Kuhn 1970b, p. 151), but rather by their eventually dying and a new generation growing up familiar with it.

New paradigms are followed by rising debates and controversies. Controversies are "almost non-existent during periods of normal science, but [occur] regularly just before and during scientific revolutions" (Kuhn 1970b, p. 48).

Externals

For some new paradigms, a second major source of rejection and suppression can be brought into play. Kuhn refers to these as *externals*—outside-of-science cultural, societal, and political factors that affect the knowledge process. External factors can turn an anomaly into a crisis: Ptolemaic failure to predict the position of the planets became a source of acute crisis because the calendar was in shambles [and planting seasons were affected] (Kuhn 1970b). Externals can also hasten the transfer of knowledge, that is, the invention of the printing press or establishment of trade routes and travel.

Externals can also suppress a new paradigm for reasons that have nothing to do with its truth or utility. In the seventeenth century Galileo contributed to the development of physics, built a telescope that made it possible to see the moons of Jupiter, and believed the Copernican heliocentric paradigm (Gruber 1974). However, he did so under the hostile stare of the Inquisition, which eventually imprisoned and condemned him to death for his ideas. He escaped immolation only by recanting and swearing: "I, Galileo, being in my seventieth year, being a prisoner and on my knees, and before your Eminences, having before my eyes the Holy

Gospel, which I touch with my hands, abjure, curse, and detest the error and the heresy of the movement of the earth" (Gruber 1974, pp. 36–37).

Copernicus delayed publication of *Concerning the Revolutions of the Heavenly Spheres* for *thirty years*, until 1543 — the year of his death — and even then with a "preface added by a friend pretending that Copernicus had not actually believed the heliocentric heresy" (Gruber 1974, p. 37). In 1600, almost 40 years later, Giordano Bruno, one of the earlier adherents of the Copernican theory, was burned at the stake by the Inquisition.

> If the decision between the Copernican and the traditional universe had concerned only astronomers, Copernicus' proposal would almost certainly have achieved a quiet and gradual victory. But the decision was not exclusively, or even primarily, a matter for astronomers, and as the debate spread from astronomical circles it became tumultuous in the extreme. [Kuhn 1957, p. 188]

When externals enter a paradigm clash, the controversies become intense. The most heated external arguments were religious. Martin Luther, his principal assistant Melanchthon, and Calvin quoted Scripture against Copernican ideas and were joined in 1610 by the Catholic Church (Kuhn 1957). Kuhn wrote that the churchmen's dogmatism disguises their motives, but it did not eliminate them because Christian life and morality could not easily adapt to a universe in which the earth was just one of a number of planets. Cosmology, morality, and theology were interwoven. "The vigor and venom displayed at the height of the Copernican controversy, three centuries later, testifies to the strength and vitality of the tradition" (Kuhn 1957, pp. 192–193).

Darwin delayed publication of his work on natural selection, *On the Origin of the Species*, for twenty years specifically *because* he feared persecution. There has been speculation that Darwin delayed so long because he was neurotic and unable to write or publish. Whatever the state of his mental health, he was able to publish extensively in other areas, including an eight-volume work on barnacles that remains the standard reference! But his private notebooks reveal that he anticipated persecution for his ideas about evolution and chose to suppress this aspect of his work. It was only when Alfred Wallace informed him that he was going to publish an outline on natural selection did Darwin work feverishly to bring out his own work. However, he understood and feared the power of factors external to science, even referring to the fate of the astronomers in his private notebooks (Gruber 1974).

He had witnessed societal retaliation at the University of Edinburgh as a teenager when an acquaintance presented a paper on a scientific matter that challenged religious precepts. It was struck, along with all discussion and even notification of its reading, from the records of the Plinian Society.

Externals rarely affect small, technological paradigms. However, if a paradigm is big, and especially if it challenges values that are central to a civilization, societal institutions mobilize to suppress the paradigm and to retaliate against its leading adherents. Society rejects a paradigm to maintain core values and beliefs. The historian Fernand Braudel (1987) has written that civilizations have superficial manifestations (plays, artwork, fashion) and periods (the Romantic era or the Renaissance), as well as turning points, signaled by important events or "heroes." But civilizations also have "deep structures"—foundations that are simultaneously conscious and subconscious (e.g., "religious beliefs, . . . or a timeless peasantry or attitudes towards death, work, pleasure and family life (p. 28). These structures are enduring, distinctive, and original. They give civilizations their characteristic qualities. For example, "The role of women is always a structural element in any civilization . . . it is a long-lived reality, resistant to external pressure, and hard to change overnight. A *civilization generally refuses to accept a cultural innovation that calls in question one of its own structural elements*" (Braudel 1987 p. 29, my emphasis). These structures change, but very slowly and always reluctantly. When large paradigms are attacked by externals, it is because they have impinged on a society's deep structures. Then the paradigm may be suppressed for a time. The solutions offered by the paradigm are not recognized and the problems must be denied and forgotten as problems. But these problems remain; the anomalies eventually resurface, and the pattern is repeated until the civilization begins to tolerate seeing what the anomalies uncover.

MPD AND CONTROVERSIES SURROUNDING THE TRAUMA PARADIGM

In light of intellectual history, the controversies surrounding MPD should not be a surprise; they could have been predicted. They are part of the controversies associated with the emergence of a larger paradigm—the trauma paradigm.

The development of the trauma paradigm shows a point-for-point correspondence with the development of other large paradigms. It has great explanatory power, surprisingly wide applicability, and the ability to attract large groups of active researchers and clinical practitioners. The psychophysiological trauma syndrome continues to be investigated and elaborated. Bessel van der Kolk's work (1987, van der Kolk and van der

Hart 1991) would be an example of exploring and extending the basic trauma paradigm. As with other paradigms, basic early discoveries and problem solutions have been applied to other problem areas, for instance, responses to the trauma of combat or of rape. These applications generate *component* paradigms and disciplinary matrices in each of these areas as well. The basic trauma paradigm and the component paradigms have also been resisted, rejected, repressed, and suppressed both by adherents of the old paradigm and by Kuhnian externals. For instance, the recently completed *DSM-IV* Field Trials for posttraumatic stress disorder (PTSD) investigated complex responses to chronic trauma including affect dysregulation, dissociative phenomena, somatization, and characterological adaptations. The syndrome is called *Disorders of Extreme Stress - Not Otherwise Specified* (DESNOS) (Herman 1992, van der Kolk 1993a). Among chronically traumatized people, there was a very high prevalence of the DESNOS symptoms, and DESNOS was slated to be included in the appendix to the *DSM-IV* under the heading of "Complicated Post Traumatic Stress Disorder" (van der Kolk, 1993a). When the *DSM-IV* was published, DESNOS had been inexplicably dropped from the appendix. Apparently, there was considerable controversy about it among *DSM-IV* committees for two reasons. Any role for external trauma with regard to the character or personality disorders was protested by adherents of the older intrapsychic paradigms. Also, even among those individuals convinced by the robust empirical link between external trauma and character problems, it was felt that inclusion of DESNOS would have more of an impact on the present diagnostic nomenclature than they were prepared to tolerate (van der Kolk, personal communication, April 1994). Including DESNOS would entail a reconstruction of the nomenclature, or as Kuhn (1970b) puts it, the reconstruction of prior theory and the reevaluation of earlier data. In this particular paradigm clash, the adherents of the older paradigm prevailed. If adherents of DESNOS continue to amass data, this issue will reemerge for *DSM-V*. This appears probable. The robustness of the data on the basic psychophysiological trauma response and the number and usefulness of the applications into special areas makes it unlikely that the trauma paradigms will simply evaporate, or be suppressed. The emergence of this major paradigm does appear to be a revolution in the mental health field.

The factors that make individuals and institutions draw back from awareness and acknowledgment of trauma make them even less likely to acknowledge the existence and causes of MPD. MPD can be seen as the apotheosis of traumatic processes. Here we see the effects of severe trauma on human beings with unnerving clarity, precisely because the trauma that is etiologically linked to MPD is severe, repetitive, and often intentional. To understand the MPD controversies, we need to understand the controversies surrounding the other trauma paradigms as well; it will become apparent the MPD controversies are more of the same. Understanding the entire complex of controversies, however, provides a perspective from which we can draw conclusions.

Trauma—The Basic Paradigm

Pierre Janet originated the early findings and conceptualizations related to dissociative (or posttraumatic) psychopathology (Ellenberger 1970, Putnam 1989a, 1989b, 1993, van der Kolk and van der Hart 1989). As such, his work began the modern trauma paradigm. Conventional wisdom held that when things became "too much," people simply needed a brief period of rest and they would soon be "as good as new." Janet noted that the effects of experiences did not always dissipate with time. Some experiences could be overwhelming to an individual, particularly if they produced "vehement emotion," could not be encompassed by the person's existing cognitive schema, and appropriate action was not possible (van der Kolk and van der Hart 1989). This feeling of being overwhelmed did not end when the overwhelming event ended. Nor did the person return to his or her way of being prior to the experience. Janet had noticed an anomaly— a violation of expectation.

Janet viewed memory as the central organizing apparatus of the mind (van der Kolk and van der Hart 1991). He noted that the ease with which experience is integrated into existing mental schemas depends on the subjective assessment of the experience. While familiar and expectable experiences are automatically assimilated into memory—Janet coined the term *subconscious* for these automatically stored memories (Ellenberger 1970)—frightening or novel experiences do not easily fit into existing cognitive schemas. They are therefore remembered with particular vividness—*hypermnesias*—or they may totally resist integration, becoming dissociated from conscious awareness—(*amnesias*)—and voluntary control (van der Kolk and van der Hart 1991).

In addition to identifying the linkage between traumatic antecedents and dissociation, Janet recognized the role of state-dependent memory processes in dissociative amnesias and the altered states of consciousness in disturbances of identity characteristic of the dissociative disorders (Putnam 1989b). He recognized that dissociation was the underlying mechanism in a broad range of disorders now categorized in *DSM-IV* as dissociation, somatization, conversion, borderline personality, and posttraumatic stress disorders (van der Hart and Friedman 1989).

In accordance with Kuhn's model, Janet came somewhat out of left field. His training was in philosophy and psychology (when the latter was still a branch of philosophy). He held a position as professor of philosophy at the Lyceum in Le Havre (Putnam 1989a), only beginning his training in medicine some years later.

The Etiology of Hysteria

Freud's use of Janet's work on dissociation for the etiology of hysteria constituted the first application and extension of this new paradigm. Janet and Freud had studied with Charcot at La Salpetrière in Paris. They hoped, as did most followers of Charcot, to solve the riddle of the cause of hysteria (Herman 1992). (The etiology of hysteria constitutes Kuhn's second type of anomaly—the intractable problem that attracts attention.) While in Paris, Freud had also been exposed to contemporary work attesting to the reality and severity of childhood sexual abuse, including autopsies at the Paris morgue performed on the young victims of such abuse (Masson 1984). By 1896, in *The Aetiology of Hysteria*, Freud wrote that hysteria was caused by psychological trauma, but he went further than Janet and identified that trauma as childhood sexual abuse. He had established a component paradigm—an application of the basic trauma paradigm to a new problem—and transformed the way it was seen.

In his groundbreaking 1896 work on the etiology of hysteria, Freud put forth his thesis that "at the bottom of every case of hysteria there are one or more occurrences of premature sexual experience, [during] . . . the earliest years of childhood" (p. 203). He felt he had shown his colleagues "the solution to a more than thousand-year-old problem—*a caput Nili*" (Masson 1984, p. 3). In fact he had, since the etiology of hysteria had been an intractable problem for centuries; he and Breuer had been able to see the problem in a new way. This paper established Freud's position that the sexual abuse of children was real, not derived from fantasies, and that these experiences had a damaging and lasting effect (Masson 1984).

Freud obtained objective confirmation of the details of the child sexual abuse in two of his eighteen cases by "fortunate accident," not because he was attempting to ascertain the historical accuracy of his patients' accounts (Masson 1984). Masson notes that Freud's language in the 1896 paper— abuse, rape, attack, seduction, assault, aggression, and traumas—strongly suggests that Freud considered them to be sexual violence directed against children. Only one term used—seduction—is ambiguous in that it implies some degree of participation on the part of the child; probably not coincidentally, this is the term under which Freud's insight came to be known—the "seduction" theory.

Combat and PTSD

The second area to which the trauma paradigm was extended was war, and ironically, it was Freud again who recognized and wrote about it. During World War I, he noticed a striking anomaly within his own psychoanalytic system—the persistent tendency of combat veterans to repeatedly talk about or reexperience aspects of their experiences in combat. (According to the Freudian pleasure principle, these men should have avoided all consideration of their profoundly aversive experiences, but they were doing precisely the opposite.) Freud posited a *repetition compulsion*—a drive to master these overwhelming experiences.

The trauma paradigm was neglected and then resurrected in World War II. Kardiner (1941) conceptualized posttraumatic stress syndrome, which he called a *physioneurosis* because of its strong physiological components. His descriptions coincide with contemporary formal diagnostic criteria for PTSD (van der Kolk 1987). Kardiner pointed out that many individuals with PTSD continue to live in the emotional environment of the traumatic event with "enduring vigilance for and sensitivity to environmental threat" (van der Kolk 1993b, p. 2). He described the persistence of startle response and irritability, the outbursts of aggression, fixation on the trauma, personality constriction, and recurrent dreams (van der Kolk 1987, p. 2). Grinker and Spiegel (1945) and Kardiner and Spiegel (1947) noted that close interpersonal ties within the fighting unit helped its members better resist combat fatigue (thus identifying the importance of secure attachments as a source of resistance to trauma).

Kardiner attempted to develop a theory of trauma within the framework of psychoanalysis but found this impossible to do (Herman 1992)—an example of incommensurability between paradigms. He left psychoanalysis for anthropology and it was "only then . . . that he was able to return to the subject of war trauma, this time having in anthropology a conceptual framework that recognized the impact of social reality" (Herman 1992, p. 24).

Other Applications of the Trauma Paradigm

The trauma paradigm has been applied to a wide range of precipitants including: accidents and natural disasters, the physical, sexual, and incestuous abuse of children, rape, sadism, POW and concentration camp experience, and political torture.

Erich Lindemann's (1944) work after the infamous Coconut Grove fire identified trauma as a consequence of accidents and natural disasters. Mardi Horowitz (1976) clarified the bi-phasic presentation of the trauma response—chronic numbing punctuated by repetitive intrusions of some part of the trauma. Kempe and his colleagues (1962) documented child battering. Green (1985), Eth and Pynoos (1985), Goodwin (1985a), and Terr (1990) demonstrated that children experience the full trauma response, including PTSD.

Burgess and Holmstrom (1974) identified the rape-trauma syndrome—a pattern of reactions that included insomnia, nausea, startle responses, and nightmares as well as dissociative or numbing symptoms. They noted that some of the victims' symptoms resembled those previously described in combat veterans.

The rediscovery of childhood sexual abuse (Goodwin 1989, Goodwin et al. 1979, Herman 1981, Peters 1976, Rush 1980), particularly incestuous abuse (Gelinas 1983, Herman 1981, Meiselman 1978) followed soon after. I (Gelinas 1983) identified incest as a trauma that produced characteristic sequelae of PTSD, continuing risk of interpersonal exploitation, and an increased risk of intergenerational incest. Incest survivors were described as clinically resembling soldiers with combat fatigue. Others have subsequently elaborated the linkages between incestuous abuse and PTSD (Blake-White and Kline 1985, Briere and Runtz 1987, Donaldson and Gardner 1985, Goodwin 1984, Lindberg and Distad 1985).

Responding to increasing referrals of severely abused children, Goodwin began to study sadism (1993a,b) in a range of phenomena, including severe child abuse, family violence, torture, the Holocaust, prostitution, pornography and sex rings, ritual abuse, and sadistic criminals.

The trauma paradigm has also been applied to treatment with victims of organized violence, including concentration camps (Danieli 1984), political torture (Basoglu 1992), and combat POWs.

Rejection and Controversy Vary by Content of the Trauma

Herman (1992) has pointed out that

> the study of psychological trauma has a curious history—one of episodic amnesia. Periods of active investigation have alternated with periods of oblivion. Repeatedly in the past century, similar lines of inquiry have been taken up and abruptly abandoned, only to be rediscovered much later . . . Though the field has in fact an abundant and rich tradition, it has been periodically forgotten and must be periodically reclaimed. [p. 7]

She (Herman 1992) dismisses as the cause of this "intermittent amnesia" the ordinary changes in fashion that affect any intellectual pursuit. The study of psychological trauma has not suffered because of lack of interest. Rather, the *subject itself* "provokes such intense controversy that it period-ically becomes anathema. . . ." The study of psychological trauma "has repeatedly *led into realms of the unthinkable* and *foundered on fundamental questions of belief*" (Herman 1992, p. 7; my emphases).

More specifically, the nature of the trauma appears to influence the responses of individuals and institutions. Three trauma clusters emerge: (1) accidents and natural disasters, (2) combat, and (3) interpersonal violence. The last of these—interpersonal violence—can be differentiated into two important subsets: institutionalized (prisoner of war, concentra-tion camp, political torture) and personalized (physical and sexual abuse of children including incest, rape, and other assaults, battering, pornography rings, sexual, and homicidal torture).

Each of these component paradigms—applications of the basic trauma paradigm—has been resisted or rejected by adherents of the preexisting paradigms in classic Kuhnian fashion. Similarly, they have been repressed and suppressed by externals. However, the degree of paradigmatic rejection and the type of externals differ depending on the type of trauma involved.

Accidents and Disasters

Recognition of trauma in accident and disaster is usually unambivalent. The situation is readily comprehensible and it is all too easy to identify with the victim. Nevertheless, identification and acknowledgment quickly turn into impatience. The victim is soon admonished to "put it behind you," as though that were possible. Continuing reference to the trauma frequently precipitates attacks on the character of the individual despite his or her continuing symptomatology. This is especially true if there are fears that the individual is seeking unjust compensation. If monetary claims are being made, this may be a legitimate concern. These are external factors which foster resistance to the recognition of trauma. These cases need to be evaluated on a case by case basis by someone with expertise in the area. The historical tendency of health-care professional to treat physical injuries but overlook or minimize psychological sequelae constitutes a paradig-matic form of resistance.

Combat

In this society, the ability to acknowledge combat trauma shows a clear cyclic pattern (Herman 1992). Kardiner complained about this in 1941.

> The subject of neurotic disturbances consequent upon war has, in the last 25 years, been submitted to a good deal of capriciousness in public interest and

psychiatric whims. The public does not sustain its interest, which was very great after World War I, and neither does psychiatry. Hence these conditions are not subject to continuous study . . . but only to periodic efforts which cannot be characterized as very diligent. [p. 1]

In this statement, he concisely identifies both external and paradigmatic resistance to the trauma paradigm. Society's amnesia for the lessons derived from the study of combat fatigue is poignantly illustrated by our involvement in the Vietnam War, during which men were transferred in and out of units as *single individuals* despite our having learned in *both* world wars that the strongest protection against the overwhelming terror of combat was the degree of relatedness within the immediate fighting unit (Grinker and Spiegel 1945, Kardiner and Spiegel 1947). Paradigmatic resistance arose from adherents of the dominant biomedical paradigm which, during World War I, insisted that PTSD—then referred to as "shell shock"—was a physical result of the concussion of exploding shells.

Interpersonal Violence

The most intense and, at times, irrational resistance and rejection—both paradigmatically and externally—are evident in relation to the effects of interpersonal violence. Paradigmatic attacks come from the biomedical paradigm and also from the psychoanalytic paradigm. Rejection of the interpersonal trauma paradigms take three forms: 1. denial (sometimes to the point of denying the existence of the phenomenon itself), 2. attacking the credibility of the victim, and 3. attacking the clinicians who treat trauma survivors.

Not coincidentally, the more severe the trauma, the more vituperative the attack. This partially explains why controversy about MPD is especially tumultuous; because MPD results from the most horrific forms of interpersonal violence, it is the least tolerated.

The first such attacks were directed at the progenitor of the trauma paradigm, Pierre Janet, and, as we will see, are eerily similar to attacks on clinicians treating trauma today. This is particularly so for clinicians treating MPD.

ATTACKS ON THE PARADIGMS CONCERNING INTERPERSONAL VIOLENCE

Attack and Suppression: Pierre Janet

Janet's work was attacked by several groups and was actually suppressed. Herman (1992) notes that, unlike his rival Freud, Janet "never abandoned his traumatic theory of hysteria and . . . never retreated from his hysterical patients, [so] lived to see his works forgotten and his ideas neglected" (p. 18). Janet's work was attacked by the "rigidly organicist" French neurologists and by psychoanalysts, Freud among them (Ellenberger 1970).

The zeitgeist of the times, which ignored the position of the powerless and devalued (Herman 1992) and suppressed voluminous information about horrendous child physical and sexual abuse constituted a powerful external factor contributing to resistance to Janet's findings. For example, men such as Ambroise Tardieu, Alexandre Lacassagne, R. Garraud, and Paul Bernard presented graphic evidence of physical and sexual abuse based on autopsies of murdered children, only to have their findings ignored (Masson 1984). Also, the credibility of the child victims was challenged by Alfred Fournier and others (Masson 1984). Society had tired of looking at atrocities and having to do something about them; public opinion shifted and these problems were no longer held to exist. Ellenberger (1970) notes that the suppression of this work "was as irrational and sudden as had been the fashion that had caused its rise to fame in the 1880s. It occurred in spite of great [efforts] on the part of certain adherents . . . who were discovering new and promising facts" (p. 17).

Attack and Repudiation: Freud.

Freud also became the target of both paradigmatic and external attack. Significantly, this occurred only after he left neurology and began to work with the effects of interpersonal violence. Herman (1992) points out that *The Aetiology of Hysteria*'s "triumphant title and exultant tone suggest that Freud viewed his contribution as the crowning achievement in the field" (p. 13), but within a year, Freud had repudiated the trauma-based paradigm about the etiology of hysteria (Masson 1984).

Paradigmatic attacks came from practitioners working within the dominant biomedical paradigm who utterly rejected Freud's theory. In a letter to Wilhelm Fliess days after his "Aetiology" lecture at the Society for Psychiatry and Neurology, Freud (Masson 1984) reports that his presentation was "met with an icy reception from the asses, and from Krafft-Ebing the strange comment: 'It sounds like a scientific fairy tale'." (p. 9). This must have been especially shocking as Freud had chosen that night to present his paper *because* the eminent Krafft-Ebing was to chair the meeting. Less than two weeks later, Freud wrote to Fliess (Masson 1984), "I am as isolated as you could wish me to be: the word has been given out to abandon me, and a void is forming around me" (p. 10). In fact, ten days later in the professional journal *Wiener klinische Wochenschrift* he found that his presentation was listed by title alone, without the customary summary and discussion (Masson 1984). This is eerily similar to the fate of Darwin's friend, whose presentation to the Plinian Society was struck from the official record, as was notice of its impending presentation. Freud published the paper a few weeks later and continued to explore the seduction theory in his clinical work, centering more and more on the role of abusive fathers. ("My confidence in the father-etiology has risen greatly" [Freud to W. Fliess, December 12, 1897, Masson 1984, p. 114]). *But he refrained from speaking or writing publicly about this work.* This is precisely what both Copernicus and Darwin did (and perhaps Galileo wished he had done?) in relation to their revolutionary formulations. Freud was also attacked by external forces. Many professionals were shocked by what Freud's paradigm suggested about Viennese society, the functioning of the family, and the behavior of men.

Finally, Freud had more personal reasons to step back from his trauma formulation. From 1887 until about 1903, Freud turned to Wilhelm Fliess for support and intellectual discourse, but this was a disastrous association for Freud (Masson 1984).

> Freud continued to write to Fliess about his new discoveries. He was the one person to whom Freud was willing to tell everything he knew about the evidence slowly emerging from his clinical practice supporting the reality of seductions and their psychological impact. . . . However, Robert Fliess (1895–1970), Wilhelm Fliess's son, believed that his father had sexually molested him, and this at precisely the time Freud was writing to Fliess about seduction. [p. 138]

Robert Fliess's perceptions of his father as having suffered from an ambulatory psychosis and having sexually abused him were "clarified . . . in two . . . thorough analyses" (Fliess, 1956, p. 17, quoted in Masson 1984, p. 141), and were discussed with Freud himself. Masson (1984) notes the irony in the intellectual sharing between Freud and Wilhelm Fliess. "Freud was like a dogged detective, on the track of a great crime, communicating his hunches and approximations and at last his final discovery to his best friend, who may have been in fact the criminal (p. 142).

In 1905, Freud publicly repudiated the seduction theory and launched psychoanalysis in the direction of the oedipal formulation, with its emphasis on intrapsychic fantasy and conflict rather than the impact of reality. Despite confirmatory evidence for some of his patients' histories of abuse, and *without offering any clinical documentation of false complaints or accounts,* Freud decided that his hysterical patients' accounts of childhood sexual abuse were untrue and, moreover, that they were wishful fantasies (Herman 1992). Thus, Freud defined sexual and incestuous abuse out of existence. The psychoanalytic paradigm became the greatest intellectual impediment to seeing such abuse. Although his formulations grew increasingly convoluted to accommodate his oedipal formulation, attacks and controversy surrounding Freud's work waned. Across Europe the willingness to acknowledge the existence of trauma waned (Ellenberger 1970, Herman 1992, Masson 1984); leading practitioners of the paradigm were discredited or ignored, and a wealth of material became intellectually and clinically invisible.

This triad of denial, attack the victim, and attack the clinician continues into the present time. These type of attacks swirl around all of the interpersonal violence paradigms: physical, sexual and incestuous abuse of children, rape, battering, sadism, the Holocaust and political torture, and the sadistic abuse that is etiologically linked to MPD. Adherents of the biomedical and psychoanalytic paradigms again provide powerful sources of paradigmatic resistance. External factors also contribute.

Denial

Denial of the effects of interpersonal violence is pervasive and deeply rooted in both professionals and society. They deny with all the active and willful obliviousness of the dynamic meaning of this process. Several writers have pointed out the active quality of both the paradigmatic and external denial of interpersonal violence. Goodwin (1985) refers to the insistence on overlooking child sexual abuse as a shared negative hallucination. According to Goodwin (1985), "Incredulity can be understood as an intellectualized variant of derealization; and, like the dissociative defenses, incredulity is an effective way to gain distance from terrifying realities" (p. 7). Summit (1989) stresses the power of this stance.

> This sort of unknowingness is not simply a lack of knowledge; it is an entrenched, religious ignoring. There is no modern word to recognize this unthinkable concept. The proper word, as obscure now as the concept, derives from a medieval doctrine. . . . That word translates literally from the Latin (*nescire*) as not to know. The word for deliberate, beatific ignorance is *nescience*. In our historic failure to grasp the importance of sexual abuse and our reluctance to embrace it now, we . . . are not naively innocent. We seem to be willfully ignorant, nescient. . . . The complementary derivatives of the same [word] root are *conscience, conscientious, conscious, consciousness, science* and *omniscience*. [pp. 418–419]

This is one reason why the individuals who are most seriously abused are least believed—they tell the most terrible stories. (They are also the most symptomatic and easily dismissed as less credible by those who wish to remain nescient.) Similarly, the paradigms that investigate or treat the most seriously abused survivors are most likely to be targets of persisting and extreme attacks that literally deny the existence of the trauma itself. These include the sadistic abuse of children, MPD, and the Holocaust.

Detailed consideration of the denial of the Holocaust is beyond the scope of this chapter. But denial of child sexual abuse and of the Holocaust share a great deal: in the pattern and motivations for attack, in the role of the sensationalistic media, and in the success with which detractors can recruit the gullible and prejudicially motivated (Ellen Ogintz, personal communication, August 1993). While it is patently absurd to argue that the Holocaust never occurred, these arguments are being promulgated largely by American anti-Semites and Middle European Neo-Nazis seeking to rehabilitate Nazism (Lipstadt 1993). Lest we think denial or attempts at rehabilitation so ludicrous that we can afford to dismiss them, we should remember that, when surveyed, 22 percent of Americans thought "it was possible" that the Holocaust never occurred. Lipstadt's prescient analysis was published *before* the "ethnic cleansing" we are currently witnessing in the former Yugoslavia.

Paradigmatic Denial and Controversies

There is a long history of denying child abuse, particularly child sexual abuse (Goodwin 1985b, 1989, Herman 1981, 1992, Masson 1984, Rush 1980, Summit 1983, 1988, 1989). Masson (1984) documents the chronic reinterpretation of injuries in children, to protect the psychological comfort of adults in the late nineteenth century when recognition of child abuse was suppressed. In the modern era, prior to Kempe and colleagues' work (1962) on the battered child syndrome, "it had been thought that infants who presented with bruises, bleeding around the brain, and multiple bone fractures might be suffering from a genetic syndrome" (Goodwin 1993b, p. 90). As recently as 1972, pediatricians in New York City accounted for only *eight* of 2,300 child abuse reports in that year (Goodwin 1985).

Symptoms of early trauma are ignored and denied in adults as well, squarely within the mental-health disciplines. Goodwin and colleagues (1988) studied ten consecutive members of an incest survivors' group for very symptomatic and very seriously abused women. *All* ten survivors met PTSD criteria and showed *extreme* symptomatology (e.g., flashbacks to the sexual abuse), but *none* had been diagnosed as having PTSD. All had at least one major dissociative symptom (e.g., fugues, no memory for important life events, recurrent experiences of not recognizing persons, places or objects which should have been familiar, and voluntary anaes-thesias). One patient met all criteria for multiple personality disorder. All ten had attempted suicide (nine more than once); nine had multiple somatic complaints. Although these individuals had received mental-health care for appreciable lengths of time, not one was accurately diagnosed or treated.

The psychoanalytic paradigm has served as the primary intellectual and emotional impediment to seeing or believing in incestuous abuse (De-Mause 1994, Goodwin, 1985b, 1993a, 1993b, Herman 1981, 1992, Masson 1984, Putnam 1989a, Ross 1989, Rush 1980). Believing a patient's accounts of childhood sexual abuse was viewed derisively as naïveté in the clinician. Since Freud's repudiation of the seduction theory, analysts have routinely reinterpreted patients' account of incestuous abuse as unconscious wishes. Analysts of children have neglected to ascertain whether their patient's reports were real or not. This is illustrated in DeMause's discussion (1994) of a case described by Melanie Klein (1960) in which she pointedly avoided asking a 10-year-old boy whether his reports of sucking his dog's penis and having his own penis sucked might be cover memories for real incest. The avoidance occurred despite the boy's timid suggestion that "perhaps this had happened in the past with his brother."

The refusal to see the reality of abusive trauma continues among psychoanalytic adherents to this day. Wilson (1994) writes, "Naturally Freud knew that some of his patients were sexually seduced by a family member. He soon realized however, that it was implausible for all his hysterical patients to have been sexually seduced as children" (p. 215). Why was it implausible? All these patients were "hysterical," that is, they showed the same symptom cluster and clinical presentation. Why should they not have the same precipitant to their common symptoms? But Wilson feels that regarding these accounts as screen memories removed an impasse in the development of psychoanalysis. The incommensurability of paradigms is unmistakable here.

Interestingly enough, a few women analysts, including Marie Bona-parte, Edith Jacobson, Phyllis Greenacre, and Annie Reich believed their patients' accounts of incestuous abuse (DeMause 1994). They were, in a sense, coming out of left field in that they were women, which in psychoanalysis left them out of the political and conceptual mainstream. Furthermore, personal factors influence who can see trauma. Kardiner cited his own traumatic childhood (Herman 1992) as facilitating his recognizing trauma in combat veterans. As women, these analysts also may have appreciated the reality of sexual victimization in a way which most men could not.

As a result, mental-health professionals have operated with a highly distorted conceptual framework regarding the prevalence of child sexual abuse, particularly incestuous abuse.

> Writing in the authoritative *Comprehensive Textbook of Psychiatry, (2nd Edition)*, Henderson (1975) estimated that the true prevalence of incest was 1 per 1 million population. Recalling Russell's (1986) data [prevalence rate of over 16% among women in the general population] . . ., means that the mental health professions were proceeding with prevalence figures that represented 1/160,000 of the overall population of incest victims (.00000625%) and 1/45,000 of those who suffered father-daughter incest (.0000222%). [Kluft 1990, p. 3]

Freud's incredulity despite corroborated cases modeled a stance toward disclosures of incestuous abuse that later psychoanalysts were to emulate for decades. Goodwin (1985b) writes that this was brought home to her "when a psychoanalytic colleague staunchly refused to believe that sexual abuse existed in a family where three daughters, one granddaughter, and one grandson had complained, and where medical evidence was available" (p. 6).

Denial Generated by Externals

External forces have also attacked the interpersonal violence paradigms; those victims and situations who exemplify the most severe abuse are the targets of the most vituperative attacks. The credibility of sadistic abuse accounts have been attacked and the phenomenon denied, particularly if the patient describes ritualized elements (Gardner 1991, Hicks 1991, Lotto 1994, Matzner 1991, Noll 1989, Richardson et al. 1991, Victor 1993).

Some authors have raised thoughtful issues. For instance Young (1991) suggests that patients may have developed satanic metaphors to explain forms of severe abuse actually suffered. Ganaway (1992b) complains that the media blitz has reached the point that complex MPD cases not contaminated by the expectation of finding satanic ritual abuse may soon be the exception. While both are raising good points, unfortunately they do so not to differentiate some cases from others but to argue against the existence of *any* form of ritualized sexual abuse.

This flies in the face of documented cases. For instance, a cult called the Children of God has clearly been shown to practice ritualized sexual and incestuous abuse of the children (McFarland 1994). McFarland traces the origins of this cult and its history in the United States, Europe, and South America, documents their history of criminal involvement, and cites the

1974 report by the Attorney General of New York that the cult's activities included neglect, starvation, kidnapping, imprisonment, virtual enslavement, religious prostitution, polygamy, rape and sexual abuse of children, and incest. The existence of some sexually sadistic cults has been documented, but this evidence is ignored in the rush to denial.

Sadistic abuse is often, though not invariably, ritualized. This can range from the individual ritualized behavior of the serial murderer who stalks, kidnaps, tortures, and kills in a *particular way* (Goodwin 1993a), through the familial sadistic abuser who uses certain implements, schedules, and procedures (Gelinas, under review), through extended family or affinity groups who (for profit, sex, power, or ideology) practice formal or informal ritualized abuse (Burgess et al. 1984, Goodwin 1993b). Accounts of sadistic abuse are given by a wide range of victims, including survivors of rape, child physical and sexual abuse, POW and concentration camp internment, and political torture. Accounts of sadistic abuse *with ritualized aspects* emerge primarily from *two independent groups*—children abused in daycare and patients with MPD (Goodwin 1993b, Summit 1989). For this reason, denial of ritual abuse is an important issue when considering denial of the existence of MPD.

Individuals who wish to deny the existence of ritualized sadistic abuse continue to call for physical evidence. This is not inappropriate. But, when physical evidence has been documented both historically and currently, *it does not seem to make a difference* (Goodwin 1993b). A pattern emerges in which some individuals who do not want to know either argue around the evidence or ignore its existence and continue to call for it.

An example of this historically concerns the fifteenth-century French nobleman Gilles de Rais, who was condemned by the Inquisition for the sexual murders of over 100 latency-aged boys. There is unmistakable physical evidence of ritualized sadistic abuse by Gilles de Rais, yet there have been numerous attempts to exculpate him and his activities. "The child skeletons found in his castle are glossed over, as is his detailed confession (torture . . . [was] not applied) as are the affidavits of numerous family members . . . and the confessions of his accomplices." (Goodwin 1993b, pp. 480–481).

In current cases, the same pattern of calling for physical evidence, and then ignoring or suppressing such evidence when it is available, occurs. A case in point is the Miami Country Walk case. In this case, Francisco Fuster, a 36-year-old Cuban immigrant who had previously been convicted of manslaughter and sexually abusing a 9-year-old girl in New York, and his 17-year-old Honduran wife, Ileana, were convicted of ritual sexual and physical abuse. Individuals who deny the existence of sadistic ritualized abuse present this case as a miscarriage of justice in which convictions were obtained with no corroborating evidence except for the testimony of very young children (Lotto 1994). However, there was both physical evidence and the confession of the co-defendant wife.

> Investigators found physical evidence, including photographs of unmistakable fecal fetishism showing Frank Fuster's wife and child soiled with feces. The crucifix described by the children as the instrument of Fuster's bloody demonstrations of the rape of Ileana was found under the mattress of their bed. Frank Fuster's own child described the private, utterly sadistic tortures he and Ileana endured apart from the other children in their care. . . . Ileana's dramatic turnabout was not the pivotal element for the jury. Ileana decided to testify, at the urging of her attorney and with no plea bargain with prosecutors, only after jurors were reduced to tears in response to viewing the entirety of the videotaped interviews with the children. [Summit 1994, p. 399]

The jury found Frank Fuster guilty and he was sentenced to six life sentences plus 165 years, but this case continues to be used to argue against the existence of ritual abuse.

Controversy about the existence of sadistic ritual abuse is then heightened by some journalists who, for whatever reasons, take distorted but adamant positions. In the Miami Country Walk case, Summit (1994) points out that in attempting to deny the existence of ritualized abuse itself, some investigative reporters appear to be engaged in a "mission to debunk 'satanic panic' [and] have proclaimed Fuster innocent" (p. 400). Another investigative reporter, who lived in the Country Walk community and was a participant/observer in the case, saw the situation very differently and wrote *Unspeakable Acts* (Hollingsworth 1986). The Miami Country Walk case had admissible physical evidence, the confession of the co-defendant, and the videotaped testimony of victims. It even had photographs. But a nescient stance preserves emotional equilibrium and controversy apparently sells newspapers.

Reasonable adults can be expected to have doubts about accounts of ritualized sadistic abuse, but once detailed information and physical evidence are available, the existence of such abuse is demonstrated. It may be distasteful or anxiety-provoking, but its existence as a phenomenon has been established. However, the availability of physical evidence in the Miami Country Walk case appears to have made no difference to a minority of attackers who continue to reject the existence of ritual abuse. Perhaps this should be the primary criterion for the identification of a powerful Kuhnian external—*the evidence makes no difference*.

The most infamous case involving allegations of ritual abuse, to date, is the McMartin preschool case. Individuals who deny the existence of ritual abuse present this case as having no physical evidence. However, there was a great deal of physical evidence. This included medical evidence. The forensic medical examiners of the original thirteen children who were scheduled to testify reported "scars, tears, enlarged body openings or other evidence indicating blunt force trauma consistent with repeated sodomy and rape" (October 1988 *Los Angeles Times*, quoted in Rockwell 1994, p. 460). One of the children bled from the anus; some had contracted venereal disease (Rockwell 1994).

The children described tunnels and a secret room under the floor of the preschool, one leading to an outside exit under a rabbit hutch and another to a neighboring building. They described being loaded into vehicles in the garage of that building for transport to other locations where they were also abused. A rift developed between the parents and prosecutors. The latter faced a dilemma—the more improbable the charges sounded, the more difficult to get a conviction. They decided not to pursue the ritual elements of the case and settle for sexual molestation. The parents, for a number of reasons, wanted to know if these tunnels existed.

After 33 months of trial, the jury found for the defense that (as Summit [1994] mordantly describes) "a demonstrably crazy woman had initiated a satanic witch hunt which was swept into absurd illusion through leading questions from therapists and hysterical reinforcement by parents eager to put themselves in the limelight of the case of the century" (1994, p. 403). A few parents protested the failure of the prosecution and were then scapegoated by a small group of investigative journalists.

> So now the McMartin parents can triumphantly torture poor Ray Buckey again, abetted by the cowards and opportunists in the justice system. . . . A few well-publicized sentences of imprisonment of parents (along with "therapists" and social workers, it goes without saying) and we would see a speedy end to these disgusting miscarriages of justice. [Quoted in Summit 1994, pp. 403–404]

However, in 1990, with permission from the new owner of the preschool site, some parents commissioned an independent archeological study to pursue the children's reports of tunnels. Summit (1994) notes that the results of this definitive excavation are detailed in the 185-page *Report of the Archaeological Excavation of the McMartin Preschool Site* by E. Gary Stickel, Ph.D., the UCLA archeologist commissioned to do the excavation. Following detailed descriptions from one of the children, they found tunnels, a secret underground room, various exits, and unequivocal evidence of concealment and deception. They found that the dirt that filled the tunnels was different in color, texture, and compaction from the surrounding soil, and was different itself along different sections of the tunnel. One tunnel contained the features described by the 12-year-old girl—a metal waste pipe, protruding roots, a passage under concrete foundation worn smooth in contrast to the rest of the concrete, a "room-like potential space" 6 feet 8 inches high and at least 9 feet in diameter now filled with contrasting earth fill "bearing remnants of timber, plywood and tar paper which appeared to have shored up the ceiling" (Summit 1994, p. 407). Beneath the floor of the exit a plastic lunch bag was found bearing its distribution date: "Disney Class 82/83." Nothing in this location should have postdated September 1966, when the foundation was poured.

> The most conspicuous and naturally inexplicable items were found placed exactly under the concrete arch between the two classrooms. These were four large containers, two enameled iron pots, a crockery jar, and a cast iron cauldron, arranged together in an upright position, resting not where the floor would have been but halfway up to the ceiling. There was no theoretical explanation for such location except that they were placed deliberately within a pre-existing, half-filled trench or tunnel. If all the artifacts represented random scatter of trash on an earlier dump site, as some skeptics have asserted, there is no justification for their exclusive delineation within a discrete pattern of tunnels or trenches. And if such conspicuous items as the four large containers had been littered on a dump site, they would not have survived clustered, upright and unbroken through the subsequent grading and leveling of the preschool site. [Summit 1994, p.408]

Obviously, these containers were planted to give the appearance that the surrounding soil was old and undisturbed. There can be no doubt, upon reading this evidence, that the tunnels the children had been describing did exist, which lends further credence to the ritualized aspects of their abuse.

The power of nescience is formidable, however. *People* magazine sent a reporter to interview Dr. Stickel, the project archeologist. The journalist reported to headquarters the remarkable misunderstanding that the project found nothing. Dr. Stickel was dumbfounded: " 'I told her the children said there were tunnels and we found tunnels. It was as simple as that' " (Summit 1994, p. 410). Apparently it was not that simple, because the story about the physical evidence of the tunnels at the McMartin preschool never reached print. The existence of these tunnels does not in itself prove that abuse took place but it adds significant credibility to what seemed to be fantastic or outlandish accounts. However, like the bodies of murdered children examined and reported by Tardieu and his colleagues in France, the existence of this concrete physical evidence has been rendered invisible by paradigmatic and external forces. In the media, a small number of extreme detractors can generate a great deal of controversy and attract a lot of attention, while the more moderate majority do not enter the fray or find that their material is not printed. The result is that the more sensationalistic elements in the media begin to define the parameters of the debate.

Finally, *formalized* ritual elements have been found in sadistic abuse for centuries but their existence continues to be denied by professionals and society alike. The Children of God cult practiced sexual abuse with "religious" trappings. In 1987, in Oude Pekela, a village in the Netherlands, a small boy was taken to his family physician with anal bleeding. About half the children aged 4–11 in that physician practice panel made clear complaints about having been sexually abused by adults in costumes. This included urinating and defecating on them, threatening them, and many other sadistic behaviors. All children making abuse complaints had behavioral symptoms and about 80 percent had physical or physiological disturbances. *"Yet the problem was judged by law enforcement and public opinion to have been mass hysteria"* (Goodwin 1994, p. 486, my emphasis). The ritual elements were clear here too, and denied.

Attacks on the Victim

Attacking the credibility of the victim is a time-honored tactic of defense attorneys in rape cases. The present author treated a woman who was the target of attempted rape by a burglar. The assailant was apprehended and tried; *because* there was so much evidence that he was the assailant, his attorney tried to attack the character of the victim. Their defense was scuttled, however, when the assistant district attorney revealed that the victim was a woman religious (i.e., a sister or nun) and a "virgin intacta." It was a rare but rather wonderful moment in court. However, victims of interpersonal violence rarely have such an impeccable defense against character assassination.

Credibility of the victim is especially at issue in child sexual abuse cases. It is in these cases that we see particularly clearly the sequence described by Herman (1992): "it never happened; the victim lies; the victim exaggerates; the victim brought it upon herself; and in any case it is time to move on and forget the past" (p. 8).

Attacking the credibility of the victim in child sexual abuse cases occurred historically and continues as a form of rejection.

A century ago, Freud's contemporary, Iwan Bloch wrote children's declarations before the law are, for the truly experienced knower of children, downright *null* and *hollow*, absolutely worthless and without significance; all the more insignificant and all the more hollow the more often the child repeats the declaration and the more determined he is to stick to his statements. [Masson 1984, p. 220]

Bloch also blamed children for their own sexual abuse. "Frequently there is no question of the 'seduction' of children, but rather the instigation derives in the first place from the children themselves." (Bloch 1909, quoted in Masson 1984, p. 220)

Any behavior of the child during the postdiscovery or disclosure phase can and has been interpreted as evidence of lying. Fortunately, Summit (1983) has systematized children's characteristic postdiscovery behavior in order to assist clinicians and the courts in recognizing this profile and avoiding misinterpretation. However, even after convictions of sexual abuse, 20 to 50 percent of parents persist in alleging that the child lied (Defrances 1969).

False Memory Syndrome

The most spectacular example of attack on the victims is what is called the "False Memory Syndrome." The False Memory Syndrome Foundation was established by Peter Freyd and his wife Pamela immediately after Peter was confronted by his grown daughter, Jennifer, and accused of incestuous abuse (Fried 1994). Although Jennifer, the daughter, had not made her accusations public and had no plans to do so, both parents publicly attacked her credibility—as well as her competence, memory, mental health status, and her marriage (Fried 1994). The parents also contacted the university department in which the daughter is a faculty member, and attacked her *professional* credibility in an attempt to derail upcoming decisions about her tenure (Fried 1994). The FMSF actively enlists other accused parents and coaches them in ways to attack their children's credibility.

Their most striking innovations include the fabrication of a hypothetical disorder—the "false memory syndrome"—and their intentional manipulation of a willing press. The purported FMS syndrome has no definition, no criteria for inclusion, and is not recognized by cognitive psychologists. As Bloom (1994) points out, "The use of the medical term 'syndrome' is interesting since it lends credibility to something that has not yet been shown to exist, for which there have been no clinical trials, no scientifically controlled comparison groups, no research to document or quantify the alleged phenomenon" (p. 470).

The journalist Stephen Fried (1994) notes that, although most of the accusations had not led to litigation,

membership and media interest in the FMSF grew steadily until July, when the *New York Times* did a story called CHILDHOOD TRAUMA: MEMORY OR

INVENTION?, which read almost as if it had been packaged by Pam Freyd. Every expert quoted about "false" memories was on the FMSF board—except one, who was immediately invited to join. Pam was identified in the article as a psychologist, which, while incorrect, immediately established her as an expert in the field. . . . Suddenly, the phones at the FMSF office started ringing off the hook. [p. 155]

The Freyd family has been called "the most influentially dysfunctional family in America" (Fried 1994), but with the exception of Stephen Fried's detailed article on them, the media has uncritically cited their positions and stirred up the controversy around credibility of incestuous abuse accounts.

One of the leading advocates and beneficiaries of this controversy is a cognitive psychologist, Dr. Elizabeth Loftus, an active member of the FMS Foundation's Board of Directors. She has undeniably been able to create false memories in the minds of college volunteers (Loftus 1993) by having each volunteer's family tell a detailed but fictitious story of how the volunteer was lost in a shopping mall as a very young child. In most cases, the volunteers then said they "remembered" the event. Loftus then generalized this finding to attack the concept of "repressed" memories, the credibility of patients, *and* the technique of therapists. Her work ignores several crucial elements, however. Neither Loftus nor anyone else has re-created the traumatic situations that characterize patient's experiences. It is scientifically invalid to generalize from research findings on innocuous, artificial events to traumatizing events. A growing body of research data, based on both human and animal studies, indicates that the mechanism of memory that functions during states of terror and hyperarousal is very different from that during normal memory storage and retrieval. Narrative memory (everyday, innocuous experiences) appears to be processed in the hippocampus whereas traumatic memory (from overwhelming experiences) is processed in the amygdala (van der Kolk 1993b).

Attack the Mother

A variant of attacking the victim is to attack the mother. For example, the credibility and character of Judy Johnson, the mother who first drew attention to the McMartin preschool, has been repeatedly attacked, and often misrepresented. Cockburn's *Wall Street Journal* op-ed piece (1990) described the McMartin case as one in which "the allegations . . . had been extorted from her two-year-old by a mother—now dead—with a history of mental illness" (Summit 1994, p. 413). Cockburn neglects to mention that Johnson's mental-health history began only *after* the allegations (Summit 1994). Lotto (1994) emphasizes Johnson's alcoholism and hospitalization (although he mentions that these occurred after her complaints about the preschool). Summit (1994) challenges the tactic of attacking this mother without overlooking the complications of her situation or the circumstances of this case.

> If an author is to be equally empathic with all the players, one might consider that McMartin whistle blower Judy Johnson's psychotic break and alcoholic toxicity were precipitated by, rather than precipitants of, her desperate concern that she and her not-quite three-year-old son were victims of unfathomable treachery. [Summit] met Ms. Johnson in February, 1984. . . . Judy Johnson was quite sane and emotionally contained even as she described the improbable complaints of her child. [p. 398]

Summit describes Johnson as alienated from her husband and increasingly reclusive in a small house with her two children, one sexually abused in his preschool and the other dying of a brain malignancy. Her hyperprotective stance toward her two children warranted protective service and mental-health intervention and Johnson was hospitalized briefly. He regards her as the embodiment of the individual who is suspicious enough to uncover a "perfectly hidden evil" (p. 399) and then blamed for the chaos that follows.

In many multivictim cases, there is a "pattern of parental group denial before an eccentric outsider triggers a threshold of recognition" (Summit 1994, p. 411). Concerned parents are reassured by "reasonable explanations" for possible indicators of abuse.

> Conventional, well-socialized parents (and professionals) receive . . . reassurances with relief, repeating and reinforcing them among one another. . . . It remains for the odd one, the unsocialized outsider, to pursue the nagging suspicion that the authorities could be wrong. . . . Such a person is easily stigmatized as eccentric and unreliable, if not crazy. [Summit 1994, p. 412]

Johnson was an irritant in the Manhattan Beach community, battling with the local school board to acquire home care for her ailing son. She subscribed to holistic ideas about diet and health, and this is what prompted her to go out of town for university evaluation of her sexual abuse fears after local doctors had dismissed them. Johnson is not a simple figure, but she deserved a balanced presentation, not attack and dismissal as the Chicken Little responsible for a witch hunt. But the tradition of attacking the victim, or the mother, in child sexual abuse cases is an enduring one.

Attacks on the Therapists

The third major type of attack are attacks on the therapists who treat trauma survivors. This is true of all the component paradigms. Thus, Henry Kempe was severely criticized by many of his colleagues for provoking "hysteria" with his "speculation" about battered children (Ruth Kempe, personal communication to Roland Summit, in Summit 1989). Similarly, psychoanalysts, led by Freud and Jones, persecuted Sandor Ferenczi when he published his findings regarding incestuous abuse (Masson 1984, Summit 1989).

These attacks are directed particularly toward clinicians who treat child sexual abuse. Some of the detractors write that therapists are merely naïve, and that reports of sadistic or ritual child abuse are urban myths or screen memories which the therapist is, essentially, too dumb to recognize. Some of these detractors serve the valuable function of reminding clinicians to evaluate patient's accounts carefully, but their opinions are destructive when they distort the evidence, ignore patient's symptomatology, and deny the very existence of sadistic or ritualized abused. For example, Lotto (1994) presents the Ingraham case in Olympia, Washington as follows:

> Paul Ingraham . . . was sentenced to 20 years in prison for sexually abusing his two daughters, in large part based on his own confession. This confession followed months of questioning by police interrogators, as well as sessions with several therapists and a pastor who knew of and believed in the literal truth of the increasingly fantastic allegations that kept coming from the two daughters in the family. [p. 375]

Clearly, the import is that undue influence and protracted interrogation led to a false confession and subsequent miscarriage of justice. This is a distortion of some important elements of the case. Paul Ingraham, a former chief civil deputy for the sheriff's office,

> *within minutes* of his advisement confessed to ritual abuse occurring over many years . . . which allegedly involved two other law enforcement officers. Ingraham has been sentenced, but charges against the other two were dismissed because the victims were too traumatized to appear in court. . . . In September, 1992 the Washington State Supreme Court rejected Ingraham's motion to withdraw his guilty plea. [Rockwell 1994, p. 454; my emphasis]

Some of the allegations in this case were too fantastic or contaminated for anyone to believe. But, it is very odd that a grown man would enter trance states so readily and admit guilt to long strings of accusations. There has been no reasonable explanation for this behavior. He even admitted to a series of events that did not exist.

Richard Ofshe, a social psychologist, has attacked therapists, accusing them of "implanting" false memories of abuse. He gained access to Mr. Ingraham and performed an experiment. Ofshe suggested a fabricated situation in which Ingraham was encouraging his son and daughter to have sex with each other. "After some time in which Paul engaged in his usual process of meditating on the suggested events while in a trance state he did in fact 'recover' a series of detailed and plausible sounding 'memories' which conformed to the suggested scenario" (Lotto 1994, p. 378). Ofshe's experiment is useful in its demonstration that an extremely dissociated and suggestible man could be induced to conjure up a memory to a nonexistent event. It is quite possible that inexperienced and unskilled therapists can do this inadvertently with patients upon occasion. However, Ingraham's propensity to dissociate so thoroughly raises the question of whether he is a survivor of some type of trauma. Also, his denial of many of his accounts attests to the temporary quality of confabulated memories. His case also highlights a point rarely discussed—the patient bears some responsibility for his/her own memories and "productions" whether in therapy, everyday life, or criminal proceedings.

The reminder to all therapists regarding suggestibility is useful. But the uses to which the Ingraham case and Ofshe's experiment have been put are destructive. The case is inaccurately used to argue that Ingraham was wrongly convicted, that *none* of the accusations were true, and that he was induced under long careful coaching to confess. Ofshe's experiment is used to argue that accounts of ritual abuse are implanted by therapists.

Calof's (1993) examination of the subject is far more helpful. He proposes a clinical stance in which the therapist tries always to stay half a step behind patients as they wrestle with the conflict between believing and not believing their memories. The clinician's job is not to advocate for any version of reality but to provide a forum where they can examine all sides of their conflicts and experience.

The most concerted attacks on therapists come from the False Memory Syndrome Foundation. They deny the reality of repressed memory, deny reports of sadistic and ritual abuse, and charge that therapists—through a variety of methods (suggestion, hypnosis, drugs)—are implanting pseudo-memories of abuse in thousands of unwitting patients' heads (Bloom 1994). Lawsuits against therapists are actively encouraged (Bloom 1994), as are complaints to Boards of Registration, not for breaches of professional conduct, but for implanting memories of childhood sexual abuse. The false memory controversy, and the lawsuits against individual therapists, constitutes a backlash against the private realization and therapy and the public discourse about childhood sexual abuse. It is also a backlash against some of the excesses of the self-help movement, and undertrained and careless therapists.

There are, however, no documented, controlled studies that support any of the FMSF claims. Scientific terminology is used to describe anecdotal events, and studies done on trivial events and normal people are generalized to traumatic situations. Most members of the FMSF Board have little clinical experience in trauma or the dissociative disorders. Bloom (1994) has written, "Nor is there any explanation for how perfectly normal, supposedly healthy human beings could be influenced, sometimes within a session or two, by a perfect stranger, to suddenly and spuriously believe that someone in their family had molested them as a child" (p. 472). Jennifer Freyd, the woman whose parents founded the FMSF, experienced "waking 'visions' of rape scenes and male genitalia" (Fried 1994, p. 86) at home after her *second* therapy session. It is very unrealistic to think that any therapist could implant memories of any kind that quickly, and the notion is demeaning to both therapist and patient. DeMause (1994) notes that "therapists are a timid group at best, and the notion that they suddenly began implanting false memories in tens of thousands of their clients for no apparent reason strained credulity. Certainly, no one has presented a shred of evidence for massive 'false memory' implantations" (p. 505). Nor have those accusing therapists of implanting memories addressed the obvious question of why thousands of psychotherapists across the country would simultaneously and similarly begin implanting just such material in patient's heads. Or how, technically, they could accomplish this. If clinicians are motivated by greed, why are they all manufacturing ideas specifically about child sexual abuse; why not include other topics to purportedly implant in the memories of their patients. Perhaps a more realistic explanation relates to Diana Russell's (1986) data which documents a 16 percent prevalence rate of incestuous abuse among women in this country. Patients are telling their therapists about their childhoods, and the therapists are believing them.

Clinicians are beginning to defend themselves from these attacks in a number of ways. One form of defense is to examine the motivations of the attackers, particularly those individuals within the FMSF, since the Foundation has been so central to these attacks. Rockwell (1994) writes that "the 'False Memory Syndrome' is a sham invented by pedophiles and sexual abusers for the media" (p. 450). Rockwell documents his assertion by drawing our attention to Ralph Underwager, a Lutheran minister and psychologist, and his wife Hollida Wakefield, prominent members of the FMSF Advisory Board for several years. Underwager routinely testifies as an expert witness against children in sexual abuse cases.

> In an interview with Underwager and Wakefield which appears in the Winter 1993 issue of *Paedika*, a pedophile journal published in Holland, they were supportive of pedophilia. They also blamed the trauma of interrogating child abuse victims as being the cause of the children's symptoms and suggested that therapists are implanting memories of ritual abuse in children's minds. [pp. 450–451]

Rockwell describes Peter and Pamela Freyd, founders of the FMSF, as initiating a massive public relations effort in which they present themselves as a falsely accused couple.

He notes that Shirley and Paul Eberle, authors of the *Pity the Little Children: The Politics of Child Abuse* and *The Abuse of Innocence: The McMartin Preschool Trial*, also assert that accounts of child sexual abuse are implanted by therapists. *Abuse of Innocence* was taken quite seriously by reviewers and widely quoted as authoritative. It claims that the over 100 McMartin children who reported they had been ritually abused were all "brain-washed," the mothers were "hysterical," and that it was meaningless that physicians documented that three-quarters of the children bore physical evidence corroborating their stories. None of the media who repeated the Eberles' assertions examined the authors. If they had, they would have discovered that the Eberles have a long and public history as commercial child pornographers and every reason to attempt to discredit the credibility of victims, mothers, and therapists. "In the 1970's they were publishers of an underground child pornography journal in Los Angeles called *Finger*, which contained nude photographs of them and their children" (Rockwell 1994, p. 451). DeMause (1994) notes that the Eberles had been called the most prolific publishers of child pornography in the United States. "Their kiddie porn material that I have seen and the articles they have published such as 'I was a sexpot at five' and 'Little Lolitas' included illustrations of children involved in sodomy and oral copulation and featured porno-graphic photos of the Eberles" (p. 506).

Those individuals and groups or foundations who attack the credibility of survivors of child sexual abuse and therapists who treat such survivors, are obviously comprised of different types of people with various motiva-tions. That these include advocates of pedophilia and child pornographers is demonstrable, and their motivations for discrediting therapists obvious. Similarly, many others have chosen aggressively to attack their children for private confrontations of childhood sexual abuse and have enlisted the media in their accusations against child and therapist. Before any other individuals jump on the bandwagon attacking therapists, they might re-examine the company they would be keeping. Some authors have raised good points about suggestibility, narrative memory, the role of hypnosis, and therapist influence. Clarification of these important issues is best done carefully and empirically, by those trained in the relevant field. The gullible and intellectually uncritical media has no constructive role to play, despite their rather self-important protestations. They are functioning as a Kuhnian external that is impeding the growth of knowledge. Perhaps when they are more careful, and more fair, they will have firmer ground to stand on.

THE MPD CONTROVERSIES

The controversies surrounding MPD are distinguished from those around the other trauma paradigms only by their heat and vituperativeness. In the present analysis, this is predictable since the MPD paradigm treats individuals who have been the most seriously abused.

Attacks on the MPD paradigm tend to be directed toward the existence of MPD itself and the clinicians who treat and research MPD. The clinicians are usually accused of naïveté and/or iatrogenically creating MPD and here especially, they have become the target of numerous FMS Foundation-backed civil lawsuits. Attacks on the victims do not enter into controversy so clearly in MPD as in other interpersonal violence paradigms, so they will be reviewed only briefly.

Other authors have recognized that a Kuhnian paradigm clash is at the root of the MPD controversies (Kluft 1993, Ross 1994a). Loewenstein (1993) also noted the utility of Kuhn's framework for our ability to see patients with MPD.

> Many of us believe that the apparent "explosion" in the diagnosis of MPD and dissociative disorders is really a result of the recognition of patients who have always been with us but simply were not "seen" before there was a paradigm to allow us to do so. . . . [Kuhn] notes that "skeptics" of his view "might remember that color blindness was nowhere noticed until John Dalton's description of it in 1794." [p. 192]

MPD as a Trauma-Based Disorder

MPD is etiologically linked with severe early childhood trauma, almost invariably in the form of severe abuse. Some reports place the prevalence of childhood abuse among MPD patients to be approximately 90 percent (Coons and Milstein 1986, Frischholz 1985). The National Institute of Mental Health study of 100 MPD cases reported a 97 percent prevalence rate of significant childhood trauma (Putnam et al. 1983, 1986). Putnam (1989a) notes, "Incestuous abuse was the most commonly reported trauma (68 percent) but other forms of sexual abuse, physical abuse, and a variety of forms of emotional abuse were reported" (p. 47). Most of these MPD patients described three or more *different* types of trauma during childhood. When he compared the accounts of MPD patients with other sexual abuse survivors, Putnam (1989a) was struck by the quality of extreme sadism reported.

> Bondage situations; the insertion of a variety of instruments into vagina, mouth, and anus; and various forms of physical and sexual torture are common reports. Many multiples have told me of being sexually abused by groups of people, of being forced into prostitution by family members, or of being offered as a sexual enticement to their mother's boyfriends. [p. 49]

Physical abuse ranged from beatings to bizarre forms of torture, assault with implements, enforced confinements and/or burials, and other ritualized abuse. Enforced confinements included: "tying the child up; locking the child in closets, cellars, or trunks; stuffing the child in boxes or bags; or even burying the child alive" (Putnam 1989a, p. 49). It was Putnam's impression that the physical abuse experienced by multiple personality patients also "was far more sadistic and bizarre than that suffered by most victims of child abuse" (p. 49). Others have demonstrated or described the links between MPD and early multimodal abuses as well (Bliss 1980, Boor 1982, Braun 1985, 1990, Braun and Sachs 1985, Coons 1980, Coons and Milstein 1986, Frischholz 1985, Greaves 1980, Kluft 1984, 1985, 1992, Putnam 1984, 1989a, Putnam et al. 1986, Saltman and Solomon 1982, Spiegel 1984, Stern 1984, Wilbur 1984, 1985).

A few cases of MPD are caused by childhood trauma that is not abuse based, particularly from war zones (Putnam 1989a). In every case, the child had seen the massacre of several family members because of military or terrorist actions. "One adolescent multiple, for example, reported seeing her parents blown to bits in a minefield and trying to piece their bodies back together. This same child later witnessed her grandfather being shot to death and a sibling being beheaded" (Putnam 1989a, p. 50). In rare instances, sustained pain, repeated surgeries, and isolation during early childhood or near-death experiences have been associated with the development of MPD. But overwhelmingly, the data demonstrate that individuals with MPD grew up in highly disturbed and violent homes (Putnam 1989a).

The severe and sustained trauma that the child experiences during early to middle childhood promotes the development of MPD through several interconnected mechanisms. The first is a disruption of the normal developmental tasks of consolidation of the self across behavioral states and the acquisition of control over modulation of stimulation and internal states (Putnam 1989a). The recurring trauma instead creates a situation in which it is adaptive for the child to heighten the separation between behavioral states, to compartmentalize overwhelming affects and memories generated by the trauma; children in such circumstances may use their enhanced dissociative capacity to escape from the trauma by the only means at their disposal, entering into dissociative states (Putnam 1989a). The dissociative states are adaptive in the face of unremitting abuse or what Kluft has called "vicious torment" (personal communication 1992) because they provide: escape from the constraints of reality, containment of traumatic memories and affects outside of normal conscious awareness, alteration or detachment of sense of self (so that the trauma is happening to someone else or to a depersonalized self), and finally analgesia (Putnam 1989a).

Putnam (1989a) noted that few attempts at independent verification of accounts have been made. When these attempts are undertaken, however, MPD patients' accounts have been verified (Kluft 1986 personal communication to Putnam, Bliss personal communication to Putnam 1984, cited in Putnam 1989a).

The MPD paradigm is subject to the same pattern of interest and suppression shown by other trauma paradigms. Both Putnam (1989a) and Ross (1989) have documented interest in MPD during the latter half of the nineteenth century, then decline in interest after the turn of the century. This was prompted by changes in the zeitgeist, introduction of the term schizophrenia (see especially Rosenbaum 1980), and the discrediting of leading adherents in the MPD paradigm. Beginning in the 1970s however, forgotten knowledge from Janet and Morton Prince was rediscovered, laboratory investigations began, and Cornelia Wilbur and her colleagues at the University of Kentucky began studying MPD. She participated in the lay publication of *Sybil* because scholarly journals rejected her MPD papers (Greaves 1993, Kluft 1992); Wilbur was then criticized by her peers for not publishing in the professional forum! In 1980, MPD was codified in *DSM-III*.

Attacks on the Victim

Public challenges to the credibility of MPD patients have been relatively muted, except in criminal cases where individuals with MPD are portrayed as malingering. But forensic cases of *all types* must take malingering into account, so this concern is neither unwarranted nor unique to MPD. The muted nature of the public attacks appears to be related to confusion so deep that even the sensationalizing media cannot find a foothold from which to launch itself. They appear to hold the symptoms of MPD in some awe. The media provides accounts of MPD symptoms, but they have not tended toward concerted attack.

Another reason for the relatively muted public attack is that the press has not sufficiently realized the etiologic link between MPD and early sadistic abuse. They are still at the descriptive phase of reporting MPD symptoms. When the press realizes the link between MPD and early abuse, they will very probably participate in the sort of attacks they already direct toward individuals describing sadistic and ritualized abuse. However, the mental-health professions are attacking the credibility of MPD patients. Goodwin (1985b) notes that "most present-day psychiatrists were confidently taught . . . that multiple personality did not occur, but might be mentioned at times by female patients who were malingering or attention-getting" (p. 2). (Lest we single out psychiatrists, the present author notes that MPD patients were not brought up at all during her training in clinical psychology. Other professions are probably similar.) MPD patients are likely to be ignored, derided, or in some way treated negatively in the mental-health systems. They are regarded as attention-seeking (Merskey 1992) and suffering from screen memories and promulgating urban myths (Ganaway 1992); MPD patients' accounts of ritual abuse are put down to mutual deception between patient and therapist, "wherein the therapist has either a conscious or unconscious investment in finding the cult memories" (Ganaway 1992, p. 121). Here, we see the transition that is so quickly made in the MPD controversies, from looking at the patients and their symptoms to accusing the therapist of naïveté or iatrogenesis.

Denial of the Existence of MPD and the Issue of Iatrogenesis

Despite interest and clinical investigation of MPD for more than a century (Ellenberger 1970), some individuals continue to argue that it does not exist. Putnam notes that two thorough review articles (Sutcliffe and Jones 1962, Taylor and Martin 1944) sought to establish criteria and determine whether or not MPD was a real entity. Although both concluded that MPD was a real clinical entity that could not be discounted as fad or fraud, they set a stance of defensive skepticism that later authors were forced to adopt for purposes of credibility. Many of the articles on MPD over the next two decades focused on proving that MPD existed rather than on contributing new clinical knowledge. The field is only now beginning to extricate itself from the consequences of this defensive position and to rise above the "frequent and often ignorant challenges to prove that MPD exists" (Putnam 1989a, p. 32) It is curious that MPD, one of the oldest psychiatric disorders on record, is still continually called upon to prove its existence while other newly defined disorders are routinely accepted. Such broadside calls for proof of the existence of MPD is an example of nescience in both the professions and society. Professional nescience contributes to the fact that it takes mental-health professionals an average of 6.8 years to diagnose MPD patients once the patient has become involved with the mental-health system (Bliss and Jeppsen. 1985, Putnam et al. 1986, Ross et al. 1989).

Putnam's points are well taken. A very recent Harvard Mental Health Letter is emblazoned "Does multiple personality disorder really exist?" Among the biomedical detractors, we again see the attempts to depsychologize the results of trauma. Early in the century, the brain was felt to be at fault; later "head injury, marked intoxication, extreme fatigue, lowered general energy, unbalanced urges, severe conflicts, and excessive learnings and forgettings" were held responsible (Taylor and Martin 1944, quoted in Ross 1989, p. 41). Trauma is notably absent, except for physical head injury.

Sometimes the history of trauma is denied altogether. Mary Reynolds, the first documented American case, was described by her medical biographer Weir Mitchell as having had a childhood "marked by no extraordinary incidents" (Goodwin and Fine 1993, p. 368). In fact, her family was religiously persecuted and the focus of two sets of religious riots in Birmingham, England. During these riots, their home was ransacked and their church burned, following which they fled to North America. Eight younger siblings were born during Mary's first sixteen years, one of whom died between the first and second riots. Her older sister died of smallpox; she had measles encephalitis at age 5 and witnessed at age 7 a cholera epidemic that killed her father and almost killed her mother and sister. She worried about rumors of war between her adopted and native countries and in fact the War of 1812 broke out (summarized from Goodwin and Fine 1993). Even for the times, this is an unusual number of childhood traumas, yet they were ignored or denied in the explanation of her MPD.

Paradigmatic denial of the existence of MPD is particularly acute in the psychoanalytic paradigm. Freud's repudiation of the seduction theory directly contributed to the discrediting of MPD (Ross 1989). Following repudiation, Freud was compelled to erect an elaborate theoretical explanation for symptoms, and for many decades MPD patients were not seen as suffering the adult consequences of childhood trauma. In fact, both Ross (1989) and Loewenstein (1993) make persuasive arguments based on symptoms, Breuer's clinical notes, and family of origin information, that Anna O./Bertha Pappenheim is most appropriately diagnosed as MPD. But, she was viewed through psychoanalytic filters, and the MPD diagnosis was avoided.

The combined medical and psychoanalytic paradigms made it impossible for clinicians working with MPD to publish in mainstream journals, instead publishing in obscure journals or the lay press (Greaves 1993). Practices withered, referrals slowed dramatically, and colleagues criticized clinicians making the MPD diagnosis (Greaves 1993).

Psychoanalytic clinicians continue to use highly convoluted formulations to explain symptoms while denying MPD. Thus, Merskey (1992) reviewed classic MPD cases to deny the existence of MPD, but he distorts other authors' positions. For example, Merskey cites Putnam's patient profile for MPD and then describes Putnam's approach thus.

> Some patients declare their diagnosis. Otherwise, says Putnam (1989, p. 90), the therapist who wishes to "elicit alter personalities" should ask gentle questions about whether the patient has ever felt like more than one person, searching for another part, and ultimately asking "Do you ever feel as if you are not alone, as if there is someone else or some other part watching you?" In the event of a response the therapist looks for "any . . . attribute, function or description to use as a label to elicit this other part directly" This is a very clear and honest statement, but with such an approach there is a likelihood that the therapist will produce the phenomenon. [p. 327]

However, Putnam (1989a) actually uses this sequence as a final assessment tool, and *only after* a number of far more general and less leading evaluation procedures including: mental status examination including time loss, depersonalization and/or derealization and Schneiderian first-rank symptoms, the use of sequential tasks and observations, extended interviews, psychological testing, and a physical examination. The section Merskey quotes from is specifically titled "Meeting the Alter Personalities," and it occurs only if all the other parts of an evaluation lead the clinician to believe the patient has MPD. Merskey has presented a distorted view of the evaluation procedure Putnam has advocated in order to suggest he is iatrogenically producing MPD.

Merskey proposes that "MPD is created" by therapists in four ways: misinterpretation of organic or bipolar illness; the conscious development of fantasies as a solution to emotional problems; development of hysterical amnesia, followed by retraining; creation by implicit demand under hypnosis or repeated interviews. Here we have the familiar physiological hypothesis, attack on patient credibility, and two different attacks on the therapists. Also, Merskey does not carefully use the cases in an integrated way to prove particular points. Instead, a large number of cases are excerpted, illustrations are taken out of context, and the resulting enterprise to deny the existence of MPD is a strained jumble.

The current rejection of the MPD diagnosis by accusing the therapist of iatrogenesis collapses two forms of attack into one. For instance, McHugh (1993) has written, that MPD is created by therapists and it is often based on the crudest form of suggestion. The iatrogenic rejection could hardly be stated more baldly. In Kuhnian terms, Dr. McHugh's position as the Director of the Department of Psychiatry at Johns Hopkins would not be irrelevant; instead, he would be regarded as an established figure in an older, incommensurable paradigm, who was unwilling or unable to see the new paradigm.

Professional skepticism about MPD continues (Aldridge-Morris 1989, Fahey 1988). Dell and his colleagues (1988, and under review) have documented a significant *decrease* in overall professional skepticism about MPD during the past five years, but the presence of an active minority of skeptics whose actions are described by other clinicians in "worst incident" accounts. (Clinicians working with dissociative disorder patients were asked about all, and mild to worst, incidents regarding professional skepticism and MPD that they had experienced.) Dell and colleagues found that when asked to review worst skeptical incidents (e.g., treating the patient with sarcasm or contempt, telling the patient they were faking or attention seeking, professional behaviors that adversely affected treatment), clinicians identified psychiatrists in this role 189 times, psychologists 78, social workers 63, and "others" 29 times (p < .001). In Kuhnian terms, the most established, most powerful segment of the mental health group is the most invested in the old paradigm, and thus the most resistant to MPD. Dell and colleagues comment that the behavior of the majority of these skeptics would appear to cross the boundaries from counter-transference into unethical professional behavior. Less expected is the fact that profession does not seem to *protect* MPD adherents; that is, psychiatrists who work with dissociative disorder patients are just as likely to have experienced the professional skepticism of other mental-health professionals as were psychologists, social workers, and individuals in the "others" category. Only for MPD do some clinicians feel free not to believe in a *DSM-III, DSM-III-R,* and *DSM-IV* diagnosis. They are not arguing with some of the criteria, the link with trauma, or its associated features. They simply allow themselves to not believe. These "extreme skeptics" are an example of Summit's nescience.

Two subgroups that deny the existence of MPD are more careful and deserve more attention. One group writes that MPD is an artifact of hypnosis. Martin Orne probably exemplifies this group (Orne et al. 1984). Orne's involvement in forensic work has had a significant influence on his thinking about MPD. He has had a long-standing concern about the potential for hypnosis to influence forensic cases, and is preoccupied with the idea that a diagnosis of MPD results in the patient not being held accountable for his or her behavior (Ross 1992). In forensic cases, his points are well taken. But malingering is a differential diagnosis in all forensic situations. Orne has generalized beyond the forensic into the purely clinical and taken the position that MPD is rare, and that most cases diagnosed in the 1980s are iatrogenic artifacts created by naïve therapists and suggestible patients (Ross 1992).

The second group draws attention to the irrefutable fact that features of MPD can be created in the laboratory. The question raised by Ross (1989) is what the significance of these experiments might be. None of them resulted in the creation of MPD.

> MPD is not a transient phenomenon existing only in cross-section. Nor does it exist in isolation from a wide range of signs and symptoms that accompany it. There is no doubt that one can get college students to act as if they have alter personalities quite easily. But these students do not have a history of childhood abuse, numerous psychiatric symptoms, extensive involvement with the mental health system with limited benefit, and specific primary and secondary features of MPD stretching back for decades . . . None of the experiments with normal college students have resulted in the creation of anything even remotely approaching full MPD. [p. 58]

Ross thinks that these experiments creating analogues of isolated features of MPD are valuable because they help us to understand MPD, especially the notion that normal individuals can easily create (at least temporary) alters or alterlike states in the right demand situations. Lifton (1986) has described this in his work on Nazi doctors as *doubling*. MPD is not a fantastical curiosity. It is an extension of the normal developmental abilities to become intensely involved in play, books, or movies, that are used adaptively to escape terrible abuse or trauma (Ross 1989). As such, MPD should be far from rare, either in its classic or partial forms.

One particularly intense form of attacking the therapist is the current number of civil lawsuits directed against MPD clinicians, not for unprofessional conduct, but allegedly for memory implantation. Ross, then president of the International Society for the Study of Dissociation has written (1994b) that "the most pressing issue for the ISSMP&D membership, early in 1994, is that of false memories and the many lawsuits expected over the next few years against therapists for allegedly implanting false memories. . . . We should not take a polarized position. . . . Our role . . . should be to study false memories as a serious clinical problem. We also need to counter flagrant acting out against our membership" (p. 1).

These lawsuits against therapists constitute the intrusion of an intense external on the MPD paradigm; the FMSF-advocated lawsuits function to suppress MPD clinicians in precisely the same way the Inquisition persecuted the astronomers to suppress their ideas. The present author knows three reputable, leading figures in the MPD field who are currently the target of FMSF-backed lawsuits. Although several of the suits directed at one individual are about to be dismissed, this clinician has had to live with the pressure, expense, and professional consequences of what amounts to persecution.

Ross (1994b) reminds us that while distortions in memory are biologically normal and we have known about them for centuries, they are not necessarily a therapist's fault. Patients and therapists must be responsible for their own memories, just as they are responsible for their own feelings and behaviors. The therapist is a consultant to the recovery process, not a boss or persuader. The patient should lead and the therapist follow.

He further points out that false memory suits are reinforced by massive secondary gain that far exceeds any that could be derived from therapy. These include major financial awards for the patient and/or parents, and pseudoreconciliation with the family, with a sealing over of family lies, secrets, and conflicts (Ross 1994b).

Finally, Ross (1994b) points to an inherent paradox in all false memory suits. "They are based on a claim that the client is weak, suggestible, vulnerable, easily persuaded, swayed by secondary gain, and not responsible for her own memories. This is a demeaning characterization. *But, if it is accurate, it means that the memories of therapy could be as false as the memories recovered during therapy* (p. 3; my emphasis).

> The constant in the equation is the person who tells fantastic stories for secondary gain, in changing social contexts. Therefore, therapists should be able to launch false memory suits against the parents, lawyers, and background organizations suing them. I am considering doing so. The media should also be liable for damaging professional reputations through sensationalizing false memories of therapy, thereby generating ratings, circulation, and advertising revenues for themselves. [Ross 1994b, p. 3]

Clearly, the climate is changing and clinicians are preparing to go on the offensive if they are personally attacked. At this point in history, the level of controversy has become so heated it has become irrational, persecutory, nonproductive, and at times actionable. It is time to sit back and be far more careful in how we engage in such controversy. Does this mean that the extreme skeptics about MPD will disappear? Probably not; we will continue to see motivated misperceptions, duplicity, and mendacity, as people argue positions, sometimes for ulterior personal motives. We also continue to see people deny the existence of the Holocaust, and argue that natural selection does not occur and should not be taught. Their engaging in argument does not necessarily mean that they should be paid attention to. This is a radical notion in this day and age. Some people are unable or unwilling to distinguish between genuine history and ideology (Lipstadt 1993); but we should not provide them a soapbox. To raise ideological arguments to the level of debate is dangerous and destructive. While Kuhnian externals exist, if they are destructive they should not be encouraged. The growth of knowledge sometimes proceeds *despite* externals.

As with Copernicus and Darwin, controversy about MPD has left the universe of scholarly debate and is now being radically influenced by externals. The flash point that provoked the intrusion of externals is the issue of child sexual abuse, particularly sadistic incestuous abuse. Sadistic abuse represents the convergence of power, sex, need, and attachment—forces our society does not yet have adequate ways of considering or handling. The subject has touched a raw societal nerve. In our society, over 16 percent of women in the normal population have been incestuously abused as children (Russell 1986). The deep structure that MPD and many of the other interpersonal violence paradigms are calling attention to is this sexual abuse of children. This has implications for our treatment of children and other powerless segments of the society, for the functioning of the family, and for the intersection of power and gender. Our society neither wants to know nor change in regard to these issues.

The continuing attacks on the trauma paradigm, particularly the uglier ones targeting MPD clinicians, should be recognized for what they are. Even fifteen years ago, a Kuhnian rejection could be respected. At this point, with the wealth of information available and the presence of controversy so visible that all clinicians must know something about it (the public certainly does), it would seem that it is time for clinical professionals to reengage on a scholarly, data-based level, and look at the evidence.

In the future when challenged about the existence of MPD, I will take the route Frank Putnam (1989a) takes.

It is difficult to convince another professional who has never "seen" an MPD patient of the existence of the disorder. Even eminent therapists such as Cornelia Wilbur have been publicly accused by ignorant professionals of perpetuating a *folie à deux* with their patients. . . . I have learned to stop arguing with those who, either out of ignorance or malice, attempt to deny the existence of MPD. At the present time, it is sufficient to point them gently toward the *DSM-III-R* and a list of references (Boor and Coons 1983, Damgaard et al. 1985) and let the sheer volume of evidence argue on its own behalf. [p. 195]

Finally, when I think of some of my patients, I remember what Ross (1989) wrote about MPD.

What is MPD? MPD is a little girl imagining that the abuse is happening to someone else. This is the core of the disorder, to which all other features are secondary. This imagining is so intense, subjectively compelling, and adaptive, that the abused child experiences dissociated aspects of herself as other people. It is this core characteristic of MPD that makes it a treatable disorder, because the imagining can be unlearned, and the past confronted and mastered. [pp. 55–56]

REFERENCES

Aldridge-Morris, R. (1989). *Multiple Personality: An Exercise in Deception*. London: Lawrence Erlbaum.

Basoglu, M., ed. (1992). *Torture and Its Consequences: Current Treatment Approaches*. Cambridge, England: University of Cambridge Press.

Blake-White, J., and Kline, C. M. (1985). Treating the dissociative process in adult victims of childhood incest. *Social Casework: The Journal of Contemporary Social Work* 66:394–402.

Bliss, E. L. (1980). Multiple personalities: a report of 14 cases with implications for schizophrenia and hysteria. *Archives of General Psychiatry* 37:1388–1397.

Bliss, E. L., and Jeppsen, A. (1985). Prevalence of multiple personality among inpatients and outpatients. *American Journal of Psychiatry* 142:250–251.

Bloom, S. L. (1994). Hearing the survivor's voice: sundering the wall of denial. *The Journal of Psychohistory* 21:461–478.

Boor, M. (1982). The multiple personality epidemic. *The Journal of Nervous and Mental Disease* 170: 302–304.

Boor, M., and Coons, P. M. (1983). A comprehensive bibliography of literature pertaining to multiple personality. *Psychological Reports* 53:295–310.

Braudel, F. (1987). *A History of Civilizations*, American ed. New York: Allen Lane-The Penguin Press.

Braun, B. G. (1985). The role of the family in the development of multiple personality disorder. *International Journal of Family Psychiatry* 5:303–313.

——— (1988a). The BASK model of dissociation. *Dissociation* 1:4–23.

_____ (1988b). The BASK model of dissociation: Part II—Treatment, *Dissociation*, 1:16–23.

_____ (1990). Dissociative disorders as sequelae to incest. In *Incest - Related Syndromes of Adult Psychopathology*, ed. R. P. Kluft, pp. 227–246. Washington, DC: American Psychiatric Press.

Braun, B. G., and Sachs, R. G. (1985). The development of multiple personality disorder: predisposing, precipitating, and perpetuating factors. In *Childhood Antecedents of Multiple Personality Disorder*, ed. R. P. Kluft, pp. 37–64. Washington, D. C.: American Psychiatric Press.

Briere, J., and Runtz, M. (1987). Post sexual abuse trauma: data and implications for clinical practice. *Journal of Interpersonal Violence* 2:367–379.

Burgess, A., Hartman, C., McCausland, M., and Powers, P. (1984). Response patterns in children and adolescents exploited through sex rings and pornography. *American Journal of Psychiatry* 141:656–661.

Burgess, A. W. and Holmstrom, L. L. (1974). Rape trauma syndrome. *American Journal of Psychiatry* 131:981–986.

Calof, D. (1993). Facing the truth about false memory. *The Family Therapy Networker* 17:38–45.

Cockburn, A. (1990). The McMartin case: indict the children, jail the parents. *The Wall Street Journal* February 8, p. A17.

Coons, P. M. (1980) Multiple personality: diagnostic considerations. *Journal of Clinical Psychiatry* 41:330–336.

Coons, P. M., and Milstein, V. (1986). Psychosexual disturbances in multiple personality: characteristics, etiology, and treatment. *Journal of Clinical Psychiatry* 47:106–110.

Damgaard, J., Benschoten, S. V., and Fagan, J. (1985). An updated bibliography of literature pertaining to multiple personality. *Psychological Reports* 57:131–137.

Danieli, Y. (1984). Psychotherapists' participation in the conspiracy of silence about the Holocaust. *Psychoanalytic Psychology* 23–24.

Defrances, V. (1969). *Protecting the Child Victim of Sex Crimes Committed by Adults*. Englewood, CO: American Humane Association.

Dell, P. F. (1988). Professional skepticism about multiple personality disorder. *Journal of Nervous and Mental Diseases* 176:528–531.

Dell, P. F., Cohen, B., Courtois, C., and Turkus, J. (under review). Current professional skepticism about multiple personality disorder.

DeMause, L. (1994). Why cults terrorize and kill children. *The Journal of Psychohistory* 21:505–518.

Donaldson, M. A., and Gardner, R. (1985). Diagnosis and treatment of traumatic stress among women after childhood incest. In *Trauma and Its Wake*, ed. C. Figley, pp. 356–377. New York: Brunner/Mazel.

Eberle, P., and Eberle, S. (1986). *Politics of Child Abuse*. Secaucus, NJ: Lyle Stuart.

_____ (1993). *The Abuse of Innocence: The McMartin Preschool Trial*. New York: Prometheus.

Ellenberger, H. F. (1970). *The Discovery of the Unconscious: The History and Evolution of Dynamic Psychiatry*. New York: Basic Books.

Eth, S., and Pynoos, R.S., eds. (1985). *Post-Traumatic Stress Disorder in Children*. Washington, DC: American Psychiatric Press.

Fahey, T. A. (1988). The diagnosis of multiple personality disorder: a critical review. *British Journal of Psychiatry* 153:597–606.

Fliess, R. (1956). *Erogeneity and Libido: Addenda to the Theory of the Psychosexual Development of the Human*. New York: International Universities Press.

Freud, S. (1896). The aetiology of hysteria. *Standard Edition* 3:191–221.

Fried, S. (1994). War of remembrance. *Philadelphia*, January, pp. 61–64, 71, 143, 150–157.

Frischholz, E. J. (1985). The relationship among dissociation, hypnosis and child abuse in the development of MPD. In *Childhood Antecedents of Multiple Personality*, ed. R. P. Kluft, pp. 99–126. Washington, DC: American Psychiatric Press.

Ganaway, G. (1989). Historical versus narrative truth: clarifying the role of exogenous trauma in the etiology of MPD and its variants. *Dissociation* 2:205–220.

—— (1992). On the nature of memories: response to "A reply to Ganaway." *Dissociation* 5:120–122.

Gardner, R. (1991). *Sex Abuse Hysteria: Salem Witch Trial Revisited*. Philadelphia: Center for Applied Psychology.

Gelinas, D. J. (1983). The persisting negative effects of incest. *Psychiatry* 46:312–332.

—— (under review). Abuse with malevolent intent and the traumatic development context.

—— (1993). Relational patterns in incestuous families, malevolent variations, and specific interventions with the adult survivor. In *Treatment of Adult Survivors of Incest*, ed. P. Paddison, pp. 1–35. Washington, DC: American Psychiatric Press.

Goodwin, J. M. (1984). Incest victims exhibit post traumatic stress disorder. *Clinical Psychiatry News* 12:13.

—— (1985a). Post-traumatic symptoms in incest victims. In *Post-Traumatic Stress Disorder in Children*, ed. S. Eth and R. Pynoos, pp. 155–169. Washington, DC: American Psychiatric Press.

—— (1985b). Credibility problems in multiple personality disorder patients and abused children. In *Childhood Antecedents of Multiple Personality*, ed. R. P. Kluft, pp. 1–12. Washington, DC: American Psychiatric Press.

—— (1989). Recognizing dissociative symptoms in abused children. In *Sexual Abuse: Incest Victims and Their Families*, ed. J. Goodwin, 2nd ed., pp. 169–181. Chicago: Year Book Medical Publishers.

—— (1993a). Sadistic abuse: definition, recognition, and treatment. *Dissociation* 6:181–187.

—— (1993b). Human vectors of trauma: illustrations from the Marquis de Sade. In *Rediscovering Childhood Trauma: Historical Casebook and Clinical Applications*, ed. J. M. Goodwin, pp. 95–111. Washington, DC: American Psychiatric Press.

Goodwin, J., Cheeves, K., and Connell, V. (1988). Defining a syndrome of severe symptoms in survivors of severe incestuous abuse. *Dissociation* 1:11–15.

Goodwin, J., and Fine, C. (1993). Mary Reynolds and Estelle: somatic symptoms and unacknowledged trauma. In *Rediscovering Childhood Trauma: Historical Casebook and Clinical Applications*, ed. J. M. Goodwin, pp. 119–132. Washington, DC: American Psychiatric Press.

Goodwin, J. M., Sahd, D., and Rada, R. (1979). Incest hoax: false accusations, false denials. *Bulletin of the American Academy of Psychiatry and the Law.* 6:269–276.

Greaves, G. B. (1980). Multiple personality: 165 years after Mary Reynolds. *Journal of Nervous and Mental Disease* 168:577–596.

—— (1993). A history of multiple personality disorder. In *Clinical Perspectives on Multiple Personality Disorder*, ed. R. P. Kluft and C. G. Fine, pp. 355–380.

Green, A. H. (1985). Children traumatized by physical abuse. In *Post-traumatic Stress Disorder in Children*, ed. S. Eth and R. Pynoos, pp. 133–154. Washington, DC: American Psychiatric Press.

Grinker, R., and Spiegel, J. P. (1945). *Men Under Stress*. Philadelphia: Blakeston.

Gruber, H. E., with Barrett, P. H. (1974). *Darwin on Man: A Psychological Study of Scientific Creativity and Darwin's Early and Unpublished Notebooks*. New York: E. P. Dutton.

Henderson, D. (1975). Incest. In *Comprehensive Textbook of Psychiatry*, ed. A. M. Freedman, H. Kaplan, and B. Sadock, 2nd ed., Baltimore: Williams & Wilkins.

Herman, J. L. (1981). *Father–Daughter Incest*. Cambridge, MA: Harvard University Press.

—— (1992). *Trauma and Recovery*. New York: Basic Books.

Hicks, R. (1991). *In Pursuit of Satan: The Police and the Occult*. Buffalo: Prometheus Books.

Hollingsworth, J. (1986). *Unspeakable Acts*. New York: Congdon and Weed.

Horowitz, M. J. (1976). *Stress Response Syndromes*. New York: Jason Aronson.

Kardiner, A. (1941). *The Traumatic Neuroses of War*. New York: P. Hoeber.

Kardiner, A., and Spiegel, H. (1947). *War, Stress, and Neurotic Illness*. New York: Hoeber.

Kempe, C. H., Silverman, F., Steele, B., et al. (1962). The battered child syndrome. *Journal of the American Medical Association* 181:17–24.

Klein, M. (1960). *Narrative of a Child Analysis: The Conduct of the Psycho-Analysis of Children as Seen in the Treatment of a Ten Year Old Boy*. New York: Basic Books.

Kluft, R. P. (1984). Treatment of multiple personality disorder. *Psychiatric Clinics of North America* 7:9–29.

―――― (1985). Childhood multiple personality disorder: predictors, clinical findings and treatment results. In *Childhood Antecedents of Multiple Personality*, pp. 167–196. Washington, DC: American Psychiatric Press.

―――― (1990). Introduction. In *Incest–Related Syndromes of Adult Psychopathology*, pp. 1–10. Washington, DC: American Psychiatric Press.

―――― (1992a). Editorial: Cornelia B. Wilbur. *Dissociation*:71–72.

―――― (1992b). Hypnosis and multiple personality disorder. Paper presented at conference at Daniel Brown, Ph.D. & Associates, Cambridge, MA.

―――― (1993). Foreword: on paradigms and the legitimization of myopia. In *Rediscovering Childhood Trauma: Historical Casebook and Clinical Applications*, ed. J. M. Goodwin, pp. xv–xxii. Washington, DC: American Psychiatric Press.

Kuhn, T. S. (1957). *The Copernican Revolution: Planetary Astronomy in the Development of Western Thought*. Cambridge, MA: Harvard University Press.

―――― (1970a). Reflections on my critics. In *Criticism and the Growth of Knowledge*, ed. I. Lakatos and A. Musgrave, pp. 231–278. London: Cambridge University Press.

―――― (1970b). *The Structure of Scientific Revolutions*, 2nd ed., enl. Chicago: University of Chicago Press.

Lifton, R. J. (1986). *Nazi Doctors: Medical Killing and the Psychology of Genocide*. New York: Basic Books.

Lindberg, F. H., and Distad, L. J. (1985). Posttraumatic stress disorders in women who experienced childhood incest. *Child Abuse and Neglect* 9:521–526.

Lindemann, E. (1944). Symptomatology and management of acute grief. *American Journal of Psychiatry* 101:141–148.

Lipstadt, D. E. (1993). *Denying the Holocaust: The Growing Assault on Truth and Memory*. New York: The Free Press.

Loewenstein, R. J. (1993). Posttraumatic and dissociative aspects of transference and countertransference in the treatment of multiple personality disorder. In *Clinical Perspectives on Multiple Personality Disorder*, ed. R. P. Kluft and C. G. Fine, pp. 51–86. Washington, DC: American Psychiatric Press.

Loftus, E. (1993). The reality of repressed memories. *The American Psychologist* 48:518–537.

Lotto, D. (1994). On witches and witch hunts: ritual and satanic cult abuse. *The Journal of Psychohistory* 21:373–396.

Masson, J. M. (1984). *The Assault on Truth: Freud's Suppression of the Seduction Theory*. New York: Farrar, Straus, and Giroux.

Matzner, F. (1991). Does Satanism exist? *Journal of the American Academy of Child and Adolescent Psychiatry* 30:848.

McFarland, R. B. (1994). The children of God. *The Journal of Psychohistory* 21:497–499.

McHugh, P. R. (1993). Multiple personality disorder. *Harvard Mental Health Letter* 10:4–6.

Meiselman, K. (1978). *Incest: A Psychological Study of Causes and Effects with Treatment Recommendations*. San Francisco: Jossey-Bass.

Merskey, H. (1992). The manufacture of personalities: the production of multiple personality disorder. *British Journal of Psychiatry* 160:327–340.

Noll, R. (1989). Satanism, UFO abductions, historians and clinicians: those who do not remember the past . . . Letter to the editor in *Dissociation* 2:251–253.

Orne, M. T., Dinges, D. F., and Orne, E. C. (1984). On the differential diagnosis of multiple personality in the forensic context. *International Journal of Clinical and Experimental Hypnosis* 32:118–169.

Peters, J. J. (1976). Children who are victims of sexual assault and the psychology of offenders. *American Journal of Psychotherapy* 30:398–432.

Putnam, F. W. (1984). The psychophysiologic investigation of multiple personality disorder. *Psychiatric Clinics of North America* 7:31–40.

––––––– (1989a). *Diagnosis and Treatment of Multiple Personality Disorder*. New York: Guilford.

––––––– (1989b). Pierre Janet and modern views of dissociation. *Journal of Traumatic Stress* 2:413–429.

––––––– (1993). Dissociative phenomenon. In *Dissociative Disorders: A Clinical Review*, ed. D. I. Spiegel, pp. 1–16. Lutherville, MD: Sidran.

Putnam, F. W., Guroff, J. J., Silberman, E. K., et al. (1986). The clinical phenomenology of multiple personality disorder: a review of 100 recent cases. *Journal of Clinical Psychiatry* 47:285–293.

Putnam, F. W., Post, R. M., Guroff, J. J., et al. (1983). 100 cases of multiple personality disorder. Paper presented at the meeting of the American Psychiatric Association, May, New York.

Richardson, J., Best, J., and Bromley, D. (1991). *The Satanism Scare*. New York: Aldine De Gruyter.

Rockwell, R. B. (1994). One psychiatrist's view of satanic ritual abuse. *The Journal of Psychohistory* 21:443–460.

Rosenbaum, M. (1980). The role of the term schizophrenia in the decline of diagnoses of multiple personality. *Archives of General Psychiatry* 37:1383–1385.

Ross, C. A. (1989). *Multiple Personality Disorder: Diagnosis, Clinical Features, and Treatment*. New York: John Wiley and Sons.

––––––– (1992). Anne Sexton: iatrogenesis of an alter personality in an undiagnosed case of MPD. *Dissociation* 5:141–149.

––––––– (1994a). DSM-IV: Dissociated from Trauma. Paper presented at the Eastern Regional Conference on Abuse and Multiple Personality, June, Washington, DC.

––––––– (1994b). President's Message. *ISSMP&D* (International Society for the Study of Multiple Personality and Dissociation) *News*, April, pp. 1–3.

Ross, C. A., Norton, G. R., and Wozney, K. (1989). Multiple personality disorder: an analysis of 236 cases. *Canadian Journal of Psychiatry* 34:413–418.

Rush, F. (1980). *The Best Kept Secret: Sexual Abuse of Children*. New York: McGraw-Hill.

Russell, D. E. H. (1986). *The Secret Trauma: Incest in the Lives of Girls and Women*. New York: Basic Books.

Saltman, V., and Solomon, R. (1982). Incest and the multiple personality. *Psychological Reports* 50:1127–1141.

Spiegel, D. (1984). Multiple personality disorder as a post-traumatic stress disorder. *Psychiatric Clinics of North America* 7:101–110.

Stern, C. R. (1984). The etiology of multiple personalities. *Psychiatric Clinics of North America* 7:149–159.

Summit, R. C. (1983). The child sexual abuse accommodation syndrome. *Child Abuse and Neglect* 7:177–193.

––––––– (1988). Hidden victims, hidden pain: societal avoidance of child sexual abuse. In *The Lasting Effects of Child Abuse*, ed. G. E. Wyatt, pp. 39–60. Newbury Park, CA: Sage.

––––––– (1989). The centrality of victimization: regaining the focal point of recovery for survivors of child sexual abuse. *Psychiatric Clinics of North America* 12:413–430.

_____ (1994). The dark tunnels of McMartin. *The Journal of Psychohistory*, 21:397–416.

Sutcliffe, J. P., and Jones, J. (1962). Personal identity, multiple personality, and hypnosis. *The International Journal of Clinical and Experimental Hypnosis* 10:231–269.

Taylor, W. S., and Martin, M. F. (1944). Multiple personality. *Journal of Abnormal Social Psychology* 39:281–330.

Terr, L. (1990). *Too Scared to Cry*. New York: Harper and Row.

Underwager, R., and Wakefield, H. (1993). Interview: Hollida Wakefield and Ralph Underwager. *Paidika: The Journal of Paedophilia* 3:2–12.

van der Hart, O., and Friedman, B. (1989). A reader's guide to Pierre Janet on dissociation: a neglected intellectual heritage. *Dissociation* 9:3–16.

van der Kolk, B. A. (1987). *Psychological Trauma*. Washington, DC: American Psychiatric Press.

_____ (1993a). PTSD field trials for *DSM-IV*. *Traumatic stress points* (News for the International Society for Traumatic Stress Studies) 7:5.

_____ (1993b). Biological considerations about emotions, trauma, memory, and the brain. In *Human Feelings: Exploration in Affect Development and Meaning*, ed. S. L. Ablon, pp. 221–240. Hillsdale, NJ: Lawrence Erlbaum.

van der Kolk, B. A., and van der Hart, O. (1989). Pierre Janet and the breakdown of adaptation in psychological trauma. *American Journal of Psychiatry*, 146:1530–1540.

_____ (1991). The intrusive past: the flexibility of memory and the engraving of trauma. *American Imago* 48:425–454.

Victor, J. (1993). *Satanic Panic: The Creation of a Contemporary Legend*. Chicago: Open Court.

Wilbur, C. (1984). Multiple personality and child abuse. *Psychiatric Clinics of North America* 7:3–7.

_____ (1985). The effect of child abuse on the psyche. In *Childhood Antecedents of Multiple Personality* ed. R. P. Kluft, pp. 21–36. Washington, DC: American Psychiatric Press.

Wilson, N. (1994). Some psychoanalytic commentary on the deMause and Kahr papers. *The Journal of Psychohistory* 19:215–217.

Young, W. (1991). Patients reporting ritual abuse in childhood: a clinical syndrome. Report of 37 cases. *Child Abuse and Neglect* 15:181–189.

8

A Developmental Model
for Trauma

Mark R. Elin

As a psychotherapist, neuropsychologist, and student of psychoanalysis for the past twenty years, I find that a significant portion of my clinical work is focused on and influenced by the deepening range of trauma disorders within my patients. Few researchers and clinicians have attempted to integrate a developmental model (Braun 1984, Cole and Putnam 1992, Engel et al. 1978, Hartman and Burgess 1993, Putnam 1991, Trickett and Putnam 1993).

The effects of trauma on development will be reviewed in case studies identifying dissociative identity disorders (DID) and posttraumatic stress disorders (PTSD) as influencing the normal course of information processing in neuropsychological development. Parallel memory systems will be discussed as alternative avenues for integrating trauma experiences. Implications for treatment will also be outlined.

This chapter offers a comprehensive development model for identification and treatment of dissociative identity disorders (DID). The developmental model integrates the domains of developmental relevance for motor, memory, language, cognition, affect, self, and object representations. It is my position that DID develops as a result of pathology to an individual's developmental schema. DID has been challenging, perplexing, and often fear-provoking for therapists. Often I hear from my colleagues a sense of apprehension, unwillingness, and anxiety in treating these character disorders, which are often rationalized away as iatrogenic, malingering, and factitious, or as reasons to avoid responsibility for criminal activities. This chapter focuses on trauma and violence as being the precipitant stimuli contributing to DID.

Traumatic memories challenge the most skilled psychotherapist. The developmental model will help in the treatment of trauma patients by decreasing tension and anxiety in both the therapist (who is subject to projective identification and countertransference issues) and the patient. Placing dissociative identity disorders in a developmental context will help to understand the patient's trauma history better. Interventions by the therapist and therapeutic style may differ depending upon the context in which personalities develop.

The dissociative identity disorders patient imposes history to integrate mind, body, and neurophysiological events from overwhelming trauma such as child abuse, rape, victimization, and subjugation. These patients suffer from an overwhelming loss of self and identity formation. Dissociation functions as a silent defense against overwhelming trauma, but contributes to a disintegration of development. It can be represented by unconscious projections and projective identifications.

DID mirrors developmental psychopathology and evidences symptoms contributing to disregulation of information processing systems, releases of episodic discontrol, disaffective states, and dissociative features. I am sure that each one of us can cite many examples of episodic discontrol, disaffective behavioral states, and sadomasochistic relationships aggravating dissociative phenomenon and severe psychopathology. Tied to these affective states are projective rage, anger, irrational belief systems, erratic and unmodulated behaviors, all of which set the stage for acts of aggression.

Cognitive, affective, memory, and language systems are information processing substrates that contribute to neuropsychological development. These substrates are responsible for sequential, hierarchical development and integration (Gedo and Wilson 1993, Piaget 1971). Gedo writes (1979):

> Human personality is a hierarchy of personal aims. . . . The entire hierarchy, in both conscious and unconscious aspects, will form the person's primary identity, or as I would prefer to call it, the "self-organization." The formation of the self-organization and its later transformation, especially through the acquisition of systems of values, should be viewed as the core of personality development. [pp. 139]

Researchers have found that even single events of trauma can disrupt normal information processing. In a study by Wilkinson (1983) of the survivors of a disaster, 36 percent mentioned an inability to feel deeply about anything, 34 percent reported apathy, and 29 percent mentioned feeling detachment. Valent (1984) reported that among the survivors of a fire there was an absence of emotions and a sense of being dazed or stunned. Feinstein and Spiegel (1989) reported that after an ambush in Namibia, 41 percent of the direct and indirect combatants showed markedly diminished interest in usual activities, and 24 percent expressed feelings of detachment or estrangement one week after the attack.

Denial, dissociative memories, repression, cognitive distortions, lost dissociative linkages to preconscious and conscious events needs further clarification. Femina and colleagues (1990) interviewed sixty-nine incarcerated adolescents. Twenty-six gave histories of abuse, discrepant with histories obtained from records and interviews conducted during adolescence. Eight individuals had records documenting abuse but denied it, and three individuals had records indicating no abuse had occurred but they told the researchers they had been abused. These challenge our diagnostic abilities and belief systems concerning the nature of dissociative identity disorders.

SKEPTICS AND BELIEVERS

Most clinicians accept the relationships between dissociation and trauma. However, there are skeptics who believe that DID is an iatrogenic condition prompted by clinical suggestion and psychosocial phenomenon. Without going into an exhaustive review of these controversies, it is worthwhile to discuss some of the controversies in the field.

Fahy (1988) asserts that an iatrogenic factor may contribute to the development of the syndrome and that there is little evidence from genetic, physiological, or psychiatric studies to suggest that DID represents a distinct psychiatric disorder. He views DID as a hysterical syndrome. Merskey (1992) asserts that DID is a North American phenomenon, and that suggestion contributes to this iatrogenic disorder. However, Boon and Draijer (1991) conducted a study in the Netherlands using the structured clinical interview for *DSM-III-R* dissociative disorders (SCID-D). Information about childhood trauma symptoms and borderline pathology as well as histrionic character disorders was collected. Twelve patients were categorized as having DID and eleven with dissociative disorder not otherwise specified. The researchers concluded that dissociative disorders are clearly not only an American phenomenon.

Benschoten (1990) asserts that the validity of preschoolers' memories of satanic abuse and the accuracy of the diagnosis of DID should be critically evaluated. Frankel (1993) documented studies of memory both with and without the use of hypnosis. He found that there was minimal corroboration in the adult reports of childhood abuse. Memories brought up by hypnosis were considered undependable because of the inaccuracies produced by the hypnotized subjects. He asserts that suggestibility in psychotherapy and the use of hypnosis may distort information and be an antagonizing factor for accurately recalling childhood abuse.

Dell (1988) surveyed therapists who treat DID patients. Seventy-eight percent of those surveyed reported that they encountered intense skepticism from other professionals. The skepticism was due mainly to: (1) the decline of interest in dissociation, (2) underappreciation of the prevalence of individuals with dissociative ability, and (3) misconceptions about the clinical presentation of patients with DID.

There is not enough room in this chapter to review in great detail the history of dissociation; however, it is important to discuss some of the recent literature and research. The position of this chapter is as follows: (1) dissociation and DID are symptoms consistent with Developmental Psychopathology from trauma, and (2) there are multiple levels of information processing taking place across different modalities of brain function and behavior. Braun (1984) reports that dissociation is a defensive process against trauma. He asserts that under extremely stressful circumstances, most often due to child abuse, the multiple personality develops as a result of repeated dissociative episodes. Alter personalities can develop a history of memories, events, ideas, beliefs, perceptions, and behavioral response patterns.

A number of authors have recently corroborated the relationship between dissociative symptoms and traumatic events (Coons et al. 1989, Coons and Milstein 1992, Frischholz 1985, Putnam 1986b, Spiegel 1984).

There are numerous physiological studies supporting state-dependent memory, cognitive, and visual differences found in alter personalities. Trauma symptoms in alter personalities may be expressed in the forms of developmental idiosyncrasies, pathognomonic responses, and neurological-like symptoms. Miller (1989) gave an ophthalmologic examination to nine DID patients and nine controls. The DID patients showed more variability across alter personalities than did the controls, averaging 4.5 times the number of changes in optical functioning. In one DID case, the person exhibited better than average acuity without muscle balance problems, but a second personality evidenced deteriorated acuity with left exotropia (turning outward of the left eye), which resolved completely when the person switched back to the first personality.

In a study of the autonomic nervous system activity in DID patients, Putnam and colleagues (1990) established that eight of nine DID patients manifested physiologically distinct alter personality states that were consistent over five testing sessions spaced one or more days apart. Alter personalities were tested for skin conductance, respiration, skin temperature, and heart rate. A repeated-measures design was used to measure for variability across alter states. DID patients showed physiologic patterns in differentiated personality states. Further neurophysiological studies conducted by Ludwig and colleagues (1972) demonstrated significant differences to the same stimulus across the alter personalities of two patients. Ludwig believed that in DID patients encoding of learned information was state dependent but that neutral stimuli was more available across personalities than emotional information.

How learning in one state of consciousness is related to another was also studied by Ross and colleagues (1979). A supporting article by Nissen and colleagues (1988) concluded that "the degree of compartmentalization of knowledge (in DID patients) appears to depend on the extent to which that knowledge is interpreted in ways that are unique to a personality as well as the extent to which processes operating at the time of retrieval are strongly personality-dependent" (pp. 117–118).

In a review of dissociation and trauma, Spiegel and Cardena (1991) noted that "antecedents of dissociative phenomenon include reactive dissociative symptomatology, psychogenic amnesia, atypical dissociative disorders, and, most extremely, multiple personality disorders due to physical, sexual, emotional, human made, or natural disasters" Amnesia due to sexual, physical, and verbal abuse in childhood was also noted by Coons and colleagues (1989). They found that in patients diagnosed with atypical dissociative disorder, 82 percent were also diagnosed with psychogenic amnesia.

The one striking difference between the critics and supporters of DID is that the supporters have begun to operationalize and empirically evaluate, through statistical analysis and controlled experiments, the symptoms, diagnosis, and profile for DID. There are no studies by the critics to disprove DID; their criticisms are largely based on narrative critiques of DID research and anecdotal behavior. I do not know of one scientific study disproving that DID results from childhood trauma. The critics have reviewed narrative ccounts of classical psychoanalytic cases and critically evaluated the history of DID that they believe is iatrogenically based, culturally predetermined, and suggestible.

In summarizing this section, despite skepticism about the phenomena and diagnostic considerations, research has documented the presence and importance of trauma related events in precipitating dissociative features. On the one hand Fahy (1988), Merskey (1992), and Frankel (1993) raise significant doubts about the diagnosis of DID. Other clinicians and researchers, on the other hand, have empirically and scientifically researched this phenomenon and believe in the veridical diagnostic benchmarks of this personality disorder. Missing from recent conceptualization, however, is a comprehensive model of the role of development in the expression of trauma-related dissociative symptoms.

Before this model is presented and elaborated upon, I will present two extensive case studies, which will illustrate (1) the provocative clinical presentation of trauma disorder patients, and (2) the multiple symptoms characteristics in previously traumatized adult patients.

CASE STUDIES

Case 1

The first case is of a 40-year-old female with two preadolescent children who was admitted to the hospital following an overdose of medications (Prozac, Clonopin, Navane, and Premarin). She was on the ICU unit for approximately 2 weeks and had undergone several dysrhythmias until she was stabilized. On admission, the patient reported a 2-week history of suicidal symptoms prior to her overdose. She reported that her four personalities, a child alter, a malevolent alter, a protector, and a core personality, were in conflict with each other. Her fifth personality was killed during the suicide attempt by the malevolent alter, who wanted to kill off other personalities as well.

Recent stressful events in the patient's life included concerns that she would be laid off from her position as an office manager. Conflicts with her children, husband, and over a recent termination with her former therapist also caused significant stress and turmoil in her life. Approximately eighteen months earlier, the patient's father left her a message reporting "that he had her once and that he would have her again." She had not heard from her father in ten years. During convalescence from facial surgery, to be described below, a plethora of images, feelings, events, sensory and perceptual impressions, and brief flashbacks (frames of disparate and fragmented information) were brought to consciousness. She demonstrated dissociative features such as depersonalization, derealization, memory impairment, loss of time, and poor impulse control. It was clearly outside her ability to navigate and monitor the psychological material that she was attempting to integrate. Over the course of treatment she was hospitalized four times for suicidal ideation or attempts. She was able to take responsibility for coming into the hospital when she had suicidal thoughts expressed by the malevolent alter.

In this case, the patient's deepening depression was exacerbated by realizations of sexual abuse by her father. She began to recall the abuse following a delicate facial surgical procedure for injuries she originally sustained when she was a child. This recent procedure required reconstructive surgery, which took a time period of several months for complete convalescence. During this phase of surgical reconstruction her expressive language abilities were restricted due to the nature of the surgical intervention. The significance of her physical limitations became more meaningful as it affected her psychologically, lifting previously repressed material. Early childhood memories pertaining to oral sex, sexual intercourse, and beatings became more vivid and detailed. She was unable to verbalize the newfound memories to her therapist. As her flashbacks became more detailed, complicated, and profound, she managed to write detailed notes about internal thoughts, images, and beliefs. When her son used a fork to cut a sausage, she remembered her father stabbing her with a fork during sex acts. Cruel and sadistic themes emerged from the past, which contributed to deepening depression, confusional state, isolation, loss of control, and disorganized thinking with loose articulation of boundaries.

Her memory is patchy for the first years of life with serious deficits in declarative and implicit memory functioning. Reporting family historical events was marked by constrictive repressive defenses blocking information that she simply did not have access to.

Eventually she was able to report being abused by her father from the age of 2 through 18. She recalled memories of her father taking her out to the toolshed in the back of their house and placing objects in her vagina, including his fingers and penis. He also inflicted multiple lacerations to her head. At the age of 12 she attempted to report this child abuse to a psychiatrist, who allegedly raped her as well. She described her mother as ineffectual, malevolent, and physically abusive.

Following six to eight months of therapy, she recalled splitting off a child alter from the age of 4, who contained many of the memories and details about the child abuse. During latency, a lethal alter emerged who wanted to get rid of the wimpy core personality. Her father's sadistic behavior continued, and she remembered him taking out his pistol, placing a bullet in the chamber, spinning it, pointing it at her head, and pulling the trigger. Meanwhile, her lethal alter became enraged, fueled, and in more control, hoping to condense a "meaner and more aggressive" personality that would dominate the patient's internal life.

The patient began dating her future husband at age 16. When she went into the hospital for an appendectomy he impregnated her while she was convalescing in the hospital. The child was placed for adoption against her wishes, although she did manage to hold her son for a brief period of time in the hospital. She never told the boyfriend about their child. Several years after this incident he contacted the patient and they were married. Three years into the marriage she told him about their son. Approximately three years before her coming into therapy her husband began placing kitchen implements into her vagina. She reports that "it felt just like Dad." She has not had any sexual contact with her husband for the past six years.

Following three and a half years of psychotherapy, this patient is integrated and no longer uses alter states to express her trauma history. The alters had represented different developmental, psycho-pathological benchmarks in her life, identifying periods of abuse and encapsulating biographical information, memories, and emotions. This case will be discussed in the context of the developmental paradigm in the section on treatment implications.

Case 2

I have been seeing a 47-year-old male who initially appeared to be psychotic. He presented as a well-nourished, disheveled man, with conjugate eye gaze, who navigated into my office using a cane. He demonstrated compensatory visual and ocular motor symptoms and spoke in short phrases admitting his confusion, feelings of isolation, loneliness, and lack of integration of the past.

He had a history of seizure disorders, right hemiparesis, right hemisensory loss, and right visual field defect arising from a sus-pected arterial venous malformation in the basal ganglia region of his brain. He had one abnormal electroencephalogram, and a 2.5 centi-meter occult AVM in the left basal ganglia was noted on CT scan. During initial evaluation, it was difficult to tie together the patient's presentation and history since he had a paucity of memory (holo-phrastic, telegraphic speech formations) and poor recall for specific periods and events in his life. Episodic, implicit, and declarative memory was impaired due to a closed head injury from ten years previously. His memory was further clouded due to an injury in which he had fallen off of a ladder.

The patient had family in the area, but remained independent. He describes his mother as ineffectual, and his father (deceased) as abusive and out of control.

Later in therapy, it became clear that he had suffered early childhood sexual, physical, and psychological abuse by his father and siblings. He was repeatedly tortured, thrown out of a second floor window, sodomized, and used as an object for sadistic gratification. Initially in therapy it was clear that he was having amnestic episodes. He was able to describe briefly that he was in the military, but had little reference or linkages to historical events. I changed his diagnosis to PTSD disorder with amnestic and/or fugue states. He was clearly dissociating in the office and barely able to maintain an integrated level of speech.

The patient reported reaching all developmental milestones at appropriate benchmarks. He reported a history of dyslexia and may have also had Gilles de la Tourette's Syndrome (i.e., patient describes barking as a child). He enlisted in the military and lost track of his memory, associative linkages, and connections to his past as well as subsequent events. He reports that he experienced horrors "beyond the imagination." The patient said that he was involved in hundreds of fire fights (the usual number being about twenty per serviceman). He experienced burning of villages and people, dismemberment, torture, and the annihilation of children and women. Emerging from this situation, he was able to complete college and become an electrical engineer.

As an adult, he often worked at menial positions. He was unaware of the actual depth of his technical knowledge. Further along in therapy, he revealed that he had several academic degrees and was responsible for operating power generators that required significant skill, application of visuomotor functioning, and visuospatial memory. He complained that the left side of his body would "shut down." In a previous hospitalization following loss of consciousness, doctors noticed there was an old lesion in the left hemisphere of the brain; however, there was no correlation between his symptoms and the location of the lesion. The etiology of this lesion still remains somewhat of a neurological puzzle, and no neurosurgeon is willing to investigate this problem further.

THE DEVELOPMENTAL MODEL

The developmental model for trauma takes a neuropsychological and psychodynamic approach to treatment of dissociative disorders. It is a six-tier model for hierarchical integration, identifying psychopathology from single and repetitive incidences of sexual, physical, and emotional abuse, from natural and human-made disasters, and from illnesses, diseases, or accidents.

The first stage requires knowledge and training in normal development from gestation to senescence in motor, memory, language, cognition, affects, self, and object relations theory. The second stage recognizes the effects of trauma on altering neurochemical, biological, and physical disruptions in brain functions, and the deployment of neurotransmitter substances coming from the locus coeruleus to limbic (amygdala) and cerebral cortex, innervating higher cortical systems and their neurosubstrates.

The third stage identifies the neuropsychological information processing system sensory systems and their pathways for carrying olfaction, taste, audition, visual, tactile, kinesthetic, propioceptive, visceral, and gustatory reactions. This sensory, nonverbal stimuli is deposited into implicit, procedural, and perceptual representational memory systems (Schacter 1990, Tulving and Schacter 1990) and language-based memories.

The fourth stage places all of the aforementioned levels of development, maturation, and memory along multiple parallel information processing units (using computerized models) representing multiple distributed systems (cortical and subcortical interactions), each containing vectors of neurological and psychological development (including objects, affects, and object representations). In a nontraumatized individual, the parallel systems communicate in a flexible manner. In stage five, when trauma is experienced, communication among the levels of development becomes encapsulated. It contains incomplete, yet crystallized, forms of a person's identity, personality, and neurophysiological functions. These are dissociated from higher and lower levels of development. These separate, rigid, and contained representations of an individual's personality may be understood as being DID.

The sixth stage of the developmental model is reparation through treatment. Psychodynamic psychotherapy, behavioral therapy, and medication are used singly or in combination. Through the use of dreams, projective identifications, and other techniques, the therapist becomes the bridge to unearth rigid defenses and constrictive cognitions.

DOMAINS OF DEVELOPMENTAL RELEVANCE

There are six critical domains of developmental relevance: motor, memory, language, affect, cognition, and self–object representations. The complete development of the neurophysiological, neuropsychological, and psychological developmental stages are found in Elin (1994). The influence of external trauma events affecting endogenous psychophysiological responses from assaults can be devastating to normal psychological growth and development

Motor

To support this notion, the interconnectedness between central nervous system development and activities in the external world influences heavily on the development of motor systems. Injury, accidents, and diseases to the central nervous system can directly halt, circumvent, postpone, or critically damage the normal myelination process and the intricately connected and woven supportive motor systems. Psychological development can easily influence this system if injured and may become state dependently bound in memory.

The investigations of Riddle and colleagues (Gardner 1973) in ninety-one foundling-home infants found incidences of anxiety and sadness. They failed to gain weight and even lost weight. There were periods of stupor and insomnia; and they reported that thirty-one infants died between the seventh and twelfth month of life in spite of good food and meticulous medical care. Infants who did survive the first year of life showed severe physical retardation.

Motor development may be easily altered, interrupted, or suppressed due to external trauma on the central nervous system and neurohormonal networks that contribute to growth. Strong associative links may be established within an individual's developing psyche to react to threatening stimuli via motor movements, expression (tics), blindness, weakness, and even hemiparesis and hemiplegias associated with earlier psychogenic traumas. This may establish a protective shield against physical and emotional violence. The benchmarks of trauma to an individual's body ego will readily be seen in the treatment setting. Distinguishing among the neurological disorders and/or neuropsychological dysfunctions (i.e., ADD, LD, conduct disorders, etc.) is the task of the therapist for identifying an illness/disease process or subsequent injury, accident or dissociative state that is well encapsulated over time due to trauma.

Memory

From motor development we move into higher levels of human behavior and brain development focusing on memory development and the development of neurotransmitter receptors (Nelson 1994). It is important to understand the neurophysiological and neuropsychological development of memory. These are intricate and detailed systems requiring a clear understanding to best identify with what the patient is experiencing in dissociative identity states.

The development of the self involves neurophysiological, cognitive, and affective linkages as well as integration of memory systems in the infant and toddler. The integration of these developmental areas is also important for effective and sequential information processing, which is the bedrock of neurodevelopmental growth, development of language, psychosocial and brain activations. Meltzoff (1990) posited there is a kernel of higher level memory system from the earliest phases of infancy and that changes in memory structure occur throughout childhood.

Deloache (1989) reports that as myelination increases and develops over time a rapid change in representational memory occurs between 2½ and 3 years of age. Thompson and Meyers (1985) studied inferences and recall at ages 4 and 7. The 7-year-olds displayed more logical or constrained emotional interferences than the 4-year-olds.

Bjorklund (1985) posited that associative interconnections are formed relatively early and do not change significantly from the elementary school years through adulthood. Age-related changes are believed to be due to categorical relationships that can be used subsequently to structure recall.

As maturation of memory develops, certain neurophysiological and chemical reactions occur. DeWied and Croiset (1991) report that "synapses that participate in the processing of information (memory traces)" (p. 168) cause a physiochemical change causing electrical activity and release of neurotransmitters and other neuromessengers in neuronal pathways which carry sensory, motivational, and emotional stimuli. Reticular formation, limbic, mid-brain structures, and neuropeptides contribute to memory processes and association areas, and parietal, temporal, and neocortex structures provide storage sites for long-term memory. The frontal cortex is a major site for organization of memory processes and lower brain centers are readily connected to frontal systems involved in learning, memory, and emotional processing of information.

In the preceding section experimental research supports findings that memory begins earlier on in childhood development than previously thought to be the case. The maturation of brain development for registration and consolidation of short-term, intermittent, and long-term storage is variable under certain experimental and psychosocial conditions.

Early trauma memory experiences are condensed into complex memory units coming from multiple levels of sensory, perceptual information and linked to representational images, beliefs, feelings, and ultimately impressions concerning the trauma experience. Therefore, memory, under normal conditions, may operate in an organized and flexible manner, but under stress and trauma, events may coalesce and exhibit fluctuations in information processing. This will have a disorganizing effect on memory consolidation.

DID and dissociative features are symptoms not unlike other forms of memory disorders that manifest as a result of trauma. The disorganization of memory may be considered to be a diagnostic indicator for trauma and should not be used as an argument to undermine the fact that trauma experiences are contained in complex memory banks and are not believed to be falsified experiences.

Language

The unfolding of language systems is directly related to phonology, memory, and learning. These may be seriously undermined in the development of neurocognitive and maturational development in children who show early language and learning disabilities or dissociative memory processes. The patient's language style may not only be purely of a dissociative defense to ward off unwanted thoughts and feelings, but may signal the presence of early trauma and identify the age of the patient when the abuse occurred to neurocognitive substrates. This is particularly noteworthy for individuals who were abused before language development.

In alter identities or fugue states, individuals often report memories in one word utterances. They use telegraphic speech style, early sentence structures, and agrammatical semantic and syntactical usage. Often intonations, gestures, and articulation differences occur that take on the vernacular characteristics and mannerisms of an unfamiliar accent or language system. Disguised language is also similar to that seen in twin language. Written expressive language may assume a discursive, loose, associative style, and manual writing styles are significantly altered depending upon the personality represented. In some cases, permanent injury to linguistic competency may occur during critical periods of language development in which it is bypassed, blocked, or severely repressed as a result of physical, sexual, and psychological abuse.

Abused children exhibit neuropsychological, neurocognitive, and neurophysiological deficiencies in normal development and language systems. Together with motor and distributed memory modalities, we can identify the child and adult who has undergone serious physical, sexual, or emotional abuse during critical phases of linguistic development.

The following symptoms may be characteristic of a trauma history: stuttering, telegraphic speech, word-finding difficulties, poor sentence structure, specific learning disabilities, and difficulty with early language reproductions. Metaphorical and symbolic representations of trauma experiences compete for visual, verbal, and spatial configurations and images. Hence, a tapestry of motor, language, affective, and memory systems communicate a latent history of events that occurred during critical periods of language development and other systems modalities. To further explore the complexity of these systems let us turn our attention to the neuropsychology of affect and memory consolidation.

Affect

The neurophysiological basis for affects of behavior are created by the neurohypophyseal hormones and related peptides. These may be mediated by a receptive complex in the ventral hippocampus for which vasopressin and related peptides are considered agonist and oxytocin and related peptides as "inverse agonist" (DeWied and Croiset 1991). There are numerous brain structures responsible for processing and integrating affects.

Affects may also be mediated by the amygdala. McGaugh and colleagues (1992) suggest that the amygdala may be a locus of neural changes underlying the memory of affective experiences. The amygdala may have a role in mediating stimulus response and reward or punishment experiences (Weiskrantz 1956). This structure may be especially sensitive to trauma events and may be considered a gauge for alerting an individual to external threats to the organism.

As Basch (1976) points out, affect conditions are automatic, and not voluntary. They are under direct control of the subcortical centers. He asserts that in traumatic conditions, affects are not integrated into synchronous and well-organized modules. Affects are the signals to assume a defensive or reactive posture for human beings to protect, defend, or respond to state-dependent learned and unconscious threatening material. Affects are linked to personal development and contribute in trauma states to fragmented memories, disorganized thinking, as well as dampened and disaffective qualities of mood.

Affect tone, attunement to self-objects and their representations are coupled with important caregivers and influenced by environmental conditions. Children react intuitively to safety and predictable outcomes and behaviors by adults. Tomkins (1963) posits that a negative affective linkage to a previously painful experience may be "admitted to the possibility of pain stimulation" (p. 28). This provokes anticipatory avoidant behavior in the absence of the actual drive stimulus. He linked facial, visceral, and motor responses to affectively heightened states of experience. Therefore, affects represent a biological response to psychological material. Over time this material is identified by more complex hierarchical and representational systems (i.e., through symbols, dreams, memories, and important objects in the child's real world).

Cognition and Self-Object Representation

In trauma, words are suppressed and cut off from consciousness. Symbols are lost, embedded, or dampened, and the world of objects remains less available for affective linkages in a traumatic state. Reality testing is impaired and feelings of meaninglessness, isolation, and loneliness pervade an individual. Disregulation of affect, loss of impulse control, sad facies and labored speech all offer diagnostic considerations into a patient's trauma history. In DID and other dissociative states objects, affects, ideas, and accompanying linguistic provisions for labeling internal events and external reality may be imprecisely linked to memory systems. In trauma states, memory information processing is directly altered by the underlying neurological systems and threatening external and ideational material experienced following trauma. Therefore, dissociation is not only in response to trauma but is also experienced as a dissociative phenomenon activated among internal memory and representational systems usually responsible for integrating part objects, part-whole objects, and their affect connections, which do not communicate successfully across information processing systems in a precise manner due to trauma. Therefore, it is my position that DID and trauma disorders are also a dissociative memory disorder that is a symptom of previously experienced trauma states and conditions.

Cognition is the mantelpiece on which rest motor, memory, language, affect, and self-object development. It is supported by the structure and interconnectedness of the neurophysiological, biological, and biochemical systems. Cognitive maturation begins at birth, and early infant memory studies support the developing nature of the infant's neurological system for retaining and integrating information. In the early months of human infant development, a complex instinctual process develops whose function is to ensure that the infant obtains sufficient parental care for its survival. Ainsworth (1964) suggests that at least two cognitive acquisitions of the human infant are necessary conditions for social bonding. These are the ability to discriminate between figures, and the notion of object permanence.

Cognitive development in children is an organized hierarchical process related to brain development. The construction of mental representations, images, and words is highly dependent on the structure of the cortical network. It is also important for integrating successive learning experiences into coherent functional systems such as language and memory.

Effects of Trauma on Neurophysiological Functioning and Memory

I have presented briefly the domains of developmental relevance and now will focus more fully on how trauma effects neurophysiological functioning and performance as well as consolidation and integration of memory via affect memory and the different modalities in which memory is retrieved, registered, encoded, and recalled.

Silberman and colleagues (1985) report that memory processes are of central interest in DID. Apart from behavioral changes, the various personality states of DID patients are most prominently distinguished by amnesia-related events that take place in disparate states. A further clinical feature of DID is that while the various alters may behave as though they do not share one another's memories, they may also appear to have photographic recall of events that happened to them even in the distant past. These results are similar to Ludwig and colleagues (1972) who found evidence that material learned in one state influenced its processing in other states. Emotionally laden words were processed in memory differently in alter personalities although emotionally neutral material was processed similarly. Emotionally neutral material apparently lacked compartmentalization in these patients. Ross and colleagues (1994) found that primary emotions are modulated by the right hemisphere and positive emotions are modulated by the left hemisphere while negative emotions are modulated by the right. Hence, a compartmentalization in recall of information suggests, once again, the compartmentalization of neuronal specific activities and their substrates.

In patients with trauma disorders, visual and verbal images contain trauma memories that build on threatening feelings to body ego. The process of assimilation and accommodation toward equilibration requires that the child adapt to the world by changing its internal structure or schemata. In DID, early developmental structures are blocked. Cognitive and emotional development are arrested, creating alternative memory, language, and affect systems for coping and adjusting. It is this failure to move along normal lines of development that according to Noam (1992) accounts for aspects of development that remain unaccommodated.

During a trauma event, in consequence of overwhelming anxiety and brutality waged against the self, plasticity of cognitive functioning and of schemata are isolated and compartmentalized. This is similar to what Glover (1979) perceived as ego nuclei, or islets, of executive function of object-related awareness that form coherent structures of the ego. Depending upon the developmental phase, a specific period of cognitive and psychological behaviors toward the self will be reenacted to include burnings, slashings, stealing, and conduct disorders. The trauma victim has no choice but to attempt to survive a chaotic internal world often dissociated and unrelated to external activities and events that are walled off due to an amnestic condition.

There have been no research studies to identify how trauma memories are stored and integrated among different alter personalities. The response to trauma is distinctive with observable, biological, and psychological reactions.

Grant and Redman (1981) identified the locus coeruleus as exerting a hierarchical control over the autonomic nervous system, and therefore involved in stress response syndromes. A single cell in the locus coeruleus may divergently innervate the hippocampus, amygdala, and temporal cortex.

Charney and colleagues (1993) suggest that neurophysiological dysfunction in PTSD disorders may involve the amygdala, locus coeruleus, hippocampus, noradrenergic, dopamine, opiate, and corticotrophin neurochemical systems. This results in an array of behavioral and physiologica¹ responses necessary for survival. The amygdala has rich connections for neurocognitive functioning with neocortex and visceral brain stem activity (Halgren 1992). Halgren and colleagues (1978) found that amygdala stimulation has included such symptoms as hallucinations, emotions (almost always fear), déjà vu, visceral sensations (usually epigastric), autonomic changes, hormonal secretions, and loss of contact. Trauma patients exhibit similar symptoms when experiencing a traumatic event or memory. Hence, the amygdala is involved in emotional qualities as it relates to the cognitive systems. This may be one reason why it is difficult to dissociate emotional from cognitive processing.

In my own work with PTSD and DID patients, they represent neurophysiological changes to motor (tics), behavior, prosody of voice, posture, gait, and station as in the case study previously described. Grinker and Spiegel (1945) described autonomic and extra-pyramidal events following acute stress similar to Parkinson's disease which involves the substantia nigra, basal ganglia, and control of movement and memory. These patients exhibited reduced eye blink, cogwheel rigidity, coarse tremor of hand and lips, postural flexion, propulsive gait, startle reactions, and speech abnormalities associated with catecholamine depletion. Dopamine is a neural transmitter that is depleted in Parkinson's disease. Dopaminergic systems supply basal ganglia and limbic system structures.

This mediates memory, learning, olfaction, visceral functions, and control of limbic structures to include the hippocampus, amygdala, and limbic cortical association areas and cingulum to the frontal, temporal, and parietal lobes. These centers send information to and from the cortex receiving sensory information from higher sensory areas in the temporal lobe and other input from the prefrontal association cortex in the association area on the lateral side surface of the parietal lobe.

Depletion of noradrenergic supplies to the hippocampus, amygdala, and higher cortical centers may create a disorganizing effect on memory and prevent it from successfully being encoded. In infancy, there is also evidence of a surge of synaptic density throughout the cortex. Cortical substrates in child development are flexible and plastic in nature. Ontogenically, the brain may undergo significant trauma. However, restorative cognitive, psychological, and memory systems may be reconditioned to approximate normal development.

In trauma, disconnections, interruptions, and disorganization of memory occur in neurocognitive performance. In dissociation and dissociative identity disorders, information is dislocated, in part, due to neurotransmitter depletion. A weakened information processing system contains encapsulations of childhood thoughts, memories, dreams, and experiences that remain encapsulated as a branch off the normal parallel stages of development.

Neuromodulatory systems, the amygdala, locus coeruleus, hippocampus, and sensory cortex are all involved during traumatic experiences and memory processing. Most evidence points to the amygdala as centrally important for processing neurocognitive material associated to trauma (Charney et al. 1993). The prefrontal cortical dopaminergic systems are also involved in a number of higher level functions including attention and memory. Traumatic memories may be encoded via sensory, motor, language functions, and so forth, with subsequent negative and/or positive reinforcement for conditioning and extinction of neurocognitive memories and associations. It is important to review some of the input, integrative, and output systems for how memory information is received, integrated, consolidated, and expressed through output channels. This will give us a greater appreciation for how information is encapsulated and dissociated from the original trauma events. The following is an introduction to the neuropsychology of memory.

NEUROPSYCHOLOGICAL PRINCIPLES FOR MEMORY CONSOLIDATION

It has already been well documented that memory storage is regulated by neuromodulatory systems activated by experiences. Acute stress increases dopaminergic release in a number of specific brain areas. The medial prefrontal cortex is believed to be involved in higher level cognitive functions including attention, concentration, and "working memory" (Baddeley and Hutch 1974) appears to be especially sensitive and vulnerable to stress.

Gold and von Buskirk (1978) suggest that neuromodulatory systems influence memory storage based on interactions affecting the release of norepinephrine within the amygdala. "The amygdala may be selectively involved in modulating memory storage and other brain regions" (p. 838). Mishkin (1978) demonstrated that lesions in the amygdala or hippocampus alone were not sufficient to produce amnesia whereas lesions in both structures did result in memory loss. This was also noted by Warrington and Weiskranz (1982) who believed that the involvement of two systems connecting temporal neocortex and mesial-basal frontal lobes were required for development of amnesia.

Memory disturbances have been encountered by epileptologists who have identified many of the common features cited by Janet (1920) who found that psychogenetic amnesia included abnormal mood, extreme arousal, and alcohol use. Janet concluded that extreme states of arousal would interfere with memory registration as would alcohol or an intense traumatic event.

Epileptologists Rowan and Rosenbaum (1991) reported memory loss as a frequent complaint by their patients including increasing forgetfulness, forgetting commonly placed items, appointments, schedules, and what they were about to do or say. They identified this condition as *ictal amnesia*, which they believed was caused by seizures or by its aftereffect. They looked at transient global amnesia consisting of anterograde and retrograde memory loss associated with relatively normal behavior. Similar to dissociative patients, their patients were able to converse and perform normal complex acts but they appeared to be bewildered and repeatedly asked questions such as "Where am I? What day is it? What is happening?" There was no sign of associated clinical seizure activity such as automatisms. These events may last up to 24 hours and an average of 7 to 8 hours.

MEMORY-INFORMATION PROCESSING MODELS

There are two popular human memory processing developmental models. In one model, Atkinson and Shiffrin (1968) present three types of memory storage: (1) sensory registered, (2) short-term, and (3) long-term. Information is received through auditory, visual, and tactile modalities in the sensory registers. The sensory registrar can hold a large volume of information before it is transferred to long-term storage. Information may be easily blocked from reaching long-term storage. Input systems determine how information is organized, stored, and encoded.

In an equally compelling model, Cowan (1988) proposes that short-term memory is a subset of long-term memory. Sensory memory and executive controls are believed to be separate functional units from long-term memory. The central executive performs a conglomeration of functions to include: (1) maintenance of information and short-term memory through rehearsal, (2) search of long-term memory to accomplish more elaborate storage of items than short-term memory, and (3) problem-solving activities.

It is important to discuss some of the basic pathways of memory information processing systems for encoding of information and affect systems. Encoding is a process that converts an event into a memory trace or its representations. This represents a consolidation of memory information in working memory (Baddeley and Hutch 1974, Crossin 1992), explicit memory, implicit memory, procedural memory, and declarative memory (Squire and Butters 1992).

Implicit memory (Butters and Stuss 1989) suggests a prior experience is unconsciously represented. Procedural memory is the encoding of operations or procedures involved in producing a motor task. Declarative memory includes "facts, episodes, and routines of everyday life" (Squire 1986 p. 1614). Linguistic, affective, visual, propioceptive, kinesthetic, and sensory data enter into this multiple memory system and forms cells of memories with interconnections and interdependence on words, physical events, and affective levels of responding for processing clear, exact, and well-modulated memory systems.

Traumatic events are believed to enter and/or block memory from entering into specific storage modalities. Memory remains encapsulated, distorted, or isolated due to the influx of a highly stressful environment. Associated affect connections draw distinctions as to what memories are recalled either through words, life experiences, events, or motor activities from specific developmental stages when repetitive trauma occurs.

When individuals are in a state of fear, panic, or numbness (opioid states), information is drawn in selectively for memory storage. These memories may remain isolated, repressed, and dissociated from consciousness during everyday activities. However specific perceptual, motor, and sensory stimuli can evoke affective linkages to these underlying memory substrates. This may also occur through higher cortical levels of processing information across memory systems.

Putnam (1986a) found evidence of amnesia in 98 percent of 100 cases of DID. He asserts that unexplained memory lapses occur in everyday life as a frequent presenting symptom of patients who were subsequently given a diagnosis of DID and that there has been remarkably little investigation of memory function in these patients (Schacter and Kilstrom 1989).

Ludwig and colleagues (1972) compared associate-learning tests from two alternate forms of the Wechsler Memory Scale in a patient who had four personalities. Two personalities studied a particular list from the learning trial, and the list was given to each of the other personalities. Transfer of information from one personality to some of the others was noted as was evidence for "cross-personality" vacillation of performance on the block design subtest of the WAIS. In two additional tests, transfer was observed only from one personality to the other and not vice versa. Ludwig suggested that effectively charged material transferred only from one personality to the other, whereas affectively neutral material transferred among all personalities. This would be an example of implicit memory phenomenon (Schacter and Kilstrom 1989).

Research has focused primarily on neuropsychological tests for language functioning and learning across personalities (Nissen et al. 1988). Bower (1981) reported that information acquired in one emotional state is inaccessible to another. To support this position in amnestic studies, Schacter and Kilstrom (1989) reviewed extensively amnestic conditions occurring from traumatic events and concluded that cueing procedures can be useful in covering "preserved islands of autobiographical memories" and also suggest that the accessibility of such memories may depend on the availability of some sort of identity information (i.e., a nickname) (p. 212).

Memory systems for explicit and implicit information may remain unavailable across modalities of memory storage and under certain circumstances; functional amnesias may respond to cueing techniques for capturing previously lost memories of traumas. In DID, multiple personalities emerge that have amnestic qualities for one or more of the alters.

The essential points posited in the developmental model is as follows: (1) The domains of developmental relevance are influenced by the integrity of neurophysiological, biological, and neurochemical systems. (2) These structures and systems produce interactive effects on information processing in the human brain for the consolidation of verbal and nonverbal memory. (3) Ultimately the representation of this material is analyzed through the synthesis of symbols, dreams, evocative memory, linguistic productions, and so forth. Research has documented that encoding occurs at earlier stages of development (infancy) then previously thought to be the case. Between the ages of 2 and 3 language acquisition is elaborated. An amnestic period may develop that blocks early nonverbal memory patterns from reaching conscious recall, recognition, and by having direct access to a verbal analogue. (4) Symptomatic features from trauma and subsequent developmental psychopathology will be operationalized within the trans-

ferential relationship when the patient's developmental arrest, unconscious representations, fantasies, and motor-cognitive systems cluster
together to form encapsulations of his/her trauma history. (5) The patient's
premorbid history including extent, duration, and time of abuse during
critical phases of development will determine to what degree dissociation
or dissociative identity disorders crystallize and form rigid parallel information-processing systems and encapsulations.

As a further attempt for integrating the developmental model, information from these sections will be made through a discussion of parallel
memory systems.

PARALLEL MEMORY SYSTEMS

A review of neurophysiological consequences of trauma reveals there may
be multiple circuits that create a parallel processing system for integrating
information through separate and distinct modalities of learning.

There are multiple avenues for integrating implicit and explicit experiences and their affect connections with semantic, declarative, and procedural memory systems. Evidence for a dual memory system (Pillemer and
White 1989) suggests that the first system presents itself at birth and is
operational through life and cannot be identified by situations and affective
cues. Experiences, feelings, locations, or people are expressed through
memories of images, behaviors, or emotions. A second, socially accessible
system emerges during the preschool years. It composes the individual's
biographical history and is called the higher order system.

There are significant similarities between parallel processing in the
computer and in the brain: (1) There are processing units where the actual
decisions and calculations take place, (2) memory where information is
stored, and (3) information avenues. Parallel computers utilize numerous
CPUs (central processing units) all operating simultaneously and many
pieces of information can be manipulated simultaneously. There is great
potential for significant levels of parallelism that communicate with thousands of processors, and, in order to perform a calculation, may need to
use data from another processor (Parks 1991).

Translating this into the human information processing system, and
within the complex personality system of a DID patient, access to specific
memory functions may come only through one alter to another, since a
special predesigned system only allows information to be accessed by the
processor's memory (alter's experiences, relationship, and dissociations to
another personality system's memory bank).

From the standpoint of human development, language, memory, affect systems, and cognitive representations simultaneously, and in parallel, manage millions of units of information. These require sharing data, repressing, locating information, dissociating or dislocating sources of information. Synchronization is a primary, intervening structural task. It is required not only of individual processing systems, but also within computers. When a large number of processors try to access memory together, information processing is overloaded and slowed down. In a similar manner, neurological systems on multiple levels of interaction compete for attention in the human brain.

Mesulam (1985) suggests that multiple brain areas are involved for directing attention. These areas include parietal, frontal, and cingulate cortices, which correspond to sensory, motor, and motivational components that are influenced by the reticular activating system. Damage to all three centers produces global attention deficits while lesions to one area produce only partial deficits in attention. Interestingly, lesions in one area may produce multiple deficits because of their proportional representation with multiple areas of functioning.

Peterson and colleagues (1988) measured cerebral blood flow changes to detect brain areas showing activity during three hierarchical word-processing tasks. The authors concluded that the visual information from the occipital cortex proceeds to output coding without phonological recoding in the temporal cortex. The pronunciation of presented words does not stimulate the frontal lobes, while the semantic processing during the word usage task activated the frontal but not the temporal regions. Building on the notion of hierarchical systems in memory and psychodynamic principles, Forest (1991) discusses parallel memory systems across mental and neuropsychiatric defenses in cortical processes. He supports a parallel processing system across multiple channels that are interconnected processes of parallel process systems. Analogical interpretations within the transference, interpreting defenses, and examining the complex interplay of psychological dynamic properties are also examples of multiple parallel systems.

Another reason why patients who experience trauma in their early years of development develop dissociative identity disorders as opposed to integrating one representational system may be the plasticity of brain functioning and the adaptability of the nervous tissue. The brain is capable of modifying its organization to cope with pathological events (Konorski 1948). The impact of trauma is absorbed by creating alternate and more complex parallel processing systems, similar to reactive synaptogenesis (Cotman et al. 1981). Synaptogenesis allows for the remodeling of new neuronal systems. Sprouting enables effective synapsis to be replaced by new ones.

Alter personalities create relationships internally as an avenue for safety in a world that is not a safe place. Hence, the patient's cognitive style for investigating external objects and relationships becomes invested purely within the self, encapsulating a myriad of memories condensed into self-objects, affects, and object connections. Alter personalities may remain in their original form, multiply, or grow as maturation progresses. The hierarchy of the nervous system translates into the parallel memory systems, which may or may not intersect for communication between alter personalities. In fact, Bowlby (1958) suggests that alternative parallel paths of development occur in psychopathology.

To clarify the phenomenon of DID, imagine a three-dimensional cube representing the entire personality system and domains of developmental relevance. At each corner would be a square encapsulating self-objects, their representations, memories, affects, cognitions, psychosocial experiences, developmental tasks, and underlying neurobiological substrates for assimilation and accommodation to trauma events. When an external trauma event is introduced into this information-processing system, the lines interconnecting the encapsulations along a myriad of permutations and multiple tracks become inflexible and rigid (almost frozen in place), dislodged, and dissociated from the larger more integrated personality system. The encapsulated parallel self systems may remain totally isolated, divorced, and sequestered from other self systems. DID is viewed in this developmental model as a disorder of mounting complexity containing intradynamics of object relations, self and cognitive systems, information-processing units, and, moreover, as a multiple memory disorder. Hence, a private, secretive, and self-contained world preserves the entire personality and characterological development of the trauma victim.

Although more complete condensation of treatment implications appears in the following section, it is important to highlight, at this moment, how parallel memory systems and behavioral patterns become encapsulated cognitive representations of an individual's trauma history.

Noam (1992) proposes that particular experiences resist integration to higher order systems. This is a process he called *overassimilation*. It involves incorporating experiences into an earlier structure when a more developed structure exists. The consequences, or products, of overassimilation are encapsulations, which form a living biography. Expanding on Noam's theory of encapsulations, I propose that the psyche has an ability to incorporate different levels of development ranging from less differentiated to more differentiated, which metabolize into separate levels and systems. DID patients link together encapsulations of memory, language, affect, and self structures. Through projective identification, they can be understood in the therapeutic setting as having acquired not only characteristics of their own projections of the self but becoming identified with the objects of its projection (Malin and Grotstein 1966). Hence, the intrapsychic make-up of the trauma victim can best be understood by creating, in the transferential relationship, the level of attachment behavior to animate and inanimate objects, transitional objects to interpersonal relatedness. Separation and attachment issues are mediated affectively both within the patient and within the transference.

Encapsulations contain all of the developmental features and their corresponding affects when the trauma took place. They are represented by age-specific alters representing that period of development. This is a cognitive system based on coping and adjusting to trauma experiences that have overwhelmed the ego or interrupted cognitive development. For example, Putnam (1989) found a significant correlation between the number of different types of childhood trauma reported and the number of alter personalities a patient had suggested. The more traumatized the patient was as a child, the more alter personalities the patient's system will contain. The alters are actually banks of trauma information that is hidden, absent, and/or abandoned by the self to protect against future trauma. Isolated and compartmentalized memories remain well encapsulated and unavailable for immediate recall.

Dissociation is well defined as a way to distance oneself from the external environment. However, the internal self-objects remain available, innervated, and protected. This internalization identifies the struggle for articulation of boundary formation which was not successfully mastered in infancy and childhood. It leads to psychopathology and symptomatology (somatic complaints, eating disorders, sleep disturbances, gastrointestinal distress, suicidal ideations, etc.). The alters represent a chain of defensive systems against the external world for safety. Affectively dissociated and isolated from external traumata, DID is a psychopathological developmental process that disrupts cognitive development, behavior, and psychodynamic systems and structures.

Paradoxically, this represents developmental abilities for assimilation and accommodation. Interpretation of projective identifications and countertransference issues allow the therapist to identify the patient's internal world. Higher levels of development are demonstrated when the child's thinking is characterized by reversibility. Reversibility is also identified as a process necessary for decentering and self-reflection. Later on, abstract concepts (formal operational period of development) and the development of the basis for the hypothetical deductive reasoning processes occur. These are essential components of the psychotherapeutic process to incorporate developmental events as they are acted out and displaced into the present. They account for repetition compulsions, and provide an opportunity for self-reflection and reconstruction.

In trauma victims, the hierarchical integration of cognitive/affective and self–object relations may be seriously undermined and distorted. Hence, encapsulations of memory may take place as a way to dissociate and maintain a sense of self. The process of integrating both internal and external experiences is a motivation toward articulation of boundaries for object constancy and permanence. Within trauma victims, psychic representational and hierarchical system sensations, perceptions, memories, and affective linkages, all move along parallel lines of information processing. They reveal what appear to be separate and distinct personality features.

In less extreme forms, such as single episodes of trauma and/or war, trauma victims dissociate and separate off fragments of sensory experiences. This is in an attempt to compensate for overwhelming stimuli invading personal boundaries. The cognitive, psychological, and parallel information processing system absorb these single events more successfully than situations involving repeated trauma over critical periods of development.

TREATMENT OF TRAUMA AND DISSOCIATIVE IDENTITY DISORDER PATIENTS

Dissociative disorders are perhaps the most perplexing, engaging, and complex diagnoses challenging our clinical acumen. There is a significant amount to learn about the underlying developmental, personality, and neurological systems contributing to this disorder.

The reconstruction of trauma in psychotherapy initiates change by using the patient's highest levels of development to move toward newer and more integrated plateaus of ego development. Through the transferential relationship, parallel lines of development will loosen and become more adaptable and synchronous. The therapist creates an environment for safety, trust, and psychological growth and development for trauma victims. Trauma creates an internal state of overwhelming fear. This sends a clear message to developing internal systems to respond neurophysiologically. Encapsulation occurs in the trauma victim's sensory/perceptual, memory, cognitive, and psychological systems and appears as separate entities, identified as alters.

Psychotherapy helps the patient to grieve for pathological development as well as tolerate ambiguity and depression. A new sense of intersubjectivity is born in the therapeutic relationship free from exploitation and annihilation fantasies for a better sense of self, self-objects, and ultimately personal identity formation.

In the therapeutic transferential relationship, keen attention to bodily signals, tensions, anxieties, and loss of or weakened functioning must be considered as part of the psychogenic experiences laid down at a prelinguistic level, yet exhibiting islands of memory formations of a reflexive, unconscious, nonverbal, and state-dependent condition.

DID and dissociation disorders arise from a developmental dysfunctional psychopathological process occurring across specific modalities of information processing through infancy, childhood, and adolescence, and in some cases of adult PTSD, traumatic experience.

CLINICAL VIGNETTES AND ADDITIONAL IMPLICATIONS

In abuse there is an extensive disruption to normal development without supportive, soothing external objects to help guide or develop trust in the infant/child. Abuse victims are more internally based, creating a situation similar to an occlusion of an artery that increases blood pressure and tension. The patient creates her own environment based on the lack of reciprocity with the external world instead of creating a dialogue with the outside world. She internalizes perceptions, and external perceptions become poorly articulated, differentiated, and lack normal introjection and identification. Children internalize statements of self-reproach, "I am bad. I shouldn't live."

However, the integration of cognition and maturation usually moves forward. In states of deprivation and neglect, psychogenic amnesias, silences, dissociative content, and using others in a persecutory role damage a child's independence, mastery, and conceptualization of self. Boundaries between self and others are poorly articulated. Normal development is thwarted, and the ingredients so essential for the development of the self and articulation of boundaries between self and others exhibit perforations. Overwhelmed by external conflict and pain, trauma victims create, organize, construct an elaborate defensive operational system; they redraw their own boundaries. Bridging the separation of self, affect, and other becomes the challenge for working with severely traumatized individuals.

The treatment of individuals with DID requires a full range of psychotherapeutic skills, techniques, and experiences. Supervision, personal analysis, and inpatient hospital facilities will help structure and secure the environment for constructive, successful therapy. Self-destructive and self-defeating behaviors and acts of violence and hostility against the self are best contained within the conventional techniques of psychodynamic psychotherapy, which will offer more in-depth, comprehensive, and structural therapeutic intervention for integration. The task of therapy is to weave together the various levels of information-processing systems by moving through amnestic barriers, confronting frozen and isolated states of alter personalities, and identifying and elaborating upon developmental periods previously torn away from the self, contributing to random and varying disruptions in development.

The alter personalities represent a chain of defensive symptoms, garnering experiences from projective identification. Projective identification may also result in the self becoming identified with the object of its projection. It is through projective identification that the therapist may be seen in a range of roles and positions including omnipotence, annihilation fantasies, punitive, maternal, or paternal.

Countertransference reactions for withdrawal, disaffective states, detachment, doubts, skepticism, loss of boundaries, and eroticization may occur by paying attention to the different levels of information processing and encapsulations presented by the fantasies and memories of patients whose fears, panic, paranoia, issues of blame, shame, and humiliation all need to be expressed and interpreted.

At times, the avoidance of rejection, responding to negative transferential themes and issues, may leave the therapist feeling unimportant, unprepared, alone, overwhelmed, and continually challenged by the conduct of patients. The therapist's countertransference reactions need to be examined over the course of the work. Identifying nonverbal levels of functioning, weak affective linkages, and cognitive slippages are all available for understanding the extent of trauma and abuse. The therapeutic relationship will undoubtedly be tested over and over again. The relationship to the patient needs to be measured so that repetition of past events will not be reenacted in the treatment.

The development of psychopathology in trauma and DID offers a critical hurdle to overcome. DID is a major memory disorder that contributes to an encapsulation process. Neurophysiological systems, memories, language, learning, cognition, and self systems all enter into the transferential relationship. Brittle, fragmented, and perforated boundaries of different levels of information-processing systems blend together to create alter personalities. How successful personality development and cognitive development was at the point when the trauma was introduced will determine how successful trauma will be handled in the future. In DID and some PTSD disorders, a succession of repeated trauma experiences will tear away at normal development and move the self toward preservation and vigilance, toward remaining hidden and inaccessible to the external world and rooted in the unconscious life of the patient.

The trauma model was applied to both of the following cases. In the case presented on DID, this patient is in a stage of integration (Kluft 1993). By placing the patient's treatment within an information-processing system and utilizing psychodynamic and psychoanalytic conventional techniques, she is off all of her medications except Prozac, which is at a low dose. Treatment has taken approximately two years and six hospitalizations. The last hospitalization was in the latter part of her first year of treatment.

In both cases, psychodynamic psychotherapy and a cognitive information-processing system have assisted in the recovery of lost, impaired, and brittle psychological and cognitive systems present in early childhood relationships which were unsatisfactory, punishing, and traumatic. Placing symptoms within the context of a structured paradigm supports the cognitive work. This offers clear structure, control over impulses, and a sense of well-being for the patient, and does not interfere with the transferential relationship or work of psychodynamic psychotherapy to mend the psychological tapestry that has been frayed and fragmented from early childhood experiences and losses.

Therapists may consider how challenging it is for trauma patients to blend together in-depth levels of psychological material that is reified from dampened and blunted affect states into rich affect connections with corresponding self and other representations. To manage our patients through prolonged periods of grief, mourning, ambivalent separation/attachment themes, suicidal and annihilation gestures and fantasies, anaclitic depressions, pre- and core psychotic states of mind, and early developmental fantasized material requires supportive techniques while the frame of psychodynamic psychotherapy remains firmly in place.

All of our tools as therapists inherited from classical psychoanalytic and psychodynamic psychotherapeutic orientations are well established approaches for working through trauma material. Establishing contact with a range of personality systems and defenses (encapsulations) is an initial step into the myriad character formations in DID patients. Defense analysis is required to assess the psychodynamic quality, strength, fragility, and importance (need gratification) as this relates to the patient's developmental trauma benchmarks.

As more primitive forms of psychopathology emerge there is an equal necessity to structure, complement, acknowledge, and guide our patients in a supportive manner. Therapy requires weaving together, in a reciprocal manner, the patient's cognitive strengths with more compromised levels of character pathology. By blending weaker, less differentiated aspects of the self with more robust and integrative higher order representations contained in parallel memory (encapsulations), our patients will move from plateau to plateau. Treatment will foster a greater capacity to tolerate primitive psychological material.

Even in florid psychotic states there is some semblance of order, rigid but well defined in nonorganic conditions. Hence, through conventional psychotherapy techniques we access unconscious trauma material in an organized manner. We palpate rigid, constrictive, repressive defenses into more resilient defensive modalities and contribute to a more adaptable character style and interaction with others.

Hypnosis and psychodynamic psychotherapy helped to explore our patient's alter personalities and unearthed early childhood traumas of sexual, physical, and psychological abuse. The patient's alters developed to help her manage the overwhelming pain and fear that she experienced during the years of her abuse. It was clear that each alter contained a matrix of neurological and cognitive features, which resembled parallel developmental information-processing systems. Each line of development contained an object, its affects, representations, and neurological substrates.

For example, the patient's child alter represented a change in verbal productions, different semantic and syntactical usage (utilizing telegraphic speech), and altered gait. She appeared troubled, helpless, and remained isolated and separate from other people. She would often play with her stuffed animals, which brought her comfort. In therapy, her memories concerning oral and vaginal penetration were uncovered. She visually recalled many of the childhood memories, feelings, and experiences of being molested by her father. She clearly identified the assertive alter as protecting the core personality from these haunting memories.

The development of the relationship in therapy is the cornerstone of all healing. By establishing feelings of safety, her other personalities emerged gradually. The hateful, negative, and annihilating personality was represented by a calm, determined, and omnipotent figure. This alter wanted "full control" and developed following a rape. She contained the cognitive and developmental features required for going to school, excelling at her work, and integrating highly developed formal operational tasks and abilities. Her language was fluent, showing an expansive vocabulary. Initially she did not know about the memories contained in the child personality. She was directed toward destruction of the self and was the embodiment of the father. Her determination was so clear and cold that she thought nothing about taking handsful of pills, driving her car off of the road, and placing herself in dangerous and unpredictable situations. Treatment involved confrontation, clarification, interpretation, and working through (the four basic procedures used in psychoanalytic psychotherapy). It also entailed integrating a neurophysiological and information processing system for analyzing parallel processing systems. Finally, a supportive environment was constructed that addresses the patient's phenomenological experiences.

Melting away the boundaries across her four altered states has brought her closer to a long-lasting integration. She found psychological energy, enthusiasm, and motivation for building on her life experiences by seeking new employment, and new relationships. She ceased relying on earlier damaged and poorly integrated cognitive representations of herself. Via the transference, she is able to incorporate, introject, and identify with a resilient, permanent, and nonthreatening therapist. Even under conditions of great volatility, she was able to contract for inpatient hospitalizations whenever she needed protection.

In the case of my patient with PTSD, a psychodynamic developmental trauma model was used. Within the first six months, he lost about 20 pounds and was able to put down his cane and walk with a normal gait. He also shaved regularly. There is no evidence for hemiplegia, hemiparesis, or spastic gait. His arm no longer revealed cogwheel rigidity, and ocular motor movements were normal. He displayed no former symptoms of hysteria. This initial phase of therapy identified motor, language, affect, thinking, self-representation systems, and parallel information processing. His neurological symptoms were directly associated to trauma that took place many years ago. This information was concurrently linked to early periods of deprivation and abuse. His language functioning, depth of reflection, and associative memory capacities gradually cleared. Today, he runs his own business but continues to experience significant fugue states.

Through therapy, he is able clearly to identify childhood traumas and events, and how these prepared him for his military career. Sounds, sights, and smells initiate amnestic and fugue states. His memories are strongly linked to these different sensory modalities and filter into a range of memories. By introducing a model of information processing, he is better able to control his affect and identify with greater clarity and depth the stimuli that create a condition for amnesia or fugue states. He is working psychodynamically and integrating this cognitive model. For example, if he experiences a memory, mood shift, amnesia, or fugue state, he will report on his movements, communications, affect, sensory/perceptual experience, and memory systems (visual and nonverbal) that initiated moving into an altered state of consciousness. This has given him a way to manage his underlying dysphoria. This will ultimately enhance his self-esteem. Psychotherapy will address developmental issues pertaining to self–object representations and interpersonal relationships.

CONCLUDING REMARKS

The DID diagnosis represents multiple levels of information processing and related psychodynamic underpinnings that created the symptoms of seemingly separate and distinct personalities. Part of therapy is teaching abuse victims how to think about their inner experience and move toward integrating these different levels of development that were missed during early development. They did not develop or experience the navigation techniques or support from parents to help reintegrate their personal experience in a more organized manner. The developmental model for trauma is a system to identify patients' underlying pain, wounds, and fragmented sense of themselves in a complex and challenging world. Therefore, it is important to identify the highest levels of cognitive functioning and to utilize these structures to anchor less-developed cognitive and dynamic structures and perceptions.

A plethora of information comes into the treatment setting. The material in the transferential relationship addresses major inconsistencies, incompatible memories, trauma experiences, and so forth. The therapist is the instrument for change and the receiver of data. Within the relationship the therapist begins to weave this material together to confront and interpret the patient's experiences.

With many trauma patients, I maintain a dream journal to help document the symbols, content, and process of the psychotherapy. It is also through the unconscious dream-life of the patient that previously amnestic material, fugue states, and alternates containing trauma information may reappear in the dream and be recalled or recognized by a smell, sound, touch, or voice that brings back the memory in the domain of the dream, which is later linked more appropriately with conscious symbols, beliefs, impressions, and affects.

For example, with my patient who is diagnosed with DID, the destructive alter communicated to another personality in a dream that she was guilty of suicidal attempts, and revealed where she had hoarded medications. Previously the two alters were purported to be in an amnestic state. My patient with PTSD reported a dream in which "someone asked me about my childhood with specific reference to my father." He recalls that he was beaten and left outside with his face swollen. "I recalled having knots, bruises, and hair matted with blood as a wrench swung across my head." In another dream he relived fighting in combat and observed several companions and a loved one burning, and other aggressive acts of destruction. This dream was initiated by the taste of blood in his mouth, which he experienced as an abused child.

I firmly believe that dreams are a reflection of dissociative material and communicate important information about the dreamer's mental state. The dream communicates unconscious images and impressions to the therapist concerning the internal state of the patient. Often concrete, affectless, and psychotic themes foreshadow suicide attempts and/or recurrent major depressive episodes. Dreams may reflect the integration of language, memory, affect, self–object relations, and cognitive development before it is consciously integrated and identified to the patient as a symbol of progress.

Through the delicate process of psychotherapy, healing can be initiated, discovered, and shared with our trauma patients to help end their isolation, fear, and threats from previously perceived violence against the self. As Fairbairn (1952) suggests, the internalization of the object is a defense originally adopted by the child to deal with the original trauma. Internalization is not just a product of fantasy but is a distinct psychological process.

Over the years I have considered the neurological and medical complications that my patients who have aphasic conditions have experienced, as well as locked-in syndromes from spinal cord injuries and concomitant head injuries. I have also thought about the deaf children and adults with whom I have worked and who have used all forms of communication to express their thoughts, feelings, and beliefs. In many ways, dissociative disorders stemming from trauma closely approximate the nonverbal confusion that these other individuals have also experienced. Much like the deaf child, the aphasic patient's world often remains hidden and unavailable to the outside observer. The psychotherapist becomes the tool to help penetrate the inner world of dissociative identities and dissociative disorders.

256   DISSOCIATIVE IDENTITY DISORDER

REFERENCES

Ainsworth M. D. (1964). Patterns of attachment behavior shown by the infant in interaction with his mother. *Merrill-Palmer Quarterly* 10:51–58.

Atkinson, R. C., and Shiffrin, R. M. (1968). Human memory: a proposed system and its control processes. In *Advances in the Psychology of Learning and Motivation Research and Theory*, ed. K. W. Spence and J. T. Spence, pp. 89–195. New York: Academic.

Baddelely, A. D., and Hitch, G. J. (1974). Working memory. In *The Psychology of Learning and Motivation*, ed. G. H. Bower, pp. 47–90. New York: Academic.

Baillargeon, R. (1986). Representing the existence and location of hidden objects: object permanence in 6 and 8 month olds. *Cognition* 23:21–41.

Basch, M. F. (1976). The concept of affects: a reexamination. *Journal of the American Psychoanalytic Association* 24:759–777.

Benschoten, S. C. (1990). Multiple personality disorder and satanic ritual abuse: the issue of credibility. *Dissociation* 3:22–30.

Bjorklund, D. F. (1985). The role of conceptual knowledge in the development of organization in children's memories. In *Basic Processes in Memory Development*, ed. C. J. Brainerd and M. Pressley, pp. 103–142. New York: Springer-Verlag.

Boon, S., and Draijer, N. (1991). Diagnosing dissociative disorders in the Netherlands: a pilot study with the structured clinical interview for *DSM-III-R: dissociative disorders. American Journal of Psychiatry* 148:458–462.

Bower, G. H. (1981). Mood and memory. *American Psychologist* 36:129–148.

Bowlby, J. (1958). The nature of the child tied to his mother. *International Journal of Psychology* 39:350–373.

Braun, B. G. (1984). Towards a theory of multiple personality and other dissociative phenomenon. *Psychiatric Clinics of North America* 7:171–193.

Butters, N., and Stuss, D. T. (1989). Diencephalic amnesia. In *Handbook of Neuropsychology*, ed. F. Bollar and J. Grafman, pp. 107–148. Amsterdam: Elsevier.

Charney, D. S., Deutch, A. Y., Krystal, J. H., et al. (1993). Psychobiological mechanisms of post traumatic stress disorder. *Archives of General Psychiatry* 50:294–305.

Cole, P. M., and Putnam, F. W. (1992). Affects of incest on self and social functioning: a developmental psychopathology perspective. *Journal of Consulting and Clinical Psychology* 60:174–184.

Coons, P. M., Bowman, E. S., and Pellow, T. A. (1989). Post traumatic aspects of the treatment of victims of sexual abuse and incest. *Psychiatric Clinics of North America* 12:325–337.

Coons, P. M., and Milstein, V. (1992). Psychogenic amnesia: a clinical investigation of 25 cases. *Dissociation* 4:73–79.

Cotman, C. P., Nieto-Sampedro, M., and Harris, E. W. (1981). Synapsis replacement in the adult nervous system of vertebrates. *Physiological Review* 61:684–784.

Cowan, N. (1988). Evolving conceptions of memory storage: selective attention and their mutual constraints within the human information-processing system. *Psychological Bulletin* 104:163–191.

Crossin, B. (1992). *Subcortical Functions in Language and Memory*. New York: Guilford.

Dell, P. F. (1988). Professional skepticism about multiple personality disorders. *The Journal of Nervous and Mental Disease* 176:528–531.

Deloache, J. S. (1989). The development of representation in the young child. *Advances in Child Development and Behavior* 22:1–39.

DeWied, D., and Croiset, G. (1991). Stress modulation of learning and memory processes. *Methods Achieve Experimental Pathology* 15:167–199.

Elin, M. (1994). *Domains of Developmental Relevance from Trauma*. Manuscript in progress.

Engel, G., Reichsman, F., and Viederman, M. (1978). Monica: a 25 year longitudinal study of the consequences of trauma in infancy. *Scientific Proceedings-Panel Reports: Annual Meetings of the American Psychoanalytic Association*. Atlanta, May, 107–126.

Fahy, T. A. (1988). The diagnosis of multiple personality disorder: a critical review. *British Journal of Psychiatry* 153:597–606.

Fairbairn, W. R. D. (1952). *Psycho-Analytic Studies of the Personality*. New York: Basic Books.

Feinstein, A., and Spiegel, D. (1989). Post traumatic stress disorder: a descriptive study supporting *DSM-III-R* criteria. *American Journal of Psychiatry* 146:665–666.

Femina, D. D., Yeager, C. A., and Lewis, D. O. (1990). Child abuse: adolescent records versus adult recall. *Child Abuse and Neglect* 14:227–231.

Forest, D. V. (1991). Mental, neuropsychic, and brain patterns of defense. *Journal of the American Academy of Psychoanalysis* 19:99–123.

Frankel, F. H. (1993). Adult reconstruction of childhood events in the multiple personality literature. *American Journal of Psychiatry* 150:954–958.

Frischholz, E. J. (1985). *The Relationship between Dissociation, Hypnosis, and Child Abuse and the Development of Multiple Personality. Childhood and Descendants of Multiple Personality*. Washington, DC: American Psychiatric Press.

Gardner, L. I. (1973). Deprivation dwarfism. *Scientific American*. San Francisco: W. H. Freeman and Co.

Gedo, J. E. (1979). *Beyond Interpretation*. New York: International Universities Press.

Gedo, J. E., and Wilson, A. eds. (1993). The hierarchical model of mental functioning: sources and applications. In *Psychoanalysis*, pp. 129–152. New York: Guilford.

Glover, E. (1979). *The Technique of Psychoanalysis*. New York: International Universities Press.

Gold, P. E., and von Buskirk, R. (1978). Post training brain norepinephrine concentrations: correlation with retention performance of avoidance training with peripheral epinephrine modulation of memory processing. *Behavioral Biology* 23:509–520.

Grant, S. J., and Redmond, D. E. (1981). The neuroanatomy and pharmacology at the nucleus locus coeruleus. In *Pharmacology of Clonidine*, ed. H. Lal and S. Fielding. New York: Alan R. Liss.

Greenson, R. (1967). *The Technique and Practice of Psychoanalysis*. New York: International Universities Press.

Grinker, R. R., and Spiegel, J. J. (1945). *Men under Stress*. New York: McGraw-Hill.

Halgren, E. (1992). Emotional physiology of the amygdala within the context of human cognition. In *The Amygdala*, ed. J. T. Aggleton, pp. 191–228. New York: Wiley-Liss.

Halgren, E., Walter, R. D., and Grandall, P. H. (1978). Mental phenomenon evoked by electrical stimulation of the human hippocampal formation and amygdala. *Brain* 101:83–117.

Hartman, C. R., and Burgess, A. W. (1993). Information processing of trauma. *Child Abuse and Neglect* 17:47–58.

Janet, P. (1920). *The Major Symptoms of Hysteria*. New York: Hafner.

Kluft, R. P. (1993). *The Integration of Personalities: Clinical Perspectives on Multiple Personality Disorder*. Washington, DC: American Psychiatric Press.

Konorski, J. (1948). *Conditioned Reflexes in Neuron Organization*. Cambridge: Cambridge University Press.

Ludwig, A., Brandsma, J., and Wilbur, C. (1972). The objective study of multiple personality disorders. *Archives of General Psychiatry* 26:298–310.

Malin, A., and Grotstein, J. S. (1966). Projective identification: the therapeutic process. *International Journal of Psychoanalysis* 47:26–31.

McGaugh, J. L., Introini-Collison, I. B., Cahill, L., et al. (1992). Involvement of the amygdala in neuromodulatory influences on memory storage. In *The Amygdala*, ed. J. T. Aggleton. New York: Wiley-Liss.

Meltzoff, A. (1990). Towards a developmental cognitive science: the implications of cross-model matching and imitation for the development of representation and memory in infancy. *Annals of New York Academy of Science* 608:1–31.

Merskey, H. (1992). The manufacture of personalities: the production of multiple personality disorder. *British Journal of Psychiatry* 160:327–340.

Mesulam, M. (1985). *Principles of Behavioral Neurology*. Philadelphia: F. A. Davis.

Miller, S. (1989). Optical differences in cases of multiple personality disorder. *Journal of Nervous and Mental Disease* 177:480–486.

Mishkin, M. (1978). Memory in monkeys is severely impaired by combined but not by separate removal of amygdala in hippocampus. *Nature* 273:297–298.

Nelson, C. A. (1994). Neural correlates of recognition memory in the first post natal year. In *Human Behavior in the Developing Brain*, ed. G. Dawson and C. Fischer, pp. 269–313. New York: Guilford.

Nissen, M. J., Ross, J. L., Willingham, D. B., et al. (1988). Memory and awareness in the patient with multiple personality disorder. *Brain and Cognition* 8:117–134.

Ornstein, P. A., Naus, M. J., and Liberty, C. (1975). Rehearsal and organizational processes in children's memory. *Child Development* 26:818–830.

Parks, R. W. (1991). Parallel distributed processing and neural networks: origins, methodology and cognitive functions. *International Journal of Neuroscience* 60:195–214.

Peterson, S. E., Fox, P. T., Posner, M. I., et al. (1988). Positron emission tomographic studies of the cortical anatomy of single-word processing. *Nature* 331:585–589.

Piaget, J. (1971). *Biology and Knowledge*. Chicago: University of Chicago Press.

Pillemer, D. D., and White, S. H. (1989). Childhood events recalled by children and adults. *Advances in Child Development and Behavior* 21:297–340.

Putnam, F. W. (1986a). The scientific study of multiple personality disorder. In *Split Minds Split Brains*, ed. J. M. Quen, pp. 109–125. New York: New York University Press.

―――― (1986b). Development, reliability, and validity of a dissociative scale. *Journal of Nervous and Mental Disorders* 174:727–735.

―――― (1989). *Diagnosis and Treatment of Multiple Personality Disorder*. New York: Guilford.

―――― (1991). Recent research on multiple personality disorder. *Psychiatric Clinics of North America* 14:489–502.

Putnam, F. W., Zahn, T., and Post, R. (1990). Differential autonomic nervous system activity in multiple personality disorder. *Psychiatry Research* 31:251–260.

Ross, E. D., Homan, R. W., and Buck, R. (1994). Differential hemispheric lateralization of primary and social emotions. *Neuropsychiatry, Neuropsychology, and Behavior Neurology* 7:1–19.

Ross, V., Weingartner, H., and Post, R. M. (1979). Clinical implications of state dependent learning. *American Journal of Psychiatry* 136:927–931.

Rowan, J. A., and Rosenbaum, D. H. (1991). Ictal amnesia and fugue states. In *Advances in Neurology*. ed. D. Smith, D. Treiman, and M. Trimble, pp. 357–367. New York: Raven.

Schacter, D. L. (1990). Perceptual representation systems and implicit memory: toward a resolution of the multiple memory systems debate. *Annals of the New York Academy of Science* 608:543–571.

Schacter, D. L., and Kilstrom, J. F. (1989). Functional Amnesia. In *Handbook of Neuropsychology*, ed. F. Bowler and J. Grafman, pp. 209–231. New York: Elsevier Science.

Silberman, E. K., Putnam, F. W., Weingartner, H., et al. (1985). Dissociative states in multiple personality disorder: a quantitative study. *Psychiatry Research* 15:253–260.

Spiegel, D. (1984). Multiple personality as a post traumatic stress disorder. *Psychiatric Clinics of North America* 7:101–110.

Spiegel, D., and Cardena, F. (1991). Disintegrated experience: the dissociative disorders revisited. *Journal of Abnormal Psychology* 100:366–378.

Squire, L. R. (1986). Mechanisms of memory. *Science* 232:1612–1619.

Squire, L. R., and Butters, N. (1992). *Neuropsychology of Memory*, 2nd ed. New York: Guilford.

Thompson, J. G., and Meyers, N. A. (1985). Inferences and recalls at ages 4 and 7. *Child Development* 56:1134–1144.

Tomkins, S. S. (1963). *Affect/Imagery/Consciousness. The Negative Affects*. New York: Springer.

Trickett, P. K., and Putnam, F. W. (1993). Impact of child sexual abuse on females: toward a developmental, psychobiological integration. *Psychological Sciences* 4:81–87.

Tulving, E., and Schacter, D. L. (1990). Priming and human memory systems. *Science* 247:301–306.

Valent, P. (1984). The Ash Wednesday bush fires in Victoria. *Medical Journal of Australia* 141:291–330.

Warrington, E. K., and Weiskranz, L. (1982). Amnesia: the disconnection syndrome? *Neuropsychologia* 20:233–248.

Weiskranz, L. (1956). Behavioral changes associated with ablation of the amygdala complex in monkeys. *Journal of Comparative and Physiological Psychology* 49:381–391.

Wilkinson, C. B. (1983). Aftermath of a disaster: the collapse of the Hyatt Regency Hotel skywalk. *American Journal of Psychiatry* 140:1134–1139.

9

Diagnosis of Dissociative Identity Disorder

Colin A. Ross

To be valid, the method of diagnosing dissociative identity disorder (DID), must be the same as that used throughout *DSM-IV*, as exemplified by the decision trees for differential diagnosis contained in Appendix A of the Manual (American Psychiatric Association 1994). The decision tree method advocated by the American Psychiatric Association is based on the standard approach to differential diagnosis in general medicine taught in medical schools throughout the world. The approach to the diagnosis of DID that I will describe is traditional, conservative, academic, mainstream, scientific, and medical.

In this chapter I will describe the general principles of differential diagnosis, the use of the Dissociative Experiences Scale (DES) (Bernstein and Putnam 1986), the Dissociative Disorders Interview Schedule (DDIS) (Ross 1989, Ross et al. 1989b), and the Structured Clinical Interview for *DSM-IV* Dissociative Disorders (SCID-D) (Steinberg 1993, Steinberg et al. 1990). I will then delineate the clinical diagnosis and differential diagnosis of DID in detail.

In order to make a valid and reliable diagnosis of DID, it is not necessary to believe in any particular model or theory of the etiology or intrapsychic reality of the disorder, nor need one believe that the identities or personality states are concretely or literally real. That is not how the *DSM-IV* diagnostic system works. To make a *DSM-IV* diagnosis, one follows operationalized rules laid out in the Manual, based on clinical history and mental status examination. Debates about the "reality" of DID are irrelevant to discussion of its diagnosis and differential diagnosis: likewise,

261

disagreements about the etiology and pathological mechanisms of schizophrenia are irrelevant to the *DSM-IV* process of making the diagnosis.

The *DSM-IV* diagnostic process has been deliberately designed to remove ideology as much as possible, and to base diagnostic decisions on phenomenology. In this spirit, terms like *hysterical* and *neurosis* have been removed from the diagnostic terminology because they are derived from ideology, not scientific research, and because they introduce too much bias into the system. Someone who believes that schizophrenia is a biomedical brain illness driven predominantly by abnormal genes should diagnose schizophrenia in the same way, with the same reliability and validity, as someone who believes its causation is purely psychosocial. The *DSM-IV* system is designed to be as atheoretical as possible, and to avoid presumptions about etiology in making diagnoses.

Despite the effort to remove politics from *DSM-IV*, the pervasive influence of ideology in the Manual is still evident, and I review this further elsewhere (Ross 1994). The diagnosis of DID should be approached in the same spirit as that for any other psychiatric disorder.

DSM-IV DIAGNOSTIC CRITERIA FOR DISSOCIATIVE IDENTITY DISORDER

The most important changes made to DID in *DSM-IV*, in comparison to *DSM-III-R*, are in the textual description of the disorder. The text has been updated, clarified, and much improved based on developments in the field over the intervening seven years. In the *DSM-IV Draft Criteria* (American Psychiatric Association 1992), the name of the disorder was listed as "dissociative identity disorder (multiple personality disorder)" (p. n: 1). In *DSM-IV* itself, however, the wording is "dissociative identity disorder (*formerly* multiple personality disorder)" (p. 484). This means that use of the term MPD is now disallowed, whereas in the draft criteria it appeared to be optional.

The diagnostic criteria are:

A. The presence of two or more distinct identities or personality states (each with its own relatively enduring pattern of perceiving, relating to, and thinking about the environment and self).
B. At least two of these identities recurrently take control of the person's behavior.
C. Inability to recall important personal information that is too extensive to be explained by ordinary forgetfulness.

D. The disturbance is not due to the direct physiological effects of a substance (e.g., blackouts or chaotic behavior during Alcohol Intoxication) or a general medical condition (e.g., complex partial seizures). *Note:* In children, the symptoms are not attributable to imaginary playmates or other fantasy play. [p. 487]

Criterion C, the amnesia criterion, was introduced in the *DSM-IV* criteria set in order to narrow the definition of the disorder and reduce false positive diagnoses due to ego state disorders, incomplete forms of DID, trance-possession phenomena, and other forms of dissociation. Although this is a good idea in principle, and based in part on research data of mine (Ross et al. 1990), in fact the mere presence of amnesia does not differentiate DID from dissociative disorder not otherwise specified (DDNOS), because all subjects with both disorders report amnesia. This conclusion was demonstrated by comparing 166 subjects with clinical diagnoses of DID to 57 with clinical diagnoses of DDNOS on the DES and DDIS (Ross et al. 1992). What differentiates DID from DDNOS is the greater degree and complexity of the amnesia in DID, not the simple presence or absence of amnesia. Nevertheless, amnesia is a universal feature of DID.

There is a scholarly error in *DSM-IV* (1994) in Appendix D, where it is stated that "the DSM-III requirement that there be inability to recall important personal information has been reinstated" (p. 784). How this erroneous idea became a piece of accepted folklore within the dissociative disorders field, I don't know, but examination of the *DSM-III* criteria for multiple personality disorder reveals that there is no requirement for amnesia in the criteria set (American Psychiatric Association 1980).

The diagnostic criteria for DID have been criticized as being too vague, and complaints are made that the definition of what constitutes a personality state is too subjective. This is an erroneous criticism for two reasons: first, the way to decide whether the criteria are too vague is to examine data from studies of reliability, not to make ideological arguments. In fact, the reliability of DID is higher than that for any other psychiatric disorder. Second, the criteria are no more vague than those elsewhere in *DSM-IV*. Consider *DSM-IV* 1994 criterion B for Alcohol Intoxication, for instance:

B. Clinically significant maladaptive behavioral or psychological changes (e.g., inappropriate sexual or aggressive behavior, mood liability, impaired judgment, impaired social or occupational functioning) that developed during, or shortly after alcohol ingestion. [p. 197]

One could complain that phrases like "clinically significant maladapative behavior," "inappropriate sexual or aggressive behavior," and "impaired

social or occupational functioning" are highly subjective, not operationalized, subject to cultural bias, and really just represent the medicalization of
harmless recreation. Psychiatry could be described as a puritanical social
agency designed to inhibit people from having fun at parties. Although
this criticism would be regarded as preposterous by most psychiatrists, it
is logically and scientifically as well founded as the analogous criticism of
DID criteria.

Similar criticisms of criterion B for schizophrenia, criterion A for specific
phobia, and criterion A (1) for major depressive episode could be made.
The fact that such criticisms are made differentially against DID criteria,
when they could just as well be directed at any other psychiatric disorder,
is another example of ideological prejudice masquerading as scientific
argument within psychiatry.

DIAGNOSIS AND DIFFERENTIAL DIAGNOSIS WITHIN GENERAL MEDICINE

If a patient comes to a doctor with a sore knee, the doctor has to construct
both a differential diagnosis and a diagnosis. He does this by asking a
series of questions in a decision tree format, then conducting a physical
examination. I was taught in medical school that 90 percent of clinical
diagnoses can made by history alone, and that history taking is the major
diagnostic medical skill. The differential diagnosis is a short list of possible diagnoses that the doctor is considering seriously, and the diagnosis
is the one he favors and eventually confirms. Each disorder in general
medicine has its fixed differential diagnosis, which can be modified if
additional or unusual signs or symptoms are present. A sign is a physical
manifestation of disease directly observed by the doctor, while a symptom
is an experience reported by the patient, such as pain, blood in the urine
a day earlier, or blurry vision.

If the problem is a sore knee, the doctor will ask certain initial questions
that lead him down one or another major branch in the decision tree. For
instance, he may ask when the pain started. If the patient replies that it
started immediately upon being tackled from the left rear by a linebacker
during a football game, in the absence of any prior symptoms, the doctor
is led down an acute physical trauma branch of the decision tree, and drops
arthritis and infection from his differential diagnosis. He will then ask more
specific questions, already suspecting that the injury may be to the medial
collateral ligament.

If, on the other hand, the sore knee arose gradually over the past two days in a woman in her twenties, and the knee is described as red, swollen, and warm, in the absence of any physical injury, a tackle by a linebacker causing a tear of the medial collateral ligament is dropped from consideration. The doctor will be considering a gonorrheal arthritis more seriously, and will ask questions about sexual contacts and urinary symptoms, which he would not ask of the football player. Alternatively, if the patient is 70 years old, and the pain has been present for six years, osteoarthritis rises to the top of the differential diagnosis, and the doctor asks a different series of questions.

The general method is to ask screening questions, the answers to which force the doctor down different branches of the decision tree. As one moves down the decision tree to smaller and smaller branches, the range of possible diagnoses narrows until finally there is only one diagnostic possibility. For certain diseases such as streptococcal pneumonia, the diagnostic decision tree is relatively simple and fixed, while for others, such as systemic lupus erythematosis, is it complex and subtle. However, in all cases the principles remain the same.

In general medicine one never hears debates about the validity of streptococcal pneumonia because the diagnosis, laboratory investigation, and specific treatment of this disorder are scientifically established. Debates such as that about the reality of DID can only occur in the absence of science, and they cease to exist when scientific answers are obtained.

USE OF THE DES, DDIS, AND SCID-D IN DIAGNOSING DISSOCIATIVE IDENTITY DISORDER

The DES is a self-report screening measure with excellent reliability and validity (Bernstein and Putnam 1986, Boon and Draijer 1993ab, Carlson et al. 1993). It yields a score ranging from 0–100, with higher scores increasing the likelihood of a dissociative disorder. Patients with DID consistently have the highest scores of any diagnostic group, with average scores in the upper 30s, 40s, or 50s, compared to general population mean scores of 10–11 (Ross et al. 1991a). Patients with DDNOS tend to have average DES scores in the 20s or low 30s.

In our study comparing 166 subjects with DID to 57 with DDNOS (Ross et al. 1992), the DID group had an average DES score of 39.7 (S.D. 18.3), while the average score for the DDNOS group was 21.7 (S.D. 17.0), $(t(193) = 6.106, p\ .00001)$. This means that about 15 percent of those with DID scored below 20 on the DES. A discriminant function analysis of the

DDIS in this study demonstrated that it could correctly assign 91.4 percent of the DID subjects to the DID category, a level of performance not exceeded by any other structured interview diagnosis in psychiatry

Studies have employed DES cutoff scores of 15, 20, 25 or 30 in screening for dissociative disorders (Boon and Draijer 1993ab, Ross et al. 1991a, Steinberg et al. 1991). The decision as to what cutoff score to use is based on several considerations. The higher the cutoff score used, the fewer people will have to be assessed carefully for dissociative disorders, therefore the less time and energy required. However, the higher the cutoff score, the more low-scoring DID cases will not be entered into the intensive assessment phase.

Alternatively, the lower the cutoff score, the fewer cases will be missed, but the more people without dissociative disorders will have to be intensively assessed. Deciding on a DES cutoff score to be used in a given setting involves a trade-off between the importance of not missing cases, and the resources available for more careful diagnostic workup. Sophisticated statistical methods for analyzing these trade-offs are available (Boon and Draijer 1993a, Steinberg et al. 1991), but these are not of any use in daily clinical work. Overall, I recommend regarding DES scores above 20 as suspicious for a dissociative disorder, above 30 as strongly suggestive, and above 40 as highly suggestive.

It is possible to have full DID and a DES score in the normal range, and it is possible to have a high DES score and not have any dissociative disorder: higher scores simply increase the index of suspicion for the disorder. The DES takes ten minutes to complete and can be scored by a student or receptionist.

Once the DES cutoff score is set, clients, patients, or research subjects with scores above the cutoff can then be interviewed with the DDIS or SCID-D. The third phase of the assessment is a clinical diagnostic interview, which is always required to confirm or disconfirm the structured interview diagnosis. Data available to date indicate that if the DDIS makes a diagnosis of DID, there is only a 1 percent chance that this is not the correct diagnosis. Use of the DES, DDIS, or SCID-D in clinical work is not compulsory, and the diagnosis of DID can be made to acceptable standards of practice on a clinical basis alone.

How to Make a Clinical Diagnosis of Dissociative Identity Disorder

Three texts (Boon and Draijer 1993a, Putnam 1989, Ross 1989) and two papers (Kluft 1985, Loewenstein 1991) review the diagnosis and mental status examination of DID in detail. Further information is available in the SCID-D manual (Steinberg 1993). Although this is a brief list of references, it leads the reader into the literature.

There are a few major screening questions and considerations that lead the clinician into the differential diagnosis of DID:

1. Does the patient suffer from blank spells or periods of missing time?
2. Does she or he describe auditory hallucinations (hearing voices)?
3. Is there a history of severe, chronic childhood trauma?
4. Does she or he meet or nearly meet *DSM-IV* criteria for borderline personality disorder?
5. Can a thought disorder be ruled out?

If all of these can be answered in the affirmative, DID is the leading possibility in the differential diagnosis. Each of these items can be inquired about briefly, then the clinician can return to each one sequentially for more detailed history taking, or each can be reviewed in detail after it is first asked about—it is a matter of clinician preference which approach is used. As in all history taking, one starts with open-ended questions and gradually narrows down to more specific closed-ended questions. At least 5 percent of general adult psychiatric inpatients will meet all of these five screening criteria for DID (Ross et al. 1991a). They can be inquired about without any demand characteristics for false endorsement of DID.

The iatrogenic model of DID holds that organized signs and symptoms of the disorder do not exist prior to first contact with a clinician who generates the invalid diagnosis. This position has been broadened by Merskey (1992) who maintains that the culture in general can create invalid cases through media influence, although reinforcement by a misguided clinician is still required. He would also assert that the condition can be extinguished by a skeptic who does not reinforce it. I agree with Dr. Merskey that if the condition does not preexist contact with the clinician diagnosing it, then it is not genuine DID.

In most cases, a diagnosis of DID or a provisional diagnosis of DDNOS can be made at the first contact with the mental-health system. Most patients will give a history of DID diagnostic criteria and secondary features dating back to adolescence or childhood. Often many of these can be confirmed by a friend or relative, and quite commonly there is clear evidence of undiagnosed DID in prior medical records. One seeks collateral confirmation of the diagnosis in the same way that one does for schizophrenia or bipolar mood disorder, but not more so.

In two large DID series totaling 336 cases, the average length of time in the mental health care system prior to diagnosis of the DID was 6.8 years

(Putnam et al. 1986, Ross et al. 1989a). During this period the subjects in these two large series received two to three other psychiatric diagnoses. In a series of 102 cases of DID from four centers (Ross et al. 1990), 95.1 percent had received prior psychiatric treatment, and 86.3 percent had been prescribed psychotropic medication or ECT. Of the 102 DID patients, 26.5 percent had a prior diagnosis of schizophrenia, while out of 236 DID cases in another series (Ross et al. 1989c) 40.8 percent had a prior clinical diagnosis of schizophrenia. Putnam and colleagues (1986) reported prior diagnoses of schizophrenia in just under 50 percent of their 100 DID cases.

A not unusual situation is exemplified by a case on which I was a consultant. Another consultant had concluded that the DID had been artifactually created during a three-year psychotherapy. However, hospital records from an admission six years prior to the onset of the therapy revealed that the patient believed she had been possessed by demons since childhood, described three different sexual abuse perpetrators, wanted to get the parts of herself integrated in treatment, and reported amnesia for parts of a sexual assault. She reported that the demons had originally protected her but were now abusive toward her, and a note describes a demon taking executive control and frightening a social worker. Another note describes the patient being amnestic for a letter she wrote to a social worker that was signed with a different name. A dissociative disorder was not mentioned in the differential diagnosis in the record, and there was no evidence that her sexual trauma had been discussed with her at any time during the hospitalization, other than on intake history.

A history of many different prior diagnoses and failure to respond to a variety of different treatments is a soft indicator for undiagnosed DID. Any adequate model of the disorder must account for the frequent prior diagnoses of schizophrenia, the frequent hospitalizations and suicide attempts, the fact that up to 16 percent of DID patients have received ECT prior to diagnosis, and the clear indicators of chronic complex dissociative symptoms in prior medical records. It is not rare for the names of alter personalities to be recorded in nursing notes of previous admissions, with no discussion of dissociation by the attending physician. These objective empirical facts about undiagnosed DID patients are not consistent with a hysteria-based model of the disorder, unless the vast majority of psychiatrists are unable to differentiate hysteria from psychosis and vegetative depression

In a study of 774 emergency department consultation reports by the Department of Psychiatry at St. Boniface Hospital in Winnipeg, Canada from 1985 to 1991, amnesia was not commented on in 96.1 percent of cases. A history of childhood physical abuse was not commented on in 89.7 percent of cases, and of sexual abuse in 87.7 percent of cases, indicating that such information was not considered important, asked about, or recorded. By comparison, depressed mood was not commented on in 29.3 percent of cases, suicidal ideation in 26. 6 percent, and auditory hallucinations in 61.2 percent (Ross and Clark 1992). These figures indicate sloppy clinical consultation work in general, and almost complete absence of any attempt to assess for dissociative disorders. There is no reason to think that performance in this department, where I was a full-time academic staff member from 1985 to 1991, is inferior to the norm for North America. This study could be replicated in the medical records of any Department of Psychiatry in the world, and I'm sure the findings would be similar.

Assessment of Amnesia

Most people are amnestic for well over 99 percent of the information they have consciously registered during their lifetimes. This is self-evident if one tries to list everything eaten at all breakfasts since birth. One would think that the differentiation of normal from pathological amnesia would therefore be impossible due to a ceiling effect, but this is not the case. Individuals with DID report forms of amnesia that do not occur in the absence of that diagnosis.

A general principle in differentiating DID from DDNOS, borderline personality disorder, or other conditions is that dissociative symptoms exist on a spectrum of increasing severity and complexity linked to increasingly severe childhood trauma. Boon and Draijer (1993a) and my research group (Ross et al. 1992a) have provided empirical support for this model. Clinically, DID patients exhibit forms of amnesia that span the full range of the continuum, from normal to those pathognomonic for the disorder.

In a classic, fully crystallized, active case of DID, the person describes recurrent periods of missing time. For instance, the person may be at home at 10:00 in the morning, and suddenly it is 7:30 P.M., and the person is downtown in a bar, unaware of how she got there. The period of missing time is completely blanked out and the onset and offset of the amnesia are instantaneous. During the period of amnesia the person has been engaging in complex, purposeful, organized, socially unremarkable behavior, and has not appeared to be disoriented, mentally ill, or in a trance. It is not difficult to obtain collateral history about the person's mental status during at least some of the amnestic periods—the behavior may be out of character in comparison to that which is usual for the individual, but would not be unusual for someone of a different character type.

The periods of missing time most commonly last minutes or hours, but can last days or weeks. In some cases a period of several years may be completely missing, and this may include important events like marriage, graduation, or childbirth, with no concurrent substance abuse. Usually the person has been experiencing blank spells since childhood, and often she will describe being accused of things she did not do, or accused of lying repeatedly as a child. Not uncommonly, however, the person is not directly aware of missing time, though it can be inferred from secondary features to be described below. Some people don't realize that it is abnormal to miss blocks of time, and assume that everyone experiences such amnesia.

When the blank spells get very short, they can be difficult to differentiate from normal lapses of attention and concentration. For instance, some patients report suddenly coming to and finding themselves in a different room in the house, unable to remember walking there. This in and of itself is not an indicator of DID, unless numerous other symptoms are also present.

Blank spells can also vary in their degree of density. If one thinks of blank spells as caused by a screen imposed between the person and the world, the screen can gradually be made more and more transparent—the blank spells may be patchy and incomplete, and difficult to differentiate from episodes of depersonalization. In fact, if one starts with a full, dense blank spell, and gradually reduces the density, one will arrive at classical descriptions of depersonalization, such as looking at the world through a fog. I mention this to point out that the relationship between amnesia and depersonalization is complex.

Another form of amnesia is massive amnesia for childhood which has no discrete onset or offset. This is an indicator of childhood trauma of some kind, though not necessarily sexual abuse, and can occur in people without DID or DDNOS. The *DSM-IV* criteria for psychogenic amnesia disorder have been broadened from the *DSM-III-R* criteria for psychogenic amnesia to include this common form of traumatic amnesia for childhood. Since it is normal not to remember most of one's childhood, there is a gray zone in which it is difficult to differentiate traumatic amnesia from normal forgetting.

In one case, a woman reported to me that she had 100 percent amnesia for her childhood and that her memories suddenly begin during her fourteenth birthday; this is clearly not normal forgetting. A variant is for someone to report apparently normal memory up to age 9, complete amnesia from age 9 to 12, than apparently normal memory thereafter. If the person exhibits the full DDIS profile for DDNOS or DID, reports no childhood sexual abuse, but remarks that an alcoholic stepfather lived with her and her mother during this period, before being jailed for sexual abuse of a cousin of the patient's, the clinical implications are clear.

One way to attempt to differentiate traumatic amnesia from normal forgetting is to inquire as to whether younger siblings remember major events like vacations for which the person has no recall. Amnesia is a common symptom and should be inquired about routinely in psychiatric assessments.

Assessment of Voices

DID patients are great teachers about the assessment of auditory hallucinations. They have taught me that the conventional mental status assessment of voices in psychiatry is like a cardiology in which the doctor takes the pulse, but does not listen to the chest with a stethoscope. A vast amount of information about voices is simply left out of the standard history and mental status examination.

I like to describe voices as being controlled by two dials, one for volume, and one for ego-alienness. In DID patients, both dials are turned all the way up. DID patients classically describe chronic auditory hallucinations going back into childhood in the absence of thought disorder or other features of psychosis, and continuing during long periods in which they are neither depressed nor manic. The voices are fully ego alien, that is, they are experienced as not coming from the self, and they are fully out loud, although heard inside the head. The voices are unequivocally experienced as being just like the voices of separate human beings, except that they come from inside the head. Sometimes they are heard as external, but not usually. Skeptics seem to doubt the validity of DID voices, while accepting the ego-alien nature of obsessions and compulsions in obsessive-compulsive disorder, which is another example of differential ideological bias against DID.

If one gradually turns down the volume on voices, they shade into thoughts, which are like quiet voices. On the other hand, if volume stays full, but the ego-alien dial is gradually turned down, the voices change into an inner dialogue of the self with the self, such as everyone experiences. All possible combinations of settings of the two dials can occur in DID. DID patients will describe inner dialogs with themselves, and be unsure whether the other half of the dialog feels like self or other, and they will describe voices that are "not really voices" but "more like thoughts" except that "they're out loud but not as loud as voices." When one or the other dial is turned down low, it can be difficult to differentiate the DID person's internal experience from DDNOS, or even normal. The differentiating feature is the extreme symptom and its frequency.

Voices have other characteristics. They may be male or female, young or old, angry or sad, friendly or hostile. Sometimes a DID patient will say, "I don't hear voices, but I hear children crying inside." One has to explore the meaning of the word *voice* to the individual, because one person may have full auditory hallucinations yet report not hearing voices, while another may report hearing voices, but the phenomenon is normal internal self-dialogue. The characteristics of voices are inquired about initially with open-ended questions such as, "What can you tell me about the voices?" or "Do the voices have any special characteristics?" Patients may be reluctant to describe voices for fear of being thought crazy, which is a realistic concern.

Voices may be described somewhat vaguely or in detail. A person may say, "I have a 16-year old voice called Mary who always wants to go out and party." Usually the person is familiar with more than one voice, and can give at least a gender and an approximate age range in the form of child, adolescent, or adult. The voices may talk to the person, or to each other, they may comment on the person's actions, and they may command the person to do things such as shop or self-mutilate. The person will often know parts of herself in detail but only be aware of others as "voices" heard coming from far back in the psyche. As the person progresses through the active phases of MPD therapy, these voices are engaged, take executive control, achieve co-consciousness, and are integrated.

Voices in DID are also accompanied by affect. When a certain voice is talking, the host personality may be flooded with ego-alien fear, sadness, or anger, and not know the origins or motives behind the feelings. There is also often a palpable sensation of the presence of an internal entity, as in a possession state, as the voice comes near and becomes more forceful. The voice, in other words, is more than just an auditory hallucination, and is in fact an alter personality.

DID patients may also hear voices that do not come from alter personalities. These can be memories of the voices of other people that are revivified during abreactions, or alter personalities can make the host personality have auditory, visual, or somatic hallucinations. Additionally, it is always possible that a given voice is due to anticholinergic delirium, hallucinogen psychosis, or some other cause that requires differential diagnosis.

Since the voices are manifestations of alter personalities in DID, they interact with each other like members of a family. One takes a history about the family interactions, alliances, secrets, and conflicts of the voices. If a spontaneous switch occurs during the assessment, it will be evident that the perspective on the voices and their origins and interactions has shifted, and that a second history, so to speak, must be taken. All of this inquiry will arouse the horror of extreme disbelievers, but is simply history taking.

Another quality of DID voices is that one can have a rational indirect conversation with them. This is called *talking through*. In this technique, without making any suggestions about DID or other persons or personalities inside, one simply asks the person for permission to ask the voices a few questions, commenting casually that this is something that is sometimes done as part of a psychiatric assessment. The undiagnosed DID patient usually thinks this is a bit weird, but usually complies. I then explain that I will ask the voice a question, the voice will answer inside the person's head, and the person will pass on the answer. Permission granted, I will then ask whether the voice is listening, hears me, and understands what I am saying.

The response to this may be silence, "yes," or expletives. Or the person might answer, "He said there's no one here."

To this, as a skilled trance logician, I might reply, "Thank you for letting me know that you're not there. Do you have any questions you want to ask me?"

The response to this might be, "He said he's keeping an eye on you."

Shifting into a therapeutic mode briefly, I might then say, "I think it's smart to keep an eye on me, and on people in general. Based on what you've told me, you've been abused by a lot of people in your life, and many have seemed trustworthy at first. I think it's smart not to trust too much, and I think you're lucky to have a voice inside helping you not to trust too much. You've gotten into trouble too many times by trusting people too much. So I don't expect the voice to trust me, and in fact I think that would be a bad idea if he did. What do you think of what I've just said, voice?"

Looking a bit tranced out, the person might say, "I'm watching you." This would indicate a partial intrusion of the alter personality into executive control, as indicated by the trance expression, change in gestalt, and grammatical shift. Often, talking through evokes a spontaneous switch without any suggestions having been made about DID, alter personalities, or other people inside.

Although the ability of the voices to engage in rational indirect conversation should weigh in favor of DID and against schizophrenia in the differential diagnosis, this property of DID voices raises the question of whether voices could be contacted psychotherapeutically in true-positive schizophrenia.

In DID work the attitude of the clinician toward the voices is fundamentally different from that in standard psychiatric work with schizophrenia. I was taught in my psychiatry residency that auditory hallucinations are a *symptom* with which the patient is afflicted. One tries to form a treatment alliance with the patient to work together on getting rid of the voices with medication. This is analogous to prescribing an antibiotic for fever. Fever is one of a cluster of infectious disease symptoms one eradicates with antibiotics, while voices are one of a cluster of psychotic symptoms one eradicates with neuroleptics.

In DID work, however, one forms a treatment alliance with the voices, and they are just as much the patient as the presenting part of the person who experiences them as auditory hallucinations. In fact the current host personality, in some cases, was previously a voice before the host functions were abdicated by "the person," who is now "a voice." Naïve concepts of the host personality being the person and the alters being illusions founder on the facts that different alters can function as host personality at different stages of life, that a host personality can be created *de novo* in adulthood, and that some patients have executive groups of alters that share host functions, with no one alter personality being "the person." Undiagnosed DID patients sometimes get nervous when I start talking to their voices.

Partial Intrusions of Alter Personalities

Full switches of executive control in which alter A is out, then alter B, then alter A again, with one-way amnesia between A and B, is the classical characteristic of DID, but partial intrusions are probably more common. These give rise to Schneiderian first rank symptoms of schizophrenia (Ross 1989), which are similar to the *DSM-IV* diagnostic criteria for schizophrenia. Schneiderian symptoms are listed in the DDIS and include voices arguing in the head, voices commenting, having your thoughts made or controlled by someone or something outside you (made thoughts), made feelings, made actions, external influences affecting the body, thoughts being taken out of your mind, thinking someone's else's thoughts, thoughts out loud, other people being able to hear your thoughts, and delusional thinking. The average number of Schneiderian symptoms out of 11 in a series of 166 cases of DID was 6.5 compared to 3.8 for DDNOS $(t(221) = 6.281$, p .00001) (Ross et al. 1992). Schneiderian symptoms are actually more common in DID than in schizophrenia, and are more common in clinically diagnosed schizophrenics who report childhood abuse than in those who do not.

These symptoms occur when alters in the background influence the thoughts, feelings, and perceptions of the one in executive control. At times alter personalities may be copresent, and the person may be unsure who is out—during therapy, as the DID system moves gradually toward integration, differentiation of who is out becomes more difficult both subjectively for the patient and for the clinician.

Assessment of Childhood Trauma

Over 90 percent of DID patients can give a history of childhood physical and/or sexual abuse on first diagnostic assessment (Ross et al. 1990). The idea that DID patients are supposed to enter treatment fully amnestic for their trauma, then be susceptible to the recovery of confabulated memories simply doesn't fit the data. What actually occurs empirically in the clinic is that much of the trauma is blocked out, but enough is remembered to yield positive findings. As is true for the signs and symptoms of the disorder, disclosures of childhood sexual abuse are often available in medical records long antedating contact with the clinician who first diagnosed the DID.

One patient I worked with had her disclosure of paternal incest recorded in a chart from another hospital, in addition to the names and functions of her alter personalities, but a DID diagnosis had not been made. When I met with this patient and her father he denied incest, and during several years of work with her and her family she recanted and redisclosed both her incest and her DID several times over in cycles lasting three to six months. In three years of further follow-up she has taken a position of stable recantation of the incest, has a good relationship with her family, continues to have DID, and has now recovered memories of apparent medical experimentation by aliens. I mention this case to illustrate that confabulated memories can occur in true DID cases, and that these can antedate the diagnosis of DID.

In a case referred to me for inpatient treatment of DID and satanic ritual abuse I made a sole diagnosis of schizotypal personality disorder. In this instance I could not uncover a single symptom, confabulated memory, or indicator of abuse of any kind, and sent the patient home after four days in the hospital, much to the surprise of both the patient and the referring therapist.

In another case referred for inpatient treatment of DID I made a diagnosis of classical medical-surgical Munchausen's syndrome (factitious disorder with combined psychological and physical signs and symptoms in *DSM-IV* terminology). I listened to an account of a self-inflicted shotgun wound to the chest made with the barrel touching the skin, and the gun at a 90 degree angle to the chest wall, which resulted in near death from exsanguination while the patient lay in a field for over twelve hours before being rescued—the wound, according to the patient, healed with no visible scarring. My judgment was that this woman probably had had a traumatic childhood, and that she had a mild form of DDNOS in addition to her factitious disorder. I told her directly that my diagnosis was Munchausen's syndrome, explained the disorder to her psychoeducationally, formed a good treatment alliance with her, kept her in the hospital for three weeks on the Dissociative Disorders Unit, and referred her back to her psychologist, who agreed with and was pleased by my diagnosis and treatment.

In another DID case the father had been convicted and jailed for incest with the patient when she was a teenager. In another case described to me by a law enforcement officer, a confiscated videotape made by the father showed the patient doing a hypnotic eye roll and going into a trance while her father had intercourse with her.

I mention these cases to counter all-or-nothing cognitive errors, also called dichotomized thinking, which occur too frequently in popular media commentaries on the problem of the reality of recovered trauma memories. One can diagnose DID in the absence of a trauma history, but a trauma history can be obtained on first assessment in over 90 percent of cases. DID patients can have objectively verified trauma memories, confabulated memories, dreams which they mistake for memories, screen memories in the classical Freudian sense, and fantasies that they mistake for memories. In this regard they are like everyone else on the planet.

SECONDARY FEATURES OF DISSOCIATIVE IDENTITY DISORDER

In the DDIS there are sixteen secondary features of DID: 166 DID cases averaged 10.2 secondary features each compared to 5.2 for DDNOS $(t(221) = 9.534, p .00001)$. The amnesia secondary features were secondary with respect to *DSM-III-R* diagnostic criteria for MPD, but technically are now primary features with the inclusion of an amnesia criterion for DID in *DSM-IV*. I retained them in the secondary features section of the *DSM-IV* version of the DDIS for continuity and comparability in research findings. These features are: objects missing that cannot be accounted for, objects present, changes in handwriting, strangers knowing the person, people describing disremembered events and behavior, blank spells, coming out of blank spells in unfamiliar locations, extensive amnesia for childhood after age 5, flashbacks, depersonalization, voices (specifically coming from inside the head) referring to oneself as "we" or "us," another person or persons inside, another person inside having a name, and another person inside taking control of the body.

These symptoms follow logically from the intrapsychic structure of the disorder, which are imbedded in the *DSM-IV* diagnostic criteria. Like voices and amnesia, they occur on a continuum from normal to full DID, and no one symptom is necessarily pathological if it occurs infrequently or in isolation. For instance, it is perfectly normal to forget where one put something. When an as yet undiagnosed DID patient reports her treasured diary missing, then finds it stuffed under a pillow on a couch two days later, with angry block letter printing as the last entry, and reports hearing a voice swear at her and insult her while she was looking for it, this represents three secondary features of DID.

Similarly, anyone can find objects at home that they can't remember buying. This is not the same as opening the bedroom closet and finding six sets of hooker's clothing that one can't remember buying, that were not there yesterday, and that coincide with a blank spell of three hours' duration, unaccounted-for mileage accumulated on the car, and a charge card bill arriving a month later signed in an unfamiliar script.

Secondary features can be reported in an obvious or a subtle fashion. One patient said that she must have a "very familiar face," because strangers were always claiming to know her. In a big city it was hard to tell if this was a DID symptom or simply having a familiar face. Later, an alter personality described encounters with these people for which the host personality was amnestic. It is normal to forget meeting someone in the past, but it is out of the range of ordinary experience to be completely amnestic for a two-hour luncheon with a person who seems to be a stranger, when the luncheon took place the previous week, and no drugs or alcohol were consumed.

Undiagnosed DID patients will report these secondary features with concern and bewilderment, and when asked what they think is going on, will often not postulate DID as an explanation for their experiences. A more detailed discussion of the secondary features of DID can be found in Putnam (1989) and Ross (1989). The greater the number of secondary features, the more likely it is a case of DID. On the DDIS, secondary features are scored as positive only if they occur fairly often or frequently — like all rater decisions on the DDIS, the decision as to what represents fairly often or frequently is made by the interviewee, not by the interviewer, in order to reduce interviewer bias.

Out of 102 DID patients, most of whom received the DDIS at initial diagnostic assessment for a dissociative disorder, 90.2 percent reported another person existing inside, 81.4 percent another person taking control of the body, and 70.6 percent another person inside having a different name (Ross et al. 1990). These data must be accounted for in any model of the disorder. The majority of diagnosed DID patients have been aware of having other people inside prior to diagnostic assessment for a dissociative disorder, yet have not concluded that they have DID.

COMORBID SYMPTOM CLUSTERS
AND DIAGNOSES

All studies of DID have found extensive comorbidity. When we interviewed 107 DID patients with the SCID-I (Spitzer et al. 1990) we found that the average number of lifetime comorbid Axis I disorders was 7.3 (S.D. 2.5), while the average number of Axis II diagnoses in 103 subjects interviewed with the SCID-II was 3.6 (S.D. 2.5) (Ellason et al. under review). This makes an average of 10.9 comorbid diagnoses not including the DID, which is not diagnosed by the SCID. When one considers that the SCID does not diagnose posttraumatic stress disorder, sleep disorders, or psychosexual disorders, it is evident that the average DID inpatient meets lifetime criteria for about fifteen different *DSM-IV* disorders. This is a preposterous and invalid finding within the dominant conceptual system of late-twentieth-century psychiatry.

Given the supposed baseline frequency of these disorders in the general population, the fact that they are by and large supposed to be independent disease entities, and the number of subjects carrying the DID diagnosis today, our findings on comorbidity are statistically impossible. The only two possible interpretations are that DID patients are impressionable hysterics who overendorse interview items, and therefore the findings are not valid, or that the conceptual system of late twentieth century is fundamentally flawed.

I support the latter hypothesis. I see the comorbidity of DID as part of an all-inclusive normal human response to severe chronic childhood trauma, and I see trauma as a major etiological factor in psychiatric disorders throughout *DSM-IV*, to varying degrees depending on the disorder. I see childhood trauma as psychiatry's germ. In general medicine, all doctors learn a great deal about germs, their effects, interactions with the immune system, and treatment. Some doctors specialize in infectious diseases and some become radiologists and rarely deal with infectious diseases. However, germs can complicate transplant surgery, hip replacements, AIDS, blood transfusions, or virtually any medical condition and its treatment. Germs can cause illnesses ranging in severity from the common cold to catastrophic sepsis, and there is a wide range of susceptibility to germs across individuals and at different stages of the life cycle. Many psychiatrists are functioning like internists who don't want to know about germs. DID is the great teacher about psychiatry's germ theory.

Depression, anxiety disorders including panic disorder and posttraumatic stress disorder, eating disorders, somatoform disorders, substance abuse, personality disorders, and psychosexual disorders are particularly common forms of comorbidity. This list of disorders encompasses much of

DSM-IV. Also common by SCID criteria are psychotic disorders including schizophrenia. Unlike the other forms of comorbidity, however, the psychotic diagnoses are usually false positives.

It is noteworthy that there is no mention of childhood sexual abuse or dissociation in the two major sections of *DSM-IV*, Schizophrenia and Other Psychotic Disorders, and Mood Disorders. The differential diagnosis between psychosis and dissociation is actually subtle, difficult, and of profound clinical importance for both diagnosis and treatment. The fact that this differential diagnostic problem is treated by *DSM-IV* schizophrenia experts as if it doesn't exist is a measure of their resistance to a paradigm shift already in process.

Therapists often ask me if it is possible for one alter personality to be psychotic, while the others are not. My reply is that this is not a meaningful question to me. By convention, I regard the word *psychotic* as referring to symptoms arising from some general morbid brain process, and being like *delirium* in that regard. Therefore the psychotic alter is by definition manifesting conversion or dissociative symptoms or pseudopsychosis. The main point is that a lone "psychotic" alter personality is serving an interpersonal and intrapsychic defensive function, and cannot be treated successfully with neuroleptics. For a response to neuroleptics to be likely, it appears that psychotic features must pervade the entire personality system, rather than being limited to one personality state.

The problem of the relationship between dissociation and psychosis, and the differential response of symptoms to DID-like psychotherapy and neuroleptics is a research challenge of great interest. In this regard I have just applied to a pharmaceutical company for financial support for a double-blind randomized placebo controlled trial of a new antipsychotic medication in the treatment of DID.

The question of the relative weight that should be given to different comorbid diagnoses in the treatment plan is also difficult and subtle and lacks adequate data. As a general principle, the greater the degree of comorbidity, and the more false-positive diagnoses that have been made by prior clinicians, the more likely it is that one has an undiagnosed case of DID.

Finally, I would like to comment on extrasensory and paranormal experiences, which are inquired about in the DDIS. These include precognition, mental telepathy, telekinesis, possession experiences, and contact with ghosts and poltergeists. ESP experiences are very common in DID patients, and they endorse more of these items than patients in any other diagnostic group studied to date. ESP experiences should raise the index of suspicion for a dissociative disorder.

Because of its extensive comorbidity, DID is the only condition with which one can practice general psychiatry while being a subspecialist. It is important to have as broad a grounding in general psychopathology as possible in order to diagnose and treat DID. I have not found another disorder that taxes my skills at differential diagnosis, psychotherapy, psychopharmacology, case management, and behavioral management to the same degree.

The Relationship of Dissociative Identity Disorder with Borderline Personality Disorder

To summarize briefly, data gathered with the DDIS show overwhelmingly that borderline diagnostic criteria are a checklist of posttraumatic symptoms characteristic of individuals who have experienced chronic childhood trauma. Borderline personality disorder is not a disease entity which one either has or does not have, rather it is a symptom checklist; the more traumatized a group of individuals, the more positive items on the checklist it is likely to have on average.

For the first time, a ninth diagnostic criterion has been included in the *DSM-IV* criteria set for borderline personality disorder—now, instead of having five out of eight symptoms, as was the case in *DSM-III-R*, one can have five out of nine symptoms. It has become easier to be borderline. The new criterion is (American Psychiatric Association 1994): "(9) transient, stress-related paranoid ideation or severe dissociative symptoms" (p. 654).

However, typically for *DSM-IV*, dissociative disorders are not mentioned in the text for borderline personality disorder, either in the differential diagnosis or as an exclusion criterion. Additionally, there is no discussion of acute stress disorder, so one is provided no rules for deciding whether a given dissociative symptom represents a criterion for borderline personality disorder, dissociative amnesia disorder, or acute stress disorder.

When initially proposed, acute stress disorder was called *brief reactive dissociative disorder* and was to be included in the dissociative disorders section. It was switched to the anxiety disorders section and renamed for political reasons. Dissociative disorders are also not mentioned in the differential diagnosis of acute stress disorder, although the B criteria for acute stress disorder are:

B. Either while experiencing the stressor or after experiencing the distressing event, the individual has three (or more) of the following dissociative symptoms:

(1) a subjective sense of numbing, detachment, or absence of emotional responsiveness

(2) a reduction in awareness of his or her surroundings (e.g., "being in a daze")

(3) derealization

(4) depersonalization

(5) dissociative amnesia (i.e., inability to recall an important aspect of the trauma). [p. 432]

It is not possible, using *DSM-IV* criteria, to make differential diagnostic decisions about the relationship between dissociative disorders, borderline personality disorder, and acute stress disorder. The problem is further complicated when one considers that neither acute stress disorder nor dissociative disorders are discussed in the section for brief psychotic disorder.

A person could be in a trance state due to an acute-onset adult trauma and be diagnosed as DDNOS, acute stress disorder, or brief psychotic disorder, based on criterion A (4) for brief psychotic disorder, which is "grossly disorganized or catatonic behavior" (p. 304). I mention these problems with the *DSM-IV* system to illustrate that it cannot account coherently for the effects of trauma on mental state.

In terms of the relationship between DID and borderline personality, this should be conceptualized in the same way as the relationship between depression, panic disorder, or any other Axis I disorder and borderline personality; DID and borderline personality disorder can coexist and are not mutually exclusive. In a number of series, 30–44 percent of DID patients have not met criteria for borderline personality disorder (Ellason et al., under review). Therefore borderline personality disorder is neither necessary nor sufficient for the existence of DID. Most often, DID patients are called borderlines simply as an expression of hostile countertransference.

THE ABSENCE OF A THOUGHT DISORDER IN DISSOCIATIVE IDENTITY DISORDER

On the Positive and Negative Syndrome Scale (PANSS), a scale developed to measure symptoms of schizophrenia, DID patients report more positive and fewer negative symptoms of schizophrenia than do schizophrenics (Ellason and Ross, in press). Despite this very interesting overlap between dissociative symptoms and positive symptoms of schizophrenia, the vast majority of DID patients are not psychotic.

The thought processes of the DID patient are basically intact, coherent, and logical. Given their internal experience, what they say makes sense. Additionally, the condition can be treated to stable long-term remission with psychotherapy. The absence of a thought disorder in the presence of positive symptoms of schizophrenia should raise the index of suspicion for DID and DID should be an exclusion criterion in the *DSM-V* diagnostic criteria set for schizophrenia.

Complex Partial Seizures as a *DSM-IV* Exclusion Criterion for Dissociative Identity Disorder

Complex partial seizures (temporal lobe epilepsy) should not have been listed as an exclusion criterion for DID in *DSM-IV*. The idea that temporal lobe epilepsy poses a serious differential diagnostic problem for DID is an artifact of biomedical reductionism and has no scientific basis. I did a study in which twenty subjects with DID and no abnormal EEGs, twenty subjects with clinical diagnoses of temporal lobe epilepsy and abnormal EEGs, and twenty-eight controls with other neurological conditions were compared on the DES and DDIS (Ross et al. 1989a). The seizure patients did not differ from controls, and neither group differed from general population norms gathered in later research.

Complex partial seizure disorder does not look anything remotely like DID clinically. Loewenstein and Putnam (1988) and Putnam (1986) have provided further data confirming the lack of any substantial overlap or interaction between the two conditions. This piece of clinical folklore should be laid to rest in *DSM-V* unless divergent, replicated data are published in the interim.

CONCLUSIONS

The diagnosis of DID can be made in an orderly fashion using a decision tree format. When there is a history of recurrent blank spells in the absence of substance abuse during which behavior has been organized and socially focused, with a normal mental status; chronic auditory hallucinations in the absence of psychosis or mood disorder; a childhood trauma history; and borderline or other personality disorder criteria, then DID is by far the most likely diagnosis. The presence of extensive comorbidity and a history of prior treatment failures is suggestive but nonspecific. The secondary features of DID are probably pathognomonic when present in sufficient number.

For DID to be valid, the signs and symptoms must antedate contact with the diagnosing clinician, as is true of all *DSM-IV* disorders. The reasons most clinicians fail to diagnose DID are ideological opposition to the diagnosis, inadequate training in the signs and symptoms, and failure to ask the relevant questions. If the full DES and DDIS profile is present, and *DSM-IV* criteria are met, the only diagnostic possibilities besides DID are malingering and factitious disorder. No scientific evidence exists to suggest that DID is malingered more often than other psychiatric disorders, or that it is a more common presenting feature of factitious disorder than other conditions. Lastly, the statement that DID is a cultural artifact is like informing the body of a deceased victim of an *amok* attack that *amok* is a culture-bound syndrome.

REFERENCES

American Psychiatric Association (1980). *Diagnostic and Statistical Manual of Mental Disorders*, 3rd ed. Washington, DC.

———— (1992). *DSM-IV Draft Criteria*. Washington, DC.

———— (1994). *Diagnostic and Statistical Manual of Mental Disorders*, 4th ed. Washington, DC.

Bernstein, E. M., and Putnam, F. W. (1986). Development, reliability, and validity of a dissociation scale. *Journal of Nervous and Mental Disease* 174:727–735.

Boon, S., and Draijer, N. (1993a). *Multiple Personality Disorder in the Netherlands*. Amsterdam: Swets Zeitlinger.

———— (1993b). Multiple personality in the Netherlands: a clinical investigation of 71 patients. American Journal of Psychiatry 150:489–494.

Carlson, E. B. (1994). Studying the interaction between physical psychological states with the Dissociative Experiences Scale. In *Dissociation: Culture, Mind, and Body*, ed. D. Spiegel, pp. 41–58. Washington, DC: American Psychiatric Press.

Carlson, E. B., Putnam, F. W., Ross, C. A., et al. (1993). Validity of the dissociative experiences scale in screening for multiple personality disorder: a multicenter study. *American Journal of Psychiatry* 150:1030–1036.

Ellason, J., and Ross, C. A. (in press). PANSS data on dissociative identity disorder. *Journal of Nervous and Mental Disease*.

Ellason, J., Ross, C. A., and Fuchs, D. (under review). Axis I and II comorbidity in dissociative identity disorder. *Journal of Nervous and Mental Disease*.

Kluft, R. P. (1985). Making the diagnosis of multiple personality disorder (MPD). In *Directions in Psychiatry*, ed. F. F. Flach, 5(24), pp. 1–10. New York: Hatherleigh.

Loewenstein, R. J. (1991). An office mental status examination for multiple personality disorder. *Psychiatric Clinics of North America* 14. 567–604.

Loewenstein, R. J., and Putnam, F. W. (1988). A comparison of dissociative symptoms in patients with complex partial seizure, MPD, and posttraumatic stress disorder. *Dissociation* 1:17–23.

Merskey, H. (1992). The manufacture of personalities: the production of multiple personality disorder. *British Journal of Psychiatry* 160:327–340.

Putnam, F. W. (1986). The scientific investigation of multiple personality disorder. In *Split Minds/Split Brains*, ed. J. M. Quen, pp. 109–125. New York: University Press.

_____ (1989). *Diagnosis and Treatment of Multiple Personality Disorder.* New York: Guilford.

Putnam, F. W., Guroff, J. J., Silberman, E. K., et al. (1986). The clinical phenomenology of multiple personality disorder: review of 100 recent cases. *Journal of Clinical Psychiatry* 47:285–293.

Ross, C. A. (1989). *Multiple Personality Disorder: Diagnosis, Clinical Features, and Treatment.* New York: John Wiley & Sons.

_____ (1994). Pseudoscience in the *American Journal of Psychiatry.* In *Pseudoscience in Biological Psychiatry,* ed., C. A. Ross and A. Pam. New York: John Wiley & Sons.

Ross, C. A., Anderson, G., and Clark, P. (1994). Childhood abuse and the positive symptoms of schizophrenia. *Hospital and Community Psychiatry* 45:489–491.

Ross, C. A., Anderson, G., Fleisher, W. P., & Norton, G. R. (1991a). The frequency of multiple personality disorder among psychiatric inpatients. *American Journal of Psychiatry* 148:1717–1720.

Ross, C. A., Anderson, G., Fraser, G. A., et al. (1992a). Differentiating multiple personality disorder and dissociative disorder not otherwise specified. *Dissociation* 4:87–90.

Ross, C. A., and Clark, P. (1992b). Assessment of childhood trauma and dissociation in an emergency department. *Dissociation* 5:163–165.

Ross, C. A., Heber, S., Anderson, G., et al. (1989a). Differentiating multiple personality disorder and complex partial seizures. *General Hospital Psychiatry* 11:54–58.

Ross, C. A., Heber, S., Norton, G. R., et al. (1989b). The dissociative disorders interview schedule: a structured interview. *Dissociation* 2:169–189.

Ross, C. A., Joshi, S., and Currie, R. (1991b). Dissociative experiences in the general population. *American Journal of Psychiatry* 148:1547–1552.

Ross, C. A., Miller, S. D., Reagor, P., et al. (1990). Structured interview data on 102 cases of multiple personality disorder from four centers. *American Journal of Psychiatry* 147:596–602.

Ross, C. A., Norton, G. R., and Wozney, K. (1989c). Multiple personality disorder: an analysis of 236 cases. *Canadian Journal of Psychiatry* 34:413–418.

Saxe, G. N., van der Kolk, B. A., Berkowitz, R., et al. (1993). Dissociative disorders in psychiatric inpatients. *American Journal of Psychiatry* 150:1037–1042.

Spitzer, R. L., Williams, J. B., Gibbon, M., and First, M. B. (1990). *User's Guide for the Structured Cyclical Interview* for DSM-III-R. Washington, DC: American Psychiatric Press.

Steinberg, M. (1993). *Interviewer's Guide to the Structured Clinical Interview for* DSM-IV *Dissociative Disorders (SCID-D).* Washington, DC: American Psychiatric Press.

_____ (1994). Systematizing dissociation: symptomatology and diagnostic assessment. In *Dissociation: Culture, Mind, and Body,* ed. D. Spiegel, pp. 59–88. Washington, DC: American Psychiatric Press.

Steinberg, M., Rounsaville, B. J., and Cicchetti, D. V. (1990). The structured clinical interview for *DSM-III-R* dissociative disorders (SCID-D): preliminary report on a new diagnostic instrument. *American Journal of Psychiatry* 147:76–82.

_____ (1991). Detection of dissociative disorders in psychiatric patients by a screening instrument and a structured diagnostic interview. *American Journal of Psychiatry* 148:1050–1054.

10

Cultural Variations in Multiple Personality Disorder

Deborah Golub

PART I: INTRODUCTION

Years ago, my grandmother described to me her childhood memory of secretly watching the exorcism of a *dybbuk* from her ailing infant brother. She did not elaborate his symptoms or the presence in the home of an abusive stepfather. Instead, she recounted peeking into the bedroom of their walk-up on New York's Lower East Side, where rabbis shouted commands to the possessing spirit and poured hot lead into a bucket of cold water in order to make determinations from the shapes of hardened metal.

The whispered and abbreviated telling by an old woman recaptured her earlier fear although my grandmother had never professed a belief either in possession or the transmigration of dead souls to the newborn. Nor did her vocabulary include such notions as trauma and dissociation. In fact, I don't recall that the incident ever was discussed or interpreted in our rationalist, agnostic household, where spirit residues from the old country, nevertheless, seemed to linger.

Each of us carries a deep, poetic, yet private language of our culture's narrative, a language that is separate from the technical terminology of science and is capable of communicating that which cannot be explained rationally. The profound difference reveals one reason why any cross-cultural discussion of illness or dissociation, including multiple personality disorder (MPD) in the case of this chapter, requires a more comprehensive vocabulary than that offered by Western psychological theory. Such a discussion necessitates language that is understandable to Western psychiatry while expanding the conceptual boundaries of those paradigms. The dilemma for a contributor to a scientific book such as this is not an uncommon one—how to describe experience that is outside the writer's experience, using terms that are unavailable in his or her language.

The fact that we would even discuss the subject of MPD in diverse cultural settings implies the generalization and application of a structure created by members of one culture to others who may not share the same ideas about the naming, etiology, dynamics, and treatment of disease and illness. Clearly, cross-cultural comparison is difficult when behaviors are understood and described by societies in uniquely meaningful ways. An *etic* process—one that studies behavior from outside the cultural system— carries with it the risk of imposing upon those being analyzed certain externally constructed and culturally circumscribed criteria that the outside interpreters consider universal. The danger of creating categorical fallacies is obvious and the challenge formidable: to suspend momentarily our own categories as much as we possibly can in order to discover inductively how others construct their world, and then to try accurately to translate human experience from one world view to another.

Other chapters in this book consider a more fundamental controversy— that of the very existence of MPD. This chapter highlights questions about the universality versus culture-boundedness of a pattern of behaviors that at this moment in time Western psychiatry has named *multiple personality disorder*. The following pages do not offer new research or suggest novel interpretations. Nor is it my intention to advocate a particular point of view in the heated debate. Rather, this chapter attempts mainly to place MPD in the broader context of cultural dissociation and the embodiment of alternative identities, focusing on the relationship between MPD and possession states. This cross-cultural perspective provides a framework in which readers can make their own assessments about the inventory of reports from the MPD literature of cases outside North America (including the continental United States and Canada, for the purposes of this chapter), as well as among ethnically diverse groups in North America. Finally, the chapter summarizes various issues and perspectives expressed by writers in the field about the cultural construction and distribution of MPD.

PART II: DISSOCIATION ACROSS CULTURES

Cultural Constructs of Multiplicity

It is impractical to discuss MPD across cultures without first talking about cross-cultural dissociation in general. Ideas about self, soul, and the nature of reality influence the way a society views the etiology of multiplicity and, therefore, its appropriate treatment and healers. A culture that believes in the self as continuous but the relationship between what is internal and external to self as distinct, will regard multiplicity differently than will a society that considers a continuous self illusory, and self and universe one. Similarly, a culture that does not give credence to the existence of a separate and parallel universe inhabited by external entities probably must discount supernatural factors like possession as a cause of multiplicity. The etiology of entities resides, instead, within the individual who is a single person with split-off parts (Goodman 1988, Krippner 1987). Reintegration of this self-contained unit rather than the invitation or expulsion of external spirits is an implied psychotherapeutic treatment goal.

Goodman (1988) proposed that there is no room for soul in a paradigm that views this self-contained unit as a source of all experience. Soul theory, on the other hand, hypothesizes that humans consist of a shell that is inhabited by an ephemeral substance called the soul. Occasionally, the body surrenders to an alien entity whose nature is culturally determined.

The psychophysiological basis of multiplicity, particularly favored in today's ascendant biological psychiatry, not only mirrors Western dualism and its notion of separate selfhood, but also supports the tendency to universalize Western theory based on the idea of a common human physiology; that is, biology determines while culture merely influences (Kleinman 1987). Culture must be pared away in order to determine the true underlying disease. Kleinman warned against the hubris of psychiatry to medicalize the human condition and to exaggerate biological dimensions while de-emphasizing cultural aspects.

Although anthropology and psychiatry may share a positivist Western-oriented belief about the biopsychological source of entities (Mulhern 1991), they differ traditionally in the way they compare illness among diverse cultures. Anthropology prefers an *emic* approach wherein illness categories are discovered through observation within the society rather than by imposition of an external structure. Cross-cultural comparisons are arrived at anthropologically as a final step (Kleinman 1987). Psychiatry, on the other hand, often establishes general categories initially and focuses on locating similarities rather than differences. Whereas psychiatry asks how psychological disorders are similar across cultures, anthropology wonders how they differ (Kleinman 1987).

Psychological research currently supports the bias to universalize and to test newly formulated illness categories within culturally distinct populations (Kleinman 1987, Mulhern 1991). The desire for a single universal explanation of illness suggests a belief that there is one ultimately correct answer, a proposition that, in turn, implies the existence of a single objective truth about reality and self. The assumption itself must be regarded as culture-bound since reality is culturally relative and unprovable (Goodman 1988).

On occasion, behaviors associated with an MPD-like presentation cannot be explained by Western concepts of reality. An example is xenoglossy, the ability of a person to speak an unlearned language. Xenoglossy is distinguished from a syndrome of changing dialects (Hsia and Tsai 1981), from those instances when a specific alter has studied the language or learned it from an abuser, or when, like Cory's (1919–1920) patient, Spanish Maria, the personality speaks only fragments and idiosyncratic linguistic constructions. In xenoglossy, language acquisition cannot be attributed to prior exposure by any alter to the new language.

The phenomenon is observed and described rarely in the psychiatric community (Krippner 1987, Oesterreich 1966, Stevenson 1974, 1976, 1984, Stevenson and Pasricha 1979) and, as much as I can discern, is not listed in any dissociative disorders assessment instrument. Contemporary scholars who do detail cases of xenoglossy are likely to be regarded as on the fringe of psychiatry even though some of their more conservative colleagues acknowledge the researchers' seriousness, sincerity, and appropriate caution (Favazza 1985). Ross (1989), a well-known supporter of the MPD diagnosis, has written eloquently about the prejudicial exclusion of extrasensory perception from mainstream psychiatry. However, while he states that he neither believes nor disbelieves in the existence of xenoglossy, he adds that he has never seen a case (personal communication, April 30, 1993).

The paucity of attention to this phenomenon could indicate that the behavior is either nonexistent, extraordinarily unusual, unrecognized; not researched in a stringent manner that would merit credibility; the result of hypnotic suggestion or fraud; or that it must be disregarded, as its explanation can only be in the realm of the paranormal. To accept a paranormal cause means to admit the existence of a separate reality; xenoglossy, in fact, is quite believable within the context of reincarnation, possession, transmigration of souls, extrasensory perception, or telepathy. To accept MPD means to exclude all of the unexplainable and untestable phenomena associated with it (Taylor and Martin 1944). The example of xenoglossy highlights a larger question relevant to the cross-cultural diagnosis of MPD, namely: To what extent do the culturally constructed delimitations of any theoretical model require that it exclude phenomenology incompatible with its world view?

MPD and Possession Worldwide

The ability to dissociate appears to be a fundamental, ancient, and universal psychobiological capacity of human beings that is necessary for their healthy functioning, and multiplicity a normal condition present in all people (Beahrs 1982, Bourguignon 1973, Crabtree 1985, Goodman 1988, Kenny 1981, Kleinman 1988, Krippner 1987, Lampl-de Groot 1981, Ross 1991a). This ubiquitous "genetic endowment" (Goodman 1988) allows some members of all cultures to embody alternative identities (Mulhern 1991); themes of fragmentation of self and transformation of identity can be traced throughout history (Lifton 1968, Ross 1989). The expressive content of dissociative behaviors both in possession and in nonpossession states such as trance, ecstasy, soul loss, and spirit journeys, seems to be "exquisitely and always mediated by cultural expectations" (Martinez-Taboas 1991a, p. 131) and by the society's explanatory system, regardless of the underlying physiological source (Bourguignon 1968).

Some writers consider MPD and possession as two forms of dissociation. They are parallel dissociative disorders with similar etiologies and different clinical pictures (Adityanjee et al. 1989, Castillo 1991, Saxena and Prasad 1989). What currently is called MPD reflects a secular version of the same mental structures that characterize possession states (Kluft 1993, Ross 1989). If the syndrome of multiple personality were "externally validated and ritualized in psychotherapeutic procedure, it would function as an existential equivalent of possession" (Kenny 1981, p. 355).

Possession has been considered by different scholars either as hysterical dissociation or as a variety of "multiple personality" (Adityanjee et al. 1989, Akhtar 1988, Bilu and Beit-Hallahmi 1989, Ellenberger 1970). Were early cases of possession reviewed today, they might be diagnosed as dissociative disorders (Goodwin et al. 1990). Still others (Adityanjee 1990) interpret MPD as a culturally influenced presentation of possession. Despite obvious similarities in the phenomenology, however, some concerned clinicians and anthropologists warn that it is an invalid projection to equate dissociative disorders or MPD with possession (Castillo 1991, Ross 1989). MPD and possession have roots of their own in the discrete theories that shape them (Kenny 1981). Spirit possession cannot be reduced to underlying pathology (Mulhern 1991); it is not MPD misdiagnosed. Likewise, misinterpreting dissociative disorders as possession is "both bad medicine and bad religion" (Ross 1989, p. 26).

The belief in possession by discarnate entities occurs throughout human time and is present in most cultures today (Allison 1985, Kleinman 1988, Kluft 1993, Mulhern 1991, Putnam 1989). Bourguignon (1968, 1973, 1976) identified various forms of institutionalized, culturally patterned altered states of consciousness in 90 percent of 488 societies, possession beliefs in 74 percent, and possession trance in 52 percent of the same group. Such a high incidence and prevalence makes one wonder why reports of MPD are so dramatically fewer than those of possession (Kenny 1981), and why the Western self is more vulnerable to MPD whereas other countries show greater susceptibility to possession (Martinez-Taboas 1991a).

One reason may be that polytheism and reincarnation are conducive to spirit possession (Daie et al. 1992, Kluft 1993, Varma et al. 1981), and possession does tend to be inversely proportional to MPD worldwide (Bourguignon 1979, Daie et al. 1992). Scholars predict that where indigenous possession states remain strong MPD will be uncommon (Kluft 1993). Similarly, MPD will rise in polytheistic, preindustrial societies as the belief in evil spirits declines and Westernization and industrialization increase (Adityanjee et al. 1989, Alexander 1956).

The "internalized critical observer" of many Westerners creates a self that is inaccessible to possession by gods or ghosts (Kleinman 1987, 1988); nevertheless, the natural ability to dissociate remains, regardless of culture. Goodman (1988) proposed that when a society no longer needs this everpresent genetic capacity to enter religious trance and to "switch brain maps," individuals may wander accidentally into the "genetic endowment," particularly those people whose self-integrity has been violated by trauma or whose personality structure already is damaged. They experience disordered multiplicity when they relinquish their "personality map," and have neither the knowledge nor cultural rituals to assist their safe return.

Ross (1991a) argued that pathological multiplicity may develop more frequently in cultures that are hostile to multiplicity. Modern industrial "man" suppresses normal multiplicity via a "cultural dissociation barrier" and develops an unhealthy disconnection from other part selves. The dissociated executive self denigrates spirits, polytheism, extrasensory perception, and deeper intuitive selves as primitive, superstitious, and threatening. Likewise, Western culture may label similar related behaviors in other cultures as pathological; for example, shamanism might be considered schizophrenic or possession trance, hysterical (Mulhern 1991).

The cultural dissociation barrier is not the creation of idiosyncratic experience, Ross continued, but rather the product of sociocultural forces. It reflects a cultural pathology that is a trance state in itself, and one from which our society must awaken if it is to regain health (Tart 1987, cited in Crabtree 1992). In a sense, then, the Western self perceives itself as "an entity with a congenital taint" (Kenny 1981, p. 355), and is pathological in the way it relates to normal multiplicity. The problem in MPD is not the multiplicity but the extent of pathological dissociation (Ross 1991a). Furthermore, if the individual fails to suppress aspects that are unacceptable to Western thinking, he or she risks feeling discordant with what the surrounding culture accepts as real (Crabtree 1992).

The Historical Relationship between MPD and Possession

The history of multiple personality diagnoses does reveal a rather close relationship between psychology, parapsychology, and religion. Contemporary writers have applied a hindsight MPD diagnosis to some historical accounts of possession. For example, Bliss (1986) cited the first documented case of "multiple personality" as reported in 1646 by Paracelsus, involving a woman whose unremembered alternate personality stole her money. Putnam (1989) went back even further to "MPD archetypes" during paleolithic times. Cave paintings at Lascaux and Les Trois Frères have been interpreted as human beings experiencing shamanistic transformations or dissociative trance states (Bourguignon 1979, Putnam 1989).

Other historical cases of possession have not been reinterpreted by the psychiatric community. Reports of "demonic possession" appear in ancient texts: a fourth-century B.C. temple inscription at Thebes, the biography of Apollonius of Tyana in classical Greece, and the Kabbala and biography of St. Gall in the Middle Ages (Oesterreich 1966). The biblical account from the Book of Mark, which named possession and described its healing by exorcism, was not claimed in this century as an example of MPD although some behaviors are reminiscent of multiple personality.

> A man who lived in the tombs, it is written, had an unclean spirit. He screamed and tore his own flesh, and his strength defied restraint even by chains. Demons spoke from the man's mouth identifying themselves as Legion for they claimed to exist in great numbers. Upon a command from the healer, the demons agreed to depart but only if the exorcist, Jesus, would allow them to enter a grazing herd of swine.

In the early nineteenth century, the German physician, Justinius Kerner, attempted to treat another case of demonic possession medically (Goodman 1988). He resorted to exorcism only when his modern medicine failed.

> Anna Maria Uz, born in 1799, apparently led a normal and happy life until the onset of her symptoms in 1830. She, too, convulsed, cursed, thrashed, hit herself, and spoke with an unrecognizable voice. Each episode was followed by headaches and the claim of complete amnesia.
>
> Kerner prescribed St. John's wort, an herb with supposed antidemonic properties. He employed magnetism, which resulted in Anna Maria's ability to hear the voice of a protective spirit but also aroused the demons. Hypnosis, concluded Kerner, was useful but inade-

quate. Ultimately, one demon reluctantly agreed to depart on the condition that it could confess all of its sins with the help of an exorcist. Relapses continued until Kerner located Jacob Dürr, a mysterious German "shaman" who rid Anna Maria of the demons once and for all, and whom Kerner used thereafter in all his similar cases.

In another classic case, "demonic possession" was cured using psychological principles—in Janet's words, a "modern exorcism" (Oesterreich 1966, p. 110, Crabtree 1985).

A man named Achille returned from a business trip one day in 1890 and unexpectedly began to exhibit highly uncharacteristic behaviors. He contorted grotesquely, uttered blasphemies, screamed that he was being cut and burned, and claimed the devil was controlling him.

Achille was taken to Saltpêtrière Hospital, "the most propitious place to-day for the exorcism of the possessed and the expulsion of demons" (Janet, cited in Oesterreich 1966, p. 112), where Janet instantly recognized the signs of possession. When Janet's attempt at hypnosis failed, the psychologist induced automatic writing. He successfully engaged the "devil" in conversation and, by challenging the entity to prove its power, tricked it into placing Achille under hypnosis, whereupon Janet learned that Achille had had an extramarital liaison during his business trip. The psychologist surmised that in his guilt-ridden state, Achille had created the demon. Resolution of the problem and complete departure of the possessing entity occurred when Janet hypnotically evoked Achille's wife to whom the patient confessed and asked forgiveness. The exorcism was a "psychological exorcism not of the demon but of the memory that resulted in creation of the demon" (Ross 1989, p. 24).

In former times, psychiatry often accepted varieties of human experience that involved mysterious and untestable realities more consonant with non-Western cosmologies. Between 1800 and the first decades of the twentieth century, when the new diagnosis of schizophrenia appeared, mainstream Western psychiatry hypothesized a supernatural basis of multiple personalities as well as the physiological, psychological, or sociological causes (Stern 1984). During this era, exorcism continued to be sanctioned for what Western society recognized as Judeo-Christian forms of possession (Kluft 1993).

Before an era when possession came to be viewed by some as MPD, MPD-like cases probably were diagnosed as possession. At the turn of the century, William James described hysterics as incipient mediums and along with other psychical researchers regarded multiple personality as occurring on a continuum with mediumship, trance, possession, and religious ecstasy (Kenny 1981). The English Society for Psychical Research investigated telekinesis, hypnosis, clairvoyance, apparitions, and mediumship. Multiple personality was a primary intersection of psychical interests and abnormal psychology, although the relationship between multiple personality theory and spiritism was somewhat ambiguous and uncomfortable at the time (Kenny 1981).

James's patient, Mrs. Piper, was "the most oracularly powerful medium of the period," whose abilities James accepted (Kenny 1981, p. 342). (Even after his death, it is said, subsequent clinicians like Hyslop consulted the ghost of James through mediums in order to confirm the diagnoses of their own patients; however, reports from séances indicate James's apparent lack of cooperation.) Some contemporaries of Morton Prince felt that Prince's patient, Miss Beauchamp, might have become a medium—her abilities seemed to exceed those of their host. Prince's colleagues concluded that certain skills belonging to Sally, one of Miss Beauchamp's alternate personalities, were not physically but telepathically derived. In accordance with contemporary thinking, mind was not necessarily connected to matter, that is, brain (Kenny 1981).

Since 1920, few cases of multiple personality have been attributed to the supernatural, although even today patients cite paranormal experiences in their constellation of symptoms (Stern 1984). In the United States, spirit or demon alters are more prevalent in religiously fundamentalist or rural sections of the country (Putnam 1989, Ross 1989), and throughout North America demon alters emerge in 28.6 percent of MPD cases, and alters claiming to be dead relatives occur in 20.6 percent (Ross et al. 1989).

Clearly, the mere claim of spirits does not prove their existence. Furthermore, the etiology of unexplainable phenomena is clinically irrelevant—all that can be taken as real is the individual's experience as that person describes it. What we can see throughout history and despite psychiatry's movement toward intrapsychic and psychobiological explanations, however, is the continuing perception among some individuals who experience illness of a causal connection between their symptoms and the supernatural.

Transmodal and Transcultural Treatment

Today, a small number of psychiatrists and exorcists treat psychiatric patients with exorcism or other spiritually based indigenous methods.

Allison (1980), a California psychiatrist who claimed to believe in the possibility of spirit possession, has treated MPD with "exorcism." He works within the MPD patient's belief system which, for many, includes the idea of reincarnation. Allison did not contend that the patient actually is possessed or that the clinical intervention gets rid of real evil spirits. However, he stated that he has encountered "aspects" or "entities" that do not comply with the classic pattern of MPD, that are not true alters, and that do not fulfill any recognizable psychological purpose. Allison's unorthodox treatment incorporates hypnosis, commands, and suggestions, for example, that a patient "push" evil energy from his or her own body into an external object. Through these rituals, often lasting a mere few minutes, the psychiatrist has reported complete and long-lasting disappearance of symptoms following banishment.

When patients present with complaints of otherworldly spirits, McAll, a contemporary British psychiatrist with experience as a war surgeon in China, advised initially ruling out neurosis and psychosis (Crabtree 1985). However, he acknowledged that possession sometimes exists unrelated to mental illness, and that it can be unresponsive to standard psychiatric methods. According to McAll, such cases require prayer and religious rites in order to help the spirit find peace, and he directs follow-up treatment to the underlying spiritual illness of the host, which may have created the patient's dependency on the possessed state.

Crabtree (1985), a Toronto psychotherapist, claimed to have worked with fifty cases of apparent possession over a seven-year period. He felt that neither the therapist nor client need believe in the objective reality of possession in order for treatment to be efficacious. What is of primary importance is that the therapist be flexible enough to move beyond the closed framework of his or her theoretical training; listen seriously to patients' descriptions; and treat the cases "as if" they are exactly what they appear: bona fide instances of possession.

Various spiritually based treatments for possession by alien entities are used generally, according to Crabtree (1985). The possessor may be commanded to leave, as in exorcism, or persuaded to depart, if the spirit appears as a higher entity with which one can reason. The possessing agent can be dissolved with highly concentrated positive energy, the evil power neutralized by its opposite. The entity can be driven back whence it came. Or, it can be bound and isolated from its energy source—in essence, "starved out" when the host shifts attention to more mundane activities.

This latter technique is reminiscent of Fahy and colleagues (1989) in England who withdrew attention from the alters of their dissociated patients and focused, instead, on other aspects of psychodynamics. The logic of such treatment is that symptoms will disappear if they are not engaged. Some might argue that diminished reports of symptoms in such cases relates more to the reluctance of MPD patients to disclose to a therapist whom they perceive as nonsupportive. However, from the point of view of occultists, the theory makes sense, albeit for different reasons. When the therapist sanctions alternate entities, that attention gives energy to the intruder, reinforces the spirit's foothold, diminishes the host's spiritual strength, and exacerbates the pathology.

Psychotherapy involving living or discarnate human possessors often involves treatment of both host and intruder as two separate individuals in a relationship (Crabtree 1985). Sometimes it is necessary to treat the entity in order to liberate it from its unhealthy attachment, or "neurotic bond," to the host. In such cases, the possessor is drawn into the therapeutic process and information gathered about its purpose. Ultimately, resolution is sought between the possessor and possessed so that both can move on. Once resolution is achieved, the entity and host usually either sever all contact or maintain a friendly relationship that allows the entity to return when the host needs its assistance or advice.

Crabtree's background and practice consist largely of family cases, thus he encounters possession in the context of family systems. However, some puzzling possessions have occurred that Crabtree could not understand in terms of family systems and in which the treatment methods were less classically psychodynamic. One striking case involved Charles, the son of a German war bride and English serviceman, who was raised in England.

At the age of 18, Charles began having feelings in which he seemed to hear, see, and "remember" places and events that had occurred in Germany before his birth. He became increasingly fearful of impending death. During hypnosis, Charles, who had never learned the language, conversed fluently in a local German dialect and narrated in the first person the life stories of two people, Horst and Hans.

Horst was a sensitive, artistic, nonobservant Jew who was deported in his teens to Theresienstadt concentration camp. During a forced march along a railroad track, he had fallen and was shot in the back of the head. Hans, a naïve young German guard on the railroad eventually stationed at Theresienstadt, had pleaded with Horst to get up and continue marching. When Hans failed to shoot, an older German officer killed Horst.

Crabtree, convinced that Hans and Horst were trying to resolve unfinished aspects of their lives through Charles, treated Charles by allowing the spirits to emerge and receive help. In hypnosis, Horst accepted his death and realized that it did not annihilate him but rather brought peace. Hans acknowledged his guilt and realized that his final "act of kindness" to Horst was atonement. As the spirits' problems resolved, Charles no longer feared his own imminent death, and his obsession with wartime Germany ceased.

Treatment of psychiatric patients with dissociative responses can be transcultural as well as transmodal. Israeli psychotherapists diagnosed a severe anxiety reaction in an Israeli Druze patient who was inhabited by the spirit of a dead Syrian Druze man (Daie et al. 1992). Transmigration of souls is a normal phenomenon in Druze culture, so treatment that conformed to the patient's belief system acknowledged that his pathology derived not from his memory of the incarnation but from the anxiety that those memories produced. Appropriate cure consisted in helping the man reunite with the living family of his previous incarnation. An emotional one-time-only meeting at the Israeli-Syrian border was arranged, and attended by relatives of both the Israeli patient and his Syrian former soul.

Therapists applied another culturally prescribed ritual in a case of major depressive disorder with dissociative and psychotic features (Witztum et al. 1990). The patient, an Israeli Jew of North African descent, felt tormented by a personal angel similar to a *maggid* who conveys secrets to kabbalists via automatic writing or speaking through a host's body. One relative wished to drive out the entity while the therapists chose, instead, to convert the angel into an ally.

Culturally relevant techniques were incorporated with an elderly Native American medicine man who manifested eleven "subpersonalities," four human and seven nonhuman (Smith 1989). The animal alters were embedded in the patient's cultural belief system about the spirit world and its powerful medicine, wherein tribal shamans are known to embody animal entities. In order to be effective, the treatment had to protect the spiritual needs of the Indian community. Initial attempts at fusion resulted in the complaint that the medicine man was losing his spiritual powers. Therefore, a treatment plan required that some alters remain as "spiritual traces" in case they were needed for his work at a later time.

Occasionally, I have taken a small number of Khmer adolescents who were being treated in the United States to a distant, revered Cambodian monk for Buddhist exorcism (Golub 1989). The adolescents felt themselves possessed by ghosts, the dead, or frightening spirits from the forest through which they had fled Khmer Rouge and Vietnamese invaders. Prior to exorcism, one young girl spoke in an unrecognizable voice and her countenance and manner changed dramatically from moment to moment. More commonly, the teenagers reported being visited in dreams by the benign spirits of their dead parents who offered them advice. Such visitations provided great comfort to the surviving children and at these times therapy consisted not of exorcism but of listening together to the words of the dream-spirits.

In Brazil, exorcism combines with psychotherapy (Krippner 1987). There, both *Kardecismo* spiritists and psychiatrists use exorcism to treat "MPD." Some hospitals are administered by spiritist practitioners and a number of psychologists and psychiatrists are spiritists themselves. Most Brazilian practitioners who are familiar with MPD regard spirit possession or past-life evocation as a possible explanation of the problem.

The spiritist concept of MPD differs from the psychiatric notion in part because the spiritist concept of self allows for entities and reincarnation. According to one practitioner, a medical doctor whom Krippner (1987) interviewed, the psyche is like an onion, each layer consisting of the same fundamental spirit in different forms. He claimed to have treated over 1,000 cases of spirit possession of which 3 percent he identified as MPD. A second practitioner who has diagnosed thirty cases of "MPD" viewed the etiology as problems from this life, past lives, or the spirit world.

Spiritist practitioners often refer MPD cases to psychiatrists when they determine that the etiology is abuse rather than spirit intrusion, although they acknowledge that childhood trauma can lead to spirit possession as well. If the intruder is malevolent, exorcism is indicated. Otherwise, treatment consists of attempts at merging: "Each personality 'lives in its own apartment' but all are encouraged 'to enter the dining room'" (Krippner 1987, p. 279). In cases where the patient is a medium or potential medium, alternate personalities are retained after treatment so that they can emerge on occasion to assist the medium's work.

On the whole, Western-trained psychiatrists rarely attempt exorcism, no matter how they understand that term and regardless of whether they ascribe a diagnosis of possession or MPD (Goodwin et al. 1990, Putnam 1989). Ross (1989) agreed that exorcism generally is not an appropriate treatment (although he claimed to have exorcised, together with a chaplain, a discarnate entity from a woman), "not because there are no demons, but because dissociative states are part of the whole person" (p. 26). The demon alter, Ross continued, ultimately is a frightened and posturing child to be reintegrated rather than banished.

It makes little sense to expel what is part of the personality, Greaves concurred (Krippner 1987). Often, such attempts at driving out are followed by exacerbation of rage and acting out by the persecutor alter. Exorcism, in such instances, produces the opposite of integration. However, other writers point out a paradox (Goodwin et al. 1990). They argue that exorcism is inherent in the contemporary concept of integration in which the healer refuses to accept that a person has more than one body and psyche, and insists that the patient regain unity. It is unfortunate that exorcism is not applied more often, lamented Goodman (1988), because exorcism is the only strategy incorporated cross-culturally against demonic possession, and it can help sufferers regain ritual control over the entities.

Similarities and Differences between MPD and Possession

Various typologies of possession suggest that some of its forms are more closely akin than others to modern MPD. Bourguignon (1968) distinguished between trance and possession in a way that clarifies the possible relationship between those states and multiple personalities. Dissociation or trance may or may not be regarded by the community as possession. Trance, according to Bourguignon's model, consists of conditions that are explained locally by naturalistic or supernatural causes. Naturalistic explanations of trance include hypnosis, biochemical changes, and somatic or psychological illness, for example, the latter of which includes a subcategory called multiple personality. Not all trance is possession and not all possession is demonic.

Supernatural explanatory systems subdivide into possession, such as spirit presence, and nonpossession, such as soul absence. Possession may be voluntary or involuntary, manifest or latent, lucid or somnambulistic. Voluntary possession is desirable and often benign, differing in that respect from MPD. Shamans, mediums, and spiritists regularly enter into this positive, consciously induced state. Involuntary possession, on the other hand, is demonic. Intruders are uninvited and must be manipulated and expelled.

The similarities between MPD and involuntary possession are apparent. Manifest, latent, lucid, and somnambulistic possession also share features with MPD. Alternative personalities can emerge during possession spontaneously (manifest) or they can be brought out by hypnosis (latent). In lucid possession the host is aware of two souls struggling within and retains memory of the simultaneous cohabitation by self and outsiders. Perhaps more like MPD is somnambulistic possession, during which the host experiences amnesia between alternative personalities and loses consciousness of self when the intruder enters.

While there are numerous commonalities and differences between MPD and possession (see Tables 10–1, 10–2, 10–3), it might be useful to mention briefly just two of the shared characteristics from the point of view of spirit possession: the role of trauma and risks to the healer. "If there are devils, if there are supernormal powers, it is through the cracked self that they enter," wrote William James in 1896 (Kenny 1981, p. 341). Many indige-

TABLE 10-1
Similarities and Differences—Nature of the Experience*

MPD	Possession (nondemonic)
Condition is considered pathological. A disorder.	Condition is culturally normative. Fostered and stimulated.
Pathology is reflected in condition itself.	Pathology occurs when ritual possession fails. Person who can't switch is viewed as defective. Deviance not because of possession but because of anxiety that possessed person may feel. Possession itself is healing and resocializing.
Capacity to dissociate often is understood as a defense mechanism. Ultimately discouraged.	Capability is explicitly encouraged, structured, and controlled by society (except in children when spirits viewed as harassing; rituals to prevent interference by spirits until adulthood).
Person is socially isolated and dysfunctional.	Person is well adjusted in everyday life. Formalized ritual behavior requires that the individual be able to comply with culturally prescribed behaviors.
Individual is viewed as a deviant without cultural support.	Possessed individual is supported within a formally organized public event, during which consensually agreed upon beliefs are routinely embodied.

Internal origin of alters.
  Alters are split-off parts of principal personality, private and personal creations.
	External origin of spirits.
	  Personality is created by entity other than the individual. Separate being possesses.

Embodied alter is a personality.	Spirits emerge from historical context of a specific human group. Parameters are the shared historical memory of the group.
Society questions existence of spirits. Alters are "real" only as they aid integration of self.	Spirits are "real" and viewed as honored guests.
Neither community nor therapist believe in separate existence of alters.	Socially accepted. Teach and foster expression by alters.

Interpreted by some as role playing or faking.

Extraordinary feats substantiate authenticity in locally meaningful ways.

---

*Tables 10-1, 10-2, and 10-3 have been compiled from the untabulated texts of various authors, including: Bourguignon 1968, 1989, Daie et al. 1992, Downs et al. 1990, Goodman 1988, Goodwin et al. 1990, Kenny 1991, Krippner 1987, Mulhern 1991, Ross 1989, Varma et al. 1981.

TABLE 10–2
Similarities and Differences—Phenomenology*

MPD	*Possession (nondemonic)*
Episodic disturbance of identity.	
Invasion by a new personality that is distinct and separate.	
Stable alternative identities. Each set of traits is a coherent separate personality.	
Identities have own name. Identifiable by actions and transformations.	
Alters may have no resemblance to any known person. Idiosyncratic.	Personality is a concrete, known person or deity with characteristics agreed upon by society. Spirit must be recognizable to group and act characteristically.
	Spirit must establish its genealogical relationship to pantheon.
	Spirit must establish its identity by routinely taking possession.
Life span of alternate personality is that of one human body. Life span of host circumscribes the personalities.	Spirits circumscribe the life span of the host.
Helper personalities	
Persecutor personalities	

Embodiment of alters is an everyday action.
  Alters may emerge and depart at any time.
	Embodiment of spirits is a ritual occurrence.
	  Possession begins and ends within confines of ritual.

No ritual help or control.	Ritual control. Occurs within well-defined rules and under specific circumstances.
Alter is not invited.	Spirit is invited, although person can be possessed "accidentally" by an unruly, unauthorized spirit. Supplicant asks a being who possesses no body to enter his/her body for the duration of ritual and use as sees fit. Owner soul watches or leaves.
Can enter by a breach.	
Painful childhood experiences or trauma can create proclivity, vulnerability to condition. Spontaneous manifestation is a response to current stress.	

(continued)

TABLE 10–2 (continued)

MPD	Possession (nondemonic)
Body of host undergoes physiological changes.	
Biological aspects are seen as validating real existence of alternative identities within body of the multiple.	Changes are seen as guarantee of supernatural origins.
Behavior of host changes under special circumstances.	
Many similar though not necessarily identical behaviors, e.g., switching, amnesia.	
Trance and out-of-body experiences are common.	
Culture does not formally or directly "teach" patient how to enact role of alter.	Host learns under controlled conditions to embody and carry spirit correctly. Acts according to what he perceives as appropriate to possessing spirit.
Alters respond and give expression to felt stress.	
Alters express feelings divergent from core personality.	
Host feels no responsibility for alters' actions.	
Can induce condition in others.	
Host remembers only dimly.	
Patient often conceals or minimizes symptoms.	Ostentatious rather than hidden behavior.
Limited number of reports.	Commonplace occurrence.
Vast majority of hosts are women.	
More women are victims of violence. Incarcerated men possibly underidentified.	Male dominated societies. Woman more vulnerable to diesase and trauma, e.g., poverty, beating, mutilation, starvation.

*Compiled from the untabulated texts of Bourguignon 1968, 1989, Daie et al. 1992, Downs et al. 1990, Goodman 1988, Goodwin et al. 1990, Kenny 1981, Krippner 1987, Mulhern 1991, Ross 1989, Varma et al. 1981.

nous healers worldwide would agree with the statement's literal reading, and add that different kinds of experience make a person vulnerable to intrusion: mental or physical illness, spiritual weakness, curiosity, destructive thoughts, ingestion of drugs, or childhood trauma. Hatred of an abuser is "one of the strongest magnets attracting . . . 'evil entities' " (Allison 1985, p. 47). Practitioners in various cultures believe that very painful events in childhood enhance a person's proclivity to dissociation or possession by spirits (Fahy 1988, Krippner 1987, Martinez-Taboas 1991b, Mulhern 1991). Trauma causes hypersensitivity, which in turn makes one available and triggers the emergence of alien identities.

TABLE 10-3
Similarities and Differences—Treatment*

MPD	Possession (nondemonic)
Healer must establish credibility whether views forces as endogenous or external.	
Healer views relationship with client as finite and leading to independence.	Healer's relationship with client is a permanent commitment. No fear of dependency.
No contextual relevance in individual therapy.	Healing is a creative and public act.
A treatment goal is to help overcome pathological splits.	Treatment: to come to terms with spirit world. Possession trance holds central place.
Healer supports belief that alters exist only as aspect of self.	Healer supports belief that other spirit entities exist.
Preparation of safe or sacred space for healing.	
Healer may induce altered state of consciousness.	
Personalities sometimes are produced in therapeutic interaction.	
Therapist does not intentionally induce, at least the initial appearance of an entity.	Healer suggests and provides models of spirit personalities.
Diagnostic concern about authenticity.	
Healer addresses spirits/alters as discrete.	
Focus on patient's life history.	Focus on past lives of spirits.
Find alter's name, age, reasons for being, history.	Identify spirit. Demonic possession: Who sent you? How many are you? Why are you in this person? How long have you been inside?
Negotiate, persuade, bargain, contract with hostile personalities.	
Therapist focuses on integration. Expulsion of hostile alters generally is not recommended.	Exorcist focuses on expulsion of malevolent spirits.
Therapist can't always cause to disappear.	Upon ritual cue, possession will unfailingly dissolve. Community ensures host's safe return and preserves memory.
Cure occurs when person reintegrates.	Cure occurs when host successfully carries spirits. Repeated possessions are normal.
Grave risks to healer.	
Necessary characteristics of healer.	

*Compiled from the untabulated texts of Bourguignon 1968, 1989, Daie et al. 1992, Downs et al. 1990, Goodman 1988, Goodwin et al. 1990, Kenny 1981, Krippner 1987, Mulhern 1991, Ross 1989, Varma et al. 1981.

Stevenson (1984) proposed a relationship between xenoglossy and reincarnation that involves the notion of trauma, not necessarily as experienced within the life span of the host, but rather of its disembodied personality. Trauma, he postulated, can produce a bonding together of traumatic memories and their associated emotions. This cluster becomes somewhat autonomous from the more integrated structure of an individual's other subpersonalities, and the festering pressure to find a conduit or outlet persists after death. In other words, an alter personality in a living person can arise from the traumatic residue of a former life as well as from trauma to the host.

Prior sexual penetration such as among abused children or women following marriage makes those individuals more vulnerable to *dybbuks*, the malevolent spirits of the dead found in Jewish folklore (Bilu and Beit-Hallahmi 1989). At times, a possessing *dybbuk* publicly identifies sexual transgressors among observers of the exorcism ceremony, and makes evident the sexual trespasses of his own lifetime. Analyzing such cases and noting that adolescents often were present in the household, some analytically oriented therapists claimed that the possession relates to the expression of forbidden sexual impulses of the otherwise "culturally sealed" (Mulhern 1991) host by means of the creation of a culpable external agent—*dybbuks* among Jews (Bilu and Beit-Hallahmi 1989), *duendes* in Colombia (León 1975), or possessing spirits in India (Akhtar 1988, Alexander 1956). In Alexander's paper, cited as the first MPD description in the modern era (Bowman 1990), it is interesting to note that his interpretation does not focus on aspects of the case that suggest actual incest in the Indian girl's history. Nor does León's analysis in Colombia take into account the fact that the sufferer had experienced sexual abuse not only prior to the possession but from a priest who was treating her.

One must be cautious about making cross-cultural comparisons about childhood abuse, warned Korbin (1981). The nature of abuse may vary in different areas of the world. There is no universal standard; practices considered acceptable in one culture might be regarded as abusive elsewhere. However, no culture sanctions extreme harm, and idiosyncratic behaviors do exist outside that which the culture condones.

Healers also face potential risks as a result of their contact with MPD, posttraumatic stress disorder, and other traumatized or dissociatively disordered patients. Discussions in the literature often frame the dangers in terms of countertransference, secondary traumatization, or vicarious traumatization rather than in the language of possession. Therapists are not taught how to prepare, detoxify, or self-exorcise following interaction with certain patients in the same way that mediums, medicine men, and other traditional healers learn techniques from their masters.

Therapists may find themselves both fascinated and terrified, particularly when they are confronted by unexplainable entities in patients (Allison 1985). The clinicians may be "infected" with a "demonic chill" from demon alters (Ross 1989) that is similar to the infection experienced by exorcists. Psychiatrists and exorcists differ about whether this contagion is psychic or demonic in nature. The philosopher Oesterreich (1966) analyzed the untimely demise of four exorcists of the famous seventeenth-century possessions at the convent of Loudun and concluded, "It is hardly necessary to remark that the true source of this infection [was] not the mere sight of the possessed but the concomitant lively belief in the demoniacal character of their state and its contagious nature" (p. 92).

Both psychotherapists and exorcists agree that it is mandatory to protect oneself from these forces (Ronquillo 1991); however, exorcists are more precise than Western therapists about the necessary prerequisites for undertaking such curative work. The indigenous healers know they must always remember that their power comes from a higher source and avoid engaging in a personal struggle with the entity. Failure to do so can lead to possession of the exorcist by the spirit (Crabtree 1985). Jewish exorcists must be able to distinguish the evil in the possessed from the evil within themselves (Baker 1975, cited in Goodwin et al. 1990). Work must not be undertaken because of personal motives or a sense of urgency (Winkler 1981, cited in Goodwin et al. 1990). Rabbis must be masters, strong enough to withstand insults, accusations, physical attacks, and the demon's attempts to seduce or to cause them to lose their faith (Goodwin et al. 1990).

Despite their personal qualities, extensive training, and experience, exorcists and mediums still encounter great danger. Jacob Dürr, the powerful German healer whom Justinius Kerner sought, barely ate, trembled from the least bit of drink, and was in nearly perpetual communication with demons, angels, and souls of the dead. "What am I to do? . . . Where am I to get the strength for my cures?" the old man despaired (Goodman 1988, p. 105). Eventually he lost (but later regained) his strength and his healing powers. Taoists believe that for each person freed, a specific number of years is taken off the life of the exorcising monk (Goullart 1961, cited in Goodwin et al. 1990). Every exorcist in every culture risks the "irreparable pillage of his deepest self" (Martin 1987, cited in Goodwin et al. 1990, p. 97).

Summary

MPD shares aspects of its phenomenology with non-Western forms of dissociation, particularly involuntary possession states. The ontological basis of alternate identities differs across cultures as do the identification, naming, dynamics, treatment, and social context of multiplicity. Rather

than evaluate possession states with psychiatric criteria, Part II attempted
to view MPD from a non-Western orientation. It is hoped that this broader
perspective will provide an alternative lens through which to interpret
critically the following cross-cultural case reports.

PART III: MPD CASES ACROSS CULTURES

Experts disagree greatly about the incidence and prevalence of MPD
worldwide, some claiming that it is nonexistent, others that the syndrome
occurs rarely, seldom, frequently, or even in epidemic numbers. Among
the possible reasons for this discrepancy are the conditions under which
cases have been identified. The previous section gave examples of ways
that similar phenomenology is understood and categorized differently
across cultures. The shared features of MPD and possession states may
account for each sometimes being diagnosed as the other. Within the field
of psychiatry, the nosology has transformed and produced a variety of
diagnostic labels: co-consciousness, secondary personality, conversion
hysteria—amnesic type, hysterical neurosis—dissociative type, multiple
personality, MPD, and dissociative identity disorder. The validity of either
a transcultural or retroactive diagnosis remains dubious and produces
questions about whether any current nomenclature can be applied to
behaviors that may have arisen in another spaciotemporal context.

Additional considerations complicate cross-cultural identification of
MPD. For one thing, MPD has been claimed in the literature by individuals
other than psychiatrists and psychologists. Anthropologists, spiritists, and
various traditional healers, for example, sometimes use the same psychiatric terminology but different diagnostic criteria or explanatory systems.
Furthermore, cases outside North America have been diagnosed both by
members of the client's culture and by North American MPD experts
working overseas. Some patients are members of the culture and others are
North Americans living in another society and described as cases of MPD
from that country.

Within North America there are a few reports of MPD among migrant,
immigrant, and native populations. In addition, transcultural manifestations appear among alters themselves in the form of their declared cultural
identity or language preference. Part II identified clinicians who borrow
culturally diverse treatment theories and methods that are consonant with
the client's belief system but to which the treaters themselves do not
necessarily subscribe.

The following citations include mainly cases termed MPD or any of the
corresponding diagnoses from previous *Diagnostic and Statistical Manuals*
(*DSM*) of the American Psychiatric Association. They have been located

primarily in English-language sources published since 1956. Thus, this discussion gives limited attention to early cases reported throughout Europe and among North American patients who emigrated from other countries at the beginning of the century. Examples from outside the United States and Canada are presented first, followed by accounts of ethnically diverse patients in North America, and transcultural variations among alters themselves.

MPD outside the United States and Canada

In 1944, Taylor and Martin located seventy-six cases of "multiple personality" in the literature and postulated that there were at least that many more examples throughout the world. Their survey revealed that 57 percent of the cases had occurred in the United States, 18 percent in France, 16 percent in Britain, and the remainder in Germany and Switzerland. By 1980, 200 cases of MPD had been described in the world literature (Ross et al. 1989), and by 1986 (Bliss) the figure was estimated at 300. A recent literature search (Coons et al. 1991) discovered case reports in thirteen countries outside the United States and Canada—including Australia, Brazil, Czechoslovakia, England, France, Germany, Holland, India, Italy, Japan, New Zealand, South Africa, Switzerland, and the territory of Puerto Rico. Questionnaires from the same study found fifteen clinicians who claimed a total of thirty-two new cases of MPD in Belgium, Bulgaria, Colombia, Guatemala, Israel, and Mexico as well as the formerly identified England, Holland, Japan, and Puerto Rico. The researchers interpreted dissociative disorders not otherwise specified (DDNOS) among the responses from Brazil, Germany, India, Japan, and Mexico. My own literature review located reports of possible MPD cases in Scotland, Russia, and in North America among Native Americans, Puerto Ricans residing on the mainland, and immigrants or refugees from Latin America, Cambodia, Hong Kong, and Lebanon.

Some authors note racial differences among MPD patients (Coons et al. 1991, Putnam 1989) and their alters (Ross 1989, Ross et al. 1989); however, the literature offers few epidemiological findings based on ethnicity. Putnam (1989) stated that Asian clients, primarily Cambodians, make up 2 percent of his MPD practice. Cross-cultural case reports continue to be sporadic although studies are under way in India, The Netherlands, France, and Puerto Rico (Putnam 1989, 1991).

Not all cases are described in detail; Putnam (1989) alluded to several instances of MPD in children and adolescents from war-torn Cambodia and Lebanon. It is unclear where or when the pathology appeared and what the cultural context of diagnosis and treatment was. In some areas of the world, situations of extremity such as war, natural disaster, famine, religious persecution, thought reform, or indoctrination during captivity by terrorists or cultists might contribute to dissociative states (Ross 1989). Ethiopian children, Cambodian boat people, Brazilian street children, and adults who were children in Vietnam during the 1960s may be among those who experience chronic complex dissociative disorders, although the nature of the dissociation most likely varies according to the trauma and culture (Ross 1991b).

Cases from Asia and the Pacific have been recorded in India, Japan, Australia, and New Zealand. Generally, identified MPD is quite unusual in India whereas possession states are common. In a study of 2,651 psychiatric patients, 2.3 percent, or sixty-two, fit the *DSM-III* dissociative disorders category, and of those, 90.3 percent were atypical type and none were multiple personality (Saxena and Prasad 1989).

The literature from India presents a total of six examples of MPD. In the earliest of these accounts, Alexander (1956) described an adolescent Indian girl, Soosan, who complained of possession by two evil spirits, or secondary personalities as Alexander called them, for which the host had total amnesia. Each of the discrete personalities disclosed physical violence in its own lifetime. The male indicated incest in both his and Soosan's histories and professed his ongoing sexual desire for Soosan. Alexander interpreted the case not as one of dissociation but rather of repression of the patient's sexual impulses, a defense mechanism that he felt expresses itself easily in a culture that believes in evil spirits.

Another instance of secondary personality with xenoglossy led to a different theoretical formulation (Stevenson 1984, Stevenson and Pasricha 1979). The core personality, a Marathi-speaking Indian woman, frequently transformed into a nineteenth-century Bengali whose genealogy, language, and descriptions of the period and locale were verified. The authors compared the case with typical secondary personality and concluded that this situation was reminiscent of reincarnation and involved a paranormally acquired skill.

Varma et al. (1981) related an instance of "multiple personality" in India to hysterical possession states that are more commonly manifested in the culture. Three additional examples of "multiple personality disorder" were outlined in 1989 by Indian psychiatrists Adityanjee, Raju, and Khandelwal. These authors attributed to cultural factors differences between their cases and those of Western patients in, for example, the number of alters and mode of switching. When at least one Western physician (Rathbun 1990) questioned the diagnostic accuracy of two of the latter three cases, Adityanjee (1990) defended the assessments on the basis of subtleties of patient presentation, speed of intervention, and the need for clinicians to be flexible when applying classification systems cross-culturally.

MPD cases in Japan likewise spark controversy and journal commentary. Takahashi (1990) cited two earlier Japanese-language reports of MPD that were ignored by colleagues in that country, and noted that two patients mentioned in a third article might well have experienced MPD but were diagnosed as schizophrenic. Based on his own review of 489 patients, which revealed seven cases of dissociative disorders and no MPD, Takahashi concluded that MPD, indeed, is rare in Japan; however, he proposed that investigations of cross-cultural incidence should continue.

Supporters of the MPD diagnosis from the United States (Frischholz and Braun 1990), Puerto Rico (Martinez-Taboas 1990), Canada (Ross 1990), and The Netherlands (van der Hart 1990) responded to Takahashi. Generally, they wondered about the extent of confirmation bias in the research whereby new data are construed in a manner consistent with original hypotheses, in this case, reinforcing the initial skepticism among the Japanese evaluators. They also questioned the skill of the Japanese team in recognizing and diagnosing MPD, and suspected that their possible misdiagnoses of schizophrenia were due in part to currently inadequate diagnostic instruments. In Japan, which has a tradition of belief in spirits and demonic possession, complex dissociative disorders may be fairly common today in forms other than MPD (Ross 1990). Finally, the respondents took issue with Takahashi's assertion of extremely low child abuse in Japan, suspecting, instead, cultural proscriptions against its disclosure.

Australia communicates much skepticism and few accounts of MPD: one early report (Maddison 1953), plus reports among six clinicians from an admittedly biased sample who described ten cases (Coons et al. 1991). New Zealand recorded minimal numbers of MPD cases (Chancellor and Fraser 1982) although Altrocchi (1992), an American, "quickly located" multiple MPD cases during a four-month trip to New Zealand. In one instance, three hours of consultation (far less time than many evaluators consider necessary) with the attending clinician alone were sufficient to convince Altrocchi of the accuracy of an MPD diagnosis. He anticipated a high frequency of MPD in New Zealand, an individualistic society with "frequent" child abuse, and looked for possible cases at crisis services for abuse victims. A number of clients self-diagnosed in response to media presentations about his work. Clinicians who had conferred with Altrocchi began identifying their own cases and started training others to do so. Altrocchi then described the emergence of previously undetected patients, and, contradicting mainstream New Zealand professionals, predicted that an explosion of MPD was imminent in that country.

A 1928 case (Laubscher) appears to be the only English-language reference to co-consciousness or multiplicity in South Africa or on the entire African continent for that matter. Simpson (1989), a psychiatrist from Johannesburg, did not specifically address MPD in South Africa, but in a letter to the *British Journal of Psychiatry* he articulated his conviction that the disorder is largely culture-bound and iatrogenic in nature.

Nor does the Middle East report many instances of multiple personality disorder, although literature from the region describes dissociative states related to possession or the transmigration of souls. The questionnaire of Coons and colleagues (1991) uncovered five cases of MPD in Israel. Since that study, S. Noy (personal communication, October 22, 1993) observed one MPD patient, and diagnosed and treated two others, a North American immigrant and a native-born Israeli.

Belief in spirits and possession is common in Latin America. Some medically trained spiritist practitioners in Brazil have diagnosed "MPD" among their dissociated clients. Krippner's paper (1987) cited a total of 360 MPD cases diagnosed by three individuals. Coons and colleagues (1991) found one new case in Guatemala, one in Colombia, and two in Mexico. An intriguing account of a rural Chinese-Mexican man possessed by four autonomous spirits may be an instance of DDNOS (Cramer 1980), as possibly are Goodman's (1988) example from Mexico, the *duende* cases in Colombia (León 1975), and numerous other descriptions of discrete personalities taking over their host. Dissociative reaction associated with *santería*, a syncretic religion that combines African and Catholic elements, was identified in 127 Cuban patients using *DSM-I* criteria (Bustamente 1968).

Martinez-Taboas (1989, 1990, 1991a,b) writes prolifically about MPD in Puerto Rico, where he and his colleagues detected and treated fifteen patients. Despite differences between Puerto Rican culture and that of the mainland United States and Canada, patient profiles were very much alike. One exception was the universal presentation of intense headaches and frequent "convulsions" among Puerto Rican patients, which the author explained in terms of a cultural tendency to somatize. Surprisingly, in a culture where many believe in spiritism, only 13 percent of alters—fewer than their mainland counterparts—claimed to be supernatural. The striking similarity of most MPD features between Puerto Rican and mainland patients, however, led Martinez-Taboas to conclude that MPD probably is not that rare throughout Latin America; what is uncommon is a general interest in dissociative disorders among Latino professionals.

The majority of MPD cases reported outside North America appear to have occurred in Europe and primarily in the Netherlands. At one point in 1989, a single psychiatric outpatient clinic in Holland treated fifteen patients (van der Hart and Boon 1989). Dutch researchers observed core symptoms that were notably similar to those of North Americans in seventy-one MPD patients referred by sixty clinicians who had diagnosed the MPD previously or suspected a dissociative disorder (Boon and Draijer

1993). Van der Hart (van der Hart and Boon 1990) observed his first case of MPD in 1980. He and a group of Dutch clinicians began training in 1984 with Braun, Kluft, and Sachs from the United States, after which the Dutch participants reported seeing "many more" MPD patients. Other colleagues confided that they, too, were treating MPD but had not shared this because of the great resistance among Dutch psychiatrists to the MPD diagnosis. Boon and Draijer (1991) concluded that dissociative disorders, and particularly MPD, are not culture-bound and exclusive to North America.

A 1991 study (Vanderlinden et al.) about dissociative experiences in the general populations of Belgium and The Netherlands reinforces the Dutch findings, as well as eleven other assertions of MPD in Belgium the same year (Coons et al. 1991). Vanderlinden and colleagues reasoned that dissociation occurs quite commonly, based on their estimate that 3 percent of the Flemish and Dutch populations report serious dissociative disorders, 1 percent at a level as high as patients with MPD.

Nineteen (3 percent) out of 679 Swiss psychiatrists indicated that they currently were examining, treating, or managing one or more *DSM-III* MPD cases (Modestin 1992). Ten percent of the same group responded that they had seen at least one MPD patient in their career. Proportions of psychiatrists who answered questionnaires corresponded exactly with German-, French-, and Italian-speaking regions of Switzerland. Based on his findings, Modestin argued that MPD genuinely exists and is distributed widely in space and time; however, the condition is relatively rare.

In recent years, only three accounts of MPD have emerged from England (Cutler and Reed 1975, Fahy et al. 1989, Miller 1989), along with a fourth case that showed features suggestive of multiple personality disorder (Bruce-Jones and Coid 1992). Apparently, more British cases of multiple personality appeared before 1944 than since—twelve according to Taylor and Martin (1944). Aldridge-Morris (1993) conducted an informal survey through the letters' columns of British journals and did not come up with any clear case of MPD among the responses. At the other extreme, a colleague from Scotland claimed to have been involved with "many" MPD cases in that country (Macilwain 1992).

Czechoslovakia's single report of MPD appeared prior to the 1950s (Boleloucky 1988); however, Bulgarian accounts have pointed to two recent patients (Coons et al. 1991). During an official visit to Moscow and Leningrad by American psychiatrists, their Russian hosts denied awareness of any case of MPD in that country and claimed ignorance about child sexual abuse, although one Soviet psychologist wondered in private about the possible MPD status of a female patient (Allison 1991).

Since the breakup of the Soviet Union and communist regimes in Eastern Europe, more clinicians from those former republics are presenting papers about the effects of civil strife, natural and toxic disasters, and transgenerational trauma related to massive oppression. International affiliations, research, and increased communication may begin to reveal manifestations of dissociation in the region, supplementing coded literary expressions and underground testimony which, until now, have been the principal vehicle for documenting the effects of severe trauma and coping.

MPD among Ethnically Diverse Clients in North America

No epidemiological studies in the literature describe MPD among immigrants, refugees, or their children born in the country of resettlement. Case descriptions are also rare although it is possible that authors simply have omitted cultural details from their accounts. In general, ethnocultural variables have been ignored in North American studies whether the patient or his or her family have been citizens for generations or whether they arrived recently (see Table 10–4).

Ronquillo (1991) presented the MPD case of an Hispanic woman, Dolores, who had lived in the United States for twenty-five years. She was born and raised in a rural area of an unspecified "politically unstable Latin country" to which she returned periodically as an adult

TABLE 10–4
Ethnic Diversity among Clients in North America*

Name	Observer	Date	Impression	Ethnicity
Marie	McKee and Wittkower	1962	Double personality	French Canadian
_____	Rendon	1974	Dissociation/ Schizophrenia/ Espiritismo	Puerto Rican
Mrs. B.	Alonso and Jeffrey	1988	Atypical dissociative disorder/Santería	Cuban American
(Various)	Putnam	1989	MPD	Cambodian
(Various)	Putnam	1989	MPD	Lebanese
_____	Smith	1989	MPD	Native American
_____	Ross	1990	MPD	Hong Kong
Mrs. C.	Steinberg	1990	MPD/Ataque de nervios	Puerto Rican
Dolores	Ronquillo	1991	MPD/Espiritismo	Latin American

*Information in this table derives from case descriptions. Please refer to above citations located in the reference section of this chapter for case details.

(p. 40). The woman's early life had been filled with many catastrophes: deaths, rape, and violence in the immediate family, and her own childhood kidnapping and sexual abuse over three years by a politician. Because of the potentially dangerous repercussions, family were prevented from intervening despite their knowledge of her whereabouts. During these years, she witnessed tortures and death, and experienced repeated death threats from her abductor.

Dolores believed in *espiritismo*, a widely practiced spiritist tradition in Latin America. She claimed no control over her four alters, and both she and her community regarded them as possessing spirits. Aspects of the alters' behavior were influenced by cultural folklore figures connected with *espiritismo*. Treatment in the United States necessarily involved consultation with an *espiritista* in addition to the social worker. In response to this case, Ronquillo advised further research to determine the extent to which Hispanic MPD clients who believe in *espiritismo* or *santería* personify folklore figures in the behavior of their private alters, and also to examine why Hispanics with MPD are not being identified within the United States mental-health system.

MPD should be considered in Hispanics with a history of *ataques de nervios*, proposed Steinberg (1990) in her discussion of a Puerto Rican woman in Connecticut. The patient's symptoms were classic for an *ataque* and consistent with MPD, and her history revealed severe childhood physical and sexual trauma. In this patient's case, acute *ataques* were manifested by one of her child alters. Steinberg reiterated Rendon's (1974) earlier observation about common misdiagnoses of schizophrenia among hysterically dissociated Puerto Ricans in New York. Those inaccurate interpretations, Rendon felt, were based on misunderstanding of social class, migration stressors, cultural values, and culturally determined and accepted styles of dissociation. Steinberg listed possible culturally influenced sources of the earlier misdiagnosis of her patient, including the inability of evaluators to discriminate between culturally accepted *ataques* and the underlying dissociative disorder.

Bustamente (1968) also suggested that Cuban schizophrenic patients were being misdiagnosed, in part, related to their alternation between everyday logical thinking and the religious magical thinking of *santería*, the boundary between which can become blurred. Many Cuban Americans also practice *santería*. Belief in spirit possession appears across a wide range of psychopathology and may complicate the transcultural diagnosis and treatment of mental illness among Cuban Americans (Alonso and Jeffrey

1988). Of four examples presented, none was evaluated as MPD although the authors considered atypical dissociative disorder in one case.

Asian Americans are described even less often than Hispanics in the MPD literature; references are made only in passing. One woman born in Hong Kong and evaluated in Canada presented as a "classic" case of MPD (Ross 1990, personal communication, October 28, 1993). Putnam (1989) treated several cases of MPD among Cambodians and Lebanese youths, presumably after their resettlement in the United States.

Some accounts of multiple personality make one question the observers' diagnosis and treatment. For example, a French Canadian woman born in Canada was described as a case of double personality (McKee and Wittkower 1962). Each personality had her own name and characteristic set of behaviors; however, the principal personality remained consistently aware that the second identity was a "fraud," an imaginary figure whose demise the primary personality arranged. Smith's (1989) description of a Native American man also is interesting for the age of its subject, 70, and because he was a highly respected medicine man. It would be useful to know something about the elder's medical and social history, prior interventions based on traditional Indian medicine, and how the man and his community understood the patient's self-reported inability to perform healing ceremonies because of internal fighting among spirits.

Cultural Differences among Alters

An analysis of 236 Canadian MPD patients revealed that in 21.1 percent of the cases alters were of a different race (Ross et al. 1989). One of the authors (Ross 1989) suspected that Caucasian patients in Canada have fewer black alters than do Americans. While some comparative data exist concerning racial differences, statistics about linguistic and cultural diversity among alters tend to be anecdotal. The latter two features appear to be fairly common among alternate identities and to be distributed widely throughout time and geography.

Table 10–5 presents just a sample of historical and contemporary cases in which the alter and core personalities differed. Although valid conclusions cannot be drawn from such a small sample, it is interesting to track the preponderance of specific linguistic and cultural identities. For example, Latin was more commonly spoken by alters in earlier times, and gypsies reappear as alternate personalities in Brazil. Personal, cultural, and historical forces surely influence the recurrence of specific ethnicities among alters in any given time or place. Some believers in reincarnation might

TABLE 10-5
Cultural Differences among Alter Personalities*

Name	Observer	Date	Impression	Culture or Language of Core (Alter)
(Various)	Syrian of Palestine/ Lucian/ Oesterreich	125 A.D./1922	Possession	(Greek, "barbarian tongues")
—	Gmelin/ Ellenberger	1791/1970	Exchanged personalities	Germany (French)
Esther	Fromer/ Oesterreich	1812/1922	Dybbuk possession	Polish Jew (High German, Latin, "strange languages")
Fritz	Lemaître/ Oesterreich	1906/1922	Somnambulistic possession	France (Armenian, Latin)
—	Dannholz/ Oesterreich	1916/1922	Mpepo sickness/ Xenoglossy	East Africa (Swahili, English)
Maria	Cory	1919	Dual personality	U.S. (Spanish)
Elena	Morselli/ Ellenberger	1925	Multiple personality	Italy (French)
Case #7	Bruce/Taylor and Martin	1944	Multiple personality	English (Welsh)
Jensen	Stevenson	1974	Xenoglossy	Jewish American (Swedish)
Mrs. A. B.	Cutler and Reed	1975	Multiple personality	Great Britain (German)
Gretchen	Stevenson	1976	Xenoglossy	U.S. (German)
Sharada	Stevenson and Pasricha	1979	Secondary personality/ Xenoglossy	Marathi (Bengali)
Billy Milligan	Keyes	1981	Multiple personality	U.S. (Yugoslavia, England x 3, Australia, Orthodox Jew, Arabic, Serbo-Croat, Swahili)

N.	Varma, Bouri and Wig	1981	Multiple personality	Hindi, Punjabi (English)
Leroy Jackson	Allison	1985	Possession syndrome	African American (Greece, New Zealand)
Isabel	Jacob/Krippner	1987	MPD	Brazil (French gypsy)
Fiona	Andrade/Krippner	1987	Past life/Xenoglossy	Brazil (Spanish gypsy)
Sonia	Mendes/Krippner	1987	MPD/Past lives/Xenoglossy	Brazil (France, China, Jewish)
(Two patients)	Adityanjee, Raju and Khandelwal	1989	MPD	Hindi (English)
Rafik	Daie, Witztum, Mark and Rabinowitz	1992	Severe anxiety reaction/Transmigration of souls	Israeli Druze (Syrian Druze)
——	Noy	1993	MPD	Israeli Jew b. U.S. (English, archaic Hebrew, modern Hebrew)
(Various)	Ross	1993	MPD	English (German), English (French), English (Spanish)

*Table 10–5 is compiled by the author from textual descriptions and personal communications about clinical material. Please refer to the reference section of this chapter for case details.

explain the patterns differently, hypothesizing that entities tend to incarnate to living persons whose culture is similar to their own.

Some alters who claim a cultural identity different from the principal personality are able to speak a second language. In certain cases, observers traced the appearance of the new culture or language to incidents in the patient's earlier life. The "spirit" in a French turn-of-the-century case of somnambulistic possession claimed to be Armenian. Although its host, a boy of 14, mentioned he had seen picture postcards of Armenia, the spirit's fluency in Latin remained unexplainable (Oesterreich 1966). Gmelin's 1791 case of "exchanged personalities" featured a German woman who suddenly became an aristocratic French lady speaking French perfectly and German with a French accent (Ellenberger 1970). Gmelin speculated that the German personality might have been influenced by the sight of aristocratic refugees arriving in Stuttgart at the beginning of the French Revolution two years earlier.

Cory's patient, Spanish Maria, spoke a smattering of Spanish and her English had a Spanish accent. She had known Mexican girls in her convent school and had begun a relationship with an older man whose mother was Spanish. A decade later, W. F. Prince concluded that Grace Oliver, the principal personality, had fabricated Spanish Maria from her own life experiences (Kenny 1981). The alter of Morselli's Italian patient, Elena, was French. Interestingly, whether speaking French or Italian, both personalities felt that they were communicating in Italian.

Mediums in James's day often had American Indian " 'controls' . . . from the other side" who served to introduce and speak for other entities (Kenny 1981, p. 343). Mrs. A. B. from Great Britain reported a German alter (Cutler and Reed 1975). The soul of a Syrian Druze man transmigrated into an Israeli Druze (Daie et al. 1992). An African-American forensic patient of Allison (1985) claimed a personality from Greece and a spirit originating in New Zealand. In Brazil, a woman treated for MPD described under hypnosis her former life as a French gypsy (Krippner 1987).

Taylor and Martin (1944) referred to a case in which one personality understood only English; the other spoke Welsh. In India, personalities alternated in one patient between English, Hindi, and Punjabi (Varma et al. 1981), and English and Hindi in two others (Adityanjee et al. 1989). Some alters of Noy's North American Israeli patient spoke only English, a few archaic Hebrew, and others modern Hebrew. Part of treatment involved teaching all alters to communicate in modern Hebrew. The alter of an MPD patient of Ross spoke German, the language of her abuser; other patients had French- and Spanish-speaking personalities (personal communications, April 30 and October 28, 1993). Ragen Vadascovinich, a Yugoslav personality of Billy Milligan, supposedly read, wrote, and spoke fluent Serbo-Croat (Keyes 1981). Arthur, an English alter, read and wrote fluent Arabic and claimed proficiency in Swahili. In addition, two child personalities said they were English, another was Australian, and a fourth described himself as an Orthodox Jew.

Lucian, born in 125 A.D., recounted an exorcist called the Syrian of Palestine whose patients began to utter Greek or a "barbarian tongue" when possessed (Oesterreich 1966). *Dybbuks* in a Polish ghetto commanded loudly in "strange languages" (Latin) or gave treatises sprinkled with High German during the rituals to expel them from their human hosts (Oesterreich 1966).

During the *mpepo* sickness, a form of possession affecting mainly women, East African spirits often spoke in a foreign tongue, such as Swahili or English, with which the ill person was unfamiliar (Oesterreich 1966). Observers found hysteria to be an inadequate explanation of the phenomenon. Xenoglossy appeared in Brazil as well. One medium's past-life entity, a Spanish gypsy, spoke a specific dialect of gypsies on the Iberian peninsula of which the medium had no prior knowledge (Krippner 1987). A second Brazilian under the care of a different spiritist not only spoke French as an eighteenth-century reincarnated spirit, but other alters claimed to be a Chinese man and a sixteenth-century Jewish housewife. One of the most prolific writers on the subject of xenoglossy published cases in the United States of unlearned Swedish (Stevenson 1974) and German (Stevenson 1976, 1984), and in India of Bengali (Stevenson 1984, Stevenson and Pasricha 1979).

Summary

Cross-cultural dimensions of MPD include international comparisons, ethnocultural differences within a single country, and cultural variations among alters of an individual patient. The preceding pages listed case reports in all three areas. The purpose was to identify examples rather than to examine their validity. Clearly, many colleagues disagree with the authors' assessments of their data. The concluding section of this chapter, therefore, focuses on controversies regarding the interactions of culture and pathology in MPD.

PART IV: POINTS OF VIEW

Skeptics and proponents of the MPD diagnosis arrive at different conclusions about its cross-cultural incidence. At times, the energy of the polemic seems to polarize the interpreters even further. However, a fine reading of the literature indicates that more agnosticism exists than the sometimes vitriolic debate would suggest. Strong believers agree that the disorder is constrained by historical and social forces and that its universality cannot simply be assumed. Doubters accept that cases have appeared beyond the North American continent and that further investigation is warranted. Still, it is quite easy to enumerate contrasting opinions about the incidence and culture-boundedness of MPD.

MPD has been called either nonexistent or a clinical rarity in Great Britain, Sweden, most of continental Europe, Russia, India, South and Southeast Asia, Japan, and New Zealand. According to some, it is an iatrogenic, largely culture-bound disorder specific to North America (Aldridge-Morris 1993, Fahy 1988, Fahy et al. 1989, Simpson 1989). Others point to a similar set of core symptoms across cultures and the striking resemblance of clinical phenomenology among MPD patients in the United States and Canada, Puerto Rico, The Netherlands, and other parts of Europe (Boon and Draijer 1993, Martinez-Taboas 1989, 1991b, Putnam 1991). They claim that the disorder is not culture-bound and exclusive to North America, but emerges in diverse cultures and distributes widely across geography and time (Boon and Draijer 1991, Coons et al. 1991, Macilwain 1992, Martinez-Taboas 1991a, van der Hart and Boon 1989, 1990).

Despite the similarities, it may be premature to regard MPD as universal because psychiatric categories always must be understood within their own unique cultural and historical contexts (Martinez-Taboas 1991a, Ross 1989). Symptoms arise within a specific milieu; even though individuals from different settings may share trauma as an etiological factor and dissociation as a defense, the explanatory systems, dynamics of the pathology, and method of treatment will be rooted in and maintained by local culture (Bourguignon 1989, Smith 1989).

Scholars attribute the variation in MPD rates around the world to numerous factors. One reason for the discrepancy relates to diagnostic classification systems. Possession syndrome currently is unavailable as a diagnosis to Western clinicians, and atypical dissociative disorders or DDNOS have been the next appropriate category available to non-Westerners. It is quite possible that until the *DSM* broadens its nosology, cases that otherwise might be classified as possession or a culture-specific form of dissociation are being mislabeled as MPD in North America, thus inflating its numbers there. *DSM-III-R* criteria are criticized as excessively vague. More accurate differential diagnosis might show that reports of MPD in the West, in fact, may be DDNOS instead, just as clearer discrimination could reveal a higher frequency of borderline personality disorders and, consequently, diminished rates of MPD.

Other explanations for the frequency differential are cited. Psychiatric traditions vary throughout the world, providing an inherited diagnostic convention within which to frame cases, and milieus that support the MPD diagnosis to different degrees. In the United States, psychotherapy may be more highly integrated into psychiatry, making patients less anxious about being labeled or judged and, therefore, less reluctant to reveal their disorder (Macilwain 1992). A more supportive social environment contributes to greater numbers of cases, in part, because it gives more approval to role playing (Adityanjee et al. 1989, Varma et al. 1981) and accords high status with sick-role privileges (Fahy 1988). The atmosphere in North America also is one that demonstrates great interest in child abuse, trauma, hypnosis, and dissociative disorders.

Training workshops and media presentations increase awareness which, in turn, fosters popularity of the diagnosis and the emergence of new cases. Media tend to sensationalize accounts of MPD, and North American patients may incorporate aspects of media stories into their own constructions. Furthermore, American psychiatric journals, unlike their European counterparts, promote more publication of articles pertaining to MPD (Bruce-Jones and Coid 1992). Private clinics are establishing specialized treatment units, and more experts are collecting and reporting data about groups of patients. Presumably, the intense focus, funding, and publication space given MPD by North American professionals and mass media increase the tendency to shape perceptions and behaviors according to a popular new paradigm; of course, they also may educate people to recognize what, in fact, may be a real, previously unidentified syndrome.

It is posited that certain cultures do not provide all the necessary factors for a total configuration of MPD (Martinez-Taboas 1990, 1991a, Takahashi 1990). The disorder is unlikely to develop in a culture where the self is collective and interpersonal, the society is interdependent, children are valued, and dissociative states "split off into semiotic systems of gods, ghosts, or ancestors" (Martinez-Taboas 1991a, p. 131). Conversely, MPD's emergence is catalyzed by an individualistic society in which the self is autonomous and isolated, children are abused or neglected, and dissociation assists in defending the individual self.

Childhood abuse emerges as a common topic in discussions about cross-cultural incidence of MPD. North America reports more childhood physical and sexual abuse, associated with higher rates of MPD. Outside North America other forms of severe chronic trauma and the culturally shaped dissociative responses to these events may be overlooked in the

MPD literature. Takahashi (1990) claimed that child abuse was nonexistent among his patients in Japan, where family bonds are more strongly maintained and supervised by extended kin. Data from India do not support the charge that abuse may be hidden there (Adityanjee et al. 1989). Nevertheless, many believe that cultural constraints do inhibit the disclosure of sexual abuse in certain areas of the world. Political ideology may not allow for the revealing of patient histories or for diagnoses that would admit to an imperfect social order. It also is conceivable that therapists who come from a more traditionally psychoanalytic orientation will assume that sexualizing alters are based in the patient's hysterical neurosis rather than in trauma history.

Many of the explanations for the higher rates of MPD in the United States and Canada also account for its low incidence elsewhere. A smaller number of international cases might be the result of less interest, less funding, fewer clinicians and trained experts, lack of public awareness and professional education, less child abuse or its disclosure, slower rates of Westernization and industrialization, broader belief in polytheism and spirit possession, ambiguous diagnostic criteria, and inadequate cross-cultural diagnostic instruments. In series of cases outside of North America, large numbers of MPD patients are diagnosed by few clinicians.

Misdiagnosis or underdiagnosis sometimes occurs when behaviors similar to MPD are identified according to different criteria. MPD may not be the primary diagnosis and differential diagnosis may not consider MPD. Some dissociative behaviors are not viewed as pathological by the patient or local community, hence treatment is not sought. If help is requested, first family and then indigenous healers may be the treatment of choice, with the patient appearing at Western-oriented clinics only when illness is critical and all other options have been exhausted. Certain countries do not permit hospital admission with an MPD diagnosis (van der Hart and Boon 1990), and MPD patients who go to providers other than hospitals and clinics do not appear in the statistics.

Some clinicians do not focus on or sanction certain symptoms of MPD. They may deny the syndrome or be uninformed, inexperienced, or not clinically sensitized to recognize it. They may fail to see aspects of the disorder unless behaviors are pronounced. Some evaluators assume that diagnosis of MPD can be made with relative ease despite the disorder's covert complexities (Kluft 1990). Clinical interviews alone are insufficient (Ross 1990), and short hospital stays offer too little time to uncover the syndrome and all of its subtleties and personality networks (Martinez-Taboas 1991b). Interviewers may not ask important questions about related symptomatology that would help to clarify the disorder.

Attitudes of the practitioner can account for lower frequencies of MPD.

Skepticism and a conservative proclivity to diagnose more respectable disorders prevail in parts of the world (Kluft 1990). Professionals often fear ridicule if they make a diagnosis of MPD, particularly if they practice in a social milieu that does not support the MPD diagnosis. Where MPD is reported in burgeoning numbers outside North America, skeptics refer to possible selection bias, to the fact that many of those reporting new cases have been trained by believers from North America, to zealousness coupled with inexperience, and to the eagerness for professional recognition that comes of being the first in one's country to report a case of MPD.

PART V: CONCLUSIONS

This chapter considered theories of self and reality that underlie a culture's explanation about multiplicity and the embodiment of alternative identities. It discussed the relationship between MPD and possession, showing how similar behaviors might be interpreted differently, and describing subtleties of cross-cultural translation of illness and its treatment. Transmodal and transcultural approaches to the healing of dissociative disorders portrayed ways that some clinicians have moved beyond the limitations of their own theoretical framework in order to respond to the diverse world views of patients. These approaches suggest possibilities for ethnic-sensitive compromise rather than dichotomization of treatment paradigms.

Awareness of cultural variation in the naming of normal and pathological dissociative states provided a perspective from which to view cases of MPD from around the world and among ethnically diverse immigrant, refugee, and native populations. Cultural variation among idiosyncratic alters is a topic that has not been described in the literature, although it appears to be a common occurrence and probably is influenced by cultural and historical forces as well as individual history. Finally, the chapter presented arguments based on cross-cultural findings that might explain from the points of view of skeptics and supporters the high incidence of MPD in North America and its lower frequency worldwide.

Many topics have yet to be investigated. Ethnographic features are notably absent from the demographic data in large-scale North American studies. Cultural dimensions of MPD cannot be considered in any society separate from issues of race, class, and gender, and theoretical formulations need to address the interplay among these factors.

Acculturation surely affects diagnosis, treatment, and the dynamics of dissociative pathology. Studies have not compared MPD among immigrants or migrants, with those people who experience illness in the country of origin. It would be useful to consider transformations of dissociative phenomenology in terms of their meanings to patients, and to compare preferred treatments among newcomers with those of first- and second-generation immigrants. Ethnopharmacological interventions might contribute to a broader understanding of the biological bases of dissociation.

Clearly, we can learn much more about MPD from cross-cultural research. However, Western clinicians must continue to remain open to the many discrete non-Western categories of illness, as well as to the ways that indigenous explanatory systems might understand and treat what we call MPD. Familiarity with the range of opinion among Western-trained clinicians about other cultures is insufficient to understand multicultural dimensions of multiplicity; it is necessary to hear directly from individuals within those diverse systems. Unfortunately, the people from whom we might best learn—the child peeking through the door at the exorcism by rabbis, the German shaman, the Cambodian monk, the Brazilian medium, the Indian medicine man—are not likely to be found in professional publications where the language must conform to Western scientific culture.

Once, a famous rabbi whom I had not met before, suddenly approached me and declared, "You must continue to read the white words on white paper." I understood him to mean that answers lie not in easily discernible forms but in the invisible. Perhaps it is in silent, original language rather than calcified idioms of science—perhaps through our invited presence at living ceremonies rather than our scientific inquiry about them—that we can begin to understand.

REFERENCES

Adityanjee. (1990). Dr. Adityanjee replies [Letter]. *American Journal of Psychiatry* 147:1260–1261.

Adityanjee, Raju, G. S. P., and Khandelwal, S. K. (1989). Current status of multiple personality disorder in India. *American Journal of Psychiatry* 146:1607–1610.

Akhtar, S. (1988). Four culture-bound psychiatric syndromes in India. *International Journal of Social Psychiatry* 34:70–74.

Aldridge-Morris, R. (1993). Professional scepticism towards multiple personality disorder [Letter]. *British Journal of Psychiatry* 162:569–570.

Alexander, V. K. (1956). A case study of a multiple personality. *Journal of Abnormal and Social Psychology* 52:272–276.

Allison, R. (1980). *Minds in Many Pieces*. New York: Rawson, Wade.

_____ (1985). The possession syndrome on trial. *American Journal of Forensic Psychiatry* 6:46–56.

_____ (1991). In search of multiples in Moscow. *American Journal of Forensic Psychiatry* 12:51–65.

Alonso, L., and Jeffrey, W. (1988). Mental illness complicated by the santeria belief in spirit possession. *Hospital and Community Psychiatry* 39:1188–1191.

Altrocchi, J. (1992). "We don't have that problem here": MPD in New Zealand. *Dissociation* 5:109–110.

Baker, R. (1975). *Binding the Devil: Exorcism Past and Present.* New York: Hawthorne Books.

Beahrs, J. (1982). *Unity and Multiplicity.* New York: Brunner/Mazel.

Bilu, Y., and Beit-Hallahmi, B. (1989). Dybbuk-possession as a hysterical symptom: psychodynamic and socio-cultural factors. *Israel Journal of Psychiatry and Related Sciences* 26:138–149.

Bliss, E. (1986). *Multiple Personality, Allied Disorders, and Hypnosis.* New York: Oxford University Press.

Boleloucky, Z. (1988). Minohocetna disociovana osobnost—navy zajem o stary problem [Multiple personality—a new interest in an old problem]. *Ceskoslovenska Psychiatrie* 82:318–327.

Boon, S., and Draijer, N. (1991). Diagnosing dissociative disorders in the Netherlands: a pilot study with the Structured Clinical Interview for *DSM-III-R* dissociative disorders. *American Journal of Psychiatry* 148:458–462.

———— (1993). Multiple personality disorder in The Netherlands: a clinical investigation of 71 patients. *American Journal of Psychiatry* 150:489–494.

Bourguignon, E. (1968). World distribution and patterns of possession states. In *Trance and Possession States,* ed. R. Prince, pp. 3–34. Montreal: R. M. Bucke Memorial Society.

———— (1973). *Religion, Altered States of Consciousness, and Social Change.* Columbus: Ohio State University Press.

———— (1976). *Possession.* San Francisco: Chandler and Sharp.

———— (1979). *Psychological Anthropology.* New York: Holt, Rinehart and Winston.

———— (1989). Multiple personality, possession trance, and the psychic unity of mankind. *Ethos* 17:371–384.

Bowman, E. (1990). Adolescent MPD in the nineteenth and early twentieth centuries. *Dissociation* 3:179–187.

Bruce-Jones, W., and Coid, J. (1992). Identity diffusion presenting as multiple personality disorder in a female psychopath. *British Journal of Psychiatry* 160:541–544.

Bustamente, J. A. (1968). Cultural factors in hysterias with schizophrenic clinical picture. *International Journal of Social Psychiatry* 14:113–118.

Castillo, R. (1991). Culture, trance and mental illness: divided consciousness in South Asia (yoga meditation). Ph.D. diss., Harvard University.

Chancellor, A. M., and Fraser, A. R. (1982). Dissociative disorder, conversion disorder, and the use of abreaction in a 22-year-old male. *New Zealand Medical Journal* 95:418–419.

Coons, P. M., Bowman, E. S., Kluft, R. P., and Milstein, V. (1991). The cross-cultural occurrence of MPD: additional cases from a recent survey. *Dissociation* 4:124–128.

Cory, C. E. (1919–20). A divided self. *Journal of Abnormal Psychology* 14: 281–291.

Crabtree, A. (1985). *Multiple Man: Explorations in Possession and Multiple Personality Disorder.* New York: Praeger.

———— (1992). Dissociation and memory: a two-hundred-year perspective. *Dissociation* 5:150–154.

Cramer, M. (1980). Psychopathology and shamanism in rural Mexico: a case study of spirit possession. *British Journal of Medical Psychology* 53:67–73.

Cutler, B., and Reed, J. (1975). Multiple personality: a single case study with a 15 year follow-up. *Psychological Medicine* 5:18–26.

Daie, N., Witztum, E., Mark, M., and Rabinowitz, S. (1992). The belief in the transmigration of souls: psychotherapy of a Druze patient with severe anxiety reaction. *British Journal of Medical Psychology* 65:119–130.

DISSOCIATIVE IDENTITY DISORDER

Downs, J., Dahmer, S., and Battle, A. (1990). Multiple personality disorder in India [Letter]. *American Journal of Psychiatry* 147:1260.

Ellenberger, H. (1970). *The Discovery of the Unconscious.* New York: Basic Books.

Fahy, T. (1988). The diagnosis of multiple personality disorder: a critical review. *British Journal of Psychiatry* 153:597–606.

Fahy, T., Abas, M., and Brown, J. C. (1989). Multiple personality: a symptom of psychiatric disorder. *British Journal of Psychiatry* 154:99–101.

Favazza, A. R. (1985). Unlearned language: new studies in xenoglossy [Review]. *American Journal of Psychiatry* 142:1218–1219.

Frischholz, E., and Braun, B. (1990). Comment on "Is MPD really rare in Japan?" *Dissociation* 3:60–61.

Golub, D. (1989). Cross-cultural dimensions of art psychotherapy: Cambodian survivors of war trauma. In *Advances in Art Therapy,* ed. H. Wadeson, J. Durkin, and D. Perach, pp. 5–42. New York: John Wiley and Sons.

Goodman, F. D. (1988). *How About Demons?: Possession and Exorcism in the Modern World.* Bloomington: Indiana University Press.

Goodwin, J., Hill, S., and Attias, R. (1990). Historical and folk techniques of exorcism: applications to treatment of dissociative disorders. *Dissociation* 3:94–101.

Goullart, P. (1961). *Le Monastrere de la Montagne de Jade.* Paris: Fayard.

Hsia, Y. F., and Tsai, N. (1981). Transcultural investigation of recent symptomatology of schizophrenia in China. *American Journal of Psychiatry* 138:1484–1486.

Kenny, M. G. (1981). Multiple personality and spirit possession. *Psychiatry* 44:337–358.

Keyes, D. (1981). *The Minds of Billy Milligan.* New York: Random House.

Kleinman, A. (1987). Anthropology and psychiatry: the role of culture in cross-cultural research on illness. *British Journal of Psychiatry* 151:447–454.

—— (1988). *Rethinking Psychiatry.* New York: Macmillan.

Kluft, R. (1990). An introduction to Takahashi's "Is MPD really rare in Japan?" *Dissociation* 3:56.

—— (1993). Multiple personality disorder. In *Dissociative Disorders: A Clinical Review,* ed. D. Spiegel, pp. 17–44. Lutherville, MD: Sidran.

Korbin, J. (1981). *Child Abuse and Neglect: Cross-Cultural Perspectives.* Berkeley: University of California Press.

Krippner, S. (1987). Cross-cultural approaches to multiple personality disorder: practices in Brazilian spiritism. *Ethos* 15:273–295.

Lampl-de Groot, J. (1981). Notes on "multiple personality." *Psychoanalytic Quarterly* 50:614–624.

Laubscher, B. J. (1928). A case of co-conscious personalities. *Journal of the Medical Association of South Africa* 2:115–117.

León, C. A. (1975). "El duende" and other incubi: suggestive interactions between culture, the devil, and the brain. *Archives of General Psychiatry* 32:155–162.

Lifton, R. J. (1968). Protean man. *Partisan Review* 35:13–27.

Macilwain, I. F. (1992). Multiple personality disorder [Letter]. *British Journal of Psychiatry* 161:863.

Maddison, D. C. (1953). A case of double personality. *Medical Journal of Australia* 1:814–816.

Martin, M. (1987). *Hostage to the Devil.* New York: Harper and Row.

Martinez-Taboas, A. (1989). Preliminary observations of MPD in Puerto Rico. *Dissociation* 2:128–131.

—— (1990). Reflections on Takahashi's methodology and the role of culture on MPD. *Dissociation* 3:62–63.

—— (1991a). Multiple personality disorder as seen from a social constructionist viewpoint. *Dissociation* 4:129–133.

_____ (1991b). Multiple personality in Puerto Rico: analysis of fifteen cases. *Dissociation* 4:189–192.

McKee, J. B., and Wittkower, E. D. (1962). A case of double personality with death of the imaginary partner. *Canadian Psychiatric Association Journal* 7:134–139.

Miller, M. (1989). A case of MPD in London [Letter]. *Dissociation* 2:251.

Modestin, J. (1992). Multiple personality disorder in Switzerland. *American Journal of Psychiatry* 149:88–92.

Mulhern, S. (1991). Embodied alternative identities: bearing witness to a world that might have been. *Psychiatric Clinics of North America* 14:769–786.

Oesterreich, T. K. (1966). *Possession: Demoniacal and Other Among Primitive Races, in Antiquity, the Middle Ages, and Modern Times.* 1922. Reprint. New Hyde Park, NY: University Books.

Putnam, F. W. (1989). *Diagnosis and Treatment of Multiple Personality Disorder.* New York: Guilford.

_____ (1991). Recent research on multiple personality disorder. *Psychiatric Clinics of North America* 14:489–502.

Rathbun, J. M. (1990). Multiple personality disorder in India [Letter]. *American Journal of Psychiatry* 147:1260.

Rendon, M. (1974). Transcultural aspects of Puerto Rican mental illness in New York. *International Journal of Social Psychiatry* 20:18–24.

Ronquillo, E. B. (1991). The influence of "espiritismo" on a case of multiple personality disorder. *Dissociation* 4:39–45.

Ross, C. (1989). *Multiple Personality Disorder: Diagnosis, Clinical Features, and Treatment.* New York: John Wiley and Sons.

_____ (1990). Comments on: Takahashi's "Is MPD really rare in Japan?" *Dissociation* 3:64–65.

_____ (1991a). The dissociated executive self and the cultural dissociation barrier. *Dissociation* 4:55–61.

_____ (1991b). Epidemiology of multiple personality disorder and dissociation. *Psychiatric Clinics of North America* 14:503–517.

Ross, C. A., Norton, G. R., and Wozney, K. (1989). Multiple personality disorder: an analysis of 236 cases. *Canadian Journal of Psychiatry* 34:413–418.

Saxena, S., and Prasad, K. V. (1989). DSM-III subclassification of dissociative disorders applied to psychiatric outpatients in India. *American Journal of Psychiatry* 146:261–262.

Simpson, M. A. (1989). Multiple personality disorder [Letter]. *British Journal of Psychiatry* 155:565.

Smith, S. G. (1989). Multiple personality disorder with human and non-human subpersonality components. *Dissociation* 2:52–56.

Steinberg, M. (1990). Transcultural issues in psychiatry: the ataque and multiple personality disorder. *Dissociation* 3:31–33.

Stern, C. R. (1984). The etiology of multiple personalities. *Psychiatric Clinics of North America* 7:149–159.

Stevenson, I. (1974). Xenoglossy: a review and report of a case. *Proceedings of the American Society for Psychical Research* 31:264.

_____ (1976). A preliminary report of a new case of responsive xenoglossy: the case of Gretchen. *Journal of the American Society for Psychical Research* 70:65–77.

_____ (1984). *Unlearned Language.* Charlottesville: University Press of Virginia.

Stevenson, I., and Pasricha, S. (1979). A case of secondary personality with xenoglossy. *American Journal of Psychiatry* 136:1591–1592.

Takahashi, Y. (1990). Is multiple personality disorder really rare in Japan? *Dissociation* 3:57–59.

Tart, C. (1987). *Waking Up: Overcoming the Obstacles to Human Potential.* Boston: Shambala.

Taylor, W. S., and Martin, M. F. (1944). Multiple personality. *Journal of Abnormal and Social Psychology* 39:281–300.

van der Hart, O. (1990). Commentary on Takahashi's "Is MPD really rare in Japan?"
    Dissociation 3:66–67.
van der Hart, O., and Boon, S. (1989). Multiple personality disorder [Letter]. *British Journal of
    Psychiatry* 154:419.
_____ (1990). Contemporary interest in multiple personality disorder and child abuse in The
    Netherlands. *Dissociation* 3:34–37.
Vanderlinden, J., Van Dyck, R., Vandereycken, W., and Vertommen, H. (1991). Dissociative
    experiences in the general population in The Netherlands and Belgium: a study with the
    Dissociative Questionnaire (DIS-Q). *Dissociation* 4:180–184.
Varma, V. K., Bouri, M., and Wig, N. N. (1981). Multiple personality in India: comparison
    with hysterical possession state. *American Journal of Psychotherapy* 35:113–120.
Winkler, G. (1981). *Dybbuk*. New York: Judaica Press.
Witztum, E., Buchbinder, J. T., and van der Hart, O. (1990). Summoning a punishing angel:
    treatment of a depressed patient with dissociative features. *Bulletin of the Menninger Clinic*
    54:525–537.

11

Allegations of Ritual Abuse

David K. Sakheim

The psychiatric phenomenon of patients presenting and being labeled by therapists as "ritually abused" and/or "satanic cult survivors"[1] is fairly new and quite controversial. The allegations made by such individuals tend to be very extreme and the field is struggling with how to approach this area. Clinicians and researchers take strong emotional positions despite the absence of sufficient empirical data to do so in an educated fashion.

INCIDENCE/PREVALENCE

There have been no well-controlled studies on the incidence or prevalence of satanic ritual abuse reports. However, it is clear that more and more reports of such atrocities are emerging throughout the world (Braun 1989a). Estimates vary tremendously, with some assuming that this phenomena is nonexistent or extremely rare, and others suggesting that it is a common occurrence. Dr. Bennett Braun, a noted researcher in the dissociative disorders field, has stated that based on his experience and research he estimates this phenomenon to be as frequent as 28 percent of all patients with multiple personality disorder, or even as high as 50 percent of all inpatients with multiple personality disorder (Braun 1989b, Braun and Gray 1987). Clearly, there is a need for more empirical research to address even such basic questions as how common these reports are in clinical settings.

---

[1]This term will be used to refer to individuals who present for psychotherapy and describe atrocities that were inflicted upon them by secret organized groups of people as part of satanic rituals. Female pronouns will be used throughout this paper when referring to ritual abuse survivors, as it appears that the vast majority of survivors in therapy are women.

This chapter attempts to discuss and clarify some of these issues and to give an overview of what is currently known in the field.

CLARIFICATION OF TERMS

In order to maintain a scientific orientation, it is essential to be precise about how terms are defined and used. *Ritual abuse*, a new term, has already gone through a number of permutations in meaning. It was originally coined by Lawrence Pazder to describe his patient's cult abuse experiences (Smith and Pazder 1980). As others began disclosing similar stories, the phrase *satanic ritual abuse* began to be applied in the literature. However, it was quickly pointed out that virtually any group can as systematically and ritually abuse a child as can someone practicing satanism (Lanning 1989). Thus, the *satanic* has been dropped in most uses. In a task force summary report the Los Angeles County Commission for Women (Ritual Abuse Task Force 1989) defined ritual abuse as follows:

> A brutal form of abuse of children, adolescents, and adults, consisting of physical, sexual, and psychological abuse, and involving the use of rituals. Ritual does not necessarily mean satanic. However, most survivors state that they were ritually abused as part of satanic worship for the purpose of indoctrinating them into satanic beliefs and practices. Ritual abuse rarely consists of a single episode. It usually involves repeated abuse over an extended period of time. [p. 1]

Recently, Jean Goodwin recommended using the term *sadistic ritual abuse* to capture better the fact that the phrase applies to the effects of deliberate and repeated sadism (Goodwin 1993). Current usage of the term *ritual abuse* has broadened somewhat from the original meaning, and usually refers to the extremes of human cruelty, in which an individual has experienced the combination of repeated physical, sexual, psychological, and spiritual abuse.

In discussing this area it is critical not to lose sight of the fact that most children who are severely and repetitively abused experience this abuse in nonsatanic situations. Although child abuse in satanic cults is an important area, it would be a terrible error to focus solely on cults and miss the far greater problem of everyday child abuse in America. Thus, it may be useful to have a broadened definition of ritual abuse that speaks to the more extreme, encompassing, and repetitive kinds of abuse that can occur.

However, despite all of the above caveats, understanding the motivations of the perpetrators can be an important factor in working through the experiences of someone abused in a satan-worship context. It clearly has a different impact for a patient if the trauma experienced was accidental, random, deliberate, sanctioned by society, inflicted in the name of religion, blamed on the victim, committed by multiple perpetrators, and so forth. Thus, it probably makes the most sense in attempting to categorize such experiences to attend to the severity of what was experienced as well as to note the context in which the abuse occurred. Jean Goodwin's term *sadistic ritual abuse* is probably the most useful generic term for repetitive and brutal abuse of children that is on the extreme end of the sexual, physical, emotional, and spiritual abuse continua. One can then specify the context by stating that the patient was ritually abused as part of a Satan-worshiping group, as part of a multidimensional child sex ring, within an organized crime family, by a psychotic parent, and so forth.

Despite the broadened definition, many ritual abuse survivors who seek out psychotherapy describe an involvement with satanism among their tormentors. This has made for some confusion about just who those groups of perpetrators are.

Satanism

A definition of *satanism* is not a simple matter. The term can be used to refer to many types of legal and illegal groups, and it is clearly an error to categorize all of these groups together. As Kenneth Lanning (1992) has pointed out, it does not make sense to label a crime with the religion of the perpetrator. For example, in speaking about child abuse in the recent Waco Texas cult of David Koresh, people did not describe such abuse as a "Christian crime," and it would not have been useful to do so. It is also important to realize that satanism as a religion does not necessarily imply illegal activities and that the individuals and groups that get labeled as satanic are heterogeneous. Thus, it is important to be cautious in using the term satanism.

The label satanism can be applied by one group to another or be a self-applied designation, and it can refer to both legal and illegal practices. Usually it is used to justify censure, oppression, or warfare, and is a way of saying that the individual or group in question is immoral and evil. For example, the Ayatollah Khomeini labeled the United States "The Great Satan" and informed his followers that it was their moral duty to fight this evil enemy.

On the other hand, satanism can be used as a self-definition. There are legal, constitutionally protected religions that practice satanism (e.g., the Church of Satan and the Temple of Set) that do not espouse any illegal activities. It is important to note that these legal and open religious groups are rarely named by ritual abuse survivors as being involved in their abuse.

Even among those who do break the law, satanism is still a heterogeneous grouping. There are individuals who become fascinated with satanism or the occult and who may dabble in some homespun version (e.g., an alienated high-school student who dabbles in black magic and drugs). There are groups (such as youth gangs) who get involved in satanism, often as part of their rebellion against authority. There are even organized crime groups that get involved in such practices, such as Adolfo Constanzo's drug ring in Matamoros, Mexico. This group practiced satanism, believing that it would protect them from being caught by the police. However, none of these individuals or groups is typically described by "satanic cult survivors" in their therapies.

Public discussions of satanism often confuse these various groups. For example, in presenting coverage about this controversy, the media frequently use examples of legal organized religions, individuals with preexisting psychological problems, or dabblers in satanic practices to support survivors' reports in therapy or to provide evidence that satanism exists. There is no question that it exists. In fact, the only controversial groups are secret, illegal satanic cults. No one disputes that the other groups are present and active in our society. What is controversial is the description provided by ritual abuse survivors in therapy of highly organized intergenerational satanic cults and the extreme atrocities that these groups are alleged to commit.

The Allegations

There are primarily two ways in which these extreme reports come to light. The first result from daycare abuse investigations, and the second from individuals in psychotherapy. What is typically described has nothing to do with any more commonly known types of satanism. Instead, there is usually a description of a family or group of families that secretly have been practicing satanism for generations. These cults are alleged to commit extreme abuse and violence and to go to great lengths to cover up their activities. The allegations regarding illegal practices within these groups almost always include the murder of children and adults, child sexual and physical abuse, drug use and sales, forced impregnations and subsequent abortions, creation of child and adult pornography, cannibalism, and other extreme violence and deviance. Thus, it is important to understand that survivors are not discussing the known varieties of satanism in our culture. They are discussing an entirely different type of totalist group experience.

These descriptions of secret yet well-organized intergenerational satanic cults are what many in the field dispute, and there is very little evidence of them or information about them.

One factor that has led many clinicians to believe the stories of their patients is that their allegations are quite detailed and consistent and often match those of other survivors who have never met, sometimes from different parts of the world (Braun 1989a). The reports consistently describe extremely violent paramilitary cults, which indoctrinate their children from birth to become part of this belief system. The belief system tends to stem from a gnostic view in which the world is believed to be under the influence and control of hostile spirits. Thus, a person's primary goal in life is to become as powerful as possible (through learning *magick*) in order to control these entities (Katchen and Sakheim 1992). It is also believed that a person can become more powerful by being possessed by such a spirit. For example, a person might be forced to hold something burning without flinching. The cult view is that the person must be possessed by a strong demon or spirit to be able to handle such pain without reaction. A psychological explanation, on the other hand, would posit that the person dissociates from the pain involved and hypnotically shuts off his/her feelings in order to stand without flinching. (Of course, it should also be assumed that somewhere inside the pain was being registered.) The psychological view would see this event as traumatic and likely to create problems, while the cult view would be that this is a strengthening experience for the person involved, as it connects him/her with a powerful spirit. Many of the events described appear designed to create such a possession experience.

In general, the rituals described by survivors appear to have one of three purposes. These are indoctrinating someone into the group, helping someone in the group to attain increased power through possession or other magick, or intimidating a member never to disclose cult-related activities.

Indoctrination Rituals

There are rituals undertaken at certain ages to convince the child that she is evil and a part of the group. For example, most survivors describe death and rebirth rituals in which the child is first tortured and then placed in a box or coffin, being told that she is being killed and buried. After being left for an extended period of time, she will be dug up (sometimes put inside and then pulled out of an animal carcass) and is then told that she is "being reborn unto Satan." There are many other types of tortures described by survivors, usually with the goal of getting the person into an altered state of consciousness so that dissociation (what they regard as possession) can occur. The person's dissociation is encouraged and the split-off parts of the self are even given new cult names. Another way that the cults are reported to attack a survivor's sense of identity is to force her to commit atrocities upon others. This confounds any sense of being a good person, and is reinforced by messages to the contrary, such as telling the person that she is evil and therefore a part of the group.

The descriptions of rituals make it clear that in order to survive, the person must either become an exquisite liar or must learn to dissociate. For example, patients have described being beaten until they agreed to participate in a ceremony. However, if they finally agreed they were told that this wasn't good enough because they were only doing so to avoid further beating and not because they "really wanted" to participate. The beatings then continued until the person either convinced the group that she really wanted this, or until she could split off a part of herself that is able to identify with the group's agenda. This is what the group is hoping to accomplish. If the person can dissociate and create a willing group member, the cult views this as possession, and therefore success.

Many survivors describe *magic tricks* that are used to convince members of the group's power. For example, some patients have described having what is supposed to be holy water (but is actually acid) thrown on them. The high priest secretly makes the switch. Thus, when the altered holy water burns the person's flesh, both she and the other group members are convinced that she truly must be evil and, therefore, has become part of the group.

Acquisition of Power

Many of the descriptions of rituals involve reversals of traditional Christian practices and symbols. Survivors typically report that these groups see such desecrations as additional ways to attain the power to do magick. Thus, backward prayers, backward writing (e.g., "nema" instead of "amen" or "natas" instead of "satan"), desecration of church property, inverted symbols (e.g., upside-down crosses), and reversals of most Christian holidays and practices are deliberately embraced. This includes reversals of Christian rites of passage such as baptism. In the cult version, the goal is the opposite from the Christian one, and is meant to make the person impure. For example, *satanic baptism* has been described by many survivors as a ceremony in which leeches are put on the person as well as a variety of other disgusting substances.

Most survivors also speak about having been forced to participate in rituals involving animal and/or human sacrifices. These are believed by the group to be a way of obtaining the life force (power) of the organism being sacrificed. Aleister Crowley (1976) explains,

> It would be unwise to condemn as irrational the practice of those savages who tear the heart and liver from an adversary and devour them while yet warm. In any case it was the theory of the ancient Magicians, that any living being is a storehouse of energy varying in quantity according to the size and health of the animal, and in quality according to its mental and moral character. At the death of the animal this energy is liberated suddenly. [pp. 94–95]

In other words, the younger, or more innocent and pure, the victim, the more power is believed to reside there. It is also believed that the more physiological arousal present, the more energy there is to obtain. Thus, survivor descriptions often include not only killing, but the deliberate induction of maximal fear and/or sexual arousal in the victim just prior to its death. Many survivors describe elaborate rituals in this regard, with the sacrifice usually performed inside a drawn circle, which is believed to help contain the released energy until it can be channeled to the desired recipient. Some of the cult groups described in therapy appear to be greatly involved with the elaborate details of these practices, believing that numbers, colors, shapes, symbols, and specific practices all contain important magical significance. Other groups appear far less engrossed in such detail and seem much more involved in the sadism, power, and/or monetary aspects of the various activities.

Prevention of Disclosure

It is not difficult to confuse or terrify a child. Nonetheless, these cults are described as going to great lengths to terrorize the members into complete obedience and silence. Everything from tricks and illusions to blackmail and direct threats are used. Most survivors also describe sophisticated uses of hypnosis (programming) to insure such loyalty to the group. For example, it is commonly reported that a child is drugged and upon awakening is informed that a bomb was surgically placed inside her that is programmed to explode if she ever tells anyone about the group, killing her and the person she tells. This kind of suggestion is very clever as it capitalizes on the person's physiology to enhance its effects (i.e., if the child even thinks of telling someone, her nervous increase in heart rate may be misconstrued as the bomb's ticking).

Some clinicians have reported incredibly sophisticated and intricate programming involving elaborate attempts at mind control. What makes some of these reports even more controversial is that they often include connections to CIA and other government intelligence agencies and typically relate to efforts by these groups to study mind control in an effort to develop the perfect assassin, soldier, messenger, and so forth, by using deliberately created dissociation. Although many of these reports sound far-fetched, numerous clinicians have validated running into similar detailed descriptions of mind-control strategies, even down to the same unusual code words and techniques being utilized and the same individuals being named (Hammond 1993). Although American and other intelligence agencies have revealed that they have carried out secret mind-control experiments on unsuspecting civilians (Shefflin 1993), the present allegations suggest a far more elaborate and organized effort involving long-term experimentation using a variety of tortures on hundreds of nonvolunteers, mostly children. If confirmed, it undoubtedly would be the biggest scandal in American history.

The Black Mass

Some of the most controversial allegations made by survivors include reports of infanticide and cannibalism. These usually have to do with the *black mass*. Such depictions have emerged throughout history and are usually quite similar. However, historians and current researchers are divided as to the significance of these reports. Some believe that these stories are fictional accounts designed to titillate (as in the writings of the Marquis de Sade). Others believe that they are primarily the text of tortured confessions produced by inquisitions. Some historians believe that these are reports of genuine criminal acts, but are the actions of isolated groups of disturbed individuals who happened to demonstrate similar bizarre behaviors in acting out their perversions. Finally, there are those historians who suggest that these reports are merely tips of the iceberg of an ongoing satanic conspiracy that has been unmasked from time to time (Hill and Goodwin 1989, Noll 1989, Raschke 1990). Descriptions of the black mass usually include the murder of an infant or the use of an aborted fetus in the ceremony (many survivors report being raped in previous ceremonies so that they will be pregnant and so that the fetus can be aborted in this ritual), the reciting of backward prayers, the consumption of blood and flesh, the use of drugs, and a sexual orgy where children and adults are all involved. As noted above, some occult writers such as Crowley (1976) state that sacrifice, especially of an infant, is an important way to enhance magick and that it is possible to obtain the life energy from this organism by consuming it. Thus, the black mass allegedly is designed to combine the various practices that the group believes can enhance its power.

Whatever the rationales, it is clear that almost all allegations from survivors are of terrible abuses and tortures by the very people who are supposed to protect them. In fact, virtually every survivor also describes sadistic abuses at home, in addition to the traumas that occurred at rituals and cult ceremonies. The families appear completely focused on wielding power in every sphere of life and the survivor's experience universally includes feeling completely helpless in such a sadistic, controlled, and power-oriented environment.

CREDIBILITY ISSUES

At present the most common area for discussion about satanic cults is to debate the reality of their existence. Opinions vary from assuming 100 percent accuracy of survivors' recall to assuming that all of the descriptions of atrocities are delusional. Clearly, until more investigative work is completed there cannot be any definitive resolutions to this debate. In fact it seems likely that there will not be one single answer. Patients will probably range from those who are malingering for secondary gain; to those who are delusional or who were tricked and confused; to still others for whom descriptions of satanism are screen memories, metaphoric communications, or exaggerated memories; and finally, to those who have truly experienced extreme and ritualized forms of abuse. The situation becomes even more complex when one sees that not only is it likely that patients will differ in these ways, but that even for one individual, different memories may have different meanings. For example, a patient who was actually abused in a cult may have some memories that are distorted, due to tricks, confusion, or drug use at the time, and other memories that are more clear and unmistakable.

How do we make sense of the two conflicting facets of our knowledge about these claims? The first is that survivors and clinicians from all over the world are coming forward with very similar descriptions and reports of abusive practices by these groups. The second is that there has not been sufficient forensic evidence found to date that would validate these allegations, especially the more extreme charges of infanticide and adult murders. George Greaves (1992), in an excellent discussion of this issue, points out that in the presence of such conflicting information and the absence of clear data, clinicians, police, sociologists, historians, anthropologists, and other researchers in this area tend to take one of four positions. He calls these the Nihilists, the Apologists, the Heuristics, and the Methodologists.

Nihilists

Greaves (1992) refers to the first group as the *Nihilists*. This group suggests that reports by survivors cannot be true. Some members of this group simply cannot conceive of the possibility that human beings can be so violent and cruel to each other. However, the majority of this group's membership are police who have become skeptical of survivor reports and researchers who are investigating the area in order to make sense of it as a social phenomenon (e.g., historians and anthropologists). The police in the group point out that in addition to the lack of sufficient physical evidence, ritual abuse reports are usually different from what is currently understood about other types of criminal activity. For example, the reports typically describe as many female as male perpetrators and involve multiple victim–multiple perpetrator conspiracy crimes in which very dysfunctional individuals are alleged to go for long periods of time maintaining tightly controlled secrets and group loyalty. It is also alleged that these individuals are able to commit massive conspiracy crimes and yet cover up all forensic evidence (Lanning 1992, Van Benschoten 1990).

Interestingly, there is a small group of therapists and client advocates who take this position as well. They are fearful that the more extreme reports of ritual abuse survivors will not be verified and that this will harm the hard-won credibility of other abuse survivors and of the trauma recovery movement itself.

The Nihilists tend to do a good job of pointing out the lack of important forensic evidence to date (e.g., Hicks 1991, for an excellent critique of much of the evidence that has been used to support patient allegations). However, they generally tend to come up with unsatisfying arguments to explain the allegations themselves. Some of the hypotheses generated by this group include: reports of bizarre atrocities being screen memories for more typical kinds of abuse; patient memories incorporating material to which they have been exposed from lectures, books, or other media; patients being delusional; therapist influence/suggestion; memories uncovered under hypnosis being unreliable; selective reinforcement by society of more extreme abuse reports; misunderstanding by therapists of aspects of the collective unconscious; and patient communications in metaphor that get taken literally. This group also points out ways in which communities can become involved in believing reports of satanism. Examples include: rumor panics that affect small rural areas, or "urban legends" where the descriptions given by survivors are simply interesting but untrue stories that rapidly spread through a population. The Nihilists believe that this type of social contagion is occurring in the psychotherapeutic community, so that as satanism is more widely reported, therapists believe they are seeing it more and/or patients are jumping on the bandwagon (Brunvand 1986, Hicks 1991, Mulhern 1990, Richardson et al. 1991, Victor 1989, 1990). In a very important paper, George Ganaway (1989) compared the phenomenon of patients reporting ritual abuse to those reporting UFO abductions, suggesting that the same psychological mechanisms (the creation of dissociative fantasies and distortions) may be at work for both populations. Of the various writers in this group, he offers the most plausible psychological explanations of why some survivor reports may not be accurate. Although it is certainly the case that each of the above hypotheses can account for some cases, most clinicians working in the field do not see them as satisfactory explanations for the vast numbers of cases or for the similarities in reported detail (e.g., unrelated patients describing detailed practices performed on certain dates or knowing various coding systems and words to specific prayers that have not been published).

Apologists

The second group described by Greaves are the *Apologists*. They believe that patient reports must be true and then set out to account for the fact that so little validating data has been made available. It is noteworthy that this group is primarily made up of the clinicians who work with this population. These therapists tend to work with other trauma survivors as well, especially incest victims, and many have been politically active in trying to get the field to understand the impact of such trauma. Thus, they tend to approach abuse reports from an advocacy stance. Many in this group feel that an injustice has been done to trauma survivors in the past because of the field's disbelief in reports of incest and other family abuses, and they caution that we not make the same mistakes again.

Some Apologists argue that there is forensic evidence to support survivors claims, that numerous cases have even been won in court, but that this data is often unavailable because there is currently no organized police mechanism for collecting such case information (Boyd 1991, Raschke

1990, Tamarkin 1993). The Apologists point out that most ritual abuse survivors are too intimidated and afraid to go to the police in the first place, and even if they do, they are often not taken seriously because of a psychiatric history and/or because of the bizarre nature of the allegations. It is also noted that police are usually very hesitant to investigate claims in which the statute of limitations has already run out. In addition, some Apologists have even suggested that local or state police may be infiltrated by cult members who sabotage any attempts to explore cult-related charges. The Apologists claim that the police are not trained to investigate these types of groups (just as special units have been needed to investigate organized crime), and that the cults use very sophisticated mechanisms to destroy evidence, such as portable crematoriums. Thus, the Apologists claim that it is not surprising that more evidence has not been found. In addition, most people in the field agree that the cases that have gone to court have been terribly mishandled, making it almost impossible to discover what really happened. Errors have included leading interviews, contamination between witnesses, premature notification of potential perpetrators, lost evidence, poorly trained therapists and police, and so on. Rather than saying that no confirming evidence has yet been found, it might be more fair to say that there have not yet been adequate investigations.

Many Apologists also believe that frequently the cases that reach the court system are "sanitized" so that claims of satanic cult activities are dropped or restated in more traditional legal language. This has been done by prosecutors who are afraid that juries will become incredulous at the more extreme charges; they prosecute instead for "child abuse," "murder," "cruelty to animals," "child pornography," and so forth. The result is that any convictions obtained do not appear to be convictions of satanic cult cases.

The above explanations account for some cases being inadequately examined; however, these arguments still cannot sufficiently explain why these cases, in which thousands of survivors allege multiple murders, abortions, stabbings, kidnappings, and so forth, have not resulted in more substantive forensic evidence being found to document the most extreme of these crimes.

Heuristics

The next group that Greaves describes are those clinicians who claim that it really doesn't matter if this phenomenon is real or not. He calls this group the *Heuristics*. They believe that all that is important is that these patients get better when they are treated like other trauma survivors. In other words, if a clinician acts as if the reports are real and helps the patient to work through her feelings, the patient can recover. Unfortunately, this is not a tenable social position because it does matter if the reports are real or not. It may be an arguable clinical attitude, but it certainly is not an arguable social one. The veracity of allegations about children and adults being raped, killed, cannibalized, used to make pornography, and so forth, certainly matters in terms of society's obligation to protect its members and prevent these crimes.

Methodologists

The last group described by Greaves are the *Methodologists*. This group is made up of people who base their views on the data. Unfortunately, at the present time this group has no members! There is not sufficient forensic data yet available to form any solid conclusions about this area.

RITUAL ABUSE SURVIVORS AS A HETEROGENEOUS POPULATION

Even in the absence of clear research data, it would appear that patients presenting as ritual abuse survivors are actually a very heterogeneous group. Memories can vary across individuals and even within a single person.

Some people clearly malinger for secondary gain (e.g., attention, increased psychotherapy time, availability of staff and monetary support, etc.). It is unfortunate but true that current practices in the mental health field differentially reinforce certain types of problems so that patients can be pushed toward defining themselves in more dramatic and severe terms. For example, more resources are often expended for a satanic ritual abuse survivor than for someone who is "merely" disclosing a history of family violence. It can also tremendously complicate these issues when allegations are made as part of a custody battle or when other legal matters are involved.

Some patients present with clear delusional disorders and it is very important to assess their thought processes (e.g., primary process vs. secondary process thinking). Psychotic patients can frequently incorporate satanism into a delusional system, although such a presentation is usually fairly easy to assess clinically.

Occasionally, a ritual abuse memory is a screen for family incest experiences. However, this is mostly inadequate as an explanatory mechanism because most ritual abuse survivors also describe severe abuses within their families. Thus, the idea of a screen to protect them from such overwhelming betrayal does not make sense (Greaves 1992).

Some survivors appear to be speaking in a language of metaphor. They usually do not describe details of holidays, coding systems, or the content of prayers. However, their descriptions of rape and other abuses by satan worshipers may speak to how their nonsatanic childhood abuse experiences felt to them. For example, Ryder (1992) presents a case in which the client described trauma in a past life. Although some clinicians would work with this as a real experience, as did Ryder, most would see it as a way to distance psychologically from more painful (albeit likely less sensational) feelings and experiences from this life. It is certainly conceivable that some ritual abuse memories serve a similar distancing function through psychological metaphor.

Some trauma survivors have defended themselves by minimizing the abuses they experienced. To convey the horrors of what they felt (and often feel while remembering) there may be some need to exaggerate or to engage in "projective empathy," describing events so that the listener will empathize with their helplessness, rage, or degree of overwhelming feelings. For example, describing cannibalism may convey the degree of horror and taboo they felt as a child being molested by a parent.

Some trauma memories become confused or distorted. This is not surprising if one considers how inaccurate most people are as witnesses even under ideal circumstances (Orne 1979). If one is hearing the retrieval of a dissociated twenty-year-old memory that was created under the influence of torture, trickery, fear, pain, terror, and sometimes a variety of drugs, it would be inconceivable to imagine that some distortions do not occur. In fact, this confusion of perception is often one of the most painful aspects for any torture survivor in his/her struggle to sort out what is real.

Memory can be influenced by hypnosis to fill in gaps. These can be accurate or inaccurate reconstructions, but the person involved usually increases his/her belief in the material in either case (Bliss 1986, Orne 1979). Many survivors also describe deliberate hypnotic procedures as part of their abuse in which all sorts of distortions of experience were suggested to them. Thus, many survivor memories may have hypnotic distortions or hypnotic artifacts that have occurred from the traumas themselves or from the memory recovery process.

Another interesting phenomenon, about which very little is known, is known as *Pseudo-PTSD* (Post Traumatic Stress Disorder). This refers to clinical situations such as the Vietnam veteran who presents with combat-related PTSD, but who, upon investigation, turns out never to have been in the military. It would be very useful to follow such patients to see if their symptoms reflect some other type of trauma, or if they are instead more like some form of delusional disorder, and if their psychotherapy follows a similar or different course from that of other patients with PTSD symptoms. It is certainly possible that some ritual abuse survivors fall into this category.

Last, for anyone working with this group of patients, some are very convincing about the experiences they describe. They present a clinical picture fitting the profile of a torture survivor, and the course of treatment often supports this view. A few patients have even been able to present concrete evidence to support their claims, with a small minority being able to find forensic data to support them.

It is essential to appreciate the complexity of this area, and to understand that even for any particular patient, different memories that surface may fit into different categories and it is probably fair to say that most patients will present with a combination of factors. Unfortunately, our field has a tendency to become polarized in such situations, with some clinicians claiming that every patient's story is true and that the rest of the field is heartless, while others claim that every patient's story is delusional and the rest of the field is merely too gullible. Neither of these polarized positions takes into account all of the data, and neither will help us to move forward in our understanding of this complex group of patients.

The fact that trauma survivors can give very accurate accounts, can speak in metaphor, can lie, can be confused, and so forth, should not be all that surprising to clinicians. The need to see survivors as either accurate or as having false memories misses this complexity. This creates many problems clinically as well as legally. There is no reason to think that the testimony of an abused person is more or less subject to the distortions and contaminations found in other people's testimony. In addition, it appears that severe abuse can create confusion and a need for distance, which can result in additional distortions. It would be tragic to disallow such testimony, but it would be equally mistaken to assume perfect veracity. Just as we might assume that a crime victim can make errors in identification due to his/her state of emotional arousal at the time of the crime, we must assume that this is also possible for severe child-abuse survivors. However, we do not disallow the testimony of all crime victims just because we know that they can make errors. Instead, we insist that there be a combination of evidence (including witness testimony) that helps to rule out reasonable doubts about the allegations. The same principles should apply when it comes to the reports of sadistic abuse survivors.

Juries should be educated about the kinds of errors and inaccuracies that can occur with such memories, and should then be allowed to assess the whole of the evidence presented.

To understand this area it is important to maintain both a scientific skepticism and an empathic clinical orientation. We need to avoid the hysteria of overreaction, yet equally to avoid the natural denial mechanisms that are triggered when one is confronted with horrible material. Despite humanity's clearly documented history of interpersonal violence, and despite our psychological understanding of posttraumatic stress reactions, we tend to approach most victims with disbelief. Much as our field has approached the area of incest and other forms of child abuse for years, we demand tremendous amounts of proof before we are willing to believe that people can be that cruel to one another. Although we know that such practices have occurred throughout history, each time they come to light we try to avoid the pain of knowledge. Recent history is full of such events. Examples include the Holocaust, Stalin's mass killings, KKK and Mafia violence, the massacre at My Lai, activities of the Ceaucescu regime, Noriega's "dignity battalions," Jonestown's mass suicide, recent reports of "wilding" and "gay bashing," capital punishment, the use of chemical weapons, the massacre at Tiananmen Square, the Nazi killings of mental patients, the murders of Brazilian street children, CIA drug experiments, and the recent reports of rape camps and "ethnic cleansing" in Bosnia. The list could easily go on for pages. These are not only examples of the extremes of human cruelty, but are also examples of the extremes to which human denial can go. People do not want to look at how sadistic our species can be.

It is also easy to point to hysterical overreactions throughout history. Hysteria can be as dangerous as denial. It is no coincidence that the term *witch hunt* implies going after innocent people as part of a mass hysteria, as in the Salem witch trials. The days of Senator Joseph McCarthy provide a telling example. Many in the Jewish community are particularly sensitive to this issue since allegations of "ritual murder" of Christian children have been used for centuries as a way to justify pogroms against Jews. From the false allegations and subsequent murders in Roshana, Lithuania in 1657 to the similar use of such allegations by the Nazis in this century, charges of ritual murder have been used repeatedly to justify oppression.

Over the years the mental-health profession has been immune neither to hysterical overreactions nor to the denial of interpersonal violence. It will be very sad if the internal disagreements in our field about how to approach ritual abuse force therapists to take sides before information is available to do so in an educated fashion. If premature judgement occurs, each side will misdiagnose important clinical situations. It would be a major loss to our field if hysteria allows us to go far beyond our data, since our credibility rests on maintaining a scientific approach. However, it would be equally tragic for ritual abuse to become the "incest" of the 1990s, in the sense that we end up blaming the victims and attributing their stories to fantasy, rather than confronting the horrors of their experiences (Masson 1984).

It is very important to learn from careful clinical observation if completely fantasized trauma (as opposed to real trauma or a screen memory that does, in fact, have a traumatic etiology) can produce a PTSD syndrome. It is also important to study how treatment approaches will need to differ for different subpopulations. Clearly, as we learn more about the subtypes of patients who present with PTSD symptoms, as well as about the prevalence, symptom pictures, course, and so on, of each type of subgroup, we will be able to make a more credible assessment and offer more helpful treatment approaches. We do not yet have this information.

Unfortunately, we have a difficult time believing that patients have been severely traumatized even when there is corroborating data. This is especially striking since nothing they describe is really unknown to us. Taken separately, the crimes that ritually abused patients report (child abuse, torture, infanticide, cannibalism, child pornography, drug abuse and sales, cruelty to animals, murder, and so forth) are all crimes that we know to occur. In part, it is our difficulty in imagining the combination of horrors that makes us so skeptical. However, by working to understand this far end of the continuum of human cruelty, through research and treatment with survivors, we will probably become far better able to understand and treat less severe forms of abuse and trauma. A focus on Satan or other more mystical and sensational aspects of this area can take us away from the sad reality of the extreme sadism and cruelty that are truly behind the problems that these patients experience.

The therapist must not be seduced by his or her own needs or by the compelling material and the intensely projected affects to give up a therapeutic role and become an active agent for either side of the patient's ambivalence. The therapist's role is to help the patient better to understand her own doubts and certainties. A major part of the trauma involved for these patients is the very fact that their perceptions and memories have been so distorted by the abuse. Healing is made far more difficult and painful by the confusion, dissociation, and nonsequential memories that the abuse created. For a therapist to appoint himself- /herself as an arbiter of reality, especially if that entails taking one side of the patient's ambivalence as truth, does not help this process. It probably only adds to the patient's already profound distrust of her own perceptions in her struggle to sort out what is real and what is not.

At present, the degree to which intergenerational satanic cults exist, conspire, and are organized is not at all clear. However, there is no disagreement that many of the patients in question have experienced severe forms of abuse and that as therapists we need to find ways to help them to heal. Even if we discover that there is no global conspiracy, we will still need to develop ways to investigate and prosecute the criminal acts that do occur (e.g., develop nonleading yet effective interview techniques), as well as to develop and provide treatment for the victims.

Walter Young (1990) pointed out that if even a small fraction of what these patients report turns out to be true, this would clearly warrant further investment of resources to aid with investigation, prevention, and treatment. If, on the other hand, all of the reports are completely fabricated, it would confront the field with an unprecedented social and psychological phenomenon that would also require the investment of resources to understand both the cultural and the dynamic significance, as well as to find ways to help these survivors to explore and resolve their delusions. In either case, or in the more likely and complex middle ground, the field clearly must do more to understand and deal with this phenomenon.

REFERENCES

Bliss, E. L. (1986). *Multiple Personality Disorder, Allied Disorders and Hypnosis*. New York: Oxford University Press.

Boyd, A. (1991). *Blasphemous Rumors: Is Satanic Ritual Abuse Fact or Fantasy?* London: Fount.

Braun, B. G. (1989a). Ritualistic abuse and dissociation. Paper presented at 2nd Annual Conference for the California Society for the Study of Multiple Personality and Dissociation,–April, Costa Mesa, CA.

————— (1989b). Letters to the editor. *Newsletter of the International Society for the Study of Multiple Personality and Dissociation* 2:11. p. 11.

Braun, B. G., and Gray, G. (1987). *Report on the 1986 questionnaire:* Multiple personality disorder and cult involvement. Paper presented at 4th International Conference on Multiple Personality Disorder/Dissociative States, at Rush Presbyterian-St. Luke's Medical Center, Chicago, IL.

Brunvand, J. H. (1986). *The Choking Doberman and Other "New" Urban Legends*. New York: Norton.

Crowley, A. (1976). *Magick in Theory and Practice*. New York: Dover, 1924.

Ganaway, G. (1989). Historical truth versus narrative truth: clarifying the role of exogenous trauma in the etiology of multiple personality and its variants. *Dissociation* 2:205–220.

Goodwin, J. (1993). Sadistic abuse: pitfalls for victims and therapists. Paper presented at 5th Regional Conference on Abuse and Multiple Personality, June 7, Alexandria, VA.

Greaves, G. (1992). Alternative hypotheses regarding claims of satanic cult activity: a critical analysis. In *Out of Darkness: Exploring Satanism and Ritual Abuse*, ed. D. K. Sakheim and S. E. Devine pp. 45–72. New York: Lexington.

Hammond, C. (1993). Treatment approaches to ritual abuse and mind control. Paper presented at 5th Regional Conference on Abuse and Multiple Personality, June 8th, Alexandria, VA.

Hicks, R. (1991). *In Pursuit of Satan: The Police and the Occult*. Buffalo: Prometheus Books.

Hill. S., and Goodwin, J. (1989). Satanism: similarities between patient accounts and pre-Inquisition historical sources. *Dissociation* 2:39–44.

Katchen, M. H., and Sakheim, D. K. (1993). The history of satanic religion. In *Out of Darkness: Exploring Satanism and Ritual Abuse*, ed. D. K. Sakheim and S. E. Devine, pp. 1–19. New York: Lexington Books.

Lanning, K. V. (1989). *Satanic, Occult, Ritualistic Crime: A Law Enforcement Perspective*. Quantico, VA: FBI Academy.

_____ (1992). A law-enforcement perspective on allegations of ritual abuse. In *Out of Darkness: Exploring Satanism and Ritual Abuse*, ed. D. K. Sakheim and S. E. Devine, pp. 109–146. New York: Lexington Books.

Masson, J. M. (1984). *The Assault on Truth: Freud's Suppression of the Seduction Theory*. New York: Harper Collins.

Mulhern, S. (1990). Training courses and seminars on satanic ritual abuse: a critical review. Paper presented at 7th International Conference on the Treatment of Multiple Personality and Dissociative Disorders, November at Rush Presbyterian-St. Luke's Medical Center, Chicago, IL.

_____ (1991). Satanism and psychotherapy: a rumor in search of an inquisition. In *The Satanism Scare* ed. J. T. Richardson, J. Best, and D. G. Bromley, pp. 145–172. New York: Aldine De Gruyter.

Noll, R. (1989). Satanism, UFO abductions, historians and clinicians: those who do not remember the past. . . . *Dissociation* 2:251–253.

Orne, M. T. (1979). The use and misuse of hypnosis in court. *International Journal of Clinical and Experimental Hypnosis* 27:311–341.

Raschke, C. (1990). *Painted Black: Satanic Crime in America*. San Francisco: Harper and Row.

Richardson, J. T., Best, J., and Bromley, D. G., eds. (1991). *The Satanism Scare*. New York: Aldine De Gruyter.

Ritual Abuse Task Force (1989). *Ritual abuse: Definitions, Glossary, the Use of Mind Control*. (September 15). Los Angeles County Commission for Women.

Ryder, D. (1992). *Breaking the Circle of Satanic Ritual Abuse*. Minneapolis: CompCare.

Shefflin, A. (1993). Mind control and hypnosis. Paper presented at Daniel Brown & Associates Annual Seminars and Workshops on Psychotherapy & Hypnotherapy, October 23, Center for Integrative Psychotherapy, Cambridge, MA.

Smith, M., and Pazder, L. (1980). *Michelle Remembers*. New York: Pocket Books.

Tamarkin, C. (1993). Investigative issues in ritual abuse cases. Paper presented at 5th Regional Conference on Abuse and Multiple Personality,–June 7, Alexandria, VA.

Van Benschoten, S. C. (1990). Multiple personality disorder and satanic ritual abuse: the issue of credibility. *Dissociation* 3:22–30.

_____ (1990). The spread of satanic cult rumors. *Skeptical Inquirer* 14:287–291.

Victor, J. (1989). A rumor-panic about a dangerous satanic cult in western New York. *New York Folklore* 15:22–49.

Young, W. (1990). President's Report. *International Society for the Study of Multiple Personality and Dissociation*. Ottawa, Ontario.

12

Current Controversies Surrounding Dissociative Identity Disorder

Richard P. Kluft

INTRODUCTION

Controversy is no stranger to the study of dissociative identity disorder (DID), formerly known as multiple personality disorder (MPD). The often dramatic and always thought-provoking nature of its symptoms, the disquieting questions about identity and responsibility raised by the presence and activities of alter personalities, the problematic concerns about memory posed by its alternate constructions of reality and its amnestic barriers, and the unsettling picture of the world painted by these patients' accounts of their traumatic pasts combine to evoke strong and not infrequently polarized reactions in the lay public and among mental-health professionals and scientific investigators alike.

Neither fascination nor skepticism (both of which are intellectualized varieties of countertransference misperception) is associated with objectivity or clarity of insight. Invariably the enthusiast and the naysayer alike find ample ammunition for their causes, and, armed with unacknowledged confirmatory bias (Baron et al. 1988), never fail to find support for their original hypotheses. They demonstrate an inclination to search for material that confirms their hunches instead of attempting to discover all available evidence, some of which might disconfirm their original hypotheses. This is especially likely to occur when the matters at issue are affectively distressing: one's opponents are declared to be incorrect and/or misguided, and denied credibility. As Goodwin (1985) has observed in connection with society's tendency to disregard accounts of the mistreatment of children, "Incredulity can be understood as an intellectualized variant of derealization; and, like the dissociative defenses, incredulity is an effective way to gain distance from terrifying realities" (p. 7).

In order to illustrate this principle at work, we may turn to a recent article by Frankel (1992) challenging the allegations of childhood traumatization made by DID/MPD patients. Frankel points out that few of the articles he has reviewed document alleged abuses. However, he has failed to cite several articles in which abuse has been documented, particularly in childhood cases. Since it is difficult to work with the assumption that a Harvard Medical School professor cannot do a literature search, the omission of the citations in question raises the issue of confirmatory bias. Likewise, Fahy (1988) adds me to the list of those who are rather negative about the use of hypnosis in the treatment of MPD/DID, referring to a decontextualized sentence or two and disregarding the fact that I have advocated the careful use of hypnosis with DID/MPD patients in numerous articles.

To the irrationality of confirmatory bias we must add what has been learned from cognitive dissonance theory (Festinger 1957). This teaches us that when we hold a belief strongly and encounter information that disconfirms it, we are more likely to discard the disconfirmatory evidence than the theory that we cherish. Therefore, it is not uncommon for adherents of one point of view to systematically disregard and/or dismiss data that is inimical to their original points of view. Thus, those therapists who genuinely believe that a good therapist must believe his or her patients tend to discount the ample laboratory and clinical evidence that memory is a reconstructive process subject to many distortions, including confabulation and pseudomemory. As a result, their treatments fail to take into account findings of profound relevance for work with the traumatized. An honest and informed therapist will find occasion to wonder about his or her own memory, as well as that of his or her patients.

The above observations are complicated by what we know of the history of ideological change in science, mainly through the seminal work of Thomas Kuhn (1970). In science we tend to view the world through a series of paradigms, which replace one another as we subscribe to successive views of the world and how it is best understood. Scientific revolutions occur when an older paradigm is replaced in whole or in part by a newer one. When scientists view the world under the influence of a new paradigm they see new and different things, even if they are examining familiar subjects with familiar instruments. In fact, Kuhn (1970) states, "In so far as their only recourse to that world is through what they see and do, we may want to say that after a revolution scientists are responding to a different world" (p. 111). Kuhn goes on to say that "the proponents of competing paradigms . . . see different things when they look from the same point in the same direction. Both are looking at the world, and what they look at has not changed. But in some areas they see different things, and they see them in different relations one to the other" (p. 150). Therefore, in order for them to communicate, "one group or the other must experience the conversion we have been calling a paradigm shift" (p. 150). Because the transition is between "incommensurables" it can not be stepwise or logical, it must occur in a gestalt manner, "all at once (though not necessarily in an instant) or not at all" (p. 150).

Therefore, we should not be surprised to find that many of the most vehement skeptics with regard to DID/MPD are very senior persons who had long and distinguished careers before the rise in the mid-1980s of what Loewenstein (1993) has described as the " 'Wilburian Revolution' in the understanding of MPD" (p. 52); that is the understanding of DID/MPD as a complex dissociative process with the potential of having a complex system of alters, an etiology related to trauma, a structure involving complex dissociative defenses, and a transference pattern related to the many alters. Such authors feel comfortable discussing DID/MPD without attending to the "Wilburian" paradigm except to attack it (e.g., Mersky 1992; Orne and Bates 1992, Orne and Bauer-Manley 1991), regarding it unscientific and incompatible with the alternate hypotheses they endorse.

Given these and numerous other concerns, controversy is inevitable. One could wish that the din would cease and sweet reason prevail, but this is impossible because different paradigms dictate alternative conceptualizations of what is reasonable (and what is sweet). As Boring (1963) has observed, more with philosophic resignation than enthusiasm: "After much thought on the matter, I have come reluctantly to the conclusion that scientific truth . . . must come about by controversy. . . . It seems that scientific truth . . . lies in its greatest minds being brilliantly and determinedly wrong . . . with some third, eclectically-minded middle-of-the-road nonentity seizing the prize. . . . I hate this view, because it is not dramatic and it is not fair; and yet I believe it is the verdict of the history of science" (p. 68).

Acknowledging in advance that my attempts to discuss some of the controversial areas in regard to DID/MPD will be regarded as biased and inflammatory by some, I will attempt to introduce the reader to some of my baseline attitudes, so that they may be taken into account when my remarks on specific subjects are encountered. One of my most characteristic attitudes is a distrust of paradigms and theories, and of those who regard them with awe and reverence. I am often reminded of Freud's 1893 obituary of Charcot. Freud (1962) said, "Charcot never tired of defending the rights of purely clinical work, which consists of seeing and ordering things, against the encroachments of theoretical medicine" (p. 13). On one occasion a student challenged Charcot about an aspect of his clinical work, maintaining that it could not be true because it contradicted a famous theory. To this, Charcot replied, " 'La théorie, c'est bon, mais ca n'empeche pas d'exister' ('Theory is good, but it does not prevent things from existing')" (p. 13). The reader can expect that when there is a conflict between theory and clinical findings, I will value the latter over the former, in the belief that the theory must expand to encompass the facts, rather than the facts be sacrificed in veneration to the theory.

I also think that since science is always trying to refine its understanding, no insight is definitive, and no insight should be disregarded a priori if it is based on relatively crude information or studies with unsophisticated methodologies. Therefore, any article that implicitly or explicitly makes a peremptory dismissal of the clinical literature will not gain my respect. Such apparent respect for scientific method all too often is recruited in the service of making an a priori dismissal of observations with which one disagrees, but cannot disprove, so that the incapacity to disprove one's opponent is bypassed and the opponent is discredited under the rubric of a scrupulous pursuit of "the truth."

For example, I had harbored severe doubts about the work of the late Nicholas Spanos, Ph.D., which is often cited to demonstrate that DID/MPD is iatrogenic. When I met Dr. Spanos several years after the publication of these studies and asked if he had ever seen the clinical phenomena of DID/MPD that he indicated he had replicated in his social-psychological experiments (Spanos et al 1985, Spanos et al. 1986), I learned that he had never seen a patient with this disorder, was unfamiliar with its actual manifestations, and considered these informational deficits irrelevant to his work.

However, if there is a conflict between findings from studies with poor methodologies and those with more advanced methodologies, those from the better studies should prevail if it can be proven that all other factors comparing the groups of studies are equal. Otherwise, it might be that the two groups of studies may be observing and exploring somewhat different phenomena. I also tend to look very closely at publications that are overtly contemptuous of those who do not share the authors' point of view. Such papers almost inevitably suffer from confirmatory bias.

The reader should be aware that I am very highly involved with the modern study of DID/MPD and, on the basis of my experiences and research, have reached the conclusions that DID/MPD is a naturalistically occurring disorder, associated with overwhelming (but not necessarily abuse-related) childhood experiences, and that its active treatment is often followed by good to excellent clinical results (Kluft 1984a 1993a). Recent review articles summarize my findings and conclusions (Kluft 1991a, 1993a).

THE MODERN HISTORY OF DID/MPD

The diagnosis of DID/MPD has been made more frequently in the last decade than in the entire prior recorded history of psychiatry. A condition long considered a rarity, and declared extinct by Stengel in 1943, is now a diagnostic commonplace. This has led to one of the most heated controversies in the dissociative disorders field, with many offering the opinion that the condition is rare or does not even occur naturalistically, and that the recent upsurge in the frequency of the making of this diagnosis is due to iatrogenic factors or the misapplication of loose diagnostic criteria. Others counter that the recent increase in the diagnosis is the result of the increased awareness of clinicians and improved diagnostic approaches.

This controversy overlaps with many others, which will be addressed below. Here, I will reflect only on the narrow issue of why the diagnosis might be made with increased frequency at one point in time than another. Certainly it is undeniable that at certain moments in history certain diagnoses become more fashionable, and are even promoted by various social trends and pressures. There is no a priori reason to discount the skeptics' concern that this might be occurring with DID/MPD. In my opinion and experience, overdiagnosis is occurring, and may be occurring frequently in isolated circumstances, but this is not a universal occurrence. It is most common when clinicians in a given location begin to become aware of DID/MPD and have not yet acquired sufficient experience with such patients to have an accurate searching image for the condition. As a result, patients who demonstrate dissociative tendencies or manifest symptoms that fall short of DID/MPD diagnostic criteria are called DID/MPD by clinicians making earnest mistakes about the boundaries of the condition, unaware that DDNOS (dissociative disorder not otherwise specified) is a preferable designation for patients with vaguer findings. Also, it is possible for the inexperienced and/or those inclined be accepting of all that a patient alleges to take at face value a patient's misperception and/or misidentification of his or her situation. Furthermore, many clinicians new to work with hypnosis may mistake findings that are not uncommon in the highly hypnotizable as indicators of DID/MPD, such as the demonstration of "hidden observer" phenomena described by Hilgard (1986) and ego-states as described by Watkins and Watkins (1993). However, it has been my personal experience that most neophytes and clinicians inexperienced with DID/MPD tend toward caution and underdiagnosis, reluctant to make the more controversial DID/MPD diagnosis. I have encountered a number of clinicians who do not understand that the mind is not a unity, and consider every manifestation of dissociated executive function DID/MPD, and a number whose understanding of DID/MPD is so idiosyncratic or suffused with a belief system that makes DID/MPD considerations more likely to be promoted.

A common situation occurs when a clinician in an area begins to develop an interest in dissociative disorders and makes this type of diagnosis in patients who have received other diagnoses from local colleagues. It is predictable that the word will go out that "Dr. X thinks everybody has MPD." Those who are upset with the proliferation of DID/MPD diagnoses will attack Dr. X, while those who are concerned with whether patients of their own have this condition will seek out Dr. X for consultation. It is possible that Dr. X will be both guilty and innocent. As Dr. X grows in experience, he or she will undoubtedly find more subtle signs of dissociation with greater facility, and make the diagnosis on the basis of more subtle findings, which probably should not be called DID/MPD at that point in time even though the patient may deserve the diagnosis by life history (see Kluft 1985a, 1991b). In all likelihood Dr. X's wide-spectrum DID/MPD diagnoses will include both DDNOS patients who are over-diagnosed by the DID/MPD label and patients for whom the diagnosis is quite apt. Both Kluft (1985a, 1991b) and Boon and Draijer (1993) have demonstrated that most DDNOS patients with some features of MPD go on to demonstrate overt DID/MPD if sequentially reassessed.

In the interests of objectivity, it should be noticed that when interest in DID/MPD begins to rise in an area in which there previously had been little curiosity about or awareness of DID/MPD, there should be a period of apparent overdiagnosis as clinicians begin to recognize the previously undiagnosed DID/MPD patients who have accumulated in the local mental-health care delivery system. In my own experience, I found many more DID/MPD patients in my first few years of practice in a medium-sized city outside of Philadelphia than I found in my subsequent years there, despite my increasing experience and clinical sophistication. A backlog of undiagnosed DID/MPD patients had been recycling through the psychiatric unit of the local hospital. Those having been found and treated, new cases were identified frequently, but at a much slower rate.

Having commented on some of the factors that may promote real or apparent overdiagnosis at this point in history, let me turn to the alternative stance. It is useful to observe that it is commonplace for conditions to be diagnosed more frequently when increasing and/or systematic efforts are made to make the diagnosis in question. Prior to the 1980s there was little systematic effort to consider the DID/MPD diagnosis on a routine basis. Therefore, it stands to reason that the likelihood of the condition's being recognized has been tremendously enhanced by recent developments. Elsewhere I have observed (Kluft 1991b):

When MPD was considered a rarity, and, moreover, a rarity with dramatic and flamboyant manifestations, little attention was paid to its recognition and treatment. Given the prevailing wisdom of the era, it was reasonable to assume that sooner or later, the condition would declare itself. When MPD was thought by many to emerge as an iatrogenic artifact . . . the notion of making systematic inquiry about its manifestations on a routine basis was implicitly discouraged. . . . Alone among illnesses and mental disorders, the clinically approved approach to MPD . . . has been to conduct the diagnostic interview without making efforts to discern its presence lest it be created thereby.

Therefore, the emergence of systematic efforts to diagnose and discern the epidemiology of MPD is a relatively recent phenomenon, which could not occur before there existed (1) a recognition that the condition is sufficiently frequent to merit such inquiries; (2) an awareness that the condition occurs naturalistically apart from interventions that might be seen to induce it; and (3) effective treatments so that it is useful to discern its presence or absence. [pp. 606–607]

What has made it more likely that DID/MPD will be diagnosed and recognized? There are several factors, which I have reviewed elsewhere (Kluft 1987a). Foremost has been the rise of feminism, with its sensitization of the professions to the widespread exploitation of women and children. It helped to create an atmosphere in which complaints of abuse could be heard more sympathetically, and in which posttraumatic conditions became associated with women's issues. Also, the tragic aftermath of the Vietnam War, which forced the mental-health professions to look carefully at posttraumatic stress disorder (PTSD), brought about fruitful cooperation and collaboration between the students of PTSD and DID/MPD, enriching both fields and making many PTSD scholars interested in the dissociative disorders. The rise of biological psychiatry teased apart many overlapping syndromes—out of the study of those who did not respond to treatment with available measures many proved to be both traumatized and highly dissociative. *DSM-III* (American Psychiatric Association 1980) distinguished the dissociative disorders as a freestanding group, emphasizing their legitimacy as mental disorders. Increased interest in hypnosis led to a growing number of clinicians who became familiar with hypnotic and dissociative phenomena, many of whom, when they encountered these phenomena in patients, began to appreciate the importance of dissociative psychopathology.

The efforts of pioneers in the DID/MPD field, most notably Ralph B. Allison, M.D., the late Cornelia B. Wilbur, M.D., and David Caul, M.D., led to the availability of workshops on DID/MPD and an increasing number of clinicians able to diagnose and treat this condition. By 1980, the literature began to explode with pioneering publications on DID/MPD. Greaves's (1980) classic review article, Bliss's (1980) landmark study of fourteen patients' phenomenology, Coons's (1980) systematic discussion of making the diagnosis of DID/MPD, Braun's (1980) treatment recommendations, and Marmer's (1980) psychoanalytic study laid a strong foundation and put many important contributions in the literature for the first time. At long last, a contemporary literature about DID/MPD was available.

The modern history of the study of DID/MPD is discussed at length by Greaves (1993). Suffice it to say that building on what has been discussed above, the field rapidly learned the natural history of the condition (Kluft 1985a), enhanced its sophistication with regard to diagnosis (Coons 1984, Kluft 1985b, 1987a,b), and developed specialized approaches to diagnosis including relatively novel interviewing approaches (Putnam 1989), a specialized mental status examination (Loewenstein 1991), screening instruments (Bernstein and Putnam 1986), and structured diagnostic instruments (Ross 1989, Steinberg 1993a,b). Given this wealth of information, it would be most remarkable if an increase in the number of DID/MPD patients being diagnosed had not occurred. The objection that this may be related to unduly lax diagnostic criteria is unlikely. Most experts who have reflected on whether the more stringent *DSM-IV* criteria would stifle the increasing use of the DID/MPD diagnosis have concluded that no more than 5 percent of contemporary cases diagnosed by *DSM-III-R* criteria would be excluded thereby.

In conclusion, it appears most likely that the modern increase in the diagnosis of DID/MPD patients, while most likely involving some instances of overdiagnosis, is the natural outcome of the mental-health professions' increasing sophistication with regard to the diagnosis of this group of patients.

THE ETIOLOGY OF DID/MPD

Arguments surrounding the etiology of DID/MPD have been one of the most characteristic and consistent of the modern controversies. Here I will address only some of the areas of dispute. A more thorough exploration of models and theories of etiology is available elsewhere (Kluft, in press).

Is DID/MPD a Mental Disorder or a Syndrome?

Controversies exist as to whether DID/MPD is a freestanding mental disorder or a syndrome that develops in the context of other mental illnesses. Unfortunately, this important issue has not received the sophisticated treatment that it deserves because most of the articles that address it have been flawed by the unproven assumptions made by their authors. Here I will try to address several issues without attempting a critical review of prior publications.

DID/MPD may coexist with a wide range of other symptomatology, which may, in a given case, represent epiphenomena of the DID/MPD, independent comorbid conditions, or both. At this point in time, it often is not possible to determine the relationship of the dissociative disorder to the other phenomena in a given case without longitudinal observation and study and careful attention to the response of those phenomena to various treatment interventions. If one assumes a priori that a particular condition is primary, and that fluctuations in DID/MPD phenomenology that parallel the fluctuations of the condition assumed to be primary indicate that DID/MPD is a symptom of the other condition, it will be easy to make a case for DID/MPD's being a syndrome alone. However, if one appreciates that it is very normal for the vicissitudes of one condition to impact on another, even if both are separate conditions, such inferences must be discarded or qualified. Kluft (unpublished data linked with 1985a) found that although the responses to treatment of affective disorders in patients with MPD/DID phenomena did lead to changes in the DID/MPD phenomena, and might be associated with a transient waxing and waning of dissociative symptoms, there were no instances in which the control of the affective disorder led to the complete cessation of DID/MPD manifestations.

One confusing aspect of this problem is that MPD/DID can occur in patients with many forms of Axis 2 psychopathology (Fink 1991), some of which are associated with brief psychotic episodes, and that highly hypnotizable individuals are vulnerable to the development of what have been called hysterical psychoses. This, in addition to the coexistence of MPD/DID with affective disorders that may involve psychotic features, and with schizoaffective disorders in uncommon situations, leads to the possibility that DID/MPD may be encountered in patients with neurotic, borderline, and psychotic levels of ego strength and defenses. Again, in this context only the a priori assumption that one psychopathology is primary will lead to the second disorder's being considered a syndrome by comparison.

In considering this particular controversy, it is important to appreciate its complexity in order to demonstrate that a particular set of findings constitutes a freestanding disorder. To do so, it is essential to demonstrate that they constitute a unique pattern of characteristic symptoms and have a characteristic natural history over time. Furthermore, any postulated hypotheses must hold up on follow-up, rather than appear accurate only for a brief period of observation (Woodruff et al. 1974). Kluft (1985a) followed over 210 MPD patients in order to determine the natural history of DID/MPD. He was able to discern a characteristic pattern for the DID/MPD manifestations (1985a) and a typology of presentations (1991a) that was unrelated to the waxing and waning of other comorbidity. He also noted that in some patients with both affective disorders and dissociative disorders the dissociative disorders were refractory and could not be controlled until the affective disorders had been treated successfully (1988a). He found that DID/MPD rarely responded to treatment that did not address the condition specifically (1985a, 1993a). No untreated patients lost their DID/MPD without treatment, and only 2–3 percent of the patients in therapies that addressed other problem areas but did not address the DID/MPD directly were relieved of their dissociative symptoms in a definitive manner (1993a).

The above observations are most consistent with the hypothesis that DID/MPD is a disorder rather than a syndrome, but they do not rule out the possibility that at times the manifestations of the disorder can occur as a syndrome associated with another disorder.

Is DID/MPD a Naturalistic Mental Disorder, or Is It an Iatrogenic Condition?

It is not uncommon for clinicians (Merskey 1992), clinical investigators (Kampman 1976), and scientific investigators (Spanos et al. 1985, 1986) to state that DID/MPD is an iatrogenic artifact, limited in distribution to those areas in which clinicians evoke these artifacts on a fairly regular basis. It was in this spirit that Fahy (1988) described DID/MPD as a North American culture-bound condition. Hypnosis is often thought to play a major role in the genesis of such artifactual states, along with the deleterious impact of the interest of the clinician, who is assumed to be an enthusiast whose rapt investment in making the diagnosis creates cues and expectations that explicitly or implicitly induce the patient to manifest its characteristic stigmata.

Before proceeding, it is important to explore certain problems inherent in the assessment of iatrogenesis allegations. In order to demonstrate that an allegation of iatrogenesis is more substantial than a statement of opinion, it is necessary to demonstrate that the helping professional(s) has (have) indeed brought to bear influences that are sufficient to have brought about the condition in question (and not simply the appearance of the condition in question) for long enough to demonstrate that the particular condition is present and following the characteristic course of that condition. For example, if an allegation is made that a patient is suffering an iatrogenic cardiac difficulty due to a low potassium level induced by the prescription of diuretics, it would be useful to recheck the potassium level and be sure that the level is in fact low, rather than a laboratory error or a mislabeled sample from another source. It would be necessary to demonstrate that the problem in question is indeed a recognized consequence of low potassium. Furthermore, it is necessary to demonstrate that a higher baseline potassium level existed previously, that the drug was prescribed, that active medication was obtained, and that in fact it was administered, ingested, absorbed, and absorbed in sufficient quantity to have had the effect it is alleged to have had. In addition, it would be important to ascertain and demonstrate that other medications, supplements, and foodstuffs that might have been prescribed to preserve and provide compensatory potassium have not been prescribed, administered, taken, absorbed, and absorbed in sufficient quantity to call the allegation into question. Without such proofs and demonstrations, it remains possible that the low potassium and its consequences have causes other than the prescribed diuretic. Even with the demonstration that potential iatrogenic factors are present, it still remains necessary to rule out other contributions to the problematic potassium level so that a false attribution of iatrogenesis is not made, and the patient, believed to be safe after the correction of the medication regimen, is left at the mercy of an additional undiagnosed condition or risk factor. Succinctly put, it is far easier to allege the iatrogenic reduction of a patient's potassium level than it is to prove it.

In a similar spirit, the allegation that DID/MPD has developed after a mental health professional has made inquiry about its manifestations or whether the patient has endured abuse is easy to make, but difficult to sustain. First, it must be demonstrated that neither DID/MPD nor a condition known to be associated with more covert manifestations of DID/MPD, such as DDNOS, was present before the interventions that are questioned. Second, it must be demonstrated (rather than decreed) that DID/MPD indeed can be created by the interventions that are alleged to have created it. Third, it must be shown that the interventions that are alleged to have created the DID/MPD have indeed occurred, have been registered by the patient, and are sufficiently potent to have been capable of having created the alleged effect. Fourth, it must be demonstrated that efforts to prevent such an outcome have not been made, or have been insufficient or unsuccessful. Fifth, the absence of alternative credible explanations for the presence of DID/MPD phenomena must be demonstrated. As a corollary, sixth, even if it is agreed that the conditions necessary to produce iatrogenic DID/MPD are present, it must be demonstrated that they and not some other factors were the definite causative agent rather than a minor contributing factor.

In view of the covert and clandestine nature of DID/MPD's natural history, it is very difficult to prove that the condition was not present before becoming manifest. What makes a condition manifest is not necessarily what has caused it. For example, it is not unusual for an unsuspected bipolar disorder to become clinically manifest when a psychiatrist prescribes an antidepressant for what was thought to have been depression alone, or for a cardiologist to find evidence of an unsuspected cardiac condition by administering a stress test, but the psychiatrist and the cardiologist have not created de novo disease by their interventions. Likewise, it is not credible to argue that beginning psychotherapy or administering a comprehensive diagnostic evaluation in which questions about dissociative disorders have been asked has created DID/MPD without being vulnerable to the counterargument that one has indulged in a post hoc, propter hoc type of fallacious reasoning.

In order to allege an intervention has created a condition, there must be some proof that this is indeed possible. Nowhere in the literature is there a demonstration rather than an allegation of the iatrogenesis of the full and sustained picture of DID/MPD. In 1982 I reported repeating elements of earlier iatrogenesis experiments and finding that the phenomena that were evoked had little in common with clinical DID/MPD. Instead, they lead to transient situation-dependent and often uncooperative permeable ego-state manifestations (Leavitt 1947), enactments of past life suggestions (Kampman 1976), and dissociative phenomena such as automatic writing (Harriman 1942). Spanos, unfamiliar with DID/MPD, created transient amnestic and role-playing phenomena, not the full clinical condition (Spanos et al. 1985, Spanos et al. 1986). He never addressed the pars pro toto fallacy built into his expectations and criteria for success. If mere enactment of certain aspects of a role establishes the legitimacy of a condition, then certainly it is fair to reason that the subject of a stage hypnotist who can be induced to cluck like a chicken should be cooked for dinner! It may be instructive to appreciate that Estabrooks, one of the great hypnotic practitioners of the last generation, was involved in the efforts to create "hypnotic couriers" for the military (Ross 1994). The goal was to induce military subjects to be able to be hypnotized and receive information in an altered state that they would not know they knew in their waking states, and therefore could not reveal. However, if hypnotized by an indicated individual, they would be able to reveal their information and receive a reply, of which they would also be unaware. It took months to establish such phenomena in cooperative good military subjects. If such heroic effort was necessary to achieve such modest dissociative goals, it is difficult to argue that DID/MPD can be established with a small number of questions. In the absence of a single credible demonstration of the iatrogenesis of DID/MPD, any allegation of the iatrogenesis of DID/MPD must be regarded with great caution and misgiving.

The failure of iatrogenesis experiments to create this disorder makes it difficult to demonstrate that interventions alleged to have created an iatrogenic version of the disorder are potent enough to do so. Also, it is a rare clinician (with an exception to be noted below) who is not alert to the risks of misdiagnosis, and who does not take steps to prevent leading the patient to endorse phenomena that may not have been present in the first place. Unfortunately, there are substantial groups of clinicians about whom this cannot be said, because their paradigm implicitly and explicitly assumes that their patients will try to deny their psychopathology and require vigorous confrontation about being in denial. Here I refer to the many twelve-step programs and those whose treatment models are informed by them. Most of these models are derived from the Alcoholics Anonymous program, which was developed to reach a group of patients whose capacity for denial can be olympic in magnitude. Therapists who apply the vigorous confrontations and interventions necessary to reach the alcoholic or drug addict to other groups may overstep all reasonable limits that clinical experience and memory research would dictate as prudent, and virtually force acknowledgment of phenomena and experiences down the throats of the pliable, suggestive, and desperate.

It is essential to appreciate that no effort to argue for iatrogenesis has shown that no alternative explanation is possible. In fact, Janet's initial arguments about iatrogenesis were made about a patient who had shown florid dissociative phenomena for years before the intervention that was alleged to have created her condition (Braun 1984, Kluft 1982). Finally, no study or clinical vignette put forth as a demonstration of iatrogenesis has shown that the interventions alleged to have brought this about were the sole or major causative agent as opposed to being one of many contributing factors.

Because it often is stated that hypnosis can create DID/MPD and that experts make patients into DID/MPD with astonishing facility, it is important to appreciate that Ross and his colleagues have explored both of these issues. Ross and Norton (1989) found that hypnosis did not appreciably influence the phenomena of these conditions, although more child personalities and accounts of abuse were found in patients who had been approached with hypnosis. Ross and colleagues (1989) also compared the phenomena of DID/MPD patients assessed by those who were avowedly interested in these conditions and those who were not. No appreciable differences were discovered. Certainly, if either hypnosis or enthusiasm is to be alleged to be a factor in causing iatrogenic DID/MPD, one would think that these factors would have some impact on the phenomena elicited. Although it cannot be assumed that this could not have occurred in individual cases, it is clear that it cannot be assumed to be a prevalent occurrence. In the absence of solid proof of the reality of iatrogenesis, and in the presence of an increasingly voluminous literature documenting the phenomena and natural history of DID/MPD, it seems most parsimonious to regard the iatrogenesis hypothesis for the etiology of this condition unproven, a hypertrophic and egregious expression of the post hoc, propter hoc fallacy, and move on to study more important issues. Because only a keen appreciation of the impact of our procedures upon our patients will keep us honest and alert, the iatrogenesis hypothesis should not be discarded, but should serve as one of the many guardians of the scientific conscience of the field.

The Iatrogenic Worsening of DID/MPD

Although the iatrogenic creation of DID/MPD may prove to be an ironic myth, it is critical to appreciate that the iatrogenic worsening of DID/MPD is neither myth nor epidemic, but it is a very serious clinical problem that cries out for attention. Unfortunately, it has been relegated to a minor place in the dissociative disorders literature due to the furor that all too often surrounds the largely empty debate that has surrounded de novo iatrogenesis.

In 1982 I reported a patient whose complexity was very much increased by the inept use of hypnosis by a practitioner who was untrained in its use and had never used it before. The David Caul Memorial Symposium (1989), with contributions from Braun, Coons, Fine, Greaves, Kluft, and Torem (all 1989), was replete with examples of treatments gone awry. All too often the only way the dissociative patient can protect him or herself from the overwhelming onslaught of a maladroit or poorly paced treatment is by dissociating, often to the extent of forming additional alter personalities.

The practitioner who refuses to address the DID/MPD may create pressures that impel such patients either to dissociate, further sequestering that for which they will receive no help, or to create even more dramatic "proofs" that the condition is, in fact, present. In the former case, the alters will be kept far from the therapy and the therapist, who will see no trace of what is occurring, and feel confirmed in the belief that his or her policy of nonreinforcement is reducing the disorder. In the latter, the therapist will feel confirmed in his or her opinion that the patient is a mythomaniacal and narcissistic character disorder patient, probably of the borderline variety, and that such turmoil is a protest against the withholding of inappropriate gratifications and interventions. Either the patient will subside or leave treatment.

What of the therapist who does not deny the disorder, but who is either fascinated with it or mistakes scoptophilic exploration of the alter system for treatment? Such a therapist conveys that he or she is more interested in the panoply of psychopathology than the patient as a person, or the patient's recovery. In order to please the therapist, in response to suggestions—implicit and explicit, direct and indirect—and in the erroneous impression that they are proceeding well in therapy, patients may over-label their phenomena as additional alters, or even create some. What of the therapist who makes a beeline for the traumatic material without doing the necessary preparatory psychotherapy? The patients of such therapists may need to form new alters to handle the overwhelming pressure of such premature uncovering, to provide alters and memories as material for the therapist, and to create alters that appear to cope well in order to help them escape the pressure of the therapy.

It is crucial to appreciate the triphasic nature of the treatment of the traumatized (Herman 1992) and its implications for the treatment of DID/MPD patients (Fine 1991, Kluft 1988a, 1989b, 1993a,b). It is necessary to create a situation of safety in the therapy before going into the remembrance of trauma and the mourning of its impact, which in turn must occur before successful intrapersonal and interpersonal reconnection. Therapists who do not respect these observations and the principles of pacing that follow from them (Fine 1991, 1993, Kluft, 1991a, 1993a,b,c) are likely to retraumatize their patients and give them little recourse but to dissociate further.

Not only should the treatment be carefully paced to avoid such untoward events, but the therapist should abstain from imposing his or her beliefs about the structure of alter systems and from going on vigorous trauma hunts. Both have high potential for iatrogenic complication of the alters system and the generation of pseudomemories which may be sufficiently formidable to verge upon pseudologia fantastica. For example, leading DID/MPD patients to believe that they must have a particular type of alter may cause them to generate same. It has been a curious experience to witness that DID/MPD patients who come from areas in which therapists often have been trained by experts who believe that certain types of alters are invariably encountered are more likely to manifest them, while such alters are found less frequently in areas in which the major experts do not endorse the ubiquity of such phenomena. Two egregious examples are the inner self-helper (ISH) first described by Allison (1974) and the central core personality, described by a number of practitioners in Ohio and Canada. Luckily these two types of alters, even if artifactual, are often constructive and useful. However, in areas where religious beliefs endorsing the actual presence of the devil and his minions on earth are prevalent, patients in treatment with therapists holding such beliefs can be done a major disservice by being encouraged to believe they have, and thereby generating, demonic alters.

Likewise, although it is useful to take histories, it is important to respect amnestic barriers early in treatment unless there are firm clinical indications to the contrary. Taking the history of a number of alters certainly may uncover more traumata than the patient can manage. When it seems possible that this could occur, usually it becomes important to curtail exploration except in the most general terms until the treatment has addressed what has already emerged. The resolution of one layer of pathology is often sufficient to prompt the emergence of the next, and is less associated with overwhelming the patient or generating pressures toward pseudomemory formation, and with it, the potential of instigating alters to contain traumata that never occurred but conceivably might be believed in forever.

Although I could cite many areas of difficulty associated with the misuse of basically constructive techniques, I will restrict myself to commenting on two very common misadventures: the overuse of journaling and excessive preoccupation with mapping the personality system. Journaling was suggested by the early pioneers because (1) many alters identified themselves for the first time in writing; (2) for many alters telling was prohibited, but writing was not understood to be; (3) journaling often was a valuable outlet between sessions; and (4) by contributing to and reading a joint journal, alters could begin to become aware of one another and breach dissociative boundaries. However, if a patient journals excessively, not only will he or she generate too much for the therapist to read, but there is danger that autobiography and intercommunication can degenerate into a solipsistic fantasy game in which imagination replaces reality. I advise against my patient's journaling more than 20–30 minutes per day. However, I know that an occasional patient will journal for hours, and become lost in the vicissitudes of his or her internal worlds. Alters can be created to fill in the roles necessary in these inner worlds, a complication I described in 1988(b). Many therapists and patients appear unaware of this potential hazard.

Closely related is excessive mapping of the alter system. When correctly done (e.g., Fine 1991, 1993), mapping is a useful exercise. It is done early in therapy, and perhaps occasionally thereafter to assess intrapsychic changes and alterations in amnestic barriers and alter systems. However,

I have seen countless instances in which patients have spent hours of time daily for weeks and months in such pursuits. Several therapists have come to me in consultation and shown me maps including upward of 10,000 alters, asking me what to do. They usually are not happy when I explore the possibility that the map is the record of imaginative play perverted into a fantasy game in which both patient and therapist have left reality far behind and created a new shared reality in which the therapy takes on the features of a game of "Dungeons and Dragons" run riot.

A Problem of Substance: Factitious DID/MPD

As vigorously as I have argued against the widespread allegations of iatrogenesis in the de novo etiology of DID/MPD, I insist quite forcefully that factitious DID/MPD and the factitious elaboration of legitimate dissociative disorders are problems of genuine concern, although of uncertain incidence and prevalence. A series of such patients has been reported by Coons (1994). Elsewhere (Kluft, in press) I have outlined some of the many dynamics that can motivate the use of a false or factitious history and alter system as a defense. Here I will restrict myself to observing that for many individuals, manifesting the features and histories of DID/MPD patients is preferable to their own baseline realities. One of my patients warned me about a friend of hers who was trying to evade difficult life circumstances and enter a dissociative disorders program by presenting herself as suffering DID/MPD, mimicking my patient's symptoms and history. My patient was irate for two reasons. First, she protested: "That bitch is trying to get in here on my life story!" Second, she resented the friend's calumny of the friend's parents, because she had always run to her friend's house as a refuge from her own abusive childhood (confirmed to me by her abusive mother's confession in a family therapy). Although I must admit that I was disappointed in some of the first descriptions of factitious DID/MPD situations, because they have not been very convincing, I believe it is a significant problem that will be studied in greater depth in the near future.

A Painful Clinical Reality: Naturalistic, Iatrogenic, and Factitious Features Can Be Found in the Same Patient

It is always tempting to try to smash an adversary with whose point of view one disagrees. If life were played by the same rules as a formal debate, this might be a functional stance. Unfortunately, assuming one's adversary is completely out of touch with reality is rarely either accurate or helpful. I find it useful to study the adversary's point of view, and to try to discern how it could be inferred in good faith from phenomena that are actually present. When I pursued this approach in my 1987(c) study of "The Simulation and Dissimulation of Multiple Personality Disorder," I discovered that since naturalistic MPD phenomena superficially mimicked the behavior that forensic experts associate with malingerers it was only natural that such authorities, by using their customary paradigms, would be very likely to dismiss most DID/MPD patients as malingerers.

When we examine the iatrogenesis argument in a similar spirit, it is enlightening to observe that many characteristic DID/MPD phenomena are very much like those one would expect to encounter in a iatrogenic or factitious situation. This circumstance, combined with the factors described above, would be sufficient to convince many colleagues that any and all DID/MPD manifestations can be attributed to iatrogenic or factitious etiologies. Space does not allow an extensive exploration of this subject, but a few observations on the deconstruction of some of these patients' manifestations may be instructive.

DID/MPD patients vary widely with respect to their abilities to control switching and the creation of new alters. Some DID/MPD patients have alters that more or less determine which alters will assume executive control of the body. In some patients particular alters have been assigned the role of creating new alters. Regardless of the degree of volitional control in a given patient, it is clear that the process of alter construction draws heavily upon external influences, both with regard to the instigation of new dividedness and the form taken by the new dividedness. Consequently, we should not be surprised to find that DID/MPD patients can rapidly form new alters in response to their external circumstances, and that a readiness to do so could be construed as evidence for iatrogenesis by those who do not appreciate the adaptational value of such a capacity.

As Spiegel (1986, 1991) has observed, dissociation involves the segregation of certain bits of information from others in a relatively rule-bound manner, and dissociation is an ad hoc and on-line defensive process rather than a retrospective defensive operation with regard to trauma such as repression. These patients developed alters in response to intercurrent stressors in childhood, and may retain this capacity as adults, forming alters to adapt to evolving situations. It is not unusual to find that a child has formed an alter to cope with a traumatic experience and/or another to manifest behavior that will propitiate an abuser. Nor is it unusual to find that a hospitalized adult DID/MPD patient has formed a new alter to cope with the stress of the hospital stay, and/or to manifest the type of behavior that will allow him or her to appear ready for discharge.

Imagine such behavior from the perspective of a person who enters the situation strongly inclined to perceive the condition as iatrogenic. Such a person might be likely, even predisposed, to conclude that the patient in question rapidly learned that alter formation was encouraged and prized by the psychiatric staff of the hospital, and is complying with the cues and demand characteristics of the situation.

DID/MPD patients, along with most who have been abused as children, become skilled at reading others in order to figure out how to behave in order to anticipate and avoid difficulties. They become capable of manipulating themselves and others to achieve at least an illusion of safety or control of their circumstances. In this they inevitably overlap with that group of patients who feign or produce symptoms in order to achieve and maintain the patient role, those who suffer the factitious disorders. It is not uncommon for DID/MPD patients to become demoralized about their prospects for recovery, and to dedicate themselves to finding and holding on to some facsimile of safety and connectedness in their often difficult and complex lives. Consequently, it should not be surprising that an unknown but significant percentage of DID/MPD patients spend a great deal of effort in achieving and maintaining the patient role, including the development of attention-demanding symptoms and behaviors designed to create, protect, or enhance their patient roles. They have been encouraged in this by the increasing inroads of models of health-care delivery systems that attempt to minimize the utilization of services by patients, creating incessant fears of abandonment and the loss of their relationships with their therapists. We should expect to see an increase in factitious components to mental illnesses as attempts are made to deprive very needy and unstable patients of the level of therapy that serves to contain and support them. It should not be surprising that the motivation to preserve the patient role, for both good reasons and bad, will generate some DID/MPD behaviors that make both specialists and skeptics shake their heads in astonishment and amazement.

A woman who appeared to have genuine DID/MPD became concerned that her therapist was losing interest in her, and that her managed care company was trying to curtail her use of her hospital care benefits. Between the time that her doctor told her that she probably would be discharged within a few days and her next review, she began to complain of the presence of numerous previously unknown alters, and flashbacks of dramatic and repugnant traumata of a type she had not reported before, but which had been reported by another patient on the same unit. Confronted with these new problems, her doctor felt manipulated and uncertain about what he was observing, but concluded he had to spend more time with her, and argued her case for an extended stay with her insurer's review personnel with force and vigor.

It is useful to appreciate that the phenomena of the DID/MPD patient, like the patient suffering from any other type of mental disorder, do not develop in a vacuum. Imbricated within findings that have been characteristic of this condition from its first descriptions in the clinical literature will be the flotsam and jetsam of contemporary culture and the residues of experiences and interactions with the mental health care professions. Within the alter system of one of my patients were alters based upon Jacqueline Kennedy Onassis, Madonna, Anna Freud, and a former therapist. A young boy I assessed sixteen years ago had alters based on his parents and characters from the "Flintstone" and "Jetson" cartoon families; while one I interviewed two years ago had several alters based on the more contemporary "Mutant Ninja Turtles."

OTHER CONTROVERSIES IN BRIEF

Are the Traumata Alleged by DID/MPD Patients Actual Recollections or Fantastic Pseudomemories?

This issue is highly polarized and politicized. It is also usually unresolvable. Like most pursuits of ultimate truth, it is doomed to frustration except when conducted by those who either by dint of ignorance and/or arrogance and/or overzealous application of a paradigm of belief outside its area of validity presume to have more wisdom than their colleagues. Memory is imperfect and vulnerable to decay and distortion by postevent information and all varieties of contaminants, including the retrieval cues under the aegis of which the search of memory is conducted. Confabulations and pseudomemories are not new discoveries, they are classic findings. Human memory, however vulnerable and potentially flawed, is serviceable enough to address most of the daily and long-term needs of the species. Recently Loftus (1993) reviewed the subject of repressed memory in a less than complete manner, but lucidly raised many important concerns about the accuracy of recovered memories. She raised the issue of whether long-delayed recovery of memories from childhood could be given credence. It is commonplace to assert that true traumata are not forgotten—they are all too present. However, it has long been appreciated that combat soldiers are often amnestic for some of what they have been through (e.g., Sargent and Slater 1941), and Kooper and colleagues (1994) have demonstrated that it is not uncommon for memory to be affected by trauma due to natural disasters in nonpatient populations. Briere and Conte (1993) and Feldman-Summers and Pope (1994) have shown that it is not uncommon for people to have periods during which they did not remember childhood traumata that they generally recall. Herman and Schatzow (1987) demonstrated that of women alleging incest, including those who only recalled the incest after it had long been repressed or dissociated, 74 percent could get good confirmatory evidence, and 9 percent could find suggestive but less persuasive evidence. Bliss (1984) investigated some allegations by DID/MPD patients and could get confirmation for aspects of the accounts of twelve out of thirteen subjects. Williams (1992), 1994) has shown that 38 percent of women interviewed seventeen years after documented childhood trauma did not recall the documented trauma at the time of the study. In a recent study, Coons (1994b) was able to document child abuse in eight of nine adolescent cases of DID/MPD and in all twelve cases of childhood and adolescent DDNOS. These findings suggest that the allegations made by DID/MPD patients both on the basis of consciously available memories and recovered memories should not be dismissed out of hand.

Clinical circumstances often make it impractical, impossible, or contraindicated to play detective or to interview ancillary sources. I have had the experience of following many DID/MPD patients for a decade or more. This has allowed me to observe that often families that deny all allegations of a DID/MPD patient change their story once the significant alleged perpetrators have passed away or become separated from the family. Two examples may suffice. In one instance, the mother of one woman was alcoholic from the patient's childhood until nearly a decade after the patient integrated. The mother called her after making a solid connection with Alcoholics Anonymous, and told her that as part of her recovery, she had to tell my patient that all of her allegations of abuse by her father were accurate. She apologized for having "crawled into the bottle" because she had lacked the courage to stand up for her daughter and to face her own shame over the part she had played in some aspects of the abuse. In another, the sister of a woman who alleged massive intrafamilial abuse had maintained for eleven years that the patient was lying about what had occurred in the family. However, upon the death of their parents, the sister began to discuss their past openly, and admitted that she, too, had suffered similar mistreatment.

Yet clinical experience also allows us to see that some allegations are simply dead wrong, and are based on either lies, fantasies, the doings of the alter system, pseudomemories, or other influences. For example, one hospitalized woman alleged that she was receiving telephone calls from a satanic cult, whose members were instructing her as to how and when to kill the author and a colleague. It was possible to restrict the patient from all access to a telephone for forty-eight hours, during which she stated that she had received two calls from "the cult." It was possible to determine that the assassination issue had begun to come up when the patient was fearing termination of treatment by the colleague. When this and the fact that calls had been alleged when the patient had not been able to receive any calls were brought to the patient's attention, I was able to access an alter who claimed to have given most of the personalities the hallucinated experience of such calls by means of autohypnosis. Another patient had given an elaborate history of mistreatment to a prior therapist who had used aggressive hypnotic inquiries and leading questions extensively. After extensive experience with this patient I reached the conclusion that much of the history I had been given consisted of pseudomemories, but that I could not determine which accounts were reasonably accurate, and which were artifactual. In yet a third instance a patient of mine was hospitalized elsewhere and returned to me with a conviction that she had been involved in satanic ritual abuse, which was openly discussed by patients at the other facility. Luckily, it was possible to demonstrate that irrefutable evidence existed to make it clear that these "memories" could not have occurred because she was in Philadelphia when her satanic abuse in California was supposed to have taken place.

Polarized stances of skepticism toward recovered memories, on the one hand, and believing implicitly whatever patients recount, on the other, both fly in the face of strong scientific and clinical evidence, are without credibility, and are capable of generating more misadventure and mischief than any caring professional would wish to visit upon his or her patient (and more than any circumspect professional would wish to visit upon him- or herself). To pretend otherwise demands that we place our beliefs, theories, and politics above data. Charcot's axiom remains a most useful caution to those who verge upon becoming true believers. Elsewhere (Kluft, in press) I address the clinical implications of working within an atmosphere of "informed uncertainty" that acknowledges both the limitations of our capacity to determine the truth and the fact that recovery can occur without its being determined.

Does Active Treatment of DID/MPD Phenomena Reinforce or Resolve DID/MPD?

The development of systematic approaches to the treatment of DID/MPD (e.g., Braun 1986, Kluft 1991a, Putnam 1989, Ross 1989) has not been greeted with unabashed enthusiasm. Instead, voices have been raised to suggest that such approaches reify and reinforce the disorder, complicate its management, and prolong the patient's morbidity. Fortunately, there is data to suggest a resolution of this debate, and face-saving acknowledgment of the importance of the concerns raised by the point of view that can be questioned if not disproven.

In a series of articles (Kluft 1982, 1984a, 1985a, 1986, 1993a) I traced aspects of my longitudinal study of over 210 DID/MPD patients. I was able to compare both treated and untreated patients; among the treated groups I was able to follow patients treated by therapists who disagreed with the diagnosis, who accepted the diagnosis but did not treat it directly, and those who treated it specifically and directly. The findings were unequivocal. Of the patients treated by those who disagreed with the diagnosis and would not treat its manifestations actively, all retained active DID/MPD on reevaluation. Of those treated by therapists who did not dispute the DID/MPD diagnosis but who did not address it specifically and relied on what they considered good therapy ultimately to resolve the dissociative disorder, only approximately 3 percent did not have the condition on follow-up. These results are inconsistent with the frequently voiced advice that the condition ceases if not reinforced.

In contrast, Coons (1986) followed twenty such patients in therapy with twenty therapists for an average of thirty-nine months. Nineteen of the twenty therapists were working with their first DID/MPD patient, and many were trainees. Two-thirds of the patients were considerably improved, and 25 percent had integrated. Kluft, working with data drawn from the patients from his own practice and a few from the practice of the late Cornelia B. Wilbur, M.D., found that of patients who were in treatment at least three months, 90 percent remained in treatment and 90 percent of them integrated. Neither the Coons study, based on the work of trainees, nor the Kluft study, based on the work of experts, can serve as the basis of any generalizations, because neither represents the work of the average therapist and the average patient. Also, there are data to indicate that Kluft was studying a much healthier group than Coons (Kluft 1994). However, these studies demonstrate that trainees doing specific active DID/MPD with their first cases do better than experienced therapists who do not address the condition directly. This is a powerful argument in favor of active direct treatment of DID/MPD.

That having been said, the active and direct treatment that proves effective always builds in a number of safeguards to discourage the reification and further elaboration of the dissociative psychopathology (Kluft 1993a,b). Most of the major figures in the treatment of DID/MPD have always been aware of and sensitive to the risks of inadvertent iatrogenic complications and regressive dependency, and conducted their clinical work with as much scrupulousness as the give and take of clinical work allows.

Does the Use of Hypnosis Facilitate or Compromise the Treatment of DID/MPD?

The very existence of this venerable debate is based upon a host of misconceptions, most of which are relatively recondite to all but a small group of students of hypnosis. Here I will note only a few relevant issues. The first is that it often is possible to treat DID/MPD patients without ever inducing hypnosis, but it is completely impossible to treat them without hypnosis. This is not clever wordplay—it is an acknowledgement of clinical and theoretical reality. Following the observations of Spiegel and Spiegel (1978), hypnosis comes in three forms: spontaneous trance, autohypnosis, and heterohypnosis (following a ritual of induction performed by another person). Breuer and Freud (1955) noticed spontaneous trance and autohypnosis in their DID/MPD patient Anna O. Bliss (1986) has attributed this disorder to the unwitting abuse of autohypnosis. Given that the patient will experience naturalistic trance and autohypnosis, the decision to abjure the use of heterohypnosis deprives the clinician of the opportunity to help the patient restructure his or her autohypnotic proclivities and patterns toward therapeutic ends, and leaves the patient's psychopathologies with an often insurmountable home field advantage (Kluft 1992a,b). While some patients' dissociative defenses and barriers can be treated without the use of formal hypnosis, some patients are encountered for which this is not possible for prohibitively prolonged periods of time (if at all), and their treatments may founder (Kluft 1987d).

The real issue here is not whether to use hypnosis, which is inevitably a part of these patients' treatments, but rather which uses of hypnosis are likely to be helpful and which are potentially detrimental. This is a point on which authorities who are usually at odds often agree. There is considerable consensus that the use of hypnosis for integrative and supportive purposes is appropriate. There is dispute over whether the use of hypnosis for the exploration of the alter system and for the retrieval of historical materials is appropriate. While there remains considerable room for debate, it is clear that excellent clinical results have been achieved by psychotherapists who employ hypnosis in this manner. It is also clear that the cautions of those who fear iatrogenic increases in the complexity of the alter system and the generation of confabulations and pseudomemories are not without substance. At this point in history, it appears that the decision as to whether hypnosis should be employed for these purposes in a given clinical situation is a matter for experience and clinical judgment to decide. My own experience has demonstrated that since most clinical stalemates are related to the presence and activities of as yet undiscovered alters, as are many other troubling symptoms, there is often substantial justification for such explorations (1988c). For example, a DID/MPD patient in treatment with me for only three weeks began to have apparent grand mal seizures. I induced hypnosis and asked to speak to the alters behind the seizures, and soon had them in conversation. The seizures were both defenses against the revelation of certain traumatic events and representations of them. I told these alters that I was in no rush to unearth upsetting material before the overall patient was prepared to face them, and saw no reason to force them to speak until they were ready. They agreed to stop creating the seizures and to discuss their concerns in treatment when they were ready.

My experience has taught me that unless there is reason to suspect that the patient will be involved in legal proceedings, which might contraindicate any use of heterohypnosis, I can consider the judicious use of hypnosis to revisit material that has already been offered for therapeutic purposes. However, I tend to be very circumspect and cautious when the issue is the accessing of memories de novo. I generally try to avoid such explorations unless there are specific clinical indications to do so. If the patient and I elect to proceed, it is only after we have explored the pluses and minuses of such a decision and the patient has come to a position of genuine informed consent. Usually I have found alternative methods to approach the material in question. A frequent approach is to discuss the situation with an alter who is protesting the revelation, and press for an ample exploration of the rationale for withholding. Usually a process evolves in which the material is revealed by a concerned alter without hypnosis. In my experience, one fairly frequent indication for such hypnotic explorations is therapeutic stalemate in an uncomfortable but otherwise cooperative and accessible patient who is without forensic entanglements, who has given informed consent, and who has demonstrated the capacity to contain him or herself rather than to push immediately to take action on what has emerged in the therapy. The latter is a prerequisite, because the patient who will move to act on materials before they have been processed in therapy is too labile to work with in this manner. Such a patient may damage his or her own life and the life of others by making unwise accusations and confrontations based on materials of uncertain veracity, and of unestablished psychodynamic significance.

Are Specialized Dissociative Disorders Units a Therapeutic Advance or Hotbeds of Contamination and Contagion?

This is a most interesting controversy, with intriguing arguments being offered on both sides. McHugh (1993) argued against such units. He drew his reasoning from the experience of Babinski in addressing the iatrogenic hystero-epilepsies at Charcot's ward of the Salpêtrière. In essence, since the condition in question (hystero-epilepsy) was iatrogenic, and clusters of patients who would be vulnerable to such influences would in all likelihood begin to manifest the symptoms that are of interest to the doctors who provide such suggestions and implicit inducements, the patients would reinforce one another's psychopathology. It stood to reason that one should disperse rather than concentrate such patients, and take pains not to demonstrate potentially reinforcing attention to the symptomatology. Indeed, this is consistent with my own limited experience with symptom contagion.

Unfortunately for McHugh's argument, the evidence that DID/MPD is completely iatrogenic is nil. Unfortunately for those who argue for such units, that the condition is not iatrogenic does not demonstrate that its complications and elaborations cannot be iatrogenic, which restores some legitimacy to McHugh's vastly overstated concerns.

In favor of such units is the often dismal track record of general units in working with such patients, and the problems that may surround the treatment of DID/MPD patients in general settings (Kluft 1991c). In years of consultation to hospital milieus, it has been my experience that unless a general psychiatric unit is willing to prioritize achieving excellence in working with dissociative disorder patients, and accord such expertise the same respect that is given to expertise in working with the traditional patient populations, it is unlikely that the DID/MPD patient can be treated with equal effectiveness in a nonspecialized setting.

Although the specialized unit can be a wonderful resource, it certainly can fall prey to some of the problems that concerned McHugh. Not all specialized programs are equal in quality, and often their differences in quality are related to the adroitness with which the staff can contain the potential for chaos and contamination when such patients, with their potentially incendiary and explosive issues and concerns, are brought together.

Granted the competence of the staff of a specialized unit in addressing the concerns above, there is little doubt a specialized unit can do a much more reliable job in containing the DID/MPD patient's distress and providing support for specialized interventions than a unit that has not been trained to deal with the procedures that are useful and the myriad nuances of such situations (Kluft 1992c). In my five years of experience as the chief of a specialized dissociative disorders program, I have found it has provided an unparalleled opportunity to work rapidly and effectively with DID/MPD patients, and I have been able to achieve results more quickly and efficiently than I had been able to in general hospital psychiatric units or general adult units in psychiatric hospital settings.

Virtually all of the patients treated on this unit who have had prior experience in nonspecialized settings have found themselves better able to focus on their therapeutic work in a dissociative disorders unit in which their concerns were not strange, unique, or special.

In considering the usefulness of the specialized program, it is important to bear in mind that most of the treatment of a DID/MPD patient will take place in the outpatient setting. Therefore, with rare exceptions, the major goal of a period of hospital treatment is to build a better outpatient. The enhancement of stability, mastery, and coping is a significant focus, even in hospital stays designed to support intensive exploratory and/or abreactive work, or to deal with problematic alters (Kluft 1991c). In our program we try to monitor every treatment to assure that uncovering and potentially destabilizing interventions are balanced with stabilization efforts, and that reasonable pacing is observed.

CONCLUDING COMMENTS

I am painfully aware that these brief remarks are at best a superficial and cursory attempt to address a number of important controversial concerns, all of which deserve more extensive exploration. Literally dozens of important controversies could not be addressed due to considerations of space. For example, I have bypassed the weighty concerns raised by *DSM-IV*'s (American Psychiatric Association 1994) decision to change the name of the disorder, a change from *DSM-III-R* (American Psychiatric Association 1987) that I consider undesirable and problematic. It is unlikely that any arguments, however potent, will resolve the polarized debates and frequently impassioned controversies that continue to swirl about dissociative identity disorder (multiple personality disorder). Those currently writing on both sides of these disputes often appear too caught up in the fervor of the situation to achieve dispassion and objectivity.

To draw a biblical analogy, perhaps the current major contributors to the field and their critics can be understood as a generation that, like Moses, has matured under the oppression of circumstances and events that preclude their ever reaching the promised land of a clearer understanding, and that it will require the rising of a new generation untainted by those circumstances and the controversies that arose from them to allow the completion of this journey.

REFERENCES

Allison, R. B. (1974). A new treatment approach for multiple personalities. *American Journal of Clinical Hypnosis* 17:15–32.

Baron, J., Beattie, J., and Hershey, J. D. (1988). Heuristics and biases in diagnostic reasoning: congruence, information, and certainty. *Organization Behavior and Human Decision Processes* 42:88–110.

Bernstein, E., and Putnam, F. W. (1986). Development, reliability, and validity of a dissociation scale. *Journal of Nervous and Mental Disease* 174:727–735.

Bliss, E. L. (1980). Multiple personalities: a report of 14 cases with implications for schizophrenia and hysteria. *Archives of General Psychiatry* 37:1388–1397.

_____ (1984). Spontaneous self-hypnosis in multiple personality disorder. *Psychiatric Clinics of North America* 7:135–148.

_____ (1986). *Multiple Personality, Allied Disorders, and Hypnosis*. New York: Oxford University Press.

Boon, S., and Draijer, N. (1993). *Multiple Personality Disorder in the Netherlands: A Study on Reliability and Validity of the Diagnosis*. Amsterdam: Swets & Zeitlinger.

Boring, E. (1963). The psychology of controversy. In *History, Psychology, and Science: Selected Papers*. New York: Wiley.

Braun, B. G. (1980). Hypnosis for multiple personalities. In *Clinical Hypnosis in Medicine*, ed. H. Wain, pp. 209–217. Chicago: Year Book Medical.

_____ (1984). Hypnosis creates multiple personality: myth or reality? *International Journal of Clinical and Experimental Hypnosis* 32:191–197.

_____ (1986). *Treatment of Multiple Personality Disorder*. Washington, DC: American Psychiatric Press.

_____ (1989). Iatrophilia and iatrophobia in the diagnosis and treatment of MPD. *Dissociation* 2:66–69.

Breuer, J., and Freud, S. (1955). On the psychical mechanisms of hysterical phenomena: preliminary communication. *Standard Edition* 2:259–333.

Briere, J., and Conte, J. (1993). Self-reported amnesia for abuse in adults molested as children. *Journal of Traumatic Stress* 6:21–31.

Coons, P. M. (1980). Multiple personality: diagnostic considerations. *Journal of Clinical Psychiatry* 41:330–336.

_____ (1984). The differential diagnosis of multiple personality disorder: a comprehensive review. *Psychiatric Clinics of North America* 7:51–67.

_____ (1986). Treatment progress in 20 patients with multiple personality disorder. *Journal of Nervous and Mental Disease* 174:715–721.

_____ (1989). Iatrogenic factors in the misdiagnosis of multiple personality disorder. *Dissociation* 2:70–76.

_____ (1994a). Factitious or malingered multiple personality disorder: eleven cases. *Dissociation* 7.

_____ (1994b). Confirmation of childhood abuse in child and adolescent cases of multiple personality disorder and dissociative disorder not otherwise specified. *Journal of Nervous and Mental Disease* 182:461–464.

Diagnostic and Statistical Manual of Mental Disorders (1980). 3rd ed. Washington, DC: American Psychiatric Association.

_____ (1987). 3rd ed., rev. Washington, DC: American Psychiatric Association.

_____ (1994). 4th ed. Washington, DC: American Psychiatric Association.

Fahy, T. A. (1988). The diagnosis of multiple personality disorder: a critical review. *British Journal of Psychiatry* 153:597–606.

Feldman-Summers, S., and Pope, K. (1994). The experience of "forgetting" childhood abuse: a national survey of psychologists. *Journal of Consulting and Clinical Psychology* 62:636–639.

Festinger, L. (1957). *A Theory of Cognitive Dissonance*. Stanford: Stanford University Press.

Fine, C. G. (1989). Treatment errors and iatrogenesis across therapeutic modalities in MPD and allied dissociative disorders. *Dissociation* 2:77–82.

_____ (1991). Treatment stabilization and crisis prevention: pacing the therapy of the multiple personality disorder patient. *Psychiatric Clinics of North America*, 14:661–675.

_____ (1993). A tactical integrationalist perspective on the treatment of multiple personality disorder. In *Clinical Perspectives on Multiple Personality Disorder*, R. P. Kluft and C. G. Fine, pp.135–153. Washington, DC: American Psychiatric Association.

Fink, D. (1991). The comorbidity of multiple personality disorder and *DSM-III-R* axis II disorders. *Psychiatric Clinics of North America* 14:547–566.

Frankel, F. H. (1992). Adult reconstruction of childhood events in the multiple personality disorder literature. *American Journal of Psychiatry* 150:954–958.

Freud, S. (1962). Charcot. In *The complete psychological works of Sigmund Freud*, vol. 3, ed. and trans. J. Strachey, pp. 7–23. London: Hogarth.

Goodwin, J. (1985). Credibility problems in multiple personality disorder patients and abused children. In *Childhood Antecedents of Multiple Personality*, ed. R. P. Kluft pp. 1–19. Washington, DC: American Psychiatric Press.

Greaves, G. B. (1980). Multiple personality: 165 years after Mary Reynolds. *Journal of Nervous and Mental Disease* 168:577–596.

_____ (1989). Observations on the claim of iatrogenesis in the promulgation of MPD: a discussion. *Dissociation* 2, 99–104.

_____ (1993). A history of multiple personality disorder. In *Clinical Perspectives on Multiple Personality Disorder*, eds. R. P. Kluft and C. G. Fine pp. 355–380. Washington, DC: American Psychiatric Press.

Harriman, P. (1942). The experimental production of some phenomena of multiple personality. *Journal of Abnormal and Social Psychology* 37:244–255.

Herman, J. L. (1992). *Trauma and Recovery*. New York: Basic Books.

Herman, J. L., and Schatzow, E. (1987). Recovery and verification of memories of childhood sexual trauma. *Psychoanalytic Psychology* 4:1–14.

Hilgard, E. R. (1986). *Divided Consciousness: Multiple Controls in Human Thought and Action*. New York: Wiley.

Kampman, R. (1976). Hypnotically induced multiple personality: an experimental study. *International Journal of Clinical and Experimental Hypnosis* 24:215–227.

Kluft, R. P. (1982). Varieties of hypnotic interventions in the treatment of multiple personality. *American Journal of Clinical Hypnosis* 24:230–240.

_____ (1984a). Treatment of multiple personality disorder. *Psychiatric Clinics of North America* 7:9–29.

_____ (1984b). Aspects of the treatment of multiple personality disorder. *Psychiatric Annals* 14:51–55.

_____ (1985a). The natural history of multiple personality disorder. In *Childhood Antecedents of Multiple Personality*, ed. R. P. Kluft, pp. 197–238. Washington, DC: American Psychiatric Press.

_____ (1985b). Making the diagnosis of multiple personality disorder (MPD). In *Directions in Psychiatry*, ed. F. F. Flach, New York: Hatherleigh.

_____ (1986). Personality unification in multiple personality disorder (MPD): a follow-up study. In *Treatment of Multiple Personality Disorder*, ed. B. G. Braun, pp. 29–60. Washington, DC: American Psychiatric Press.

_____ (1987a). An update on multiple personality disorder. *Hospital and Community Psychiatry* 38:363–373.

_____ (1987b). Making the diagnosis of multiple personality disorder. In *Diagnostics and Psychopathology*, ed. F. F. Flach, pp. 207–225. New York: Norton.

_____ (1987c). The simulation and dissimulation of multiple personality disorder. *American Journal of Clinical Hypnosis* 30:104–118.

_____ (1987d). Unsuspected multiple personality disorder: an uncommon source of protracted resistance, interruption, and failure in psychoanalysis. *Hillside Journal of Clinical Psychiatry* 9:100–115.

_____ (1988a). On treating the older patient with multiple personality disorder: "race against time or make haste slowly?" *American Journal of Clinical Hypnosis* 30:257–266.

_____ (1988b). The phenomenology and treatment of extremely complex multiple personality disorder. *Dissociation* 1(4):47–58.

_____ (1988c). On giving consultations to therapists treating MPD: fifteen years' experience - part 1 (diagnosis and treatment). *Dissociation* 1(3):23–29.

_____ (1989a). Iatrogenic creation of new alter personalities. *Dissociation* 2:83–91.

_____ (1989b). Playing for time: temporizing techniques in the treatment of multiple personality disorder. *American Journal of Clinical Hypnosis* 32:90–98.

_____ (1991a). Multiple personality disorder. In *American Psychiatric Press Annual Review of Psychiatry*, vol. 10, ed. A. Tasman and S. M. Goldfinger, pp. 161–188. Washington, DC: American Psychiatric Press.

_____ (1991b). Clinical presentations of multiple personality disorder. *Psychiatric Clinics of North America* 14:605–629.

_____ (1991c). The hospital treatment of multiple personality disorder. *Psychiatric Clinics of North America* 14:695–719.

_____ (1992a). The use of hypnosis with dissociative disorders. *Psychiatric Medicine* 10:31–46.

_____ (1992b). Hypnosis with multiple personality disorder. *American Journal of Preventive Psychiatry and Neurology* 3:19–27.

_____ (1992c). Enhancing the hospital treatment of dissociative disorder patients by developing nursing expertise in the application of hypnotic techniques without formal trance induction. *American Journal of Clinical Hypnosis* 34:158–167.

_____ (1993a). The treatment of dissociative disorder patients: an overview of discoveries, successes, and failures. *Dissociation* 6:87–101.

_____ (1993b). The initial stages of psychotherapy in the treatment of multiple personality disorder patients. *Dissociation* 7:145–161.

_____ (1993c). Basic principles in conducting the psychotherapy of multiple personality disorder. In *Clinical Perspectives on Multiple Personality Disorder*, ed. R. P. Kluft and C. F. Fine, pp. 19–50. Washington, DC: American Psychiatric Press.

_____ (1994). Treatment trajectories in multiple personality disorder. *Dissociation* 7.

_____ (in press). An overview of the treatment of patients alleging that they have suffered ritualized or sadistic abuse. In *The Phenomenon of Ritualized Abuse*, ed. G. A. Fraser. Washington, DC: American Psychiatric Press.

Kooper, C., Classen, C., and Spiegel, D. (1994). Predictors of posttraumatic stress symptoms among survivors of the Oakland/Berkeley firestorm. *American Journal of Psychiatry* 151:888–894.

Kuhn, T. S. (1970). *The Structure of Scientific Revolutions*, 2nd ed. Chicago: University of Chicago Press.

Leavitt, H. C. (1947). A case of hypnotically produced secondary and tertiary personalities. *Psychoanalytic Review* 34:274–295.

Loewenstein, R. J. (1991). An office mental status examination for complex chronic dissociative symptoms and multiple personality disorder. *Psychiatric Clinics of North America* 14:567–604.

_____ (1993). Posttraumatic and dissociative aspects of transference and countertransference in the treatment of multiple personality disorder. In *Clinical Perspectives on Multiple Personality Disorder* ed. R. P. Kluft and C. G. Fine, pp. 511–85. Washington, DC: American Psychiatric Press, 1993.

Loftus, E. (1993). The reality of repressed memories. *American Psychologist* 48:518–537.

Marmer, S. S. (1980). Psychoanalysis of multiple personality. *International Journal of Psychoanalysis* 61:677–693.

McHugh, P. R. (1993). Multiple personality disorder. *The Harvard Mental Health Letter* 10 (3):4–6.

Mersky, H. (1992). The manufacture of personalities: the production of multiple personality disorder. *British Journal of Psychiatry* 160:327–340.

Orne, M. T., and Bates, B. L. (1992). Reflections on multiple personality disorder: a view from the looking glass of hypnosis past. In *Mosaic of Contemporary Psychiatry in Perspective*, ed. A. Kales, pp. 247–260. New York: Springer-Verlag.

Orne, M. T., and Bauer-Marley, M. K. (1991). Disorders of self: myths, metaphors, and the demand characteristics of treatment. In *The Self: Interdisciplinary Approaches*, ed. J. Strauss and G. R. Goethals, pp. 93–106. New York: Springer-Verlag.

Putnam, F. W. (1989). *Diagnosis and Treatment of Multiple Personality Disorder*. New York: Guilford.

Ross, C. A. (1989). *Multiple Personality Disorder: Clinical Phenomenology, Diagnosis, and Treatment*. New York: Wiley.

Ross, C. A. (1994). Debating myself. Paper presented at the Eastern Regional Conference on Abuse and Multiple Personality Disorder, Alexandria, VA., June 10.

Ross, C. A., and Norton, G. R. (1989). Effects of hypnosis on the features of multiple personality disorder. *American Journal of Clinical Hypnosis* 32:99–106.

Ross, C. A., Norton, G. R., and Fraser, G. A. (1989). Evidence against the iatrogenesis of multiple personality disorder. *Dissociation* 22:61–65.

Sargent, W., and Slater, E. (1941). Amnestic syndromes in war. *Proceedings of the Royal Society of Medicine* 34:757–764.

Spanos, N. P., Weekes, J. R., and Bertrand, L. D. (1985). Multiple personality: a social psychological perspective. *Journal of Abnormal Psychology* 94:362–376.

Spanos, N. P., Weekes, J. R., Menary, E., and Bertrand, L. D. Hypnotic interview and age regression in the elicitation of multiple personality symptoms: a simulation study. *Psychiatry* 49:298–311.

Spiegel, D. (1986). Dissociating damage. *American Journal of Clinical Hypnosis* 29:123–131.

_____ (1991). Dissociation and trauma. In *American Psychiatric Press Annual Review of Psychiatry*, vol. 10, ed. A. Tasman and S. Goldfinger, pp. 261–266. Washington, DC: American Psychiatric Press.

Spiegel, H., and Spiegel, D. (1978). *Trance and Treatment*. New York, Basic Books.

Steinberg, M. (1993a). *Clinical Interview for the Diagnosis of DSM-IV Dissociative Disorders*. Washington, DC: American Psychiatric Press.

_____ (1993b). *Interviewer's Guide to the Clinical Interview for the Diagnosis of DSM-IV Dissociative Disorders*. Washington, DC: American Psychiatric Press.

Stengel, E. (1943). Further studies on pathological wandering (fugues with the impulse to wander). *Journal of Mental Health Science* 89:224–241.

Torem, M. (1989). Iatrogenic factors in the perpetuation of splitting and multiplicity. *Dissociation* 2:92–98.

Watkins, J. G., and Watkins, H. H. (1993). Ego-state therapy in the treatment of dissociative disorders. In *Clinical Perspectives on Multiple Personality Disorder* ed. R. P. Kluft and C. G. Fine pp. 277–299. Washington, DC: American Psychiatric Press.

Williams, L. M. (1992). Adult memories of childhood abuse: preliminary findings form a longitudinal study. *The APSAC Advisor* (Summer):19–21.

_____ (1994). Recall of childhood trauma: a prospective study of women's memories of child sexual abuse. *Journal of Consulting and Clinical Psychology*.

Woodruff, R. A., Goodwin, D. W., and Guze, S. (1974). *Psychiatric Diagnosis*. New York: Oxford University Press.

13

Misalliances and Misadventures in the Treatment of Dissociative Disorders

Seth Robert Segall

The psychotherapist who is treating his/her first complex dissociative case is plagued by doubt and uncertainty almost every step of the way. At first the therapist wonders whether the client really has a dissociative disorder, or whether the client is dissembling. The therapist may wonder whether he/she is creating implicit demands for the client to behave as if the client had multiple identities. The therapist may also worry over whether dwelling on dissociative phenomena may perhaps reinforce them. Perhaps the therapist should treat them with benign neglect in the hopes that they will extinguish. The therapist is also perplexed over how to understand the ego states that present themselves: What, really, is an ego state, alter, or "part"? Are these spurious enactments, or do they reflect the deep underlying organization of the client's psyche in a profound way?

If the therapist decides to interact with and attend to these ego states, a new set of dilemmas arises. Should the therapist respect their assertions of individuality, or undermine those assertions? Should child ego states be treated as real children? How should one treat ego states that are belligerent and contentious? Should the therapist work toward integration or internal cooperation? Should the therapist work toward cure or symptom abatement? Should the therapist do "traditional" psychotherapy, or should he/she be doing hypnotherapy, reparenting, deprogramming, or even exorcism?

At some point these ego states may report images and other sensations that are purported to represent traumatic memories. How should the therapist understand the memories of trauma that the client presents? Are these memory-like images and sensations that the client reports veridical or are they fantasies, or some combination of the real and the fantastic? Should the client confront his/her alleged abusers with these memories? Should the therapeutic work with these purported memories focus on blood-and-guts abreactions, or should it focus on correcting cognitive errors and integrating sequestered information? What is an abreaction, anyway, and how does it work? How does a hypnotically induced fusion work?

The therapist is also faced with uncertainties about whether to maintain the same boundaries that he/she does with other clients. The client may present with a multitude of unusual requests, some of which appear perhaps to have face validity. Should these be indulged, or rejected? Who should be in control of the therapy? Should the therapist direct the therapy from an authoritative stance, or is the client capable of self-directing the healing process through some sort of deep unconscious wisdom? Do posttraumatic dissociative clients require a special relationship different from the normative psychotherapeutic relationship in order to heal? How supportive/nurturant should the therapist be, and how confrontive/limit setting should he/she be?

Not only can the therapist be plagued by doubts concerning diagnosis and therapeutic strategy, but the nature of the traumatic material that may be presented can also challenge the therapist on a deeper existential level. The therapist may find himself/herself asking basic questions about the moral structure of the universe: How could such things happen? If there is a God, why does He permit children to be harmed? What are people really like? How can one understand the nature of evil? These existential issues may also involve questions about the moral value of suffering, the value of continued human existence in the face of extreme suffering, and the ability and limitations of the human spirit to transcend suffering and heal the most grievous wounds. Finally, there are almost inevitable metaphysical questions about the nature of consciousness itself: Is it unitary, or is its unity an illusion?

I do not want to suggest that the complex dissociative disorders, including dissociative identity disorder (DID) and its variants, are unique in raising perplexing questions. The treatment of a disorder such as schizophrenia can evoke similar questions in the mind of the thoughtful therapist; for example, is schizophrenia a unitary disorder, several disorders, or a spurious wastebasket category? Is there a role for traditional psychotherapy in the treatment of schizophrenia? What is the role of family psychopathology in the etiology of schizophrenia? How prominent are biological factors in the emergence of these disorders? What is the actual likelihood of recovery, and how can good prognosis be identified early on? In the field of schizophrenia treatment there is a dominant paradigm, which includes both medical and rehabilitative elements, that is accepted by most treating agents (although substantial criticisms of that paradigm exist, e.g., Bentall 1990, Breggin 1991, Karon and VandenBos 1981). The training that most psychotherapists receive during their graduate education prepares them, rightly or wrongly, to accept the existence of schizophrenia as a real entity, to accept theories of at least predominantly biological causation, to treat delusions and hallucinations as symptoms requiring management rather than as meaningful phenomena to be explored, to stress the importance of medications in the treatment, to minimize the use of any uncovering approach to psychotherapy, and so on. While critics of the normative model act as gadflies and prevent premature closure on these issues, most therapists are able to avoid having to make fundamental decisions about treatment by adhering to the dominant paradigm. These same therapists have received little or no training, however, about how to understand, diagnose, or treat the complex dissociative disorders, hence their vulnerability to doubt, uncertainty, vacillation, and sometimes tragic misalliances and misadventures.

There is a remarkable paucity of outcome research in the area of the treatment of the dissociative disorders, and not a single assertion concerning their treatment can be said to have achieved objective near-validation through tolerably well-controlled experimental or quasi-experimental studies. All of the work in this field is still in the prescientific phase; for instance, the most often-cited outcome data in the field are taken from Richard Kluft's (1986) retrospective examination of his own extensive case files. It may be some time before studies are done with multiple therapists comparing multiple methods using systematic measurement and random assignment. Recently, Beutler and Hill (1992) have discussed many of the prominent methodological issues involved in doing this type of outcome research, and Kluft (1993a) has stressed the need for multicenter/ multitherapist prospective outcome studies using standardized measures.

Over two decades ago when May (1971) tried to compare the efficacy of psychotherapy and neuroleptics in the treatment of schizophrenia, he could point to sixteen studies that had tried to address the question. Today, many major mental disorders have treatments that have at least a paucity of outcome research to back them up. One only needs to look at the work that Barlow and his colleagues (Barlow and Cerny 1988) have done in the field of anxiety disorders or that Beck and his colleagues (1979) have done in the field of depression. I mention this because I think it is important to realize how far behind the field of dissociative disorders treatment is, and how far it still has to go before authoritative statements about how to do psychotherapy with this population can be made.

In the face of chronic uncertainty and doubt, in the absence of even moderately well-validated scientific outcome data, and buffeted by powerful transference and countertransference forces in the therapy hour, it is no small wonder that therapists in this area are likely to lose their bearings and drift into error. As it will be some time before one can answer most questions of proper tactics and strategy on a strictly scientific basis, some sort of prescientific normative model of how to conduct these therapies is needed to provide the neophyte therapist with guidelines that will prevent him/her from going too far astray, and to provide future researchers with hypotheses that are worthy of testing. A review of contemporary books and articles on the psychotherapy of dissociative and posttraumatic stress disorders (e.g., Braun 1986, Chu 1988, Courtois 1988, Greaves 1988, Horevitz 1993, Kluft 1993b, Loewenstein 1993, McCann and Perlman 1990, Putnam 1989, Ross 1989) suggests that specialists in the field have been recognizing the problems and limitations inherent in earlier models of understanding dissociation and its treatment, and have been attempting to establish a normative model that could serve as a guide for therapists. These proposed models share many similarities, and at times differ at various crucial points, but there does seem to be an emerging consensus on what constitutes grave error. In fact, many of these points of consensus have been incorporated into a recently issued draft of "Recommendations for Treating Dissociative Identity Disorder" which is under consideration by the Committee on Standards of Practice of the International Society for the Study of Multiple Personality and Dissociation (ISSMP&D 1993). In this article I hope to illuminate the nature of several common pitfalls in the treatment of the dissociative disorders, and propose some simple rules of thumb to help therapists struggling with their first dissociative cases to steer clear of avoidable error.

PITFALL #1: FAILURE TO RETAIN THE TREATMENT FRAME

The primary goal of therapy with the dissociative client is the integration, assimilation, and transformation of information about past traumatic events into ordinary consciousness in a way that allows the client to contemplate such information without self-duplicity or excessive affective distress while permitting the client to develop a less negative self-evaluation. Along the way, work is done to help the client correct cognitive errors about these events and to develop means of regulating the experience of affect so that the client can rely less on dissociative defenses. In addition, the experience of the therapeutic relationship provides the client with a model of a nonexploitative relationship in which the patient is valued as a human being of equal existential worth, and in which boundaries are properly adhered to. This model is radically different from the exploitative relationships in which the traumatic events that disturb many patients occurred. In pathogenic past relationships proper caretaker–child boundaries were not observed, and the client may have served primarily as a need-gratifying object of the exploiter without any concern for the client's existential worth, or readiness or tolerance for certain experiences.

The role of the therapist in this process is primarily to assist the client in the work he/she must do if the goals of therapy are to be achieved. The therapist maintains the treatment frame (cf. Langs 1976, 1982), helps the client to become increasingly aware of his/her habitual avoidances, helps the client to deepen his/her experiencing of him/herself, corrects the client's cognitive errors, helps modulate the rate of self-discovery so that it is not retraumatizing, encourages an internal dialogue that allows for the mutual assimilation/accommodation of contradictory schemas, and supports the client's efforts to experiment with new and less pathological means of controlling and soothing distressing affect and the development of new instrumental behaviors to meet interpersonal goals. Anything that distracts the focus of therapy from these purposes or undermines the role of the therapist in directing therapy toward these goals derails the course of the therapy.

The first goal of the therapist is the maintenance of the therapeutic frame for the simple reason that if the frame is not maintained, none of the other aims will be achieved. Violations of the therapeutic frame usually serve as detours from the tasks of therapy, with therapist and client colluding to avoid the work that needs to be done (e.g., failing to deal with transference and countertransference issues). Every time the therapist allows a lapse in the frame of treatment, he ignores an opportunity to explore the process in the client that has helped to generate that lapse. This often occurs because the therapist feels he must act to fill a need in the client, rather than to reflect on that need, and assist the client in understanding and coping with it. In addition, once the frame has been violated, the sense of safety the client formerly had in the therapeutic relationship may be altered, and the client may no longer feel safe enough to proceed with the difficult work ahead. The therapist who treats dissociative disorders will find that there are many reasons why the client may try to divert the therapist from the therapeutic task, or why the therapist might chose to join with the client in that diversion.

Chief among these reasons is the client's belief that he needs more than the standard therapeutic relationship to improve. A client may believe, for example, that he requires the love and caring he never got from his parents, or that he needs a rescuer of some sort who will play a role in his life outside of the therapist's office. Another client may believe that the horror of his childhood entitles him to special caring and consideration from the therapist as recompense. The problems with such beliefs is that they are based on cognitive errors. The facts are that: 1) the client is now an adult and does not really need a parent, 2) by relying on a rescuer that client never has to develop his own internal resources, and 3) there is no evidence that a friendship with the therapist facilitates the dissolution of the client's internal dissociative barriers. Being parented, rescued, befriended, or beloved are all attempts to feel better without getting well, as opposed to being pathways to getting well.

Dissociative clients will try to stretch the limits and boundaries of the treatment frame in myriad ways, sometimes showing a great deal of ingenuity and resourcefulness in this regard. One way they may try to do this is by encouraging the therapist to lengthen the therapeutic hour. They may, for example, become suddenly productive at the end of the session, producing material that is sure to intrigue the therapist. They may choose the last minute of the session to make a statement about suicidal intent. They may initiate a spontaneous abreaction, or enter a spontaneous trance and become nonresponsive at the end of the session. The therapist cannot let a possibly suicidal client walk out the door, or send a patient out the door while he/she is actively reliving a childhood rape, but, once the immediate problem has been addressed, in the next session the client's wish to prolong the session must be an explicit topic of the therapy hour. The reason for this wish must be understood, and the importance of maintaining boundaries within each hour needs to be reemphasized.

None of this should necessarily be seen, by the way, as a contraindication of a planned longer session, for example, a longer session to do particularly difficult abreactive work. The point is that such deviations should be prompted by the dictates of treatment and not by a need to gratify the client. Even in these instances, however, the unconscious meanings of the planned longer session can complicate the course of therapy.

Another common way of stretching the limits of the therapy hour is through seeking contact with the therapist between therapy sessions, usually by telephone. Emergency or quasi-emergency telephone calls may, if not addressed, become a chronic problem. The therapist needs to address why there are so many crises, and should not assume that the therapy of dissociative disorders is naturally crisis filled, and that he/she should expect that the client will need this amount of time. Perhaps the pacing of a therapy is too rapid and destabilizing and ought to be slowed down. Perhaps the client's social support network is so weak that it would be best not to do uncovering work at the point. Perhaps the client needs an extra session each week that he will pay for. Or perhaps a client is trying to stretch the therapeutic relationship, to find evidence that the therapist cares for her/him more than for other clients, and enact the fantasy that she/he is part of the therapist's life and not just a client. Once again, this should become the topic of the therapeutic dialogue, and not a problem that the therapist colludes with, or reacts angrily against.

Another common area in which the client will try to stretch the relationship is to ask the therapist implicitly or explicitly to be his/her friend. The client may begin calling the therapist by the therapist's first name, or a child ego state may emerge, which asks directly, "Are you my friend?" The child ego state may request that the therapist engage in activities that have nothing to do with a therapeutic task, but which are activities that a friend or parent might engage in with a child. These requests from a child ego state can confuse a therapist who makes the cognitive error of assuming that the child ego state is in some way really a child and must be treated as one would treat a genuine child. The child ego state is not a genuine child who requires parenting, but an aspect of a client in therapy that needs psychotherapy just as much as other aspects of the client do. In other words, the therapist must interact with the child in the same way he/she interacts with the host—by focusing the session on the therapeutic dialogue and maintaining the frame of treatment.

Not all therapists agree with the formulation I have been giving in terms of the value of adhering to limits. Philip Kinsler (1992), for example, has upheld the view that dissociative clients require more of the therapist than do other patients. He states that "the goals of therapy with the severe abuse survivor are different, and *this therapy requires a different degree of engagement and availability* than does a traditional therapy" (p. 168) (Emphasis in the original). Kinsler then goes on to advocate for "availability to clients after 'normal' hours," and "allowing extremely strong attachments to form towards the therapist" (p. 168). He also stated that "virtually every therapist I know who does this kind of work reaches out further in this work than he does in any other. The patients simply require it if we are to really do our jobs" (p. 168).

Richard Kluft requested that a number of well-known therapists respond to Kinsler's article, and these responses (Comstock 1992, Fine 1992,

Olson 1992, Sachs 1992, Torem 1992, and Young 1992) appeared in the same issue of *Dissociation* as Kinsler's article and a rejoinder to their responses by Kinsler. The consensus of the responses was largely negative to Kinsler's views. The respondents essentially saw Kinsler as overemphasizing relationship issues and setting the stage for difficulty in therapy by advocating excessive flexibility in boundaries. This debate is in some degree isomorphic with a long-standing debate within the larger field of psychotherapy in general, namely the relative value of the therapeutic relationship itself, in contrast to the various techniques recommended by disparate schools of psychotherapy.

Irvin Yalom (1989), a leading exponent of the existential approach to psychotherapy, makes a similar case to Kinsler's in his semifictionalized account of the treatment of a DID patient he identifies as "Marge." In thinking through the way he works with traumatized patients today, Yalom notes:

> When I first began to work as a therapist, I naively believed that the past was fixed and knowable; that if I were perspicacious enough, I could discover that first false turn . . . and that I could act on this discovery to set things right again. In those days I would have deepened Marge's hypnotic state, regressed her in age, asked her to explore early traumas—for example, her father's sexual abuse—and urged her to experience and discharge all the attendant feelings, the fear, the arousal, the rage, the betrayal. But over the years I've learned that the therapist's venture is not to engage the patient in a joint archeological dig. If any patients have ever been helped in this fashion, it wasn't because of the search. . . . No, a therapist helps a patient not by sifting though the past but by being lovingly present with that person; by being trustworthy, interested; and by believing that their joint activity will ultimately be redemptive and healing. The drama of age regression and incest recapitulation . . . is healing only because it provides therapist and patient with some shared interesting activity while the real therapeutic force—the relationship—is ripening on the tree. [p. 227]

Yalom's implicit recommendations as to the therapist's role are the polar opposite of Langs's (1976) admonitions to maintain the treatment frame and technical neutrality. Rather than being a technician who cures through the proper application of a method, Yalom uses his own person in forming a real relationship with the client as a way of nurturing and expanding the client's mode of being-with and being-in-the-world. A reading of the case history of Marge indicates a willingness to take late night telephone calls and answer personal questions about himself. Far from being deviations from the therapist's role of interpreter, these fully characterize what Yalom believes to be helpful. His patient's ability to ask personal questions is seen as a sign of her personal growth rather than a means of avoiding the work of therapy or stretching a therapeutic boundary. When Marge asks him, "How did you decide to get into this field? Have you ever regretted it? Do you ever get bored? With me? What do you do with your problems?" Yalom decided it was important to "be receptive and respectful of each of her questions" and to answer "each one as fully and honestly as possible" It was a sign of Marge's growth that she began to treat Yalom as an equal and flirt with him a bit: "When we finish, how will you get along without me? I'm sure you'll miss my little late-night calls" (p. 228).

As is usually the case with these acrimonious debates within psychology (e.g., nature vs. nurture, phenomenology vs. behaviorism), the best solution involves an integration of these opposing positions through some type of Hegelian dialectic. Truth rarely resides within one extreme, and I would think there is variance in a successful psychotherapy that can be parceled out to the therapist–client relationship, and variance as well that can be attributed to specific techniques used in the right place and time.

My own view is that the dissociative client does require a certain type of relationship with the therapist, but that relationship does not differ from the kind of relationship that every client requires. That relationship is the therapist–client relationship and not a parent–child relationship, a protector–ward relationship, a friendship relationship, or an erotic relationship. It is not a special relationship in the sense that it is different from the special relationship that every therapy entails. That relationship is one of caring enough about the client in the sense that the therapist wishes the client well and hopes he/she can be of benefit to the client. That relationship is one of respect for the client as a person, respect for the client's defenses, and respect for the client's own capacity for growth, change, and healing. It means the therapist's commitment to listen genuinely to the client and to understand what the client has to say on both overt and covert levels. It means that the therapist will make trial identifications with the client to try to get the feel of the client's experiential world. It means that the therapist will try not to use the client to get his/her own needs gratified, and will try not to be exploitative or manipulative, or involve the client in a dual relationship. It means that the therapist will not gratify the client's attempts to reestablish pathological past relationships. It means that the therapist is committed at the deepest level to making the therapy a success, and that part of doing this is safeguarding the frame of therapy to make sure that therapy progresses and that serious misalliances and misadventures do not occur. It means the therapist will not try to mollify his/her own anxieties and be a nice guy in order to avoid dealing with aspects of the negative transference. As Walter Young (1992) puts it so aptly, massive overinvestments in caring for the patient reflect these therapists' confusion about what really might help in terms of encouraging a patient's personal growth and sense of mastery through encouraging independent behaviors in other instances. We may mistake gratification for a mode of therapy instead of a countertransference enactment when we, as therapists, feel overwhelmed, accept a patient's burden in treatment as our own, and feel impotent to help in more clearly defined ways that might also lead to our patient's healing and trust. What a patient needs and what a patient wants are often different things, a fact that is not always recognized by patients, and may not be appreciated by naive therapists. [p. 172]

Kinsler (1992), in believing that dissociative clients require a relationship different from that with other clients, is colluding with the client's erroneous view of what is wrong, namely that the client is too weak and helpless to do the work of therapy without a therapist's apparently limitless giving and caring. If a therapist accepts this premise, a prosthetic relationship develops in which the therapist fills in the lacunae that exist within the patient; this relationship substitutes for getting well rather than facilitating it. Instead of assuming that the client needs a special relationship to tolerate the therapeutic work, the therapist might be better off examining whether his/her approach to treatment may be overwhelming the client, and whether he/she needs to adopt a new therapeutic strategy that the client can tolerate without requiring that the therapist play a role that evokes greater dependency. In addition, the client's unrealistic expectations of the therapist need to be made explicit and empathically explored, rather than responded to in the sphere of action.

Flagrant violations of therapeutic boundaries are readily apparent in the literature, and sometimes touted as positive prescriptions for how to do treatment. A good example of this is the late Lynn Wilson's (Casey and Wilson 1991) successful reparenting therapy of Joan Casey described in *The Flock*. In that book the client tells the therapist, "If you spend some time with me outside of the office I think I would know that you care about me in a real, nonprofessional way. You've been trying to convince me for a year that I should have more of a sense of my worth, but how can I believe people could really want to be with me if you aren't?" (p. 92). The therapist seems convinced that it is an important therapeutic goal to prove to Ms. Casey that she does care about her in a more than professional way. She allows the client to visit her at her home, and visits the client at hers. When she is anxious about the client's condition, she goes to the client's home and spends hours with her. Therapy sessions regularly run overtime. The therapist spends time cuddling the client's child ego states, feeling that she is providing them with maternal love. The therapist involves her husband in the client's treatment. Eventually, both the therapist and her husband begin to think of the client as family, and the therapist tells the client that she loves her like a daughter. The client is keenly aware of this change from psychotherapy to reparenting and writes: "Being a family with Gordon and Lynn [the therapist and her husband] was different from being in therapy" (p. 180). The therapists also take the client with them on trips to their cottage on weekends to do more intensive work.

The fact that this was, in the end, a successful treatment is a testament to many factors, including the fact that this client's wish to be independent was relatively stronger than her dependency strivings; that the relative strength of the more prosocial aspects of her character was greater than the borderline or antisocial aspects of her character; that the therapist was able to give up her time, energy, and privacy without feeling resentful and angry about being drained; that the therapist's need to give and nurture was not overly contaminated by masochistic needs, or needs to control or exploit; that the therapist's family was not resentful of the loss of her time or their privacy and was willing to accommodate an extra member; that the therapist did not become inordinately jealous of the client's flirtatious behavior toward her husband; that the therapist's agency did not become upset by her devoting too much time to one part of her caseload without, one assumes, commensurate financial recompense; and so on. One can easily imagine, however, a very different and less happy ending to this type of therapy. The treatment frame exists not only, or even primarily, to protect the therapist from being overwhelmed by client demands, but also to prevent the treatment from being harmed by the nontherapeutic motives of the therapist.

The recent newspaper accounts of the suicide of Harvard medical student Paul Lozano one month after his termination of therapy with Dr. Margaret Bean-Bayog (Butterfield 1992a,b,c, Butterfield and Mydans 1992) provides a good example of how easily a well-intentioned reparenting therapy can become a fatal misadventure. While these newspaper accounts contain allegations, counterallegations, and conjectures of uncertain validity, several elements seem reasonably clear. It would appear that Dr. Bean-Bayog viewed Mr. Lozano, correctly or incorrectly, as a survivor of childhood trauma, and one informant to the newspaper reported that at some point after the termination of Dr. Bean-Bayog's treatment he presented with a child ego state: "His voice would change, it was like he was speaking like a 6-year old. . . . He even walked like a little boy" (Butterfield 1992a, p. 14). "He started clinging to his stuffed animal and he started talking to me in his infantile voice" (Butterfield and Mydans 1992, p. 38). Dr. Bean-Bayog, after trying a more conventional approach with Mr. Lozano, decided that conventional psychotherapy had failed and decided to "put herself in the role of 'a benevolent mother who would not abuse him,' giving him a stuffed bear, children's books, and flashcards with messages directing him to think of her as his mother" (Butterfield and Mydans 1992, p. 38). The flashcards would contain statements, arrived at in conjunction with the client, such as "I'm your mom and I love you and you love me very, very much" (p. 38). At some point in the therapy, Dr. Bean-Bayog became aware that the treatment was not going well, and while the patient was hospitalized she terminated treatment with him. About one month later he committed suicide by a lethal injection of cocaine. Shortly before his death he reportedly told a nurse in his hometown that he "missed Margaret" (p. 38). He then told her that he was hearing his former psychiatrist's voice and that the voice was telling him to kill himself. There are a variety of other complications to this tangled and convoluted tale, which I have omitted for the sake of brevity, including unproved allegations of sexual involvement between the client and his therapist. In the wake of the suicide, the family brought a malpractice suit against Dr. Bean-Bayog, which was settled for one million dollars. Dr. Bean-Bayog was also placed on leave from her appointment with the Harvard Medical School, and the Massachusetts Board of Registration in Medicine accused her of treatment that did "not conform to accepted standards of medical practice" (Butterfield 1992b, p. 16). Rather than defend herself against the board and endure what she thought would be a "media circus" at a public hearing, Dr. Bean-Bayog relinquished her license to practice medicine. Prior to this case, Dr. Bean-Bayog had a twenty-year reputation as a highly regarded specialist in alcohol addiction. The case stands as a clear warning of the dangers involved in departing from established standards in the area of maintaining the frame of treatment both to client and to therapist.

It would be comforting to be able to state that serious boundary violations in the therapy of trauma survivors and dissociative clients are quite rare, but this is not the case. Kluft (1990a), for example, has documented twelve case histories in which incest victims were sexually revictimized by their psychotherapists. The phenomenon of sexual revictimization of sexual-abuse survivors was common enough for Kluft to give it a name: *sitting duck syndrome*. It would appear that the potential for sexual-abuse surviving clients to establish new relationships with therapists that replicate the pathological relationships of childhood is reasonably strong. Therapists must therefore scrutinize every request to vary the treatment frame with this in mind, and the cautious therapist will maintain a clear treatment frame and clear boundaries.

The main problem with the therapy conducted in *The Flock* is not that any harm was done to the client, or that the therapist behaved in an unprofessional way. The therapist had, after all, obtained consultation and support from the late Connie Wilbur, the historic pioneer in the field of dissociative disorders, who had engaged in similar (although less dramatic) boundary violations, which were depicted in *Sybil* (Schreiber 1973). Also, the therapy described in *The Flock* was begun in 1981 before much of the current clinical lore about appropriate therapy for dissociative clients had been developed or disseminated. The main problem is rather with the underlying premise of the therapy: that in order to get well the client needs to know that you care for him/her in a way that goes beyond the bounds of normal professional caring. What kind of therapy, for example, would Lynn Wilson have provided for a patient who was less lovable and appealing than Joan Casey? Ms. Casey presents herself, and is represented, as an exceptionally bright, thoughtful, attractive, articulate, and appealing person. A generous and gifted therapist may be able to take such a patient into the bosom of his/her family under special once-in-a-lifetime circumstances, but what does one do with dissociative clients who are less attractive, not very intelligent, and who have ego states that are predominantly borderline, narcissistic, and/or antisocial? Can a therapist love such a patient like a son or daughter? Can a therapist consistently maintain such love as the client proceeds to wreak havoc with the therapist's private and personal life? If the answer to either of these questions is no, does that mean the client cannot be successfully treated? Fortunately, those therapists who pay considerable attention to the therapeutic frame also report positive therapeutic outcomes, so that there is no reason to believe that loving a patient into health is the only route to recovery. In fact, some might argue that giving someone love in return for money is the hallmark of another profession, not the hallmark of psychotherapy.

Indeed, if the client receives the special caring he seeks from the therapist, it does not at all follow that the client will therefore internalize the loving therapist as a benevolent introject, and come to the realization that he himself is, in essence, lovable. On the contrary, it is more likely the client will become dependent on that special caring as a source of his well-being, and will do all he can to ensure that it is genuine, boundless, and eternal. The client may then be motivated to undertake investigations to see that the therapist loves him even if he does not pay for his sessions, or that the therapist will love him at all hours of the day and night, and love him better than all of his other clients. Perhaps the client will need to engage in endless manipulations to make sure that he will not lose the therapist's love and interest. Perhaps he will also need to suppress negative transference feelings to prevent such a potential loss.

In her afterword to the book, Frances Howland (Casey and Wilson 1991) asserts that the Wilsons' treatment of Joan Casey was "ideal," and goes on to state that "anything less than six hours per week [of therapeutic contact] is difficult for both patient and therapist" (p. 302). I would agree with Dr. Howland that a frequency of more than once a week over an extended period of time is desirable (although I find her "at least six hours" excessive), but if this frequency of contact were necessary for cure, only the wealthiest DID clients could be cured. Very few clients can afford this kind of treatment, very few third-party payers would allow it, and very few therapists could afford to see clients for reduced rates at such frequencies. It is my impression, however, that most DID clients are seen at frequencies less intense than six hours a week and, fortunately, still make good progress toward cure. Colin Ross (1989) has written, for example, that "I rarely see an outpatient more than twice a week" (p. 211). Putnam and Loewenstein's (1993) survey of 305 clinicians found that the average DID patient was seen twice weekly. The recent proposed ISSMP&D (1993) draft recommendations on DID treatment also suggest that the "usual frequency for therapy is one or two sessions per week" (p. 15). In my own practice I see mostly blue-collar clients, many of whom have managed-care type health coverage. Clients are most often seen on a once or twice a week basis, although they may be seen more frequently during periods of crisis or for certain abreactive work. There are even clients I am seeing on a once every other week basis because of their limited income and circumscribed health-care benefits. While I do not recommend this sparse frequency, and believe that treatment is taking place under adverse circumstances, I do believe that with the right client and with proper attention to not overwhelming defensive structure and proper pacing, this kind of treatment can be done. In a similar vein, Richard Kluft (1992) tells of a client he sees once monthly who is making progress in treatment, which I suspect is probably a record of sorts.

Several authors who have written on the topic of errors in the psychotherapy of dissociative disorders and who advocate strict maintenance of the treatment frame (e.g., Chu 1988, Greaves 1988, Kluft 1993a, Torem 1992) have approvingly cited the work of Langs (1976, 1982) as a basic reference. None of these authors has discussed some of the problems inherent in applying Langs's approach directly to the treatment of dissociative disorders, however. Langs believes in the strictest adherence to both therapist neutrality and to a frame of treatment in which the therapist's role is essentially restricted to the interpretation of unconscious derivatives in the client's free association. It is a treatment frame that is perhaps appropriate to a certain school of psychoanalytic psychotherapy, but which may be inappropriate to other types of therapy including hypnotherapy, cognitive therapy, behavior therapy, humanistic psychotherapy, existential psychotherapy, and a whole variety of other therapies. For better or for worse, it certainly is not the way that most therapists work with their DID clients. Most therapists in the field support a therapeutic model in which the therapist is both warmer and more active (e.g., Kluft 1993b) rather than being neutral and passive, and in which the therapist may play a variety of roles other than interpreter of unconscious derivatives. The therapist may, for example, do some instructing of the client around the client's role in therapy, may engage the client in cognitive disputation, may write a therapeutic contract, may induce a hypnotic trance, and may suggest the client experiment with new behaviors ranging from journal writing to trying some types of internal compromises. All of these behaviors would be serious violations of the treatment frame in Langs's conception of the conduct of psychotherapy. What Langs does say that is universal to all therapies, however, is that the frame of therapy must be consonant with the aims of the type of therapy one is doing, and that all interventions must be carefully scrutinized in terms of whether they maintain or violate that frame. Whenever one feels motivated to violate that frame, countertransference motives need to be analyzed and consultation ought to be obtained.

PITFALL #2: FAILURE TO RESPECT DEFENSES

One way to understand complex dissociative disorders is to see them as defensive systems that initially arose to preserve and protect the developing child from overwhelming sensations, emotions, and intolerable conflict, thereby enabling the developing child to survive in a relatively enduring no-win, double-binding environment. These are essentially disorders of "double bookkeeping" in which the client both knows and does not know something simultaneously. The hallmark of these disorders are amnesias for traumatic events or aspects of those events in the ego state(s) which most often occupy the social interface.

As stated in the previous section, I believe the primary goal of therapy with dissociative clients is "the integration, assimilation, and transformation of information about past traumatic events," but therapists sometimes ignore the admonition that this be done "in a way that allows the client to contemplate such information without . . . excessive affective distress." Therapists often have their own needs for therapy to be stimulating and interesting, to experience themselves as potent and effective, and, often enough, to have their own voyeuristic wishes gratified. For some therapists, the most gratifying therapy sessions can be those in which the client is in touch with powerful feelings that were formally dissociated and when the therapist believes that "now we are really getting to the bottom of things." While the literature warns of clients becoming addicted to abreactions, a similar danger exists for the therapist. While in the previous section I mentioned the danger of therapists colluding with clients to avoid painful emotional states, in this section I wish to discuss the danger of the therapist's overeagerness to breach resistance and defenses. The therapist's wishes to push ahead and work harder and faster than the client can tolerate are often as destructive, if not more destructive, than the therapist's failure to maintain the treatment frame. Indeed they show a similar disrespect for the client's tolerance for disturbing affective states as the original abuser of the client, and a parallel placing of an authority figure's needs above the needs of the vulnerable and dependent client's. In the instance of the original abuse, the abuser too may have had the mistaken belief that what he was doing was in the client's own interest.

The point cannot be made clearly enough: *it is not the therapist's job to tear down dissociative barriers*. The client will allow them to dissolve if and when they are no longer required. The process of making those barriers unnecessary is a lengthy and painstaking one, and it occurs only if certain conditions are met: (1) if the client is currently out of the abusive situation that necessitated the dissociation, (2) if the life-space the client occupies is sufficiently stable and supportive so that no concurrent crises are impinging on the therapy, (3) if the therapy hour is established as a safe and secure place, (4) if the therapist can be sufficiently trusted to place the integrity of the therapeutic dialogue above his/her own nontherapeutic wishes for gratification of his desire to be powerful or loved, and (5) if the therapist is able to listen to what the client has to say, both in its overt and covert meanings. If these conditions are met, the client will tell the therapist everything that must be known in its own due time. The process of therapy will unfold by itself. The therapist need do nothing to extract or pull out information, or tear down or remove barriers. The client will continue to tell as long as he/she is heard and not manipulated, as long as the therapist does not collude with the client to avoid issues that make the therapist uncomfortable, and as long as the affect associated with the telling is tolerable for the client and does not overtax his/her coping resources. As the client says more, there is a gradual process of desensitization to the affective components of his/her story that enables the client gradually to go further, as long as there are no untoward events within the therapy. It is the therapist's job to see that untoward therapeutic events are kept to a minimum.

As a matter of fact, far from needing to hurry the client up and extract information, it is the therapist's job to slow the client down and make sure that traumatic material enters consciousness at a tolerable pace. Clients will often try to uncover material on their own between sessions with an obsessive intensity, and ask the therapist's assistance in tearing down internal barriers, with the thought that the sooner they get to traumatic material, the faster they will get better. The truth is just the reverse: tearing down barriers results in relapses, therapeutic drop-outs, suicidal crises, and the reemergence of borderline-type impulsive behavior as a means of controlling intrusive unpleasant affects. Hence, the famous dictum attributed to Richard Kluft that "the slower you go, the faster you get there" (Goodwin and Attias 1993, p. 7).

There are myriad ways in which the therapist can slow things down. The therapist may suggest that protective forces within the client will continue to be protective and not allow troublesome material to emerge too quickly. The therapist may ally with defensive ego states, indicate how much he/she values the role they play, and urge them not to give up their function unless and until they are truly convinced that the time is right. The therapist may also utilize a variety of hypnotic techniques that emphasize containment, fractionation, distancing, grounding, "safe place," time distortion, and attenuation/modulation of affect to make the pacing of therapy more tolerable (Brown and Fromm 1986; Fine 1991; Kluft 1989, 1990b, Sachs 1993; Turin 1991). These techniques enable the client to develop a sense of mastery over intrusive affective states, and enhance the ego's ability to tolerate and manage affects without feeling overwhelmed. This experience of agency, efficacy, being in control, and mastering affect is precisely what was missing in the original traumatic event(s) that were experienced by the client as an imposition from outside the ego, and involved an intensity of unpleasant affect that the ego was unable to contain, attenuate, or tolerate. Recovery involves the growth and strengthening of ego-functions, and not the passive reexperiencing of that which the ego is not yet strong enough to endure. Similarly, therapy should emphasize growth, mastery, and autonomy in the present, and is not simply, or even primarily, an historical excavation.

The debate over the relative importance of ego-enhancing versus uncovering aspects of the treatment of dissociative disorders is played out in a variety of ways in the literature. Nowhere is this more prominent than in the debate over the role of emotional catharsis in what has been called the abreactive process. Some writers in the field stress the crucial role of a cathartic abreaction of affect in the treatment of posttraumatic disorders. John G. Watkins (1992), for example, writes:

> One either starts an abreaction or one does not. There is no half-way. When the decision is made to do it, go into it with all the feeling possible. Don't get part-way into the release of affect and then decide it is too violent. This usually means the therapist can't take it. Once you open up the patient's

bound affect you must continue until it has been fully released. A good surgeon does not open up his patient and then decide that he/she is not prepared to cope with what he/she finds there. [p. 56]

In contrast, Catherine Fine's (1991) recommendations on how to perform an abreaction differ dramatically from Watkins's suggestions. Whereas Fine advocates a role for catharsis, her approach emphasizes a greater degree of ego-involvement, self-control, and titration of affect:

A second precautionary technique to dilute affect and decrease the negative impact of abreactive work is to do frequent "fractionated" abreactions rather than full abreactions. . . . The fractionated abreaction involves achieving this goal in small increments. Rather than doing one complete abreaction in one (extended) or several therapy sessions, the feelings are slowly reconnected to discrete aspects of the history with cognitive restructuring throughout. This process parallels using systematic desensitization to achieve mastery over a phobic stimulus rather than flooding procedures. [p. 672]

In yet a third approach to the question of abreaction and catharsis, van der Hart and Brown (1992) have reexamined the entire concept of abreaction, and questioned to what degree emotional catharsis plays an important role in memory work. They deemphasize the role of affective expression and instead emphasize the cognitive, structural, and integrative aspects of treatment: "While controlled re-experiencing of the trauma appears to be an essential part of almost every treatment approach, the goal has become more the facilitation of the gradual processing of all relevant aspects of the traumatic experience, and the re-integration of previously dissociated aspects of the personality" (p. 137). Their argument has been strongly influenced by Brown and Fromm's (1986) suggestions regarding the treatment of PTSD. Brown and Fromm comment that abreaction is based on an outdated hydraulic model of affect. They state that

although hypnotic abreaction may be of limited use in certain cases of acute stress symptoms, we do not recommend this treatment; in particular, we do not recommend that the therapist intentionally encourage dramatic emotional expression. . . . Since most PTSD patients fear loss of control, the therapist's encouragement of emotional displays merely intensifies the fear and does not facilitate the working through of trauma. In the transference, the therapist is seen as trying to retraumatize or otherwise inflict pain on the patient. The prevalence of negative therapeutic reactions is extremely high in abreactive hypnotherapy of PTSD. [p. 273]

The debate over the relative role of a complete emotional catharsis as opposed to the cognitive/integrative function of abreactive work is far from over, and is, again, a question that can only be resolved empirically by future research. There does seem to be a general movement within the field of trauma-oriented therapy, however, toward a greater respect for defensive processes, and an enhanced emphasis on cognitive processing and affective control.

PITFALL #3: PLAYING FAVORITES

In a fictionalized account of a real psychotherapy, Yalom (1989) described his decision essentially to suppress a dissociated ego state in a patient with DID due to his principled adherence to *therapeutic monogamy*. In his account, Yalom identified the host personality as "Marge" and the encroaching ego-state as "Me": "I had promised myself to Marge. If I consorted with 'Me' it would be catastrophic for Marge. . . . So I stayed faithful and when I sensed 'Me' approaching—for example, when Marge closed her eyes and began to enter a trance—I was quick to jar her awake by shouting 'Marge, come back!' " (pp. 225–226). In a similar vein, Middlebrook (1991) has described Martin Orne's psychotherapy of Pulitzer Prize-winning poetess Anne Sexton. During her therapy sessions Ms. Sexton began to manifest an ego state named Elizabeth at around the same time that she began to report a "memory or fantasy" about an incestuous experience with her father. Elizabeth asked to be put under hypnosis, stating, "If you give her time to get dissociated enough she will be willing. . . . I know a lot" (pp. 55–56). Dr. Orne thought that Ms. Sexton's desire to personify certain of her personality traits was a dangerous tendency, however. Middlebrook notes that "discussing Elizabeth later, he commented that after a brief initial interest in this manifestation, he observed that Sexton was dangerously close to developing multiple personality disorder, so he disengaged himself from acknowledging Elizabeth as a person distinct from Anne" (p. 60). Middlebrook then quotes Orne as saying: "Once my interest dropped, so did hers, and no doctor ever saw Elizabeth again" (p. 61).

Both Yalom and Orne make principled arguments for dealing directly only with the initially presenting ego state. Orne is fearful that interacting with a split-off ego state will increase the degree of dissociation, whereas Yalom is fearful of the depleted presenting ego state feeling neglected if he attends to a far more interesting and vivacious newly emergent ego state. Both represent examples of a policy of alliance with one ego state, as opposed to a policy of forming alliances with as many ego states as possible. Yalom and Orne provide an answer to the question "Who is the client?" by positing that the presenting ego state is the client. This solution is analogous to a family therapist deciding that the "identified patient" is his client, and that other family members are only in therapy to help the client get well.

Other therapists have recommended an even-handed policy in interacting with ego states, however. Frank Putnam (1989) has written that "every alter must be treated as an equal. Every personality was created for a reason and with a purpose. To selectively encourage some and ignore or suppress others is to ask for trouble" (p. 162). Similarly, Richard Kluft (1993b) has written: "The therapist must be even-handed to all of the alters and must avoid 'playing favorites' " (p. 37). Indeed the idea of not forming exclusive alliances with any one ego state against another is implied, if not overtly stated, in every normative model of the psychotherapy of DID written by someone who has claimed to be a specialist in the field. This is not terribly different from the therapeutic principle often espoused in the therapy of nondissociative clients, namely that one should not take sides with one polarity or another of a client's ambivalence. In this solution, the presenting ego state is not the client, but the whole system of ego states is seen as the client, much as a family therapist sees an entire family system, rather than an identified patient, as the client in a family therapy.

Parenthetically, it seems important to state that the idea of working with enacted or personified representations of ego states is not at all unique to the psychotherapy of DID. For example, one need only think of Moreno's (1946) psychodramatic techniques, Perls's enactments of polarities (Polster and Polster 1973) using the "two-chair technique," or Federn's (1952) theory of ego-states, which is reflected both in Berne's (1961) transactional analysis and Watkins's (1992) ego state therapy. John Rowan (1990) has done a fascinating job of summarizing and analyzing the role that the theoretical construct of ego state has played in the history of psychology and psychotherapy, and has pointed out parallels in the work of Freud and Jung, as well as in the work of Roberto Assagioli (1975), Alvin Mahrer (1978), and others.

The presenting ego state will often express fear of loss of control and even fear of nonbeing if the therapist establishes rapport with other ego states. While that fear needs to be taken seriously and not cavalierly disregarded, it cannot be the determining factor in the choice of therapeutic goals. The therapist cannot and should not go ahead with contacting other ego states without the presenting ego state's permission, but an educational project needs to be undertaken to help allay the presenting ego state's fears, and help it to understand why opening a dialogue with other parts of the system is really in the presenting ego state's own best interest. If permission is never given, then the time and situation are not right to begin this type of therapy. Usually, if therapy is being well conducted, and if the client's life situation is sufficiently stable/supportive to begin this type of work, permission will eventually be forthcoming.

An inappropriate alliance with the presenting ego state is not the only or even the most common type of therapist/ego state misalliance in the treatment of DID. Some ego states are simply easier to ally with than others. Dependent, compliant, pacific, or vulnerable ego states, and those that share the therapist's overall view of the therapeutic process, are easier to deal with than counterdependent, resistant, grandiose, paranoid, narcissistic, borderline, antisocial, sadistic, suicidal, or histrionic ego states. These ego states are enactments of a variety of defensive operations that have historically helped to keep the client from being overwhelmed by painful affect. These include identifications with the aggressor, grandiose feelings of omnipotence, the use of one's sexuality to gain a sense of being valued or powerful, the use of self-inflicted pain to distract oneself from feelings associated with being victimized and abused, the need to be hyperalert and suspicious, and the knowledge that one has ultimate control over the degree of pain one feels by having ultimate control over whether one lives or dies. In order to work more effectively with these ego states, the therapist needs to get over seeing them as a nuisance and come to view them with the degree of respect they deserve for having successfully helped the client cope with his/her burden of pain through the years.

The therapeutic process is almost certain to be derailed if the therapist chooses to ally against these more difficult ego states, or chooses to put off dealing with them. Therapists sometimes wish to take a battering ram and obliterate these defenses in order to get to the split-off information (images, affects, ideas, sensations) that is hidden behind them. This is just another variation on the failure to respect defenses that was discussed in the previous section. One must remember that in any psychotherapy, dealing successfully with resistances must precede the exploration of conflictual material. Just as one should not breach these defensive ego states, one should also not ignore them, because if one spends all one's time with more tractable states and never works with the more difficult ones, one will never get to the more truly traumatic and troublesome material, which the more difficult states serve to contain.

Ego states that resist the integration of dissociated content, whether they take the form of guardians, walls, big brothers, or demonic figures, must be respected, and the therapist must succeed in making an alliance with them. Their concerns and fears must be taken seriously by the therapist. The therapist can often cement an alliance with them by prescribing the symptom, in other words, urging them to watch carefully and scrutinize the therapist for signs that he/she may be just another abuser, a reckless incompetent, or a bull in a china shop. These protective states have their own woes, and need the assistance of the therapist just as much as the more amiable parts of the system. Indeed, it becomes much easier for the therapist to ally with and identify with these ego states if he/she can focus on the knowledge that these protective ego states are really hurt or frightened child ego states that are wearing scary costumes to ward off further harm.

It is even more difficult to deal with ego states that represent the impulsive, abusive, or self-destructive aspects of the self-system. When an ego state threatens suicide or homicide, the client and third parties need protection from their behavior, and yet the therapist still needs to find a point of alliance with these states. Therapeutic failure is almost certainly guaranteed if the therapist tries to deal with them by killing them, banishing them, imprisoning them, or exorcising them. After all, they are not really corporeal entities, and cannot really be expelled or killed. They are schemas, however, which can both assimilate and accommodate to new information from outside the system, and to information encapsulated in other schemas that they begin to interact with. The therapist may suggest that he/she knows better ways for the destructive ego state to accomplish the ends they both agree are desirable. The therapist may suggest substitute activities for the ego state to experiment with. The therapist may give the ego state specific tasks to carry out within the system that entail an elevated status, but that are prosocial within the system. (For example, self-abusive ego states, which exist to create physical pain to distract the client from psychic pain, can be given the job of pain-monitors who inform the therapist when psychic pain is becoming too intolerable.) At the same time, however, the therapist must be blunt: the overall system is responsible for controlling destructive behavior; and other ego states must make sure that the destructive behavior does not get acted out, or the therapist will have to ensure the client's safety by exerting external controls. The process of reaching these internal compromises and helping the system to control its excesses is not at all magical, but is simply a process of negotiation and contracting, which starts with the therapist's respect for, and ability to ally with, all the interested parties. A therapist who has established his/her untrustworthiness by allying with one ego state against another cannot be a successful negotiator, just as a biased mediator can never successfully conclude a labor contract negotiation.

Some normative models of the treatment of dissociative disorders stress the establishment of therapist–client trust as one of the first orders of business (cf. Braun 1986). In reality, the self-system of dissociative clients can never develop the kind of trust that nontraumatized clients can until the therapy is very nearly almost complete. There is no trust phase that is completed early on in the treatment so that one can move on to another phase. At any given moment in the therapy trust is always in the process of either waxing or waning. All of the pitfalls elaborated in this article have an effect on the degree of trust the client can experience toward the therapist. A therapist who violates boundaries loses trust, just as a therapist who fails to respect defenses loses trust. Therapy then begins to feel like an unsafe place. The same is true with the issue of the rejection of an ego state by the therapist. Clients live with the fear that they are, in the last analysis, unlovable and undeserving. When therapists fail to respect an ego state, they are rejecting a secret but valued part of the person, one that is hidden from the rest of the world, and that rejection is a narcissistic wound that reinforces the client's worst fears. It strengthens the core assumption that only the facade of the presenting ego state is socially acceptable, and that the client has been correct all along to hide all these other personality potentials. It also lets the client know that he/she must be on guard with this therapist to prevent future feelings of rejection.

Sometimes therapists may ally with a particular ego state because the relationship with that ego state is gratifying for the therapist. Adults who were chronically abused as children know how to accommodate themselves to meet a caregiver's wishes in order to keep safe. They can easily turn therapy into a situation where the client keeps the therapist happy in order to keep the therapist from being angry with them, hurting them, or abandoning them. They can inflate the therapist's ego by making the therapist feel wise, kindly, and protective. They can be charming and fascinating. They can use their sexuality as a way to keep the therapist's interest. They can fabricate information by telling the therapist what they think the therapist wants to hear. They can also remain sick so as to keep the therapist at their beck and call. If the therapist allies with one of these accommodating ego states, both therapist and client will feel good about the "work" that is being done, but no work will actually get done.

Sometimes therapists may ally with an ego state because they hope for a magic way to resolve their uncertainties and insecurities. The client may present, for example, with an ego state that claims to be an internal guide, spirit guide, or internal self-helper who is omniscient and benevolent. These higher selves often seem disconcertingly similar to the ego states William James (1890) noted in his observations on the spirit guide in mediumships and possession states:

> If he ventures on higher intellectual flights, he abounds in a curiously vague optimistic philosophy-and-water, in which phrases about spirit, harmony, beauty, law, progression, development, etc., keep recurring. It seems exactly as if one author composed more than half of these trance messages, no matter

by whom they are uttered. Whether all sub-conscious selves are particularly susceptible to a certain stratum of the zeitgeist and get their inspiration from it, I know not; but this is obviously the case with the secondary selves which become 'developed' in spiritualist circles. [p. 394]

While the spiritualists and theosophists who influenced the mediums of James's age are no longer around, one does not have to go very far to find parallel cultural beliefs today, for example, in New Age thought and contemporary Christian thought regarding angels.

These higher selves may at times provide useful information, and may at times present useful ideas, but it ought to go without saying that their claims to omniscience and infallibility can no more be taken at face value than the claims of demonic powers made by less affable ego states. The therapist cannot allow himself/herself to be led about by these ego states, and can only take their pronouncements under advisement. There is never an excuse for abdicating one's own professional judgment.

Sometimes the therapist may spend inordinate amounts of time with an ego state, not simply due to fear or flattery, but due to a misunderstanding of the nature of ego states. In these instances the therapist joins with his client's delusion that the ego states are persons. Thus therapists may believe that child ego states are really children and must be treated as real children, or they overempathize with ego states' fears that integration/fusion will bring about their death. This, of course, inevitably leads to the question: "What are ego states?" The most complete definition to date is the one offered by Richard Kluft (1991) in his discussion of what he calls the *disaggregate self state*:

A disaggregate self state . . . is the mental address of a relatively stable and enduring particular pattern of selective mobilization of mental contents and functions, which may be behaviorally enacted with noteworthy role-taking and role-playing dimensions and sensitive to intrapsychic, interpersonal, and environmental stimuli. It is organized in and associated with a relatively stable . . . pattern of neurophysiological activation, and has crucial psychodynamic contents. It functions both as a recipient, processor, and storage center for perceptions, experiences, and the processing of such in connection with past events and thoughts, and/or present and anticipated ones as well. It has a sense of its own identity and ideation, and a capacity for initiating thought processes and actions. [p. 611]

The ego state concept has much in common with the traditional psychoanalytic concepts of introjects and internal objects, with the additional understanding that these schemas may be activated as objects or as subjects. A critical introject may, for example, be enacted as an executive self who criticizes external (or other internal) objects, or may exist as an internal object who criticizes the current executive self. This dual nature of the ego state as both object and subject has been previously explored by Watkins (1987) in his discussion of the concept of the *identofact*, and by Kernberg (1984) in his discussion of dissociated ego states in the borderline disorders.

Ego states are really not personality fragments because once one of these schemas is executive, it has control over most of the psychic structure (except for those specific schemas that remain disaggregated from it by dissociative barriers or failures of integration). A child ego state is, therefore, only a partial enactment of a child, since it really still has access to the adult lexicon and many other adult structures that can be put in its service. On the other hand, the child ego state also has at its command certain primitive atavistic structures that are normally inaccessible when other ego states are exercising executive control. Consequently, while a child ego state may have access to certain memory schemas and linguistic and behavioral schemas that the adult states (and other child states) do not, the child state still can understand whatever the therapist says that the adult states would understand. The therapist does not have to limit his/her vocabulary when talking to these ego states. In addition, while a therapist might choose to use art therapy or play therapy techniques with these ego states, he/she is not limited to these techniques and should feel free to use the same sort of verbal psychotherapeutic techniques that he/she would with the adult states. Similarly, hypnotic age-progression techniques can work with ego states to help them grow older, whereas such techniques would obviously be of no assistance to real children engaged in the same task. It follows from this that the therapist does not have to play disparate roles with different ego states (e.g., parenting or playing with the children, while maintaining more normal treatment boundaries with the adult states). In fact, it seems contraindicated for the therapist to enact different aspects of himself with the different ego states. This reenacts the client's experience with primary caregiving figures during early development. Often these caregivers were themselves highly dissociated, and clients will often have different names for their parents' different ego states (e.g., Daddy, Dad, Father, George). Therapist inconsistency also encourages borderline splitting of the client's internalized representation of the therapist. The client's efforts to internalize the therapist as a constant object is, therefore, assisted by therapist constancy.

Lastly, if the therapist understands that ego states are not people, he/she is much less likely to join inadvertently with the resistance to integration of ego states. When ego states are reluctant to integrate because they do not want to die, the therapist can make a number of points. First, that he/she will not do any forced integrations—that an ego state will not be integrated with other ego states until or unless it is ready. Second, that integration is not like dying, but more like blending and joining. Third, that the ego state is not a person, and is mistaken in thinking of itself as a person. Instead, it is indeed a part of a system, once fragmented and incoherent, now increasingly interactive and organized, that constitutes the person.

PITFALL #4: FAILURE TO UNDERSTAND THE NATURE OF MEMORY

From Bartlett (1932) through Loftus (1993) psychologists have understood that memory is reconstructive rather than reproductive. A recalled memory is the product of a variety of cognitive processes and social influences rather than a veridical reproduction. Concepts such as leveling and sharpening, proactive and retroactive inhibition, and confabulation are familiar concepts to psychologists of memory. As Loftus (1993) so ably summarizes, the literature on the use of hypnosis to assist in memory recall assures us that there is no magical or royal road to accurate recall, and that the process of hypnosis may amplify problems in the contamination of memory traces through suggestibility and the use of active imagination. Neither the recaller's subjective sense of certainty about a memory, nor the amount of affect accompanying a purported recall adds to the likelihood that a particular memory is veridical. Psychologists who ignore this do so at their own peril. The suggestibility of persons with hysterical conversion and/or dissociative disorders is legendary, and has been well known at least since Janet (1924) who was already aware of the flights of fancy of which hysterics were capable, especially in the hands of an incautious therapist. Many contemporary therapists who treat dissociative disorders are also keenly aware of this problem (Chu et al. 1991, Chu et al. 1992).

How then is one to know when a recall of a past trauma is essentially accurate and when it is an elaborate fiction? The answer, unfortunately, is that there is no gold standard for judging these memories. Sometimes we are fortunate enough to have court or pediatric records that substantiate portions of an account, and, at other times, there may be relatives who report similar acts of being victimized by the same abuser, or can vouch as eyewitnesses for the authenticity of certain events. Even these corroborative records and witnesses can never give us complete certainty, however. Wright (1993a, b), for example, documents an incident of alleged abuse in which two sisters corroborated each other's stories, and the alleged abuser confessed to his crimes and was sentenced to prison, and yet the events alleged most probably never occurred. In my own practice, a middle-aged patient whose father was arrested, tried, and convicted over three decades ago for molesting her at the time when she was still a preadolescent, and whose mother corroborated many tales of horrific violence within the family, is also a patient who has memories of a U.F.O. abduction, intrauterine experiences, past-life experiences, and astral travels. Dissociative clients become dissociative at least partly because of their capacity for a rich and vivid fantasy life, one that is strong enough to maintain the delusion of multiplicity against the dictates of common sense and consensual social reality. It makes no sense then to insist that their productions within trance states cannot be enriched and altered by that capacity.

Some therapists throw up their hands at this, and state that what really happened is not the therapist's concern, and that the therapist must only deal with the client's subjective reality. If a client believes, for example, that he participated in the sacrificial killing and subsequent cannibalizing of a baby, it does not matter whether he really did so if he believes he did so. The therapist must help the client work through his guilt as if it were real. If a client falsely believes she was raped, the therapist must help her to abreact her terror, anger, and shame as if this were a real event. This professional stance is an extremely dangerous one, however. Our profession is one that necessarily insists on making a distinction between the moral nature of thought and action. It makes a rather significant difference whether one once thought about killing one's father, or actually did so. In the first instance, we reassure our clients that such thoughts are commonplace and tolerable; in the latter, we urge our clients to turn themselves over to the authorities. In the instance of the client who believes he had complicity in a ritualistic murder, it makes a rather large difference whether he must struggle over the course of a lifetime to live with a legitimate burden of unpardonable guilt, or whether we can convince him that this murder was a fantasy that never occurred as a real action, and must be interpreted and understood as reflecting unconscious dynamics.

Given the fact that we cannot be certain of the truth of our clients' recollections, and given a belief that it does matter whether these accounts are objectively true, what is a reasonable stance for the therapist to take? First the therapist must be willing to live with uncertainty and ambiguity and to resist the client's pressure for premature closure and validation of an alleged recollection. When a client states he/she recalls a past event that is credible to the therapist, and asks the therapist whether it really happened, the only defensible stance the therapist can make is to say, "It is possible that it happened, but I wasn't there and I can't know for sure." This is a long way from the now infamous quote in an often helpful book called *The Courage to Heal* (Bass and Davis 1988) that asserts, "If you think you were abused, and your life shows the symptoms, then you were" (p. 22). If the client tells a tale of past trauma that sounds incredible to the therapist, there is nothing wrong with the therapist letting the client know that "I do not think it is likely that this happened in just the way that you told it." Therapists are often afraid to risk the client's anger by offering their own common sense, and yet they can be setting the stage for disaster in therapy if they do not. I am not asserting here that the therapist will always be right in judging the accuracy of a client's memory, and in most instances the therapist would best serve the client by observing "a respectful neutral stance." (ISSMP&D 1993, p. 17). Nevertheless, some clients' memories are obviously wrong, and it does not help the therapy if the therapist hides his/her own incredulity.

Sometimes therapists are afraid of their own common sense judgments, fearful that their disbelief is a pathological denial, analogous to the denial of many contemporary citizens that the Holocaust happened, or to the denial of those therapists who wrote off their clients' memories of suffering genuine child sexual abuse for many years as mere oedipal fantasies. Therapists must learn, however, to make a distinction between disbelieving well-documented horrors in the face of clear evidence, and retaining some degree of skepticism about poorly documented horrors in the remarkable absence of evidence. Kenneth Lanning (1992), for example, has summarized the results of investigations by the Behavioral Science Unit of the FBI Academy into the existence of large-scale organized satanic child-abusing cults, and finds no credible evidence at this point for their existence. This is not to deny that there are child sex rings, or satanic religious sects, or religious or criminal organizations that do engage in sexual abuse. We are all aware of the Charles Mansons, Jim Joneses, and David Koreshes that exist all too frequently within our society. Lanning's review of the evidence suggests, however, that there is no widespread organized nationwide pattern of secret organizations that perform ritual human sacrifice at the level that would need to exist to account for all of the clients who believe they recall committing human sacrifices.

In addition to the question of whether a particular recollection is essentially true, there is also the somewhat separate question of whether treating that recollection as true or false has a pragmatic and utilitarian value within the therapy. If we treat this recollection as true, does it help the client to get better or worse? If the therapy is getting bogged down, for example, in endless abreactions of ever more fantastic and sordid recollections, as the client continues to act out and decompensate, it is evident that therapy has taken a very wrong turn. If, on the other hand, dealing with these memories as true has a salutary effect on the client's level of functioning, the process of dealing with these memories as true may have clinical validity even while its objective truth value may be undetermined.

At present, there is no good empirical evidence as to whether treating recollections of ritual abuse (RA), for example, as true leads to a more positive or negative therapeutic outcome. In his review of the literature, George Greaves (1992) notes:

> Almost no one has systematically analyzed the empirical validity of the many competing hypotheses that have been generated in the field, examined the methodology of data gathering, looked carefully at the assumptions being made by various authors and presenters, or looked at the reports themselves from a validity perspective. [p. 46]

I have heard one nationally respected expert who believes in the actuality of RA accounts (Sachs 1993) state that there are, as of yet, no published case histories of polyfragmented RA-type clients being brought successfully to a successful final integration of all their ego states. While some might argue that this serves as evidence that the trauma these clients have experienced is worse than that of other DID clients and that they are therefore harder to treat, others might argue that this is evidence for not treating these recollections as being objectively true. In any case, the therapeutic value of treating these recollections as true is an empirical question that hopefully will be resolved by careful and thoughtful research: it cannot be answered by partisanship and earnest belief based on single case studies and anecdotes.

In discussing the danger of false memories, there is also the danger that real memories of abuse will again be discounted by therapists as has historically been the case. At times the literature on false memories seems to go too far, impugning the validity of the concept of repressed memory itself. The human ability to compartmentalize and sequester information, and to disattend to certain aspects of experience, is so familiar (not only to psychotherapists, but also to students of hypnosis and state-dependent learning), that one would hardly think that it needs to be reaffirmed at this date. The mechanics of this process may be subject to debate, and one may well quibble over the existence of the hypothesized mechanisms underlying repression, denial, dissociation, splitting, and allied processes, but the existence of some form of sequestration as a genuine phenomenon seems well documented (cf. Hilgard 1977).

Again, the final resolution of this issue is one best addressed by research rather than speculation. Research of the type done by Saywitz and colleagues (1991) should be helpful in appreciating the likely magnitude of

Type I and Type II errors in believing in memory reports. In that study, 5-and 7-year-old children were questioned about a physical examination given to them by a physician one week to one month earlier. Half of the children had experienced a vaginal and anal examination as part of the physical examination and half had not. The children were then interviewed using a three-part procedure: first, their memories were assessed in a free-recall situation; then they were asked to demonstrate the physical examination using an anatomically correct doll; and last they were directly asked seventy questions about the examination, including twenty-one misleading questions. Of those children who were vaginally examined, only 22 percent reported the genital examination during free recall, and only 17 percent reported it using the dolls to demonstrate the examination. Upon direct questioning (e.g., pointing to the vagina on the doll and asking, "Did the doctor touch you there?"), 86 percent of the children who were genitally touched answered yes to the question. (It is noteworthy that even with direct questioning there is a 14 percent underreporting.) None of the children who were not genitally examined falsely reported such an examination during free recall or during their enactments using the dolls. There was, however, a 2.86 percent false-report rate among children who were not genitally touched when direct questioning was used. In other words, underreporting is a problem of greater magnitude than false reporting in this study, but false reports do occur at a low frequency. The results for reports of anal touch parallel those of vaginal touch, with 11 percent of those children touched reporting it under free recall, 11 percent of those children touched reporting it under the enactment with dolls condition, and 69 percent reporting it under direct questioning. Of those children not anally touched, none falsely reported it in free recall or the demonstration condition, but there was a 5.56 percent false-report rate with direct questioning. In general the 7-year-olds were more accurate reporters, and children were more likely to be misled by direct questions when interviewed one month after the examination than when interviewed one week after the examination. Memories weakened by time were more easily swayed by a misleading questioning technique. This study suggests that direct questioning increases both correct and incorrect information: more correct information is recalled, but more confabulation occurs as well. This result is very similar to what the hypnosis literature suggests: that hypnosis increases both accurate and inaccurate recall (Nadon et al. 1991). It may be that any directive method that enhances the likelihood of recalling more accurate facts also encourages a certain degree of confabulation. While the study is encouraging in that the rates of confabulation about genital touch are low, there are reasons not to be too complacent about these results. First, the children were not placed in an emotionally charged environment where questions about genital touch were asked repeatedly, as sometimes occurs during psychological examination or criminal investigation. Second, the interview was conducted relatively close to the physical examination in time. What would the rate of confabulation have been two months later, or one year later, or thirty years later? Finally, the memory was a nontraumatic memory. Are traumatic memories coded or stored in the same way as nontraumatic memories? Many questions need to be explored and studied before we will have a better appreciation of these issues concerning memory.

CONCLUSIONS

While few authoritative statements can be made about the treatment of dissociative disorders, what should be clear by now is the need for the therapist to exercise due caution in an area where much remains uncertain and controversial. The physician's prime directive is first to do no harm, and psychotherapists in general would do well to abide by this obligation. Due caution implies that therapists will not depart from a normative model of how to conduct therapy without appropriate forethought and consultation, and an ongoing awareness that when they do so they are treading on thin ice. All of the cautions in this chapter to maintain the treatment frame, to tread gently on defensive structures, not to take sides in internal disputes but to maintain one's neutrality, and to maintain one's scientific understanding of the memory process, are extensions of rules that would be broadly endorsed within the larger community of psychotherapists. In other words, good therapy with dissociative clients follows the same rules as good psychotherapy in general.

Therapists are at greatest peril when they forget the knowledge that they have already acquired in working with nondissociative clients. Richard Loewenstein (1993) has written cogently on the bipersonal field that arises between therapist and dissociative client. Within that field therapists often experience dissociative phenomena that parallel the internal process of their clients. The therapist can become "entranced" with the phenomena that are being manifested in the client's behavior, with all the concomitant features that "trance" implies: a narrowing focus of attention onto what is immediately present and a fading of one's usual frame of reference. It is probably a combination of this enthrallment factor together with the powerful countertransference phenomena already alluded to in earlier sections of this chapter that account for the amnesia for already-acquired skills and knowledge so often encountered in experienced therapists when they begin to work with dissociative clients.

REFERENCES

Assagioli, R. (1975). *Psychosynthesis: A Manual of Principles and Techniques*. London: Turnstone.

Barlow, D., and Cerny, J. (1988). *Psychological Treatment of Panic*. New York: Guilford.

Bartlett, F. C. (1932). *Remembering: A Study in Experimental and Social Psychology*. New York: Cambridge University Press.

Bass, E., and Davis, L. (1988). *The Courage to Heal*. New York: Harper and Row.

Beck, A., Rush, A. J., Shaw, B. F., and Emery, G. (1979). *Cognitive Therapy of Depression*. New York: Guilford.

Bentall, R., ed. (1990). *Reconstructing Schizophrenia*. London: Routledge.

Berne, E. (1961). *Transactional Analysis in Psychotherapy*. New York: Castle Books.

Beutler, L., and Hill, C. (1992). Process and outcome research in the treatment of adult victims of childhood sexual abuse: methodological issues. *Journal of Consulting and Clinical Psychology* 60:204–212.

Braun, B. (1986). Issues in the psychotherapy of multiple personality disorder. In *Treatment of Multiple Personality Disorder*, pp. 3–28. Washington, DC: American Psychiatric Press.

Breggin, P. R. (1991). *Toxic Psychiatry*. New York: St. Martin's.

Brown, D., and Fromm, E. (1986). *Hypnotherapy and Hypnoanalysis*. New York: Lawrence Erlbaum.

Butterfield, F. (1992a). Panel orders a hearing in bizarre Harvard case. *The New York Times*, March 31, Section A, p. 14.

———— (1992b). Therapy in suicide case defended by psychiatrist. *The New York Times*, April 1, Section A, p. 16.

———— (1992c). Therapist told of desire for client, court is told. *The New York Times* April 2, Section A, p. 14.

Butterfield, F., and Mydans, S. (1992). Paths of patient and his therapist cross on dark journey leading to death. *The New York Times*, April 12, Section A, p. 38.

Casey, J., and Wilson, L. (1991). *The Flock*. New York: Fawcett Columbine.

Chu, J. (1988). Ten traps for therapists in the treatment of trauma survivors. *Dissociation* 1:24–31.

Chu, J., Curtis, J., and Ganaway, G. (1991). The critical issues task force report: strategies for evaluating the validity of reports of childhood abuse. *ISSMP&D News* (December):5–7.

Chu, J., Hornstein, N., Putnam, F., and Ganaway, G. (1992). The critical issues task force report: the role of hypnosis and amytal interviews in the recovery of traumatic memories. *ISSMP&D News* (June):6–9.

Comstock, C. (1992). Response to the centrality of relationship: what's *not* being said. *Dissociation* 5:171–2.

Courtois, C. (1988). *Healing the Incest Wound: Adult Survivors in Psychotherapy*. New York: W. W. Norton.

Federn, P. (1952). *Ego Psychology and the Psychoses*. New York: Basic Books.

Fine, C. G. (1991). Treatment stabilization and crisis prevention: pacing the therapy of multiple personality disorder. In *The Psychiatric Clinics of North America: Multiple Personality Disorder*, Volume 14, Number 3, ed., R. J. Loewenstein, pp. 661–676. Philadelphia: W. B. Saunders.

———— (1992). Response to the centrality of relationship: What's *not* being said. *Dissociation* 5:173.

Goodwin, J., and Attias, R. (1993). Marginalia. *ISSMP&D News* (April):7.

Greaves, G. (1988). Common errors in the treatment of multiple personality disorder. *Dissociation* 1:61–66.

_____ (1992). Alternate hypotheses regarding claims of satanic cult activity: a critical analysis. In *Out of Darkness: Exploring Satanism and Ritual Abuse*, ed. D. K. Sakheim and S. E. Devine, pp. 45–72. New York: Lexington.

Hilgard, E. (1977). *Divided Consciousness: Multiple Controls in Human Thought and Action*. New York: John Wiley and Sons.

Horevitz, R. (1993). Hypnosis in the treatment of multiple personality disorder. In *Handbook of Clinical Hypnosis*, ed. J. Rhue, S. J. Lynn, and I. Kirsch, pp. 395–424. Washington, DC.: American Psychological Association.

International Society for the Study of Multiple Personality and Dissociation (1993). Draft of "Recommendations for treating dissociative identity disorder." *ISSMP&D News* (October), pp. 14–19.

James, W. (1890). *The Principles of Psychology*, vol. 1. New York: Henry Holt.

Janet, P. (1924). *The Major Symptoms of Hysteria: Fifteen Lectures Given in the Medical School of Harvard University*, 2nd ed. New York: MacMillan.

Karon, B. P., and VandenBos, G. R. (1981). *Psychotherapy of Schizophrenia: The Treatment of Choice*. New York: Jason Aronson

Kernberg, O. F. (1984). *Severe Personality Disorders: Psychotherapeutic Strategies*. New Haven: Yale University Press.

Kinsler, P. J. (1992). The centrality of relationship: what's *not* being said. *Dissociation* 5:166–170.

Kluft, R. P. (1986). Personality unification in multiple personality disorder: a follow-up study. In *Treatment of Multiple Personality Disorder*, ed. B. Braun, pp. 29–60. Washington, DC: American Psychiatric Press.

_____ (1989). Playing for time: temporizing techniques in the treatment of multiple personality disorder. *American Journal of Clinical Hypnosis* 32:90–97.

_____ (1990a). Incest and subsequent revictimization: the case of therapist–patient sexual exploitation, with a description of sitting duck syndrome. In *Incest-Related Syndromes of Adult Psychopathology*, ed. R. P. Kluft, pp. 263–288. Washington, DC: American Psychiatric Press.

_____ (1990b). Containing dysphoria in MPD. In *Handbook of Hypnotic Suggestions and Metaphors*, ed. C. Hammond, pp. 342–343. New York: W. W. Norton.

_____ (1991). Clinical presentations of multiple personality disorder. In *The Psychiatric Clinics of North America: Multiple Personality Disorder*, Volume 14, Number 3, ed. R. J. Loewenstein, pp. 605–630. Philadelphia: W. B. Saunders.

_____ (1992). Comment made during "Hypnosis and Multiple Personality Disorder Workshop," 4–6 December, at Daniel Brown, Ph.D. & Associates, Cambridge, MA.

_____ (1993a). Editorial: reflections on the treatment of multiple personality disorder: terminable or interminable? *Dissociation* 5:185–186.

_____ (1993b). Basic principles in conducting the psychotherapy of multiple personality disorder. In *Clinical Perspectives on Multiple Personality Disorder*, ed. R. P. Kluft and C. G. Fine, pp. 19–50. Washington, DC: American Psychiatric Press.

Langs, R. (1976). *The Bipersonal Field*. New York: Jason Aronson.

_____ (1982). *Psychotherapy: A Basic Text*. New York: Jason Aronson.

Lanning, K. (1992). A law-enforcement perspective on allegations of ritual abuse. In *Out of Darkness: Exploring Satanism and Ritual Abuse*, ed. D. K. Sakheim and S. E. Devine, pp. 109–146. New York: Lexington.

Loewenstein, R. J. (1993). Posttraumatic and dissociative aspects of transference and countertransference in the treatment of multiple personality disorder. In *Clinical Perspectives on Multiple Personality Disorder*, ed. R. P. Kluft and C. G. Fine, pp. 51–86. Washington, DC: American Psychiatric Press.

Loftus, E. (1993). The reality of repressed memories. *American Psychologist* 48:518–537.

Mahrer, A. (1978). *Experiencing.* New York: Brunner/Mazel.

May, P. (1971). Psychotherapy and ataraxic drugs. In *Handbook of Psychotherapy and Behavior Change,* ed. A. E. Bergin and S. L. Garfield, pp. 495–542. New York: John Wiley and Sons.

McCann, I. L., and Pearlman, L. A. (1990). *Psychological Trauma and the Adult Survivor: Theory, Therapy and Transformation.* New York: Brunner/Mazel.

Middlebrook, D. W. (1991). *Anne Sexton.* New York: Houghton Mifflin.

Moreno, J. (1946). *Psychodrama.* New York: Beacon.

Nadon, R., Laurence, J., and Perry, C. (1991). The two disciplines of scientific hypnosis: a synergistic model. In *Theories of Hypnosis: Current Models and Perspectives,* ed. S. J. Lynn and J. W. Rhue, pp. 485–519. New York: Guilford.

Olson, J. A. (1992). Response to the centrality of relationship: what's *not* being said. *Dissociation* 5:174–175.

Polster, E., and Polster, M. (1973). *Gestalt Therapy Integrated.* New York: Vintage.

Putnam, F. (1989). *Diagnosis and Treatment of Multiple Personality Disorder.* New York: Guilford.

Putnam, F., and Loewenstein, R. J. (1993). Treatment of multiple personality disorder: a survey of current practices. *American Journal of Psychiatry* 150:1048–1052.

Ross, C. A. (1989). *Multiple Personality Disorder: Diagnosis, Clinical Features and Treatment.* New York: John Wiley and Sons.

Rowan, J. (1990). *Subpersonalities: The People Inside Us.* London: Routledge.

Sachs, R. G. (1992). Response to the centrality of relationship: what's *not* being said. *Dissociation* 5:176.

—— (1993). Workshop entitled "Hypnotherapy and Multiple Personality Disorder" 4–6, December at Daniel Brown, Ph.D. & Associates, Cambridge, MA.

Saywitz, K. J., Goodman, G. S., Nicholas, E. and Moan, S. F. (1991). Children's memories of a physical examination of genital touch: implications for reports of child sexual abuse. *Journal of Consulting and Clinical Psychology* 59:682–691.

Schreiber, F. (1973). *Sybil.* New York: Regnery.

Torem, M. (1992). Response to the centrality of relationship: what's *not* being said. *Dissociation* 5:177–178.

Turin, A. (1991). Trauma, trance, and treatment: better psychotherapy with hypnosis. Manuscript distributed at workshop, 6 April, at the Massachusetts School of Professional Psychology, Boston, MA.

van der Hart, O., and Brown, P. (1992). Abreaction reevaluated. *Dissociation* 5:127–140.

Watkins, J. G. (1987). *Hypnotherapeutic Techniques: The Practice of Clinical Hypnosis,* vol. 1. New York: Irvington.

—— (1992). *Hypnoanalytic Techniques: The Practice of Clinical Hypnosis,* vol. 2. New York: Irvington.

Wright, L. (1993a). Remembering Satan, part 1. *The New Yorker,* May 17, pp. 60–66.

—— (1993b). Remembering Satan, part 2. *The New Yorker,* May 24, pp. 57–76.

Yalom, I. (1989). *Love's Executioner.* New York: Basic Books.

Young, W. (1992). Response to the centrality of relationship: what's *not* being said. *Dissociation* 5: 179–180.

14

Current Treatment of
Dissociative Identity Disorder

Colin A. Ross

The treatment of dissociative identity disorder (DID) is described in detail in two textbooks (Putnam 1989, Ross 1989), and additional information is available in Kluft (1985a,b), Braun (1986), and Kluft and Fine (1993). The treatment literature has continued to be updated in papers that have appeared in the journal *Dissociation* (Kluft 1988–1993), and the use of expressive therapies has been described in Kluft (1988–1993). A special issue of *Psychiatric Clinics of North America* (Loewenstein 1991), contains useful information. These references lead the reader into the literature. I have provided additional definition of my own clinical work in two books (Ross 1994, in press). Readers wishing to obtain a list of book-length case histories should consult North and colleagues (1993)

In this chapter I will not attempt a scholarly review of this treatment literature. Rather I will describe what I take to be the current mainstream treatment of DID. The approach I describe is consistent with the *Treatment Guidelines for Dissociative Identity Disorder* of the International Society for the Study of Dissociation (1994), of which I am the current president. The Society currently has about 3,100 members, and the *Guidelines* are the product of the Society membership as a whole, the current literature, and the committee that developed the material.

THE STANCE OF THE THERAPIST

The therapist treating DID needs to set the treatment frame, be responsible for it, and take a therapeutic stance. This involves not making certain treatment errors—as the director of a dissociative disorders unit I see many cases in which therapy has gone off course due to therapists' errors. The therapist is not a friend of the client, therapist and client are not on a mutual spiritual journey, they are not involved in each other's personal lives outside therapy, and the purpose of the treatment is not reparenting. The therapist cannot fill up the emptiness inside the client through indiscriminate "caring."

The therapist is neutral with respect to the reality of any given memory, and the amount and quality of the client's contact with her family of origin. The client must be responsible for her own feelings, thoughts, actions, and memories, though she may project responsibility onto the therapist. The therapist functions as a consultant to the survivor in her healing, but is not the primary cause of it, in charge of it, or responsible for it. The therapist should not work harder than the client.

The therapy must have healthy boundaries, and usually involves one to three hours a week of therapy. Therapies that involve more than five hours a week of clinical contact for prolonged periods are likely to be regressive and to foster dependency on the therapist. The therapy needs to be paced, conducted mostly on an outpatient basis, and focused on the goals of symptom reduction and improvement in psychosocial function. Recovery of traumatic memory is not a goal of treatment in and of itself, and has utility only if it leads to healing.

The therapist is active and interventionist in stance. The vast bulk of the therapy, consisting of a rational, adult conversation, is conducted in a working, problem-solving mode, and involves a blend of systems, cognitive, and psychodynamic techniques. Although useful, hypnosis is an adjuvant technique used primarily for symptom reduction and to facilitate guided imagery. I personally do not use hypnotic inductions in conjunction with efforts at memory retrieval, and never give more than brief relaxation suggestions; I have treated cases to integration without formal hypnotic procedures. I probably underemphasize hypnosis compared to other leading practitioners, and tend to work predominantly in a cognitive mode.

The healing effect of the therapy occurs at the level of process and structure, not at the content level. Therefore, within the dyad of therapy, the historical accuracy of the memories is not the primary consideration—healing occurs as a result of correcting cognitive errors, processing traumatic affect, and developing more adaptive coping skills, not as a result of remembering in and of itself. The therapist must be aware that the rules change fundamentally whenever the client steps outside the therapy dyad and begins to make public statements about past trauma. In public, the usual rules of evidence, and possibilities for lawsuits and countersuits, apply. Any client contemplating legal action needs both legal and psychological counseling as to the legal and emotional cost-benefit of any potential action. I actively discuss the problem of the historical accuracy of memories in both individual and group therapy.

Some critics make the assumption that iatrogenic amplification of dissociative disorder not otherwise specified (DDNOS) or borderline personality disorder into a DID which did not exist before the therapy is damaging and to be avoided. This assumption has no empirical basis and runs counter to my clinical experience. DDNOS patients who, in childhood, were unable to crystallize full DID as a naturalistic coping strategy may be handicapped in therapy because they have not generated sufficient internal structure. In other words, even if I conceded that most cases of DID in treatment today are artifacts, which I don't, it would not follow that this is a bad thing therapeutically. It is quite possible that amplifying DDNOS up into full DID confers a better treatment outcome. Only adequately designed treatment outcome studies could establish whether iatrogenic amplification, assuming it occurs, has a positive or negative effect.

The therapist does not, as a rule, confer names on the dissociated identities within the patient. On occasion, however, in a minority of cases and by mutual consent, therapist and client can name a personality state for management purposes, and to keep things organized in therapy. When this is done, it is understood by both parties to be a different process from the manner in which most states acquired their names prior to the onset of therapy. This is no different in principle or degree from the socialization into the vocabulary of therapy which occurs in the cognitive-behavioral treatment of panic disorder. Calling a panic attack a panic attack could reinforce and reify the phenomenon as much or more than naming a personality state.

By far the major change required in the dissociative disorders field as a whole is the tightening up of boundaries. Loose boundaries are an endemic problem, in the form of dual track relationships, confidentiality violations, therapist overinvolvement, sexual contact with clients, overidentification with clients, and alignment of the therapist with the host personality against internal and external perpetrators. None of these endemic problems is evidence against the reality of the disorder or the efficacy of well-conducted therapy.

DISSOCIATIVE IDENTITY DISORDER THERAPY IS MICRODETAILED AND STRUCTURED

Before describing specific techniques of therapy, I want to describe the gestalt of the treatment. During my psychiatry residency from 1981 to 1985,

I was taught long-term psychoanalytic psychotherapy, but received no lectures, workshops, handouts, or case conferences on childhood sexual abuse or dissociative disorders. This was despite 400 hours of individual supervision in long-term psychotherapy, a year of weekly case conferences on psychotherapy, a year of half-time training in family therapy, and six months of half-time training in short-term dynamic psychotherapy, in addition to core training in adult and child and adolescent psychiatry, and a one-year teaching fellowship.

Compared to my experience in the treatment of DID, my experience of psychoanalytic psychotherapy has been that it is vague, unfocused, and directionless. This is my personal experience, and my impression from reading the literature and listening to dozens of case presentations by residents and staff psychiatrists.

The treatment of DID is much more like the cognitive-behavioral treatment of depression, or treatment of panic disorder through systematic desensitization. It is detailed, based on a clear treatment rationale, and involves specific steps and techniques, which are directly linked to target symptoms.The treatment can be taught effectively, and the newly taught therapist can predict the interventions of the teacher in detail once the general principles are mastered.

One might compare the treatment of DID to the manufacture of a jet aircraft. Rather than being impressionistic, or based on mutual trance and hysteria, the gestalt of the therapy is predominantly one of detail and structure. The connections between different parts of the personality system, the past, and the treatment interventions have the level of detail of a wiring diagram for a jet.

A comparison I like to make is to completing a Ph.D. I tell patients that the treatment of DID to integration is one of the biggest projects human beings take on. It involves more effort and thinking than is required to complete a Ph.D. thesis. This is why the treatment takes three to five years, and sometimes longer. Progressing through the treatment involves accomplishing a specified series of tasks, and progress can be monitored in terms of internal tasks completed and external symptom reduction.

No other treatment in psychiatry approaches the positive cost-benefit analysis of a successfully treated case of DID in terms of symptom reduction, reduction in health care utilization, and improvement in psychosocial function. Other disorders that are equally treatable to long-term remission, such as panic disorder and simple phobia, do not carry equivalent morbidity, and disorders with equivalent morbidity, such as schizophrenia, cannot be treated to remission without maintenance medication.

The treatment of DID is rational in the medical sense of the word, at a psychosocial level. The etiology, which is a dissociative response to chronic childhood trauma, is known, the relationship of the etiology to a micro-detailed understanding of phenomenology is in place, and there is a direct relationship between the details of the treatment and the phenomenology of the disorder. It is because the treatment of DID is uniquely rational, in comparison to all other treatments for major mental disorders, that the disorder can be cured. DID is the one major mental disorder in which the doctor can achieve his dream of curing serious illness and take his place beside internists and surgeons. Resistance to the disorder is therefore antimedical.

THE STAGES OF THERAPY

The therapy of DID is divided into four stages which, like the stage of death and dying, overlap a great deal in actual practice. The first or initial stage of therapy involves formation of a treatment alliance, psychoeducation about trauma and dissociation, initial mapping of the personality system, setting the frame of therapy, establishing rules, limits, and boundaries, and laying a foundation for the middle phase, which is the difficult, prolonged phase of therapy.

During the initial phase, attention must be paid to social supports, ongoing relationships that may be abusive in nature, preserving function at the optimal level, and warning the patient about the lengthy, arduous work that lies ahead. The idea is to lay as secure and stable a foundation as possible before beginning memory processing work. Comorbidity may require treatment with AA groups, antidepressants or anxiolytics, eating disorder groups, or other modalities. There are no data on the circular nature of decisions about whether to treat comorbid depression by treating the DID with psychotherapy, or first treating the depression with antidepressants, so in practice both are usually done concurrently. The same logic applies to the problem of whether to suspend DID treatment until substance abuse is resolved, or treat the substance abuse by treating the DID.

The middle phase of therapy is the part that everyone would like to skip over. The problem is that no one has figured out how to get to stable integration without going through the middle phase of therapy—if such a treatment method could be devised, one which lead to true resolution of the trauma, it would be wonderful. The middle phase involves establishing interpersonality communication and cooperation, negotiating adaptive solutions to system problems, correcting cognitive errors, processing traumatic memories, and devising nondissociative coping strategies. Notice that trauma memory processing is but a small component of this work.

The late preintegration phase of therapy involves consolidation of treatment gains, strengthening and practicing nondissociative defenses, grief work, final reprocessing of the impact of the trauma, and integrations of selected alter personalities, culminating in full integration and resolution of the DID. By this phase of therapy there is clearly evident dramatic symptom reduction across Axes I and II. Most patients, other than those who continue to be profoundly characterologically impaired, should be functioning reasonably well in terms of employment and reduced health care utilization by this time.

The postintegration phase of therapy involves learning to cope with life as an integrated individual, which is a big job. Dealing with the loneliness, inner quiet, and inability to switch and "check out" when stress mounts too high, is a major treatment task equivalent to a usual course of psychotherapy. Depending on the person's position in the life cycle, grief work about lost decades and opportunities is required, and this can be very painful. The integrated person needs help and psychoeducation about normal relationships, sexuality, time sense, and stress. Often, the person cannot differentiate normal dissociation and forgetting from impending relapse.

After integration, there may be persistent Axis I and II psychopathology, which requires attention. Antidepressants or cognitive-behavioral treatment for an anxiety disorder may be required, and the person with concurrent bipolar mood disorder will continue to require lithium. In my experience, the level of Axis I comorbidity is always dramatically reduced postintegration, including the degree of insomnia and headache.

It is helpful during the most difficult parts of the middle phase of therapy to point out that many individuals have made it through this stage of therapy, that it does not last forever, and that things will improve.

USE OF MEDICATIONS IN THE TREATMENT OF DISSOCIATIVE IDENTITY DISORDER

There are no double blind placebo-controlled trials of any medication in the treatment of DID. Everyone is agreed that there is no medication that affects the core symptoms of the disorder, and that medications are used primarily for comorbid anxiety, depression, and posttraumatic symptoms. The indications for different medications are basically those for the comorbid symptoms independent of DID; in the dissociative disorders field, we import what we know from other areas of psychiatry. This being the case, everything to be said must be tentative and based on extensive but nevertheless anecdotal clinical experience.

Although it is not a medication, the indications for electroconvulsive therapy (ECT) are the same as those in general psychiatry; in a series of 102 DID cases 16.7 percent had received prior ECT (Ross et al. 1990), but my clinical experience with over 500 admissions to a Dissociative Disorders Unit tells me that the true indications for ECT are present in less than 1 percent of this population. I suspect that in the majority of undiagnosed DID cases treated with ECT, dissociative symptoms were mistaken for symptoms of a psychotic depression. In properly selected cases, ECT can be helpful for DID patients with medication nonresponsive severe depressions, and can assist the person to be more available for psychotherapy (Bowman and Coons 1992).

The indications for lithium in DID are narrow. There is no accumulated clinical experience suggesting that lithium has a mood-stabilizing effect in DID, reduces switching, or otherwise affects dissociative symptoms, beyond the level to be expected from placebo. In assessing clinical anecdotal experience with any medication, one must assume a placebo response rate of at least 35 percent, therefore one third of DID patients should improve on lithium from placebo effect alone, regardless of blood levels. The working conclusion at present is that lithium is indicated only for concurrent bipolar mood disorder. It is important not to mistake dissociative symptoms for cyclothymia, rapid cycling bipolar mood disorder, or mood disorder not otherwise specified—this differentiation can be difficult or impossible in some cases.

The antipsychotic medications have uncertain indications. In *The Osiris Complex* (Ross 1994), I describe a case of DID in a woman who previously carried diagnoses of schizophrenia and partial complex seizure disorder. This woman could not participate in exploratory psychotherapy but was partially stabilized on high doses of trifluoperazine. The percentage of DID patients who can benefit from neuroleptics is uncertain, and it is difficult for dissociative disorders specialists to form an opinion because of selection bias; we tend to see neuroleptic treatment failures, and are not referred neuroleptic responsive cases. Trials of the newer neuroleptics with fewer extrapyramidal side effects should be carried out in DID, with measurement of a full range of target symptoms.

By far the most commonly prescribed medications are antidepressants and anxiolytics. The newer serotonin reuptake blockers such as fluoxetine have all but replaced the tricyclic antidepressants and monoamine oxidase inhibitors because of their greater safety and fewer side effects. There is no specific reason to choose one of these over the other. The serotonin reuptake blockers can be extremely helpful for depression, and sometimes for posttraumatic, anxiety, and obsessive-compulsive symptoms. I suspect that these drugs work in DID, and perhaps generally, by being prodissociatives. That is, a DID or obsessive compulsive patient improves because the drug reinforces dissociative barriers, walls off other sectors of the psyche, and thereby reduces traumatic, affective, and compulsive intrusions from elsewhere in the psyche (Ross 1989). This model leads me to hypothesize that high scores on the Dissociative Experiences Scale (Bernstein and Putnam 1986) could predict which people with obsessive-compulsive disorder will respond to serotonergic antidepressants.

Trazodone is an antidepressant that is safe, but has the useful side effect of sedation. A good antidepressant in its own right, it is often very helpful in DID cases to promote sleep, repress nightmares, reduce headache, and improve overall outlook through treatment of the concurrent sleep disorder.

Another medication I have used a little in DID cases is buspirone. It has the advantage over the benzodiazepines of not being addictive or dangerous, and having no sedative side effects. Often DID patients will obtain antidepressant and anxiolytic effects at doses of 40 or 60 milligrams per day. Overall, however, buspirone does not appear to be as useful as the serotonergic antidepressants.

The benzodiazepines would be highly useful medications if it was not for their abuse, dependency, and overdose risk. DID patients are at risk for all three of these complications, but generalizations should not be made; many DID patients can take these medications responsibly with benefit for prolonged periods of time. Others cannot use them responsibly on an outpatient basis. The dosage is usually higher than a standard general practice anxiolytic dose, and more in the accepted range for panic disorder. A great deal of irrational hostility is focused on the prescribing of benzodiazepines to DID patients, and the physician is at risk for being targeted by hostile colleagues for what is actually sensible, helpful, cautious psychopharmacology. Many patients can take 4–6 milligrams per day of lorazepam for prolonged periods without abuse problems, and in my experience tapering and discontinuing the medication or continuing with low intermittent doses postintegration is not difficult.

On inpatient units, ultrahigh doses of benzodiazepines are often very helpful in maintaining safety, containing posttraumatic symptoms, reducing acting out, and helping the person benefit from psychotherapy. These dosages can be tapered prior to discharge. Unfortunately, the regulatory and medicolegal environment is becoming so hostile that patients will probably soon be deprived of this treatment modality in favor of neuroleptics with far more complications and side effects. Of all the medications prescribed to DID patients, benzodiazepines are by far the most frequent target of hostile attribution errors by reviewers and regulatory agencies.

Finally, the antiepileptic medications like carbamazepine and valproic acid are prescribed to DID patients, usually prior to diagnosis. There is no scientific evidence that they are more effective than placebo in DID. Anecdotally, some patients seem to receive nonspecific stabilization from these medications, but I am not yet convinced that they have any specific action in DID.

One commonly hears dogmatic claims for and against the use of various medications in DID. In the absence of systematic data, these are all merely opinions. The basic approach is to prescribe medications for the same indications that one would in a non-DID patient, while being aware that every prescription is always an empirical trial. This is a perfectly acceptable and conservative mode of clinical practice. One should be aware that DID patients tend to respond erratically and inconsistently to medications, indicating that they are a biologically heterogeneous group.

TRANSFERENCE AND COUNTERTRANSFERENCE ISSUES

Although I do not practice psychoanalysis, and therefore do not attempt classical transference analysis, it is impossible to treat DID to integration without being acutely aware of transference and countertransference. DID patients have taught me that transference double binds are simple structures, and that truly advanced efforts at projective identification involve quaternary binds and chains of double binds in various geometrical configurations. The basic technique for dealing with these binds, in my practice, is what I call *cognitive loop analysis* (Ross 1994). Whatever it is called, this involves analyzing the double bind, extricating the therapist from the loop, and pointing out that the bind is an externalization of a problem in the personality system.

For instance, a patient complained that her doctor did not believe her memories. On consultation, it became apparent that the personality system was divided into two warring factions; one side wanted the doctor to state that the memories were not real in order to reinforce avoidance of the traumatic affect. Simultaneously, a group of child alters was trying to hug the doctor repeatedly in order to prevent him from convincing other staff members that the memories were not real. The children reasoned that otherwise the doctor would destroy all hope of recovery and they would have to kill themselves.

My intervention was to point out that no matter what the doctor did, someone in the system would be upset, and someone would be happy. The real problem was not the doctor, but ambivalence about processing the traumatic affect. Complaining about the doctor was simply a way of avoiding the internal conflict.

All the classically described transferences and countertransferences will be experienced in the successful treatment of a case of DID. Countertransference interpretations should be used very sparingly, if at all; I restrict them to comments using myself as an example of the unavoidable human response to the person's behavior. I might say, "You can get away with that here, because I'm not going to hit you or reject you, even though your behavior is very annoying. Out in the world, though, this behavior is guaranteed to alienate people. Therefore it's a problem we need to work on. What are you going to do about these feelings, besides dump them on me?"

The transference is as fragmented as the inner world of the patient, and can oscillate instantaneously and extremely. The level of transference distortion is often delusional in proportion, though this is a dissociative, not a psychotic, form of delusion, and responds to psychotherapy. An example is the patient who concludes that her doctor or therapist is involved in a satanic cult based on the therapist's color of clothing.

By far the most common and entrenched transference problem is the effort of the patient to place the therapist in the rescuer role, while the host personality becomes the victim, and the perpetrator role is projected onto the persecutor alters internally and the actual abuse perpetrators externally. I analyze this problem in detail in *Satanic Ritual Abuse* (Ross, in press). Succumbing to this transference pressure is the most common source of therapist error.

A patient was tearful and despondent in group because her discharge was imminent and her alters were actively suicidal, according to the host personality. She viewed her physician as cold and heartless, and stated that her alters would probably try to kill her on the trip home. The alternative to discharge, her doctor had told her, was that if still too suicidal she would have to be transferred to a state hospital. Half an hour of work with her in the group setting established that in fact the satanic alter personalities were the ones who had ensured, through their self-abusive behavior, that she would meet criteria for inpatient treatment. Without them she could not have been admitted. The host was refusing to let the satanic alters out for fear of their behavior, therefore they had received virtually no direct treatment. When one, called "the master," took executive control at my request, he said that his layer of alters wanted to be engaged in treatment, was not interested in acting out further, was cutting prior to admission only to get the host's attention, and was unhappy because the other three levels of alters refused to deal with his group's memories.

The host, following this conversation with the master, and extensive feedback from other group members, decided to use her remaining time in the hospital working actively to draw up a cooperative plan with the master's layer of alters, not to bar them from therapy, and to apply skills at system communication and cooperation she had been learning during the admission. She was not actively suicidal at discharge less than a week later.

This intervention involved a blend of cognitive, systems, and psychodynamic principles. The element of transference analysis was pointing out how the doctor was simply a pawn in the patient's psychodrama and was only following the rules of the mental-health system. The doctor had no choice but to discuss transfer to a state hospital, since the patient had not demonstrated that she could benefit from acute care treatment in a short-term intensive psychotherapy unit. Once this transference acting out was interpreted and corrected, the intrapsychic problem could be addressed.

In terms of transference pressure toward boundary violations by the therapist, I believe that the child alters are the most dangerous alters in the system. They are most likely to provoke overinvolved, rescuing, nurturing responses from therapists, and since they tend to be childlike victims, they are not immediately recognized as architects of avoidance, which they often are. In group therapy I like to use the motto, "When the going gets tough, the kids get going." This is a property of DID personality systems I have observed hundreds of times; when the situation gets too threatening, stressful, confrontational, or otherwise triggering, the system throws out one of the kids to be in executive control. This is usually understood by the patient as a helpless, trauma-driven, and automatic reaction, but actually it is a system strategy.

Having stated the motto, I pose a question to the group: "Why, if the kids are the youngest and most vulnerable, does the system send out kids when things are toughest?" The answer is that the tough, frightening, vindictive perpetrator alters running the system from the background are themselves frightened children. The switch to child alters could be analyzed in transference and psychodynamic terms as a cognitive error, or as a system strategy: to my way of thinking, these are usually just alternative vocabularies for understanding the same phenomena.

The permutations of the victim-rescuer-perpetrator triad are hypercomplex in DID, and always oscillating. There are many triangles in place at once, and any given triangle can have all three, any two, or only one point located internally, with the others externalized, at any given time. What appears to be borderline splitting and idealization/devaluation is often oscillation of the triangle, and has three poles rather than two. Although I do not attempt classical analysis of transference, and work mostly in a cognitive-systems mode, in fact my work involves intricate transference analysis.

DISSOCIATIVE IDENTITY DISORDER AS OBJECT RELATIONS CHESS GAME

A curious paradox about DID is that although not accepted by many psychoanalytical psychotherapists, it in fact proves object relations theory better than any other disorder. Where else can one see identification with the aggressor behaviorally manifest in front of one's eyes, in the form of a paternal introject alter? Similarly, I heard about transient psychotic transference in my training, but never saw one until I saw the first of hundreds demonstrated to me by DID patients—I imagine that the vast bulk of so-called psychotic transference reactions in the twentieth century have actually been dissociative in nature. Most of the constructs of object relations theory, which seem to be abstract inferences about non-DID patients, become concretely behaviorally manifest during DID treatment.

A case example will illustrate the complexities of DID as an object relations chess game.

A patient had a conflict with her mother that was acted out in the transference for two years before it was fully analyzed and understood. The problem arose from a childhood scenario, verified by the mother, in which the mother was deathly ill for prolonged periods of time and nursed for extended periods by the patient. In the patient's perception, the mother was kind and warm while skeletal and deathly ill. When she would become more physically healthy, however, the mother would become emotionally, physically, and sexually abusive, and would involve her daughter in organized sexual abuse by groups of men.

The mother was split into a sick mom and a healthy, perpetrator mom. The patient was split into a compliant, caring, nursing, loving daughter, and a hostile, murderous, bad daughter. Both of these states in the patient, which were represented by large groups of alters due to polyfragmentation, were based on incorporation/identification/introjection mechanisms, and also on the normal reaction to the corresponding behavior in the mother. Both identifications were projected onto the therapist, myself, who also had projected onto him the role of the scientifically curious pedophile doctor with whom the mother had an affair.

The good daughter alters disavowed the existence of the bad alters, and denied that the two groups of identities were parts of the same person, while the angry alters viewed the good alters as wimps, and persecuted them internally. The angry alters thought that the good daughters were idiots and that it was their fault that the perpetrator mother emerged: they attributed this emergence to the good alters' nursing care. The good alters wished that Mom would get better and live, while the bad alters wished that she would die, and saw her as a lazy dog that refused to get up, assume the mother role, and care for them in a normal fashion. The good alters believed that the bad mother didn't exist. The patient was deeply ashamed of her wish that mother would die.

The system bind was that if the mother got well and lived, they would be abused, while if she died they would be at the mercy of pedophile relatives. The good alters were idiots for not killing Mom when they could, and the bad alters were evil for wanting to kill her. At the same time, the alters only existed and were real for the perpetrator mom, and were reduced to existing in the mother's eyes only as delirious hallucinations when she was ill, and took the form of the good mom. To be real the alters had to be perceived by the perpetrator mom, which was to be abused. This need to be abused in order to be real had been acted out in a series of abusive relationships over the years, and had also been acted out by certain alters on others. This acting out at times took the form of precise superficial self-laceration in sets of parallel straight lines—the number of lines had private numerological significance.

The solution to the problem was to not be in this world in order not to be driven crazy by the double binds. However, not being crazy returned her to the everyday world, which drove her crazy, and made her leave the world defensively, which relieved her from the double binds and made her not crazy. The patient had carried a diagnosis of schizophrenia for years. Whenever she made progress in therapy and started to become healthier, she panicked, because this meant that the perpetrator mom projected onto the therapist and the world would begin to emerge. The ultimate solution was to withdraw into what she called "a spiritual dot." The analysis of the acting out of the permutations of this logic in her past and current relationships, internal world, and transference, took considerable time and effort.

I invented the term *dissociative identity disorder as object relations chess gam* to capture the structure, order, and complexity of the transference mov and countermoves. Part of the skill required of the therapist is to track the endless cycles of introjection, projection, reintrojection, displacement, projective identification, reaction formation, and traumatic reenactment that characterize the therapy in order to maintain a neutral therapeutic stance and not succumb to any given idealization, devaluation, or other transference distortion. The term also highlights the simplistic nature of any bimodal splitting mechanism as a model for tracking the permutations. This is the depth psychology truth that refutes the contention that DID patients are "really just borderlines." They function several orders of complexity above any bimodal models of psychopathology.

Principles of Behavioral Management

The principles of the behavioral management of DID flow from a desensitization model of the disorder, with the traumatic memories and affect functioning as the phobic stimulus. However, for behavioral analysis and management to be meaningful, the analyst must appreciate the complexities of the object relations chess game. Failure to do so will result in simplistic behavioral management strategies that work in the reverse direction of their intended effect. Also, amnesia must be factored into the repertoire of stimulus–response options in order for the analysis to be real.

Much of the therapy can be conceptualized as a cognitive-behavioral desensitization program, with cognitive errors requiring correction along the way. DID clients phobically avoid anger, conflict, pain, memories, and many other things. The behavioral principles can be illustrated by inpatient treatment examples.

In a managed health-care system, patients cannot be admitted to the dissociative disorders unit unless they are actively suicidal and cutting or burning. As soon as they stop this behavior for a day or two, the reviewer then rates them as ready for transition to day hospital. In this system, raising levels of care to higher privilege levels for non–self-abusive behavior could be regarded as a reward designed to reinforce desired behavior. However, it could also be understood as negative reinforcement, with low levels functioning as the noxious stimulus, and the stimulus being removed when the desired behavior is carried out (stopping self-mutilation).

Either way, raising levels should reinforce non–self-abusive coping strategies. Several problems arise, however. First, and simplest, the patient may perceive raising levels as a punishment because it threatens to result in loss of the safety of the hospital. When levels are raised, this is a noxious stimulus to the patient who, through response to what she perceives as negative reinforcement, cuts in order to have her levels dropped. When this occurs, the physician reports to the reviewer that the patient cut within the last 24 hours, necessitating a reduction in levels, and more inpatient days are certified.

The patient learns that to stay in the hospital longer, she must cut more. This would be fine, except that once this has persisted too long, the managed care reviewer begins to blame the physician, the unit, and the hospital for regressive treatment, and threatens not to certify any more inpatient care. This is perceived by the physician and hospital administration as a bad thing because the managed care company is a more important customer of the hospital, in terms of bottom-line financial reinforcers, than the individual patient.

What happens is that the physician now begins to tell the patient that she will soon be transferred to the state hospital if she cannot resolve her suicidal ideation. Now dropping levels becomes a punishment to the patient, rather than a reward, because it threatens her with banishment to the place where only bad people are sent. Transfer to the state hospital proves that the patient was not working hard enough, doesn't want to get better, and is generically bad. To avoid this, the patient stops cutting, and perceives the raising of levels as a reward because it removes the noxious stimulus of the threat of state hospital. The time frame for when these shifts have to be made depends entirely on the kind of insurance the patient has, not on other clinical realities.

The management of these behavioral contingencies would be relatively straightforward if it were not for internalized reinforcement loops operating within the patient at the same time. The patient may cut or burn in order to modulate and regulate negative mood states—to reverse depersonalization, anxiety, emptiness, or depression. This internal reinforcement may override the external contingencies and make them irrelevant. Alternatively, one alter may cut or burn another because the victim alter deserves punishment and is bad. The persecutor alter may not even be oriented to being in the same body, in the same year, or in the hospital, and if so will not respond to real time reinforcers.

The masochistic victim alter may view the cutting inflicted upon her as expiation, or payment for original sin, and may feel abandoned, uncared for, and panicky if the cutting stops. If this is the case, threats to send the patient to the state hospital will be perceived as promised rewards because the threatened banishment to the bad place will relieve the guilt caused by insufficient payment for past sin. The past sin may be normal physiological arousal caused by the incest. If such a loop is in place, the patient will cut more when threatened with the state hospital.

Another permutation occurs when the persecutor alters plan to com-

plete suicide upon discharge. If they understand the rules of the health-
care system, they will stop threatening to cut the host in order to be
discharged to a setting where they have greater access to lethal methods.
If this is the major operating dynamic, settled behavior in response to an
increasing of privilege levels is an indicator of increased suicide risk, and
should rationally result in the certifying of further inpatient days on the
grounds that the patient is not overtly suicidal enough to be discharged. If
the patient was ambivalent enough to be of lower suicidal risk, she would
be giving voice to her suicidal impulses but would be able to contain them.

If the patient's levels are raised without incident, she is discharged, and
then self-mutilates within a few days, state regulatory bodies will define
this as a violation of the patient's right to safety, and will define the raising
of levels and discharge as premature. If the patient is not truly actively
suicidal, and is expressing suicidal ideation only to obtain the reward of
prolonged hospitalization, however, then she should be discharged to
prevent regression and hospital dependency, at least in the opinion of the
managed care reviewer. In this situation, if the doctor guesses incorrectly,
and the balance of forces is actually tipped in favor of early postdischarge
mutilation, then the managed care company faults the doctor for regressive
treatment causing early readmission, and the state regulatory agency faults
the doctor even more strongly. However, if the doctor does not discharge
the patient, the managed care company decertifies further care, and the
hospital reacts to the negative financial contingency of free care. Too much
free care will close the unit.

None of the players in this system is being irrational from his or her
perspective. Each merely reacts to the system of rewards and punishments
in place. The patient has an employer, who has both an employee
assistance plan and an insurance company; the insurance company employs a managed care company, which interacts with the utilization review
personnel inside the hospital, who in turn meet with the physician, who
treats the patient. There are complex rewards and punishments in place at
each interface in this loop, but there are no coherent overall principles
governing the health care system as a whole.

The way the system is structured currently, the patient gets defined as
an acting-out bad borderline and the doctor gets blamed if too many
inpatient days are generated. In fact, the patient is no more borderline than
the managed care reviewer or the state regulator.

So far, my management policy has been to raise privilege levels as
quickly as possible, and not to drop them in reaction to parasuicidal
behavior, so as to avoid entrapment in any of the contingency loops. I
simply raise levels on a fixed schedule as quickly as possible. To put a
positive spin on this strategy for managed care, I define it as designed to

foster independence and prevent regression and hospital dependency. I haven't yet solved the problem of how to avoid having the state regulatory agency define this strategy as depriving the patient of her right to safety, but I am working on it.

A problem with my system of managing levels is that it is perceived by some nursing staff as being soft on bad borderline behavior. Some nurses, doctors from other units, and reviewers, see it as failing to set limits, punish the patient for bad behavior, and take charge. These critics think I let patients get away with things. My answer is that the survival of the dissociative disorders units is threatened from many quarters, and its management requires complex, high-level analysis skills. Simple behavioral schemes simply don't work in this population. One advantage of my viewpoint is that I get to define any avoidance on my part as a subtle behavioral strategy. My hope is that by educating all players in the system to the complexity of behavioral analysis required, more rational management decisions, attributions, and behavioral regimes can be set in place.

Forming a Treatment Alliance with Persecutory Alter Personalities

One of the key interventions on our unit is making friends with persecutory alters. Too often these alters have been rejected, devalued, and hurt by the host personality and the referring therapist. Such alters have been locked in internal boxes, exorcised, feared, accused of ongoing participation in satanic human sacrifices (a claim they often make themselves), defined as "programmed by the cult," and otherwise hated. They have been defined as the problem, and usually the host personality regards the alters as the cause of her problems. From a systems perspective, the persecutor alters are like the identified patient in a family system. The behavior of the bad alters is not the problem: it is the solution to a problem. The therapist's job is to help understand what problem is being solved by the self-abusive behavior, and then to help the system find a more adaptive solution.

In doing this work I have become increasingly aware of the problem of *host resistance*. The alters were created, originally, to solve a problem, which was the overwhelming impact of the trauma on the organism's defenses, so they are the solution not the problem. The problem is that the host personality does not want to integrate the traumatic memories and their attendant affect back into herself. She therefore defines the bad alters as bad, not part of herself, and the problem, in order to avoid the real work of therapy. If the therapy threatens to center the badness inside herself she projects it out onto the unit, nurses, doctor, therapist, or hospital administration. Unfortunately, outside regulators are too often too quick to identify with these patient projections, not having been sobered by direct experience of the distortions and misattributions.

As quickly as possible, we move to form a treatment alliance with the key persecutor personalities involved in the presenting problem, reframe their behavior as positive in intention, and increase interpersonality communication and cooperation. The idea is to shift the system from a civil war mode of function to one of negotiated compromise. To do this within an average length of stay of three weeks requires focus and concentration of treatment effort and a minor emphasis on trauma memory recovery and processing.

To illustrate a few strategies, I usually point out to the host that it was the suicidal behavior of the persecutor alters that got her into hospital. I say that they have been doing their job all along, and that they are part of her overall survival strategy. One of their major functions was to hold all the anger for years so that the host, who is anger phobic, would not have to deal with it. It is hardly fair, given that fact, to fault the persecutors for being angry. I then define anger as a positive, powerful form of energy, if channeled in a healthy direction. I point out that the women's movement brought child abuse out of the closet, which in turn made the unit and the patient's current treatment possible, based on accurate, legitimate anger. I say that rage is the biologically normal response to chronic childhood sexual abuse. In fact, I say, it would be abnormal *not* to be extremely angry, given the patient's childhood.

With the persecutors listening in from the back of the system, which they usually do, I point out that the host personality has gotten into many abusive situations over the years due to trusting too much and not being assertive enough. This is a natural consequence of the dissociation that was required to survive childhood—the problem now is that the body has grown up, the abuse stopped long ago, and the defenses are not working. Explosive angry outbursts by the persecutors when boyfriends make sexual advances are destroying the possibility of a healthy marriage, for instance.

What is required is for the host and persecutors to share skills, so that the host is more cautious, self-protective, and assertive, and therefore less at risk for date rape, while the persecutors learn to tolerate normal, healthy intimacy. The persecutors are not bad for being angry any more than the host is bad for not being angry—both have skills to contribute to the whole.

I then point out to the host, sometimes through a clinical fable, that the angry alters must be feeling hurt, rejected, and lonely because of the host's devaluation of them, and I say that angry retaliation is not an unexpected reaction for traumatized children when they are subjected to further rejection. I say that the persecutors, like the host, have been hurt far too much already and don't deserve more internal abuse. If the persecutors are perceived as monsters or demons, I point out that this is their job—in order to protect the host from the bad feelings they hold, they have to take on a frightening identity to ensure that the host does not come too close. Inside the scary costume, I say, is a hurt child who is just trying to help. Although it might not be technically correct, I may say that it is unfair for the host to fault the demons for being demons, since she is the one who created them and gave them that identity—they are just doing what they have been created to do.

Working directly with the persecutors, I review all of the above, promise to undertake negotiations with the host on their behalf, and promise to work on correcting host cognitive errors, but only if they agree to no more self-abusive behavior. I agree to consult with them on devising other strategies to meet their needs, which are basically to protect the host from traumatic memories and affect. I also hire the persecutors as consultants to the therapy, stating that they have far more expertise on the internal system than I do and therefore can help me avoid needless errors and confrontations by giving me information.

Mindful of the complexities of behavioral analysis required, I also point out to the persecutors that they share the same treatment goal as I have, namely discharge as early as possible. I have discussed the workings of the health care system, our average length of stay, and financial realties with persecutor alter personalities identified as demons or Satan himself, with good results. Usually this treatment approach is a revolutionary experience for the persecutor alters, who have never been treated with respect and dignity before. To define these alters as iatrogenic artifacts is abusive, and will likely result in their transitory disappearance. In most cases, certainly in those seriously dedicated to recovery, making friends with the persecutors usually has a dramatic impact on the level of suicidal ideation within two or three weeks of inpatient treatment.

The Problem of the Historical Reality of the Trauma Memories

Although it has been highly politicized and polarized, current attention to the questionable reality of some trauma memories has been helpful for the dissociative disorders field. I am pleased to be able to say that in *The Osiris Complex* and *Satanic Ritual Abuse* taken together, I provide more clinical examples of inaccurate and confabulated memories than anyone else in the dissociative disorders field. However, the historical reality of the trauma memories is a minor concern in the planning of the therapy. I deliberately structure my therapeutic work such that the same intervention will be used no matter whether the memory is fully confabulated, partially accurate, or substantially accurate. This applies no matter how improbable the memory, as long as it is physically possible. If someone claims, for instance, that one alter has cancer while another one doesn't, I will explain that this is biologically impossible but that I understand the need some alters have to deny being in the same body. Similarly, if someone remembered walking on the moon in shorts and a shirt, I would explain that this is physically impossible, even if the cult has access to spaceships, but that this impossible memory must be serving some function in the personality system and that our task is to understand how that belief is helping.

Except with physically impossible memories, it is countertherapeutic to take either a believer or a nonbeliever stance. I have concluded that virtually any memory recovered in therapy could be real and accurate or never have happened, and that it is difficult or impossible to make the differentiation clinically most of the time. Naïve beliefs that one can validate the survivor by believing her memories are simply misguided, as is the idea that overt therapist disbelief is in any way curative.

I discuss the problem of the accuracy of trauma memories in both individual and group therapy, and explain that it is not my job either to believe or not believe. This is often responded to with protests that I therefore don't believe, and I have been angrily blamed by self-identified survivors in audiences at professional meetings for not believing the survivors. I have been fooled clinically by what seemed to be entirely real memories, which proved later never to have happened, and I have been at a crime scene with police at which a patient was naked, her hands bound with tape behind her back. This was the fifth or sixth targeted assault by an organized group of perpetrators with two other similar assaults photographed, witnessed, and reported on by police. The patient has been assaulted outside her home, outside her work, and in the restroom in my office building within the last year, all of these assaults being objectively documented by police and/or rescue personnel who attended at the scenes while her hands were still bound behind her back. Her memories of nonsatanic ritual abuse are clear, plausible, and detailed. There is no ex-husband, boyfriend, or other male figure who could be perpetrating these assaults for personal reasons, and two have involved two assailants. Since this trauma is objectively real, I take the position of believing in its reality, and it is as real as a broken leg or ruptured appendix.

SUMMARY

In this limited space I cannot possibly give an adequate account of the treatment of dissociatve identity disorder. My purpose has been to describe some of the key themes and methods of the treatment as practiced in 1994. The major changes in practice since the mid-1980s have been to deemphasize trauma memory recovery as such, shorten inpatient lengths of stay, tighten up boundaries, pace the treatment more slowly, and focus on maintaining the optimal level of function possible. The controversy about the historical reality of trauma memories, although it has involved a great deal of angry acting out in the media and the courts, has actually been healthy for the field.

My other purpose has been, as in my other two chapters, to provide a counter to straw-man arguments against DID psychotherapy mounted by Dr. Merskey and others. I have tried to show that an adequate account of the therapy requires complex and subtle analysis. In the absence of adequately designed treatment outcome studies, one cannot conclude scientifically that the treatment is harmful, beneficial, or neutral. However, extensive clinical experience treating DID cases to stable integration indicates anecdotally that the treatment is often highly effective compared to other modalities tried during prolonged baseline periods in the mental-health care system. If the therapy of DID was actually conducted as Dr. Merskey describes in his straw-man account, then it would indeed be stupid, but it is not, therefore the straw-man argument is irrelevant.

DID patients who have responded well to treatment have reached stable integration within two to three years and maintained it for five to seven years, despite prolonged involvement in the health care system for some, and initial entries into the system that would have guaranteed prolonged enmeshment with psychiatry in the absence of definitive treatment. None of the patients I diagnosed and treated in 1985 and 1986 have attended at an emergency department or been admitted to an inpatient unit at either of the two teaching hospitals in Winnipeg in the 1990s, to my knowledge. No other major mental illness can be treated as successfully as dissociative identity disorder.

REFERENCES

Bernstein, E. M., and Putnam, F. W. (1986). Development, reliability, and validity of a dissociation scale. *Journal of Nervous and Mental Disease* 174:727–735.
Bowman, E. S., and Coons, P. M. (1992). The use of electroconvulsive therapy in patients with dissociative disorders. *Journal of Nervous and Mental Disease* 180:524–528.

Braun, B. G. (1986) *Treatment of Multiple Personality Disorder*. Washington, DC: American Psychiatric Press.

International Society for the Study of Dissociation (1994). *Treatment Guidelines for Dissociative Identity Disorder*. Skokie, IL.

Kluft, E. S. (1993). *Expressive and Functional Therapies in the Treatment of Multiple Personality Disorder*. Springfield IL: Charles C Thomas.

Kluft, R. P. (1985a). *Childhood Antecedents of Multiple Personality Disorder*. Washington, DC: American Psychiatric Press.

_____ (1985b). The treatment of multiple personality disorder (MPD): current concepts. In *Directions in Psychiatry*, ed F. F. Flach, (24) pp. 1–10. New York: Hatherleigh.

_____ (1988–1993). *Dissociation* 1–5. (Available from International Society for the Study of Dissociation.)

Kluft, R. P., and Fine, C. G. (1993). *Clinical Perspectives on Multiple Personality Disorder*. Washington, DC: American Psychiatric Press.

Loewenstein, R. J., ed. (1991). *Psychiatric Clinics of North America*, 14.

North, C. S., Ryal, J. E., Ricci, D. A., and Wetzel, R. D. (1993). *Multiple Personalities, Multiple Disorders*. New York: Oxford University Press.

Putnam, F. W. (1989). *Diagnosis and Treatment of Multiple Personality Disorder*. New York: Guilford.

Ross, C. A. (1989). *Multiple Personality Disorder: Diagnosis, Clinical Features, and Treatment*. New York: John Wiley & Sons.

_____ (1994). *The Osiris Complex. Case Studies in Multiple Personality Disorder*. Toronto: University of Toronto Press.

_____ (in press). *Satanic Ritual Abuse*. Toronto: University of Toronto Press.

Ross, C. A., Miller, S. D., Reagor, P., et al. (1990). Structured interview data on 102 cases of multiple personality disorder from four centers. *American Journal of Psychiatry* 147:596–601.

15

Consequences of Arriving at the Diagnosis of Multiple Personality Disorder

Alan E. Siegel

Most authorities on the subject of MPD would maintain that the corner-stone of effective treatment is the mutual acknowledgment of the diagnosis by both therapist and patient. The clinical example in this chapter reflects some of the inherent difficulties that confront clinicians and patients who follow this treatment prescription.

DIAGNOSIS AND THE CARE SYSTEM

In the past ten years, the mental health professions have embraced the medical tradition of emphasizing the importance of the diagnosis as the primary step in determining the form of the treatment. The diagnosis is not simply a point-in-time observation of symptoms, but has become viewed as a comprehensive representation of the patient, her/his history, and her/his future. With the proliferation of managed care, clinicians have to present their diagnoses of patients as evidence that treatment is necessary, and as a prescription that dictates the form and the content of the treatment the patient requires. If we describe a patient as someone with an affective disorder to an insurer, we can be told how many times we should meet with the patient, how we should be working with the person, whether or not medications should be used, and what changes in symptoms and functional level we should expect to see over a specific period of time. With this elevation of the importance of diagnosis by those paying for treatment, it is easy to believe that we are indeed working in a field that is precise and predictable, and that we are treating patients whose illnesses follow predictable courses. We are urged to see the diagnosis as a fact of the patient's life, and not as a fancy of our clinical imagination. We can forget that these diagnoses, which we have elevated to the status of facts, are subject to fashions and fads. For patients in the 1950s, Havens (1989) tells us, the chances were that they would be diagnosed with either hysteria or schizophrenia. In more recent years, mania and the affective disorders have become the diagnoses that draw the most attention. As clinicians we have found one diagnosis or another particularly appealing because the task of understanding what is really troubling a person is a complex, elusive, and often painful process. It is not uncommon that the search for the diagnosis and its formulation can stand in the place of getting to know the patient and what she/he has been up against. Once discovered, the diagnosis is to serve as the basis for the implementation of a treatment plan. The process of working with someone to make better sense of what is within, and to be better able to recognize, bear, and put into perspective the affects associated with what is really bothering the person, is such a complex and elusive project that we may be drawn to look for ways to simplify, codify, and reify this confounding interpersonal experience. The diagnosis simultaneously structures and confounds this process.

Fashions in diagnosis have resulted in patients being misunderstood, neglected, or even harmed. As we become preoccupied with the value of the diagnosis itself and what it should do for us and our patients, we are in danger of adding a new dimension of misunderstanding and ignorance to our work. In the work with patients described as suffering with MPD, arriving at the diagnosis and involving the patient with the diagnosis are critical functions. They are so central to the work as prescribed by leading theoreticians such as Putnam and Ross that we need to think carefully about the implications of this portion of the prescribed therapeutic course. There are dangers in following that course, since the MPD diagnosis is a leading contender for the faddish diagnosis of the 1990s at a time when diagnosis is itself such a preeminent focus.

DIAGNOSIS AND THE PROCESS OF TREATMENT

Greenson (1967) tells us that the "traditional medical approach for determining the form of treatment is first to arrive at a diagnosis" (p. 52). Yet it is extremely difficult to make the process of psychological observation reliable. Greenson goes on to say: "Although the diagnosis tells us a great deal about the pathology, it may indicate relatively little about the healthy resources of the patient in question" (p. 53). Havens (1989), describing Sullivan, added yet another important dimension: "Further, Sullivan believed that diagnosis is never a matter of simply uncovering or recognizing a condition: it is also a creating of conditions together by the patient and doctor. So it becomes of central importance not to create a condition that is itself irremediable" (p. 128). These interactive effects, as Havens calls them, are part of the background of the controversy in MPD over whether MPD can be created in a patient by the therapist. We have all known clinicians who had the knack of making almost any patient they interview seem psychotic. We have known others who had the ability to make the most psychotic patient seem clear and organized in the interview. We know that there are inpatient services that have a certain mix of staff personalities and program orientation that are sure to be overwhelming to some of our patients. The reality of interactive effects is not a new and mysterious concept. It can perhaps create a diagnosis in a patient, but that is very different from creating a life condition.

Both Ross (1989) and Putnam (1989) are clear about the importance of making the diagnosis of MPD and the importance of the diagnosis for the patient. Ross is clear that diagnosis is a vital part of the initial phase of the therapy: the "major tasks include making the diagnosis; sharing the diagnosis with the patient; educating the patient about dissociation and abuse; proposing a treatment goal of full integration; negotiating a treatment contract; and beginning to map the system" (p. 219). He advises that with diagnosis the clinician should strike a balance "between matter of fact approach similar to that for any medical diagnosis, and traumatizing the patient with a flood of information" (p. 224). He tells us, clearly, "I am a strong advocate of diagnosis and differentiated treatment protocols." (p. 225). Ross connects the diagnosis of MPD with an assortment of medical treatments, including surgery for a malignancy. He urges us to identify and recognize MPD, and notes that the real dangers are in not diagnosing MPD in patients. He urges the utilization of current diagnostic criteria and states that although over the next ten years we may need to tighten up diagnostic criteria, it is not necessary now because of the "underdiagnosis of MPD . . . there are more false negative diagnoses than false positive," and that "overinclusive diagnostic criteria are in the best interest of patients" (p. 77). He continues: "I have not yet encountered a false positive diagnosis of MPD made by another mental health professional" (p. 78). For the clinician, making the diagnosis of MPD and treating patients accordingly has important meaning, and, for Ross, it is an important sign of professional competence. He states that as the year 2000 draws close everyone will be "mentioning their MPD case, in order to let colleagues know that they are competent clinicians who don't miss cases" (p. 77). Despite cautions about becoming overzealous, he is clear that the failure to accept and diagnose MPD in patients meeting current diagnostic criteria is intimately connected with the clinician's denial of the reality of sexual abuse in both his patient and in the culture. Ross states: "The charge of artifact is a second line of defense against dealing with the reality of childhood abuse in North America" (p. 61).

So for Ross, the way is clear. One must actively diagnose patients with MPD using existing diagnostic criteria, even if they are incomplete or lacking. For him, the danger in not diagnosing this illness far outweighs the danger in misdiagnosing the illness. Once the diagnosis is confirmed in the clinician's mind, he should share the diagnosis with the patient, as the diagnosis become the linchpin of subsequent treatment.

Putnam (1989) focuses less on the significance for the therapist's long-term professional credibility in diagnosing MPD and more on the clinical importance of the process of diagnosis. However, he does encourage our interest in this disorder by underscoring the uniqueness of the diagnosis. He addresses the problem identified by Ross when the therapist misses this diagnosis by noting: "A clinician will not find MPD if he or she is not willing to look for it" (p. 82). He initially appears to recognize and dismiss the interactive effects on the patient of the diagnostic process when he says: "Also, looking for MPD cannot create the disorder in a patient if it is not already there" (p. 82). He does not, however, seem to consider the effect that the therapist's belief in the disorder has on the generation of therapist expectations and on the course of the treatment. He acknowledges, however, that the process of establishing the diagnosis can be stressful on the patient and may have some effect on the patient's psychological experience. If MPD is suspected from the initial evaluation, Putnam advises that the clinician attempt to elicit alter personalities. He says: "I broach the subject gently, often first asking the patient whether or not he or she has ever felt like more than one person" (p. 90). Although it is debatable whether or not this question is as "gentle" as Putnam suggests, he continues his directions to the clinician and states:

> I try to avoid using the word "personality" when I am working with a patient at this stage. . . . I initially stick to descriptions such as "part," "side," "aspect," or "facet." . . . [Later] when the bounds of therapy are better established and the patient as a whole has achieved some degree of comfort with the diagnosis, I use the term "personality" more freely. [p. 92]

Putnam believes that if a patient is uncomfortable with the therapist's questions about alter personalities, this can be attributable to the existence of the disorder within the patient. Indeed, the imperative to establish the existence of the diagnosis through establishing the existence of alter personalities becomes superordinate. He says:

> If a patient does not appear to feel anything [concerning initial inquiries about alter phenomena] and denies any internal response to the therapist's requests, then he or she may not have MPD. A strong alter personality or group of alters who wish to conceal the multiplicity, however, can do so successfully for prolonged periods of therapy . . . Therefore the therapist should not irrevocably rule out the diagnosis of MPD based on failure of an alter to come forward on request. [p. 93]

Indeed, establishing the diagnosis is so critical to Putnam that if the patient continues to provide information suggestive of dissociative phenomena, and the therapist still cannot elicit an alter personality by direct request, Putnam advises, "it is worth considering the use of hypnotic probes or a drug-facilitated interview" (p. 93).

Once the therapist is convinced of the diagnosis, Putnam advises that it is not "necessary to convince the host or any other disbelievers in the multiple's system that the patient is a multiple" (p. 151). However, despite this statement, Putnam tells us: "I chip away at this issue [proving diagnosis] in a number of ways" (p. 151). The result is clearly for the patient to recognize the certainty of this diagnosis as a way to explain her/his emotional distress and disrupted life. Indeed, diagnosis is clearly linked to prognosis in Putnam's scheme. He states, "Failure to accept diagnosis generally leads to a stalemate early in therapy, with little productive work toward resolution" (p. 304). He believes that the acceptance of the diagnosis is the first step toward a positive outcome. In Putnam's view, the diagnosis should be known to and accepted by the patient's family members, friends, and colleagues. Putnam, however, sees as resistance the patient "going public" with the diagnosis to talk shows or the media. He warns the therapist not to participate in the patient's effort to "educate" the public at large about his or her multiplicity. Yet, since Putnam considers the acceptance of the diagnosis as a positive outcome measure for both patient and therapist, so it would seem that the therapist would be hard pressed to be reticent or more passive in this aspect of the treatment.

This aggressive pursuit of the diagnosis advocated by Putnam and Ross in their work with persons with MPD is especially problematic. There is a real possibility that the therapist may be experienced by the patient as coercive, and not simply active, in an effort to establish a diagnosis. The differences in power and authority between therapist and patient in the therapy situation is an important element in understanding the potential exploitation of patients by therapists. Yet Putnam and Ross do not appear to acknowledge how their pursuit of diagnosis through eliciting alters could be experienced by the patient as an expression of power and authority. It is important to note that while both Putnam and Ross tell us in detail the lengths they will go to establish the diagnosis, there are no detailed instructions about when the therapist should stop pursuing the diagnosis and seek alternative understandings of the patient.

Patients in psychological crisis welcome an explanation of their turmoil and inner disarray. Often they long for a reason for their pain, and are vulnerable to the therapist's convictions and beliefs about the causes. Putnam and Ross are so emphatic about the necessity for the therapist to pursue the diagnosis that it is quite possible that the therapist's convictions about the diagnosis may satisfy the patient's need for an explanation without much critical thinking. Some patients cathect to the particular explanation we have offered them, or to our role as explainer, rather than investing in their own ability to search for meaning and explanations as ways to promote growth and recovery.

Putnam (1989) calls multiples "special patients" (p. 163). This attitude must be communicated to the patient in many different ways. Yet it is not clear how each patient interprets this attitude, how they understand and experience the therapist's valuing them. A potential danger in this aspect of Putnam's and Ross's theoretical approaches is that the patient will experience the therapist's affirmation expressed most basically in the need to establish the diagnosis with the patient not in an integrative way, but in a divisive way. Is the therapist primarily interested in the multiplicity or the person containing these varied personas?

CLINICAL EXAMPLE

The patients who are diagnosed with MPD have most often suffered greatly because their privacy, control of their own bodies, and safety as children and adults have been violated by others. Therefore, we must be especially sensitive to issues of privacy when using case material. This case has been thoroughly disguised to protect the anonymity of all concerned.

The patient, Ms. K., came to the attention of the mental health system with her first hospitalization when she was a late adolescent. Initially, her difficulties were described as periods of intense depression and self-destructive activity. Yet, she was able to complete college and a two-year postgraduate program without significant interruptions or delays. Her late teens and early twenties were, however, marked by increasing periods of agitation and despair, with frequent self-mutilating behaviors including serious burning and cutting of her arms. She had a number of significant suicide attempts by drug overdose, and she made many suicidal gestures. She was in several different psychotherapies with accomplished clinicians, both male and female, and had been medicated with a variety of anxiolytics, antidepressants, mood stabilizers, and antipsychotics. She also participated in couples' therapy with her partner. After many short-term hospitalizations, she was hospitalized at a long-term treatment facility for one and a half years. There, after a rocky start with several suicide attempts and a variety of other serious self-destructive behaviors requiring seclusion, restraint, and constant observation, she settled into a treatment program.

The treatment team had decided that she was best diagnosed as having a borderline personality organization, with no Axis I diagnosis. Consequently, all medications were tapered, leaving only the occasional use of anxiolytics. The treatment was directed toward maximizing autonomy, and for the patient's gaining awareness of, and taking responsibility for, her painful affects. It was believed that the patient had substantive impairment in the psychic structures that made it difficult for her to tolerate and discharge affect.

Elvin Semrad (1969) described this intolerance of affect in persons vulnerable to psychosis:

> There is in the patient's personality structure extant at any given moment an incapacity to acknowledge, bear, put and keep in perspective and control by either ordinary or neurotic mechanisms certain distressing affects associated with aloneness, depression and the inevitable and unchangeable sources of life dissatisfactions which can become overwhelming. [p. 18]

The therapist and staff shared the goal of supporting and encouraging her efforts to bear affect, and they worked to help her face her affect when she tried to force others to be responsible for her feelings and her safety.

A certain amount of minor self-mutilation was expected and tolerated in the beginning months of the work, and periodically throughout the hospital stay. Her reports of extensive physical and sexual abuse as a child and young adolescent were validated, but were dealt with only as part of the affective burden she needed to find ways to bear and manage more effectively. She became increasingly autonomous over the course of the hospitalization, and was able to begin work and develop some of her hobbies. Her involvement with other people in adult education classes and church groups became sources of pride and comfort for her. She was able to sort out reasonable, although somewhat distant, relationships with her parents. Her relationships with siblings improved.

Some time after discharge, the patient and her partner had to move to another state because of a change in her partner's job status. She negotiated the move successfully and was able to continue psychotherapy with an experienced clinician in the new city. She made it a primary goal to seek out social contacts and activities, to continue what had been important relationships and sources of comfort.

Her adjustment over the first year was quite good, and she only required two overnight hospitalizations to support her when she felt particularly overwhelmed. Her therapist became persuaded, over the first few months of treatment, that a diagnosis of MPD was more appropriate than the diagnosis she had carried. The therapist believed that the patient was often dissociated during her self-destructive behaviors and at times in the treatment hour. The therapist proceeded to discuss this observation with the patient.

The patient, although at first uncertain, became more and more convinced that her therapist was correct. Some of her affective states were reframed now as dissociative states; alters were discovered and uncovered and became an active part of her daily life.

With this new diagnosis, the focus of treatment, and her social relationships began to change. The patient's partner and family became actively involved in learning about MPD. Although generally accepting, they found the experience of the patient's multiplicity anxiety provoking, and were not able to participate in the patient's request that they relate to selected alters and address the alters by name. Some of the patient's friends were unnerved by her presentation and insistence that they accept and understand her illness. The patient was not insisting that friends become as absorbed with her problems as she was, but only that they accept her diagnosis, and call her alters by name. Friends became increasingly uninterested in the patient, and some specifically objected to this latter request. Although her employer and co-workers understood that she had a psychiatric disability, they were not interested in hearing about her illness and its effect on her life to the extent that the patient felt compelled to discuss it.

Because of these uninterested or distancing responses from family, friends, and people in her workplace, the patient began to describe to her therapist feeling increasingly angry, misunderstood, and singled out for rejection. The therapy, she contended, was the only place where she could truly be herself. The patient began to feel more and more that the therapist was the only person who truly understood her. The therapist became increasingly uncomfortable with the patient's assertions of the therapist's primacy in her life and encouraged the patient to attend groups with other persons who suffered from MPD or dissociative disorders.

Initially, the patient responded to this referral with great fury and hurt. She felt that the therapist was becoming untrustworthy and two-faced, and that the referral was just a means to abandon her. Suspicious, angry alters emerged and dominated the treatment. The patient focused the treatment on her feelings and beliefs about the therapist and others in her outside world. She had trouble functioning at her job and ultimately could not maintain her work. She was overwhelmed by feelings of isolation and defectiveness, and was hospitalized following a drug overdose. After a short hospitalization, she was referred to a publicly funded day treatment program, having exhausted her insurance benefits.

The therapy continued at a reduced fee. She was started on medications. The day treatment program was sensitive to and knowledgeable about MPD but, because of the limits of program funding, could not develop a separate program for MPD patients. They tried to develop specialized program elements for MPD patients, but persons with many different significant psychiatric disorders were placed together for much of the day's activities. The patient found that the other day treatment members were uncomfortable with her insistence on bringing the alters into groups, and at being addressed by different names. She reluctantly agreed to participate in the program in a more contained, less overt way. She expressed disappointment that this therapeutic program could not offer her the sense of understanding she felt in individual therapy.

The differences between the sense of being encouraged to express herself and the alters in individual therapy and the discouragement of expression she felt in the other areas of life presented an irreconcilable conflict. She became even more absorbed with individual therapy and less involved with other people and other situations. Over the next several months, she pulled away from friends, family, and her social environment and her sense of alienation and estrangement increased.

Therapy became central and she asked for increased time, both in face-to-face sessions and telephone contacts. Episodes of self-destructive behavior increased, and her affects became more intense, labile, and intrusive. The patient eventually became furious at the therapist, who she felt was abusive. She required frequent hospitalizations to help manage feelings and impulses. She told the inpatient team that she had followed the therapist's advice to reveal and explore her inner experience. These efforts appeared to be at the expense of the rest of her life. She felt confused, and life and the therapy came to a standstill.

DISCUSSION

The therapist represented in this case followed a central tenet of the treatment of patients with MPD. The therapist became convinced in the early work with the patient that she had been misdiagnosed in previous treatment, and worked toward the expression and normalization of the patient's more elaborate inner life. The therapist moved carefully but actively toward the establishment of the diagnosis, and the acceptance of the diagnosis by the patient. Although the therapist continuously stressed safety and integration, the patient found the inclination to delve into her inner life irresistible. The result was a situation in which the therapist became the only person with whom the patient felt she could talk honestly. Finally, the patient became furious at the price she paid for honesty and understanding. In this case description, the therapist's commitment to a course of treatment resulted in a treatment relationship that was regressive for the patient, and the establishment of a transference that became fixed and problematic.

In reviewing this composite case, we can understand the patient's course from a variety of viewpoints. We can think of a number of dynamic and practical factors to explain the patient's regression. However, it is also important to recognize that this focus on establishing the patient's diagnosis, and encouraging the patient to acknowledge the diagnosis, can create problems that work against growth and integration. This focus can move the therapist and the therapy in a direction in which the patient is encouraged to understand what illness she has and not who she is as a person. Also, the therapist is encouraged to focus on ego deficits and symptoms more than the person's potential for growth and well-being. The therapist and patient are directed more toward the depths of the patient's internal life and less toward the ways the patient faces her world and the people in it. The therapist cannot, in all cases, be true to both the establishment of a diagnosis and to the patient as she lives in the world. In our case, this patient became fragmented and disconnected as she struggled to cope with tragic life experiences. This same fragmentation was expressed and reenacted in her life situation. She found herself alone, again, with an outer world inhospitable to her feelings, her worst fears about life confirmed. This patient suffers profound internal fragmentation and disconnection. It is a further hardship when the diagnosis and treatment add to this very same fragmentation.

The danger in believing too much in a diagnosis is that we can become committed more to whatever the current theoretical understanding of the diagnosis is than to comprehending the experience of each patient seeking help. We have seen this in the modern history of schizophrenia. We were first told that schizophrenia was surely the result of failures of parenting by the schizophrenogenic mother. Therapists inadvertently hurt a generation of parents, provided an incorrect explanation to the patients, and eroded the public's confidence in mental health professionals. Now, we are informed that schizophrenia is a biological illness like diabetes. This shift from the environmental to the constitutional may lead to its own set of problems. Hope and encouragement will be offered to those individuals who accept that they have a neuropsychiatric disease. For those persons who do not accept their diagnosis, they are labeled *resistant* or *noncompliant*.

Our need to be definite and effective threatens to overwhelm the hope and opportunities of a new group of people whom some call "Multiples." These persons, full of pain, have had to develop their own unique ways to cope and endure. Each person must be seen as a going concern, someone with possibilities and strengths. Although it is not useful to deny the obvious limitations of an illness like MPD, it may be more humane and helpful to let the patients tell us how they need to see and understand themselves. It may be more beneficial for them to participate in a therapy that reinforces ego synthesis and continued functioning in the real world than an exciting, but destructive, voyage into fragmentation and traumatic memories. In the end, it is the person who must be our primary concern, and not the diagnosis that we feel best describes her/him.

REFERENCES

Greenson, R. (1967). *The Technique and Practice of Psychoanalysis, Vol. 1*. New York: International Universities Press.

Havens, L. (1989). *A Safe Place: Laying the Groundwork for Psychotherapy*. Cambridge: Harvard University Press.

Putnam, F. (1989). *Diagnosis and Treatment of Multiple Personality Disorder*. New York: Guilford.

Ross, C. (1989). *Multiple Personality Disorder: Diagnosis, Clinical Features and Treatment*. New York: John Wiley and Sons.

Semrad, E. (1969). Teaching the clinical approach. In *Teaching Psychotherapy of Psychotic Patients*, ed. D. VanBuskirk. New York: Grune and Stratton.

16

Treatment of Character or Treatment of Trauma?

Joan Berzoff and Jaine Darwin

There has been considerable controversy over whether a client who has the diagnosis of dissociative identity disorder (DID) is actually suffering from borderline personality disorder (BPD) or whether the client who is diagnosed with a BPD also suffers with DID. Some authors assert that the diagnoses are entirely different (Kernberg 1975). Others see them as more similar than different, with trauma as the common etiology. They place BPD and DID diagnoses on the continuum of dissociative disorders (Herman 1992, Herman et al. 1991, Ross 1989), with DID residing on the extreme end of that continuum.

BORDERLINE DIAGNOSIS AND DID COMPARED

While there is overlap between the clinical pictures of borderline pathology and DID, *DSM-IV* criteria for these two diagnoses are, in fact, very different. *DSM-IV* defines borderline personality disorders as an Axis II diagnosis where five of the following must be present:

1. Frantic efforts to avoid real or imagined abandonment.
2. A pattern of unstable and intense interpersonal relationships characterized by alternating between extremes of overidealization and devaluation.
3. Identity disturbance: persistent and markedly disturbed, disordered or unstable self-image or sense of self.

4. Impulsivity in at least two areas that are self-damaging, for example, spending, sex, substance abuse, shoplifting, reckless driving, binge eating.
5. Affective instability: due to marked reactivity (e.g., intense episodic dysphoria, irritability or anxiety usually lasting a few hours and only rarely more than a few days).
6. Inappropriate intense anger or lack of control of anger.
7. Recurrent suicidal behavior, gestures, or behaviors, or self-mutilating behaviors.
8. Chronic feelings of emptiness or boredom.
9. Transient stress related to paranoid ideation or severe dissociative symptoms.

Unlike most disorders in *DSM-IV*, psychodynamic etiological explanations underlie the diagnosis of borderline personality disorder. Many object relations theorists (e.g., Adler and Buie 1979, Masterson 1976) use a deficit model to explain borderline psychopathology. Clients with borderline character structures are understood to have met phase-specific developmental milestones without the capacity to separate or individuate. As a result they lack object constancy and evocative memory. In the absence of a soothing other, they face life-threatening separation anxiety. When vulnerable, they feel intense rage, depression, anhedonia, and/or anxiety. While these clients may function well at work, they are prone to act out in impulsive and self-destructive ways through sexually promiscuous behaviors, addictions, and/or suicidal gestures.

Kernberg (1975) suggests that borderline character pathology reflects disturbed ego states as well as pathological object relations. He notes that because borderline patients cannot tolerate contradictory affective or ego states, their internal worlds are divided into all good or all bad self and object representations. Stemming from their early unmet needs, borderlines experience excessive aggression that cannot be neutralized. They have difficulty maintaining coherent identities and the boundaries between themselves and others are poorly defined and maintained. Splitting becomes a predominate defense because it helps deal with contradictory feelings and contradictory ego-states.

While the borderline diagnosis utilizes a psychodynamic framework based on ego states and object relations, the diagnosis of multiple personality disorder is not made on the basis of underlying character pathology but on the presence of symptoms. And although the diagnosis is most often clinically made on the basis of a client's description of amnesias and lost time (Bliss 1984), up until *DSM-III*, dissociative phenomena were not even mentioned among the *DSM* criteria.

Kluft (1989) suggested that four more factors need to be added to the current diagnosis of DID. These are that DID is a chronic, dissociative, posttraumatic stress disorder that originates in childhood. He would also rule in DID if a patient meets the above criteria and has not improved under conventional treatments.

Ross (1989) criticized the *DSM-III-R* diagnosis because it did not include an accurate description of alters and dominant personalities. He was instrumental in authoring the *DSM-IV* criteria specifying that two or more alter personalities need to be present who exhibit individually distinct, consistent, specific behaviors on at least three occasions. Furthermore, he argued that to make the diagnosis of DID, there should be evidence of amnesia or combinations of types of amnesia among alter personalities.

Other proposed diagnoses of DID have been more inclusive. Putnam (1989) adds a number of psychiatric, neurological, and medical symptoms to the diagnostic picture. These include depression, suicidality, fatigue, insomnia, sleepwalking, anxiety, phobic symptoms, substance abuse, and hallucinations during the day. Ross (1989) suggests that nonspecific features of DID should also be added to the diagnosis, such as childhood abuse, amnesias, blank spells, self-destructive behaviors, and somatic symptoms. These predominately occur in women, ages 20–40.

The same symptoms and behaviors, to be sure, are also found in people with BPD. Ross (1989) suggested that distinctions between borderline pathology and DID, *should* be blurred and that the diagnosis of MPD should be made when the criteria for borderline personality can be met or nearly met. In fact, he reports that most of his patients are also diagnosed as borderline. When dissociative symptoms are treated, however, "often the borderline personality will melt away" (p. 156).

Clinicians are left wondering whether all people with MPD are in fact borderlines. If that is the case, then to which diagnosis does the clinician largely and primarily attend? Does one treat the DID with attention to integration of the alters, or does one treat the client's underlying borderline character structure? What is the relationship between the alter personalities of a person with DID? Are these actually the fluctuating ego states of the person with a BPD? How does one factor in the character structure of each individual alter? The clinician who regards the client as suffering from DID will direct clinical attention primarily toward dissociative defenses and the reconstruction of trauma histories. A clinician who regards the client as suffering from BPD will direct clinical attention toward modifying and ultimately minimizing the defense of splitting, while attempting structural change. What are the consequences of attention to these different defenses? Will focusing on split-off ego states foster further dissociation? How much regression does one encourage in working with an individual who has BPD or DID anyway? How much should the therapist explore past trauma? How much containment and ego support should the therapist provide?

These became the questions that the authors struggled with, retrospectively, having treated the same patient consecutively for fifteen years. In what follows, we report on the case history of Laura from two diagnostic perspectives. Then we discuss our views of the value of these different diagnoses and of the treatments of the same patient.

DR. BERZOFF

Laura was 21 when I first saw her in the outpatient clinic of a large teaching hospital. A waiflike young woman, she had sought treatment because she was depressed. She felt she was "always accidentally hurting herself" and wanted to stop. She was quite isolated socially, felt she was drifting, and was working as a salesperson in a local department store. She complained of sleepwalking and had recently fallen off a horse and injured her neck. She thought the accident might be related to her feelings about herself.

Laura was the second adopted child of two middle-class parents. Her mother worked as a physical therapist and her father as a school principal. Adopted at age 2, she had previously been in a number of foster homes. Her earliest memories included passing an orphanage and being told by her father she'd be returned if she didn't behave. She also remembered throwing an egg at her brother at age 5, and her father taking her to the landfill, saying, "This is where you belong." He then left and didn't return for her until after sundown.

Laura remembered her mother as rigid, cold, and proper. Her mother had specifically wanted a daughter and named Laura after herself. Laura's mother was excessively concerned with physical appearance, and Laura grew up feeling that she was always overweight according to her mother's standards. At intake, she weighed around 90 lbs, and while not looking anorexic, her straight, thin, shape was androgynous.

Laura's mother was at home with her until she was 5 and then began working the afternoon shift when Laura entered school. Laura was left in her father's care after school. The family is remembered by the patient as "a sham." While they looked like a model family to the community, their home life was marked by verbal, physical, and sexual abuse. Laura remembers physical abuse first directed against her older brother Peter, who was regularly beaten by their father for doing poorly academically. Laura did well at school, both academically and athletically, but was withdrawn at home.

She remembers her father as impulsive and bizarre. He would shoot dogs who crossed his yard and killed the family cat when it tore some furniture in their home. In her suburban elementary school Laura was a tomboy and became increasingly withdrawn. Her teachers became concerned and suggested therapy. Laura remembers seeing a psychiatrist but being unable to tell him about the family violence, which continued to escalate. Her parents terminated the treatment after a month or two.

When Laura was 11, she woke up with her father's penis in her mouth. In that same year, she was raped by her brother who told her that he was doing it for her own good. She feared that if she told her parents about her brother they would kill him, and so she continued her pattern of silence. Her father would not allow her to keep her door shut. He began to listen in on her phone calls, intercept her mail, as well as call the police regularly, complaining about children in her neighborhood. He also continued to abuse her sexually at night.

As a teenager, she told her mother about the sexual abuse at the hands of her father. Her mother's response was to buy her a motorcycle. Since she was underage to drive, it sat in the driveway. As soon as she was old enough to drive, she totalled the motorcycle. She was immobilized for four months during which time she was repeatedly sexually violated by her father.

By age 16, Laura was taking significant amounts of drugs supplied both by her brother, who was dealing, and by her mother, who kept a jar of pills in the bedroom. As Laura and Peter would take the pills, their mother would replace them.

When she was 16, Laura sought help from a youth group leader who convinced her to apply early admission to a local college, where she was accepted with a full athletic scholarship. It was then that her mother "noticed" the missing pills, and both parents put Laura under house arrest for being a substance abuser. Her parents tried to fire the group leader who had offered help. They did not allow Laura any phone calls, nor was she allowed to leave the house under any circumstances. Her father even hired a guard and she spent that year taking more drugs. In the middle of the year, her mother was called away to care for her sick grandfather. Laura continued to be sexually abused by her father and her brother.

At 17, Laura ran away from home and lived with her youth group leader, who had left the town in which the family lived. During this time, her parents burned her school trophies and formally disowned her. Laura stayed with her mentor for about six months while making enough money to live independently. By the time she came to treatment, her mentor had terminated their relationship and Laura did not know why. In fact, Laura had also had a number of roommate situations and friendships that had not worked out and which had been precipitously terminated without her knowing why. She was equally puzzled about those relationships. She saw herself as quite alone in the world, slighted by acquaintances and rebuffed by her parents with whom she continually tried to reconnect.

Given Laura's self-destructive behaviors, her emptiness, impulsivity, trauma history, unstable relationships in which people were viewed as either quite loving or depriving, distorted view of her body, and the historical time in which the treatment occurred (1974), I diagnosed her as having a BPD. Probably the most compelling reason for the diagnosis was my own experience with her.

From our first encounter, there was a profound and haunting emptiness in trying to engage with her. I would often feel a boundarylessness in the room, as if, in the many silences between us, parts of herself (and even parts of myself) were fragmenting under the weight of what she had experienced. I would leave our sessions feeling empty, hungry, lost, and confused. Sometimes she would be quite devaluing; at other times, it seemed that her hopes were pinned solely on our relationship.

Given her borderline diagnosis, and my own internal responses, our therapeutic goals included: (1) helping her organize her diffuse identity; (2) attending to early relational deficits; (3) providing a different kind of relationship in which I could be experienced as present, consistent, and reliable, and in which she could internalize new kinds of self and object representations; (4) modifying her less adaptive defenses (i.e., derealization and identification with the aggressor); and (5) helping her to minimize splitting in relation to her family (whom she idealized or devalued) and in the transference.

Laura began the treatment like an open book. She literally brought in dozens of bound journals that documented her multiple traumata. My first intervention was to offer her some ways to slow down, to suggest that she might not need to relive it all again, and to help her learn to tolerate and titrate her traumatic past, given her propensity, when overwhelmed, to hurt herself. Hence, my beginning work was to set some limits on the degree to which we would allow retraumatization to reoccur in the present, to help her anticipate self-destructive behaviors, and to help her gain some insight and judgment into the meanings of these behaviors slowly and over time.

Early on in the treatment a relational pattern emerged. It was to be replayed dozens of times and had to do, in part, with whether I cared for her. Laura would call me in the middle of the night to say that she was "sleepwalking." "I turned on the gas," she would say, but she would add in a whisper, "never mind." She would then go back to sleep. Usually I did not.

Since her trust had been so violated in the past, and since she seemed desperate to try to have a sustaining relationship in the present, I made a clinical (and for me, atypical) decision to allow phone calls at home. Over time, I had to modify this with very clear limits about when she could call and how long she could talk. Over time, I also had to charge her for phone time.

In the beginning of treatment, Laura reenacted her experiences of abandonment and abuse with her parents. She would go to their house and they would criticize her. She would be disinvited for holidays; her father would make advances toward her. She would experience these relationships as deeply traumatic. As time went on, however, she began to do the same with me: experience intense longings to be cared for; feel rejected, alone, and unwanted. We worked to modify her own sense of herself—as a helpless victim or as bad and unworthy—and her views of me as a nurturer or perpetrator. In the meanwhile, she began college and found some sources for intellectual pleasure, deriving considerable self-satisfaction and self-worth in the process. We tried to examine her current relationships, including friends, family, and work associates to whom she was drawn and who rebuffed her. As with so many experiences with her, however, it always felt as if there was missing data.

She graduated from a two-year college, and then met a man who seemed to be reasonably connected to her. They were engaged to be married. She became pregnant at that time, and her fiancé made it clear he did not want a child. Laura had an abortion, which aroused significant guilt in her as an adopted child. She saw herself as murdering herself, and after the abortion had a series of accidents culminating in a broken arm.

Our work continued around her defenses; especially her identification with the aggressor (her father) in light of her self-destructive behaviors. We continued to address her difficulty regulating her own internal world, her view of herself and others where she viewed all others as powerful and malevolent and herself as weak and helpless, and her ego strengths, intellectually and in her work. After the abortion, her fiancé broke off the relationship. She was devastated and suicidal, but I decided not to hospitalize her given what seemed to me to be her very serious regressive potential. It was easy to envision Laura becoming a professional and chronic inpatient.

In fact, Laura then began to develop a number of physical disorders. She first developed a blood disease that was undiagnosable; later she contracted Legionnaire's disease for which she was hospitalized. She was somewhat proud to have stumped the medical diagnosticians who could not find what was wrong with her. My experience, too, was of how difficult it was to locate what was "wrong" with her and in her relationships.

Sessions throughout the mid-phase of treatment were marked by her intense longings. When I would leave town for a weekend, she would intuitively know, and call my service (or me) to have me experience her haunting emptiness. When I would take a vacation or change an appointment, she took to terminating the relationship, writing to me in a formal and legalistic voice, such as "Herewith please find my payment. Your services will no longer be needed. Sincerely, Laura"

She continued the relationship when not seeing me by writing to me. These prodigious letters, often written in the style of poems, would include her dreams, her fears, and her experiences of aloneness. For example, she wrote:

When I was born, I was named Anna and then put in the orphanage.
When I left there my name was changed to Laura,
    and my nickname was Lulu when I was young.
Now most people know me as Laura.
I know that I won't be any skinnier or taller.

I wonder what life would have been like for Anna.
When I was young I did as I was told.
Whether by Dad or Laura, or the nuns at school.
I never played with dolls
Because I saw no sense in it.
I preferred to be out on my bike or playing football
I won first place in every contest and played the piano
But never considered that some day I would find out
How babies were born
By two that should never should have seen what lingerie I had on.
Born in New York
and all alone at 2
For which I have not forgotten
This is why I want to know
About the year 1952

There are times in everyone's life
When they want to say time out
When push comes to shove
They wonder why isn't anyone there?

In a way I feel like the Lone Ranger.
No one knew where he came from
But he had the strength and would not let others know his past

Maybe it's normal, I don't know.
JB [me] said progress would be slow.
My behavior doesn't help too much
Especially when I go and waste a session

JB said last time that I test her
Maybe I do, but its not a conscious effort,
I wonder why I'm not any better
Why I won't get close to and trust others
Why I delay my progress
Maybe because of my ego and sense of falling apart.
I think this may be why I can't be open.

These kinds of written communications were much like her verbal communications: haunting, evocative, self-blaming, sometimes angry, and very lonely. In the hours with me, she would sometimes be cryptic, sometimes crouch, often unable to speak. She would get angry with herself or me, and following such a session, would often physically harm herself.

Usually within about six weeks, she would reconnect, concerned about whether I still cared about her, calling herself a "jerk," and sorry that she "continually tested the relationship." She graduated from college and took a responsible job as a paralegal in the largest law firm in her city. She was promoted and appeared to be a valued worker. She even moved into her own apartment and, although lonely, seemed to be able to tolerate living alone.

In this phase of treatment, she began to accept the status of a loner. There was a great sadness, accompanied by occasional pride over her individual accomplishments. She began a search for her biological mother, which was both painful but productive. Intermittently, when she would feel slighted by me, she would again terminate the treatment. I saw this work as a necessary part of mourning for what had not been and probably would not be, and as a way to integrate her fragmented identity.

Although doing well at work, her interpersonal world was peopled with casual drinking acquaintances. She continued to be confronted for behaviors she did not remember, and attributed these to drinking. Her driver's license was finally suspended for drinking while driving, but she remained uninterested in controlling the drinking.

In 1985, after eleven years of her treatment, I announced that I would be leaving the area. I was pregnant with my first child and moving to a new location two hours away. Laura met the news by saying little. I, however, felt as if I were abandoning her. Although I had offered to continue seeing her, she terminated the relationship.

After my child was born, Laura came to see me four times and wrote a number of missives. Finally, the therapy was terminated and she summed up her accomplishments. She saw herself as having gained skills she was proud of, especially at work. I noted her having sustained our relationship over a very long period of time. Laura had also been able, over many years, to identify a pattern whereby she defensively dealt with trauma by abusing herself, and sometimes by abusing others. She had become better at anticipating that, when she was scared, angry, hurt, or overwhelmed, she might hurt herself. She had developed a greater capacity to bear her aloneness.

In object relations terms, Laura had been able to establish some autonomy in her relationship with me. As she began to work, albeit falteringly, on seeing herself as separate, she gained moderate success in testing out whether she could separate without metaphorically destroying me, or being destroyed by me. By leaving me again and again, she had incrementally achieved some object constancy. The subtext in our relationship was always, would I still care about her. Could she leave and come back? Could we each survive the hate generated in the relationship? By experiencing reliability and predictability over time, we had been able to create a minimal holding environment in the treatment, and she had tentatively created one in her life.

During the therapy Laura also came to modify her expectations and grieve her many losses. She had begun to mourn her lost childhood, her parents, her own unborn baby, and some relational opportunities that now seemed lost to her.

As we worked on the traumata perpetrated by each family member in a titrated way, there was growing recognition that her trust had been violated, and that this had deeply affected her capacity for loving relationships. This resulted in considerable depression, which had to be borne by her and by me. While there was some awareness of the need to hurt herself, and even to get physically hospitalized when in psychic pain, we never succeeded in extinguishing those behaviors. I did feel, however, that Laura's chronic and vague suicidal ideation ebbed and flowed over time. Another gain was that Laura managed to stay out of a psychiatric hospital. Given her severe regressive potential, and her longings to be taken care of, it seemed a therapeutic achievement that she was able to manage, albeit with great difficulty, some autonomous ego functioning.

During the eleven years of treatment this very traumatized woman had managed to graduate from college and was supporting herself, maintaining an apartment, and holding down a responsible job. Treatment had been difficult, but had been managed on an outpatient basis. I left her with the name of my colleague in the city in which she lived.

PART II OF LAURA'S TREATMENT: DR. DARWIN

Laura first contacted me approximately three years after her original therapist's departure. She wasn't sure why she was coming to treatment or what had happened in the intervening three years. She appeared as a painfully thin, boyish-looking woman who was studied in her every gesture, as if trying to comply with rules about what was proper. Our first session was most notable for her inability to talk about the past three years. The only way she and I could construct a chronology was by medical illnesses and accidents, which seemed to anchor her in time. She was prone to bouts of bronchitis and to problems with her knees and back, which had caused her to become immobilized. She was able to give a developmental history that has already been elaborated earlier in this chapter.

Her present life consisted of work and vague references to friends. She continued to have conflictual relationships with her parents who she felt were always criticizing her. She still sought their affection and was rebuffed; often being disinvited for major family holidays at the last minute. Laura was strange to sit with. She moved around the room during the hour, pacing, perching on my desk or my file cabinet. I remember thinking to myself that as long as I sat still I'd know where one of us was. She was alternately needy and then devaluing about treatment, almost defying me to help her change her life. She discounted the importance of the trauma history as something that was over and on which one should not dwell.

Diagnostically I saw her as primitive character who relied mainly on schizoid defenses. I soon also saw both the affect storms and the flat, depressive affect that could be characteristic of a patient with borderline pathology. She would attack and often left me feeling victimized. Fortunately, she also could be verbally agile and demonstrated a keen sense of humor. In the beginning the work focused on grieving for her departed therapist, on difficulties with her boss, by whom she felt taken advantage of, and on problems with her friends. For reasons not apparent to Laura, they would stop talking to her and refuse to discuss why. One friend told her, "It was bad enough for you to do what you did; to insist you don't know what you did wrong makes it worse." The work also focused on the continuing disappointment with her parents and the constant oscillation between trying to please them or trying to convince herself that they did not deserve to be pleased.

I knew her original therapy had been successful in helping her contain and manage her affects, and I attempted to do the same. Yet, I developed a growing awareness of many dissociative symptoms. She often had time periods for which she could not account; she described sleepwalking during which she would rearrange the furniture and move around in ways which caused her to awaken in the morning with unexplained bruises. She appeared quite fragmented with little feeling of continuity between sessions. I often felt as if I was sitting with a different person from week to week.

She also was acutely sensitive to my activity level in the therapy. If she experienced me as too intrusive, she would become hypervigilant and have to leave the session, or she'd have flashbacks and retreat from therapy for weeks. Additionally, Laura would smell from alcohol, but deny that she had been drinking. She suffered from many somatic complaints—joint pain, upper respiratory infections, and incessant headaches. Laura grew more despairing that after so many years of therapy, happiness still eluded her. I began to share her despair and to think about new ways to help her. My search for a new approach coincided with a growing professional interest of mine in work with trauma survivors and I began to think about her case primarily through that lens, especially in the light of her fragmentation and severe trauma history.

Approximately nine months into the treatment two events occurred. First, Laura discovered in her closet a number of tagged outfits, which she did not remember buying and which did not suit her taste. Second, Laura could not find a number of journals she kept; as noted previously, she was a prodigious writer. She feared having thrown them out, which would have been uncharacteristic. This inaugurated a period in which Laura had more frequent flashbacks. I worked with her to find ways to control them and to guarantee her safety. We tried imagery and relaxation. When this was not sufficient, I urged her to write down their content and to put them away. She started dropping off at my office throughout the week many pages of anguished recountings of the early traumas. Since she refused to consider a medication consult to help with this heightened anxiety, I attempted to support and to contain her.

The following week I received a phone call from Laura, in a baby voice, fearing retribution for telling about the trauma; this was followed by several other "people" getting on the phone and asking to talk to me. When I saw her at the scheduled appointment time the next day, Laura began by complaining of being tired although she had gone to bed early the night before. I shared what had happened on the phone the night before when she thought she was asleep. At first she became angry as if I were trying to "gaslight" her. When I repeated one story she had told me, she looked stricken. Laura began telling me about all the people who lived inside of her—fifteen in total—whose voices she heard and whom she saw at different times reflected in the mirror as well. When I labeled this as MPD, she was surprised it had a name. Laura began to elaborate about her experiences with the others, the alters, of whose existence she had known for years.

In the following weeks, as the alters identified themselves, I could see I had met many of them before—the latency-age boy who sat on the file cabinet, the imperious and angry 17-year-old who seemed to hold most of the anger, the teenager who wouldn't eat because she was too fat, and the teenager who drank on the sly. It was a difficult period for both Laura and me. She, as the host, was not used to the alters insisting on so much body time. I was not used to patients revealing themselves to be suffering from MPD. Yet, this new diagnosis offered the most cohesive explanation for that which had been illusory and fragmented. These disparate behaviors suddenly had an explanation. This did not make the work easier, just less confusing.

I began to work on issues of safety, to have the system work better as a whole and not keep secrets from each other. When I asked Laura why she or they had revealed themselves now, she replied they had all suffered and needed to be heard. Laura had trouble regulating the whole group and they began to utilize me as an auxiliary ego. The level of energy it took to keep Laura and her alters in check was immense for both of us. It became clear how often one alter had sabotaged the goals of another alter in the past, for instance, by alienating a good friend and not telling Laura what had happened. In many ways, Laura was the victim of her alters as she had been the victim of her parents. She parented the child alters in the same punitive way she had been parented, thus becoming the abuser as well.

I attempted to encourage communication and cooperation among the alters, to find ways to document what occurred during the lost time. In this way we both learned the cause of the constant fatigue—alters watching movies on cable all night; many of the unexplained bruises—the latency-age boy tripping while playing catch; the smell of alcohol on her breath—the substance-abusing teenager who drank at lunch. At one point Laura and the alters were able to write an autobiography in which the "birth" of each alter was documented—each "birth" corresponded to a major traumatic event. I attempted to improve the self care within the system by dissuading various alters from engaging in unsafe activities, always stressing their shared body. When I suggested that the alters were indeed one person who might become integrated, they would call and accuse me of trying to kill them.

I had to remind myself not to get carried away with the specialness of the diagnosis, to try to set limits and to offer therapy as a setting for containment. The therapy was like a rollercoaster. Just because the cast with whom the character pathology resided was bigger did not mean the character pathology had disappeared. While many of the ego fluctuations could be explained by the constant switching of personalities, different alters had different levels of ego functioning within themselves. There was also the reality—the patient had to continue to function at work.

The industry in which Laura worked was threatened by layoffs because of the deepening recession, and she was under more pressure at work. The drinking, done by a 16-year-old alter, became more pronounced and she was confronted at work where she had already come to the nurse's attention because of her frequent absences due to illness and her near-anorexic appearance. Laura found it harder to coordinate the system of alters. She became involved with a man at work and began to miss more and more treatment sessions.

Then she lost her job. The system was out of control. Any efforts to facilitate interaction among the alters was dropped and Laura took a repressive stance. The alters countered by essentially rendering her immobile. She had moved to another apartment and was now living an hour away from my office. As she or they became more demanding, and I set more limits on my availability, the situation reached the boiling point. Laura, who now owed me a fair amount of money, referred herself to a local mental health facility. I spoke with them at length and they agreed to accept the case. Within two days, the mobile emergency team came to her home and committed her without her consent after one of the many phone conversations in which she made vague suicide threats. Although they discharged her promptly, it was a wake-up call. I began to see that certain of Laura et al.'s behaviors could be quickly contained in a supportive system that could set absolute limits on certain provocative behaviors.

We have had sporadic contact since then. She was once hospitalized to be detoxed and a second time to treat her anorexia. She has been in day treatment and in psychiatric inpatient units. When I reflect on our work together I think we had to attend to her dissociative defenses to begin accurately to construct both her inner and outer worlds. The extensive amnesias made it difficult to understand the context and extent of both her ego fluctuations and the alterations in the self states. Without our having focused on the dissociative phenomena, I think despair, loneliness, and disappointment would have caused growing dysfunction. This would be intensified by the consequences of her behaviors during amnestic periods. I think her decline and further fragmentation were inevitable.

DR. DARWIN'S REFLECTIONS ON DR. BERZOFF'S TREATMENT

I think what Dr. Berzoff did in her work with Laura was necessary but not sufficient. She offered Laura a place in which she could begin to be safe. In urging her to titrate dealing with the trauma, the therapy looks like any good therapy with a trauma victim. Until Laura could learn self-care and regulate her affect, she could not begin to integrate the trauma. The steadiness of her first therapist allowed her to feel cared for in a way she had been deprived of as a child. The difficulty, however, as I see it, was that the diagnosis of borderline personality disorder by definition left the "badness" residing in the patient and saw her impulsivity and self-destructive behaviors as stemming from a deficit in the patient. A trauma model would formulate her destructive behaviors as efforts to maintain the dissociation in an attempt to self-soothe. If the variants in behavior and in affect are seen only as ego fluctuations, the patient is asked to try to create a cohesive whole without knowing where the parts are. Had her difficulties resided primarily within the realm of borderline psychopathology, I would have expected her to become less fragmented after such a competent psychodynamic therapy as she had with Dr. Berzoff or during the first nine months of my work with Laura when I employed a similar approach. Laura and I needed to gain entry into her inner life, replete with alters. Only then could the therapy truly undertake the Herculean task of self-regulation.

In my work with Laura, I learned about her inner lives. We were able to co-construct a history of all the traumas by documenting the birth of each alter. We were able to see the scope of the work that lay ahead; to understand what it would take to integrate or at least make a more cohesive system of alters. We were able to remove some of the mysteries — the many injuries, the lost friendships. We were not able to move beyond the beginning stages of this work, however, because we lacked the resources to do so — the ability to meet with enough frequency, and the existence of a good emergency system that would alleviate the enormous pressures on the therapist. By reframing Laura's problems as mainly dissociative in nature, we offered her the hope of a less constricted, more interpersonally connected life.

DR. BERZOFF'S REFLECTIONS ON DR. DARWIN'S WORK

One wonders whether the degree to which Dr. Darwin attended to the multiples as separate people encouraged the emergence of more alters. When Dr. Darwin treated the alters as individuals rather than separate ego states, when she spoke to them in the hours separately, when she encouraged drawings by the child alters, this encouraged fragmentation and further regression. As the therapist attended to the fragments of Laura's self as literally different selves, she may have undermined Laura's limited capacities to keep her ego intact. Dr. Darwin's therapeutic endorsement that an inner state of fragmentation was in reality a different person in the system, was potentially disorganizing. It gratified Laura's needs to see herself as special and may have resulted in further ego fragmentation. This may have laid the groundwork for Laura's current chronic downward course.

I would also maintain that her therapist's interest in her dramatic and florid symptoms may have been overstimulating for Laura. Beginning eighteen months after the emergence of alters, Laura became chronically unemployed. She currently lives with two alcoholic roommates and is still on disability. While it is certainly fair to wonder whether this would have occurred anyway, one cannot help but question whether helping her manage conflicting ego states, regulate her object world, and minimize splitting would have been therapeutically wiser than reifying dissociative states, which encouraged her to function in a less organized way.

When I recently asked Laura's permission to use the material for this paper, she replied, "The Multiples? They were always there. I just didn't know other people didn't have them too. But I don't know. I think it's the 90s. I flip through my remote control. It's dysfunction this, dysfunction that, alcoholics, incest, multiples. It's a sign of the times." Perhaps Laura, too, is aware that the diagnosis of MPD is also a social construction which represents a particular time in culture and in history. In the postmodern times in which we now live, the self is no longer conceptualized as unitary or continuous, but is seen as made up of multiple identities where each self contains "a multiple of others, singing different melodies, different verses and with different rhythms, nor do these voices necessarily harmonize" (Gergen 1991, p. 83).

JOINT DISCUSSION

If we look in the most current trauma literature, Judith Herman, M.D., offers a viable integrative approach. She writes in *Trauma and Recovery* (1992) that both the diagnosis of borderline personality disorder and diagnosis of MPD are pejorative variants on the older label of hysteria. Both diagnoses are more similar than different; each originates from severe and early childhood trauma. Herman states, "Patients with borderline personalities lack the dissociative capacity to form fragmented alters, but they have similar difficulty developing an integrated identity." (p. 127). She sees the argument regarding borderline personality disorder and multiple personality disorder diagnosis not as about extremes but about shades of gray—that they are more related than not. She proposes a different diagnosis altogether and calls it *complex post-traumatic stress disorder*.

Herman's (1992) new diagnostic entity is directed toward those individuals who are victims for prolonged periods of subjugation. She defines the areas in which these survivors experience difficulty as originating in alterations of affect regulation, states of consciousness, self-perceptions, ability to function in relationships, and loss of faith and hope.

Reflecting on Dr. Herman's ideas, we would concur that an integrative diagnosis that included altered ego states, object relations, dissociation, *and* a trauma etiology would have made the most sense for Laura. Treatment of character *and* of trauma requires attention to competing subjectivities in the context of an empathic relationship (Schwartz 1994). We would further say that any good treatment involves attending to all of the defenses and helping the client establish better defenses that may be more serviceable to the ego. In Laura's case, this would have meant helping her integrate views of herself and others. This meant hearing and understanding her sleepwalking and lost time as dissociative phenomena and acknowledging the therapist's subjective experiences of fragmentation in the service of helping Laura integrate her own internal world.

Any good treatment requires validating a client's trauma while not retraumatizing her in the process. For Laura this would have meant helping metabolize the trauma and reducing the need for dissociation. Good treatment also involves helping a client work on interpersonal relationships via the therapeutic relationship. With Laura, this would have meant providing consistency, reliability, and predictability, while attending to the transference and countertransference. It also would have meant having a relationship which was not exploitative and where boundaries were maintained. This would have included setting limits on phone calls and out-of-session contacts. Good treatment requires knowing a client's highest level of functioning and helping her achieve it. This would have meant helping Laura find more adaptive ways to cope with her painful affects, setting limits on self-destructive behaviors, and identifying and mobilizing her strengths (i.e., her intellect, writing ability, and humor). Good treatment with severely traumatized clients also means surviving the client's affects. This would have meant that each therapist would have had to know her own limits of what she could bear and neither merge with nor distance defensively from Laura. In short, good treatment requires staying focused on the interpersonal treatment frame and on maintaining a therapeutic stance.

Work with clients who have been this damaged requires that we use integrative therapeutic models and not make therapeutic choices based on theoretical loyalties. We would both agree that Laura was lucky to have had two therapists who could invest in her difficulties and bear witness to her struggles to survive. She may have been unlucky in having two therapists each of whom was limited by the scope of her own lens. We were privileged to be able to have a longitudinal view of a person who was committed to trying to make her life work and who let us see the course of various aspects of her problem across the life span. Given the patient's difficulty integrating her own self (selves), it is essential that therapists be able to tolerate multiple theoretical points of view themselves as well.

REFERENCES

Adler, G., and Buie, D. H., Jr. (1979). Aloneness and borderline psychotherapy: the possible relevance of child development issues. *International Journal of Psycho-Analysis* 60:80–96.

Bliss, E. (1984). A symptom profile of patients with multiple personality disorder, including MMPI results. *Journal of Nervous and Mental Diseases* 172:197–202.

Gergen, K. (1993). *The Saturated Self: Dilemmas of Identity in Contemporary Life*. New York: Basic Books.

Herman, J. (1992). *Trauma and Recovery*. New York: Basic Books.

Herman, J. L., Perry, J. C., and Van de Kolk, B. (1991). Childhood trauma in borderline personality disorder. *American Journal of Psychiatry* 146:440–495

Horevitz, R. P., and Braun, B. G. (1983). Are multiple personality disorder patients borderline? An analysis of 33 patients. *Psychiatric Clinics of North America* 7:69–87.

Kernberg, O. F. (1975). *Borderline Conditions and Pathological Narcissism*. New York: Jason Aronson.

Kluft, R. P. (1989). Iatrogenic creation of new alter personalities. *Dissociation* 2:83–91.

Masterson, J. H. (1976). *Psychotherapy of the Borderline Adult: A Developmental Approach*. New York: Brunner/Mazel.

Merskey, H. (1992). The manufacture of personalities: the production of multiple personality disorder. *British Journal of Psychiatry* 160:327–340.

Putnam, F. W. (1989). *Diagnosis and Treatment of Multiple Personality Disorder*. New York: Guilford.

Ross, C. (1989). *Multiple Personality Disorder, Clinical Features and Treatment*. New York: John Wiley & Sons.

Schwartz, H. (1994). From dissociation to negotiation: a relational perspective on multiple personality disorder. *Psychoanalytic Psychology* 11(2):89–231.

17

Therapists' Responses to Dissociative Clients: Countertransference and Vicarious Traumatization

Karen W. Saakvitne

Diagnosis is a tool, not a truth. It is a construction, which both limits and augments the therapist's ability to understand and make sense of a client's clinical material. Diagnosis simultaneously reflects the progress toward and limitations of the profession in understanding the complexities of psychology and psychic function. A diagnosis provides the clinician with a framework that organizes and shapes the material the client brings to each session, and thus structures the development of the therapeutic relationship.

A therapist's position, theoretical and sometimes political, on the value and validity of the diagnosis of multiple personality disorder (MPD) will influence how she listens to and understands her dissociative client's material. Diagnosis is part of the complex set of responses the therapist brings to the therapy relationship. As with countertransference, the therapist must then be mindful of the function and influence of diagnosis in each psychotherapy.

Diagnosis is only one of many responses therapists have to clients. Dissociative clients, in particular, challenge us to notice and utilize our full range of responses: cognitive, affective, somatic, and associative; conscious, preconscious, and unconscious; syntonic and dystonic; familiar and unfamiliar. Ultimately these personal responses guide our treatments, and we must acknowledge and explore them to protect and enhance our clinical work.

This chapter addresses countertransference and vicarious traumatization in psychotherapy with severely dissociative clients. Countertransference includes our affective and ideational responses to clients and their material, and our conscious and unconscious defenses against those responses. Vicarious traumatization refers to the transformation of the therapist's inner experience as a result of her empathic engagement with clients' trauma material (McCann and Pearlman 1990a). To set the stage for the more detailed discussion of countertransference and vicarious traumatization with dissociative clients, I want to highlight some general issues in diagnosis and treatment techniques.

DIAGNOSIS

The very diagnosis of MPD is emblematic of a paradigm shift in the field. It is therefore politicized. The increased recognition of the etiological centrality of trauma and the symptomatic centrality of dissociation for clients is a recent development (or redevelopment). Because it represents a point of departure from the way in which most therapists were trained, it can evoke in them conflicts about leaving the parental figures and mentors who trained them.

Extreme levels of dissociation challenge our basic beliefs about psychic functioning. We all tend to assume a unitary personality, consistent in time and psychic space. This assumption is inherent in our professional training and life experiences. Thus, to accommodate the concept of dissociation and multiplicity, we must shift our fundamental frame of reference.

A therapist's professional identity and theoretical context is part of her therapeutic context. When a therapist feels in conflict with her observing ego and "internalized supervisor" (Casement 1991), or when a therapist is subject to criticism or professional disbelief, these conflicts can emerge in her countertransference. This vulnerability is increased when a therapist does not have access to colleagues who are working in similar ways with similar clients. When she feels embarrassment and shame, her professional self-esteem suffers, which again influences her countertransference responses. These responses can emerge in a wish to deny or eradicate a client's dissociation. Alternatively, a therapist's fascination with multiplicity can lead her to want her client to dissociate so she can learn more about it.

TECHNICAL ISSUES

Therapists often feel anxious with severely dissociative and multiple personality clients. Some believe they have to learn a special kind of therapy: the therapy one does with MPD clients. I do not concur. While it is important to understand dissociation and helpful to be familiar with effective interventions and techniques, a relational psychotherapy conducted within a consistent therapeutic frame is essential. Clients who identified themselves or are identified as MPD clients are people first, and we know about the practice of psychotherapy with people. I shall return to the specifics of trauma therapy further on in this discussion.

Another technical issue that has clinical, ethical, and political ramifications is that of working with the traumatic childhood memories of clients with dissociative disorders. Clinically, the therapist must remain open to the gradual unfolding of her clients' understanding of their experience. We cannot know before our clients what their experience is. Our task is to hold the affects associated with uncovering and to allow space for the clients to be curious and to notice their own internal process. That means we must tolerate the tension of being between knowing and not knowing.

The ethical issues are critical to the field. The imposition of a therapist's preconceived notions and assumptions about the client is unethical and potentially harmful. The ethics of appropriate therapeutic technique in trauma therapies is a growing concern. While some arguments critical of trauma therapies have relied on insufficiently defined and operationalized constructs such as suggestibility and implantation, and are thus misleading and irresponsible, the issue of therapeutic technique, stance, and responsibility is valid. Therapists have an indisputable responsibility to practice within the standards of rigorous technique, theory, and ethics.

Finally, these controversies are not limited to our consulting rooms. Just as the traumatic experiences of childhood sexual, physical, and emotional abuse occur in a cultural and political context (Herman, 1981 1992), the treatment of the sequelae to trauma also occurs in a political and social context. A constructive outcome of the current controversies in the professional literature and popular media is the renewed commitment by therapists that our work be grounded in solid psychotherapy theory and technique (and by researchers that clinical research—or research applied to clinical populations—be conducted in an ethically and scientifically responsible manner). Organizations concerned with the potential for erroneous recall of childhood sexual abuse seize upon instances of inappropriate, unprofessional, or unethical therapeutic technique; the field, our clients, and our society are diminished by improper and unethical practice. At the same time, we have a responsibility to educate the public, media, and ourselves about the empirical and clinical bases for understanding the impact of trauma on individual's development and adaptations (McCann and Pearlman 1990b). We need to publicize the effective work of psychotherapy with survivors of traumatic life events and the value to society of addressing the costly effects of child abuse through prevention for children at risk and treatment for adult survivors.

PSYCHOTHERAPY AND THE THERAPIST

Clinically, I operate from the basic premise that what is healing about psychotherapy occurs within the therapeutic relationship. The therapeutic relationship includes transference, countertransference, traumatic reenactments, as well as the here-and-now real relationship between the person of the therapist and the person of the client. The client has received much attention in the literature; this chapter focuses on the person of the therapist.

As clinical director of an independent mental-health organization of psychologists which offers psychotherapy services, conducts research, and provides education and training in the field of traumatic stress, the ideas presented in this chapter reflect my own clinical experience, supervision of many clinicians treating dissociative clients, and the theoretical frameworks of psychoanalytic theory and constructivist self-development theory (McCann and Pearlman 1990b). As a psychoanalytic trauma therapist, my current work is on the integration of psychoanalytic theory and technique with trauma theory and therapy (Pearlman and Saakvitne in press, Saakvitne 1990, 1992, 1993).

THE COMPONENTS OF TRAUMA THERAPY

Any therapist working with survivors of childhood trauma needs a firm grounding in psychotherapy theory and technique. Good trauma therapy is first and foremost good theory-based psychotherapy. However, there are several arenas in which effective trauma therapy may differ from traditional psychoanalytic psychotherapy.

Trauma therapy makes greater use of *psychoeducation*. Clients often need information about normal responses to traumatic events, including dissociation; they need education about child development and children's developmental needs and abilities, and sometimes about resources for survivors. This information, the language and concepts, can help clients notice and make sense of their own experiences and symptoms and, thus, helps to interrupt the cycle of self-blame and self-denigration. Although dissociative processes are common for them, survivor clients often have limited understanding of the process of dissociation, its value, and its management, and often feel intense shame and fear that they are crazy. When we convey to a client a view of her dissociation and other posttraumatic stress symptomatology as originally adaptive, we give her tools to understand without shame or self-pathologizing her experience and choices.

Similarly, for the therapist, a solid *understanding of dissociation* and dissociative processes provides her with an invaluable tool for understanding. With this knowledge, the therapist can interpret intrapsychic and interpersonal events in the psychotherapy much more effectively and successfully (Davies and Frawley 1991). Understanding the adaptive function of dissociation eliminates the need for such client-blaming explanations as resistance, negative therapeutic reaction, or the unanalyzable patient. It opens the door to an interpersonal recognition of the need for safety and affect modulation in the challenging work of psychotherapy.

Because of the prevalence of dissociation and other defenses and symptoms that serve to protect the client from overwhelming affect, these therapies often emphasize the *development of self capacities*, that is, development of self-soothing skills, object constancy, and stability of benign self-regard. The therapeutic relationship is the site of this work, through the development of object constancy with the person of the therapist, the internalization of the therapist as a benevolent object, and the development of specific self-soothing skills.

The *management of transference* is integrated into work on the therapeutic relationship. In trauma therapy, the interpretation of transference should occur early in the work and in the context of inviting the client to notice the therapeutic relationship and the impact of the past on the present. Because the transferences are often malevolent, it is generally not useful to invite a negative transference reaction to reach full affective force as advocated in earlier psychoanalytic literature (Pearlman and Saakvitne, in press). These transferences can evoke in the client feelings of terror, dread, or shame and serve to disrupt rather than enhance the development of a therapeutic alliance. For example, to reintroduce the real relationship, a therapist may ask a client, "Do you want to check that out?" when the client describes her fantasies about the therapist's reaction or intent.

In therapies with survivors of trauma, *the therapist is called upon to be genuine and affectively present* in a way that may differ somewhat from other therapies (Davies and Frawley 1991, Jordan et al. 1991). Therapists whose preferred demeanor is that of distant professional or uninvolved expert will be less effective with this population. Being genuine and affectively available means being open to our own and our clients' observations, acknowledging our mistakes, making countertransference disclosure when helpful, and being willing to be known by and vulnerable to a client as the work unfolds. It does not mean abandoning the role of therapist, asking the client to take care of us, or bringing our needs into the relationship at the expense of our clients. Out of our countertransference horror at the pain experienced by survivors of severe child abuse, therapists can misinterpret authenticity to mean impulsivity or all-givingness. This loss of role and boundaries deprives our clients of the opportunity to make use of the healing potential of a boundaried and respectful therapeutic relationship.

These therapies require *clear frames and boundaries* whose development should be a respectful *process* between client and therapist. Psychotherapy builds a foundation of safety, established through trust, predictability, role clarity, respect, and clear communication. Clients with severe damage in trust and safety in interpersonal relationships will struggle to have some ability to monitor closeness and distance, and to develop ways to maintain some control over their terror and their vulnerable self-esteem. Therapists need solid theoretical understanding of the complexities and levels of meaning in order both to maintain the fundamental therapeutic frame and to be flexible and emphasize appropriate mutuality in the negotiation of boundaries.

In summary, the context of the therapy with adult survivors of trauma is the therapeutic relationship. The therapeutic relationship is a uniquely bounded relationship in which interactions can be noticed, named, and understood. This process of noticing and respectfully interpreting interpersonal events is reparative. It challenges, contradicts, and ultimately transforms interpersonal experiences from those familiar to most survivors in their family of origin to new relational paradigms.

When psychotherapy with dissociative clients is grounded in a developmental psychological theory, a therapist is better able to see and hold the client as a person, located in time and context, and not a collection of symptoms and crises. Without this grounding, therapy can too easily lose its focus and become a series of techniques and interventions prompted by "countertransference desperation" (Olio 1993).

When the premise of therapy is a fundamental respect for our clients, their personhood, and their capacity for survival, then it will provide rewarding experiences for both therapist and client. Clients heal and reclaim their lives, their bodies, their right to be alive and to experience joy and love. The work of psychotherapy is rewarding intellectually, interpersonally, and emotionally for the therapist. In therapy we address topics long denied by society, and by working to heal survivors, we help to break the intergenerational and personal cycles of abuse and victimization.

Davies and Frawley (1991) emphasize that treatment requires the therapist to integrate clinical experience and sophistication with a thorough working knowledge of psychological responses to trauma. The work of psychotherapy can be extraordinarily difficult and complex. The therapist is the tool of the work; she is one half of the therapeutic relationship, and her person and her responses are key factors in the unfolding work.

THE THERAPIST IN THE THERAPEUTIC RELATIONSHIP

The therapist brings her self to the therapeutic relationship. Her self includes her personality, defenses and defensive style, personal history—traumatic and otherwise—professional identity, ideals, and theoretical orientation. Into each session she also brings her current circumstances, life circumstances (e.g., personal relationships, living situation, family issues) and immediate daily circumstances (e.g., the client she saw the previous hour, the administrative hassle she just worked out). She brings her body, in whatever state it is in: health and well-being, illness, fatigue, discomfort, comfort, arousal, and whatever relationship she has with her body. She brings her countertransference and her vicarious traumatization.

A therapist relies on self-awareness. When she is aware of her responses, and free to bring her genuine, authentic self into the relationship, it is her greatest resource.

Challenges for Therapists with Dissociative Clients

When the therapeutic relationship is the context of healing, dissociation in a session is an interpersonal event as well as an intrapsychic one. The client is responding in part to what is happening in the room in the relationship between herself and her therapist. For adult survivors of childhood sexual abuse, whose current distress arises from early and often repetitive interpersonal traumas of betrayal, violation, and abuse, the new interpersonal context of the therapeutic relationship contains both hope and terror. That dichotomy is always present. The therapeutic situation then replicates the most painful dilemma of childhood for those who spent their childhood in an abusive home—that is, the dilemma of yearning accompanied by dread and fear. Dissociation is a familiar solution to that dilemma.

As a client moves forward in the relationship toward the therapist, whether slowly and tentatively like some, or rapidly and counterphobically like others, or alternating between those styles, the resulting anxiety for the client can be profound. This anxiety will be managed through a range

of strategies for modulating distance, often reflected in PTSD symptomatology of numbing and flooding, and paralleled in a client's approach and
avoidance or alternation between desperate clinging and angry rejection.
Early in the treatment, the therapist may represent a dangerous authority
figure, someone with power and credibility, which the survivor has been
told that she lacks. As the relationship develops and the opportunities of
the relationship begin to evoke in the client long-buried but powerful
wishes for closeness, nurturance, and mutuality, the sense of danger
intensifies. These are often the very needs associated with abuse in the
past. The defensive function of dissociation is again called into action.

There is a paradox here. As the therapeutic relationship and the
therapeutic alliance develop, dissociation in the therapy may increase. The
paradox can be confusing if we let ourselves forget how dangerous
connection and trust are for the survivor of childhood sexual abuse. Often
this association of fear is accompanied by powerful transferences, transferences to us as perpetrators, as dangerous, as untrustworthy. These
transferences can feel narcissistically insulting or hurtful to the therapist.
They may seem amazing or inconceivable to her. When the therapist is
defensive in response, or takes transference personally and works to
disprove it, she loses an important opportunity for exploring the feelings,
slowly building trust and working through mistrust.

Waites (1993) discusses the analogy between the survivor's dilemma and
that described in the literature on "double binds" in schizophrenia (Bateson
et al. 1956). The solution to a double bind situation is to leave the field,
which can be accomplished through dissociation. However, when in
response to the danger of closeness a client needs to leave the field through
dissociation, the therapist is left behind. The therapist is affected by the
space between her and her client, the sense of emptiness, or void, that can
emerge. This retreat from the relational context can evoke in the therapist
defenses around her fears of loss or abandonment, and affect how
competent and effective she feels as a therapist.

Dissociative clients do not bring an integrated complete sense of self to
the therapeutic relationship. The client's fragmentation can affect the
therapist's ability to feel authentic and connected in the relationship. In
response to dissociative dynamics, a therapist can become restricted,
cautious, and disconnected from herself and from the client. When we are
afraid of a client's dissociation, we can become overly cautious and
tentative so as not to provoke a dissociative response. The therapist may
move into a caricatured role, transferential, projective, or countertransfer-
ential.

These countertransference responses are also informative. One may
become aware of a split-off, developmentally immature part of a client by

the therapist's complementary maternal protective response. Noticing such a shift in herself allows the therapist to pay attention to which parts are being magnified, shut out, or denied. When a client cannot integrate her vulnerability and her anger, she invites us to respond to only certain parts of her, and to own the complementary aspect of ourselves as the whole truth. Thus the client who experiences herself as a helpless victim may invite us to assume the identity of protector or bully, and to remain unaware of our and her contradictory feelings and identities. With dissociative clients, it is important to "keep it complicated" and remember that for any response we have, its opposite may also be true.

A specific pitfall in psychotherapy with these clients is the danger that the therapist will be so fascinated with the concept of multiple personalities or so engrossed with the relationships among parts, alters, or personalities that she ignores the interpersonal events of the therapeutic relationship. The relationship between the client and oneself, between parts of the client and oneself, and the variety of feelings toward the therapist that can be represented by different aspects of the client's self all need to be named and understood over time.

COUNTERTRANSFERENCE TO DISSOCIATION

There are five contributory factors to countertransference with dissociative clients who have suffered severe childhood trauma. First is our response to the client's abuse history; the content of a client's abuse story has meaning to the therapist. We must hold our own horror about incest, about child sexual abuse, about child physical abuse, and emotional abuse and neglect. We cannot hear these stories without having them affect us; the cumulative effects of these stories across clients are addressed later in the chapter. The details of a given client's story and the way it affects us is a key part of our countertransference.

Second is our response to dissociative and posttraumatic stress disorder symptomatology, which is difficult to manage and painful to witness. The alternating of numbing and flooding, the extremes of depression, anxiety, the intrusive symptoms, flashbacks, the commonality of dissociative symptoms, the frequency of suicidality, the whole spectrum of enormously difficult and anxiety-provoking symptoms can be daunting for the therapist. They are challenging symptoms relationally. They make us anxious, angry, frightened, and horrified. All these feelings inform our countertransference and affect the treatment.

Third, we have strong responses to our trauma survivor clients' transferences to us; these transferences are challenging in their intensity and at times disturbing or dystonic in their content. Whether they are idealized or frightened or malevolent, they can challenge our identities and self-ideals. These transference can evoke concordant (identificatory) or complementary (responsive) responses from the therapist (Racker 1968).

Alternatively, transferences can awaken in us old feelings and relational paradigms from our past. With an angry and envious transference, a harshly critical client, or a client feeling victimized in the therapy, the therapist can respond as she did to an envious sibling, a critical father, or a guilt-inducing mother. This fourth countertransference reflects our transference to this client. Of whom does this person remind us? What part of ourselves do we see in our client? What do we put on this client that isn't about who she really is? This category is influenced by our history, including histories of trauma, neglect, loss, and our family context. Our personalities and defensive styles also contribute to the transferences to our clients.

Fifth, an influence on countertransference is vicarious traumatization (McCann and Pearlman 1990a, Pearlman and Saakvitne, in press). Therapists are profoundly affected and changed by work with traumatized clients. Our inner experience of self and other is irrevocably altered by our empathic exposure to clients' trauma material. The cumulative effect of working with trauma survivor clients will also inform our responses to a particular client.

Overall, countertransference is an extremely valuable tool. It is not a problem. In fact, it can be a solution to a problem. Countertransference can help the therapist become aware of an affect that the client is not, a dissociated affect. Our countertransference responses are invaluable sources of information about dissociation, about clients, about ourselves, and about the therapeutic relationship. In a compelling way, the client's projective identification provides significant information about her familiar affective experiences.

FUNCTIONS OF DISSOCIATION

Dissociation can be conscious, but is often unconscious, automatic, and divorced from context for our clients. Clients often experience intense shame as they become aware of their dissociation or realize that someone else has noticed it. Historically, it may have been imperative for dissociation to be secret. Dissociation occurs originally to allow an individual to cope with overwhelming affect, bodily sensations, and psychic betrayal. Over time other functions of dissociation evolve.

In order to focus on specific countertransference issues with dissociation, it is helpful to examine these different functions of dissociation. For the purposes of discussion, I identify four functions and discuss the different countertransference responses. Obviously these functions are theoretical and will overlap.

The functions of dissociation are as follows:

1. To separate oneself from feelings, particularly intolerable affects.
2. To separate oneself from traumatic memories, images, and knowledge.
3. To separate from oneself, or aspects of oneself, by fragmenting into different parts.
4. To separate oneself from the other, that is, the relational context, people, the world, and at times from one's membership in humanity.

DISSOCIATION FROM AFFECT

Many survivors have learned to fear their experience of affect. Strong affect may lead to intense self-loathing and fears of abandonment or annihilation. Strong feelings are often associated with danger because they evoke traumatic memories. A client may remember being flooded with overwhelming feelings and left alone at a time when her child's mind and body could not hold or make sense of the affective and bodily sensations. A client may remember times in the past when to show feelings made him more vulnerable to harm, torment, or degradation. Survivors may fear certain affects that are unbearable or dangerous for particular reasons. For one it may be unacceptable to feel fear, for another to feel longing or any kind of desire may be intolerable, for others eroticism, anger, sorrow, or shame may be intensely distressing.

Yet, of course, it is inevitable that feelings will be evoked in therapy. In fact, it is our goal to invite and address affect in therapy. Emotions are evoked in the therapy by direct material and by the therapeutic relationship itself. Difficult feelings arise for many survivors from the very experience of being in relation with the therapist as well as from specific interpersonal events or interactions with the therapist. Some clients then dissociate in response to their awareness of feelings of fear, longing, sadness, arousal, or love in relation to their therapist.

COUNTERTRANSFERENCE

For the therapist the client's dissociation means being left, often abruptly, either aware or unaware of the emerging feelings or their precipitant. The experience of being left or abandoned is evocative for all of us. When abandoned, people often feel lonely, anxious, angry, or frightened. A therapist may consciously or unconsciously associate to childhood experiences of being left or shut out. She may connect with other significant abandonments in her life. To the extent that we cannot tolerate being left or abandoned, we may be at risk to act out of our own needs and not consider the defensive needs of the client. We can be at risk to violate boundaries, to demand connection, or to try to control the situation to offset our sense of loneliness or powerlessness. This countertransference is evident if, when we invite a client to return to the relationship, we are forceful rather than gentle, and insistent rather than respectful. For example, when a therapist crosses the room to touch a client in order to "bring her back," she may be changing the frame in response to her countertransference anxiety or anger.

Alternatively, it is possible to become defensively withdrawn or angry, to shut down ourselves, to dissociate ourselves, or actively to abandon the client to regain a sense of mastery. One client reported that a former therapist told her when she was silent, as she often was, "Well, if you have nothing to say then there is no point in us meeting." The client reported feeling shamed, punished, and abandoned because she could not overcome her terror and anxiety. She experienced an internal "blankness" in sessions that was never explored but was interpreted as hostility, resistance, or passive aggression. Thus the threat to end the relationship was a punishment for her silence or abandonment of the therapist. At that point, the therapist loses sight of an important premise of therapy—that a client has a right to find a safe way to feel protected and in control. Our task is to note the apparent need for safety and control, to explore the precipitant for the need, and to address other ways that the therapist and client can work together to achieve those goals. Safety and control are reasonable goals.

When a client dissociates from feelings, another effect on the therapist is that we are left with the feelings while the client presents as numb or with "la belle indifférence." The therapist can feel with great intensity those affects from which the client fled. One can be left—both in and after the session—with enormous anxiety, often life and death anxiety, particularly with clients who play their dilemma out on the plane of suicidality. We can be left with feelings of profound grief, overwhelming rage, painful helplessness, arousal, or despair and powerlessness. Those intense feelings are exhausting when they are felt for two. It is easy to feel burdened and angry at the client's lability, at her difficulty putting words to her immediate emotional experience.

It is also possible for the therapist to be left with strong feelings disconnected from their context. As we strive to create meaning out of our experience, we will create meaning to attach to these affects. For example, if a therapist feels despair, to make sense of that feeling she may conclude that she is despairing in the therapy, that the therapy, her client, or she is hopeless. If the therapist feels shame, to make sense of that feeling she may decide she is unworthy. A therapist may need to project that feeling onto the client and see the client as bad or crazy. If we are left with strong sexual feelings we may decide the client was being seductive, or feel shame, or feel tempted to show some special attention or tenderness to the client to make our behavior consistent with our feelings.

When the feelings we are holding tap into old affective conflicts of our own, these conflicts and related defenses will influence how we manage the feelings and process the current interpersonal context. To the extent that our feelings conflict with our identity as a person or a therapist, or conflict with our ego-ideal as a therapist, we can be faced with a painful intrapsychic dilemma. We all carry in our mind an ideal of the perfect therapist we want to be. This ideal is influenced by one's mentors, supervisors, historical and fictional characters (such as, Sigmund Freud, Dr. Berger in *Ordinary People*, Dr. Fried in *I Never Promised You a Rose Garden*), and by one's own therapist. Any conflict between our experience of ourselves and our professional ego-ideal can lead to feelings of shame, guilt, lowered self-esteem. and disappointment or anger.

The danger posed when we hold feelings from which our clients have dissociated is that we will use projection to rid ourselves of intolerable feelings or an unacceptable identity (e.g., perpetrator transference, failure). We can then become caught in a dangerous cycle of unanalyzed projective processes in which we are the recipient of projective identifications followed by dissociation. The client projects an affect, then leaves by dissociation, and we are left holding the affect. In order to manage that affect we unconsciously project our response back onto the client. This cycle is not uncommon, but can be disturbing and confusing to the therapist. When unrecognized, clinicians can respond by diagnosing the client borderline personality disorder or multiple personality disorder, rather than recognizing a powerful transference–countertransference cycle within the therapeutic relationship. Therapists can feel compelled to invoke a theoretical construct like negative therapeutic reaction or unanalyzable patient, or they may abandon themselves and feel self-critical and diminished as a therapist.

Alternatively, Davies and Frawley (1991) suggest that these unconscious processes are often the greatest hope for transformation in psychotherapy.

It is ultimately the analyst's ability to both participate in and interpret the unfolding historical drama and to relate this history to current interpersonal difficulties, that encourages the progression of insight, integration, and change. . . . Our belief is that the interpretive process within the analytic experience is the only way to end the constant cycle of dissociation, projection, projective identification, and reintrojection that makes the history of abuse not only a painful memory, but an ongoing reality. [p. 30]

The connection between projection and dissociation needs more study; we are just beginning to unravel these complicated patterns of unconscious processes.

This cycle is complex and by definition involves unconscious processes of both therapist and client. It offers another reason why we cannot do this difficult and complicated work alone. We need a colleague or supervisor outside the therapeutic dyad to help us stay grounded in what is real in the relationship, in order that we do not become mired in a swamp of mutual projection or cut adrift in a sea of dissociation. Such a relationship requires safety, where we are treated respectfully by the colleague with whom we are consulting. This respect is necessary to create freedom for an honest examination of countertransference, in order to allow the therapist to use her feelings constructively in the therapy.

Another therapeutic response to dissociation is to keep the affect in the session and to keep its expression in an interpersonal context. It is critical to notice the retreat or exit from the shared space of therapy, and to begin to work with the client to establish and understand the context and precipitant of that flight. Survivors have learned not to be in the present moment when they feel frightened. For many clients, it takes considerable relearning to remain with an affect and another person at the same time. As one comes to know a client one can query in response to her dissociation, "Why now? What was the trigger? What happened just before you left?" Dissociation is not a random event, but because it is unconscious and automatic it takes work to identify the particular precipitant.

DISSOCIATION FROM TRAUMATIC MEMORIES AND IMAGERY

Another important function of dissociation is to protect one from traumatic memories. Dissociation is a key process in the compliance with the historical edict not to know. That mandate is potent and it becomes an organizing principle of an internal system that ensures survival. When not knowing and not remembering are required for both psychological and physical survival, the threat of memory or knowledge is intolerable. When a client dissociates to get away from a memory, that includes separating from the affect associated with the memory.

Dissociated memories are stored in a variety of ways. We cannot assume that all memory is verbally mediated or necessarily chronological and narrative. Traumatic memories are also stored as visual imagery memories, as somatic or body memories, as sensory memory, and as affective memory (floods of feelings with no apparent context). All of these can be experienced as separated from affect, knowledge or understanding (Braun 1988a,b).

There is another type of memory, which I call interpersonal memory. This type of memory emerges through both interpersonal and intrapersonal reenactment. Interpersonal memories represent unconscious encoding of interpersonal sequences that can emerge as automatic responses or behavior in a relational or object relational context. Janet referred to a process he called "habit memory," an automatic synthesis of information encoded in traumatic situation, which is now referred to as traumatic memory (Janet 1928, in van der Kolk and van der Hart 1992). Habit memory included, although was not limited to, behavioral reenactments. The concept of interpersonal memory is simply an integration of object relations theory concepts of transference with a current understanding of traumatic reenactments in interpersonal realms.

To the client, interpersonal enactments or behaviors can seem confusing, dystonic, or compulsive. For example, a survivor can find herself responding to the departure of a partner with such intense panic and rage that it leads to intense self-loathing and the expectation of punishment or abandonment and loss of love. Despite the cognitive intervention (e.g., "I know this person is coming back"), this cycle can repeat again and again with no modification. A survivor can be tormented by anxiety in a sexual situation that leads her to become emotionally distant and simultaneously feel frightened, alone, and fearful that her partner will reject her. These examples, as well as more general reenactment patterns of choosing abusive partners or accepting demeaning roles in relationships, can reflect the unconscious reenactment of earlier abusive and traumatic events and relationships.

Interpersonal memories can also emerge in a survivor's intrapersonal relationship to herself, that is in her "self-talk" or characteristic ways of responding to needs, feelings, and experiences. Often a survivor's harsh, critical, and punitive response to her experience of fear, weakness, or illness can reflect interpersonal experiences from childhood. For example, a client tormented with obsessive ruminations after any decision finally recognized that through her tortured self-recriminations she did to herself what her endlessly critical father had done throughout childhood. The identification of reenactment as a form or aspect of memory, that is, the idea that memory could be held as an interpersonal sequence, integrates the concept of reenactment with memory, and elaborates psychoanalytic concepts of transference and internalized object relational paradigms.

This reenactment emerges also in the therapeutic relationship. When a therapist is sensitive to the presence of dissociated interpersonal memory fragments in the therapeutic relationship, it provides a helpful framework for both client and therapist. For some clients, the concept of interpersonal memory is helpful as it allows them to have a framework within which to understand their behavior. Many clients have experienced these fragments and felt isolated, confused, and crazy because they could not make sense of their experience.

COUNTERTRANSFERENCE

When a client dissociates to get away from a memory the therapist can be left with fragments of that memory. These fragments may include disturbing imagery. The therapist can feel confused, crazy, or unsure about what is real or true. She may feel reluctant to know more and she may feel fragmented herself. One can feel the urge to probe for details or to ignore the fragment and change the subject to move away from the discomfort of a partial memory. As memories begin to emerge and the client maintains an ambivalent relationship with her own memories, the therapist will also hold that ambivalence. The therapist may find herself feeling confused about what she knows to be true, thus simultaneously holding the experience of knowing and not knowing. The images or fragments of the client's memory may stay with the therapist. They may appear in the therapist's dreams or internal landscape.

A common countertransference response to this situation is for the therapist to wish for premature knowing, that is knowing before the client knows and then telling the client her own story or history. It is essential that therapists do not ask leading questions or assume we know a client's truth better than she does. We must tolerate being left in the dark. A client can start to remember something, then "disappear," and the therapist is left frustrated and curious. The therapist can start to imagine what memories the client may have and what might have happened to her. This dynamic, in fact, can reenact an aspect of abuse; in effect the client may unconsciously be inviting the therapist to violate a boundary by imagining her in a sexual situation.

We have all experienced the frustration and wish to act when a client remembers two events and we imagine we can see how they are connected—like the wish to close a circle so powerful in optical illusions. It can be very difficult to hold the tension, the suspense, and wait for the client to fill in the blank, to make the connection, and close the circle. The therapist may have to grit her teeth to keep from blurting out the connection she perceives. As we continue to practice, trauma stories may become more familiar to us; we more easily anticipate certain patterns. It can then be harder to remain present with the client's gradual process of remembering her truth.

DISSOCIATION FROM THE SELF

A client's dissociation from self, the need to flee from her identity or aspects of her identity, reflects a fragmentary internal experience of self. This fragmentation can leave the therapist confused and anxious. A therapist may struggle to determine what is real about this client, as though the alternative is what is false. In response to the unpredictability, therapists can feel abandoned by the original self of the client, or feel manipulated, tricked, or lied to. Denying the client's subjective experience of split-off parts or selves, some therapists insist there is one true self and any other presentation of the client is untrue. This insistence is counter-transferential and prevents empathic connection with the client, and thus blocks therapeutic action.

Within the framework of dissociation, if a therapist finds these changes in ego-states or states of consciousness intolerable, she may respond internally with feelings of emptiness, sleepiness, boredom, or irritation. She might respond behaviorally by confronting the client or withdrawing. She may feel abandoned by the self of the client with whom she felt a connection.

Perhaps a related aspect of dissociation from self is represented by the client who never presents a core sense of self. Some clients create an "as if" (Deutsch 1942) or false (Winnicott 1971) self by adapting to the needs of the other—in therapy, the therapist. Trying to know someone when they are accommodating to every clue we give, consciously and unconsciously, overtly and covertly, is like trying to hold a sunbeam. A therapist can easily feel frustrated, disconnected, and cheated of the real relationship of the therapy. It is an illusion that one is connecting; the words sound right, and yet there is no spark, no contact, no connection between the authentic selves of the therapist and client. Part of what is emotionally and intellectually rewarding in the practice of psychotherapy is being involved in a relationship. When we are deprived of that, not only is our work less rewarding and fun, we may collude in shaping a client's identity just to have someone in the room with us. Alternatively we may distance from the client and the relationship by seeing the resistance as being located simply in the client without recognizing interpersonal reenactments.

COUNTERTRANSFERENCE

When a client maintains distinct unintegrated aspects of self or identity (alter selves), or when a client identifies herself as having multiple personalities or identities, the experience for the therapist is complex. On the one hand, when a client speaks in a different identity, especially if it is the first time, or if the therapist is inexperienced with clients who presented in this way, a therapist may respond instinctively in a complementary way. For example, when a client speaks as a child, one tends to respond as a protective adult. When a client speaks as an angry or sullen adolescent, one tends to respond as a calm, rational adult. When a client responds in a defensive, protective self, one tends to respond cautiously, trying to be protective of the boundaries. On the other hand, the therapist may simultaneously experience a range of feelings: confusion, anxiety, embarrassment, bewilderment, loss of continuity with herself, with the client, and with colleagues in the profession. There are complex countertransference responses to MPD clients for the same reasons that this volume exists; there is controversy in the field about the diagnosis and its treatment.

Other countertransference issues include attachments to different aspects of the self or to different alters. Often the attachment to the original presenting host personality is the one to whom we form our initial attachment—the person whom we got to know initially and with whom we feel familiar. Therapists can have intense countertransference to particular alters, for example, to vulnerable children; angry adolescents; harsh, punitive alters; murderous or suicidal alters; and mute or nonverbal alters.

A final countertransference danger to this dissociative function is for the therapist to slip into an overly concrete or literal interpretation of multiple personality as truly meaning many complete selves rather than fragmented and dissociated aspects of self and memory. This loss of a theoretical frame is dangerous, as it reflects the therapist's collusion with the client's defensive experience of self, which is based in a developmentally early concrete operations level of thinking. The development of multiple personalities represents a failure of symbolic thought; that is, it is a concretization of the experience of dissociated affect and knowledge in the face of stressors that overwhelm an individual's developmental capacities for affect modulation and self-soothing. This understanding clarifies the therapeutic task as one of self-capacities development.

DISSOCIATION FROM THE OTHER

Dissociation serves the purpose of flight from the other, which in an interpersonal context of therapy means leaving the therapist. One must question why the client had to leave, at this particular moment. What made it no longer safe in the interpersonal therapeutic space? What was the client feeling, and what did she imagine we were feeling, thinking, or doing? While there is always an interpersonal component to dissociation, that does not mean the client experiences it that way. The client's experience is more often intrapersonal. Thus, when we raise the question, "What was going on in here between us?" we may well be met with a blank stare. It is often a new concept for the client to be invited to notice her surroundings as a context to her psychological experience. In therapy, we offer the idea (novel to many survivors) that feelings and intrapsychic events occur in a context, usually interpersonal. Concomitantly, we invite the client to think about the original context for her dissociative defenses. One goal of psychotherapy with trauma survivors over time is to make the intrapersonal into interpersonal. We thus shift from the complex world of introjects, internalizations, and identities into the relationship between therapist and client, so they can be sorted through in safety. This ideal reflects the psychoanalytic goal of analysis, to make the unconscious conscious.

ORGANIZATIONAL COUNTERTRANSFERENCE

Dissociative clients evoke countertransference not only in the particular clinician working with them, but in the entire system involved in the work. This can include consulting clinicians, the hospital or clinic, or the partial hospitalization program. Organizationally, we must be willing to step back and look at our organizational countertransference process. While this often overlooked issue needs more elaboration than is possible in this chapter, it warrants acknowledgment.

VICARIOUS TRAUMATIZATION

A final element in the effect of dissociation and trauma therapy on the therapist is in the cumulative effects of exposure to traumatic material across clients. The term vicarious traumatization was coined by McCann and Pearlman (1990a), and others have identified similar phenomena (Figley in press, Herman 1992). Vicarious traumatization refers to the transformation of the therapist's inner experience and subsequent changes in the therapist's behavior resulting from empathic exposure to clients' traumatic material. It is significant that this exposure occurs as we are trying to understand a client's experience; our empathic connection makes us particularly vulnerable to transformation, both positive and negative.

Vicarious traumatization is based on constructivist self-development theory (McCann and Pearlman 1990b), a theory of personality that describes the impact of trauma on an individual's development and sense of self. It integrates psychoanalytic theories, specifically object relations theory and self psychology, with cognitive, developmental, and social learning theories. There is an emphasis on adaptation, relation to self and others, and the development of a sense of meaning in the world. Vicarious traumatization refers to McCann and Pearlman's conviction that exposure to trauma material across clients over time will affect the therapist in the same realms that constructivist self-development theory posits trauma affects an individual. The cumulative effect of this exposure is to change the therapist's self in the same ways that a traumatic event or context affects an individual's sense of self.

The general signs and symptoms of vicarious traumatization are decreased sense of energy, no time or energy for yourself, increasing disconnection from loved ones, social withdrawal, increased sensitivity to violence, threat, or fear, or the opposite—decreased sensitivity, cynicism, generalized despair and hopelessness. These are the endpoints of a gradual erosion of one's beliefs and at times of dramatic shifts in beliefs and schemas. Specific alterations include changes in one's frame of reference, that is, changes in identity, world view, and spirituality. World view reflects an individual's generalized beliefs about the world, that is, whether it is basically good or bad, just or unjust; whether people are fundamentally good or bad; whether things happen for a reason or randomly. Identity includes basic beliefs about oneself as basically an effective, worthwhile person or basically worthless or ineffectual. Spirituality includes one's capacity for hope and wonder and one's sense of meaning and connection to something beyond oneself.

Changes in self-capacities, that is, the ability to tolerate affect, to maintain a relatively positive sense of oneself, and to maintain an internal sense of connection to others, are also a sign of vicarious traumatization. The latter refers to object constancy, being able to keep a sense of positive connection to others and to yourself that stays with you over time and separations. Changes in the therapist's ego resources can be reflected in changes in her ability to do things she used to be able to do. These resources include sense of humor, intelligence, ability to make self-protective judgments, to have insight, to assess accurately social situations, and to feel empathy.

Another area of disruption from vicarious traumatization is in the area of the therapist's basic psychological needs and related cognitive schemas. Everyone has basic needs for *safety* (your belief that you are safe in the world and that loved ones are safe), *trust and dependency* (that you can trust others and trust yourself), *esteem* (your belief that you are worthwhile and that others are worthy of esteem), *control* (your belief that you can control key aspects of your life and exert some control over others and your environment), and *intimacy* (that you can be intimate and connected with yourself and with others). Each individual carries core beliefs about these areas that inform her ways of being in the world. These beliefs can be profoundly changed by chronic exposure to trauma, horror, the reality of humans' capacity for inhumanity, cruelty, and indifference.

There may also be alterations in the therapist's sensory experiences, including intrusions of a client's traumatic imagery. Many therapists who work with survivors of sexual violation have intrusive imagery from their clients' material emerge outside of sessions. It is not uncommon for a therapist to have her sexual experiences interrupted by images or memories of clients' experiences. In addition, these images can affect a therapist's relational life, sleep, ability to go to the movies, watch TV, read the news, or walk in a park and see parents and children together.

There are many ways to notice and assess the process of vicarious traumatization in oneself. One may notice subtle shifts in expectations or fantasies about things, or see profound changes in symptoms of anxiety, depression, sleeplessness, chronic fatigue, anhedonia, loss of zest for life, despair, loss of meaning. Trauma therapists must take vicarious traumatization and its effects seriously. Vicarious traumatization is a very real danger not only to therapists but potentially to our clients and the field. Every therapist will be changed by this work; our best safeguard is our self-awareness and commitment to self-protection.

Contributing Factors

One set of contributing factors to vicarious traumatization is *situational*. These factors include the kind of work a therapist does, the population with whom she works, how much she works, the support or lack thereof in the workplace, the context. Major changes, for example, in the administration of the country or in national health care, can have a major effect on our hope or despair. When we feel that our work is recognized and supported at a national, state, or local level, it makes a difference. We do not feel so alone or unrecognized in the work.

The other contributing factors are the *individual* factors that make us more or less resilient. These factors include the therapist's personal history, personality and defensive style, current personal situation and context, professional context, level of training, confidence, experience, professional history, and personal therapy. All of these factors can make a difference.

Ways to Address Vicarious Traumatization

Awareness, acknowledgment, and attention to vicarious traumatization are essential. There are three arenas in which to address and ameliorate vicarious traumatization: professional, organizational, and personal. (Pearlman and Saakvitne, in press).

Professional

Attention to balance in one's work is a necessity. This concept includes balance in the amount of clinical work one does compared to other kinds of work, including teaching, writing, supervision, research, and administration. In addition, there is a critical limit to how many clinical hours a therapist can do in a day, in a week, in a row, and still be emotionally present and effective. When the clients with whom one is working are trauma survivors, those numbers go down. Alternating individual work with group work or clinical supervision can be helpful, because different tasks call for different kinds of energy.

Ongoing supervision is an absolute necessity for every therapist. It is helpful, clinically and personally, to talk about this work; it cannot be done in isolation. Creating a supervisory relationship that, like a therapeutic relationship, is bounded, has confidentiality, and provides a safe context of respect is crucial. Peer supervision groups are effective models to get support and help. Trauma supervision needs to include specific components, including attention to vicarious traumatization (Pearlman and Saakvitne, in press). When a supervisor is also the boss, it is important to address the roles and create ground rules that allow for effective supervision. Sometimes it is necessary to change the framework and provide additional external or alternative supervision. If a work setting holds the view that therapists shouldn't have feelings about their clients or about the work, or subscribes to the belief that it is unprofessional to be emotionally affected by the work, therapists and clients will be at risk.

Therapists often need to be creative about getting what they need. They need to pay attention to their hours, and to self-care at work. This care includes their physical space and physical well-being. A therapy office should be comfortable and pleasant for the therapist. Many therapists keep things in their offices that connect them to important aspects of their past, and important people in their lives. These items are not necessarily meaningful or disclosive to a client (e.g., family photographs), but are things that help the therapist remain grounded in her identity and important relationships. When a therapist makes her space attractive and comfortable to her, the space reinforces and reminds her that she matters. It is also important for a therapist to pay attention to her body at work. Does she get up and walk around during the day? Does she eat lunch? Or does she schedule everything back to back so as to have no down time?

Being respectful of oneself and one's limits is part of being genuine in the relationship; none of us is truly caring, concerned, and giving all of the time. We have our own needs. Establishing a therapeutic frame and relationship that acknowledge the therapist's needs is essential to protect both client and therapist. Therapy with dissociative clients whose histories and current symptomatologies are distressing can be enormously challenging and taxing; both therapist and client need safety and respect. Therapist limit setting and acknowledgment of needs also models self-care and self-respect. We can acknowledge a client's need for much support and know that we cannot meet those needs at all times. Clients often do not know that they're allowed to say no, or, if they have said yes, that they are allowed to reevaluate and change their commitment. When we separate our clients' real needs from our responsibility to meet them, we support our clients' limit setting and self-care as well.

It is important that therapists take time to celebrate therapeutic successes, large and small; we all tend to talk more about the anxiety-provoking clients, the despair we fall into, the therapeutic impasses. However, there are many moments of success and triumph in this work. It is valuable for therapists to set aside time each day to acknowledge and think about the successes of the day.

Organizational Interventions

Organizationally, there are several structural decisions that can help staff members address issues of vicarious traumatization. For example, organizational support for continuing education, and for ongoing supervision and consultation convey a recognition of the challenges of the work and a commitment to providing the necessary component for ethical treatment. Structuring the physical space to be safe and as comfortable as possible is important. Acknowledging vicarious traumatization and having places and time within the organization that allow the expression of feelings makes a difference. To illustrate, we spend the first hour of case conference in an open, unstructured format for discussion of countertransference, vicarious traumatization, and any feelings that may arise in the context of work. This time is defined as a time for clinicians; it is not a therapy session, but it is a time for support and acknowledgment of the affective elements of the work. If someone moves into problem solving or intellectualizing, we refocus to the feeling level. This structured time reflects an organizational acknowledgment that the work of trauma therapy is personally meaningful and emotionally challenging. We have come to identify this time as our most important meeting of the week. Likewise we commit time out of every staff retreat (two a year) for a vicarious traumatization exercise.

Supervision and consultation are arenas in which to address vicarious traumatization, and it is possible to arrange a specific vicarious traumatization consultation for an individual or an organization. For an organization to have a sense of vision and mission also makes a difference for the individual therapist. It helps one stay grounded in the bigger picture, to remember the social, political, and professional context and impact of the work. This vision helps address and alleviate the sense of randomness and despair that can emerge over time in the field.

Personal Strategies

Finally, we need to include strategies in our personal lives to address the effects of vicarious traumatization. First, it is essential to *have* a personal life; this work can start to take over a therapist's life and she must not let it. It is vital for a therapist in her personal life to think about and address many aspects of herself, not solely her caretaking functions and capacities or her analytic mind. Therapists need to include their creativity and their bodies. Rest, exercise, nutrition, and relaxation are all important aspects of a balanced life. It can be helpful to spend time outdoors to connect with nature and with the strength and beauty that is larger than oneself and not entirely under human control. This larger context allows us to hold on to perspective.

Spirituality is important. By spirituality, I do not mean only organized religion. This work profoundly assaults our spiritual selves. We need to tend and make space for our spirituality. In the mental health field, not only do we not have a good language to address spirituality, but it is often a topic of some embarrassment and is frequently avoided. We need to operationalize the concept and help develop a language through which it can be discussed (Neumann and Pearlman, ms. in preparation). The most insidious effects of vicarious traumatization are evident in the loss of hope, wonder, and other spiritual aspects of the self. There are certainly many aspects of this work that evoke sadness, despair, frustration, and fatigue. This fact needs to be balanced by the recognition that psychotherapy is fundamentally about hope, connection, and healing.

INTEGRATION

A common identified goal in psychotherapy with dissociative and MPD clients is integration. I am proposing that the same goal is in the best interest of the therapist. We need to treat ourselves as integrated selves, to nurture all aspects of ourselves, and not become only one part of what we can be. That means addressing our physical, intellectual, emotional, psychological, spiritual, interpersonal, pragmatic, and visionary selves.

Further, as a field we need to keep lines of communication open within and between disciplines and theoretical orientations. Debates like those presented in this volume and in the popular media stir strong emotions. When we resist becoming polarized into reactive and dichotomous positions, we have an opportunity to challenge our assumptions, increase our knowledge, and deepen our understanding of complex processes. While critical thinking is essential to the field, these debates need to be conducted in a way that is respectful both to professionals and clients.

REFERENCES

Bateson, G., Jackson, D., Haley, J., and Weakland, J. (1956). Toward a theory of schizophrenia. *Behavioral Science*, 1:251–264.

Braun, B. G. (1988a). The BASK model of dissociation. *Dissociation* 11 (1):4–23.

_____ (1988b). The BASK model of dissociation. part ii: treatment. *Dissociation* 11(2): 16–23.

Casement, P. J. (1991). *Learning from the Patient*. New York: Guilford.

Davies, J. M., and Frawley, M. G. (1991). Dissociative processes and transference–countertransference paradigms in the psychoanalytically oriented treatment of adult survivors of childhood sexual abuse. *Psychoanalytic Dialogues* 2(1):5–36.

Deutsch, H. (1942). Some forms of emotional disturbance and their relationship to schizophrenia. *Psychoanalytic Quarterly* 11:301–321.

Figley, C., ed. (in press). Secondary Traumatic Stress *Disorder: Trauma and Its Wake*, vol. 3. New York: Brunner/Mazel.

Green, H. (1964). *I Never Promised You a Rose Garden*. New York: Holt, Rinehart, & Winston.

Herman, J. L. (1981). *Father–Daughter Incest*. Cambridge, MA: Harvard University Press.

———— (1992). *Trauma and Recovery*. New York: Basic Books.

Jordan, J. V., Kaplan, A. G., Miller, J. B., et al. (1991). *Women's Growth in Connection: Writings from the Stone Center*. New York: Guilford.

Maroda, K. (1990). *The Power of Countertransference*. New York: Guilford.

McCann, I. L., and Pearlman, L. A. (1990a). Vicarious traumatization: a framework for understanding the psychological effects of working with victims. *Journal of Traumatic Stress* 3(1):131–149.

———— (1990b). *Psychological Trauma and the Adult Survivor: Theory, Therapy, and Transformation*. New York: Brunner/Mazel.

Neumann, D. A., and Pearlman, L. A. (manuscript in preparation). Toward a psychological understanding of spirituality in adult survivors of childhood sexual abuse.

Olio, K. (1993). Countertransference desperation: impact on treatment choices—magic cures, inherent obstacles and misuse of effective techniques. Workshop offered at conference, Countertransference in Therapy with Survivors of Childhood Sexual Abuse, Sept. 23, 1993 at Holyoke Hospital, Holyoke, Massachusetts.

Pearlman, L. A., and Saakvitne, K. W. (in press). *Trauma and the Therapist: Countertransference and Vicarious Traumatization in Psychotherapy with Incest Survivors*. New York: W. W. Norton.

Racker, H. (1968). *Transference and Countertransference*. New York: International Universities Press.

Saakvitne, K. W. (1990). Psychoanalytic psychotherapy with incest survivors: transference and countertransference paradigms. Paper presented at the 98th Annual Convention of the American Psychological Association, Boston, Massachusetts, August 14.

———— (1992). Incest and feminine identity: shame, sexuality, and rage. Paper presented at the 100th Annual Convention of the Americal Psychological Association, Washington, DC, August 18.

———— (1993). Eroticized maternal transference: psychoanalytic treatment of female incest survivors. Paper presented at the American Psychological Association Annual Convention, Toronto, Canada, August 24.

Saakvitne, K. W., and Pearlman, L. A. (1993). The impact of internalized misogyny and violence against women on feminine identity. In *Women, Relationships and Power: Implications for Counseling*, ed. E. P. Cook, pp. 247–274. Alexandria, VA: American Counseling Association.

Saakvitne, K. W., Pearlman, L. A., and Courtois, C. (1992). Psychological trauma and the therapist: vicarious traumatization and clinical supervision. Paper presented at the American Psychological Association, Washington, DC.

van der Kolk, B. A., and van der Hart, O. (1991). The intrusive past: the flexibility of memory and the engraving of trauma. *American Imago* 98:425–454.

Waites, E. A. (1993). *Trauma and Survival: Post-traumatic and Dissociative Disorders in Women*. New York: W. W. Norton.

Winnicott, D. W. (1971). *Playing and Reality*. New York: Basic Books.

18

Treatment of Multiple Personality Disorder in a Community Mental Health Center

Ellen Nasper and Tracy Smith

This chapter presents our experiences first encountering and then introducing the diagnosis of multiple personality disorder (MPD) into a state-financed community mental health center. The usefulness of the MPD diagnosis became apparent through a sequence of clinical events as well as a change in the general diagnostic climate. Increased recognition of the role of trauma in the etiology of severe mental illnesses led us to inquire more comprehensively about trauma histories. Thorough inquiries about trauma led us to hear reports of dissociative symptoms more clearly. None of our more commonly used diagnostic categories (post-traumatic stress disorder recurrent major depression, and borderline personality disorder) adequately accounted for the symptoms that we saw.

Contemporary writers conceptualize MPD as a disorder on the dissociative continuum (Putnam 1989) that has its foundation in childhood trauma (Kluft 1985, Putnam et al. 1986, Ross 1989). Dissociative disorders arise in contexts of extreme trauma, taking shape according to the age and developmental level of the traumatized person, the nature of the trauma, and the response of the environment to the trauma (Spiegel 1993). Kluft (1984) describes a four-factor theory of the development of MPD. It postulates that MPD develops in an individual (1) who has the capacity to dissociate, (2) who experiences overwhelming trauma, (3) in an environment that shapes the dissociative response, and (4) in which there is inadequate soothing. Each aspect contributes to the fragmentation of memory, identity, and experience. There was little diagnostic controversy as we identified clearly remembered trauma histories and diagnosed PTSD or borderline disorder (although some staff did articulate discomfort with the severity of trauma uncovered). The diagnosis of multiple personality disorder has been more controversial.

We have found that diagnosing MPD has a considerable impact on the nature and course of treatment. Most significantly, it directs a clinician's attention to the narrative or historic meaning of symptoms that might otherwise be considered signs of psychosis. It is a diagnosis that is best treated through supportive and exploratory psychotherapeutic intervention, which includes and addresses all aspects, parts, or self-states of the personality (Loewenstein 1993). The psychotherapeutic transference and countertransference demands on the therapist are unique: the work involves engagement with many, sometimes rapidly shifting, personality fragments, and at times involves projective reenactments of past trauma (cf. Lyon 1992, for a vivid illustration of this). The traumatic memories encountered may be horrific and without clear narrative context, since this is the nature of the memory fragmentation. Medications are often of less central, if not equivocal, value in treatment.

In addition to the particular demands of working with the patient who has MPD, the community mental health center setting presents both significant advantages and unique challenges. The advantage in our agency is the capacity to develop an array of treatment interventions that are targeted to meet the supportive, exploratory, posttraumatic needs of the patient. These include the capacity to hospitalize, to provide twenty-four hour crisis intervention services, to provide combinations of individual, group, and art therapies, and to provide ready access for sharing of information among therapists.

The primary disadvantage of the community mental health center in the treatment of MPD results from its ignorance and resistance to the diagnosis. We maintain that this resistance has been inadvertently supported by the agency's focus on the provision of case management services. Case management primarily attends to symptoms and adaptation, while deemphasizing the role of the individual's history as a focus of treatment. In so doing, traumatic histories in general, and dissociative symptoms in particular, are often neglected. Overt PTSD, depressive, and self-abusive symptoms are observed and lead to diagnoses of PTSD, affective, and borderline personality disorders. Underlying dissociative processes and the dynamics of the MPD system, which serve to mask and buffer traumatic histories (Loewenstein 1993), go undetected.

The patient population of a community mental health center is often extremely poor; street violence is a regular part of daily life. Paradoxically, these circumstances cause therapists to resist formulating trauma-related diagnoses (see Putnam 1993). Long-term treatment relationships with this patient population conservatively affect diagnosis, increasing resistance to new diagnoses and to the rediagnosis of well-known patients. We have found, however, that appropriate diagnosis of MPD has contributed to patient stabilization and enhanced collaboration within the treatment relationship, principally because it has offered a cogent and coherent explanation of presenting symptoms to both clinicians and patients.

We will start by presenting material from the two MPD cases we first identified. The case material will then provide the basis for illustration and discussion of some of the conflicts and complexities in introducing a new diagnosis into a community mental health center system. We will discuss some of the differential diagnostic questions these patients raise and review some of the treatment interventions that have been established for them. We will follow this presentation of textbook MPD patients with a presentation of some case material from patients who seem to us to present with a psychotic multiple identity disorder. We will raise questions about whether there may be a group of patients who have psychotic MPD or a dissociative schizophrenia, who have traumatic histories and whose treatment as schizophrenics has proved inadequate. The following histories are disguised.

CASE #1

B was referred to the center by a counselor from a job training program. She was Hispanic, 24 years old, had a 3-year-old daughter, and lived with her older sister in a two-family house. Her aunt and uncle, who had raised her, lived in the other half of the house. B's chief complaint at presentation was as follows: "I need help. The problems with my uncle are bothering me. I don't know what to do. I'm scared and alone. I need somebody to guide me."

B's uncle was sexually abusing her, as he had been doing since her childhood. She was fearful that her family would retaliate against her if they learned that she was coming for help. Her primary concern was for her 3-year-old daughter's safety: "I don't want her to go through what I did growing up." She was particularly concerned that she would be seen as an inadequate mother and lose custody of her child to her uncle and aunt.

B had fragmentary recall of her history, and virtually none before age 9. At age 15 she had reported the abuse to a school counselor, which resulted in her being placed in foster care for a year. During the investigation, her uncle had denied abusing her. She returned to the home a year later hoping the situation had changed. It had not.

At presentation B was depressed and tearful. It was difficult for her to talk about the abuse. She reported that she had been cutting herself following episodes of abuse. We encouraged her to move and assisted in placing her in a battered women's shelter. Shortly after moving, B "disappeared" for several hours, eventually calling the crisis service from a motel. B had no idea how she had arrived at the motel nor what she had been doing prior to going there. (She reported a headache and extreme anxiety about this blackout.)

Also during this early assessment stage, B reported that she had run into a man who claimed to have met her at a ballgame. She had no recollection of this. He described what she had been wearing and their conversation. She realized it must have been she. Upon further inquiry B acknowledged that she had been experiencing blackouts for the last eight months. Because we routinely screen new patients for substance abuse, we knew this was not substance-abuse related. Diagnostically, we had been thinking of B as having a major depression, PTSD, and perhaps a borderline personality disorder. The introduction of significant amnesia, possible fugue states, and some significant identity disturbance suggested that none of these diagnoses fully accounted for her symptom picture.

B started treatment with one of the more experienced clinicians at the agency. A short time into her therapy, B brought her therapist a letter in her handwriting, but signed with another name. She was as perplexed as he was by this event. She claimed not to have written the letter and not to know anyone by that name. Within the next few weeks, the crisis team received phone calls from various of B's alters. Often the call was from a child alter who found herself on the street, sometimes with B's daughter, frightened and unsure how to get home.

CASE #2

C is a 45-year-old, never married mother of a 20-year-old son. At the time of her presentation to the mental health center, she was unemployed and living in her parents' home along with several aunts, cousins, and siblings. Initially C complained of depression and vague, imagistic flashbacks, which she thought related to sexual abuse. She was observed to have a circumstantial speech pattern, but she reported no psychotic symptoms.

C had briefly been seen at the mental-health center ten years earlier. At that time she was also depressed, concerned about some behavior problems with her son, and was apparently thought to have had problems with alcohol. She was seen only twice, and was diagnosed with dysthymia and a "hysterical personality" disorder.

C is the third of ten siblings. Her father was in the military, and the family relocated several times when she was a child. Her most vivid childhood memories are of living on a military base in Asia. She believes that at times during childhood she may also have lived with extended family. C's father was a severe alcoholic and verbally abusive of all members of the family. (This verbal abuse continues to the present, and is a daily occurrence in C's life.) However, although C has frequent experiences of terrifying physical sensations, visual images, and extreme emotional distress, she has virtually no clear, narrative memory of specific instances of physical or sexual abuse.

During her assessment, C reported a poor memory for childhood events. She reported, with astonishingly bland affect, a self-induced abortion at age 17. She noted that during high school she called herself another name. She further reported that it felt as though there were "four of her": a little child, a "bitch" who said things she would never say, "baby," and "Corey." C talked about these experiences reluctantly, describing that her body became rigid and that she was frightened when "baby" was trying to "come out." The interviewer observed as C physically curled up, her voice became child-like in tone, and she sobbed hysterically. C was ashamed of these episodes, knowing that something had happened but unable to describe what had occurred.

After a time C acknowledged frequently getting lost while driving, losing track of where she was going, and losing time. The Dissociative Experiences Scale (DES) indicated significant memory loss, withdrawal into fantasy, derealization, depersonalization, and identity disturbance. C described herself as frequently "spacing out" or "not being there."

C was referred to one of the authors (EN) for psychotherapy, carrying the diagnosis of dysthymia, rule out PTSD, rule out a dissociative disorder. Several things were impressive about C. She often appeared to be silly, self-deprecating, superficial, "ditzy." Her speech was intermittently hard to follow; she did not exhibit a full-blown thought disorder, but spoke in a circumstantial, hidden way, as though she was trying to conceal the meaning of her thought.

When this communication problem was pointed out, C was able to speak more clearly and directly. During an early session, C spoke of herself using the pronoun we. Over the first few months of treatment she presented several classical personality alters, each one marked with characteristic voice, accent, physical posture, dominant affects, specific memories, and concerns.

DIFFERENTIAL DIAGNOSTIC ISSUES

Loewenstein (1993) delineates several categories of dissociative symptom clusters, including amnesia, autohypnotic symptoms, and "process" symptoms. Each of these symptom clusters presented particular problems for acceptance of the MPD diagnosis. We will discuss these problems separately, focusing first on the problems posed by the amnesia and autohypnotic symptoms.

Both B and C reported significant periods of "blackouts" and "lost" time. Both reported finding themselves in locations without knowledge of how they had gotten there. Both exhibited self-hypnotic behaviors such as eye flutters; both evidenced periods during which they "tranced out" and were briefly unaware of their surroundings. These symptoms were discomfiting to the patients.

Still, members of the clinical staff were skeptical about the existence of MPD, complained that the behaviors were "attention seeking," and disbelieved the abuse histories (objections cited by Dell 1988). Some argued that if one accepted the MPD diagnosis, the patient was relieved of responsibility for her behavior (see Halleck 1990, for a discussion of this issue).

Staff often responded to the symptoms as though they were too dramatic to be believed (although neither patient was particularly dramatic in her self-presentation). These objections may have been based in countertransference responses: fears of being manipulated by the drama of the illness itself, perhaps fears about the extent of trauma reported (which in one case was current and ongoing), feeling it must be an act, that the patient must be exercising conscious control, or that the symptoms had come about to please (perhaps fascinate) the clinicians. Other clinicians appeared to use denial in response to the patients' trauma histories.

Dissociative process (Loewenstein 1993) symptoms proved, if anything, more difficult for some staff to accept. Loewenstein defines dissociative process symptoms as "complex dissociative multimodal hallucinations, passive-influence experiences, the presence of distinct personalities or personality states, switching phenomena (transitions between these states), and linguistic changes such as referring to the self in the first-person plural or third-person singular" (p. 591).

Process symptoms stimulated disbelief, and a conviction that the patient was faking or manipulating the clinician. In addition, the process symptoms presented diagnostic problems because clinical staff continued to maintain that the patient was psychotic (usually schizophrenic).

The confusion presented by MPD process symptoms is explored in several articles (Kluft 1987, Ross et al. 1989, Ross et al. 1990). They describe the frequency of Schneiderian symptoms, historically considered pathognomonic of schizophrenia, among MPD patients. Indeed, Ross and colleagues (1990) conclude with the finding that "Schneiderian symptoms are more characteristic of MPD than of schizophrenia" (p. 111). Ross and colleagues' (1990) study also comments that previous work on schizophrenia may be limited because investigators did not consider either dissociative disorders or MPD when making assessments of their patients.

Kluft (1987) describes Schneiderian symptoms in MPD as "pseudopsychotic." Loewenstein (1993), citing Kluft (1987) describes the phenomenology of MPD as "psychotic-like," citing "pseudohallucinations of voices (other alters), passive-influence experiences such as thought insertion and withdrawal, influences on the body, and 'made' feelings, thoughts, and volitional acts" (p. 591). However Loewenstein and Ross (1992) conclude that MPD patients rarely exhibit a true thought disorder.

Indeed, neither B nor C presented with a thought disorder, although both reported "hearing voices" in their heads. Both women complained of pain for which there was no physical explanation and "made" thoughts.

Loewenstein cities data he obtained with Judith Armstrong (Armstrong and Loewenstein 1990) from psychological testing protocols of MPD patients. Their data indicate that MPD patients are capable of self-observation and able to perceive whole objects. Their disturbed reality testing, when it emerges, reflects intrusive images of past trauma (Loewenstein 1993).

This capacity for self-observation was noted early in both B and C's treatment. Their impairments in reality testing seemed largely to emerge as posttraumatic reliving as well as in the "hearing" of the voices of alters as the dissociated parts of the self.

When B's case was identified, no clinician in the agency had any experience treating MPD. B's therapist received supervision from our most senior consultant. He, however, also had no experience with MPD. Apart from frequent switching, B's most prominent symptom was her extreme self-mutilation and emotional lability. She did not appear to have a thought disorder. The supervisor advised treating her as though she were borderline. Fearful that addressing the separate alters would promote regression, he advised the therapist to refuse to acknowledge the alters and to insist on speaking only with the initially presenting host. Under these treatment conditions, the patient expressed a great deal of distress and continued to be significantly unstable. Once the second MPD patient was identified, the agency approved hiring an outside consultant to provide supervision for the two therapists. Advised to accept and welcome the alters into the treatment, B (and her therapist) expressed significant relief. This resulted in the promotion of a more collaborative treatment alliance.

B's treatment served as a great stimulus to staff education about MPD, since it demanded significant coordination between the crisis and outpatient units. Crisis staff needed to be educated about how to handle the many telephone calls from various of B's alters. B's clinician met regularly with the crisis team. These repeated contacts, and the increasing effectiveness of the crisis team's interventions, educated the entire agency about MPD and about dissociative defenses.

Some argued that we shouldn't treat MPD in the agency, that it was outside of our mandated patient population. This interpretation reflected a view that the "chronically mentally ill" of our mandate exclusively referred to schizophrenics and affect-disordered patients. It became apparent that no matter how we diagnosed these patients, their severe symptomatology, frequent suicidality, utilization of crisis resources, and lack of other resources made them ours. Thus it behooved us to try to identify their disorders accurately, and to develop appropriate treatments.

DEVELOPMENT OF APPROPRIATE TREATMENT PROGRAMS

The groundwork for treatment targeted to MPD had already been laid in the development of programs focused on persons with trauma-related disorders. We had already established a group for incest survivors and an art therapy group that served as an adjunct to the verbal incest survivors group. Each of these became vehicles that we could use for our MPD patients if they so wished.

The incest survivors group was offered to B. She attended for a few sessions but found it too emotionally stimulating and decided not to continue. C, who presented as much more fragmented than B, in contrast expressed a wish to join the group. Both group leaders and C's individual therapist were hesitant about her participation. We feared that participation in such a group would foster further fragmentation in her and potentially disrupt the group process. C, however, was persistent in her wish to join.

While joining the group did provoke stimulation of some traumatic memories, for C it has been an extremely useful treatment intervention. The group has served as a support and as a normalizing experience. C had often felt "like a freak." The group accepted her and her diagnosis, even though they did not fully understand it. They had all experienced times of feeling crazy and alienated. The group was able to tolerate and support C through several abreactive episodes. C expressed feelings of shame and embarrassment because she did not recall what had happened. These feelings of shame and loss of control were familiar to all the group members.

C also asked to join the art therapy group. Art therapy (both individual and group formats) is an integral part of our trauma treatment. All the incest group members are also in an art therapy group. C has used art therapy as an invaluable route to discover, explore, and work through traumatic memories (see Greenberg and van der Kolk 1987). It was especially useful as a format in which to piece together fragmentary memories of early childhood before C had adequate language with which to contextualize her experience. Art has provided a means to match visual images with affective and body memories and with the fragments of facts which she can recall.

Our experience with C is that, on the whole, her presence has not seemed detrimental to the group process of the predominantly non-MPD group. There have been occasions when she has excused herself, feeling a need for emotional containment that the group was unable to provide. In this need, however, she is not different from other group members.

We had also been concerned that the group would foster further fragmentation in the patient. Interestingly, we have observed that C has developed several transient alter fragments that seem related to other group members. For example, one of the group members is hearing impaired and a sign interpreter attends group to assist her. For a brief period (several weeks), C developed an alter who signed. This alter "had the body" for only short periods of time, and she was responsive to spoken language (and thus apparently not deaf). Another group member is bulimic. Shortly after this member discussed her bulimia, C presented in individual therapy claiming that she was bulimic and had the urge to vomit. These alter fragments seem to manifest brief, literal fragmentary introjects of her peers. We suspect that this is a usual adaptive process for C, and not an artifact of treatment. These transient alters represent what Loewenstein (1993), describes as "a *secondary* phenomenon related to the shaping and structuralization of the dissociation" (p. 589; emphasis in the original). The development of transient alters is a means by which C structures and incorporates her experience.

Coordination of treatment among individual, group, and art therapists has proved invaluable. We have held a weekly mutual supervision group for the past several years, during which C is a frequent focus. Through this shared meeting, C's enormous strengths have emerged; she is a talented artist, a valued and courageous member of the incest survivors group, and a supportive friend to other group members. She set an example in her willingness to self-reflect and explore, and has become less fragmented through her willingness to confront difficult interpersonal issues.

PSYCHOTIC MPD

We now turn to the issue of what we shall call *psychotic MPD*. In this section we will speculate about what the appropriate diagnosis might be for a group of patients who seem to fit neither the schizophrenic nor the conventional MPD diagnosis.

Our recent experience with deinstitutionalization has given us the opportunity to raise differential diagnostic questions about some of these patients. Several of the recently deinstitutionalized patients present with what appears to be a psychotic multiple personality organization. This group may correspond to what Ross and colleagues (1990) postulate as being a "dissociative subtype of schizophrenia" (p. 117).

CASE #3

Y reports with flattened affect that she is continuously being anally and vaginally raped by "invisible penises." Now in her early 50s, Y has been institutionalized virtually continuously since her early 20s. She came from a middle-class family, graduated high school, and briefly attended college. Her father died when Y was 15, following a long illness. Y's psychiatric history began in her late teens. Her social adjustment prior to this is unknown. No trauma history has been identified, although in early records suspicion of abuse is mentioned.

While neuroleptics have helped to calm her, Y presents much as the patients described by Putnam (1989) and Quimby and colleagues (1993). She has not "burned out," she is intensely, if oddly, interpersonally related. For over a year, whenever hospital discharge approached she had major, dramatic crises. She stated that she was afraid that if she were to live in the community she would be sexually assaulted or that she would be "forced to become a prostitute." Spontaneously, she describes various "parts" or "persons" who act "using" her body and have distinct functions and names. These parts (a sexual one, a chaste one, several little girls) resemble the parts described by MPD patients.

Putnam (1989) describes several features that distinguish chronically hospitalized MPD patients from schizophrenics. MPD patients tend to be more related and involved with ward staff than schizophrenic patients; their levels of privilege vary greatly as their social functioning changes, and when they are close to discharge their behavior often regresses. Quimby and colleagues (1993) describe similar characteristics. Chronically hospitalized MPD patients do not seem to "burn out." They continue to have repeated crises; their interpersonal interactions are charged and intense. Finally, discrete behavioral states are often noted by treatment staff.

These features certainly describe Y. She usually functions at a psychotic level, and no alter or personality fragment has been able to organize the personality to adequately perform reality-based executive functions. Y has very recently moved into the community, living in a supervised group setting, and this has been achieved only with a great deal of support. For brief periods Y is able to be rational, relevant, and reality oriented. For example, she maintains socially appropriate behavior during shopping excursions with a case manager. However, no alter is capable of managing complex and novel situations encountered independently in the community.

How shall we understand Y? She is medicated with high doses of neuroleptics, but her "psychosis" is untouched. Does she have a true process psychosis? Or is Y's inability to function the result of years spent in an institutionalized environment, in which she has been so heavily medicated with neuroleptics and deprived of the psychotherapeutic opportunity to discuss a trauma history because the content of her preoccupations was seen as delusional? Presently the material Y produces is delusional in nature, and resembles schizophrenic distortion rather than the reliving of a cogent, if horrific, set of traumatic events. But perhaps the iatrogenesis has been the elaboration of a psychotic presentation, in the service of an environment that favored bizarre psychotic material over more cogent stories of abuse. From this perspective, the same patient who is seen as suggestible to the development of alters, might also be suggestible to the elaboration of more wildly psychotic delusions to mask the actual traumatic experience. If so, is a psychotherapeutic intervention appropriate now? Or is there a time when it becomes too late to unravel the fragments, clarify the history, and help someone to become more whole? We have no answers with regard to Y, or several other patients like her. But the questions her case raises need to be asked.

CONCLUSION

Our clinical experience with MPD places this diagnostic group within the context of the treatment of severe and prolonged posttraumatic illnesses. A substantial literature persuasively argues that the prevalence of childhood abuse among the chronic psychiatric population is significantly higher than previously thought (see Beck and van der Kolk 1987, Bryer et al. 1987, Carmen et al. 1984, Craine et al. 1988, Den Herder and Redner 1991, Gunderson and Sabo 1993, Herman et al. 1989, Jacobson 1989, Kluft 1990, Landecker 1992, Muenzenmaier et al. 1993, Ross et al. 1991, Stone 1990). This suggests that trauma may play a significant role in the etiology of many patients' psychiatric illnesses. The recent literature on the psychiatric consequences of trauma also suggests ways to understand the meanings of posttraumatic behaviors (for example, see Herman 1992, and van der Kolk 1994). These writings help frame posttraumatic symptoms as meaningful representations that may be explored with the patient, rather than as behaviors that need to be controlled by the clinician. We see the identification and treatment of MPD within this context. We believe that public sector institutions can accommodate MPD patients. Because of the degree of their distress, these patients will request our services. Correct diagnoses should have the effect of facilitating improvement, and a small body of literature (Ross and Dua 1993) proposes that appropriate treatment of MPD is also cost effective.

Our experience suggests that patients with MPD require a range of treatment services that includes both exploratory and supportive components. These patients benefit from individual psychotherapy that accepts the phenomenology of MPD as the patient experiences it and works with the entire patient. Loewenstein (1993) describes such treatment as follows:

> The MPD alter system as a whole is seen as the focus of treatment and all aspects of the mind are asked to participate. Internal cooperation, respect, tolerance, empathy, and coordination are initial goals....The dissociative barriers are gradually eroded from within, ultimately leading to coalescence of all alters and the appearance of a psychologically unified individual. [p. 600]

We have found that a multidimensional approach combining individual, group, and art therapies promotes these treatment goals.

Thus far the rehabilitative and case management needs of MPD patients have been neglected in public sector treatment. MPD patients pose interesting challenges in these areas because they may have alters with widely varying abilities. Many MPD patients have had significant periods of successful vocational functioning. Vocational rehabilitation services should target patient's strengths, some of which may still be accessible within competent dissociated alters. Rehabilitation and psychotherapy teams can work together during the recovery process to assist the patient to resume a productive work life. Within the current CMHC system, such success is rarely assumed, and programs are targeted to patients whose skill levels tend to be both more consistent, and lower, than the typical MPD patient.

A major task for the MPD patient is to discover her capacities for self-regulation. The nature of dissociation causes this to be a particularly difficult task, and MPD patients sometimes require inpatient hospitalization. Within the context of current public sector treatment, we recommend utilization of hospitalization for safety and stabilization, but not for exploratory work. Staff on units that treat MPD patients need to be trained to support MPD patients' skills in self-containment and self-soothing.

Treatment of MPD should include psychotherapeutic, supportive, and rehabilitative services. We believe that the specialized training of clinicians is necessary. Our experience suggests that treatment may be integrated into a wider program for treating the psychiatric consequences of childhood physical and sexual abuse. Such an approach offers MPD patients a conceptual context for understanding their disorder, and promotes a collaborative, productive treatment alliance.

REFERENCES

Armstrong, J. G., and Loewenstein, R. J. (1990). Characteristics of patients with multiple personality and dissociative disorders on psychological testing. *Journal of Nervous and Mental Disease* 178:448–454.

Beck, J. C., and van der Kolk, B. A. (1987). Reports of childhood incest and current behavior of chronically hospitalized psychotic women. *American Journal of Psychiatry* 144:1474–1476.

Bryer, J. B., Nelson, B. A., Miller, J. B., and Kroll, P. A. (1987). Childhood sexual and physical abuse as factors in adult psychiatric illness. *American Journal of Psychiatry* 144:1426–1430.

Carmen, E. H., Rieker, P. P., and Mills, T. (1984). Victims of violence and psychiatric illness. *American Journal of Psychiatry* 141:378–383.

Craine, I. S., Henson, C. E., Colliver, J. A., et al. (1988). Prevalence of a history of sexual abuse among female psychiatric patients in a state hospital system. *Hospital and Community Psychiatry* 39:300–304.

Dell, P. F. (1988). Professional skepticism about multiple personality. *Journal of Nervous and Mental Disease* 176:(9)528–531.

Den Herder, D., and Redner L. (1991). The treatment of childhood sexual trauma in chronically mentally ill adults. *Health and Social Work1 16:(1)50–57.*

Greenberg, M. S., and van der Kolk, B. A. (1987). Retrieval and integration of traumatic memories with the "painting cure." In *Psychological Trauma,* ed. B. A. van der Kolk, pp. 191–215. Washington, DC: American Psychiatric Press.

Gunderson, J. G., and Sabo, A. N. (1993). The phenomenological and conceptual interface between borderline personality disorder and PTSD. *American Journal of Psychiatry* 150:(1)19–27.

Halleck, S. L. (1990). Dissociative phenomena and the question of responsibility. *International Journal of Clinical and Experimental Hypnosis* 28:(4)298–314.

Herman, J. L. (1992). *Trauma and Recovery.* New York: Basic Books.

Herman, J. L., Perry, J. C., and van der Kolk, B. A. (1989). Childhood trauma in borderline personality disorder. *American Journal of Psychiatry* 146:(4)490–495.

Jacobson, A. (1989). Physical and sexual assault histories among psychiatric outpatients. *American Journal of Psychiatry* 146:755–758.

Kluft, R. P. (1984). Treatment of multiple personality disorder: a study of 33 cases. *Psychiatric Clinics of North America* 7:9–29.

——— , ed. (1985). *Childhood Antecedents of Multiple Personality.* Washington, DC: American Psychiatric Press.

——— (1987). First-rank symptoms as diagnostic indicators to multiple personality disorder. *American Journal of Psychiatry* 144:292–298.

——— (1990). *Incest-Related Syndromes of Adult Psychopathology.* Washington, DC: American Psychiatric Press.

Landecker, H. (1992). The role of childhood sexual trauma in the etiology of borderline personality disorder: considerations for diagnosis and treatment. *Psychotherapy* 29:(2)234–242.

Loewenstein, R. J. (1993). Dissociation, development and the psychobiology of trauma. *Journal of the American Academy of Psychoanalysis* 21:(4)581–603.

Loewenstein, R. J., and Ross, D. R. (1992). Multiple personality and psychoanalysis: an introduction. *Psychoanalytic Inquiry* 12:(1)3–48.

Lyon, K. A. (1992). Shattered mirror: a fragment of the treatment of a patient with multiple personality disorder. *Psychoanalytic Inquiry* 12:(1)71–94.

Muenzenmaier, K., Meyer, I., Struening, E., and Ferber, J. (1993). Childhood abuse and neglect among women outpatients with chronic mental illness. *Hospital and Community Psychiatry* 44:(7)666–670.

Putnam, F. W. (1989). *Diagnosis and Treatment of Multiple Personality Disorder.* New York: Guilford.

——— (1993). Dissociation in the inner city. In *Clinical Perspectives on Multiple Personality Disorder,* ed. R. P. Kluft and C. G. Fine, pp. 179–200. Washington, DC: American Psychiatric Press.

Putnam, F. W., Guroff, J. J., Silberman, E. K., et al. (1986). The clinical phenomenology of multiple personality disorder: review of 100 recent cases. *Journal of Clinical Psychiatry* 47:(6)285–293.

Quimby, L. G., Andrei, A., and Putnam, F. W. (1993). The deinstitutionalization of patients with chronic multiple personality disorder. In *Clinical Perspectives on Multiple Personality Disorder,* ed. R. P. Kluft and C. G. Fine, pp. 201–225. Washington, DC: American Psychiatric Press.

Rose, S. M., Peabody, C. G., and Stratigeas, B. (1991). Undetected abuse among intensive case management clients. *Hospital and Community Psychiatry* 42:(6)499–503.

Ross, C. A. (1989). *Multiple Personality Disorder: Diagnosis, Clinical Features and Treatment.* New York: John Wiley & Sons.

Ross, C. A., Anderson, G., Fleisher, W. P. and Norton, G. R. (1991). The frequency of multiple personality disorder among psychiatric inpatients. *American Journal of Psychiatry* 148:(12)1717–1720.

Ross, C. A., and Dua, V. (1993). Psychiatric health care costs of multiple personality disorder. *American Journal of Psychiatry* 47:103–112.

Ross, C. A., Heber, S., Norton, G. R., and Anderson, G. (1989). Differences between multiple personality disorder and other diagnostic groups on structured interview. *Journal of Nervous and Mental Disorders* 177:487–491.

Ross, C. A., Miller, S. D., Reagor, P., et al. (1990). Schneiderian symptoms in multiple personality disorder and schizophrenia. *Comprehensive Psychiatry* 31:111–118.

Spiegel, D., ed. (1993). Dissociation and trauma. In *Dissociative Disorders: A Clinical Review*, pp. 117–131. Lutherville, MD: Sidran.

Stone, M. H. (1990). Incest in the borderline patient. In *Incest-Related Syndromes of Adult Psychopathology*, ed. R. P. Kluft, pp. 183–204. Washington, DC: American Psychiatric Press.

van der Kolk, B. A. (1994). The body keeps the score: memory and the evolving psychobiology of post traumatic stress. *Harvard Review of Psychiatry* 1:4.

19

The Role of the Client's Partner in the Treatment of Multiple Personality Disorder

Mark A. Karpel

This chapter addresses the role of the client's partner[1] in the treatment of dissociative disorders, specifically, MPD. Its concerns can be summarized with the following questions:

- Do therapists who conduct individual psychotherapy with MPD clients need to think about the client's partner? Should the therapist consider the needs, the concerns—and the influence—of the partner?
- Should the partner be involved in treatment in some manner? If so, in what way? What potential benefits and liabilities are there for such involvement?

The author acknowledges the helpful contributions of the following individuals who agreed to discuss their work with dissociative clients and their partners: Lynn Benjamin, M. Ed., Private Practice, Fort Washington, PA, and Robert Benjamin, M.D., Northwestern Institute of Psychiatry, Fort Washington, PA; Denise Gelinas, Ph.D., Private Practice, Northampton and Springfield, MA; J. Mark Hall, Ph.D., Traumatic Stress Institute, South Windsor, CT; Gerald Krieger, L.I.C.S.W., B.C.D., Private Practice, Worcester, MA.

[1]The term *partner* refers to the individual with whom the client has a primary adult relationship. Because many couples are not legally married, the term *partner* is used rather than *spouse* in this chapter. Also, the author recognizes that not all MPD clients are female and that not all couple relationships are heterosexual. However, for simplicity of presentation and in light of the fact that MPD is diagnosed roughly five times as often for women as for men (Putnam 1989), and that the majority of these relationshps are heterosexual, in this chapter the client will be referred to as "she" and the partner as "he."

- Should the partner be seen by the client's therapist or referred to another clinician?
- If the partner is to be involved, should it be in the context of couple therapy, concurrent individual therapy, group treatment, family therapy, or simply intermittent contact with the client's therapist? Are there indications and contraindications for these different methods of involving partners in treatment?

In order to answer these questions, this chapter examines underlying treatment models and characteristic patterns for couples in which one partner has a dissociative disorder. It suggests reasons for—and against—involving partners in treatment as well as guidelines for doing so.

THE FORGOTTEN PARTNER?

The professional literature on MPD has extended a compassionate understanding first and foremost (and understandably) to clients, secondarily to the therapists who treat them, then, to a much lesser degree, to the clients' children,[2] and, finally, to the clients' partners. In a literature which at the time of this writing includes hundreds of books, articles, and chapters, there are roughly a dozen articles or chapters devoted to couple and family therapy with dissociative clients and less than a handful exclusively devoted to the role of partners in the treatment of dissociative disorders. This imbalance in the literature reflects a corresponding imbalance in the cognitive set of many psychotherapists who treat dissociative disorders.

There is no shortage of reasons that the partners of MPD clients would be overlooked. The predominant treatment modality for dissociative disorders is intensive individual psychotherapy. The pervasive and lasting effects of trauma and abuse call for a therapeutic relationship that is safe and well bounded and that can focus on the internal experience of the client without being "driven" by the partner's needs. The primary focus on the internal experience of the client is particularly appropriate given what

---

[2]Braun (1985a,b) has noted the high incidence of transgenerational transmission of dissociation and MPD. Coons (1985) found a higher incidence of emotional disturbance in children of MPD patients compared to children of nondissociative psychiatric patients. In a study of seventy-five MPD mothers, Kluft (1987) classified over 45 percent as "compromised/impaired" and another 16 percent as frankly abusive. Given these findings, *routine evaluation of children of dissociative clients is recommended* by a number of experts in this area (Benjamin and Benjamin 1993, Braun 1985b, Kluft 1985, Putnam 1989, and Sachs 1986). Many of the points made in this chapter in relation to the client's partner can also be applied to children.

is known about the etiology of dissociative disorders and the rigors of psychotherapy with these clients. There is overwhelming agreement that the causes of MPD lie in childhood experiences of trauma, inadequate attachment, and abuse. In other words, they are so clearly there and then rather than here and now that current contextual factors, such as the client's relationship with her partner, seem less relevant to treatment.

Furthermore, clinicians who treat dissociative clients are faced with unusual *complexity*—given the likelihood of a bewildering array of symptoms, dissociative confusion and secrecy, and complicated relationships among alters—and *intensity*—in light of traumatic transference and countertransference, multiple crises and the risk of vicarious traumatization (McCann and Pearlman 1990) or secondary PTSD (Olson et al. 1987). Given the complex demands confronting the therapist, it is understandable that he or she might not invite even greater complexity by bringing yet another individual into treatment, especially one with whom the client may have a correspondingly complicated—and not wholly positive—relationship. The therapist may be only too ready to accept the client's possibly distorted perceptions of the partner as someone who is either ineffectual, well-meaning, indifferent, saintly, or abusive, rather than to form impressions of his or her own.

While there are therapists treating dissociative clients individually who do meet with their clients' partners or who refer partners for individual, group, or couple therapy, this is not typically seen as a routine part of treatment. Yet there are compelling diagnostic, pragmatic, and ethical reasons for doing so. Before discussing these reasons, we need to examine characteristic patterns in these relationships, the types of partners who are most often drawn to MPD mates, and the concerns most often expressed by these partners.

CHARACTERISTIC RELATIONAL PATTERNS

Chronic interpersonal trauma, which is almost invariably associated with MPD, has predictable, if variable, consequences on subsequent relationships. The discussion that follows summarizes these predictable effects as expressed in adult couple relationships formed by survivors of such abuse. The discussion is supplemented by some of what is known about the effects of such abuse on survivors' therapeutic relationships. While there are bound to be differences between a survivor's relationships with her partner and with her therapist, there are significant similarities as well.

Trauma, especially chronic interpersonal trauma, tends to distort subsequent relational patterns so that they are more likely to be driven to extremes. Interactional patterns between the partners may become organized by the reenactment of prior abuse or they may be attenuated and deadened by defenses against the physical and relational closeness with which prior abuse was associated. Krugman (1987) notes that "traumatization distorts the object world of the victim. Love and violence, sexuality and aggression become fused" (p. 137).

Judith Herman (1992) observes that, for these individuals, all subsequent relationships are likely to be organized by the theme of abuse and victimization. "The protracted involvement with the perpetrator has altered the patient's relational style, so that she not only fears repeated victimization but also seems unable to protect herself from it, or even appears to invite it. The dynamics of dominance and submission are reenacted in all subsequent relationships, including the therapy" (p. 138).

The MPD client may be revictimized by her partner. Individuals who have been sexually or physically abused appear to be more likely to be reabused subsequently (Braun 1985a,b, Kluft 1990). Alternatively, the partner may be abused by the client if he becomes a target for her "destructive entitlement" (Boszormenyi-Nagy and Krasner 1986) and her rage at the original perpetrator. Finally, the partner may serve as a rescuer or caregiver for the client, who is seen by both partners as a victim of the original abusers or of the world at large. In each of these patterns, victimization is a central theme. Herman (1992) notes that even a skillful and well-trained therapist, "drawn into the dynamics of dominance and submission, . . . may inadvertently reenact aspects of the abusive relationship" (p. 139). We can imagine how much more likely this is for the client's partner who typically does not have the benefit of specialized training, who lives with the client on a full-time basis, and who, unlike the therapist, hopes to have his own needs met in the relationship.

Attachment is more likely to take extreme forms, including either extreme dependency on the partner (or vice versa), a mutually symbiotic relationship (Karpel 1976, Searles 1965, 1973), traumatic attachment, in which the victim of current abuse helplessly clings to her abuser, or—the precise opposite of these patterns—a relationship characterized by the mutual avoidance of intimacy and closeness. In the context of treatment, Liotti (1992) observes that "patients suffering from the dissociative disorders often oscillate quickly between clinging to the therapist, emotionally withdrawing from him or her, and becoming frightened as if expecting to be assaulted by the therapist" (p. 202).

Herman (1992) notes that clients with MPD represent:

> the extreme in the complications of traumatic transference. The transference may be highly fragmented, with different components carried by different

alters. . . . Therapists working with these patients [must] prepare for intensely hostile and sexualized transferences as a matter of routine. . . . The emotional vicissitudes of the recovery relationship are therefore bound to be unpredictable and confusing for patient and therapist alike. [p. 140]

Early relational abuse may lead to idealized and unrealistic expectations which, if uncorrected, can contribute to extreme disillusionment in the inevitable human foibles of the partner. Noting the survivor's experience of utter helplessness in the original traumatic experiences, Herman (1992) observes:

The memory of this experience pervades all subsequent relationships. The greater the patient's emotional conviction of helplessness and abandonment, the more desperately she feels the need for an omnipotent rescuer. She may develop intensely idealized expectations of the therapist. . . . When the therapist fails to live up to these idealized expectations—as she inevitably will fail—the patient is often overcome with fury. Because the patient feels as though her life depends upon her rescuer, she cannot afford to be tolerant; there is no room for human error. [p. 137]

Alternatively, the MPD client may enter the couple relationship expecting virtually nothing from the partner, feeling unentitled to even minimal standards of fairness and concern—a pattern that can contribute to the evolution of abusive behavior by the partner.

Chronic relational trauma undermines the MPD client's capacity for trust. Again, Herman's (1992) depiction of dynamics in the therapeutic relationship is instructive. "Though the traumatized patient feels a desperate need to rely on . . . the therapist, she cannot do so, for her capacity to trust has been damaged by the traumatic experience. . . . The patient enters the therapeutic relationship prey to every sort of doubt and suspicion. She generally assumes that the therapist is either unable or unwilling to help" (p. 138). Furthermore, in terms of the couple's relationship, secrecy, dissociation, and switching on the part of the MPD client may make interactions highly unpredictable, undermining the partner's capacity for trust in turn.

Given that sexual abuse is the most common form of abuse reported by MPD clients (Coons et al. 1988, Putnam 1989, Putnam et al. 1986), the couple's sexual relationship may be characterized by low sexual desire or sexual aversions on the part of the client, virtual if not outright exploitation of sexual alters by the partner, or compulsive reenactment involving aspects of the original sexual abuse. (Not all couples in which one partner has a dissociative disorder report sexual difficulties. Hall notes [personal communication 1994] that therapists often hear descriptions of a positive sexual relationship until the client begins to retrieve memories of abuse in treatment. This disruption represents a profound loss for both partners in these relationships.)

The patterns described above emphasize pathological patterns, but these couples, like all others, are also characterized by personal and relational resources (Karpel 1986). Attachment after all is attachment. In spite of their difficulties, these relationships may provide safety and security for the partners, support for coping with stress, and, however complicated its expression may be, love and caring concern for both partners. More specifically, MPD clients are by definition survivors. Dissociation becomes problematic when it is ego-dystonic and pervasive but it remains a potentially helpful method of coping under some circumstances. The resources that helped the client cope with the original abuse may also benefit the partner and the partner may serve as a resource for the dissociative client.

A TYPOLOGY OF PARTNERS

Benjamin and Benjamin (in press c) have proposed seven types of partners who commonly form relationships with MPD clients. The ensuing relationships have characteristic homeostatic processes that may inhibit progress in treatment. Benjamin and Benjamin suggest that a therapist's ability to identify these partner types and their attendant homeostatic patterns may help him or her to identify possible obstacles to progress in treatment. The authors are careful to point out that this typology is intended to be tentative, informal, even whimsical, and that many partners present an admixture of these characteristics. They refer to the seven types as: New Abusers, Caretakers, "Damaged Goods," Obsessives, Paranoids, Schizotypal Roommates, and Closet Dissociatives.

With *New Abusers*—the first type of partner—the MPD client "recreates childhood trauma by choosing a partner who is much like the past abuser" (Benjamin and Benjamin in press c, p. 5). Kluft (1990) has noted the propensity of victims of abuse to be reabused in subsequent relationships. Coons and Milstein (1984) found significantly higher rates of rape in MPD clients, as did Putnam and colleagues (1986) and Putnam (1989). This type of partner will likely oppose treatment since it contributes to greater independence and assertiveness on the client's part.

Caretakers—the second partner type—relate to the MPD client as do enablers or codependents to alcoholics. (Many partners of MPD clients come from alcoholic families in which the dynamic of enabling was modeled in relation to the drinker; this pattern is recreated in the relationship between the partner and the MPD mate [Benjamin and Benjamin in press, c].) These partners are preoccupied with the MPD client's symptomatology and suffering, make excessive allowances, find it difficult to hold them accountable in the relationship, and serve as overfunctioners in relation to them. They have difficulty asking for what they need and easily lose themselves in the relationship. Often, their own sense of self-esteem is quite low so that they are unable to feel good about themselves for who they are but only for what they do; hence their strenuous efforts to rescue the suffering MPD mate.

Benjamin and Benjamin (in press c) point out that these partners may be highly educated and tend toward intellectualization as a defense; they are often therapists or members of other helping professions. (The authors note that their group for partners of MPD clients had so many nurses over the years that group members joked about being a group for "recovering, impaired RNs.") This type of partner may consciously or unconsciously sabotage treatment out of competitive feelings toward this new "rescuer" — the therapist. He may also fear losing his one-up status (as the "healthy one" or "overfunctioner") and, with it, the focus that provides meaning and a sense of self-worth in his life.

Benjamin and Benjamin (in press c) refer to the third partner type as *"Damaged Goods."*

> The partner is a "good" person who secretly believes that he is in some way "damaged" or undesirable. . . . He is thrilled that a beautiful, intelligent, articulate, artistic, educated, etc. MPD client would choose him as a mate. . . . He may not have noticed . . . that his mate had MPD, and rather, saw her as overly functional and caregiving to him. . . . The identified client is so pleased that anyone would treat her non-abusively that she is more than willing to overlook even considerable faults just to have a friend and mate. [pp. 6–7]

This type of partner may be terrified that improvement for the client will inevitably mean abandonment, just as the fear of outstripping the partner may consciously or unconsciously hold back the client in treatment.

A fourth category of partner is the *Obsessives*. Benjamin and Benjamin (in press c) suggest that the pairing of the obsessive and the MPD client is much like the classical pattern identified as the obsessive-hysteric couple (Glick et al. 1987). The obsessive partner, who is typically male, is drawn to the MPD client's expressiveness or acting out, but increasingly experiences her as out of control and tries to rein in her behavior and emotionality. The MPD client finds the partner's rationality and stability reassuring, but becomes increasingly deadened or comes to resent his efforts to tone her down. This type of partner may be threatened by the client's increasing independence as she progresses in treatment.

The fifth partner type—the *Paranoid*—shares "the view that the world is a hostile place and that outsiders threaten hurt. . . . He readily identifies with the MPD partner who takes on the victim role and may angrily crusade to 'get the abusers' both from the MPD partner's family of origin and from society at large" (Benjamin and Benjamin in press c, p. 8). Benjamin and Benjamin point out that this type of partner may view the client's individual therapist as one more outside enemy and resist therapy from this standpoint. If the client improves, the partner stands to lose his ally against the outside world.

A sixth type of partner is the *Schizotypal Roommate* and is described by the authors as withdrawn and estranged from society and lacking in social skills. He is "glad to have someone . . . with whom to share his isolated world" (Benjamin and Benjamin in press c, p. 8) and may therefore be untroubled by the impairment of the MPD mate. He "meets the MPD mate's needs to avoid painful issues" (p. 8) and may have unusual tolerance for her sexual inhibitions or aversion. The authors suggest that he "is often equally sexually disinterested or dysfunctional" (p. 8). These partners may be suffering from addictions, depression, or even psychosis. They may resist treatment because they fear abandonment if the MPD client improves or becomes more comfortable in the social world for which the "schizotypal roommate" feels ill-equipped.

Closet Dissociatives—the final partner type—may be less obviously impaired than their MPD mates but they also suffer from a dissociative disorder. The two partners may have found each other in a treatment setting. The relationship is more likely to be characterized by interpersonal fusion or symbiosis (Karpel 1976, Searles 1963, 1973). More overt problems, such as addictions, may obscure the partner's dissociative symptoms (Benjamin and Benjamin in press c, p. 9).

Finally, Benjamin and Benjamin (in press c) summarize the ways in which these varying relational patterns may inhibit or interfere with treatment.

The abusive partner helps to maintain the victim stance of the MPD client. The caretaker keeps the MPD mate in a dependent role. The dependency of the "damaged goods" partner pushes the MPD mate to overfunction. The obsessive partner needs to be available to rescue the emotional and unpredictable MPD partner in order to give purpose to his life. The paranoid partner colludes with the MPD mate against a hostile and unfriendly world. The schizotypal roommate finds the distant partnership with an MPD mate to meet his needs to maintain a superficial relationship. Finally, the closet dissociative is able to hide his own impairment because his MPD mate fails to notice or protest. [p. 9]

PARTNERS' CONCERNS

Whether the partners of MPD clients become involved in treatment or not, they are likely to share certain concerns. Being familiar with these concerns can help therapists who treat MPD clients anticipate the issues that are most often problematic for their partners. (This list derives from Benjamin and Benjamin's thorough discussion of themes in group work with partners [in press b] with additional points raised by Sachs et al. (1988) and Panos et al. (1990) and from personal discussions with Gerald Krieger and J. Mark Hall.)

Becoming aware of the diagnosis of MPD is often a shocking experience for the partners. Benjamin and Benjamin (in press b) stress the ongoing struggle between "relief at finding out what is wrong and a strong wish to deny it" (p. 2). Partners may experience grief over previous false starts and misdiagnoses. They also struggle with the losses associated with their original dreams for the relationship and family life. The partner may fear that the MPD mate will never recover, be chronically disabled, or, when she improves, ultimately abandon him.

If the client begins to share the details of her abuse with her partner, it may be difficult for him to believe that such things actually occurred. His expressions of skepticism may be intensely distressing to the client, especially if disbelief by others in the past allowed the abuse to continue. Once aware of the diagnosis, both partners must consider whom to tell and whom not to tell in the "outside world." The partner may have to cover up or make excuses for the dissociative mate socially, especially if she becomes more overtly symptomatic during treatment.

Partners often express bewilderment as to how to act in relation to their dissociative mates, both before and after learning of the diagnosis. While they are unaware of the diagnosis, they may be confused by seemingly inconsistent communication or behavior related to different alters. They may not understand why the MPD mate seems upset by seemingly unimportant incidents, which in fact reactivate prior trauma. Once the diagnosis is made and shared with the partner, he may be even more confused as to how to act. Is he dealing with one person or more? Should he call alters by name? Should he play with child alters or be sexual with highly sexualized alters? Can he hold his mate accountable for the behavior of different alters?

Coping with anger can be especially difficult. Benjamin and Benjamin (in press b) point out the dilemmas involved in anger at an alter who may provoke an issue but not be "out" later to deal with it, or fear that expressing anger will trigger a switch in personalities. Coping with anger is particularly difficult if the partner feels that he has unfairly become a lightning rod for his mate's destructive entitlement (Boszormenyi-Nagy and Krasner 1986) and rage at her abusers. Partners struggle with their anger at the whole situation and how to prevent it from poisoning relationships in the family. The challenge of dealing with anger is often inherent in the partner's relationship with his in-laws.

Trust, which depends on predictability and consistency, may be especially difficult for the partner, given the discontinuities resulting from dissociative symptomatology. It may be difficult for him to put faith in agreements with his mate when overwhelming symptomatology or switching between alters make for sometimes startling inconsistencies in behavior. Panos et al. (1990) note that several partners involved in couple therapy initially raised questions concerning their own safety with their MPD mates.

Given what is known about secondary trauma or vicarious traumatization, partners may experience symptoms of PTSD, including heightened vulnerability, helplessness, rage, anxiety, confusion, numbness, and despair. In the context of treatment, Herman (1992) succinctly points out that:

> Trauma is contagious. In the role of witness to disaster or atrocity, the therapist at times is emotionally overwhelmed. She experiences, to a lesser degree, the same terror, rage, and despair as the patient. . . . The therapist may begin to experience symptoms of post-traumatic stress disorder. . . . The therapist also empathically shares the patient's experience of helplessness. [He or she] may also become fearful of the patient. [pp. 140–143]

Partners are subject to the same spiritual and existential secondary effects as the therapists who treat trauma survivors and may become "engulfed by anguish" or experience "sinking into despair" (Danieli 1984, cited in Herman 1992). Partners must grapple with questions involving how human beings could abuse others in the ways their mates have experienced, why this happened to their partners, why they have had to suffer the consequences in their own lives.

Partners who function as caregivers for their dissociative mates may come to feel increasingly deprived and neglected in the relationship. Routinely, but especially when the dissociative partner is in treatment, the relationship may come to be dominated by her intense and shifting symptomatology, crises, and hospitalizations. The partner may feel that he must put his own needs on hold. Even while they understand and sympathize with their mates' suffering, they may come to resent the lack of reciprocity in the relationship. Partners are especially likely to feel deprived and neglected if the dissociative client's symptomatology includes inhibited sexual desire or sexual aversion. When the dissociative client is the primary parent, the other partner may inherit unusual burdens for child care, especially as the dissociative client begins to recover traumatic memories and becomes more overtly symptomatic. He may also be uncertain as to whether he can safely entrust children to her care.

The MPD client's relationship with her therapist can generate troubling feelings in her partner. He may be impatient and skeptical of the likely benefits of treatment, particularly if diagnosis and treatment for MPD follows a series of prior misdiagnoses and failed treatments. He may feel competitive, resentful, or excluded. Krieger (personal communication April 1994) points out, however, that partners may feel relieved that someone else has assumed some of the burden of caring for the dissociative mate. The partner is especially likely to feel negative toward the therapy if no attempts are made to involve him in any way.

Finally, partners often express concerns associated with the MPD client's recovery. It can be unnerving to find oneself relating to a post-integration mate. In fact, Panos et al. (1990) suggest that it may take couples four to six weeks to begin to adjust to integration. The partner may have to face the loss of favored sexualized or child alters; ultimately, he may fear that, after successful treatment, the mate will abandon him. Herman (1992) notes that "therapists who work with traumatized people require an ongoing support system to deal with these intense reactions" (p. 141). This highlights a major reason why clinicians who treat MPD clients should consider the needs and concerns of their partners and, if possible, involve them in treatment.

RATIONALE AND ADVANTAGES OF INCLUDING THE PARTNER IN TREATMENT

There are compelling diagnostic, pragmatic, and ethical reasons for clinicians who conduct individual psychotherapy with dissociative clients to extend their sympathetic interest to their clients' partners.

Gaining a Fuller Picture of the MPD Client

A meeting between the therapist and the client's partner can add depth to the therapist's initial assessment of the client. This is true for individual psychotherapy of nondissociative disorders but may be even more true with MPD clients, given the secrecy and confusion that are so often part of the client's clinical presentation. The partner's impressions may help the therapist to assess the client's level of anxiety or depression as well as potential danger if suicidal thoughts and impulses are present. Even when the partner does not think of the client as having MPD, he may be aware of behaviors that the therapist recognizes as dissociation, switching, or traumatic reexperiencing.

The client may welcome the therapist's interest in her partner. She may appreciate the therapist's effort to understand the context of her life more fully; she may be relieved to know that those who are devoted to her interests will be able to work together if need be; she may be worried about her partner's symptomatology and functioning.

Finally, given the high incidence of transgenerational transmission of dissociation and MPD (Braun 1985a,b), and findings that suggest that MPD mothers have significant difficulties in parenting (Coons 1985, Kluft 1987), a meeting with the partner may help the therapist form a truer picture of the dissociative client's functioning as a parent. Such a meeting is not, however, a substitute for clinical evaluation of the children, preferably by another practitioner.

ASSESSING THE RELATIONAL CONTEXT
OF THE MPD CLIENT

Meeting with the partner may shed light on factors that maintain symptomatology and on relational resources that may support coping and foster healing in treatment.

The importance of relational factors in the etiology of psychopathology, in relapse, and in healing, has been demonstrated for a variety of psychiatric problems (Brown and Rutter 1966, Brown et al. 1972, Hafner et al. 1983, Jacobson et al. 1989, Valone et al. 1983, Vaughn and Leff 1976, Vaughn et al. 1982), most strikingly, for depression (Florin et al. 1992, Hooley 1986, Hooley et al. 1986). For example, an individual in a discordant—that is, conflictual and unhappy—relationship appears to be 25 times more likely to be depressed than a person in a nondiscordant relationship (Weissman 1987). The most frequent event preceding the onset of depression has been found to be an increase in couple's conflict (Paykel et al. 1969). In one study, the factors that best differentiated individuals who attempted suicide from community controls were found to be feelings of isolation in one's closest relationships and little affection shown by the partner (Welz 1988). The amount of criticism directed at an individual hospitalized for depression by his or her partner in an in-hospital interview was found to be a better predictor of relapse than the initial severity of the patient's symptoms (Hooley et al. 1986, Vaughn and Leff 1976).

With psychiatric disorders such as schizophrenia and depression, there is compelling evidence that family members' excessive criticism or excessive worry and preoccupation with the symptomatic individual contribute to increased symptomatology and relapse after successful treatment with medication or hospitalization (Brown and Rutter 1966, Brown et al. 1972, Florin et al. 1992,). Hooley 1986, Hooley et al. 1986, Valone et al. 1983, Vaughn and Leff 1976, Vaughn et al. 1982. Conversely, women who had a confiding relationship with their spouses (or others) were found in one study to be three times less likely to be depressed than women without such relationships facing similar life stresses (Brown and Harris 1978). In Krugman's (1987) words, "the family is critical to vulnerability, recovery, and resilience" (p. 128).

These findings suggest that interactions in a couple's relationship may be implicated in the persistence of symptomatology. They have more immediate relevance for couples in which one partner has MPD in that the single most common presenting complaint among MPD clients is depression (Allison 1978, Bliss 1984, Coons 1984, O'Brien 1985, Putnam et al. 1986).

With dissociative clients, an initial session with the partner may enable the therapist to identify whether the partner seems to fit one or more of the partner types described earlier. This may help the therapist anticipate resistance to the client's treatment based on the homeostatic patterns associated with each type. The therapist's willingness to meet with the partner from time to time during treatment, or to refer him to another clinician for concurrent treatment, may minimize the likelihood of the partner consciously or unconsciously sabotaging treatment. Assessing the relational context of the MPD client also involves looking for resources that can support treatment and help the client cope with everyday life. A partner who is sympathetic to the client's suffering and willing to support her efforts in treatment can make a significant contribution to the client's recovery.

Enlisting the Partner as an Ally for Treatment

As long as the MPD client is involved with his or her partner, that individual has the power to support the client's treatment or to oppose or subvert it. One of the most compelling reasons for the therapist to meet with the partner involves this potential for the partner to be an ally or an opponent to treatment. Without contact of any kind, the partner is more susceptible to his or her own transferential distortions of the therapist. He is even more likely to resent, undermine, or oppose treatment if he feels that the therapist is either oblivious or indifferent to his needs and concerns.

Alternatively, by asking to meet with the partner and expressing curiosity, sympathy, and respect, the therapist greatly increases the likelihood that he or she can secure an ally for treatment and a collaborator in times of crisis. The partner may be able to provide emotional support and encouragement to the client or to help with practical necessities, like rides to and from treatment, and household responsibilities when the client is feeling overwhelmed. He may deal with health-care providers, insurance companies, or HMOs to assure continuity of treatment. The partner is especially likely to be needed in times of crisis—for example, if the client needs to be hospitalized on an emergency basis. In fact, this is probably the time when most therapists do have contact with the partner, impelled by the necessities of the crisis.

The partner can help monitor suicidality or the effects of medication. Some therapists enlist partners to help the MPD client in specific circumstances. For example, if she appears to be having a flashback in which a helpless and frightened child alter is reexperiencing abuse, the partner may be able to help her switch to a more functional alter by the use of a simple prearranged circumscribed hypnotic technique. Hall (personal communication, May 1994) points out that, in addition to benefiting the client, this benefits the partner by enabling him to feel effectual and helpful to his mate. In other words, when partners are educated about the nature of trauma and dissociation, it is often mutually beneficial for both partners.

Finally, a positive therapeutic alliance with the partner provides more potential leverage for change in the relational system and, therefore, in the daily life of the MPD client. For example, if a client's husband can understand and accept that his involvement with a sexualized alter is in fact injurious to the client (since it reenacts aspects of early sexual abuse), he may be willing to be aware of when this alter is out and to forego sexual relations under these conditions.

Identifying a Partner in Need of Services

There are several reasons for therapists to assume that the MPD client's partner may also be suffering psychologically. Putnam (1989) observes that "MPD patients often marry spouses with a significant amount of psychopathology," and notes "depression, alcoholism, character pathology, and gender identification problems" are common in the partners (p. 268).

Regardless of previous pathology, the difficulties of living with a dissociative mate may contribute to stress and symptomatology. The client's often protracted treatment history will tax the partner's trust, optimism and finances. The partner must cope with the secondary elaborations of untreated trauma in the client, which may include depression, withdrawal, anxiety, addictions, suicidal impulses and attempts, sexual dysfunctions, and eating disorders. Partners are susceptible to secondary trauma or vicarious traumatization. If skilled therapists with ample training and supervision, who meet with the client once or twice a week, need support to cope with the contagious effects of trauma, how much more so do the partners who are living with MPD clients without either training or professional support?

Once again, studies of depression support the conclusion that living with an individual who is suffering psychologically can negatively affect the partner. Studies have shown that even brief interactions between depressed persons and strangers contribute to a negative mood in the stranger (Biglin et al. 1989). Coyne and colleagues (1987) found that 40 percent of the spouses of depressed persons had serious enough distress to meet standard criteria for referral to psychiatric services and that, after the depressed person recovered, only 17 percent of the spouses met these criteria.

The therapist must recognize that, in working with the client, he or she will indirectly influence the lives of those closest to her. This involves her children, parents, siblings (to varying degrees), and, of course, her partner. Therapists have an ethical obligation to extend their sympathetic curiosity and concern to all of those who are likely to be significantly affected by their work with a client. In light of homeostatic processes, the therapist should anticipate the potential development of symptomatology in the client's partner if the client makes progress in treatment. Difficulties may include depression, anxiety or panic attacks, an increase in the use of alcohol or other substances, social or work difficulties, and, in some cases, potential violence or psychosis. This point has pragmatic as well as ethical significance. If the client's partner begins to decompensate, this imposes additional stresses with which she must now cope; it may also activate powerful feelings of guilt, which may interfere with her efforts to pursue her own treatment.

Finally, even if the partner does not have significant preexisting symptomatology or diagnosable symptoms resulting from living with the MPD client, he may still need and welcome the support and help with coping. Greater education about dissociation and trauma may help him to make sensible choices when faced with inevitable dilemmas, choices which can benefit the client as well as the partner and other family members.

POTENTIAL DISADVANTAGES OF INVOLVING PARTNERS IN TREATMENT

Endangering the Psychological Safety of the MPD Client

The client may welcome the suggestion that the therapist meet with her partner; however, this is not a foregone conclusion. For a variety of reasons, the involvement of the partner in her individual treatment—even if only for one initial session—may make her feel unsafe. She may have tried to keep much of her experience—both past and current—secret from the partner. While she may be willing to let the partner know that she has sought treatment, she may fear that his meeting with the therapist will lead to the disclosure of details of past abuse or current symptomatology, a prospect that may feel unbearable to her. Including the partner in therapy may cause the client to feel powerless over the pace of disclosure.

She may also fear that the partner will reveal information to the therapist before she feels ready to do so, or that the partner's image of her—which may differ significantly from her own—will irrevocably affect her image in the therapist's eyes. She may fear that the therapist will side with the partner against her. If the partner is brought in before sufficient trust has been established in the therapeutic relationship, the client may feel ganged up on, especially if the client is female and both the partner and therapist are male (Krieger, personal communication April 1994).

If the partner fits some of the characteristics of new abusers or is highly overinvolved in her difficulties—for example, constantly giving her suggestions from his own twelve-step program as the solution to her problems—she may simply need a separate space that she feels is her own. The idea of including the partner in any way may cause anxiety, fear, or even despair. Finally, Gelinas (personal communication April 1994) notes that the therapist's effort to involve the partner in treatment may stir up turmoil among alters.

If the client seems unable to tolerate the idea of her partner meeting with the therapist, the proposal should be dropped, at least for a time. There may be advantages to meeting with the client's partner but not if it means endangering her treatment. In cases such as these, the therapist might offer to refer the partner to another practitioner; alternatively, he might simply wait to revisit the topic at a later point in treatment.

Taxing the Resources of the Therapist

In working with dissociative clients, the therapist will probably encounter complexity, confusion, and crisis. Gelinas (personal communication April 1994) refers to the rigors of trying to "stay one step ahead of the disorganization" in work with these clients. Considering the partner's needs and concerns may tax the therapist's own psychological resources and require an additional investment of time. This does not make it any less necessary; it does make it more daunting.

Creating Problematic Triangles

Extending concern and curiosity to the client's partner makes the therapist potentially more vulnerable to triangulation between the partners. For example, the partner may reveal information to the therapist but insist that it be kept secret from the client. (For suggestions on managing secrets in clinical work with couples, see Imber-Black 1993 and Karpel 1980, 1994.) Or the therapist might be immediately presented with a clash of interests between the partners and pressured to take sides. Opening the door to the partner may invite the complications which often attend couple therapy, even if the therapist has no intention of providing them.

While there are risks associated with involving partners in treatment, my own feeling is that the advantages of such involvement clearly outweigh the dangers in most cases. Furthermore, these risks can be greatly reduced by following certain guidelines and choosing among several possible formats of involvement for the partner. The remainder of this chapter elaborates these methods and guidelines.

INVOLVING THE PARTNER IN TREATMENT

If a therapist accepts the rationale for involving the client's partner in treatment, the immediate questions are: How to do it? Who should do it and when? What methods of involvement seem most likely to be productive (concurrent couple therapy, parallel individual treatment, group therapy for the partner, or simply episodic contact with a therapist)?

Should such treatment be conducted by the client's primary therapist or by another practitioner? When should such contact take place?

Most authorities, as suggested earlier, indicate their positions only by default—by failing to address the subject at all. Others have suggested different forms of involvement and conceptualized their importance in different ways. Putnam (1989) recommends that partners be included in treatment but does not specify whether this should be done in separate sessions with the therapist or in joint sessions with the client, nor does he indicate when such involvement should take place.

A number of authors have advocated for couple and/or family therapy as an *adjunct* to the treatment of MPD client (Putnam 1989, Sachs 1986, Sachs et al. 1988). Some have insisted that couple and family therapy be viewed as an *integral* part of the treatment of dissociative disorders (Benjamin and Benjamin 1992, in press d,e,f,g, Panos et al. 1990, Williams 1991). Levenson and Berry (1983) describe one case in which couple therapy was utilized as the primary form of treatment for an MPD client. However, in this case, the couple terminated therapy prematurely and the MPD client's dissociative symptoms persisted. Benjamin and Benjamin (in press a,b,c) have described the structure, process, and themes involved in group treatment for parents and partners of MPD clients.

Various opinions have been expressed concerning the timing of treatments involving the partner and the question of whether such treatment should be provided by the client's primary therapist or by another clinician. These issues are addressed in the section "Referral to Couple or Family Therapy," which appears later in this chapter. The various questions that face the therapist and some of the considerations that guide decision making in these cases are summarized in Figure 19-1. The flowchart begins with the conviction that in all cases the therapist should endeavor to meet with the partner during the opening phase of treatment unless the client objects strongly or the partner is actively abusive to the client or to the children. Recommending concurrent individual psychotherapy or group treatment for the partner or couple or family therapy may also be indicated. Decisions among these treatment formats should be made, at least in part, on where the partner can start (Krieger personal communication April 1994)—that is, in what kind of format he feels most comfortable. The decisions therapists make among these treatment options are guided in part by underlying treatment models.

Involving the client's partner in treatment introduces questions that are more easily overlooked if the therapist limits his or her awareness to the client alone: Who is the client? To whom is the therapist responsible? Where is the problem located—within the client or between the partners? What are the goals of treatment?

Figure 19–1. Decision-making chart

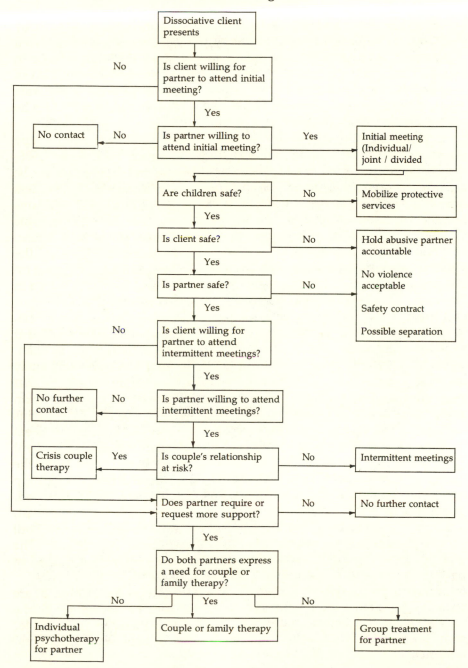

For a therapist operating from an individual treatment model, these questions have ready and clear answers. Problems are conceptualized as being within the individual, even if there is a recognition that such problems are sequelae of actual abuse by others. They are seen as being maintained by intrapsychic conflicts or defenses, character structure, or biology. The goals of treatment involve individual change; the model assumes that relational change may follow individual change. The therapist is seen as ethically responsible to the individual client alone. Most therapists who treat MPD clients operate—knowingly or unknowingly—from an individual treatment model.

Systemic treatment models answer these questions differently. Problems are conceptualized as being between people. Symptoms are seen as expressions of systemic forces, often serving protective functions for the overall system or for individuals or subsystems within it. The goal of treatment is relational change. The assumption is that individual change will follow relational or systemic change. The therapist sees him- or herself as equally responsible to all members of the relational system, a stance referred to by contextual therapists as *multidirectional partiality* or more simply *multilaterality* (Boszormenyi-Nagy and Spark 1973, Boszormenyi-Nagy and Ulrich 1981, Boszormenyi-Nagy and Krasner 1986). Benjamin and Benjamin (1992, 1993, in press a,b,c,d,e,f,g) are unusual in advocating for a systemic model in treating dissociative clients. They recognize the need for intensive individual psychotherapy for the MPD client but adopt a position of multilaterality in relation to the client's partner, children, and parents.

A third treatment model is the psychoeducational model (Anderson 1983, 1984, Falloon and Liberman 1983, Kopeikin et al. 1983). Problems are conceptualized in terms of illness, which is influenced by interactions between people. The goals of treatment are to relieve symptomatology, to support the suffering individual and those who share his or her suffering by virtue of loving and living with him or her, to enhance their efforts to cope with the illness, and to moderate the negative amplifying effects of interaction on symptomatology.

The psychoeducational model bears some resemblance to the model of spouse-aided therapy (Hafner et al. 1983), a method of treatment utilized with a range of serious psychiatric disorders that involves the client's partner in treatment. "Spouse-aided therapy engages the patient's spouse in conjoint, problem-solving therapy as a co-agent of change. . . . The patient's symptoms are the initial focus of therapy. . . . The spouse is encouraged to feel a useful and valued part of the patient's therapy, which seriously increases the likelihood of his or her serious commitment to the treatment process" (p. 388). While treatment initially focuses on the client's symptoms, the participation of both partners in treatment allows the therapist to explore "the marital contribution to symptom and problem maintenance" (p. 388).

This model is probably the most realistic one for most therapists treating MPD clients to adopt. Problems are conceptualized as both within and between people. Treatment is directed primarily toward individual and relational change. The therapist provides intensive psychotherapy of the MPD client; however, he or she is aware that interactions between the partners may perpetuate the client's symptomatology. Efforts are therefore directed toward providing support and education for the partner, whether via occasional meetings with the primary therapist, referral for individual psychotherapy or group therapy for the partner, or for couple or family therapy.

The therapist who works within this model is not functioning as a systems therapist in the traditional sense—for example, someone who conceptualizes problems in terms of current relational systems, whose efforts are designed to change current relational systems, and who is equally responsible for the welfare of all members of the system. MPD is so complex and confusing, its etiology so clearly embedded in early life experiences, and the role of trauma so central, that this type of systemic framework is ill-suited to the work that must be done.

The therapist extends his or her sympathetic curiosity to the client's partner or children, but he or she recognizes that the client needs and is entitled to a special relationship. The MPD client needs and deserves a treatment context that is well-bounded, secure, and solidly her own. She should not have to share the therapist with anyone else, including her partner (although in some case she may feel comfortable doing so). This is especially true given the likelihood of her having had negligent or unresponsive caregivers during childhood, making secure attachment with the therapist more difficult. She should be confident that the therapist is primarily responsive to *her* needs and vulnerabilities and that the agendas of others will not drive the treatment.

Williams (1991) recommends a similar approach, advocating that therapists meet with the partners and family members of dissociative clients but insisting that "the primary client, however, remains the multiple" (p. 92). In the large majority of cases, this mandate is not incompatible with concern for those who are significantly affected by their relationship with the client and by the vicissitudes of the client's treatment, most notably partners and children.

Benjamin and Benjamin (1992) consider all treatment options that involve the partner, children, or parents of MPD clients, as well as the client's individual psychotherapy, to be differing aspects of "family-centered treatment" that is aimed both at fostering integration of person-alities in the MPD client and facilitating healthy relationships in the family.

The remainder of this chapter examines indications, contraindications and guidelines for several methods of involving partners in treatment. Regardless of the method chosen, the goals are essentially the same:

• Supplementing the therapist's initial assessment of the client
• Assessing the primary relational context of the client's life (including stressors, homeostatic patterns, and resources)
• Preventing sabotage of the client's psychotherapy
• Securing an ally for treatment
• Educating and supporting the partner
• Providing further treatment for the partner if requested or required.

INITIAL AND INTERMITTENT CONTACT
BETWEEN THE THERAPIST AND PARTNER

Clinicians treating MPD clients who are in committed couple relationships should routinely endeavor to meet with their partners unless there are clear contraindications for doing so. Such contraindications include the client's inability to tolerate the meeting, current domestic violence, and an extremely unstable or ill-defined couple relationship. The first of these considerations has already been discussed.

Meeting with the client's partner is also contraindicated if the therapist suspects that the partner is violent toward the client. Therapists should be especially vigilant for signs of abuse in work with dissociative clients, given the likelihood of reenactments of abuse in these relationships. If the therapist suspects that a client is being physically abused by her partner, he or she should inquire about this in an individual session with the woman. If violence is occurring and the woman is not safe, he or she should assist her in securing safety for herself and any children. The therapist may need to help her arrange for shelter, bring in other family members to counter her isolation, educate her about her legal rights and about procedures for separating, help her to arrange for a restraining order, or, in some cases, a police escort from the office to a shelter. (For further guidelines when domestic violence is suspected in initial assessments, see Karpel 1994.)

Finally, the therapist should be more cautious about involving partners in treatment if the couple's relationship is highly unstable or on the verge of ending. An intense emotional struggle between the partners increases the likelihood that the therapist will be triangulated between them. Some of the advantages of meeting with partners (such as securing an ally for treatment) are less potent if it is questionable whether the partner is even an ally for his mate. If the partners are having difficulty deciding whether or not they are a couple, the therapist's invitation to the partner may provide an unintentional "blessing" to the relationship, which may not be in one or both partners' interests.

If there are no indications of active violence, if the couple's relationship is relatively stable, and if the client welcomes (or at least agrees to) the meeting, the therapist can begin laying the groundwork for it. Hall points out (personal communication April 1994) that the therapist should invite the participation of the client in deciding on the timing and format for the meeting as well as any guidelines concerning material she wishes not to be discussed at that time. The more active a role the client has in arranging this meeting, the less likely she, or the therapist, will regret it.

The therapist needs to explain the purposes and limitations of this meeting both to the client and to her partner. He or she should explain to the client the reasons for wanting to meet with her partner and make clear that this is not marital therapy. Usually, an explanation that emphasizes gaining a deeper understanding of the client and her life outside the office will suffice. The meeting needn't be held immediately when the client begins treatment; conducting several individual sessions first will hopefully help to build trust and make it easier for the client to tolerate the meeting involving the partner.

The therapist might meet individually with the partner or jointly with the couple. There are advantages to both formats. Meeting with both partners together allows the therapist to observe how they interact with one another and may shed light on homeostatic patterns that could subvert the client's individual treatment. Meeting individually with the partner may allow him to discuss more openly his frustrations and concerns about his mate. A useful format, which incorporates both options, involves dividing the time by meeting initially with both partners together and then spending some time with the partner individually. One to one and a half hours should suffice for this type of session. The therapist should invite the client's participation in deciding which format should be utilized.

The therapist needs to frame the meeting for the partner as well, either at the start of the meeting or by telephone beforehand. Again, the rationale given involves wanting to gain a deeper understanding of the client and to understand what things are like for the partner as well. The therapist should reiterate that this is not marital therapy and that the partner will probably meet only intermittently with the therapist—if at all—in the future. (For further guidelines and considerations involved in meeting separately with partners in a couple relationship, see Karpel 1994.)

Beyond its diagnostic purposes, the initial meeting between the therapist and the partner can serve to build a therapeutic alliance. The message
implicitly conveyed by the invitation to meet with the partner is: "I know
that you are there. I know that your partner's condition affects you and that
what goes on in this treatment will affect you. I know that this can be very
difficult to live with. I care about your welfare as well as the client's. I will
be keeping you in mind." The initial meeting can also help to educate the
partner about MPD. This is especially important if he is unaware of his
partner's dissociative disorder or poorly informed on the subject.

Once the therapist actually meets with the partner, he or she should try
to assess his strengths and coping skills, level of self-esteem, and degree
of commitment to the relationship (Williams 1991). Does he seem to fit one
or more of the partner types described earlier? Do the homeostatic
patterns associated with those types of partners appear to operate in this
relationship? If the client has clearly differentiated alters who are known
to the partner, Williams (1991) suggests asking him how the alters affect
his life. Therapists should always evaluate for secondary trauma and take
a trauma history as well. They should also try to ascertain how the partner
feels about psychotherapy for the client at this point and what his
experience has been in relation to previous treatments, if any. Williams
(1991) also suggests that the therapists assess the partner's level of hope
for the future.

If, in the meeting with the partner, the therapist becomes aware of past
or current violence, the first concern should be whether all parties are safe.
If there is no current violence, the therapist can proceed as he or she would
otherwise. If it becomes clear that children are experiencing, or are at risk
for, physical or sexual abuse, he or she must mobilize protective services.
The abusive parent—whether the client, the partner, or both—may need to
be physically separated from the children for some period of time. If the
children are safe but either the client or the partner is being abused by the
other, the abusive partner must be held responsible for his or her behavior
and the therapist must insist that no degree of violence is acceptable. If the
partners agree with this premise, a safety contract and violence-prevention
techniques, such as time-out procedures, should be established. However,
the therapist should be skeptical of the benefits of couple therapy in cases
of past domestic violence, and couple therapy is strongly contraindicated if
violence is still occurring (Bograd 1984, Coyne 1986, Dobash and Dobash
1988, Kaufman 1992, Rosenbaum and O'Leary 1986). An abusive male
partner might be referred to a program for batterers. The MPD client must
be held responsible for violence committed by any alters and the partner
supported in setting limits on such behavior. In some cases, the partners
may need to physically separate.

If both the client and her partner welcome the plan of intermittent meetings between the therapist and the partner, the nature, timing, and ground rules for these meetings should be clarified—if possible, at the end of the initial meeting. The simplest approach involves recommending (having already secured the client's agreement) intermittent meetings with the partner while the client is in treatment. These meetings are initiated by the therapist, either routinely (and probably not more often than every four to six months) or when particular issues arise in treatment that suggest that the partner's involvement might be helpful. The therapist may feel a need to schedule meetings that include the partner if, based on the client's report in her individual treatment, it seems that the couple's relationship is in danger. Occasional meetings with both partners together and with the partner individually may help to stabilize the couple's relationship. More formal couple therapy can be initiated, if necessary, in the postintegration phase of treatment. (See the discussion later in this chapter, "Referral to Couple or Family Therapy.")

The therapist may encourage the partner to call him or her (again, having already gotten the client's permission) if the partner is especially concerned about something. The partner should be informed that these calls will be discussed with the client. If the partner seems to be calling excessively and either overtaxing the therapist's resources or endangering the client's treatment, this should be discussed with him and an effort made to refer him to another therapist for more intensive support.

The same set of options is available for subsequent meetings between the therapist and the partner as for the initial meeting. The therapist can meet individually with the partner, jointly with both partners, or divide the time between these formats. Decisions regarding which format to use are made on a case-to-case basis. The format may vary from one meeting to the next, depending on: developments in the couple's relationship and in the client's treatment, the client's preferences, and the therapist's judgment as to which format is likely to prove most helpful. Ongoing contact may help in managing crises that occur over the course of treatment. Especially when issues of suicidal lethality, acute decompensation, and hospitalization are involved, a working alliance between the therapist and the partner may decrease potential risks and facilitate continuity of treatment.

If the client opposes further contact between her partner and her therapist and if the partner requests or requires further support, the therapist should refer the partner to another practitioner. If the partner is uninterested in further meetings, the therapist may have no contact with the partner and no referral is required. None of these scenarios rule out further contact in the future, but until circumstances change no contact would be expected.

REFERRAL TO GROUP THERAPY
FOR THE PARTNER

Group therapy is a potentially powerful and economical way to support partners of MPD clients. Groups for partners and parents allow family members to be included in treatment without having the MPD client give up time in individual therapy (Benjamin and Benjamin in press a). Groups provide valuable education as well as support and validation to participants. The group can help members adjust to the diagnosis of MPD for their mates in the early phases of treatment, and can function as "a component of long-term outpatient care with family participation" (p. 4). One disadvantage is the relative rarity of such services.

Benjamin and Benjamin (in press a) succinctly summarize the advantages of group therapy for partners as a component of the overall treatment of MPD.

> The . . . group provides an efficient way to help participants gain access to information, individual support, and share with others who are in a similar situation. It helps to break down a sense of isolation through the building of a community. It reduces the effects of secondary traumatization and the stigma of having a family member with MPD, while contributing to the well-being of others by bearing witness to their pain. Additionally, a group format can be a less threatening milieu in which to address partner and parent issues than in individual or couples therapy sessions. . . . Co-leaders can model both nurturing and limit-setting with group members as well as relationship-enhancing modes of communication.
>
> The partners' and parents' group is a key part of our treatment approach to dissociative disorders. From a family systems view, . . . the group helps to heal the system. From the point of view of a more traditional, individual psychodynamic and hypnotically augmented treatment schema, it can be viewed as an important adjunct and aid to the therapy by its synergistic effect on addressing and correcting the marital and family dynamics. [pp. 13–14]

Indications for referring a client's partner to group treatment include the partner's desire for further support and information and/or motivation to explore how he came to be in the relationship. A group must be available in the partner's geographical area. In addition, the group is well suited to partners who want support but are uneasy with the idea of entering into individual psychotherapy.

Benjamin and Benjamin (in press a) note certain exclusion criteria as well. Partners who are themselves dissociative or who may be abusers of the client or children should not be admitted into the group, in light of the negative effects of their inclusion on other group members. Partners who need more support than the group can provide or a one-to-one relationship with a therapist should be referred for individual psychotherapy.

REFERRAL TO INDIVIDUAL PSYCHOTHERAPY FOR THE PARTNER

This treatment option is indicated for partners who express a need for more support than the primary therapist can provide, who may themselves be experiencing symptomatology, who want help coping with difficulties related to the client's dissociative disorder, or who are motivated to explore their own feelings and relationships in psychotherapy. The goals of treatment overlap with those described for group therapy—helping the partner to explore how he came to be in the relationship and to cope with the stresses that attend it. In addition, treatment may focus more directly on the partner's psychopathology. Experience in group treatment often serves as an impetus for the partner to initiate individual psychotherapy, while movement in the other direction is less common (Benjamin and Benjamin in press a).

REFERRAL TO COUPLE OR FAMILY THERAPY

Couple therapy is indicated when both partners express a desire to focus on shared coping with stresses related to the client's dissociative disorder as well as other current problems in the relationship. Couple therapy is also indicated if this is "where the partner can start" (Krieger, personal communication April 1994), if the client agrees, and if the therapist feels reasonably comfortable that this is in the client's interests. For example, a partner who is highly dependent on the client may be threatened by her relationship with her therapist. This type of partner may wish to be involved in treatment in a way that allows him to meet conjointly with the client rather than in a group or in individual treatment by himself.

Couple therapy is contraindicated when the partner is actively abusive to the client or when the client is so overwhelmed by the rigors of her own individual treatment that she is simply unable to attend to the partner's needs. In these cases, the partner should be referred to another practitioner and couple therapy deferred, either until all abuse has ceased and the partner is involved in treatment for batterers or until the client has progressed sufficiently in treatment that she is able to focus on the needs and complaints of her partner.

Opinions differ on the question of when couple therapy should be conducted. Williams (1991), for example, indicates that couple or family therapy can be conducted concurrently with the MPD client's individual psychotherapy. Kluft and colleagues (1984) recommend that couple therapy be conducted in the postintegration phase of the MPD client's treatment. Krieger (personal communication April 1994) concurs, noting that the MPD client needs to be far enough along in her own treatment that she can tolerate hearing and responding to the needs of her partner. As Benjamin and Benjamin (in press d) indicate: "Only when both partners near the recovery stage of therapy can traditional marital therapy be effective. It is very difficult to work interpersonally until intrapsychic wholeness is achieved or nearly achieved" (p. 7). Benjamin and Benjamin do suggest however (in press d) that some couple therapy may need to be conducted intermittently during the client's individual treatment just to hold the relationship together until formal couple therapy can be conducted, if necessary, postintegration. They indicate that these sessions tend to "follow the sequence of the individual treatment" (p. 7) and should be primarily supportive and psychoeducational.

Opinions also differ on the question of whether couple or family therapy should be conducted by the client's primary therapist or by another clinician. Chiappa (1993) has spoken against one therapist conducting both the client's individual psychotherapy and family therapy. Benjamin and Benjamin (in press d) and Williams (1991) take less absolute positions, suggesting that this decision be made on a case-by-case basis. However, it should be understood that for one therapist to conduct both individual and couple or family therapy may introduce significant complications and difficulties. Probably, for most therapists who treat dissociative clients, the safest—and sanest—course of action is to refer the couple to another practitioner if couple therapy is indicated and to maintain ongoing communication with that practitioner.

There is general agreement (Sachs et al. 1988) that couple therapy should focus on here and now issues in the life of the couple or family. Sachs and colleagues (1988) suggest that couple therapy should focus on: (1) educating the partner about the nature of MPD; (2) helping the couple cope with disruptions to the homeostasis of the relational system; (3) helping them to share thoughts and feelings; and (4) preventing sabotage of the primary treatment.

When the client has clearly defined and named alters, one technical point involves how the MPD client's partner should relate to such alters.

While some authors have encouraged partners to play with child alters and to relate to them by name, many experts agree that this is not advisable. For example, Panos and colleagues (1990) suggest that "the therapist should stress to the spouse that despite having many personalities (alters), it is important to view the MPD patient as a whole person and accept that the spouse is married to this whole person, not to any one alter. At this point in therapy, it may prove helpful to refer to the different personalities as parts to reinforce this idea" (p. 11).

Similarly, Gelinas (personal communication April 1994) recommends that partners be encouraged to think of alters as different parts of the person, just as they themselves behave differently when they are sick, or very tired, or full of enthusiasm. Partners are encouraged to view the MPD mate as a whole person who is responsible for her own behavior. They are discouraged from calling alters by name, instead relating to them in an as-if way: for example, "the Andrea-part of you seemed really scared." Gelinas suggests, however, that having the partner call alters by name might be useful in a crisis, in order to help stabilize the client.

The therapist may recommend family therapy if evaluation indicates significant difficulties being experienced by one or more children (or between family members) or if the therapist feels that interactional patterns among family members exacerbate the client's symptomatology or threaten to subvert her progress in treatment. As Panos and colleagues (1990) point out: "Unless the therapist addresses the situation, the MPD patient may see herself in the bind of either sacrificing herself or her family. As one MPD woman put it, 'I don't want to resolve my past if it means I have to destroy my present'" (p. 13). Family therapy provides one way of addressing these needs.

Benjamin and Benjamin (in press b) stress that therapy directed at parenting serves "as a key intervention point for disruption of a cycle of transgenerational dysfunction" (p. 13). Elsewhere (1992), they indicate that for them the dual goals of treatment are "the traditional one of providing treatment to the individual family member with MPD in an effort to move the person in the direction of integration of personalities and also the additional goal of facilitating healthy relationships within the family" (p. 237). All forms of involving partners, children, and parents of the MPD client in treatment are designed to serve these aims.

Sachs and colleagues (1988) indicate that when the MPD client is a parent, family therapy serves to:

- Identify effects of the MPD parent on children
- Screen children for dissociation

- Help children learn how to relate to the MPD parent
- Identify stressors in the family environment that cause the parent to dissociate
- Establish appropriate boundaries between the parent and child
- Establish a strong parental subsystem.

Whether the therapist recommends couple therapy, family therapy, or individual treatment for a child or adolescent will depend on his or her initial impressions of the partner's and children's needs and his or her convictions about the efficacy of these different treatment modalities.

CONCLUSION

This chapter has encouraged therapists treating dissociative clients to try to involve the client's partner in treatment, with active participation by the client in decisions relating to this involvement. A reluctance on the part of therapists to initiate such involvement is understandable given the complexity and intensity that accompany the effort to treat dissociative clients. However, this effort on the therapist's part may help to preserve the client's primary relational context, prevent the sabotaging of treatment, support a partner in need of services, and make the tasks facing the therapist less arduous. Decisions regarding whether, when, and how to involve clients' partners in treatment should always be made on a case-by-case basis.

REFERENCES

Allison, R. (1978). Psychotherapy of multiple personality disorder. Paper presented at the annual meeting of the American Psychiatric Association, May, at Atlanta, GA.

Anderson, C. (1983). A psychoeducational program for families of patients with schizophrenia. In *Family Therapy in Schizophrenia*, ed. W. McFarlane. New York: Guilford.

_____ (1984). Depression and the family. Paper presented at the Seventh Annual Family Therapy Networker Symposium, March, at Washington, DC.

Beal, E. (1978). Use of the extended family in the treatment of multiple personalities. *American Journal of Psychiatry* 135:539–542.

Benjamin, L., and Benjamin, R. (1992). An overview of family treatment in dissociative disorders. *Dissociation* 5:236–241.

_____ (1993). Interventions with children in dissociative families: a family treatment model. *Dissociation* 6:54–65.

_____ (In press a). A group for partners and parents of MPD clients. part i: process and format. *Dissociation*.

_____ (In press b). A group for partners and parents of MPD clients. part ii: themes and responses. *Dissociation*.

_____ (In press c). A group for partners and parents of MPD clients. part iii: marital types and dynamics. *Dissociation*.

_____ (In press d). Issues in the treatment of dissociative couples. *Dissociation*.

_____ (In press e). Utilizing parenting as a clinical focus in the treatment of dissociative disorders. *Dissociation*.

_____ (In press f). Various perspectives on parenting and their implications for the treatment of dissociative disorders. *Dissociation*.

_____ (In press g). Application of contextual therapy to the treatment of MPD. *Dissociation*.

Biglin, A., Rothlind, J., Hops, H., and Sherman, L. (1989). Impact of distressed and aggressive behavior. *Journal of Abnormal Psychology* 98:218–228.

Bliss, E. (1984). A symptom profile of patients with multiple personalities, including MMPI results. *Journal of Nervous and Mental Disease* 172:197–202.

Bograd, M. (1984). Family systems approaches to wife battering: a feminist critique. *American Journal of Orthopsychiatry* 54:558–568.

Boszormenyi-Nagy, I., and Krasner, B. (1986). *Between Give and Take: A Clinical Guide to Contextual Therapy*. New York: Brunner/Mazel.

Boszormenyi-Nagy, I., and Spark, G. (1973). *Invisible Loyalties: Reciprocity in Intergenerational Family Therapy*. New York: Harper & Row.

Boszormenyi-Nagy, I., and Ulrich, D. (1981). Contextual Family Therapy. In *Handbook of Family Therapy*, ed. A. Gurman and D. Kniskern. New York: Brunner/Mazel.

Braun, B. (1985a). The role of the family in the development of multiple personality disorder. *International Journal of Family Psychiatry* 5:303–313.

_____ (1985b). The transgenerational incidence of dissociation and multiple personality disorder. In *Childhood Antecedents of Multiple Personality*, ed. R. Kluft, pp. 127–150. Washington, DC: American Psychiatric Press.

Brown, G., and Rutter, M. (1966). The measurement of family activities and relationships: a methodological study. *Human Relations* 19:241–263.

Brown, G., Birley, J., and Wing, J. (1972). Influence of family life on the course of schizophrenic disorders: a replication. *British Journal of Psychiatry* 121:241–258.

Brown, G., and Harris, T., eds. (1978). *Social Origins of Depression: A Study of Psychiatric Disorder in Women*. New York: Free Press.

Chiappa, F. (1993). Individual vs. family interventions in dissociative disorders: different pieces of the same puzzle. Paper presented at the Eighth Regional Conference on Trauma, Dissociation and Multiple Personality. Akron, OH, April.

Coons, P. (1984). The differential diagnosis of multiple personality: a comprehensive review. *Psychiatric Clinics of North America* 7:51–65.

_____ (1985). Children of parents with multiple personality disorder. In *Childhood Antecedents of Multiple Personality Disorder*, ed. R. Kluft, pp. 151–166. Washington, DC: American Psychiatric Press.

Coons, P., Bowman, E., and Milstein, V. (1988). Multiple personality disorder: a clinical investigation of 50 cases. *Journal of Nervous and Mental Disease* 176:519–527.

Coons, P., and Milstein, V. (1984). Rape and post-traumatic stress in multiple personality. *Psychological Reports* 55:839–845.

Coyne, J. (1986). Confronting the conventional wisdom. *Family Therapy Networker* 10:67–68.

Coyne, J., Kahn, J., and Gotlib, I. (1987). Depression. In *Family Interaction and Psychotherapy*, ed. T. Jacobs. New York: Plenum.

Danieli, Y. (1984). Psychotherapists' participation in the conspiracy of silence about the Holocaust. *Psychoanalytic Psychology* 23–24.

Davis, L. (1991). *Allies in Healing: When the Person You Love was Sexually Abused as a Child*. New York: HarperPerennial.

Decina, P., Kestenbaum, C., Farber, S., et al. (1980). Clinical and psychological assessment of children of bipolar probands. *American Journal of Psychiatry* 140:548–553.

Dobash, R., and Dobash, R. (1988). Research as social action: the struggle for battered women. In *Feminist Perspectives on Wife Abuse*, ed. K. Yllo and M. Bograd. Newbury Park, CA: Sage.

Falloon, I., and Liberman, R. (1983) Behavioral family interventions in the management of chronic schizophrenia. In *Family Therapy in Schizophrenia*, ed. W. McFarlane. New York: Guilford.

Florin, I., Nostadt, A., Reck, C., et al. (1992). Expressed emotion in depressed patients and their partners. *Family Process* 31:163–172.

Gelinas, D. (1983). The persisting negative effects of incest. *Psychiatry* 46:312–332.

Glick, I., Clarkin, J., and Kessler, D. (1987). *Marital and Family Therapy*, 3rd ed. New York: Grune and Stratton.

Hafner, R., Badenoch, A., Fisher, J., and Swift, H. (1983). Spouse-aided versus individual therapy in persisting psychiatric disorders: a systemic comparison. *Family Process* 22:385–399.

Herman, J. (1992). *Trauma and Recovery*. New York: Basic Books.

Hooley, J. (1986). Expressed emotion and depression: interactions between patients and high versus low EE spouses. *Journal of Abnormal Psychology* 95:237–246.

Hooley, J., Orley, J., and Teasdale, J. (1986). Levels of expressed emotion and relapse in depressive patients. *British Journal of Psychiatry* 148:642–647.

Imber-Black, E. (1993). *Secrets in Families and Family Therapy*. New York: W. W. Norton.

Jacobson, N., Holtzworth-Munroe, A., and Schmaling, K. (1989). Marital therapy and spouse involvement in the treatment of depression, agoraphobia, and alcoholism. *Journal of Consulting and Clinical Psychology* 57:5–10.

Karpel, M. (1976). Individuation: from fusion to dialogue. *Family Process* 5:65–82.

―――― (1980). Family secrets: i. Conceptual and ethical issues in the relational context. ii. Ethical and practical considerations in therapeutic management. *Family Process* 19:295–306.

―――― , ed. (1986). *Family Resources: The Hidden Partner in Family Therapy*. New York: Guilford.

―――― (1994). *Evaluating Couples: A Handbook for Practitioners*. New York: W. W. Norton.

Kaufman, G. (1992). The mysterious disappearance of battered women in family therapists' offices: male privilege colluding with male violence. *Journal of Marital and Family Therapy* 18:233–244.

Kopeikin, H., Marshall, V., and Goldstein, M. (1983). Stages and impact of crisis-oriented family therapy in the aftercare of acute schizophrenia. In *Family Therapy in Schizophrenia*, ed. W. McFarlane. New York: Guilford.

Kluft, R. (1985). The natural history of multiple personality disorder. In *Childhood Antecedents of Multiple Personality*, pp. 197–238. Washington, DC: American Psychiatric Press.

―――― (1987). The parental fitness of mothers with multiple personality disorder. *Child Abuse and Neglect* 2:273–280.

―――― (1990). Incest and subsequent revictimization: the case of therapist–patient sexual exploitation, with a description of the sitting duck syndrome. In *Incest-Related Syndromes of Adult Psychopathology*, pp. 263–288. Washington, DC: American Psychiatric Press.

Kluft, R., Braun, B., and Sachs, R. (1984). Multiple personality, intrafamilial abuse, and family psychiatry. *International Journal of Family Psychiatry* 5:283–301.

Krugman, S. (1987). Trauma in the family: perspectives on the intergenerational transmission of violence. In *Psychological Trauma*, ed. B. van der Kolk, pp. 127–152. Washington, DC: American Psychiatric Press.

Levenson, J., and Berry, S. (1983). Family intervention in a case of multiple personality. *Journal of Marriage and Family Therapy* 9:73–80.

Liotti, G. (1992). Disorganized/Disoriented attachment in the etiology of the dissociative disorders. *Dissociation* 5:196–204.

Maltz, W. (1988). Identifying and treating the sexual repercussions of incest: a couples therapy approach. *Journal of Sex and Marital Therapy* 14:142–170.

—— (1991). *The Sexual Healing Journey: A Guide for Survivors of Sexual Abuse*. New York: HarperPerennial.

McCann, L., and Pearlman, L. (1990). Vicarious traumatization: a contextual model for understanding the effects of trauma on helpers. *Journal of Traumatic Stress* 3:131–149.

O'Brien, P. (1985). The diagnosis of multiple personality syndromes: overt, covert, and latent. *Comprehensive Therapy* 11:59–66.

Olson, J., Mayton, K., and Kowal-Ellis, N. (1987). Secondary posttraumatic stress disorder: therapist response to the horror. In *Proceedings of the Fourth International Conference on Multiple Personality Disorder/Dissociative States*, ed. B. Braun. Chicago: Rush University Department of Psychiatry.

Panos, P., Panos, A., and Allred, G. (1990). The need for marriage therapy in the treatment of multiple personality disorder. *Dissociation* 3:10–14.

Paykel, E., Myers, J., Dienelt, M., et al. (1969). Life events and depression: a controlled study. *Archives of General Psychiatry* 21:753–760.

Putnam, F. (1989). *Diagnosis and Treatment of Multiple Personality Disorder*. New York: Guilford.

Putnam, F., Guroff, J., Silberman, E., et al. (1986). The clinical phenomenology of multiple personality disorder: a review of 100 recent cases. *Journal of Clinical Psychiatry* 47:285–293.

Rosenbaum, A., and O'Leary, K. (1986). The treatment of marital violence. In *The Clinical Handbook of Marital Therapy*, ed. N. Jacobson and A. Gurman, pp. 385–405. New York: Guilford.

Sachs, R. (1986). The adjunctive role of social support systems in the treatment of multiple personality disorder. In *The Treatment of Multiple Personality Disorder*, ed. B. Braun, pp. 157–174. Washington, DC: American Psychiatric Press.

Sachs, R., Frischholz, E., and Wood, J. (1988). Marital and family therapy in the treatment of multiple personality disorder. *Journal of Marital and Family Therapy* 4:249–259.

Searles, H. (1965). *Collected Papers on Schizophrenia and Related Subjects*. New York: International Universities Press.

—— (1973). Concerning therapeutic symbiosis. *Annual of Psychoanalysis* 1:247–262.

Valone, K., Norton, J., Goldstein, M., and Doane, J. (1983). Parental expressed emotion and affective style in an adolescent sample at risk for schizophrenia spectrum disorders. *Journal of Abnormal Psychology* 92:399–407.

van der Kolk, B. (1987). *Psychological Trauma*. Washington, DC: American Psychiatric Press.

Vaughn, C., and Leff, J. (1976). The influence of family and social factors on the course of psychiatric illness. *British Journal of Psychiatry* 129:125–137.

Vaughn, C., Snyder, K., Freeman, W., et al. (1982). Family factors in schizophrenia relapse: a replication. *Schizophrenia Bulletin* 8:425–426.

Weissman, M. (1987). Advances in psychiatric epidemiology: rates and risks for major depression. *American Journal of Public Health* 77:445–451.

Welz, R. (1988). Live events, current social stressors, and risk of attempted suicide. In *Current Issues of Suicidology*, ed. H.-J. Moller, A. Schmidtke, and R. Welz. New York: Springer-Verlag.

Williams, M. (1991). Clinical work with families of multiple personality patients: assessment and issues for practice. *Dissociation* 4:92–98.

CREDITS

The editors gratefully acknowledge permission to quote from the following sources:

Remarks of Dr. Lisa Uyehara at the Baystate Medical Center conference on MPD, April 1993. Used by permission of Dr. Uyehara.

"The Manufacture of Personalities," by Harold Merskey, M.D., in the *British Journal of Psychiatry*, vol. 160, pp. 327-340. Copyright © 1992 by the *British Journal of Psychiatry* and reprinted by permission of the journal and the author.

Correspondence of Harold Merskey, Maeve Lawler-Fahy, Ann Chande, Paolo Novello and Alberto Primavera, Frank W. Putnam, G. A. Fraser, Alfonso Martinez-Taboas and Margarita Francia, and David Spiegel, in the *British Journal of Psychiatry*, vol. 161, pp. 268-284. Copyright © by the *British Journal of Psychiatry* and reprinted by permission of the journal and the authors.

"A Socio-Cultural Analysis of Merskey's Approach," by Dr. Alfonso Martinez-Taboas—originally published as a correspondence between Martinez-Taboas and Margarita Francia. Used by permission.

Excerpts from "The Dark Tunnels of McMartin," by R. C. Summit, in *The Journal of Psychohistory*, vol. 21, pp. 397-416. Copyright © by *The Journal of Psychohistory* and used by permission of the journal and the author.

Poetry by "Laura," reprinted by permission of the author.

Excerpts from the articles of Lynn Benjamin and Robert Benjamin which are forthcoming in the journal *Dissociation*, used by permission of the authors.

INDEX

Abuse. *See* Childhood trauma; Ritual abuse
Accidents, trauma and, 187
Adityanjee, R., 28, 116, 289, 290, 307, 318, 319
Adler, G., 448
Affect
    developmental model (of trauma), 236–237
    dissociation from, 477
Age level, multiple personality disorder (MPD) and, 95–96
Ainsworth, M. D., 237
Akhtar, S., 289, 303
Aldridge-Morris, R., 5, 54, 96, 121, 137, 213, 310, 317
Alexander, V. K., 290, 303, 307
Allison, R. B., 5, 8, 24, 289, 294, 301, 303, 310, 353, 361, 521
Alonso, L., 312
Alter personalities
    inflation of numbers, 94–95
    intrusions, dissociative identity disorder diagnosis, 274
    treatment alliance with, object relations and, 429–431
Altrocchi, J., 308
American Medical Association (AMA), 152
American Psychiatric Association (APA), 141, 142, 153, 156, 159, 160, 162, 163, 165, 261, 262, 353, 373

Amnesia
    assessment of, 269–271
    dissociative identity disorder diagnosis, 79–80
Anastasi, A., 144
Andersen, B., 113
Anderson, B., 149
Anderson, C., 528
Anderson, J., 150
Annon, J. S., 116
Anthropology. *See* Cultural perspective
Apologists, ritual abuse, 337–338
Aristotle, 177
Assagioli, R., 398
Atkinson, R. C., 241
Attias, R., 89, 395
Azam, E. E., 6, 8, 12, 15, 25

Babinski, J., 49
Baddeley, A. D., 241, 242
Bahnson, C. B., 123
Baker, R., 304
Baldessarini, R. J., 159
Bard, J., 158
Baron, J., 347
Barrie, J. M., 109
Bartlett, F. C., 404
Basch, M. F., 236
Basoglu, M., 186
Bass, E., 405
Bates, B. L., 349
Bateson, G., 474
Bauer-Manley, N. K., 38, 349

Beahrs, J., 288
Beard, G. M., 16
Beck, A., 381
Beck, J. C., 504
Behavioral management, dissociative
    identity disorder treatment,
    426–429
Beit-Hallahmi, B., 289, 303
Benchoten, S. C., 225
Benjamin, L., 514, 515, 516, 517, 518,
    526, 528, 529, 534, 535, 536, 537
Benjamin, R., 514, 515, 516, 517, 518,
    526, 528, 529, 534, 535, 536, 537
Bentall, R., 381
Berger, P., 78
Bernstein, E. M., 69, 143, 144, 261,
    265, 354, 420
Berry, S., 526
Best, J., 91
Beutler, L., 381
Bianchi, K., 44
Bifulco, A., 151
Biglin, A., 523
Bilu, Y., 289, 303
Binet, A., 14
Bjorklund, D. F., 234
Blake-White, J., 186
Bliss, E. L., 6, 91, 93, 94, 106, 107, 116,
    125, 127, 136, 139, 142, 143, 145,
    151, 156, 159, 160, 163, 208, 211,
    291, 306, 340, 354, 367, 370, 448,
    521
Bloch, I., 199, 200
Bloch, J. P., 103, 125, 127
Bloom, S. L., 200, 204, 205
Bloor, M., 208
Bogard, M., 532
Boleloucky, Z., 310
Bonanno, G. A., 152
Bonaparte, M., 193
Boon, S., 67, 77, 94, 97, 103, 109, 225,
    265, 266, 309, 318, 320, 352
Boor, M., 6, 93, 137, 217
Borderline personality disorder
    diagnosis of, 494

dissociative identity disorder
    diagnosis and, 280–281, 447–450
    case example, 450–463
Boring, E., 349
Boszormenyi-Nagy, I., 512, 518, 528
Bourguignon, E., 288, 289, 290, 291,
    298, 318
Bower, G. H., 243
Bowers, K. S., 154
Bowlby, J., 246
Bowman, E., 303, 419
Boyd, A., 337
Bracken, P. H., 59
Braude, S. E., 95, 121
Braudel, F., 181
Braun, B. G., 90, 94, 106, 127, 136,
    138, 162, 163, 208, 223, 226, 307,
    327, 331, 354, 359, 368, 382, 413,
    481, 512, 520
Breggin, P. R., 381
Brende, J. O., 123
Breuer, J., 104, 370
Brewin, C. R., 147
Brick, S. S., 149
Briere, J., 186, 366
Bromley, D. G., 115
Brown, D., 395, 396
Brown, G., 520, 521
Brown, G. R., 149
Browne, A., 150
Bruce-Jones, W., 43, 310, 319
Bruno, G., 180
Brunvand, J. H., 337
Bryant, D., 124
Bryer, J. B., 504
Buhrich, N. A., 5
Buie, D. H., Jr., 448
Burgess, A. W., 186, 195, 223
Bustamente, J. A., 309, 312
Butterfield, F., 389, 390
Butters, N., 242

Calof, D., 204
Cameron, D. E., 79, 80
Camuset, L., 8, 15

Cardena, E., 138
Cardena, F., 227
Carlin, A. S., 150
Carlson, E. B., 69, 78, 79, 144, 265
Carlson, E. T., 9, 11
Carmen, E. H., 504
Casement, P. J., 468
Casey, J., 388, 391
Castillo, R., 289
Caul, D., 153, 353
Chancellor, A. M., 308
Chande, A., 35–38, 39, 53
Charcot, J.-M., 12, 39, 184, 349, 350, 372
Charney, D. S., 239, 240
Chiappa, F., 536
Childhood trauma. See also Ritual abuse
  assessment of, 275–276
  development and, 223–259. See also Developmental model (of trauma)
  incidence of, multiple personality disorder (MPD) and, 92, 113–114, 150–151
  therapy for, component of, 470–473
Childhood trauma and Kuhnian paradigm, 175–222
  Kuhnian paradigm attacked, 188–207
    denial, 191–199
    repudiation, 189–191
    suppression, 188–189
    therapist, 203–207
    victim, 199–202
  Kuhnian paradigm controversies, 181–188
  Kuhnian paradigm explained, 176–181
  multiple personality disorder controversies, 207–217
    attacks on victim, 209–210
    denial and iatrogenesis, 210–217
    as trauma-based disorder, 207–209
  overview of, 175
Chodoff, P., 39, 94, 159

Chodoff, R., 5, 29
Chu, J. A., 144, 149, 382, 392, 404
Clark, P., 269
Cleckley, H. M., 4, 6, 8, 20, 21, 24, 27, 40, 44, 51, 90, 138, 146
Client partner, 509–541
  couple or family therapy referral, 535–538
  exclusion of, 510–511
  group therapy referral, 534–535
  inclusion of
    disadvantages of, 524–525
    process and procedure, 525–530
    rationale and advantages, 519–520
  individual therapy referral, 535
  overview of, 509–510
  partners' concerns, 517–519
  relational context, assessment of, 520–524
  relational patterns, 511–514
  therapist contact with, 530–533
  typologies, 514–517
Coaching, multiple personality disorder (MPD), 100–101
Cockburn, A., 201
Cognition, developmental model (of trauma), 237–238
Cohen, B. M., 100, 108
Coid, J., 43, 310, 319
Cole, P. M., 223
Collins, A., 79
Combat, posttraumatic stress disorder and, 182, 187–188
Community mental health center, 493–507
  cases in, 495–498
  differential diagnosis issues, 498–500
  overview of, 493–495
  psychotic multiple personality disorder, 502
  treatment program development, 500–502
Comorbidity, dissociative identity disorder diagnosis, 278–281
Comstock, C., 385

Confabulation, multiple personality
disorder (MPD), 116–123
Congdon, M. H., 22, 153
Conte, J. R., 150, 366
Coons, P. M., 77, 93, 94, 101, 104, 106,
123, 125, 127, 137, 138, 139, 142,
145, 150, 151, 159, 160, 161, 162,
163, 208, 217, 226, 227, 306, 308,
309, 310, 318, 354, 363, 367, 369,
419, 513, 514, 520, 521
Cory, C. E., 8, 19, 26
Cotman, C., 245
Countertransference
contributory factors to, 475–476
dissociative clients and, 421–424, 474
dissociation from affect, 477–480
dissociation from self, 484–485
dissociation from traumatic memories
and imagery, 482–483
organizational countertransference, 485
informative nature of, 474–475
Coupland, W. C., 25
Couple therapy, referral to, client
partner, 535–538
Courtois, C., 382
Cowan, N., 242
Cox, J. L., 41
Coyne, J., 523, 532
Crabtree, A., 288, 290, 294, 295, 304
Craine, I. S., 504
Credibility
multiple personality disorder (MPD),
116–123
ritual abuse, 335–339
Crews, F., 87
Croiset, G., 234, 236
Crossin, B., 242
Crowley, A., 333, 335
Cultural perspective (multiple
personality disorder), 41, 60,
76–78, 88–89, 98, 114–116, 285–325
cases, 304–317
controversy, 317–320
cultural constructs, 286–288
overview of, 285–286

possession, 288–290
MPD and, 291–293
similarities and differences, 298–304
transmodal and transcultural
treatment, 293–298
Cushman, P., 60
Cutler, B., 97, 154, 310

Daie, N., 290, 296
Daily, A. H., 8, 16
Damgaard, J., 217
Danieli, Y., 186, 518
Daniels, A., 4
Darwin, C., 179, 180
Davies, J. M., 471, 472, 479
Davis, L., 405
Decker, H. S., 90, 104
Defenses, failure to respect,
dissociative identity disorder
treatment, 393–397
Defrances, V., 200
Dell, P. F., 94, 125, 151, 213, 226, 498
Deloache, J. S., 234
DeMause, L., 193, 205, 206
Den Herder, D., 504
Denial
generated by externals, 194–199
multiple personality disorder
controversies, 210–217
paradigmatic, 192–194
of violence effects, 191–192
Dennett, D. C., 126
Despine, P., 8
Deutsch, H., 483
Developmental model (of trauma),
223–259
case studies, 228–231
clinical vignettes, 249–254
domains of relevance, 232–240
affect, 236–237
cognition and self-object
representation, 237–238
language, 235–236
memory domain, 233–235
motor domain, 233

neurophysiological functioning
and memory, 238–240
memory-information processing
models, 241–244
model described, 231–232
neuropsychological principles for
memory consolidation, 240–241
overview, 223–225
parallel memory systems, 244–248
skepticism and belief, 225–228
treatment, 248–249
Dewar, H., 49
DeWied, D., 234, 236
Deyoub, P. L., 163
*Diagnostic and Statistical Manual
(DSM)-III,* 105–106, 112, 118, 143,
144, 213, 353, 448
*Diagnostic and Statistical Manual
(DSM)-III-R,* 3–4, 5, 6, 7, 43, 44,
46, 50, 93, 125, 135, 136, 137, 138,
140, 143, 146, 213, 225, 262, 270,
276, 280, 373, 449
*Diagnostic and Statistical Manual
(DSM)-IV,* 65–66, 70, 71, 73, 75,
76, 82, 106, 135, 136, 143, 213,
261–264, 270, 276, 278, 280, 373,
447, 448, 449
Differential diagnosis
community mental health center,
498–500
dissociative identity disorder
diagnosis, 264–265
Dill, D. L., 144
Dinwiddie, S. H., 137, 138, 141, 143,
144, 149, 150, 164
Disaster, trauma and, 187
Dissociation
from affect, 477
functions of, 476–477
multiple personality disorder (MPD),
126–128
from other, 485
psychoeducation, childhood trauma
therapy, 471
from self, 483–484

from traumatic memories and
imagery, 480–482
Dissociative identity disorder. *See also*
Multiple personality disorder
actual versus fantastic
pseudomemories, 366–368
combined forms, in same patient,
363–366
compartmentalization and, 34
factitious, 363
hypnosis in treatment of, 370–371
iatrogenic worsening, 360–363
mental disorder or syndrome,
354–356
modern history of, 351–354
multiple personality disorder (MPD),
3–55
naturalistic or iatrogenic disorder,
356–360
Dissociative identity disorder
diagnosis, 65–84, 261–284
alter personalities, intrusions, 274
borderline personality disorder
compared, 447–450
case example, 450–463
childhood trauma assessment,
275–276
clinical concept of, 66–68
comorbidity, 278–281
differential diagnosis, 264–265
DSM-IV criteria, 262–264
ease of false creation of, 79–81
existing data on reliability and
validity, 76–79
nonscientific/logical arguments,
68–72
overview of, 65–66, 261–262
procedure for establishing reliability
and validity, 74–76
screening measures, 265–274
secondary features, 276–277
seizures, 282
thought disorder absence in, 281–282
Dissociative identity disorder
treatment, 248–249, 413–434

Dissociative identity disorder
treatment (*continued*)
effectiveness of, 368–369
failures, 379–412
defenses, failure to respect,
393–397
memory, failure to understand
nature of, 404–409
overview of, 379–382
playing favorites, 397–404
treatment frame retention, 382–393
medications, 418–421
microdetail and structure, 415–417
object relations and, 424–432
behavioral management
principles, 426–429
generally, 424–426
historical reality problem of
trauma memories, 431–432
treatment alliance with alter
personalities, 429–431
overview of, 413
stages in, 417–418
therapist stance, 413–415
transference and countertransference
issues, 421–424
unit treatment for, 371–373
Distad, L. J., 186
Dobash, R. and R., 532
Donaldson, M. A., 186
Draijer, N., 67, 77, 94, 97, 103, 109,
225, 265, 266, 309, 318, 352
Drake, M. E., 139
DSM. *See Diagnostic and Statistical
Manual (DSM)*
Dua, V., 76, 158, 159, 160, 161, 504

Eberle, P., 206
Eberle, S., 206
Eckman, T., 156
Einstein, A., 177
Eisenhower, J. W., 94, 151
Ekman, P., 117
Elin, M., 233
Ellason, J., 278, 281

Ellenberger, H., 9, 44, 183, 189, 191,
210, 313
Ellman, R., 88
Ellsworth, P. C., 152
Engel, G., 223
Erickson, M. H., 126
Ernst, C., 150
Estabrooks, G. H., 80, 81, 358
Eth, S., 186
Ewalt, J. J. B., 41
Expense of treatment, multiple
personality disorder (MPD),
158–162

Fabrega, H., 58, 60
Fabrication, multiple personality
disorder (MPD), 116–123
Fagan, J., 95, 141, 145, 153
Fahy, T. A., 5, 33, 43, 50, 54, 72, 97,
101, 105, 141, 144, 156, 225, 227,
294, 301, 310, 317, 318, 348, 356
Fairbairn, W. R. D., 255
Falloon, I., 528
False memory syndrome, attacks on
therapist and, 204–205
False Memory Syndrome Foundation,
54, 200–201
Family therapy, referral to, client
partner, 535–538
Favazza, A. R., 288
Feather, B. W., 139
Federn, P., 398
Feighner, J. P., 144
Feinstein, A., 226
Feldman-Summers, S., 366
Femina, D. D., 225
Fernando, L., 125, 146
Festinger, L., 348
Figley, C., 486
Fine, C. G., 154, 211, 361, 362, 385,
395, 396, 413
Fink, D., 355
Finkelhor, D., 150
Fliess, R., 190
Fliess, W., 189, 190
Florin, I., 520, 521

Fode, K. L., 100
Forest, D. V., 245
Francia, M., 44–46, 52, 57
Frankel, F. H., 147, 151, 153, 225, 227, 348
Franklin, B., 177
Franklin, J., 137, 143
Franz, S. I., 8, 20
Fraser, A. R., 308
Fraser, G. A., 44–46, 50, 51, 69
Frawley, M. G., 471, 472, 479
Frazer, J. G., 41
Freeland, A., 156
Freud, S., 104, 184, 188, 189–191, 193, 194, 212, 349, 370, 398, 479
Freyd, Pamela, 200, 201, 206
Freyd, Peter, 200, 201, 206
Fried, S., 200–201, 205
Friedman, B., 183
Frischholz, E. J., 144, 208, 226, 307
Froment, J., 49
Fromm, E., 395, 396

Gahan, P., 154
Ganaway, G. K., 108, 120, 194, 210, 337
Gardner, L. I., 233
Gardner, R., 186, 194
Gedo, J. E., 224
Gelinas, D. J., 186, 195, 524, 525, 537
Gergen, K., 463
Giere, R. N., 59
Gilles de la Tourette, 8
Gilles de la Tourette's syndrome, 231
Glass, J. M., 120
Glick, I., 515
Glover, E., 239
Gmelin, E., 8, 9, 313
Goddard, H. H., 8, 19
Goettman, C., 106
Goetz, C. G., 12
Gold, P. E., 241
Golub, D., 296
Goodhart, S. P., 6, 8, 17, 26
Goodman, F. D., 287, 288, 289, 290, 291, 298, 304, 309

Goodwin, J. M., 89, 110, 112, 186, 191, 192, 193, 194, 195, 210, 211, 289, 297, 304, 328, 329, 334, 347, 395
Gould, C., 107
Goullart, P., 304
Grant, S. J., 239
Graves, S. G., 142
Gray, G., 327
Greaves, G. B., 12, 24, 93, 103, 127, 145, 155, 163, 164, 165, 208, 209, 212, 336, 337, 338, 339, 340, 354, 382, 392, 407
Green, A. H., 150, 151, 186
Greenacre, P., 193
Greenberg, M. S., 501
Greenson, R., 436–437
Greenwood, J. D., 59, 60
Grinker, R. R., 188, 239
Grotstein, J. S., 247
Group therapy, referral to, client partner, 534–535
Gruber, H. E., 179, 180
Gruenewald, D., 154
Gunderson, J. G., 504
Guze, S. B., 144

Hacking, I., 5, 6, 19, 43, 49, 52
Hafner, R., 520, 528
Hahn, R. A., 59
Halgren, E., 239
Hall, J. M., 517, 522, 531
Hall, R. C., 155
Halleck, S. L., 156, 157, 498
Hammond, C., 334
Hammond, W. A., 16
Hardy, D. W., 146, 147
Harriman, P. L., 126, 163, 358
Harris, T., 521
Hart, B., 8, 19, 396
Hartman, C. R., 223
Havens, L., 436, 437
Hawksworth, H., 8, 22, 25
Heisenberg, W., 100
Henderson, D., 194

Herman, J. L., 120, 182, 184, 185, 186, 187, 188, 189, 192, 193, 199, 361, 447, 463, 469, 486, 504, 512, 513, 518, 519
Herzog, A., 127, 163
Heuristics, ritual abuse, 338–339
Hicks, R., 194, 336, 337
Hilgard, E. R., 25, 125, 407
Hill, C., 381
Hill, S., 334
Hine, F. R., 139
Hitch, G. J., 241, 242
Hodgson, R., 8, 16
Hollingsworth, J., 196
Holmstrom, L. L., 186
Holocaust, 192
Hooley, J., 520, 521
Horevitz, R. P., 94, 127, 138, 382
Horowitz, M., 185
Horst, R., 90
Horton, P., 8, 22, 154
Howland, F. C., 148, 149, 392
Humphrey, N., 126
Hussey, D. L., 151
Hypnosis
    multiple personality disorder (MPD), 126–128, 162–163
    in treatment of dissociative identity disorder, 370–371
Hysteria, etiology of, 184

Iatrogenesis
    dissociative identity disorder, naturalistic or iatrogenic disorder, 356–360
    multiple personality disorder, 101–103, 210–217
    therapist stance, dissociative identity disorder treatment, 415
    worsening, dissociative identity disorder, 360–363
ICD-10. See *International Classification of Diseases*
Imber-Black, E., 525
Indoctrination rituals, ritual abuse, 331–332

International Classification of Diseases (ICD)-10, 65–66, 90
International distribution, of multiple personality disorder (MPD), 96–98
Interpersonal relations. *See* Client partner
Interpersonal violence, trauma and, 187

Jacobson, A., 504
Jacobson, E., 193
Jacobson, N., 520
James, W., 6, 8, 11, 16, 88, 293, 298, 401, 402
Janet, J., 8, 20
Janet, P., 6, 7, 8, 11, 12, 13, 14, 15, 20, 90, 98, 104, 126, 183, 184, 188–189, 209, 241, 292, 404, 481
Jeffrey, W., 312
Jensen, D. J., 77
Jeppsen, E. A., 6, 91, 151, 159, 160, 211
Johnson, M. K., 152
Jones, J., 7, 8, 16, 25, 95, 127, 154, 155, 163, 164, 165, 210
Jordan, J. V., 471
Joshi, S., 77
Jung, C. G., 398

Kampman, R., 126, 356, 358
Kardiner, A., 185, 188
Karon, B. P., 381
Karpel, M., 512, 514, 516, 525, 530, 531
Katchen, M. H., 331
Keane, C. B., 164
Kemp, K., 144
Kempe, C. H., 186, 192
Kendall-Tackett, K. A., 150
Kenny, M. G., 289, 290, 293, 298, 316
Kernberg, O. F., 403, 447, 448
Kerner, J., 291, 304
Ketcham, K., 152
Keyes, D., 23, 316
Khandelwal, S. K., 116
Kilstrom, J. F., 243
Kinsler, P., 385, 386, 387

Kirk, S. A., 105
Kirkland v. Georgia, 158
Kirmayer, L. J., 77
Kiser, L. J., 150
Klein, D. N., 99
Klein, M., 193
Kleinman, A., 47, 58, 287, 289, 290
Kleinman, D., 60
Kline, C. M., 186
Kluft, R. P., 5, 6, 25, 28, 94, 95, 99,
    100, 106, 108, 112, 115, 117, 118,
    119, 122, 126, 127, 137, 138, 139,
    140, 142, 143, 146, 148, 149, 150,
    153, 154, 156, 157, 159, 160, 161,
    162, 163, 194, 207, 208, 209, 266,
    289, 290, 292, 320, 350, 352, 353,
    354, 356, 359, 361, 363, 368, 369,
    370, 372, 373, 381, 382, 385, 390,
    392, 393, 395, 398, 402, 413, 449,
    493, 499, 504, 512, 514, 520, 536
Kohlenberg, R. J., 127
Konker, C., 151
Konorski, J., 245
Kooper, C., 366
Kopeikin, H., 528
Korbin, J., 303
Koresh, D., 329
Krafft-Ebing, R. von, 189
Krasner, B., 512, 518, 528
Krieger, G., 517, 519, 524, 526, 535,
    536
Krippner, S., 287, 288, 297, 301, 308,
    316, 317
Kroll, J., 110
Krugman, S., 512, 521
Kuhn, T., 175, 176–181, 207, 348
Kuhnian paradigm. *See* Childhood
    trauma and Kuhnian paradigm
Kutchins, H., 105

Lancaster, E., 103
Landecker, H., 504
Langs, R., 383, 386
Language, developmental model (of
    trauma), 235–236
Lanning, K. V., 328, 329, 336, 406

Larmore, K., 123
Larson, E. M., 93, 139
Laudan, L., 59, 61
Lauer, J., 164
Lawler-Fahy, M., 33–35
Leavitt, H. C., 126, 163
Leff, J., 520, 521
León, C. A., 303, 309
Levenson, J., 526
Lewis, A. J., 8, 20
Lewis, D. O., 158
Lewis, I. M., 115
Lewis-Fernandez, R., 60, 77
Liberman, R. P., 156, 528
Lifton, R. J., 214, 289
Lindberg, F. H., 186
Lindemann, E., 185
Lindsay, D. S., 147
Linehan, M. M., 156
Liotti, G., 512
Lipsedge, M., 115
Lipstadt, D. E., 192, 216
Lipton, S., 8, 20, 25
Littlewood, R., 115
Ljungberg, L., 5
Loewenstein, R. J., 110, 139, 140, 141,
    147, 148, 156, 164, 166, 207, 212,
    266, 282, 349, 354, 382, 392, 409,
    413, 494, 498, 499, 501, 504
Loftus, E. F., 147, 152, 165, 201, 366,
    404
Longino, H., 59
Lotto, D., 194, 196, 201, 204
Ludolph, P. S., 105, 143
Ludwig, A. M., 123, 127, 138, 227,
    238, 243
Lynn, S. J., 143, 152
Lyon, K. A., 494

Macilwain, I. F., 310, 318
Maddison, D. C., 308
Magee, B., 111
Mahrer, A., 398
Mai, F., 69, 70, 71
Malenbaum, R., 95, 138
Malin, A., 247

Malmquist, C. P., 151
Malpractice risk, multiple personality
    disorder (MPD) and, 146–149
Manicas, P. T., 47, 59
Marks, J., 79
Marmer, S. S., 354
Martin, M. F., 6, 137, 155, 164, 210,
    211, 288, 304, 305, 310
Martinez-Taboas, A., 44–46, 52, 57, 58,
    98, 289, 301, 307, 309, 318, 319,
    320
Masson, J. M., 184, 189, 190, 191, 192,
    193, 200, 203, 343
Masterson, J. H., 448
Mathew, R. J., 123
Matzner, F., 194
May, P., 381
Mayer-Gross, W., 5, 90
Mayo, T., 8
McCann, I. L., 382, 468, 469, 470, 476,
    486, 511
McCurdy, H. A., 127
McDougall, W., 18
McFarland, R. B., 194
McGaugh, J. L., 236
McHugh, P. K., 213
McHugh, P. R., 371, 372
McKee, J. B., 312
McKellar, P., 9
McMahon, P. P., 95, 141, 145, 153
McMartin preschool case, 196–198
Mead, J., 95
Medawar, P., 111, 112
Media, multiple personality disorder
    (MPD) and, 104
Medications, dissociative identity
    disorder treatment, 418–421
Meiselman, K., 186
Meltzoff, A., 234
Memory
    developmental model (of trauma),
        238–240
    dissociation from traumatic
        memories and imagery,
        480–482

Memory consolidation,
    neuropsychological principles for,
    240–241
Memory domain, developmental
    model (of trauma), 233–235
Memory-information processing
    models, developmental model (of
    trauma), 241–244
Memory systems, parallel,
    developmental model (of trauma),
    244–248
Mennen, F. E., 150
Merskey, H., 5, 7, 15, 28, 33–55,
    57–62, 69, 70, 71, 72, 74, 75, 76,
    94, 149, 155, 158, 164, 166, 210,
    212, 225, 227, 267, 356
Mesulam, M. M., 139, 245
Methodologists, ritual abuse, 339
Meyers, N. A., 234
Miller, B. F., 164
Miller, D., 8, 22, 154
Miller, M., 310
Miller, S. D., 123, 226
Millon, T., 47, 58, 139
Milstein, V., 150, 151, 208, 226, 514
Mishkin, M., 241
Mitchell, S. L., 6, 8
Mitchell, S. W., 6, 10, 26
Mitchell, W., 8, 211
Modestin, J., 91, 97, 98, 146, 310
Moore, M. S., 157
Moreno, J., 398
Morey, L. C., 58
Morreim, E. H., 165, 166
Mother, attack on, 201–202
Motor domain, developmental model
    (of trauma), 233
Muenzenmaier, K., 504
Mulhern, S., 287, 289, 290, 301, 337
Multiple personality disorder (MPD),
    3–55. See also Dissociative identity
    disorder
    age level and, 95–96
    alters in, inflation of numbers, 94–95
    case samples, 8

Multiple personality disorder
      (*continued*)
   childhood trauma and, 92, 113–114.
      See also Childhood trauma;
      Ritual abuse
   Christine (Sally) Beauchamp case,
      17–18
   client partner and, 509–541. *See also*
      Client partner
   clinical picture of, at present, 3–4
   coaching and training as factors in,
      100–101
   community mental health treatment
      of, 493–507
   conceptual presuppositions, 7–8
   correspondence on, 33–55
      from Chande, A., 35–38
      from Fraser, G. A., 44–46
      from Lawler-Fahy, M., 33–35
      from Martinez-Taboas, A. and
         Francia, M., 44–46
      from Novello and Primavera,
         40–41
      from Putnam, F. W., 42–43
      reply from Merskey, 49–55
      from Spiegel, D., 48–49
   credibility, fabrication, and
      confabulation in, 116–123
   cultural perspective on, 41, 114–116.
      See also Cultural perspective
   described, 87–89
   discussion of, 25–28
   dissociation and hypnosis related to,
      126–128
   distribution of, among clinicians,
      93–94
   early cases of
      19th century, 9–16
      turn of century, 16–17, 19
   evaluation of, 7
   expense of treatment of, 158–162
   hypnosis and, 162–163
   incidence of, 91–92
   increase in frequency of, 6, 145–146
   international distribution of, 96–98

   literature failures, 106–107, 111–113
   malpractice risk and, 146–149
   media and, 104
   overview of, 3
   pathogenesis of, conceptual
      weakness in, 3–55
   pathologizing of normal, 107–108
   patient characteristics, 103–104
   patient veracity and, 108–109
   physiological differences and,
      123–124
   politics and, 124–126
   prior treatment and incompetence,
      109–111
   race and social class distribution of,
      96
   recent cases, 20–25
   regressive and nonresponsible
      behavior encouraged, 153–158
   sex distribution of, 92–93
   skepticism, 5–6, 89–91, 135–173. *See
      also* Skepticism
   sociocultural analysis and, 57–63
   suggestion and iatrogenesis in,
      101–103
   technical issues, 468–470
Multiple personality disorder (MPD)
      diagnosis, 468
   aspects, 99–100
   care system and, 435–436
   clinical example, composite, 440–444
   criteria problems, 105–106
   ill effects of, 28–29
   methods, 98–99
   misdiagnosis and overt production
      of, 20
   problems in, 135–145
   treatment process and, 436–440
Munchausen's syndrome, 275–276
Mydans, S., 389, 390
Myers, A. T., 15
Myers, W. H. F., 8, 13, 25

Nadon, R., 408
Nakdimen, K. A., 91, 106, 138

Nelson, C. A., 234
Neumann, D. A., 491
Neurophysiology, 238–240. *See also* Physiological differences
Newton-Smith, W., 59
Nihilists, ritual abuse, 336–337
Nilchiakovit, T., 59
Nissen, M. J., 243
Noll, R., 194, 334
North, C. S., 93, 103, 104, 105, 106, 120, 123, 126, 139, 140, 144, 145, 148, 153, 154, 156, 164, 413
Norton, G. R., 141
Notestein, W., 91
Novello, P., 40–41, 49
Noy, S., 308, 316

O'Brien, P., 521
Oesterreich, T. K., 115, 288, 291, 292, 303, 313, 316
Ofshe, R., 115, 163, 204
Ogintz, E., 192
Olio, K., 472
Olson, J. A., 386, 511
Organizational countertransference, dissociative clients and, 485
Organizational intervention, vicarious trauma, 489–490
Orne, M. T., 38, 105, 117, 152, 214, 349, 397
Owen, A. R. G., 12

Pabis, R., 125, 146, 159
Panos, P., 517, 518, 519, 526, 537
Pap, A., 139
Parallel memory systems, developmental model (of trauma), 244–248
Paris, J., 150
Parks, R. W., 244
Partner. *See* Client partner
Pasricha, S., 288, 307
Patient characteristics, multiple personality disorder (MPD), 103–104

Patient veracity, multiple personality disorder (MPD) and, 108–109
Paykel, E., 520
Pazder, L., 328
Pearlman, L. A., 382, 468, 469, 470, 476, 486, 488, 491, 511
Personality, complexity in, 88
Peters, C., 8, 9, 23
Peters, J. J., 186
Peterson, G., 95
Peterson, S. E., 245
Pharmacology, dissociative identity disorder treatment, 418–421
Physiological differences, 123–124, 226–227. *See also* Neurophysiology
Piaget, J., 224
Pillemer, D. D., 244
Piper, A., Jr., 54
Pittillo, E. S., 8, 20, 21, 24
Planck, M., 179
Plumer, W. S., 6, 8, 9
Poling, J., 103
Politics, multiple personality disorder (MPD) and, 124–126
Polkinghorne, D., 59
Polster, E, 398
Polster, M., 398
Pope, K., 366
Popper, K., 59, 61, 111, 112
Possession
   cultural perspective (multiple personality disorder), 288–290
   MPD and, 291–293
   similarities and differences, 298–304
   dissociative identity disorder diagnosis, 77, 114–115
Posttraumatic stress disorder
   combat and, 185
   countertransference and, 475
   diagnosis of, 494
   Kuhnian paradigm and, 182
   pseudo form, 340–341
   therapy for, 473–474
Power acquisition, ritual abuse, 332–333
Prasad, K. V., 289, 306

Pribor, E. F., 150
Pride, M., 113, 114
Primavera, A., 40–41, 49
Prince, M., 94, 104, 209
Prince, W. F., 6, 7, 8, 17, 18, 19
Prior treatment, incompetence and, multiple personality disorder (MPD), 109–111
Proust, A., 8, 15–16
Psychoanalysis
  anti-empiricism and, 87
  seduction theory, 190–191
Psychoeducation, childhood trauma, therapy for, 470
Psychopharmacology, dissociative identity disorder treatment, 418–421
Psychotherapy, healing quality of, 470
Psychotic multiple personality disorder, community mental health center, 502
Ptolemy, 177
Putnam, F. W., 4, 6, 49, 50, 51, 69, 92, 93, 94, 96, 98, 99, 101, 102, 104, 106, 110, 111, 112, 116, 117, 121, 123, 124, 125, 138, 139, 140, 141, 142, 143, 144, 147, 148, 149, 153, 155, 156, 159, 160, 162, 164, 165, 166, 183, 193, 208, 209, 211, 212, 216, 223, 226, 242, 247, 261, 265, 266, 268, 277, 282, 289, 291, 293, 297, 306, 312, 318, 354, 368, 382, 398, 413, 420, 437, 438, 439, 440, 493, 495, 502, 503, 513, 514, 521, 522, 526
Pynoos, R. S., 186

Quimby, L. G., 502

Race differences, multiple personality disorder (MPD), 96
Racker, H., 476
Raschke, C., 334, 337–338
Rathbun, J. M., 307
Read, J. D., 147
Redman, D. E., 239

Redner, L., 504
Reed, J., 97, 154, 310
Rehabilitation, 505
Reich, A., 193
Rendon, M., 312
Richardson, J. T., 91, 194, 337
Richet, C., 8, 15
Riley, R. L., 95
Riso, L. P., 99
Ritual abuse, 327–345. See also Childhood trauma
  allegations, 330–331
  credibility issues, 335–339
    apologists, 337–338
    heuristics, 338–339
    methodologist, 339
    nihilists, 336–337
  disclosure prevention, 333
  incidence and prevalence of, 327–328
  power acquisition, 332–333
  survivors of, 339–344
  terms in, 328–335
    black mass, 334–335
    indoctrination rituals, 331–332
    satanism, 329–330
Robins, E., 144
Rochas, A. de, 8, 15
Rockwell, R. B., 203
Ronquillo, E. B., 304, 311, 312
Rosenbaum, D. H., 241
Rosenbaum, M., 209
Rosenthal, R., 100
Ross, C. A., 5, 6, 27, 28, 53, 67, 68, 69, 70, 73, 76, 77, 91, 92, 93, 94, 98, 101, 102, 105, 106, 110, 111, 117, 124, 126, 127, 137, 138, 141, 143, 144, 145, 146, 149, 150, 151, 153, 154, 155, 156, 158, 159, 160, 161, 193, 207, 211, 212, 214, 215, 217, 227, 238, 261, 262, 263, 265, 266, 267, 268, 269, 274, 277, 281, 282, 288, 289, 290, 292, 293, 297, 303, 306, 307, 308, 312, 313, 316, 318, 320, 354, 358, 359, 368, 382, 392, 413, 419, 420, 421, 422, 437, 438, 440, 447, 449, 499, 502, 504

Rowan, J. A., 241, 398
Runtz, M., 186
Rush, B., 9
Rush, F., 186, 192, 193
Russell, A. T., 95, 138
Rutter, M., 520, 521
Ryder, D., 340

Saakvitne, K. W., 470, 476, 488
Sabo, A. N., 504
Sachs, R. G., 208, 386, 395, 407, 517, 526, 536, 537
Sakheim, D. K., 331
Salkovskis, P. M., 156
Saltman, V., 208
Sandberg, D. A., 143
Sargent, W., 366
Satanism, ritual abuse, 329–330
Satel, S. L., 148, 149
Saxena, S., 289, 306
Saywitz, K. J., 407
Schacter, D. L., 143, 232, 243
Schafer, D. W., 91
Schatzow, E., 120, 367
Schetky, D. H., 112
Schreiber, F. R., 5, 8, 22, 24, 103, 391
Schwartz, T., 5, 8, 9, 22, 23, 24, 25
Schweder, R. A., 57
Science, Kuhnian paradigm and, 176–181
Searles, H., 512, 516
Secord, P. F., 47, 59
Seduction theory, 190–191
Self-object representation, developmental model (of trauma), 237–238
Semrad, E., 441
Serban, G., 147, 148, 149, 155
Sexual abuse. See Childhood trauma; Ritual abuse
Shearer, S. L., 149
Sheehan, P. W., 152, 163
Shefflin, A., 334
Shiffrin, R. M., 241
Shupe, A. D., 115
Sidis, B., 6, 8, 17, 26

Sierra, M., 61
Silberman, E. K., 127, 157, 238
Sim, M., 5
Simpson, M. A., 5, 92, 93, 94, 96, 98, 102, 109, 117, 120, 125, 126, 154, 308, 317
Singer, M., 151
Sizemore, C. C., 8, 20, 21, 24, 103
Skae, D., 8, 11, 25
Skepticism
    cultural perspective and, 317–320
    multiple personality disorder (MPD) and, 5–6, 89–91, 135–173
Slater, E., 15, 366
Smith, K., 123
Smith, M., 328
Smith, S. G., 296, 313, 318
Smith, V. L., 152
Snowden, C., 95
Sociocultural analysis, multiple personality disorder (MPD) and, 57–63. See also Cultural perspective
Socioeconomic class, multiple personality disorder (MPD), 96
Solomon, R., 208
Spanos, N. P., 27, 45, 51, 95, 122, 154, 155, 350, 356, 358
Spark, G., 528
Spencer, H., 25
Spencer, J., 95
Spiegel, D., 48–49, 69, 106, 125, 127, 138, 208, 225, 226, 227, 364, 370, 493
Spiegel, H., 53, 185, 188, 370
Spiegel, J. J., 239
Spiegel, J. P., 188
Spitzer, R. L., 73, 74
Spouse. See Client partner
Squire, L. R., 242
Steinberg, M., 67, 73, 74, 143, 266, 267, 312, 354
Stengel, E., 16, 351
Stern, C. R., 208, 292, 293
Stevenson, I., 288, 301, 307, 317
Stevenson, R. L., 127
Stickel, E. G., 197

Stoll, A. L., 159
Stone, M. H., 504
Stout, G. F., 25
Stuss, D. T., 242
Suengas, A. G., 152
Suggestion, multiple personality disorder (MPD), 101–103
Summit, R. C., 114, 191, 192, 196, 197, 198, 200, 201, 202, 203
Suppe, F., 58, 59
Suryani, L. K., 77
Sutcliffe, J. P., 7, 8, 16, 25, 95, 127, 154, 155, 163, 164, 165, 210
Swenson, C., 156
Swett, C., 150

Takahashi, Y., 5, 96, 307, 319
Tamarkin, C., 338
Tart, C., 290
Taylor, W. S., 6, 137, 155, 164, 210, 211, 288, 305, 310
Terr, L., 151, 186
Therapeutic relationship
  psychotherapy and, 470
  therapist role in, 473–475
  trauma therapy, 471–472
Therapist, attack on, 203–207
Therapist stance, dissociative identity disorder treatment, 413–415
Thigpen, C. H., 4, 6, 8, 20, 21, 24, 27, 40, 44, 51, 90, 138, 146
Thomas, G., 79
Thompson, J. G., 234
Tomkins, S. S., 236
Torem, M., 386, 392
Tozman, S., 125, 146, 159
Training, multiple personality disorder (MPD), 100–101
Transference, dissociative identity disorder treatment, 421–424
Trauma. See Childhood trauma; Developmental model (of trauma); Ritual abuse; Vicarious trauma
Treatment alliance, with alter personalities, dissociative identity

disorder treatment, object relations and, 429–431
Treatment frame retention, dissociative identity disorder treatment failures, 382–393
Trickett, P. K., 223
Tulving, E., 232
Turin, A., 395

Ulrich, D., 528
Underwager, R., 147, 152, 205–206

Valent, P., 224
Valone, K., 520, 521
Van Benschoten, S. C., 336
VandenBos, G. R., 381
van der Hart, O., 90, 97, 181–182, 183, 307, 309, 318, 320, 481
Van der Kolk, B. A., 181–182, 183, 185, 201, 481, 501, 504
Vanderlinden, J., 76
van Fraassen, B. C., 59
Van Praag, H. M., 99, 105, 124
Varma, V. K., 290, 307, 316, 318
Vaughn, C., 520, 521
Vicarious trauma, 486–491
  addressing of, 488–491
  factors contributing to, 487–488
  generally, 486–487
Victim, attacks on, 199–202, 209–210
Victor, G., 22
Victor, J., 194, 337
Violence, interpersonal, trauma and, 187
Vocational rehabilitation, 505
Voices, assessment of, 271–274
von Buskirk, R., 241

Waites, E. A., 474
Wakefield, H., 147, 152, 206
Walker, E., 27
Waller, P., 115
Ward, N. G., 150
Ware, N. C., 58
Warrington, E. K., 241
Waters, F. S., 95

Watkins, H. H., 351
Watkins, J. G., 351, 395, 398, 403
Watte, E., 115
Weinstein, H. M., 79
Weiskranz, L., 236, 241
Weiss, M., 95
Weissberg, M., 140, 148, 164
Weissman, M., 520
Welz, R., 521
Westermeyer, J., 59
Western, D., 150
White, S. H., 244
Whitman, W., 88
Widom, C. S., 151
Wilbur, C. B., 208, 209, 353, 391
Wilde, O., 88
Wilkinson, C. B., 224
Williams, L. M., 367
Williams, M., 526, 529, 532, 536
Wilson, A., 224

Wilson, L., 388, 391
Wilson, N., 193
Winfield, I., 150
Winkler, G., 304
Winnicott, D. W., 483
Wittkower, E. D., 312
Witztum, E., 296
Wood, H. C., 11
Woodruff, R. A., 356
Woolf, V., 88
World Health Organization (WHO),
   90, 92
Wright, L., 404

Yalom, I., 386, 397
Young, W., 386, 387

Zuckerman, M., 116
Zweig-Frank, H., 150